Pricing

Pricing

Making Profitable Decisions *Third Edition*

Kent B. Monroe
University of Illinois—Champaign

Boston   Burr Ridge, IL   Dubuque, IA   Madison, WI   New York   San Francisco   St. Louis
Bangkok   Bogotá   Caracas   Kuala Lumpur   Lisbon   London   Madrid   Mexico City
Milan   Montreal   New Delhi   Santiago   Seoul   Singapore   Sydney   Taipei   Toronto

McGraw-Hill Higher Education

A Division of The **McGraw-Hill** Companies

PRICING: MAKING PROFITABLE DECISIONS
Published by McGraw-Hill/Irwin, a business unit of The McGraw-Hill Companies, Inc., 1221
Avenue of the Americas, New York, NY, 10020. Copyright © 2003, 1990, 1979 by The
McGraw-Hill Companies, Inc. All rights reserved. No part of this publication may be reproduced
or distributed in any form or by any means, or stored in a database or retrieval system, without
the prior written consent of The McGraw-Hill Companies, Inc., including, but not limited to, in
any network or other electronic storage or transmission, or broadcast for distance learning.
Some ancillaries, including elecronic and print components, may not be available to customers
outside the United States.

This book is printed on acid-free paper.

domestic   1 2 3 4 5 6 7 8 9 0 DOC/DOC 0 9 8 7 6 5 4 3 2
international 1 2 3 4 5 6 7 8 9 0 DOC/DOC 0 9 8 7 6 5 4 3 2

ISBN   0-07-252881-8

Publisher: *John Biernat*
Executive editor: *Linda Schreiber*
Editorial coordinator: *Sarah Crago*
Marketing manager: *Kim Kanakes*
Media producer: *Craig Atkins*
Project manager: *Jim Labeots*
Production supervisor: *Gina Hangos*
Designer: *Matthew Baldwin*
Supplement producer: *Vicki Laird*
Senior digital content specialist: *Brian Nacik*
Cover design: *Asylum Studios*
Typeface: *10.5/12 Times New Roman*
Compositor::   *GAC Indianapolis*
Printer: *R.R. Donnelley*

Library of Congress Cataloging-in-Publication Data
Monroe, Kent B.
  Pricing: making profitable decisions/Kent B. Monroe.--3rd ed.
    p. cm.
  Includes bibliographical references and index.
  ISBN 0-07-252881-8 (alk. paper)--ISBN 0-07-119860-1 (international: alk. paper)
  1. Pricing. I. Title.
 HF5416.5 .M66 2003
 658.8'16--dc21

                                                    2002141429

INTERNATIONAL EDITION ISBN 0-07-119860-1
Copyright © 2003. Exclusive rights by The McGraw-Hill Companies, Inc. for manufacture and
export. This book cannot be re-exported from the country to which it is sold by McGraw-Hill.
The International Edition is not available in North America.

www.mhhe.com

McGraw-Hill/Irwin Series in Marketing

I dedicate this book with love and deep appreciation first to my wife and companion, Norma. Thanks for providing your unyielding support and encouragement throughout. I also dedicate the book to Scott, Karen, and Andy (son, daughter, and grandson).

Preface

This book is designed to provide the reader with an integrative framework for making pricing decisions. Economic and marketing principles are synthesized with accounting and financial information to form a basis for analyzing pricing alternatives within legal, organizational, and competitive constraints.

Pricing is a multidisciplinary and multifunctional subject. From an organizational perspective, it is a responsibility of top management that encompasses financial, marketing, and legal considerations. However, there are conceptual and operational conflicts in theory and practice between economists, accountants, financial managers, and marketing managers. Because of these conflicts and the many disciplines involved, pricing has seldom been taught as a unique course for business students. Further, most business people involved directly in the pricing activity for their organizations also have had little, if any, training in this very important business management activity. Indeed, at a recent executive training program that I conducted, not one of the 44 participants, most of whom were involved in pricing for their organizations, had any previous formal training or course in pricing.

Fortunately over the past 15 years, academics as well as managers have recognized the importance of pricing. More business schools have developed courses on pricing, at either the undergraduate or MBA level, usually in the marketing curriculum. Businesses have begun to establish separate administrative functions for their pricing analysis and decision making as they accepted an active role in pricing. In 1987, the Pricing Institute was founded to provide a mechanism for encouraging new thinking about pricing and for disseminating new ideas about pricing issues. The Institute offers training programs in pricing and sponsors annual pricing conferences. In 1992, MCB University Press began publication of *Pricing Strategy & Practice*, a journal for the dissemination of information about pricing practice and research. The Professional Pricing Society was formed by Eric Mitchell in Atlanta and Fordham University has established the Pricing Center to promote research and professional development in pricing. Further, with deregulation, privatization, and the enactment of free trade agreements between more countries, the importance of pricing has been widely recognized. Finally, not-for-profit organizations have discovered the strategic importance of pricing for their long-run survival.

BACKGROUND

This third edition represents a substantial revision of the second edition published in 1990. As with the two previous editions, the material has been developed and carefully tested in the classroom as well as in executive seminars throughout the world. In particular, much of the new material is the direct result of executive inquiry, conversations with managers, and the experiences of consultants who specialize in pricing. Every technique presented and illustrated in this book is being used by some companies in relation to their pricing activity.

THE PLAN OF THE BOOK

The objectives of this book are to systematically present the factors to be considered when setting price and to show how pricing alternatives can be developed and analyzed. As observed in Chapter 1, many contemporary practices are short-run reactions to environmental pressures, and although these short-run oriented decisions may work for some companies for a specific problem or time period, rarely are they generalizable. Thus, the thesis of this book, as outlined initially in Chapter 1, is that pricing must be long run in nature and that managers must take a proactive approach. Further, the proactive approach to pricing requires a market orientation and specifically considers how customers develop value perceptions. The proactive approach is more difficult than simply adding a profit margin to cost estimates; nevertheless, the ability to make profitable pricing decisions is substantially enhanced by taking this analytical approach.

Building on the proactive theme of the book, Sections 2 and 3 carefully analyze the price-demand relationship. The demand variable, through the way customers form value judgments, becomes an upper limit on the pricing discretion of the organization. Further, to understand how customers develop value perceptions requires an examination of how customers perceive prices, price changes, and price differences. These two sections draw heavily on newly developing thinking in economics and behavioral research.

While Chapter 2 reviews the traditional economic principles and concepts useful for understanding the price-demand relationship, Chapters 3 and 4 expand on more recent thinking and research that extends economic reasoning to understanding how contemporary markets may behave. These two new chapters introduce the important concept that information is an important resource both for understanding how markets behave, but also for implementing pricing strategies and tactics. Indeed, one important point stressed throughout the book is that effective pricing managers must continuously acquire and analyze information about competitors and customers. Furthermore, recognizing that price conveys information about the firm, its products and services, and its intentions, it is also important to manage how pricing information is communicated to the firm's internal and external constituents.

Section 3, containing Chapters 5 through 9, provides new and expanded discussion on the evidence from behavioral price research about how buyers perceive, process, retrieve, and use price information. While this area of research began in the mid-1960s, it has virtually exploded in the past decade. We now have an impressive body of research evidence on how people perceive prices and form value judgments. This evidence is reviewed and translated into implications for pricing managers in Chapters 5, 6, and 7. Chapter 8 continues the behavioral orientation by presenting some analytical methods for determining the relationship between customers' value perceptions and prices. These techniques are being used by some of the most progressively managed companies and consulting organizations. Chapter 9 then reviews many of the research approaches available to determine how customers perceive prices and to estimate the underlying price-volume relationships in different markets. These chapters also have been expanded to meet the many requests from managers and marketing researchers for material on how to do pricing research and value analysis.

Section 4 considers another major factor for developing profitable prices: cost. The vast majority of business firms are still cost-oriented in their pricing, and as a result, make some fundamental pricing mistakes. The traditional approaches to developing cost information for pricing and other decisions are, for most firms, obsolete. Therefore, a careful understanding of a better approach for developing and using cost information is developed in Chapters 10 and 11. The approach is extended beyond production or manufacturing to marketing and distribution in Chapter 12. Understanding marketing and distribution costs is very important not only for a manufacturing firm but for retailing and merchandising and service providers as well. Chapter 12 also demonstrates the need to go beyond product costing and profitability analysis to performing customer profitability analysis. Indeed the development of information technology and sophisticated information systems makes it feasible to know the relative profit contributions obtained by serving the many different types of customers with whom a firm normally does business.

Whereas Sections 2, 3, and 4 develop the analyses and techniques for considering demand and cost in pricing, Sections 5 and 6 apply this material to specific pricing decisions and price administration. Because of the intricate relationship between price and customers' value judgments, the complexity of pricing decisions is a major point of the chapters in these sections. Chapter 13 discusses the experience curve and its application to pricing. The discussion of the experience curve is placed at the beginning of the sections on decisions and administration because it provides a way of forcing managers to think in terms of the important relationships among price, volume and costs, and therefore, profits. One of the problems with the experience curve is it has been frequently misused as a pricing tool, primarily because managers did not understand the rationale of the experience phenomenon. Chapters 14 and 15 review the complexity of pricing products and services over their life cycles and the issues of developing prices for a firm selling many products and services. Illustrations are developed in these chapters to demonstrate the practical applications of the economic, behavioral and costing material developed in Sections 2, 3, and 4.

Section 6 reviews the important issues of administering prices to and through the distribution channels. Primarily, it is in the administration of the pricing function where both legal and competitive constraints must be recognized. Also, administering the pricing decisions ultimately determines the relative success of the pricing strategy. Firms often fail to pay attention to the importance of managing the pricing function; therefore, they often unknowingly (and sometimes intentionally) violate laws concerning pricing or misinterpret buyers' or competitors' responses to pricing decisions.

Section 7 covers additional topics on pricing that represent either specialized pricing issues such as auctions and competitive bidding or emerging issues such as pricing services, international pricing and pricing on the Internet. Although the pricing of services and the development of prices for international markets should follow the basic analyses and considerations discussed in Sections 2, 3, and 4, there are often additional nuances that need to be recognized. The material presented in Chapters 20 and 21 describes some of these nuances and considerations.

Finally, Section 8 reviews the material presented in the previous 21 chapters and offers some prescriptions for improving the overall pricing activity of the firm.

The book concludes with a comprehensive glossary of pricing terms.

ACKNOWLEDGMENTS

Over the past few years, a number of individuals have encouraged and supported the development of this book. The students at the University of Illinois helped in many ways, particularly by serving as "test subjects" for the material. Also, the many business people who have helped by talking with me, serving as students in executive development seminars, and asking questions have been instrumental in the gestation of this book. The reviewers of the manuscript offered positive advice, and the book reflects many of their suggestions. Larry Compeau, Clarkson University; Hooman Estelami, Fordham University; "Mick" Kolassa, University of Mississippi; Akshay Rao, University of Minnesota; Robert Schindler, Rutgers University, Camden; Joel Urbany, Notre Dame University; and Z. John Zhang, Columbia University, all read parts of the manuscript and were very helpful.

I also had some assistants who deserve special thanks. Mui (Maggie) Kung and Wei Wang helped convert the original second edition text into the foundation for the third edition. Moreover, they did research and helped develop examples and box material. They were especially helpful as we were rushing to meet production deadlines. Maggie and Wei also helped with the material and writing for Chapter 21. Wei also provided detailed comments from a student's perspective and created the first draft of the test bank. Jennifer Dolan joined us late in the development of the book, but she was very helpful in getting material to the publisher, tracking down articles, creating some outstanding illustrations, and developing supplementary materials. Very special thanks and recognition goes to Jennifer Cox, who worked in the very early stages in developing the extensive computer and filing system for the hundreds of articles that she ran down, copied, and categorized for this project. Later, Jen also helped in the development of box materials and the initial approach for Chapter 21. She was an outstanding assistant in every way, being there whenever something was needed or advice sought on how to resolve an issue. I also thank all of my current and former doctoral and master students who have worked with me on pricing research over the years and have been a constant source of stimulation and encouragement.

Over the past 15 years, it has been a pleasure to meet and grow professionally with a number of dedicated pricing professionals. I have learned much from them and they have been especially encouraging in the revision of this book. Dan Nimer led the way for all of us and it has been a delightful experience to work and learn with Dan. I am also grateful for the help in the many ways that George Cressman, John Harrison, Mick Kolassa, Mike Marn, Tom Nagle, and Gerald Smith have stimulated my thinking and writing about pricing management.

I am especially grateful to my wife and companion, Norma, for her willingness to "give me up" when I escaped to the study to work on the manuscript. She has been very encouraging and supportive throughout the entire project.

Linda Schreiber, the Marketing Editor on this book was very helpful and supportive. Sarah Crago was a very reliable and supportive contact person for the various questions and issues that came up when we were coordinating the activities between Champaign and Burr Ridge.

About the Author

KENT B. MONROE (D.B.A., 1968, Illinois; M.B.A., 1961, Indiana; B.A. 1960, Kalamazoo College) is the J.M. Jones Distinguished Professor of Marketing, University of Illinois, Urbana-Champaign. He has pioneered research on the information value of price and has presented papers before various international associations in Asia, and Europe as well as North America. His research has been published in the *Journal of Marketing Research, Journal of Consumer Research, Journal of Marketing, Management Science, Journal of the Academy of Marketing Science, Journal of Retailing, Journal of Business, Pricing Strategy & Practice,* and the *Journal of Business Research.* He has served as a consultant on pricing, marketing strategy, and marketing research to business firms, governments, and the United Nations. He has conducted executive training programs for business firms, nonprofit organizations, and universities in North and South America, Europe, Asia, Australia, and Africa. He served as chairman of the American Marketing Association's Development of Marketing Thought Task Force, 1984–88, served as a director of the Association for Consumer Research, 1989–91, was the editor of the *Journal of Consumer Research,* 1991–1993, is a member of the Advisory Board of the Pricing Institute, and a Fellow of the Decision Sciences Institute. He also serves as Editor of *Pricing Practice and Strategy,* is associate editor of the *Journal of Consumer Research,* and serves on the Editorial Review Boards of the *Journal of Marketing Research, Journal of Consumer Psychology,* and the *Asian Journal of Marketing.* He received the Pricer of the Year award from the Pricing Institute of the International Institute for Research, April 1999, and the Pioneer of the Year Award for Lifetime Achievement in pricing research by the Central Illinois Chapter of the American Marketing Association, April 2002. In October 2000, Fordham University's Pricing Center annual pricing conference was held in his honor as recognition of his contributions to the field of pricing research.

He also has taught at the Universities of Iowa and Massachusetts, Virginia Polytechnic Institute and State University (Virginia Tech), and at Glenville State College, Glenville, WV. He has won many teaching awards including the W. E. Wine Award for Teaching Excellence in 1989 while at Virginia Tech, and the Graduate Student Mentor of the Year Award from the University of Illinois in 1998. He served as Head of the Department of Business Administration at Illinois, 1994–1999 and as Head of the Department of Marketing at Virginia Tech, 1980–1984. Doctoral students under his direction at Massachusetts, Virginia Tech, and Illinois have won dissertation proposal competitions, dissertation competitions, and research paper competitions.

BRIEF CONTENTS

SECTION FIVE
DEVELOPING PRICING STRATEGIES   345

SECTION SIX
MANAGING THE PRICING FUNCTION   431

SECTION SEVEN
SPECIAL TOPICS ON PRICING   545

SECTION EIGHT
RECOMMENDATIONS   617

GLOSSARY   634

CONTENTS

Introduction

Section 1 introduces the topic of pricing and develops the strategic importance of the pricing variable. In Chapter 1, we define price and illustrate several ways price may be changed. After discussing some important environmental pressures on pricing decision makers, we present some approaches that have been used to cope with these pressures. Chapter 1 concludes with a brief overview of the implications of these current pricing practices.

CHAPTER ONE

Effective Pricing Management

There are two fools in any market:
One does not charge enough.
The other charges too much.

Russian Proverb

Recently a potential car buyer was looking for a new car. Although his first choice was just what he wanted, its price of $28,000 was simply too much. He was about to settle for a smaller model that seemed to offer the features he wanted for $5,000 less when he noticed the prices of some used cars. He found a one-year-old full-size model with only 5,000 miles and almost a full warranty for $20,000. He could not ignore the $8,000 difference between his first choice and a similar one-year-old car, and he purchased the used car. This example illustrates a theme that will be repeated throughout this book: buyers respond to price differences rather than to specific prices. Thus, it is *relative* prices that are important to buyer choice.

Although this basic point about how prices influence buyers decisions may seem complex and not intuitive, this very point drives how businesses are learning to set prices. You may observe that the buyer was really responding to the lower price of the used car. And you would be correct—up to a point. This buyer was responding to a *relatively* lower price, and it was the difference of $8,000 that eventually led him to buy the used car.

Now consider the automobile maker who has to set the price of new cars. This pricing manager must consider how each price will compare (1) to prices for similar cars by other car makers, (2) with other models in the seller's line of cars, and (3) with used car prices. The car maker must also consider whether car dealers will be able to make sufficient profit from the sales of the cars to be motivated to promote them in the local markets. Also, if the number of cars sold at the price set is insufficient to reach the market and profit objectives of the manufacturer, price promotions in the form of cash rebates or special financing arrangements for buyers might be necessary. Besides these pricing decisions, the car maker must decide on the discount in the price to give to fleet buyers such as car rental companies. Within one year these new rental cars will be sold at special sales to dealers and individuals like the buyer above. Further complicating the pricing problem for the car manufacturer is the predominance of leasing as an alternative to purchasing a car outright. Leases may require down payments ranging from nothing to a few thousand dollars, with very affordable monthly payments. They generally expire within a two- to four-year span and the leased cars may become available for resale in the used car market.[1]

As this example illustrates, a modern organization's pricing decisions are complex and important. Although pricing practice remains somewhat routine, the pricing literature has now produced sufficient new insights and approaches to provide most businesspeople opportunities to change their methods of setting prices. Yet many good managers still make bad pricing decisions.[2] Managers may make bad pricing decisions because they have inadequate or incorrect information about their customers, their competitors, or the relevant costs of the decision. In addition, they may rely on traditional thinking, invalid assumptions, or wishes that become accepted as reality. The most common result of these incorrect pricing decisions is that firms receive less revenue than some or all of their customers would be willing to give them.

---

[1]See "Why Auto Companies Can't Win for Leasing," *Business Week* (May 20, 1991), 104; "Leasing Fever: Why the Car Business Will Never Be the Same," *Business Week* (February 7, 1994); Earle Eldridge, "Expiring Leases Lift Used Car Supply," *USA TODAY* (July 13, 2000), B1.

[2]George E. Cressman, "Snatching Defeat from the Jaws of Victory: Why Do Good Managers Make Bad Pricing Decisions?" *Marketing Management* 6 (Summer 1997), 9–19.

This chapter defines price and illustrates the complexities of pricing decisions. To amplify the importance of these decisions, we discuss some environmental pressures influencing management and pricing. Then the chapter reviews how businesses have attempted to cope with these environmental pressures, the implications of current pricing strategies, and some major pricing errors that have resulted from these attempts.

The Role of Price

The basic problem of an economic society is to allocate resources among the members of the society so as to maximize the welfare of the society as a whole. To achieve this welfare objective, each resource should be used to perform the function by which it contributes most efficiently to society. In a market economy, the price system allocates these resources. That is, prices furnish the guideposts that indicate how resources should be used. Prices determine *what* products and services should be produced and in what amounts. Prices determine *how* these products and services should be produced. And prices determine *for whom* the products and services should be produced.

Thus prices affect both incomes *and* spending behavior. For the consumer with a given income level, prices influence what to buy and how much of each product to buy. For business firms, profits are determined by the difference between revenues and costs, with revenues determined by multiplying price per unit sold by the number of units sold.

Price changes also play a major role in a market economy. When the quantity demanded for a product or service is greater than the supply available, buyers bid the price up. If costs remain the same per unit sold, the higher price leads to greater profits and an incentive to invest in resources to produce even greater quantities of the product. Thus, the producers are able to bid more for raw material resources, thereby directing resources into their industry. In addition, higher prices may also stimulate a greater rate of innovation and the development of new technology. On the other hand, if available supply is greater than demand, pressures build to decrease prices and reduce output. These pressures lead producers to convert their resources to alternative uses. Thus, rising prices direct resources to the bidder of greatest desire (stimulating supply) and curtail demands of the least urgent bidders (rationing supply). Declining prices have the opposite effects.

The Definition of Price

Within this economic context, it is usual to think of price as the amount of money we must sacrifice to acquire something we desire. That is, we consider price as a formal ratio indicating the quantities of money (or goods and services) needed to acquire a given quantity of goods or services:

$$\text{Price} = \frac{\text{Quantity of money or goods and services received by the seller}}{\text{Quantity of goods and services received by the buyer}}$$

Thus, when the price of a box of cereal is quoted as $3.89, the interpretation is that the seller receives $3.89 from the buyer and the buyer receives one box of cereal. Similarly, the quotation of two shirts for $45 indicates that the seller receives $45 and the buyer receives two shirts.

Pricing Terms

Over time, many terms have evolved that are used instead of the term *price*. We pay a postage *rate* to the Postal Service. *Fees* are paid to doctors, dentists, lawyers, architects, and consultants. We pay *premiums* for insurance coverage, *rent* for apartments, *tuition* for education, and *fares* for buses, taxis, and airlines. We pay *tolls* to cross a bridge or use a highway and an *admission* to go to a movie, sporting event, concert, or museum. Banks may have *user fees* for credit charges, *minimum required balances* for a checking account service, *rents* for safety deposit boxes, and *fees* or *interest charges* for automatic teller machine (ATM) use or cash advances. In international marketing, *tariffs* and *duties* are paid to import goods into another country. The problem that this variety of terms creates is that we often fail to recognize that setting a rent, interest rate, premium, fee, admission charge, or toll is a pricing decision exactly like setting the price of a product purchased in a store.

Ways to Change Price

Organizations change prices in a variety of ways—strategically and tactically, knowingly and unknowingly—that have important implications for their ability to achieve their objectives. Suppose a seller wishes to change the price quotation. A major error made by many organizations is to pay attention only to the numerator of the ratio (the amount of money to be received), and ignore the denominator. Focusing attention on the numerator encourages their customers to think of price only in monetary terms. However, firms that take a value orientation to pricing consider both sides of the ratio. For example, the price of a first-class hotel room in a major southeastern city might vary between $59 and $225 for a one-night single occupancy. Airlines sell the same service, a coach seat between two cities on the same flight, at different prices. These different dollar prices reflect differences in the value of the product or service as perceived by the buyer (the denominator in the ratio).

Some time ago a shortage of cocoa beans resulted in a shortage of chocolate for candy manufacturers. This shortage of chocolate resulted in an increase in the price of chocolate. Prior to this shortage, a multipack of six candy bars was priced at $0.89. One candy company increased its price to $1.19 for six candy bars. Thus, one way to change price is to *change the quantity of money or goods and services to be paid by the buyer*.

However, another candy company changed the price by decreasing the number of candy bars in a multipack to five and charging $0.89 for the five bars. Therefore, a second way to change price is to *change the quantity of goods or services provided by the seller*. A seller may change the quantity of goods and services by changing the number of items or the weight (contents). For example, sugar-free Velamints reduced the size of its mints and kept the price the same—the 12-piece packages were reduced in weight from 0.85 ounces to 0.71 ounces. Similarly, Brut deodorant spray reduced the size of its can from five ounces to four ounces while maintaining the price of the can.[3] Scott Paper Co. raised price by reducing the number of paper towel sheets in a roll from 96 to 60 (a 40 percent reduction), while reducing the price by 10 cents per roll.[4] See Box 1.1 for another example of this way of changing price.

A third way a seller can change price is by *changing the quality of goods and services provided*. If the quantity ratio remains unchanged, but the quality has been decreased, then the price has actually increased because the buyer receives less. If quality is raised without changing the quantity ratio, then the price has decreased.

Price can be changed by *changing the premiums or discounts to be applied for quantity variations*. Suppose a seller

---

[3]See "New and Improved Twaddle," *Business Week* (November 1, 1993), 8.
[4]See "Will Consumers Take a Hike?" *Business Week* (August 21, 1995), 27.

FRITO-LAY TAKES CHIPS OFF THE TABLE

BOX 1.1

Sometime during late fall 2000, Frito-Lay began putting up to an ounce less in each bag of its market-leading salty snack products, including Fritos, Chee-tos, Ruffles, Cracker Jack, Lay's, Tostitos, and Doritos. The prices remained the same. For example, the popular 7.5 ounce bag of Lay's potato chips priced at $1.99 was reduced to 7.0 ounces (about three or four less chips per bag). Defending the action, a Frito-Lay spokesperson said the bags continue to be clearly marked by weight and price. She said that the company was "committed to providing consumers with the best-tasting snacks at the best value." Finally, she indicated that reducing the package size was preferable to increasing prices as consumers would be less likely to purchase the chips if prices go beyond the "magical price points of $2.29, $3.29, $1.99 and 99 cents." (See Chapter 5 for a discussion about odd pricing.)

Industry people call the practice of raising price by reducing the size of products "weight out." They believe consumers are less likely to notice this form of price increase because they may not check and remember the price per ounce (unit price) from their last purchase. If they have a reference price it will be the actual shelf price, which of course does not change.

Source: Katie Fairbank," Frito-Lay Cutting Back on Snacks," *The Champaign-Urbana News-Gazette* (January 5, 2001), C10.

quotes a 5 percent discount for all quantity purchases of 100 units or more. If each unit sells for $4.00, then anyone who purchases 1 to 99 units pays $4.00 per unit. However, if a customer buys 150 units, then the price is actually $3.80 per unit. Price can also be changed by offering premiums with purchases, such as trading stamps, toys, glasses, or frequent purchase rewards. In each case, if the quantity ratio remains constant, a premium serves to reduce the actual price paid, because the buyer receives additional goods or services.

Changing the time and place of transfer of ownership is a fifth way to change price. A concept in the retailing of furniture provides for inventory to be stored at the retail store, thereby allowing the buyer to take immediate possession instead of waiting several months for delivery. These furniture stores generally have three different price tags on the furniture. Buyers who wish to pay cash and take the item home pay a lower price than buyers who pay cash and have the store deliver it. Buyers who prefer an installment purchase and delivery pay the highest price. These different price tags explicitly recognize the differences in selling costs and services; the furniture store, in effect, transfers the delivery costs to the buyer.

Often the actual price is changed if the *place and time of payment are changed*. Being able to purchase a product and having 90 days to pay without interest is a reduction in price over paying at the time of purchase. Many credit accounts charge no interest if the balance is paid within 25 days. Because money has a time value, permitting customers to have the merchandise for a time without paying for it reduces the price.

Changing the acceptable form of payment is a seventh way of changing price. Some stores do not accept checks, other stores operate on a cash-only basis, and still others accept credit charges for regular customers. As we just discussed, being able to buy on credit without interest being charged may reduce price if the formal ratio does not change because of the additional service.

Thus, *price is the amount of money and services (or goods) the buyer exchanges for an assortment of products and services provided by the seller.* The variety of ways to change price makes pricing a very important marketing decision. Paying attention to both the numerator and denominator of the price ratio provides opportunities to make the offer unique, even if the product otherwise is considered a commodity. There is more to the determination of price, then, than simply establishing a monetary amount to be exchanged for goods and services provided.

Importance of Price Decisions

Pricing a product or service is one of the most vital decisions management makes. Price is the only marketing strategy variable that directly generates income. All the other variables in the marketing mix generate costs: advertising and promotion, product development, selling effort, distribution, packaging—all involve expenditures. Often firms determine prices by marking up cost figures supplied by the financial division and, therefore, are left with only their promotion and distribution decisions. But the pressures of adapting to today's economic environment place additional burdens on the profits of a firm.

Surveys have been conducted (in 1982, 1984, 1986, and 1994) to determine relative changes in pricing strategies.[5]

[5]Barbara Coe, "Perceptions of the Role of Pricing in the 1980's among Industrial Marketers," *Proceedings of the Summer Educators' Conference*, Chicago: American Marketing Association, 1983, 235–40; Barbara Coe, "Shifts in Industrial Pricing Objectives," *Proceedings of the Summer Educators' Conference* (Chicago: American Marketing Association, 1988), 9–14; Hermann Simon, "Some Remedies for Price Headaches," *Pricing Strategy & Practice* 2 (no. 2, 1994), 25–27.

The 1986 survey indicated that profits were the number one objective of pricing, as opposed to market share and growth. By 1994, pricing was viewed as the major pressure point for managerial decision making. We will discuss these environmental pressures next.

Faster Technological Progress

The revolution in industrial science has several important effects on pricing. First, accelerating technological progress has reduced the gap between invention and innovation, that is, the time lag between invention and commercialization. Today, a new idea is translated into a commercial product in only a few years. Technological progress also has reduced the average age of products. Thus, a new product does not have much time to become profitable, and any pricing mistakes made during introduction will make it more difficult to become profitable. Finally, in technologically advancing societies, people have been freed from many of the mundane activities associated with their basic needs. As a consequence, they spend more time and money on skiing, weekend trips to resorts, travel, or other forms of recreation. One result of this intensified competition from alternative uses of income is that demand for many goods and services is more sensitive to relative prices and shifts in prices.

Proliferation of New Products

Product innovation has also resulted in a literal "population explosion" of new products. As a result, product lines have been widened, and often the distinctiveness of products has been blurred. Widening the range of choice has blurred market segments and made it possible for small price differentials to produce relatively large shifts in demand. Thus, the process of determining prices for an entire product line has become more delicate, more complex, and more important.

Increased Demand for Services

Clearly, the developed economies of the world have become service oriented, and the demand for services in these economies as well as in developing economies is still increasing. In virtually all instances increased demand has led to increased prices because pure services consist mainly of labor, and productivity gains have been low. Such price increases for services (many of which are now regarded as necessities) have led to public concern and increased governmental activity (e.g., in health care). Many of these price increases have resulted from a naive approach to pricing without regard to underlying shifts in demand, the rate at which supply can be expanded, prices of available substitutes, consideration of the price–volume relationship, or the availability of potential substitutes.

Increased Global Competition

Since the 1980s we have witnessed a substantial increase in the flow of foreign-made products into countries around the globe due to the liberalization of foreign trade and the reduction of trade barriers, the narrowing of superiority in productivity, and the emergence of new industrialized nations. Established firms typically have responded by lowering their prices instead of finding other ways to meet this new competition. This proliferation of foreign-made products has increased price competition for domestic producers. Today it is clear that there are few shelters from global competition.

The Changing Legal Environment

Initially, many of the environmental changes just described caused substantial public concern, resulting in legislation and new forms of regulation. Concern over the increased cost of medical services, automobile insurance, legal services, repair services, education, and foreign competition led to new and proposed legislation at the federal, state, and local levels. But from the late 1970s through the 1990s, many previously regulated industries were deregulated, while nationally owned firms in countries outside the United States were privatized. Companies suddenly were making pricing decisions previously made by regulators or economic planners, and new companies were entering the deregulated industries. Smaller companies removed the shackles of regulation and entered new markets, sometimes with lower prices and sometimes with differentiated services. These changes in the legal environment have resulted in a turbulence these deregulated industries have never before experienced. As a result, pricing decisions have become more complex, more difficult, and more important.

Economic Uncertainty

During the mid-1970s Western developed economies were beset with recurring and persistent inflation, coupled with periodic shortages of basic materials such as oil and paper.

More recently, developing economies in Asia and South America have faced depressed economies and unemployment at relatively high levels. Further, some countries have instituted strict monetary and price controls to reduce rapid inflation to manageable levels. As the rate of inflation has slowed or virtually stopped in some economies, firms have found that across-the-board price increases led to customer resistance and often exacerbated a tenuous demand relationship. As a result, many firms have discovered the need for new approaches to developing pricing strategies.

Summary

The need for correct pricing decisions has become even more important as competition has intensified. Due to the increasing rate of technological progress, the time lag between invention and commercial innovation has shortened the average life of new products and encouraged quicker competitive imitative responses. Technological progress has also widened the alternative uses of buyers' money and time and has led to a greater density of substitute products and services. The demand for pure and product-attached services remains strong, increasing pressure on pricing decisions. These environmental pressures have made product and service pricing more delicate, more complex, and more important.

Conceptual Orientation to Pricing

Five essential factors should be considered when setting prices. As Figure 1.1 shows, *demand* considerations establish a ceiling, or maximum price, that may be charged. The determination of this maximum price depends on the customers' perceptions of value in the seller's product or service offering. On the other hand, *costs* set a floor or minimum possible price. For existing products, the relevant costs are the direct and assignable indirect costs associated with production, marketing, and distribution. For a new product, the relevant costs are the future direct and assignable costs over that product's life cycle. The difference between what buyers are willing and able to pay (perceived value) and the minimum cost-based price represents an initial pricing discretion. However, this range of pricing discretion is narrowed by com*petitive factors, corporate profit and market objectives,* and *regulatory constraints.*

FIGURE 1.1 **Conceptual Orientation to Pricing**

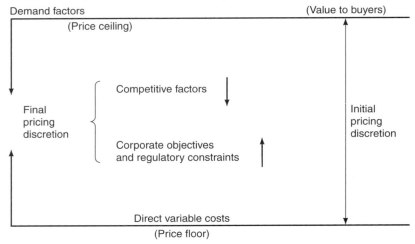

Primarily, competitive factors reduce the price ceiling, whereas corporate objectives and regulation raise the minimum possible price. Corporate objectives translate into financial requirements that necessitate higher prices to cover fixed costs and overhead and meet profit goals. Therefore, simply covering direct variable costs normally results in an insufficient price level. Government regulation (e.g., pollution controls and safety standards) often forces the costs of production up. Regulation of certain marketing practices (e.g., safe packaging) and legal regulation against predatory pricing, as well as the need to protect a product from potential liability suits, all raise the pricing floor.

Normally, these factors narrow the range of pricing discretion. Depending on the type of product and characteristics of demand and competition, this pricing discretion could still be relatively large or it could be nonexistent. Regardless, as Figure 1.1 shows, several very important factors must be considered when setting prices. Focusing only on costs obviously ignores many other important factors.

Implications of Current Pricing Decisions

As Figure 1.1, illustrates, management should analyze the effect of proposed prices on demand, costs, competition, and the other elements of marketing strategy before determining a new pricing strategy.

Demand Implications

How a firm's customers respond to a change in price is a fundamental consideration because the degree to which buyers' demands are sensitive to price differences determines the eventual effect on sales volume and revenue. However, price setters often misunderstand or overlook some basic factors. We discuss four such factors next.

Market versus Product Elasticity

Price elasticity of demand is a measure of the degree to which buyers are sensitive to price changes. In any market characterized by several functionally substitutable products there are actually two demand schedules: (1) demand for the general product (*primary demand*) and (2) demand for the firm's specific offering (*secondary demand*). Generally, it would be expected that secondary demand would be more responsive to price changes; that is, it would be more price elastic. However, as developed in Chapters 2 and 6, price elasticity varies by brand, stage of the product's life cycle, and whether the price is increased or decreased. Hence there is the danger that a seller may make an incorrect assumption about the price elasticity of a particular product.

Derived Demand for Buyers' Output

Many businesses sell their products and services to other businesses, which perform additional value-added processing before selling their output to the final users. Thus, sellers marketing to businesses need to know the degree to which the market for their customers' products is price elastic. A reduction in price in the customers' market would heighten demand for the seller. Hence, manufacturers selling to such buyers, whose product represents a significant portion of these buyers' product costs, may curtail sales opportunities by eliminating discounts or otherwise increasing prices. It is important that pricing managers know the customers of their customers.

Likelihood of Competitive Entry

An emphasis on high-price strategies may encourage the entry of competitors when entry barriers are low and when demand is price elastic. Thus buyers may quickly accept a new competitor's product because of the high prices. Moreover, continued high prices or consistent price increases may force buyers to reconsider their needs and, perhaps, actively seek competitive substitutes.

Demand Consequences of a Product Line

Most firms sell a wide range of products requiring a variety of differing marketing strategies. Generally, the firm has several product lines (groups of products that are related because they are used or marketed together). Within a product line, usually some products are functional substitutes for each other and some products are functionally complementary. For example, a photographic product line would include cameras, film, flashbulbs, projectors, screens, and accessories. Because of the demand interrelationships and because there are usually several market targets, the product-line pricing problem is a major challenge facing pricing managers.

To compound the pricing problem, complementarity may exist even if the products are functionally substitutable. Thus, continuing with the camera line example, several models of cameras, although competing for a buyer's choice, may enhance overall demand for the camera line because of the brand name, the perception of a "full line," or a positive association from one model to another. In addition, by adding new items or reducing certain prices, a firm may increase demand for existing products.

Emphasis on weeding out low-volume or low-margin products may have unanticipated consequences, depending on the effect a full line has on demand. Even though a particular product's direct profit contribution is small, it may actually "build traffic" for higher-margin products. Furthermore, prices at the low end (and often the lowest-margin product) may positively affect buyers' perceptions of the entire product line. Thus product-line decisions based only on cost considerations may weaken demand for the seller's product line. These issues are explored in greater detail in Chapters 11 and 15.

Cost Implications

It is important that a firm be aware of the composition and behavior of product costs in order to know how to evaluate a change in selling price, how to profitably segment a market, and when to add or delete products from the product line. Even so, as developed in Chapters 10 through12, costs should play a limited role in pricing. Costs indicate whether the product can be made and sold profitably at any price but not the amount of markup or markdown buyers will accept. Accurate cost information guides management in selecting a profitable product mix and in determining how much expense can be incurred without sacrificing profit.

Many current pricing decisions are cost oriented and simplistic—they elevate the role of costs while diminishing the role of demand. A survey of manufacturers of industrial capital products found that 56 percent of the responding managers mentioned cost-plus pricing as a main method of determining price.[6] Such an emphasis on costs and profit margin may lead to additional problems.

Cost-Plus Pricing

Adopting cost-plus pricing methods ignores the consideration of price–volume–cost relationships. The experience curve indicates that as cumulative production and sales volume doubles, costs decline by a constant, predictable percentage. One way to build volume is to reduce price and place managerial pressure on forcing costs down. Thus volume-oriented pricing may lead to additional reductions in cost and steady or higher profit margins. However, many firms incorrectly use a volume-oriented or market share–oriented pricing strategy because they incorrectly assume the benefits of the experience curve without understanding the very specific conditions when such a strategy can be profitable.[7] Chapters 11 and 13 will explore these issues in detail.

To illustrate the error of assuming the benefits of the experience curve, consider a large manufacturer of small electric motors who decided to reduce prices substantially. The manufacturer expected that volume would increase by a greater percentage and that this increase in volume would reduce unit production costs by an amount greater than the price reduction. Thus, the manufacturer expected to sell more units at a larger contribution margin than previously. Additional sales volume did result; however, unit costs did not decline and the firm actually lost money because of the decision. What management had not realized was that the experience curve effect, if it does occur, occurs early in the product's life cycle. The small electric motors were a 20-year-old product line!

Maximizing Margins

Elimination of low-margin products should be considered in terms of its incremental effect on costs. Many of the costs associated with a product or service are joint or common

---

[6]Peter M. Noble and Thomas S. Gruca, "Industrial Pricing: Theory and Managerial Practice," *Marketing Science* 18 (no. 3, 1999), 435–54.
[7]Joel E. Urbany, "Justifying Profitable Pricing," *Journal of Product & Brand Management Featuring Pricing Strategy & Practice* 10 (no. 3, 2001), 141–59.

costs that will persist when the product or service is deleted. Hence, the only costs relevant for the deletion decision are those costs that are directly traceable to the product or service that may be deleted. Unless the deletion decision permits increased production of other products, the net change in profit contribution may be negative. We will explore these issues in Chapters 11, 14, and 15.

Pricing with Scarce Resources

When a critical production resource is in short supply, the firm must allocate the resource across its various products. Paying strict attention to profit margins may lead to a less profitable position because high-margin items may require disproportionate amounts of the critical resource, and production capacity will be underutilized. In such circumstances, pricing should encourage sales of those products that *maximize the contribution per resource unit* used. Often, low-margin products may achieve this objective better than high-margin products. This point will be developed in Chapter 11.

Marketing and Distribution Strategy Implications

Rarely does the pricing decision occur in isolation. Generally, price interacts with other elements of the marketing strategy, and therefore several additional implications are important.

The Product Life Cycle

As products go through the product life cycle—introduction, growth, maturity, and decline—the role of price and promotion varies to meet buyer, competitive, and technological changes. As the product enters the maturity stage and competitive price differences become more important to buyers, a seller's discount and service policies become important marketing tactics. Routine elimination or cutbacks of discounts or services without regard to the product's life cycle stage could be detrimental to the seller. Further, eliminating discounts or forcing premium-priced products on distributors could produce negative distributor reactions and cost the manufacturer a portion of the reseller's support.[8] Issues of pricing over the product life cycle are covered in Chapter 14,

---

[8] See "Motorola Goes for the Hard Cell," *Business Week* (September 23, 1996), 39.

and pricing issues relative to distribution are discussed in Chapters 16 and 17.

Sales Force Management

Centralizing pricing authority and reducing or eliminating a salesperson's ability to quote prices consistent with local competition reduces the flexibility of the sales force. In effect, the sales job is significantly altered, perhaps leading to increased sales force dissatisfaction and personnel turnover. However, developing a compensation system that rewards contributions to profit and customer retention could be an effective approach to coordinate pricing and selling effort. We will return to this issue in Chapter 17.

Proactive Pricing

Pricing is one of the most important marketing decision variables. It is also a very complex and difficult decision. Traditionally, business firms and educators have paid relatively little attention to developing new approaches to making price decisions. Although many of the environmental pressures noted in this chapter have been discussed for several decades, few people have paid much attention to the issues these pressures create. Since the 1970s the full effect of these environmental pressures has become apparent and firms have been ill-prepared to develop new pricing strategies.

However, business leaders and educators have begun to search for new approaches to solving pricing problems. Some firms have been quite successful in developing new strategies and in organizing for the price decision. Unfortunately, other firms have imitated these successful strategies only to discover that the overall situation is not similar, and some undesired consequences have occurred.

Firms that have been successful in making profitable pricing decisions have taken what may be called a *proactive pricing* approach.[9] By consciously attempting to consider the effects of a pricing decision on how buyers perceive prices and how buyers develop perceptions of value, they have managed to leave less money on the table in competitive bid situations and have been able to successfully raise or reduce prices without competitive retaliation. Through deliberate

---

[9]Elliot B. Ross, "Making Money with Proactive Pricing," *Harvard Business Review* 62 (November–December 1984), 145–55.

acquisition and careful analysis of pertinent information, they have become aggressive pricing strategists and tacticians.[10]

Two prerequisites are essential for becoming a successful proactive pricer. First, it is necessary to understand how pricing works. Because of the complexities of pricing's impact on suppliers, salespeople, distributors, competitors, and customers, the basic prescriptions of traditional microeconomic theory simply do not fit the realities of a modern market system. Indeed, as indicated by this list of those on whom pricing has an impact, companies that focus primarily on their internal costs often make serious pricing errors.

Second, it is essential for any pricer to understand how customers perceive prices and price changes. As we will develop in Chapters 3 through 7, most buyers do not have complete information about alternative choices and most buyers are not capable of perfectly processing the available information to arrive at their "best" choice. Price frequently is used not only as an indicator of how much money the buyer must give up, but also as an indicator of product quality. Moreover, differences between the prices of alternative choices also affect buyers' perceptions. Thus it is imperative that the price setter know who makes the purchase decision for the products or services being priced, and how this buyer perceives price information. For example, Mobil Corp. found that only 20 percent of gasoline buyers purchased solely on the basis of price.[11]

Managerial Pricing Orientation

Although managers have identified pricing as a major pressure point or marketing headache for over two decades, organizations have been slow to develop a proactive approach to pricing. This state of affairs exists, in part, because managers have focused more on setting price than on the process of managing the pricing function. Among the consequences of inattention to managing the pricing function are that firms fail to distinguish between pricing strategy and pricing tactics, do not coordinate pricing decisions across departments, and rarely have an organizational unit responsible for regularly monitoring and adjusting prices and price policies. For

---

[10]See "The Power to Raise Prices," *Business Week* (May 4, 1998), 38–40.

[11]"Mobil Bets Drivers Pick Cappuccino over Low Prices," The *Wall Street Journal* (January 30, 1995), B1, B4.

example, a survey of the 20 largest pharmaceutical firms operating in the United States found that only four had a formally structured pricing department reporting to senior marketing executives. Firms with an organized pricing function approached pricing as an ongoing process, whereas those without a permanently assigned pricing responsibility treated pricing decisions episodically, with little or no continuity in those decisions.[12]

In a comprehensive survey about pricing practices, 49.4 percent of respondents reported changing prices on their most important products once or less in a typical year.[13] In another survey, 87 percent of the companies responding changed prices during 1996. However, only 13 percent of these price changes came after a scheduled review of pricing policy.[14] Unfortunately, these data likely underestimate the frequency that prices are adjusted during an operating period. Without managerial control of the price decision process, the net price a firm receives for its products may be substantially less than either list or invoice price.

Managerial pricing orientation involves considering how an organization sets its pricing objectives; gathers, processes, and analyzes relevant information; provides for an orderly decision process; and establishes a procedure for anticipating and responding to customer, market, and competitor changes.[15]

The Three Levels of Pricing Management

To develop an appropriate managerial pricing orientation, it is useful to think about pricing management at three levels.[16] These three levels are described next.

[12]E. M. (Mick) Kolassa, "The Appropriate Function of the Pricing Function," presented at the American Marketing Association Educators' Conference, Hilton Head, SC, February 1995.

[13]Alan S. Blinder, Elie D. Canetti, David E. Lebow, Jeremy B. Rudd, *Asking about Prices: A New Approach to Understanding Price Stickiness* (New York: Russell Sage Foundation, 1998), 84.

[14]Reported in the *Chicago Tribune*, Business Section (May 12, 1997).

[15]Gerald E. Smith, "Managerial Pricing Orientation: The Process of Making Pricing Decisions," *Pricing Strategy & Practice*, 3 (no. 3, 1995), 28–39.

[16]Michael V. Marn, "When the Price Is Not Right," *The Wall Street Journal* (February 12, 1990), A14.

Level 1: Understanding the Economic and Competitive Environment

The traditional economic view of pricing involves understanding how current and future supply and demand dynamics affect overall market prices. At this first level managers need to understand how changes in the economic and market environment affect prices. What is the likelihood and effect of new competitors entering the market? When will new production facilities—the firm's or competitors'—come online? How have buyers' tastes and preferences been changing? What is the relative influence of new product developments on market demand? As mentioned earlier, proactive pricing managers need to understand their pricing environment, especially factors that influence the dynamics of supply and demand.

Level 2: Developing Product and Market Pricing Strategy

It is important that pricing strategy be a part of the overall marketing strategy. A company's pricing strategy and tactics send a message to the market. The firm's pricing strategy provides customers with an indication of the organization's managerial orientation. Strategic pricing decisions define an organization's value image in the eyes of customers and competitors.

Developing pricing strategy within the boundaries of overall corporate and market strategy requires understanding the relationships between benefits, price, and costs. The relationship between benefits and price is defined by the firm's customers. Is the perceived "gain" embodied in the perceived benefits greater than the "give up" represented by the perceived price? By *benefits* we mean the tasks or functions performed by the product for the customer, the problems the customer solves by using the product, and the pleasure the customer derives from acquiring and using the firm's offering. In other words, does the offer represent perceived value to the customer?

The relationship between price and costs indicates how much profit the firm can make by providing that level of benefits. Finally, the relationship between benefits and costs indicates the degree to which the firm can deliver the benefits at a sustainable cost advantage relative to competition and whether it will persist over time. That is, how easily can the firm deliver the level of benefits desired by customers at a cost below that of competitors, and how long can it sustain this relative cost advantage?

Level 3: Administering the Pricing Process

The third level of price management involves determining the *actual price* to receive for each transaction. Transaction management includes setting discounts, rebates, allowances, and other reductions from the list price across customers. This level requires organizing the price administration unit, coordinating pricing across departments and functional units, establishing pricing tactics, and arranging for feedback and control. Tactical pricing decisions concern the day-to-day management of the pricing function including

- Timing of price changes.

- Amount of price changes.

- Direction of price changes.

- Administration of price changes.

- Communication of price changes to the sales force and customers.

Summary

This chapter has reviewed several contemporary environmental pressures and current pricing practices that have been used to cope with these pressures. Many current pricing practices need to be based on additional analyses, particularly cost and demand information. Moreover, a number of other important factors need to be considered when setting prices. The two necessary prerequisites for successful pricing are to know how pricing works and how customers perceive prices.

A basic role of price is to ration or stimulate supply. Thus it is important that pricing managers understand how the basic forces of supply and demand influence prices in a market economy. When demand shifts due to changes in buyers' preferences, some markets will experience shortages of what buyers are seeking, and other markets will experience excess supply (or capacity to supply) of relevant goods or services. In addition, shifts in supply due to entry or exit of competitors, addition of new productive capacity, or technological innovation will disrupt the stability of prices in the markets. Pricing managers must monitor and understand these forces influencing the general economic environment in the markets served.

The prescriptions for successful pricing articulated in this book emphasize the acquisition of correct and timely information about customers, competitors, costs, and the firm's objectives. However, this information must also be carefully analyzed prior to the determination of pricing strategies and tactics. Sections 2 through 4 present techniques for acquiring and analyzing the relevant information for pricing decisions. Section 5 explores how to use these analytical techniques for developing prices over product life cycles and for pricing multiple products or services. Section 6 discusses ways to increase pricing flexibility by developing a price structure. Section 7 discusses techniques for deciding what price to bid in an auction or in a competitive bidding situation and specific issues of pricing services for both profit and not-for-profit companies. It also explores pricing for global marketing. Finally, Section 8 offers a set of guidelines for developing and implementing a proactive approach to pricing.

Discussion Questions

1. The chapter cites two reasons for the lack of new approaches to pricing. Can you think of any additional reasons why pricing has been a neglected marketing decision variable?

2. The chapter provides the example of two candy companies changing the price of a multipack of candy bars. Assume that the strategy used by the first company resulted in a 50 percent decrease in volume during the first year after the price change, but during the second year volume was down only 30 percent from predecision levels. Assume further that late in the second year chocolate again becomes scarce and expensive. If you were the price administrator for this company, what pricing alternatives would you consider?

3. Assume that you are the price administrator for the second company in the situation described in Question 2. During the first two years after the price change described in the chapter, your multipack candy volume remained at predecision levels. Now you face the same scarcity of chocolate. What pricing alternatives would you consider? Are any of these alternatives different from those you listed in Question 2? Why or why not?

4. Before making a final decision for either of the two candy companies described in Questions 2 and 3, what additional information would you want? If the information were available, how would you use it?

5. What do you think should be the role of a pricing manager or price administrator? What type of education or training should a price administrator have?

6. In Question 5, would your answer be different if you assumed that the price administrator worked for a retail store? Would your answer be different if the price administrator worked for a service-oriented business such as a hotel or bank? Why or why not?

Suggested Readings

Coy, Peter: "The Power of Smart Pricing," *Business Week* (April 10, 2000), 160–64.

Cressman, George E.: "Snatching Defeat from the Jaws of Victory: Why Do Good Managers Make Bad Pricing Decisions?" *Marketing Management* 6 (Summer 1997), 9–19.

Dolan, Robert J.: "How Do You Know When the Price Is Right?" *Harvard Business Review* 73 (September–October 1995), 174–83.

Marn, Michael V., and Robert L. Rosiello: "Managing Price, Gaining Profit," *Harvard Business Review* 70 (September–October 1992), 84–94.

Smith, Gerald E.: "Managerial Pricing Orientation: The Process of Making Pricing Decisions," *Pricing Strategy & Practice*, 3 (no. 3 1995), 28–39.

Urbany, Joel E: "Justifying Profitable Pricing," *Journal of Product & Brand Management Featuring Pricing Strategy & Practice*, 10 (no. 3 2001), 141–57.

Economic Foundations of Pricing Theory

The discipline of economics provides the basic theory of how prices should be set. However, despite the analytical pricing solutions neoclassical economic theory provides, the theory has limited practicality. Most of the limitations of neoclassical economic theory arise because of the many necessary simplifying assumptions it makes. Nevertheless, economic theory does provide some important analytical concepts for practical pricing decisions.

This section contains three chapters. Chapter 2 briefly develops the traditional economic theory of price determination. It introduces a number of concepts that are used throughout the book and that are important in any discussion on price: revenue, elasticity, marginal revenue, and marginal costs. Chapters 3 and 4 introduce some recent important advances in economic theory. Sparked by essays by Scitovszky and Stigler, conceptual issues related to price–quality relationships, economics of information and price search behavior, and price signaling have been introduced to the pricing field. This emergence of nontraditional economic thinking about pricing represents an important recent development and provides insights into managing price competition.

CHAPTER TWO

The Economics of Price Determination

In the area of pricing a large body of literature describes how business organizations should determine their selling prices. This literature has a rich tradition and, although theoretical in nature, provides some important analytical concepts and thinking for practical pricing decisions. This chapter has two purposes: (1) to summarize the traditional neoclassical economic theory of price determination and (2) to delineate useful concepts for actual pricing decisions.

Price Determination in Theory

In our economy, pricing decisions are made by an array of private and public institutions. Many of these decisions are made within large, multifaceted, and complex profit-oriented as well as not-for-profit organizations. These pricing decisions are made in a considerably different way from the decision process traditional economic theory describes. The essentials of the economic theory of the firm tell us how a firm will decide which production technique (or method) to use and what the particular input proportions will be to produce the desired product. Given its production method and its decision as to what to produce, the firm seeks to minimize its input costs. The firm then decides the quantities of each product it plans to sell and the price per unit at which it hopes to sell each product. The objective of the firm is assumed to be profit maximization.

The economic theory that we will briefly describe is not intended to indicate how firms actually do or should make pricing decisions, or how buyers do or should respond to these pricing decisions. Economic theory is more concerned with the behavior of aggregates or markets, particularly how persistent and widespread behavior leads to stable results called *equilibrium*. One important aspect of the economic perspective is to realize that it views the firm as a pricetaker rather than a pricemaker. That is, management determines the quantity to produce, and the market sets price through the forces of supply and demand. (In contrast, a marketing perspective views price as a decision variable, rather than as a given.) Hence we should not uncritically adopt economic concepts, methods, or assumptions for the development of marketing-oriented pricing principles.

The Profit-Maximizing Firm

Figure 2.1 illustrates how a firm interested in maximizing profits determines how much to produce in the short run when price is constant; that is, when it cannot be changed. Because price is constant, the total revenue curve must go through the origin (if zero units are sold, total revenue will be zero); but because some costs are fixed in the short run, the total cost curve does not go through the origin. As long as revenue received from the sale of an additional unit of output (marginal revenue) is greater than the additional costs of producing and selling that unit (marginal cost), the firm will expand output. Because price is constant, marginal revenue equals price, and the firm will produce at the quantity level where marginal revenue (price) equals marginal cost. (In economic analysis *marginal* is defined as the change resulting from a unit increase in effort.) In Fig. 2.1 profits are at a maximum where total revenue minus total cost is the greatest, or where the slope of the total revenue curve equals the slope of the total cost curve. (In quantitative analysis *slope* measures the amount of change in the dependent variable [revenue or costs] produced by a unit increase in the independent variable [quantity].) Thus, maximum profits can be obtained when the quantity produced is Q^* units, whereas losses are at a maximum at Q' units. Should the firm produce more units than Q^*, its total cost curve is increasing faster than the total revenue curve, implying that marginal costs are greater than marginal revenues.

Figure 2.2 plots the marginal cost and average cost curves against quantity. Because the slope of the total cost curve is the increase in total cost per unit increase in quantity, the slope is marginal cost. Figures 2.1 and 2.2 summarize the key information about cost curves. As shown in Fig. 2.2,

FIGURE 2.1
Output
Determination for a
Profit-Maximizing
Firm—Short Run
(Constant Prices):
Aggregate Analysis

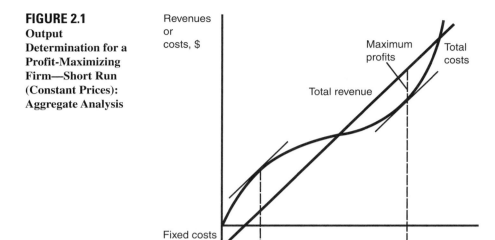

FIGURE 2.2 **Output Determination for A Profit-Maximizing Firm—Short Run**
(Constant Prices): Marginal Analysis

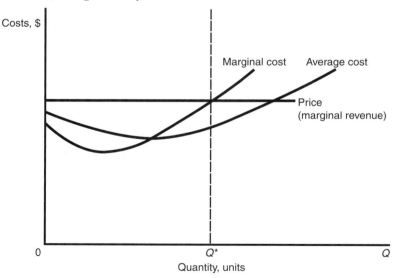

marginal cost equals average cost once, slicing up through
the average cost curve at its minimum point. The same conditions hold in the long run, but the total cost curve goes
through the origin, as does the total revenue curve.

FIGURE 2.3
Output
Determination for a
Profit-Maximizing
Firm—Short Run
(Varying Prices)

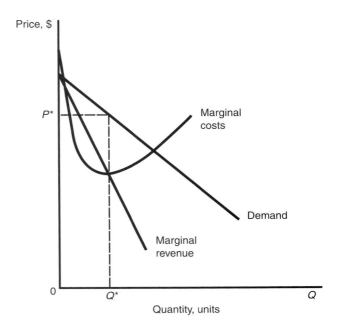

Maximum profits still occur where marginal revenue equals marginal cost.

Figure 2.3 shows the situation when prices vary. In this case the firm determines its output on the basis of where marginal revenue equals marginal cost, but the price it receives for its output is determined by the demand curve and varies according to how much is produced. Thus, as quantity produced increases, the price per unit the firm receives for its output decreases. That is, price is set at the level at which the firm can sell its entire output. The long-run solution is similar to the constant-price situation; however, when prices can vary, the total revenue curve is not linear (see Chapter 16).

Challenges to the Profit Maximization Objective

The assumption of profit maximization in this economic theory has been challenged for two basic reasons. First, profits do not appear to be managers' only objective. Second, managers who are concerned about profits may not be attempting to maximize them.

It has been argued that a business firm is a complex organization comprised of individuals with individual motives. That is, some people are working solely for the money, others are also concerned with social relationships, and some are interested in shouldering responsibility or wielding authority. Generally, the key to long-run survival is the organization's ability to adapt to environmental pressures and constraints. Hence the actual objectives of the business organization (or any organization) are determined through the interaction of a wide range of personal objectives and pressures and constraints from the organization's external environment.

The second challenge to the profit maximization assumption accepts the importance of profits but questions whether managers really attempt to maximize profits. It suggests instead that their goal is to attain *satisfactory* profits. Satisfactory profits represent a level of aspiration that the managers use to assess alternative strategies. In essence, if a strategy is predicted to generate an acceptable level of profits, then the strategy is good enough and is implemented.

Corporate and Pricing Objectives

An organization's objectives for any particular element of a marketing program should flow from three prior levels of planning. First, overall corporate objectives must be considered. Even as broad a goal as being the industry leader will affect pricing objectives. Second, the organization's specific marketing objectives are based on those corporate objectives. Finally, the third level of planning involves setting objectives for one element of the marketing mix, such as pricing. Pricing objectives should be consistent with and should advance corporate and marketing objectives. Pricing objectives can be classified according to profitability or financial goals, sales volume, and competitive factors.

Profitability Objectives

As is true of most marketing objectives, pricing objectives need to be measured precisely. Performance can then be compared with objectives to assess results. *Profitability objectives* allow such assessment; they are expressed in specific dollars or as a percentage of sales. Thus, a firm may seek average profits of $1.1 million for five years, or an 11 percent increase in total revenues before taxes.

Elements of Profitability

Four basic elements affect the profitability of any multiproduct or multiservice organization:

1. Price per unit of each product or service offering, P_i

2. Costs: variable costs per unit of each offering, VC_i, and fixed costs per period, FC.

3. Volume produced and sold of each offering, Q_i.

4. Monetary sales mix of the offerings sold.

In profitability analysis, profit measures include contribution margin per unit, total contributions per period, profit–volume ratio, contribution per resource unit, net operating profit, net income (profit after taxes), and earnings per share. Each of these profit measures will be introduced and defined in Chapter 11. Our analytical approach will be essentially the same regardless of the type of measurement used. However, preferences among profitability indicators will be distinguished in Chapter 11.

Profit Maximization

In practice, maximum profits may be realized in different ways. In some markets relatively low prices result in greater sales and higher profits. For example, Wal-mart and Kmart expect low unit profit margins because of their relatively low prices, but they attempt to maximize cumulative profits per period through high inventory turnover. In other markets, relatively high prices result in slightly decreased unit sales, but higher profits. Tiffany's and Neiman-Marcus seek to maximize their profits through a strategy of relatively high prices and high unit profit margins that offset relatively low unit sales and inventory turnover. Thus, depending on the market situation, maximum profits over a planning period may be obtained by either pricing the firm's offerings relatively low or relatively high. Which pricing strategy to follow given the objective of maximizing profits depends on the nature of market demand and competition.

Target Return on Investment

Another common pricing objective is to obtain some target percentage return on investment. *Return on investment* (ROI) is expressed as the ratio of profits to investments. For manufacturers, investments include capital, machinery, buildings, and land—as well as inventory. For wholesalers and retailers, inventory and buildings constitute the majority of their investments. An ROI objective would be specified as a specific percentage of the total capital employed. For example, a firm with $10 million in capital assets, seeking a 15 percent return on this investment, would seek to achieve net contributions to profits of $1.5 million for the planning period.

Volume-Based Objectives

Some organizations set pricing objectives in terms of sales volume. A common goal is sales growth, in which case the firm sets prices that will increase demand and therefore unit sales. Other firms may seek sales maintenance, knowing that growth does not ensure higher profits and that the organization may not have the resources needed to pursue sales growth.

Empirical evidence indicates that profitability seems to be correlated with market share. However, it has not been established that market share *causes* profits. Rather, the ability of the firm to establish a strong presence in the market, such as a reputation for quality, leads to the ability to receive price premiums that produce relatively higher profitability. In general, companies attempt to achieve a higher market share by setting relatively low prices in order to increase unit sales. Such a pricing strategy must be based on a long-term view of profitability. The company must be willing to accept lower initial profits in exchange for the profits that may be produced over time by increased volume and market share. By contrast, some companies achieve a strong position in selected markets by setting relatively high prices and offering high-quality products and service.

Competitive Objectives

In certain situations, firms base their marketing and pricing objectives on competitive strategies, most often when they seek price stability and engage in nonprice competition. When marketing a mature product whose sales growth has peaked, a company's objective may be price stability. In general, if the firm marketing such a product is the market leader, then competitors will tend to follow the leader's pricing. Competitors stay in line because the leader's objective benefits everyone.

In many cases, price stability leads to *nonprice competition* in which a firm's strategy is advanced by other components of the marketing mix. Although the goal is to maintain profitability through stable prices, the effort to increase sales through expensive promotion may erode that profitability. Still, the risks would be even greater if pricing were used to compete.

In some markets, a firm may choose to *price aggressively*—price below competition—to take advantage of market changes: when products are in early stages of the life cycle, when markets are still growing, and when there are opportunities to establish or gain a large market share. As with any objective, this aggressiveness must be considered within the context of a longer-term perspective.

Establishing Relevant Pricing Objectives

No single pricing objective is the best to pursue across market situations. Typically, firms set multiple objectives depending on the various marketing strategies that have been established. Indeed, one study found that firms seek to achieve four or more objectives.[1] Do specific market situations, then suggest certain pricing objectives?

Profitability objectives

It makes sense to use price to achieve profit objectives when

1. The firm is the low-cost supplier in the market—that is, the firm has a competitive cost advantage.

2. The firm is the price leader—other sellers follow the firm's pricing moves.

3. There is an internal required rate of return for new product introductions.

4. There is a short lead time for new products before competitors will likely enter the market.

In each of these situations, the goal would be to achieve the maximum level of profits possible in the planning period. It is not necessarily the case that a profitability objective specifies either a relative low- or high-price strategy. All four elements of profitability must be considered when developing a profit-oriented pricing strategy.

Volume Objectives

It makes sense to use price to achieve volume-oriented objectives when

1. It is known that the market is sensitive to relatively small price changes (price elastic).

[1]Peter M. Noble, "The Pricing Process: Choice of Pricing Objectives By Industrial Firms," in William M. Pride and G. Tomas M. Hult, eds., *Enhancing Knowledge Development in Marketing* (Chicago: American Marketing Association, 1997), 66–72.

2. The firm knows it is the low-cost supplier.

3. Costs decline in a predictable way as cumulative volume increases (see Chapter 13).

4. There is a strong "captive" aftermarket for replacement supplies.

5. There is an identifiable growth market segment.

6. There is little differential perceived value in the offerings of firms in the market.

7. There is a desire to limit competitive entry.

As these conditions imply, typically a volume-oriented strategy leads to relatively low prices or to a price reduction strategy. If a price reduction strategy is to be profitable, at least conditions 1 and 5 must be present (see Chapter 11). Otherwise, following a low-price, volume-oriented strategy must be viewed as an investment that may be profitable over several years. *"The significance of being the low-cost supplier is that it allows the firm to invest in non-price marketing efforts. . . .It does not give license to use price as a key competitive tool."* [2]

Competition Objectives

It makes sense to pursue a competition-oriented objective when

1. The firm is the low-cost supplier.

2. There are no perceived value differences across sellers in the minds of buyers.

3. Market share could be captured by using nonprice marketing efforts.

Summary

As this discussion shows, there is no one pricing objective that should be chosen for a specific set of market conditions. Trade-offs must be recognized and their implications carefully considered. Furthermore, objectives may change as firms recognize changes in both their organizations and the markets they serve. Errors will be made—the goal is to

---

[2]This quote is from a presentation by Dan Nimer, The DNA Group Inc., on "Pricing for Profitable Growth: Changing the Paradigm," University of Chicago (November 3–5, 1999).

BOEING CHANGES ITS PRICING OBJECTIVE

BOX 2.1

In July 1998, Boeing changed its pricing objective, increasing prices by 5 percent for most new planes. This change in focus from market share to profitability came about when corporate second-quarter profits declined to less than $47 million in July 1998 compared to $55 million reported for the same period in July 1997.

How had Boeing gotten into this situation? The firm's managers were upset that arch-rival Airbus Industrie Consortium had sold more planes than Boeing in 1995. Boeing launched a price war to recapture market share, offering discounts of up to 25 percent according to industry analysts. Boeing recaptured market share, but ended up with orders for planes that exceeded its capability to produce. Scaling up production to meet these orders sent costs spiraling upward, leading to reported losses for the commercial airplane group in 1997 of $1.8 billion and another

expected loss of $61 million for 1998. Thus, the market share focus resulted in a combined reduction in revenues per plane with an increase in costs per plane.

When announcing this change in focus from market share to profitability, then Commercial Airplane Group President Woodard said: "Overall, profits are more important than market share." However, given the fact that it takes several years from the receipt of an order for a new plane until it rolls off the assembly line, it would not be until 2000 before the planes sold at higher prices begin to influence Boeing's profitability. If Boeing can maintain its new pricing objective, it may be able to improve its profitability in the new century.

Sources: Andy Reinhardt and Seanna Browder, "Fly, Damn It, Fly," *Business* Week (November 9, 1998), 150–156; Seanna Browder, "Course Change at Boeing," *Business Week* (July 27, 1998), 34.

understand the most likely direction of that error. For example, in late 1999, Coca-Cola announced that instead of pursuing the primary objective of volume growth, it would attempt to increase profits.[3] To accomplish the profit growth objective, prices in the supermarket channel were increased. Box 2.1 illustrates a similar shift in pricing objectives by Boeing.

Market Structure: Degree of Competition

Depending on the structure of competitors within a market, firms may have considerable discretion to determine prices. In this section, we briefly review these different types of market structure. In general, markets can be classified into three broad categories by the number of competitors and the degree they have power to determine prices: perfect (or pure) monopoly; perfect (or pure) competition; and imperfect

[3]"Things Go Pricier with Coke," *Business Week* (November 29, 1999), 50.

TABLE 2.1   **Characteristics of Market Structures**

Market Structure	Degree of Competition and Product Differentiation	Examples	Degree of Power over Price
Perfect monopoly	Single seller; unique product or service	Local utilities; cable TV	Considerable; government regulations
Imperfect competition:			
Oligopoly	Few sellers; some product differentiation	Steel, chemicals, autos, computers	Some
Imperfect competition	Many sellers; some real or perceived product differences	Packaged goods; retail trade	Some
Perfect competition	Many sellers; no perceived differences in products	Primarily agricultural	None

Source: Adapted with permission from Paul A. Samuelson and William D. Nordhaus, *Economics*, 13th ed. (New York: McGraw-Hill, 1989), p. 570.

competition, which includes monopolistic competition and oligopoly. Table 2.1 sets forth the characteristics of these market structures.

Perfect Monopoly

A *perfect monopoly* occurs when only one seller supplies the product or service. If not controlled in some way, that seller could exercise enormous influence over the marketplace and its prices. As a result, the government usually institutes price restrictions to check the seller's power. The most visible monopolies in the United States have been the utility companies that supply energy. Whether owned privately or by government agencies, they alone have produced energy for specific regions of the country. Because of the costs and complexity of producing and distributing energy, a monopoly was an efficient way to provide energy. However, deregulation has begun in the energy industry, and some consumers have the option of selecting their energy provider.

Perfect and Imperfect Competition

When many sellers offer many buyers an identical product and no single seller can influence the product's price, the market structure is labeled *perfect competition*. These conditions typify the marketing of homogeneous (similar) products whose start-up costs are relatively low, thereby making it easy for new competitors to enter the market. In developed economies, some agricultural industries approach the conditions of perfect competition. In the production of soybeans and cotton and in the fishing industry, for example, so many sellers market similar products that prices tend to be set by the interaction of demand and supply (frequently via auctions—see Chapter 19).

Between the extremes of perfect monopoly and perfect competition lies the broad setting in which most businesses operate: imperfect competition. Although *imperfect competition* may be characterized by a large number of sellers and buyers, fewer sellers compete than in agricultural markets. In markets with only a few sellers, some sellers may hold relatively large market shares and thus be able to influence the prices of products they sell. Within this middle range of the competitive spectrum, economists have identified two distinct market structures: monopolistic competition and oligopoly.

Monopolistic Competition

In *monopolistic competition*, a relatively large number of firms market heterogeneous (dissimilar) products. In these markets, the degree of product differentiation is the key to price levels. Thus, consumers pay more for Stouffer's frozen dinners than dinners from Swanson and for sofas made by Knoll and Henredon than sofas from Sears. This structure is known as "monopolistic" competition because each product is perceived as unique and has an identifiable share of the market. In monopolistic competition, the greater the degree of product differentiation buyers perceive, the greater is the opportunity for competing firms to set different prices. Some firms can influence prices substantially, either because of their relatively large market share or because of the perceived quality of their products.

Oligopoly

In the second type of imperfect competition, an *oligopoly*, a few sellers dominate the marketplace and thus have substantial influence over price. Oligopolies arise primarily because the need for large economies of scale in certain industries discourages competition. The increasingly global perspective of many businesses initially moved domestic oligopolies toward monopolistic competition. However, a recent wave of global mergers and acquisitions have created a trend back toward oligopolies in a number of industries, including automobiles, telecommunications, entertainment, consumer electronics, and appliances for example.

The Laws of Supply and Demand

Whether one, a few, or many sellers are operating in a marketplace, their pricing decisions are influenced to some degree by the economic laws affecting supply and demand.

The Law of Demand

Many people misleadingly speak of demand as a number rather than as a relation. To an automobile executive, for example, demand is the number of cars that can be sold in a given period. However, it is more accurate to refer to this number as the "quantity demanded" and to define demand as the relation between this number and price. *Demand* is a relation among the various amounts of a product that buyers would be willing and able to purchase at possible alternative prices during a given time, all other things remaining the same. According to the *law of downward-sloping demand*, when a product's price is raised (while all other things are held constant), fewer units of that product will be demanded.

Typically, as shown in Figure 2.3, the *demand curve* slopes downward and to the right, where increasing quantities demanded are shown on the horizontal axis. The quantity demanded rises with diminishing price not only because current buyers may increase their consumption but also because new buyers now enter the market. The opposite also holds true. If the price rises, the quantity demanded decreases both because some buyers drop out of the market and because the remaining buyers may purchase fewer units.

The Law of Supply

Economic theory holds that, as a product's price increases, producers will be willing to supply more of it. *Supply* is a relation showing the various amounts of a product that a seller would make available for sale at possible alternative prices during a given period of time, all other things remaining the same. According to the *law of upward-sloping supply*, when a product's price is raised (while all other things are held constant), more will be produced.

TAKING ADVANTAGE OF THE LAWS OF SUPPLY AND DEMAND   **BOX 2.2**

In October 1999, Douglas Ivester, the chairman of Coca-Cola, announced that the company had been testing a vending machine that could automatically change prices for cans of soda. Recognizing that desire for a cold drink can increase while watching a sporting event or on a hot summer day, "It is fair that it should be more expensive," Ivester said "The machine will simply make this process automatic."

A spokesperson for Coca-Cola indicated that the firm had been investigating the technology for more than a year and that it was also considering adjusting prices based on demand at a specific machine. At nonpeak consumption hours, prices could be reduced; at peak consumption times, prices could be increased.

This concept of adjusting prices to meet changes in demand is really not new—it has been used for many years by the airlines and other service firms as yield management. Flexible pricing (rather than a fixed price) is becoming practical because of advances in information technology, the declining cost of computer chips, and the increasing ease of connecting with the Internet. Companies will find it easier to match daily and hourly fluctuations in price. Indeed, in Japan, some vending machines use wireless modems to adjust their prices based on the temperature outside. We can expect more of this interactive price setting in the future.

Source: Constance L. Hays, "Price Strategy in Coke Test: 'What's It Worth to You?'" *International Herald Tribune* (October 29, 1999), 20.

Equilibrium: The Intersection of Supply and Demand

In well-behaved markets, at some point the supply and demand curves intersect, establishing equilibrium between supply and demand and producing an *equilibrium price*. This equilibrium occurs after a period of adjustment between supply and demand, and prices will remain relatively stable so long as environmental conditions remain relatively constant. As we pointed out in Chapter 1, the first level of price management is to monitor these environmental conditions to know when changes in supply or demand are likely to occur. Such changes pressure the general price levels in the markets served. Box 2.2 gives an example of these changes.

Economic Theory of Buyer Behavior

We now turn to discussing how price is believed to affect demand. We begin with the neoclassical economic theory of buyer behavior, which provides the framework for most social criticism of business pricing practices. Then we will discuss various measures of demand sensitivity to price.

In this theory of how price influences buyer behavior, the buyer must decide (1) what products should be purchased and (2) how much should be purchased of each product. The quantity to be purchased depends on (1) the price of that product, (2) the prices of all other products, (3) the income of the buyer, and (4) the buyer's tastes and preferences. Given the prices of all products, and given their income, buyers make their purchases according to their own tastes and preferences. Buyers are assumed to be rational and to choose among alternative products so as to maximize satisfaction (utility).

Assumptions

As just indicated, utility means want-satisfying power, resides in the mind of the buyer, and is common to all products and services. Utility is subjective, not objective, and it is assumed that a choice of product A over product B means the buyer perceives product A as having more *utility* than product B. (In subsequent chapters we will prefer to use the term *value* rather than *utility*, but the meaning will remain the same.) Neoclassical price theory makes assumptions that do not address how people acquire and process information prior to forming preferences and making choices. The essential ideas of neoclassical theory are the maximization of utility and the law of diminishing marginal utility. This neoclassical theory of buyer behavior involves several additional assumptions about buyers:

1. Buyers calculate deliberately and choose consistently.

2. Deliberate choice rules out habit or impulse buying.

3. Consistent choice rules out vacillating and erratic behavior; buyers act predictably.

4. If buyers prefer product A to product B and product B to product C, then consistency requires that they prefer A to C.

5. Within these conditions of behavior, buyers choose as if they are maximizing utility.

6. To maximize utility buyers know all alternatives and are not ignorant about any aspect of their purchase.

7. Because of this perfect information, there never is a gap between the satisfaction buyers expect from a purchase and the actual fulfillment realized from the purchase.

8. Want and subjective utilities are not influenced by prices; that is, higher-priced products do not provide additional utility or value simply because of their higher prices.

9. Finally, total utility increases at a diminishing rate as more of a product or service is acquired.

Solution

The solution to the question of how much of a product a buyer will purchase requires the assumption of diminishing marginal returns to utility as quantity purchased increases. The quantity purchased (assuming a fixed income constraint) is where total utility is maximized.

Because it is assumed that prices serve only to indicate the amount of money buyers must give up to acquire a product, the amount of a particular product to be acquired depends on the relation between the marginal utility of acquiring an additional unit and the price of that additional unit. In addition, the assumption of diminishing marginal utility implies that buyers are capable of ranking all alternatives in terms of increasing preference and that they purchase first the most preferred product. Buyers will continue to buy additional units of the preferred product until the marginal utility of acquiring an additional unit becomes equal to or less than the marginal utility realized from purchasing a unit of the second most preferred product. This decision process continues until the amount allocated has been exhausted. The result of this decision process indicates that the marginal utility obtained from the last penny spent on product A must equal the marginal utility obtained from the last penny spent on product B, and so on for all products purchased.

To summarize, in economic theory, price is assumed to influence buyer choice because price serves as an indicator of how much the buyer must give up (sacrifice). Assuming the buyer has perfect information concerning prices and want satisfaction of comparable product alternatives, he or she can determine a product mix that maximizes satisfaction within a given budget constraint. If the buyer does not act to maximize want satisfaction, he or she is acting irrationally. The implication is that buyers should choose the low-price alternative if there is a choice between at least two differentially priced, similar products.

However, buyers really do not have complete and accurate information about the utility received from a set of products or the prices of these products. Somehow buyers do acquire sufficient information about products and about the satisfaction received from these products to decide which products to purchase with a given budget. Lacking complete information about the utility associated with the product, the buyer assesses the product on the basis of known information. Generally, one piece of information available to the buyer is the product's price. Other pieces of information about anticipated purchases are not always known, or are known less frequently than price, and the buyer cannot be sure how reliable and how complete this information is. Lack of information may introduce uncertainty about the buyer's ability to predict correctly the want satisfaction available through purchasing the product. *Hence, buyers may use price both as an indicator of product cost or sacrifice as well as an indicator of product quality (want satisfaction attributes).* This attractiveness attribute of a product's price will be explained further in Chapters 5 through 7, and the issue of lack of perfect information will be discussed in Chapters 3 and 4. Next, we discuss some important concepts that are useful when analyzing price alternatives.

Some Useful Concepts from Price Theory

The overview of the theory of the firm and the theory of the buyer so far has been primarily qualitative. That is, we have postulated that the lower the price of an item, the more a buyer is likely to buy. However, it has not been possible to say how much more likely the buyer is to buy. As shown in Figure 2.4, we can say that for a particular price, P_1, there is a greater demand for wine than for bread, and that if price increases to P_2, there will be a greater decrease in demand for bread than for wine. It is also possible to say that the demand for wine is less sensitive to changes in price, but that the demand for wine is greater than the demand for bread at any similar price. But these statements do not tell us the extent to which price and demand are related for each product or allow us to easily compare loaves per dollar to bottles per dollar. The concept of *elasticity* provides a unit-free measure of the sensitivity of one variable to another, and it provides a quantitative way of making comparisons across entities.

Demand Elasticity

In Chapter 1 and this chapter we have occasionally referred to the concept of demand sensitivity. That is, we have been

FIGURE 2-4
Concept of Price Elasticity

Note: Traditional economic texts place price on the vertical axis and quantity on the horizontal axis. However, assuming that quantity demanded depends on price, the correct procedure is to place price on the horizontal axis and quantity on the vertical axis.

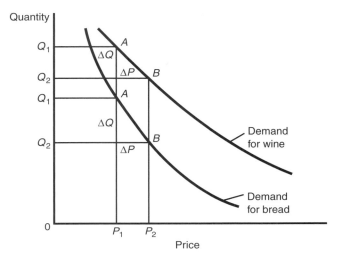

concerned with the responsiveness of demand to price changes. *Price elasticity of demand* measures the responsiveness of the quantity demanded of a product or service to a change in the price of the product or service. Specifically, price elasticity of demand is defined as the rate of percentage change in quantity demanded relative to the percentage change in price

$$E_d = \frac{(Q_1 - Q_2)/Q_1}{(P_1 - P_2)/P_1} = \frac{\Delta Q/Q_1}{\Delta P/P_1} = \%\Delta/\Delta P \quad (2\text{-}1)$$

where
E_d = price elasticity of demand

ΔQ = quantity change in demand

ΔP = change in price

Q_1, P_1 = original quantity demanded and price, respectively

If it is assumed that quantity demanded falls as price increases, then $E_d < 0$; if there is a positive relation between demand and price change, then $E_d > 0$, that is, demand increases as price increases. For the generally assumed case of a downward sloping demand curve, Figure 2.4 graphically depicts the concept of price elasticity for both bread and wine.

To illustrate the concept of price elasticity, assume that the price of a digital camera was $1,200, and annual sales at this price were 5,000 units. In 2002 the price dropped to $1,050 and annual sales were 5,500 units. In 2003, the price again dropped to $990, and annual sales were 10,000 units.

Using Equation 2.1, the price elasticity for each of these price changes can be computed:

$$E_d = \frac{(5,000-5,500)/5,000}{(\$1,200-\$1,050)/\$1,200}$$

$$E_d = \frac{-500/5,000}{\$150/\$1,200} = \frac{-500}{\$150} \times \frac{\$1,200}{5,000} = -0.80$$

and

$$E_d = \frac{(5,500-10,000)/5,500}{(\$1,050-\$990)/\$1,050}$$

$$E_d = \frac{-4,500/5,500}{\$60/\$1,050} = \frac{-4,500}{\$60} \times \frac{\$1,050}{5,500} = -14.3$$

Generally, the price elasticity of demand is not the same at all prices; nor is the elasticity of demand in any particular price range the same as the slope of the demand curve over that range of prices. In Figure 2.4 the slope of the demand curve between points A and B is $\Delta Q/\Delta P$, which is not the formula for the elasticity given in Equation 2.1. The higher the price of the product, the smaller will be the quantity demanded, and the greater will be the value of E_d; that is E_d approaches zero in value. Furthermore, if the value of the price elasticity of demand is less than -1, that is, $-\infty < E_d < -1$, then demand is elastic and sellers' revenues will rise if there is a small reduction in price. Table 2.2 summarizes the elasticity measures and their relationships to total revenue.

Often other measures of demand sensitivity are used to explore the implications of change. *Income elasticity of demand* is the responsiveness of the quantity demanded of a product or service to a change in personal income:

$$E_I = \frac{(\Delta Q)}{\Delta I} \times \frac{(I)}{Q} \qquad (2.2)$$

where

E_I = income elasticity of demand

ΔQ = quantity change in demand

ΔI = change in personal income

If E_I is negative, this implies that the product is an inferior good. That is, as income goes up fewer units are demanded. For example, as income goes up, some households will

TABLE 2.2   **Relationship of Price Elasticity of Demand to Total Revenues**

Value of E_d	Description	Effect on Total Revenues of	
		Small Price Rise	**Small Price Reduction**
0	Perfectly inelastic	Increase	Decrease
$-1 < E_d < 0$	Inelastic	Increase	Decrease
-1	Unitary elastic	No change	No change
$-\infty < E_d < -1$	Elastic	Decrease	Increase
$-\infty$	Perfectly elastic	Decrease	Increase

switch some of their meat purchases from hamburger to steak and consume less hamburger. If E_I is positive, then demand increases as income increases, but there are two different possibilities. If $0 < E_I < 1$, then the product becomes less important in households' consumption plans even though total expenditures increase. For example, necessities such as food and clothing tend to comprise less of the family's total expenditures as income increases. Finally, if E_I is greater than 1, then the product becomes more important as income increases, such as leisure and recreational activities, for example.

A third measure of demand sensitivity is *cross-price elasticity of demand*, which measures the responsiveness of demand for a product, Q_A, to a change in price of another product, P_B:

$$E_c = \frac{\Delta Q_A}{\Delta P_B} \times \frac{P_B}{Q_A} \qquad (2.3)$$

where

E_c = cross-price elasticity of demand

ΔQ_A = change in demand for product A

ΔP_B = change in price for product B

If E_c is negative, then in general the two products are *complementary*; if E_c is positive, then in general the two products are *substitutes*. For example, razor blades are complements to razors, but different brands of razors are substitute products. Now assume the price of a Kodak 35-millimeter camera is $145.00, and a comparable Minolta is $149.00. Further, assume the quantity demanded for the Kodak camera is 50,000 units, and the quantity demanded for the Minolta is 100,000 units. Suppose Kodak reduces the price of its camera to $142.00. The quantity demanded for the Kodak camera increases to 60,000 units, and the quantity demanded for the Minolta decreases to 95,000. (Because of overall increases in market demand for 35-millimeter cameras, Kodak's demand increase is not all at the expense of demand for the Minolta camera.)

The cross-price elasticity of demand for the Minolta camera can be computed using Equation 2.3.

$$E_c = \frac{-5,000}{-\$3} \times \frac{\$145}{100,000} = 2.42$$

Relationships among the Elasticities of Demand

For the moment, if the theory of consumer demand concerns the decision to buy either of two products, A and B, and the quantities to purchase of each, we can illustrate the relations among these three elasticities. Each of these products has a price, P_A and P_B; the consumer must decide how much to purchase of each, Q_A and Q_B; and the consumer has a budget or income available to spend, Y. The consumer has six elasticities of demand with respect to the three things that will influence the purchase decision: two *own-price elasticities*, E_A and E_B, two *cross-price elasticities*, E_{AB} and E_{BA}, and two *income elasticities*, E_{AI} and E_{BI} (note the subscripts of these elasticities). These six elasticities describe how buyers behave relative to changes in price of either product or changes in income.

To demonstrate the relations among the elasticities, let's trace what might happen if the price of A is reduced while everything else remains unchanged. We would expect under normal circumstances that Q_A, the demand for A, would increase. There are two basic reasons to expect this increase. First, some buyers, noting the lower price of A, would switch some of their purchases from B to A. The extent of this crossover would depend on E_{BA}, the degree that demand for product B is sensitive to changes in the price of A (this crossover is called the *substitution effect*.) Second, after the quantities usually purchased of products A and B, the buyers will have some money left over. Since the marginal utility of acquiring more units of A is now greater than P_A, buyers will increase the units purchased of A to restore the equilibrium between the marginal utility of an extra unit of A and its new, lower price, the *income effect*, expressed as E_{AI}. Thus, the ordinary price elasticity is composed of a substitution effect

EFFECT OF PRICE DIFFERENCES ON PRICE ELASTICITY

BOX 2.3

A columnist in *Forbes* reported that he had learned that his brother was paying 12 cents a minute for phone calls to Canada, whereas he had been paying 22.4 cents per minute. He complained to AT&T and was granted the 12-cent-a-minute rate. However, his readers quickly pointed out that they were paying even less for calls to Canada. The columnist responded, "For 10 cents a minute, I'll switch.

For 2 cents a minute, I won't bother." As we will observe in more detail in Chapter 6, one of the determinants of buyers' price sensitivity is their *perceptions* of price differences rather than simply *noticing* that there are different prices for purchase alternatives.

Source: "Price Inelasticity," *Forbes* (July 28, 1997), 40.

(cross-price elasticity) and an income effect (income elasticity). The income effect normally adds to the elasticity, making it a more negative number. In Chapter 6 we will provide some evidence about these relative effects on price elasticity. Box 2.3 illustrates one issue of how a price difference influences behavior.

Revenue Concepts

As mentioned in our discussion of price elasticity of demand, a relationship exists between sellers' revenues and the elasticity of demand for their products. To establish this relationship we need to define the concepts of total revenue, average revenue, and marginal revenue. *Total revenue* is the total amount spent by buyers for the product or service.

$$\text{TR} = PQ \qquad (2.4)$$

where

TR = total revenue

P = price of the product

Q = quantity demanded at price P

Average revenue is the total outlay by buyers divided by the number of units sold, or the price of the product.

$$AR = \frac{TR}{Q} = P \qquad (2.5)$$

where AR is average revenue. The average revenue curve and the demand curve are the same. *Marginal revenue* refers to the total change in total revenue resulting from a change in sales volume.

$$MR = \frac{\Delta TR}{\Delta Q} \qquad (2.6)$$

Price and Marginal Revenue

The normal, downward sloping demand curve reveals that to sell an additional unit of output, price must fall. The change in total revenue—marginal revenue—is the result of two forces: (1) the revenue derived from the additional unit sold, which is equal to the new price; and (2) the loss in revenue that results from marking down all prior salable units to the new price. If force (1) is greater than force (2), total revenue will increase; and total revenue will increase only if marginal revenue is positive. This relationship between total revenue and marginal revenue can be shown using Figure 2.5. As shown, $\Delta Q = Q_2 - Q_1$ and $\Delta P = P_1 - P_2$ where P_1 is the initial price, P_2 is the new (lower) price, Q_1 is the (smaller) sales quantity at P_1, Q_2 is the (larger) sales quantity at price P_2, ΔQ is the unit increase in sales as price falls from P_1 to P_2, and ΔP is the decrease in price necessary to increase sales by ΔQ. It can be shown that marginal revenue is

$$MR = P_2 - \frac{Q_1 \Delta P}{\Delta Q} \qquad (2.7)$$

If $\Delta Q = 1$, we see that MR is positive only when the revenue generated from the new price is greater than the loss in revenue resulting from marking down all previously salable items.

Price elasticity and marginal revenue

We can also show that the relation between marginal revenue and price elasticity of demand is given by

$$MR = P_1(1 + \frac{1}{E_d}) = P_1 \frac{E_d + 1}{E_d} \qquad (2.8)$$

This relationship between marginal revenue and price elasticity of demand has been used by the United States Postal Service to justify its postage rates. When applied to rate setting, this relation has been called the *inverse elasticity rule*.[4]

---

[4]For an informative analysis of Postal Service pricing see Jess S. Boronico, "Postal Service Pricing Subject to Reliability Constraints on Service Quality," *Pricing Strategy & Practice* 5, no. 2 (1997), 80–93; Jess S. Boronico, "Ratemaking for Postal Services: A Stochastic Marginal Cost Pricing Model," *Journal of Product & Brand Management Featuring Pricing Strategy & Practice* 7, no. 4 (1998), 342–53.

FIGURE 2.5
Price–Quantity
Demanded
Relationship

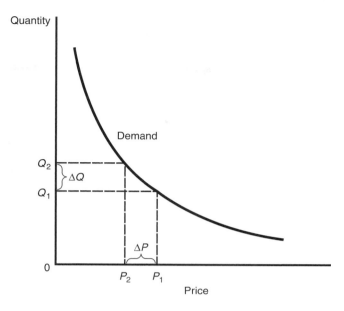

TABLE 2.3 **Relationship between Revenues and Price Elasticity**

Price–Demand Relationship	Value of Ed	Marginal Revenue When Price Increases	Marginal Revenue When Price Decreases
Negative	$-1 < E_d < 0$	Positive	Negative
Negative	$E_d = -1$	Zero	Zero
Negative	$-\infty < E_d < -1$	Negative	Positive
Positive	$0 < E_d < 1$	Positive	Negative
Positive	$E_d = 1$	Positive	Negative
Positive	$1 < E_d < \infty$	Positive	Negative

Historically, first-class mail has been the most price inelastic class of mail. Since all classes of mail have been price inelastic, price increases will result in increases in total revenue (positive marginal revenue) as shown in Table 2.2. Because first-class mail is the most inelastic, a 3-cent price increase per ounce will produce most of the needed new mail revenues. As a result, the postage rates for other classes of mail usually do not increase by as large a percentage as first-class mail.

Thus, marginal revenue varies with price and with the price elasticity of demand. Table 2.3 shows the relationship between revenues and price elasticity for both the negative price–demand relationship and the implied positive price–demand relationship from the price–quality studies discussed in Chapters 5 through 7. As Table 2.3 indicates, for the generally assumed negative price–quantity demanded relationship, revenues will increase if price increases and demand is price inelastic; revenues will fall if price increases and demand is price elastic. But, if buyers infer quality in the product or service on the basis of price and thereby perceive a higher-priced item as more attractive, a positive price–quantity demanded relationship ensues and an increase in price will increase revenues. To determine the effects of changing price on demand, a method of estimating the price–volume relationship is required. Some commonly used methods of estimating the price-volume relationship are discussed in Chapter 9.

Consumers' Surplus

As Figure 2.5 indicates some consumers are usually willing to pay more than any particular price in order to acquire a given product. This means that the price charged for the product is lower than those buyers' *perceived value* for the product. The difference between the maximum amount consumers are willing to pay for a product and the amount they actually pay is called *consumers' surplus*: the money value of the willingness of consumers to pay more than the price. This difference represents what the consumers gain from the trade. The difference is the money amounts of *value-in-use* minus *value-in-exchange*; for voluntary exchanges this is always positive. Value-in-use always exceeds value-in-exchange simply because the most consumers would pay must be greater than what they actually pay—otherwise they would not agree to the trade.

Figure 2.6 illustrates the concept of consumer surplus. In the figure, for price P_1, the amount demanded is Q_1. The area under the demand curve above the line P_1A represents the consumers' gain from acquiring Q_1 units at price P_1. Note that the total area under the entire demand curve represents the *total willingness to pay* across all consumers (value-in-use). The total willingness to pay at price P_1 is the total area under the demand curve to the left of the vertical line AQ_1. The value-in-exchange is the area of the rectangle Q_1AP_1O, while consumers' surplus is the cross-hatched area above

FIGURE 2.6
Consumers' and Sellers' Surplus

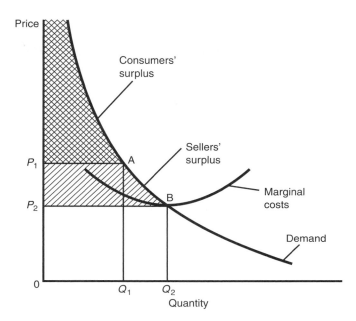

this rectangle. Consumers' surplus, then, is the consumers' net gain from trade.

Sellers, like consumers, will only engage in trade if they can realize a net gain from the transaction. Since any price above the seller's long-run marginal costs represents a profit surplus, the extent that the trade is profitable to the seller is given by P_1ABP_2, the area in Figure 2.6 above the quantity sold at the price that equals marginal cost, P_2. This area represents the seller's gain from the transactions and is called *sellers' surplus*.

We will return to the concept of consumers' surplus in Chapter 8. The important point now is that the price at which exchange takes place is not the equivalent of value as is so often assumed. Total willingness to pay (value-in-use) is comprised of value-in-exchange and consumers' surplus. This latter concept becomes an important consideration in the determination of prices. Rather than concentrating on the cost considerations when setting price, we must determine potential customers' perceived value-in-use and price accordingly. Indeed, this relationship between price and perceived value represents an important area of consumer research.

SUMMARY

This chapter has briefly reviewed the economic theory of price determination and has discussed some economic concepts useful for analyzing pricing alternatives. These concepts, in and of themselves, have limited usefulness for price determination. However, when they are extracted from the theoretical domain and applied within the constraints of reality, they are important analytical tools. The concepts of elasticity and marginal revenue are very important, but they must be applied to decisions affecting the future, where uncertainty prevails.

Two additional factors complicate the use of economic theory in pricing decisions: the assumption that all factors will remain constant and the difficulty of estimating demand. Economists often employ the Latin phrase *ceteris paribus* (literally, "other things being equal") when proposing economic models. In moving from theory to application, however, price setters find that in the real world, other things do not remain the same. Many factors change because of environmental influences beyond their control, or they change their goals, strategies, and tactics.

Estimates can be thrown off by the unexpected influence of an environmental factor. Competitors may unexpectedly change their prices or advertising expenditures; members of the distribution channel may exert pressure for additional discounts. The assumption that such factors will be constant is rarely borne out by reality; consequently, pricing decisions cannot be based on that condition. In addition to changes arising from the environment, certain factors change because of what marketers do with other elements of the marketing mix—such as improving their products, expanding their distribution systems, or increasing their budgets for advertising and promotion.

Understanding the economic environment for pricing decisions is an important part of effective pricing. No economic theory captures the complexity of practical pricing problems or provides an exact solution for solving them, but economic theory provides some useful insights and perspectives that are helpful in finding appropriate solutions.

Discussion Questions

1. If a business firm does not seek to maximize profits, what are some alternative objectives?

2. For each profit objective listed in Question 1, what do you think is the role of price? For each of these objectives, what might be the behavioral objectives of the managers of the firm?

3. Assume a firm makes three products A, B, and C. Assume also that the profit equation for this firm is given by

$$\text{Profits} = (P_1 - c_1)Q_1 + (P_2 - c_2)Q_2 + (P_3 - c_3)Q_3 - f$$

where P_i is price, c_i is variable cost, Q_i is volume sold at price P_i, and f is fixed costs ($i = 1, 2, 3$). If the firm wishes to increase profits, what elements of the equation can it attempt to change? List as many changes as possible. Holding other factors the same, what would be the impact if (a) the firm could increase price by 1 percent; (b) the firm could reduce variable costs by 1 percent; or (c) the firm could reduce fixed costs by 1 percent? Which of these three changes would have the most effect on profitability? Why?

4. A manufacturer of DVD players sold 500,000 units in year 1 at a price of $500 each. In year 2, the price was reduced to $390, and 700,000 units were sold. In year 3, the price was reduced to $250 and 1.2 million units were sold. Calculate the historical price elasticity of demand for each price change.

5. What do you think happened to the cost of producing a unit of the DVD player in Question 4 when annual production increased from 500,000 units in year 1 to 1.2 million in year 3? Explain your reasoning.

6. Can you think of some products for which demand would be (a) income elastic and (b) income inelastic?

7. In Question 6, what would be the role of price for a product that is income elastic?

8. Distinguish between the concepts of value-in-use and value-in-exchange.

Suggested Readings

Devinney, Timothy M., ed.: *Issues in Pricing: Theory and Research* (Lexington, MA: D.C. Heath, 1988).

Dickson, Peter, and Joel E. Urbany: "Retailer Reactions to Competitive Price Changes," *Journal of Retailing, 70* no. 1, (1994), 1–20.

Lindberg, Kreg, and Bruce Aylward: "Price Responsiveness in the Developing Country Nature Tourism Context: Review and Costa Rican Case Study," *Journal of Leisure Research, 31* no. 3, (1999), 281–99.

Tellis, Gerard J.: "Beyond the Many Faces of Price: An Integration of Pricing Strategies," *Journal of Marketing, 50* (October 1986), 146–60.

CHAPTER THREE

The Economics of Information

One of the most important assumptions of the economic theory we outlined in Chapter 2 is that buyers and sellers have perfect information. That is, buyers are fully informed about prices of all goods and services in the market, their tastes and preferences, and their budget constraints. Similarly, sellers are fully informed: They know the demand schedules for their products (the amount buyers will purchase at each possible price), their costs, and their supply schedules (the amount they will produce and sell at each possible price). Moreover, in a competitive environment, the seller either is just one of many sellers with no ability to influence market price or is one of a small number of sellers with an ability to influence market price. The situation with few sellers still assumes that sellers have perfect information about demand and supply conditions in setting price. Finally, sellers know who their competitors are and the likely pricing behavior of these competitors.

Usually, however, neither sellers nor buyers have perfect information—and both parties are incapable of perfectly processing the information that is available to them. As a result, we need to develop an approach for understanding how buyers and sellers might behave in an imperfect information environment. One important reason that pricing managers make incorrect decisions is because they make assumptions about how customers and competitors behave without sufficient evidence that these assumptions are valid. Some of these assumptions are based on the economic theory outlined in Chapter 2. Other assumptions are based on observations of past customer or competitor behavior that no longer reflect the way these players behave. Another reason for managers' poor pricing decisions is they misinterpret (misread) market information about their customers and competitors. In this chapter, we discuss information as a valuable resource. We will establish that the actual behavior of buyers and sellers in the market provides important information for pricing. Thus managers must learn to update this information continuously to avoid illusions about what actually is happening in their markets.

Despite evidence (summarized later in this chapter) about the extent to which buyers search for lower prices, managers tend to assume that the segment of price-vigilant, smart, or rational buyers is large and mobile. They also assume implicitly that these buyers are perfect information processors who learn quickly and efficiently where the best buys are. Because of these assumptions, managers infer that their markets are more sensitive to price reductions than they actually are. As a result, managers are more concerned with competitors' pricing decisions than with influences upon their customers' buying decisions. The prospect of losing market share may motivate them to follow competitor price reductions and to avoid price increases.[1] They also assume that customers gained through price promotions become loyal, repeat customers, leading to long-term profitability. These assumptions account for a number of anomalies in the way sellers set prices.

Some Pricing Anomalies

The laws of supply and demand introduced in Chapter 2 indicate that when demand increases, *ceteris paribus*, prices will increase until the amount demanded again equals the amount supplied. Thus when the economy experiences strong growth (that is, when demand for goods and services is increasing), when seasonal increases in demand occur, or when buyers' purchasing activities increase, (such as at Christmas or on weekends), we would normally expect price increases to reflect the increases in demand. On the contrary, however, price wars are likely to break out in boom periods, prices for food products with strong seasonal demand tend to decline at seasonal quantity peaks and rise during off-peak periods, retail price promotions tend to occur predominately on weekends

---

[1]Joel E. Urbany and Peter R. Dickson, "Competitive Price-Cutting Momentum and Pricing Reactions," *Marketing Letters 2* no. 4 (1991), 393–402.

EXAMPLES OF PRICE ANOMALIES

BOX 3.1

1. In spring 1992, the U.S. Commerce Department reported that the economy had experienced one full year of economic recovery from the previous recession. However, candy makers, supermarkets, hotel chains, car rental agencies, and many other companies in a wide range of industries were still cutting prices even as demand was increasing. Indeed, one economist indicated that companies were more interested in maintaining market share than in achieving price increases. One marketing executive said the price cuts were to "jump start" demand.

2. In June 1997, *Beverage Digest* reported that prices at supermarkets for leading soft drink brands fell an average of 3 to 4 percent in the 12 weeks ending May 4. The government's estimate of soft drink prices for April was down 2.5 percent from a year earlier—the lowest for the

month since 1994. A spokesperson for a major investment firm said that the prices were inconsistent with an economy that was growing and with the lowest rate of unemployment in 20 years.

3. Every November, supermarket managers know that nearly 100 million households in the United States will purchase a turkey for Thanksgiving. Yet, supermarkets across the country will advertise that they have the lowest turkey prices in the area. Turkey prices fall, supermarkets lose money on every turkey they sell, and managers swear they won't do it again—until next year!

Sources: Bill Saporito, "Why the Price Wars Never End," *Fortune* (March 23, 1992), 68–78; "The Latest Mad Plunge of the Price Slashers," *Business Week* (May 11, 1992), 36; "Soft Drink Price War Could Fizzle," *Chicago Tribune* (June 12, 1997).

(Friday to Sunday), and pre-Christmas markdowns tend to exceed post-Christmas markdowns.[2] (See Box 3.1.)

Figure 3.1 illustrates the pattern of retail price changes over the days of the week. The data, which show the percentage price changes, indicate that prices fall as the weekend approaches and are at their lowest levels on Fridays and Saturdays. This weekend–holiday interaction is strongest the weekend following Thanksgiving. Indeed, the researchers found that one-third of all products that experienced a markdown during the observation period were marked down the weekend following Thanksgiving and 22 percent of all price promotions occurred on Thanksgiving weekend. Overall, Thanksgiving weekend price promotions occurred over three times more often than normal promotion activity.

[2]Peter B. Pashigian and Brian Bowen, "Why Are Products Sold on Sale? Explanations of Pricing Regularities," *Quarterly Journal of Economics 105* (1991), 1015–1038; Elizabeth J. Warner and Robert B. Barsky, "The Timing and Magnitude of Retail Store Markups: Evidence from Weekends and Holidays," *Quarterly Journal of Economics 110* (May 1995), 321–52.

FIGURE 3.1   **Average Price Changes by Day of Week**

Source: Adapted with permission from Elizabeth J. Warner and Robert B. Barsky, "The Timing and Magnitude of Retail Store Mark-downs: Evidence from Weekends and Holidays," *Quarterly Journal of Economics 110* (May 1995), 321–352.

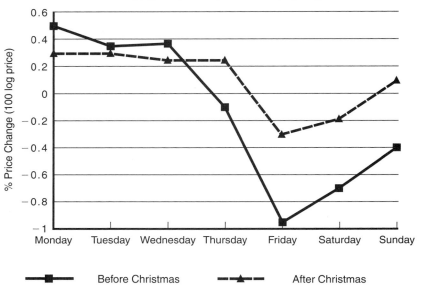

In another study covering food prices and seasonal demand peaks, for the 48 products studied feature displays were set up in 7.7 percent of the potential markets in the off-season, but in 25.7 percent of the markets during the peak months. The study used the percentage of a product's market in which promotional activity was conducted at least one week in a month as its measure of promotional activity. Mean coupon intensity also increased in the peak months—from 12.5 percent of the potential market to 30.2 percent and with 44 of the 48 products showing significant increases in coupon ads. Independent of the price reductions implied by the coupon activity, the shelf prices of 44 of the 48 seasonal products declined significantly. On average, volume increased by 199 percent and prices fell by 7.5 percent in the peak months compared to the off-peak averages. The price declines ranged between 3 percent and 15 percent. According to estimates, the mean price elasticity accounted for one-third of the seasonal demand increase. Thus 134 percent of the seasonal demand increase can be attributed to nonprice factors.[3]

[3]James M. MacDonald, "Demand, Information, and Competition: Why Do Food Prices Fall at Seasonal Demand Peaks?" *Journal of Industrial Economics 48* (March 2000), 27–45.

Possible Reasons for Observed Pricing Anomalies

Several explanations are possible for these observations: tacit oligopoly collusion, shoppers' increased search efficiencies, and changes in price elasticity of demand due to informative advertising.

Tacit Oligopoly Collusion

The kinked demand curve of oligopoly theory argues that the price setters in a market in which there are a few large competitors assume that if one of them reduces price, the other competitors will match the reduction, and no substantial increase in sales volume will occur for any seller. On the other hand, if one competitor raises price, the other competitors will not follow, and the firm raising price will lose a substantial amount of its sales volume. Thus prices are slow to change and competing firms remain in a somewhat tacit collusion.

Sellers are motivated, however, to reduce price individually and attempt to take a larger market share from their competitors. To prevent this tendency to "cheat," the other firms would retaliate by reducing their prices to the competitive level and eliminating the excess profits for all sellers. When demand increases, the market is larger and the potential rewards from cheating are greater. However, because the discounted value of the punishment remains the same (all sellers reduce prices to the competitive level), if the firm can preemptively capture a significant portion of the new growth in demand, it may achieve a net benefit from reducing price.

Shoppers' Search Efficiencies

Similar results would occur if buyers are not well informed about market conditions and, having made their best value choices, cease searching and remain loyal to a particular seller. If one firm reduces price and customers of other sellers do not know of this reduction, then there will be little increase in demand for the price-reducing firm, at least for a period of time. But if one firm raises price and its customers recognize the price increase, they will initiate a search for a better price–quality relationship, find out that other firms have not raised price, and switch to another seller. Thus, imperfect information would also make demand more elastic for price increases and inelastic for price decreases.

Informative Advertising

The economics of information explanation for pricing anomalies suggests that in periods of high demand, such as on weekends, during the Christmas season, and for seasonal products, people shop more intensively. When people are buying multiple products on weekends, multiple gifts per shopping trip, or seasonal food products, it is assumed they will invest more effort in information search to obtain the lowest price than if shopping for one product. If they search more intensively in these periods, then the price elasticity of demand should be greater. Thus sellers, believing that buyers are more vigilant at these times, increase their informational advertising and promotional expenditures. This increase in promotion and advertising provides more information for buyers, leading sellers again to perceive that demand is more price elastic. Consequently, sellers believe that price reductions will be necessary to sell successfully to these more price-sensitive buyers.

Summary

To be clear, these explanations of pricing anomalies are not mutually exclusive. We would expect that defections from collusive pricing would benefit the price-reducing firm if more buyers are aware of and respond to the price reductions. If retaliatory price reductions by other sellers occur after the demand surge has dissipated, the losses incurred by the price-reducing firm at this point will be smaller, and the net gain from the price-reduction strategy during peak demand could be positive. Because all sellers expect that at least one of them will reduce price and try to capture a larger market share, they all reduce their prices in these periods of peak demand and fail to achieve the increases in short-term profitability that would have been possible had they operated according to the laws of supply and demand.

Do Buyers Learn through Experience?

Perhaps the most intriguing aspect of this practice of reducing prices during peak demand periods is the sellers' assumption that buyers will increase their search activity, learn where the best values are, and become more price sensitive. Are buyers actually able to process the bewildering array of price and quality information provided by sellers and "learn" where to find the best value alternative? The information of economics theory that we review in the next section assumes that economic agents, buyers and sellers, can become optimal decision makers through a process of learning, or by *adaptive rationality*. This theory presumes that buyers do learn through experience and are able, perhaps over several purchase and use trials, to determine the product that best fits their needs at the lowest price in the market. That is, buyers are capable of unequivocally determining their best value.

Detecting a product's actual quality often is very difficult, however. Detecting quality by personal experience is limited by the cognitive, time and energy, and monetary resources available. Buyers typically cannot sample the variety of choices in either an exhaustive or systematic way. Some products, such as mattresses, may be purchased very infrequently and may not reveal their level of quality for a long period of time after purchase. Moreover, buyers may even experience different degrees of satisfaction with a product over separate trials. A very important limitation on their ability to use experience and external sources of quality and price information is the cognitive difficulty of integrating positive information (product attributes and benefits) with negative information (monetary cost or price) to determine the relative value of a particular alternative. Cognitively, the mental arithmetic required to integrate these pieces of information is very difficult and is subject to error and bias. In addition, given limited ability to remember details of previous experiences and the tendency to weigh recent experiences more heavily than more distant experiences, the cognitive processing of experiential information may be incomplete and incorrect.

An experiment designed to determine the ability of buyers to learn the best buys in a market situation through experience provides some important information on this issue.[4] The researchers categorized the potential market into four segments based on possible buyer learning patterns (see Table 3.1). Then, using a computerized market game, subjects made decisions to purchase a round-trip airline ticket from Los Angeles to London. Using two levels of on-time performance as the quality information (present or absent) and two levels of market share information (present or absent) for 10 airlines, the subjects were asked to make 24 decisions. After each decision, subjects were told the actual performance, the average price, the range of price, and the average on-time performance record for each airline. As Table 3.1 shows, 61.8 percent of the subjects exhibited no learning over time. Consequently, the aggregate market

[4]Jaideep Prabhu and Gerard J. Tellis, "Do Consumers Ever Learn? Analysis of Segment Behavior in Experimental Markets," *Journal of Behavioral Decision Making 13* no.1 (2000), 19–34.

TABLE 3.1 **Patterns of Buyer Learning**

Buyer Segment	Patterns of Learning Behavior	Size of Experimental Market
Learners	Buyers who begin with nonoptimal choices but move toward a best choice over trials	6.7%
Early learners	Buyers who make best choices from the beginning and continue to do so over trials	22.5
Nonlearners	Buyers who begin with nonoptimal choices and do not show significant improvement in choices over trials	61.8
Confused learners	Buyers who learn incorrect relationships or consistently use inappropriate cues or decision rules and do not show any consistent movement toward a best choice over trials	9.0

Source: Adapted from Jaideep Prabhu and Gerard J. Tellis, "Do Consumers Ever Learn? Analysis of Segment Behavior in Experimental Markets," *Journal of Behavioral Decision Making 13* no. 1 (2000), 19–34.

reflected the behavior of those who did not learn; the learners were too few to influence the behavior of the aggregate market. Experience was not cumulative; the most recent experience influenced choice.

The researchers' conclusions from this research are

1. Buyers do not make optimal purchase decisions when product quality is uncertain. They do not understand uncertain quality and misuse quality information.

2. All buyers do not behave the same way. Some buyers are able to make appropriate decisions from the beginning, and others learn with experience to make better decisions. The number of buyers who use wrong decision rules may be large enough to negate the influence of the informed buyers.

3. Buyers use heuristics and decision rules; they do not optimally integrate price and quality information. They give disproportionate weight to recent experience.

4. Limited support emerged for the hypothesis that the smart few (vigilant) buyers are able to discipline the market as generally assumed.

Economics of Information

In 1944, observing the purchase behavior of "friends and their wives," Tibor Scitovszky concluded that "more often than not people judge quality by price."[5] He also argued that judging quality on the basis of price in this way was rational behavior because it represented a belief that price was determined by the interplay of the forces of competitive supply and demand. That is, the forces of supply and demand would lead to a natural ordering of competing products on a price scale such that there would be a strong positive relationship between price and product quality.

Although buyers were assumed not to possess perfect knowledge about the capability of alternative products to satisfy their wants, it was assumed that they could process available information perfectly. Furthermore, buyers could objectively use price cues to infer product quality, assess the amount of want satisfaction derived from a given quality level, and optimize choice. Optimal choice was still determined by the trade-off between the marginal utility gained from a product choice and the utility sacrificed by paying the price. It was also implicitly assumed that buyers would acquire perfect information about actual quality after the initial choice and would continue purchasing only if the marginal utility gained was greater than or equal to utility sacrificed. Thus, it was natural for price to be an appropriate signal of product quality. Since then a number of studies have reported that the relationship between price and quality is inconsistent across products, and generally not as strong as would be expected given Scitovszky's reasoning.[6]

Stigler's Model

In 1961 George Stigler observed that economists traditionally had ignored the issue of differential information available to sellers and buyers.[7] The essence of Stigler's argument was that buyers inform themselves about prices in the

---

[5]Tibor Scitovszky, "Some Consequences of the Habit of Judging Quality by Price," *The Review of Economic Studies 12* (1944–45), 100.

[6]Eitan Gerstner, "Do Higher Prices Signal Higher Quality?" *Journal of Marketing Research 22* (May 1985), 209–215; Gerard J. Tellis and Birger Wernerfelt, "Competitive Price and Quality under Asymmetric Information," *Marketing Science 6* (Summer 1987), 240–53.

[7]George Stigler, "The Economics of Information," *Journal of Political Economy 69* (June 1961), 213–25.

marketplace until the marginal return from gathering more information equals or exceeds the marginal costs of doing the search. Because different buyers perceive different costs of and benefits from search, some buyers will be better informed than others. The existence of less-informed buyers allows some sellers to charge higher prices, leading to a spread or dispersion of prices for similar products in the market.

That is, the seller may know the quality of the product, but buyers do not know the quality until after purchase and use. In the interest of obtaining higher profits, a firm could set a high price that is not commensurate with the actual quality built into the product. Such a strategy could succeed only if buyers are unable to evaluate the product's attributes (and quality) prior to purchase or if buyers cannot completely evaluate the product after a single purchase (or even several purchases). In this situation the seller, but not buyers, has the information about a product's quality, a condition of asymmetric information. Thus an important question arises: When is it in the interest of the firm to signal to the marketplace the quality of its product using price, advertising, warranties, or other signals? We will discuss this managerial issue in Chapter 4.

Essentially, Stigler's argument provided an explanation for why we might observe a spread of prices for similar products in the market. Initially it was assumed that the products were of equivalent quality, so the buyer needed only to determine the seller that offered the lowest price. Moreover, buyers were assumed to know the distribution of prices, and therefore the lowest price. The buyers' problem was to search across sellers to find that low price. Thus, since buyers knew the cost of additional search and the lowest price, they could determine the benefit of additional search. This benefit was the difference between the currently observed lowest price and the actual lowest price. If this potential decrease in price paid (benefit of search) is greater than the cost of additional search, then the buyer would continue to search. If not, then the buyer would cease searching and buy from the seller with the current lowest observed price. In essence this theory resembles searching on the Web for the lowest price for a specific product, assuming no quality differences across sellers. That is, a buyer using an online search to find the lowest price of a specific model of a SONY four-head VCR would fit the assumptions in the original Stigler model.

Nelson's Contribution

Phillip Nelson extended Stigler's model by analyzing a market situation with joint distributions of price and quality.[8] That is, quality varies over sellers for similar products. In some cases, as argued earlier by Scitovszky, price and quality would be highly correlated and price could be used to infer quality differences across sellers. Such an inference rule would be most applicable if buyers cannot judge quality until after purchase and use. Nelson observed that quality is more difficult to determine and therefore more costly to learn through search. Thus, when quality and price are both variable, buyers must assess the relative value of alternative products in the choice set.

In essence, buyers may learn about quality through *search,* through *experience*, or not at all. The degree that buyers might be price sensitive depends on the amount and type of information they have about the products or services they are considering buying. Thus, we have the proposition that the more information buyers have, or the easier it is for them to evaluate different offerings, the more price sensitive (elastic) they will be. To observe this relationship between buyers' ability to evaluate products before purchase and price elasticity, we can separate products and services into three classes: search products, experience products, or credence products.[9]

Search products or services have purchase-determining attributes that buyers can readily evaluate before purchase. An airline's schedule, a dentist's fees, and the relative quality of a television's reception can all be determined prior to making a purchase decision. To the extent that buyers attempt to acquire such information for these products, they are likely to be aware of the attributes of substitute products and hence more sensitive to price differences than other buyers (see Table 3.2).

[8]Phillip Nelson, "Information and Consumer Behavior," *Journal of Political Economy 78* (March–April 1970), 311–29; Phillip Nelson, "Advertising As Information," *Journal of Political Economy 81* (July–August 1974), 729–54.

[9]Louis Wilde, "The Economics of Consumer Information Acquisition," *Journal of Business 53* (July 1980), S143–58; Philip Nelson, "Comments on 'The Economics of Consumer Information Acquisition, *Journal of Business 53* (July 1980), S163–65. For more information about *credence goods*, those goods for which buyers cannot evaluate quality even after "consuming" them, see Michael R. Darby and Edi Karni, "Free Competition and the Optimal Amount of Fraud," *Journal of Law and Economics 16* (April 1973), 67–88.

TABLE 3.2 Search, Experience, and Credence Attributes

	Search Attribute	Experience Attribute	Credence Attribute
Definition	Can be evaluated before purchase	Can be evaluated only after purchase	Usually cannot be evaluated after receipt or use
Examples	Dentist's fees, air travel time, TV picture quality, stereo sound	Food taste, concert performance, dry cleaning, hair permanent	Legal advice, tax advice, health care
Therefore buyers may be. . .	more aware of substitutes	less aware of substitutes	not able to compare or evaluate alternatives
Sellers likely will. . .	imitate or copy successful features	be less able to copy successful features	be more likely to customize offerings
Therefore there will be. . .	more similar substitutes	fewer and less similar substitutes	fewer and more distinctive substitutes
Cross-price elasticity will be relatively. . .	high	moderate	low

Experience products or services have attributes that can be evaluated only after purchase and use. Thus buyers do not know exactly what they are getting when they first acquire the product. However, once the product has been purchased and experienced, buyers have an idea of the attributes and the degree to which they are satisfied with the value received. Experience products are likely to be more differentiated in the marketplace, and buyers will be less sensitive to price differences than for search products.

Finally, *credence products or services* have attributes that buyers cannot evaluate confidently even after one or more purchases. For credence products such as health care products and services and legal services, buyers must rely on the reputation of the seller; external cues such as brand, store name, or price as indicators of quality; or reputable external sources of information such as professional rating agencies. Buyers will be least sensitive to price differences for credence products.

Attributes of products subject to quality assessment prior to purchase are called *search attributes*. Attributes of products or services that can only be assessed after purchase and use are called *experience attributes*. For products whose purchase determining characteristics are primarily search attributes, Stigler's search behavior theory would apply. However, for products whose purchase-determining characteristics are primarily experience attributes, the appropriate search behavior is not as simple.

Implications for Buyers' Search Behaviors

If buyers know (or assume) that the relative distribution of satisfaction they will receive from each alternative product is the same, then by examining each product sequentially they can determine product quality. Their decision rule is as stated by Stigler: Obtain information until the marginal cost of getting more information about another product exceeds the expected marginal benefit of further search. Buyers can obtain this information either by search (acquiring information before purchase), or by experience (acquiring information by trying alternative products until finding the best choice). Buyers are more likely to acquire information by experience when the cost of a poor choice is relatively low, as with frequently purchased low-price items, or when product performance is difficult to judge before purchase.

For search products the incremental costs of search are the *out-of-pocket costs* of transportation and information access fees such as Internet charges and subscriptions for magazines and newspapers, plus the *opportunity costs* of the time required to find and evaluate another product. For experience products the incremental cost of search includes the costs of obtaining price information and product and supplier information (*access cost*). An additional cost is the cost of a misfit (*fit cost*), which is the difference in satisfaction received between the best product found after sampling some of the products and the expected average satisfaction received if only one product were chosen at random.[10] For either type of product, search would continue as long as the incremental cost of search is less than the additional benefits of continuing to search.

If buyers have made a satisfactory choice of search products, then there is little if any incentive to switch to another product in subsequent purchases, at least until market

---

[10]See Brian T. Ratchford, "Cost-Benefit Models for Explaining Consumer Choice," *Management Science 28* (February 1982), 197–212; Joel E. Urbany, "An Experimental Examination of the Economics of Information," *Journal of Consumer Research 13* (September 1986), 257–71; J. Yannis Bakos, "Reducing Buyer Search Costs: Implications for Electronic Marketplaces," *Management Science 43* (December 1997), 1676–92.

conditions change. For experience products, on the other hand, buyers would likely switch products in subsequent purchases until they have found the "best" product for them. Nelson suggests that the number of experience products sampled via actual trial would be relatively large for frequently purchased products. However, as with search products, once buyers have found their "best" experience product they would not switch to an alternative in subsequent purchases as long as market conditions do not change. As the incentive to search declines, the willingness to pay a specific price increases. That is, buyers are less inclined to switch to another product or supplier because of the likelihood that the fit cost would increase.

A number of questions relative to this conceptualization about buyer search need to be considered. First, do buyers search as much as implied by the conceptualization? Second, even if buyers believe there are relatively few or no differences in satisfaction between product choices, do they continue to search for the lowest-priced product? Third, are there differences between buyer prestore search and in-store search? Fourth, what is the relative role of direct product experience versus secondhand sources such as advertising, word of mouth, or independent agencies? Fifth, if they search sequentially, what are the implications of the actual sequence of prices they encounter? For example, if each successive price encountered in the search were lower than the previous price, would they be more likely to continue search than if each successive price encountered in the search were higher than the previous price? In the increasing price situation (or even in a random price sequence), when would a buyer stop further search and accept an earlier price that had been initially rejected? These five questions address issues of whether buyers behave as conceptualized and whether the actual price information encountered while searching influences the extent of search.

Sixth, if buyers are skeptical about advertising claims for experience attributes or difficult-to-verify benefits (quality), what can pricing managers do to overcome such skepticism? Seventh, what can buyers do to prevent firms from claiming high quality but instead providing low-quality products (that is, cheating)? Eighth, given all these issues, do managers believe that they and their competitors operate in market situations in which buyers actively and consistently search for the lowest-priced alternative? That is, what is the reality of buyer search behavior, and are pricing managers' beliefs and behaviors consistent with it or only with the conceptualization of buyer search behavior?

These issues about buyer search can be categorized into three broad categories. The first five questions refer to the extent that buyers search and the nature of their search behaviors. The sixth and seventh questions concern issues that arise when we recognize that not only do buyers and sellers have less than perfect information about prices and quality, but also that the amount and nature of information these parties to a transaction have differs (*asymmetric information* problem), leading to behaviors and consequences that the conceptualization just summarized does not consider. The eighth question addresses the issue of whether pricing managers make pricing decisions based on assumptions about buyer and competitor behavior that may not reflect how these other players in the pricing game may actually behave. We will consider the first and third issues next. We will develop the problem that asymmetric information poses to buyers and to pricing managers in Chapter 4.

Nature and Extent of Buyer Search

In general, the empirical research on buyer search provides some evidence that these models of search behavior adequately describe the behavior of some buyers. However, it is also clear that buyers do not necessarily search to the extent these models imply. Additional influences on price search include buyers' knowledge about products and market conditions (knowledgeable buyers utilize information available in their memory), expertise (ability to evaluate complex information), habit (earlier search activity provides sufficient information about prices, negating new or continuing search), relative brand uncertainty (uncertainty as to which brand is best), and the social returns from the search and shopping activity.[11] Further, the empirical evidence as to whether buyers are able to remember the prices of products they have purchased seems to question the premise that buyers know the distribution of prices for different products in the market place.

---

[11]Joel E. Urbany, Peter R. Dickson and Rosemary Kalapurakal, "Price Search in the Retail Grocery Market," *Journal of Marketing 60* (April 1996), 91–104; Sridhar Moorthy, Brian T. Rachford, and Debabrata Talukdar, "Consumer Information Search Revisited: Theory and Empirical Analysis," *Journal of Consumer Research 23* (March 1997), 263–77.

Prestore versus In-Store Search

Some research suggests that there is a need to distinguish between search to select a seller (prestore search) and search for the best choice within the store (in-store search). An additional issue is whether the buyer is making a single purchase (e.g., a new automobile) or multiple selections within a store or across stores during the same shopping trip. Since buyers often make multiple purchases during the same shopping trip (e.g., groceries), the cognitive cost of obtaining and processing price, quality, and quantity information for multiple items must be considered (the number of items purchased when grocery shopping may range from 20 to 48 items).[12] Evidence seems to indicate that for many buyers the opportunity costs of search, including time and effort, are relatively high.[13] Consequently, buyers may trade off the monetary benefits of search for such things as service quality and convenience of location.

It appears that buyers' information-gathering activities may focus more on the general pricing strategy and positioning of different retailers than on specific product price information. Thus buyers may focus more on prestore search information gathering than in-store and across-store price information. A clear implication of these findings is that buyers may be more responsive to price specials within the store because they intend to purchase the item and note that it is being price promoted. A relatively small percentage of buyers shop across stores for the specific price-promoted items within the different stores.[14] Moreover, it has been found that neighboring grocery stores matching each other on price are *unlikely* to share a high proportion of customers. Thus, price differentiation as a major reason for interstore search has little effect for identifying which stores are in close competition.[15]

---

[12]See Rosemary J. Avery, "Determinants of Search for Nondurable Goods: An Empirical Assessment of the Economics of Information Theory," *Journal of Consumer Affairs 30* (Winter 1996), 390–420.

[13]Dhruv Grewal and Howard Marmorstein, "Market Price Variation, Perceived Price Variation, and Consumers' Price Search Decisions for Durable Goods," *Journal of Consumer Research 21* (December 1994), 453–60.

[14]Francis J. Mulhearn and Daniel T. Padgett, "The Relationship between Retail Price Promotions and Regular Price Purchases," *Journal of Marketing 59* (October 1995), 83–90.

[15]Robert E. Stassen, John D. Mittelstaedt, and Robert A. Mittelstaedt, "Assortment Overlap: Its Effect on Shopping in a Retail Market When the Distributions of Prices and Goods Are Known," *Journal of Retailing 75* no. 3 (1999), 371–86.

Nelson's distinction between search and experience attributes suggests that buyers will engage in different types of search behaviors depending on whether the attributes that determine the purchase decision can be known before or after use. Valid search attribute information can be obtained by actual search or from secondhand sources such as advertising, word-of-mouth communications, government agencies, or buyer-oriented publications such as *Consumer Reports*. Experience attributes can only be verified by use of the product. In general, we would expect buyers to be more skeptical of advertising claims about experience attributes than search attributes. Current research results indicate that if the determinant attributes of a purchase are search attributes, then advertising could be an effective medium to communicate these attributes to buyers. However, if the determinant attributes are experience attributes, then various forms of in-store search would be more effective. Because in-store shopping is more experiential than home shopping or shopping on the Internet, it permits more sensory assessment of the product's quality. Thus unless buyers know that quality is consistent across a set of product options, they are more likely to engage in some form of in-store search for the price–quality combination that gives them the preferred level of value for products with purchase-determining experience attributes. To overcome this disadvantage of home or interactive shopping, research has shown that interactive home shopping systems that provide accessible price and quality information, as well as across-store price information, make it easier for buyers to choose products they will like. That is, transparency of information made the shopping task more enjoyable, facilitated purchase of products buyers like, and increased customer retention.[16]

Sequence of Price Information

Another important issue is whether the sequential order of price information influences buyers' decisions to stop or continue search. That is, the economics of information theory we have sketched does not consider that buyers might use the sequence of prices encountered as evidence that further search might produce an even lower price than has been observed. The sequence of prices encountered becomes an

---

[16]John G. Lynch, Jr., and Dan Ariely, "Wine Online: Search Costs Affect Competition on Price, Quality, and Distribution," *Marketing Science 19* (Winter 2000), 83–103.

important consideration when buyers do not actually know the distribution of prices, but instead infer the distribution from the prices encountered. Thus, if the prices encountered have been successively lower than previous prices, the buyer might infer that additional search would produce still lower prices. In a situation when the prices encountered have been successively higher than previous prices, the buyer might stop searching and return to the lowest price previously encountered. However, if the sequence of prices encountered is random, some higher than previous prices, some lower than previous prices, and some neither higher nor lower than some of the previous prices, the buyer might be uncertain as to whether to stop or continue searching. Thus it is important to recognize that prices do more than constrain behavior by affecting perceived costs or sacrifice. Prices also convey information about the potential costs or benefits of future behavior. Moreover, as pointed out in Chapter 1, the strategic role of price is that it provides information about what someone (e.g., the seller) thinks is the value of the offering.

Buyers' Information Search and Pricing Decisions

Suppose that the seller has incurred an increase in costs of producing and selling a product. Or suppose that the demand for its product has increased and now exceeds the firm's ability to produce sufficient quantities to meet this demand. In either of these situations, the theory we sketched in Chapter 2 would suggest that the firm should increase its prices either to recover the increase in costs (situation 1), or to take advantage of a shortage (situation 2). Yet it has been observed that prices do not change either as readily as we might expect when there are changes in costs or demand (i.e., changes in market conditions) or in directions predicted by the theory.

There are several explanations for why prices may not change as readily as we might expect. Broadly, if all participants were ignorant of market conditions we would expect prices to change slowly. If all participants are aware of market conditions, then prices would not change and there would be situations where demand exceeds supply: (1) buyers prefer to consume some products or services as a part of the crowd (restaurant meals, sporting events),[17] (2) underpricing some products is preferable only to allow certain

[17]Gary S. Becker, "A Note on Restaurant Pricing and Other Examples of Social Influence on Price," *Journal of Political Economy 99* (October 1991), 1109–16.

higher-income buyers to have access to them (preference to loyal customers), (3) the buyer's cost of waiting for the product or service is low relative to the seller's cost of continuously adjusting prices (ski lifts), or (4) increasing prices when demand exceeds supply might be considered unfair (a surprise snowstorm leads to a shortage of snow shovels). This phenomenon of "mispricing" may also be due to sellers' desires to preserve long-term profitable relationships with their customers who are not as well informed about the change in market conditions.[18]

One of the implications of the search behavior assumed in the economics of information is that once buyers have found their "best" choice they do not need to engage in search for subsequent purchases as long as market conditions do not change. That is, they have made an investment to ascertain the best value (best quality–price relationship) across alternative choices. Once buyers have determined this best value for themselves, they have valuable information. As long as they believe their information is correct, they have no need to invest in further search. Thus it is in the seller's interest to prevent current buyers from renewing a costly search. A seller can follow a number of strategies and tactics to provide reinforcing information to buyers that they have made a "best" choice. We will review these strategies in Chapter 4 when discussing signaling.

When buyers become aware that the price of a product or service they have been purchasing has increased, they may not understand the reason. The price increase may indicate that demand has increased (or supply has decreased), or it may indicate that there has been an upward shift in costs for all similar products. However, the buyers may not know which of these reasons is correct. So only by searching again will buyers know whether the price increase is general or specific to the product or service. While searching to determine why the price has been increased, buyers may find a product with a superior quality–price relationship and switch brands or suppliers. Now these switching customers have made some product-specific investments in searching and finding this second product, and it will be more costly for the original firm to get them to switch back. Therefore, forgoing an opportunity to increase price may be an acceptable

[18]David D. Haddock and Fred S. McChesney, "Why Do Firms Contrive Shortages? The Economics of Intentional Mispricing," *Economic Inquiry 32* (October 1994), 562–81.

opportunity cost for the firm to maintain a more valuable long-term loyal buyer.

Thus if (1) the value of maintaining customer loyalty is low, (2) the buyers perceive products to be homogeneous in quality, or (3) the opportunity cost of forgoing the price increase is relatively high, then the firm would be more likely to raise its price. There may be logical reasons, then, why firms do not exhibit the profit-maximizing behavior prescribed by conventional economic theory. A compelling reason is the recognition of the value of loyal customers over a long-term period, and one way of maintaining loyalty is to communicate or signal to these customers the nature of market conditions. Similarly to maintain competitive stability in the market, short-term price decreases due to excess supply or temporary reduction in costs should be signaled to customers and to competitors to avoid either set of individuals from misinterpreting the reasons for the price adjustment.

Do Managers Misread Buyer Search?

As summarized above, buyers apparently do not search for price and quality information nearly as much as assumed in economics of information theory. Further, as we will review in Chapters 5 and 6, buyers seem to find it difficult to recall the prices they have paid for recent purchases. Recognizing this empirical evidence, theorists suggest that markets are comprised of two segments of buyers: buyers who actively search for price information (price vigilants), and buyers who do not search. This price-vigilant segment of buyers will know when price differentials across competing sellers are inconsistent with quality differentials (that is, where the "best" buys are), and they will also know when market conditions change (prices change). If this price-vigilant segment is sufficiently large, then demand for a seller's products will be relatively more price elastic. That is, the price-vigilant segment effectively disciplines the market via its price monitoring activities.

SUMMARY

It should be clear from this discussion about how buyers and sellers actually seem to behave that both parties are operating with imperfect information about prices, quality, and the reasons for the behavior of either sellers or buyers. To deal with the uncertainties created by imperfect information, sellers make assumptions about how rival sellers might behave, and sellers also make assumptions about how buyers search for and are sensitive to price information. Similarly, buyers make inferences about the sellers' behaviors based on information they acquire about prices, product quality, and the sellers themselves.

At any one point in time it is likely each participant to a transaction—seller or buyer—knows more about their own behavior and intentions than does the other party to the transaction. When one side to a potential transaction has more information than the other, it is called *asymmetric information*. While asymmetry of information is more likely to occur in relatively new situations—a firm dealing with a buyer for the first time or a buyer purchasing a difficult to evaluate product—it is likely to be present in some degree in most transactions. In Chapter 4 we will discuss the effect that asymmetry of information may have on pricing.

Perhaps the most important message of this chapter is that information has strategic value. By effectively managing information, the firm has a better opportunity to succeed in the marketplace. Another important message of this chapter is that it is necessary for firms to do more research on the role that price information plays in buyers' behaviors. Too often, pricing managers assume that buyers actively search for lower prices with a greater frequency than they actually do. Also, because managers assume that more buyers search for lower prices than actually do, they then assume that these buyers are more sensitive to price differences and to price changes than they actually are. Furthermore, without good pricing research, pricing managers do not know which of their products are truly price elastic and which ones are price inelastic.

Discussion Questions	1. What assumptions from traditional economic theory are relaxed in the economics of information theory? Why is this theoretical development important for pricing management?
	2. Why were Scitovszky's observations about buyer behavior important? What different streams of research emerged based on his observations?
	3. What were the essential contributions of Stigler and Nelson?
	4. Define the following concepts, giving examples of each, and explain the implications of each on price elasticity of demand: (a) search attributes, (b) experience attributes, (c) credence attributes.
	5. What are the different types of search costs that buyers incur?

6. What do we know about the nature and extent of buyer search?

7. What are some reasons why prices in the marketplace often do not seem to follow the laws of supply and demand? Can you provide some examples of such pricing anomalies?

8. What are some reasons why buyers might not learn the actual product price–quality relationships after purchase and use?

Suggested Readings

Lynch, John G. Jr., and Dan Ariely: "Wine Online: Search Costs Affect Competition on Price, Quality, and Distribution," *Marketing Science 19* (Winter 2000), 83–103.

MacDonald, James M.: "Demand, Information, and Competition: Why Do Food Prices Fall at Seasonal Demand Peaks?" *Journal of Industrial Economics 48* (March 2000), 27–45.

Prabhu, Jaideep, and Gerard J. Tellis: "Do Consumers Ever Learn? Analysis of Segment Behavior in Experimental Markets," *Journal of Behavioral Decision Making 13,* no. 1, (2000), 19–34.

Urbany, Joel E., Peter R. Dickson, and Rosemary Kalapurakal: "Price Search in the Retail Grocery Market," *Journal of Marketing 60* (April 1996), 91–104.

Warner, Elizabeth J., and Robert B. Barsky: "The Timing and Magnitude of Retail Store Markups: Evidence from Weekends and Holidays," *Quarterly Journal of Economics 110* (May 1995), 321–52.

CHAPTER FOUR

Signaling and Managing Competition

You do not have to blow another's light out to let yours shine.

Bernard Baruch

In this chapter we continue our development of the economics of information. We now consider the situation when one side to a potential transaction has more information than the other. Information asymmetry has important implications for both the terms of a transaction and the relationship between parties in the transaction. For example, when buyers lack information about the quality of a product that the seller knows, how can the seller communicate the level of quality in the product through its behavior? It is possible that buyers may infer the level of quality based on the price set by the seller; that is, a relatively high price would imply a relatively high-quality product. Or the buyer may infer that a warranty indicates a high-quality product, especially if similar products have either a weaker warranty or none at all.

In each of these examples the seller has provided a *signal* to the buyer about the relative quality of its products. If the seller knows that buyers infer quality on the basis of price, the reputation of the brand name or store name, or the strength of the expressed warranty, then it could set a high price for its product, invest in advertising to build a reputable name, or include a strong warranty for the product to convey the level of quality. However, providing a high-quality product may be more costly than providing a low-quality product, and complying with the provisions of an expressed warranty may be costly if the product is not of high quality. Hence if the seller believes that the short-term strategy of signaling high quality, but actually providing low quality, is more profitable than the long-term profits from providing high quality, it might decide to cheat and provide low quality even though it is signaling high quality. There are two broad solutions to this information asymmetry problem: The seller may use *signals* or behaviors that reveal the actual quality provided, or the buyers may use *incentives* to persuade the seller not to cheat.

Information asymmetry problems can occur in two forms. First, *adverse selection* occurs when one party claims that it has the capability to provide high quality, yet actually lacks the skills or commitment to do so. Adverse selection would occur when the seller's unobservable quality does not change from one transaction to another. Second a *moral hazard* may occur when the seller can change quality from one transaction to another. A moral hazard may also occur if the seller offers a full replacement warranty and the buyer does not provide proper care and maintenance of the product. Adverse selection and moral hazard problems are of concern both to buyers, who cannot evaluate the quality of a product or service prior to purchase, and for sellers whose strategies are based on quality, but whose offerings cannot be distinguished by uninformed people from low-quality ones. Adverse selection problems can be solved by signals, whereas moral hazard problems can be solved by incentives.[1] We will discuss the adverse selection problem first.

Adverse Selection

Information asymmetry exists when buyers cannot detect product quality prior to purchase and use, as is the case with experience or credence products. (See Box 4.1 for the classic example of the used car market.) If the seller cannot change quality from one transaction to another, then buyers

---

[1]Amna Kirmani and Akshay R. Rao, "No Pain, No Gain: A Critical Review of the Literature on Signaling Unobservable Quality," *Journal of Marketing, 64* (April 2000), 66–79.

THE LEMONS PROBLEM—THE MARKET FOR USED CARS

BOX 4.1

In the market for used cars, the current owners of used cars know more about the quality of cars offered for sale than potential buyers do. Some used cars are of excellent quality, but others are not—they are lemons. When the quality of a used car can be assessed prior to purchase, there will be two markets: one for high-quality used cars and one for low-quality used cars. Some buyers pay a low price and obtain a low-quality car. Other buyers pay a high price and obtain a high-quality car. We have two separate markets.

However, when the quality cannot be determined prior to purchase, buyers cannot tell the difference between the cars and will pay only a low price; only a single market emerges. Consequently, owners of high-quality cars will not offer their cars for sale, and only lemons will appear in the used car market. Adverse selection occurs when the price buyers are willing to pay is less than the price that owners of high-quality used cars are willing to supply.

Source: George A. Akerlof, "The Market for 'Lemons': Quality Uncertainty and the Market Mechansim," *Quarterly Journal of Economics 84* (August 1970), 488–500.

may learn the actual level of quality after the initial transaction, and the asymmetry information problem disappears.[2]

How can the seller provide information to the market about its product or service? Specifically, a *signal* is a piece of information that can be revealed to the market *at some cost to the provider*. A signal is an observable, alterable (by the seller) characteristic that may affect buyers' assessments of product quality. For this external cue to be perceived as a signal, there must be

1. Observable differences in the product characteristic or cue across sellers.

2. Differences between the low-quality and high-quality sellers in the cost of providing the cue.

3. Perceptions of product quality in the market that vary directly with the characteristic or cue.

---

[2]However, if the level of quality provided remains ambiguous to buyers after the initial trial, then the signals must be repeated at least until buyers are sufficiently knowledgeable about the relative quality competing sellers provide. There are several reasons why information about product quality may remain ambiguous to buyers over time. Information becomes obsolete and brand qualities change. Furthermore, buyers enter and exit to and from the market, and some buyers may have a relatively long no-buy period before purchasing again.

This third requirement is critical because if buyers know the quality does not vary as the signal varies, then the quality signal will not be credible.

Strategically, signaling is viable when a high-quality firm can be more profitable using signals than not using signals, and simultaneously, a low-quality firm cannot be profitable using signals to deceive buyers about its quality. Under these conditions, the product market naturally separates into two markets: a low-quality and a high-quality market. Then it becomes rational for buyers to infer that these signals can be used to judge the relative quality of products in the market.

To ensure that the low-quality seller cannot make short-term profits by setting a high price and falsely signaling high quality, the high-quality seller must be willing to set a high price that is less than what quality conscious buyers might be willing to pay. This sacrifice in profit margin is one type of signaling cost and is incurred as a reduction in revenues for each unit sold.

Types of Quality Signals

As Table 4.1 indicates, quality signals can be classified according to whether the seller incurs the signal cost regardless of whether it fails to perform as promised (default independent), or whether it incurs the cost only when it fails to perform as promised (default contingent). For example, investing in advertising to build a reputation, extensive unique store decorations that have the firm's insignia (which have little or no salvageable value), or a new production facility all represent expenditures that are both cash intensive and are incurred prior to any sales. Other signal costs that occur regardless of whether the firm fails to meet its promise include price reductions or temporary sales-related expenditures such as coupons or allowances.

Some signal costs are incurred only if the firm fails to deliver on its promise. Warranties and money-back guarantees are commonly used to signal quality, and the firm incurs a cost only if the product fails to perform as warranted or the customer fails to be satisfied with the product or service. Using a high price to signal quality may sacrifice revenues by limiting the quantity sold, and cheating on quality would damage the reputation of the brand, store, or corporate name, risking future revenues.

TABLE 4.1 Types of Quality Signals

	Default-Independent Signals		Default-Contingent Signals	
	Sale Independent	**Sale Dependent**	**Revenue Risking**	**Cost Incurring**
Examples	Investment in Advertising Brand equity Store name Reputation Store/facility decorations Customer contact employees uniforms Capital expenditures	Low introductory price Temporary price reductions Distribution allowances (performance related)	High price Umbrella branding Product/brand bundling	Warranties Money-back guarantees
Type	Publicly visible expenditures prior to transactions	Private expenditures related to sales transactions	Future revenues at risk	Future costs at risk
Nature of signal cost	Sunk (incurred prior to transactions)	Varies with sales or type of performance	Future (opportunity cost)	Future (varies with actual quality)
Benefits to buyers	Indirect	Direct	Indirect	Direct
Use when	Buyers cannot be easily identified	Buyer segments can be identified	Products reveal quality quickly	Products reveal quality over periods of time
Desired buyer behavior	Repeat purchase Word-of-mouth recommendations	Repeat purchase Word-of-mouth recommendations	Repeat purchase Word-of-mouth recommendations	Word-of-mouth recommendations
Potential for buyer abuse (moral hazard)	No	Yes	No	Yes

Source: Adapted with permission from Amna Kirmani and Akshay R. Rao, "No Pain, No Gain: A Critical Review of the Literature on Signaling: Unobservable Product Quality," *Journal of Marketing 64* (April 2000), 66–79.

Low Price versus High Price

Several examples of quality signals in Table 4.1 require additional explanation. When a seller without a reputable brand name initially introduces a high-quality new product to the market, it faces a dilemma, especially if the product has quality-determining attributes that are unobservable or difficult to evaluate prior to purchase and use. This seller could engage in an extensive advertising campaign to introduce the product; however, since buyers are naturally skeptical of advertised claims of superior performance, especially by an

THE AMERICANIZATION OF THE HONDA ACCORD

BOX 4.2

They slipped into the United States a few at a time. They were unobtrusively painted silver grey, desert sand, and other bland colors and blended into traffic with barely a notice. They were small and few in number at first, but their numbers grew each year. Gradually, they got bigger until they were as large as the cars that were made in the United States. After 20 years, there were many of them and it did not matter where they were made because no one could tell the difference. By 1989, the Honda Accord had become the best-selling car in the United States.

The Honda Accord was the third automobile that Honda introduced into the United States. The other two, the Honda N-600 and the original Civic, were small, undersized, underpowered, and unsafe. But, starting with the Accord, every new Honda got better and better. Over time, the perceived quality of the

Honda Accord became so strong that even Honda lawnmowers and motorcycles competed with the high-quality brands in their product categories. Now this perceived quality of Honda products enables the company to receive premium prices for its products. Despite the relatively high prices of the Honda cars, people still buy them, giving Honda exceptional profits that are invested into improving its products. Honda has gone from making cheap cars that were not very good to making cars that are very good and relatively expensive. Honda's strategy for the Accord was to first invest in producing high-quality cars at relatively low prices and then, as its reputation for quality developed, the market was willing to pay premium prices.

Source: Jerry Knight, "Detroit Can't Read Honda's Map," *Roanoke Times and World News* (January 14, 1990), F2, F5.

unknown seller, they might be leery about purchasing the product. Thus, the seller would be faced with the difficult task of using a high price to signal quality when entering the market. But, if a substantial number of buyers are willing to pay a low price for a product they believe is low quality, then this high-quality seller may enter the market using an introductory low-price tactic to get members from this relatively large market for low quality to try the product. If the actual quality is revealed quickly, then the buyers would be able to determine that the product is of high quality and transmit this information to other buyers who have not yet tried the product through repeat purchase and word-of-mouth communications.[3] Once it becomes known that the product is of high quality, the seller would be able to remove the introductory low-price offer and credibly sell and promote the high-quality product at the target high price (see Box 4.2). We will

[3]Peter W. Kennedy, "Word-of-Mouth Communication and Price as a Signal of Quality," *The Economic Record 70* (December 1994), 373–80.

return to this introductory price tactic and provide implementation guidelines in Chapter 6.

Alternatively, to introduce a high-quality product at a high price, a number of conditions must be met. First, the size of the low-price, low-quality market must be sufficiently large that it would be unprofitable for a low-quality firm to forgo profitable low-price sales in order to offer a low-quality product at a high price. Second, the high-quality product seller must set a high price that is below the actual value of the product (representing a signaling cost). Third, the seller should be reputed as a provider of high-quality products and services. In addition, several other tactics can be used to supplement the high-price strategy.

Brand Equity

Brand equity represents the value of the brand name to the buyer. Brand equity commonly has been associated with the relative level of quality provided; that is, brands perceived to be of high quality are assumed to have relatively more brand equity. However, it is perhaps more correct to think of brand as a signal of the relative quality level provided by the seller. For example, Hyatt, Marriott, and Hilton brand names may provide buyers with a signal of quality for a given level of lodging, whereas Motel 6, La Quinta, and Econo Lodge provide a signal of a different level of quality. That is, buyers have a reasonable expectation about the quality of lodging to expect from each of these providers.

As signals of relative product positions, brands may credibly signal buyers about relative quality-producing attributes. By revealing the expected quality level, a brand name reduces buyers' information search and information processing costs, as well as perceived risk.[4] Thus it is important for firms to communicate to buyers that they are committed to maintaining their brand name through a consistent marketing mix and consistent delivery of quality over time (see Box 4.3). Indeed, consumers learn more about quality through actual experience than direct or indirect communications. The consistency of current claims about quality with buyers' experiences will have an important effect on the credibility of the firm's claims and the effectiveness of its quality signals.

---

[4]Lawrence Wu, "The Pricing of a Brand Name Product: Franchising in the Motel Services Industry," *Journal of Business Venturing 14* (January 1999), 87–102.

USING CONSISTENT QUALITY SIGNALS

BOX 4.3

In 1988 and 1989, two firms introduced skin moisturizers into their line of cosmetics. Estee Lauder launched Future Perfect in spring 1988, and Ultima II launched Megadose in spring 1989. As shown in the table, both products were priced similarly, significantly higher than the other moisturizers in the market (price per ounce for five other brands ranged between $8.13 and $1.70). Future Perfect was successful, but Megadose experienced disappointing sales.

Skin moisturizers are an example of experience products because it is difficult to assess product quality even after multiple applications. Moreover, users of these products have relatively high perceived social risk because an unattractive face is undesirable. Research to determine reasons for the differential success of these two products revealed some important differences in how the two sellers implemented the tactic of signaling quality. (Chemical analysis found no significant quality differences between the seven brands in the market.)

Brand	Price ($ per oz.)	Perceived Advertising	Perceived Packaging	Perceived Brand Name	Store Display
Future Perfect (Estee Lauder)	25.10	4.6 (81%)	4.1 (72%)	Reputation for quality	Prime location, glass enclosed counter
Megadose (Ultima II)	24.20	1.8 (16%)	2.2 (22%)	New brand name	Rear location smaller space

A sample of female consumers rated the quality of the advertising and packaging of the two products. The global ratings were significantly stronger for Future Perfect. Exposure in key women's fashion magazines was 50 percent greater for Future Perfect, and the ads used four colors and two-page spreads. The ads for Megadose were in two colors and on a single page. Overall, consumers felt the black and white copy for Megadose indicated inferiority. Furthermore, the consumers' ratings of the products on three benefits and two attributes revealed that a significantly greater percentage of the women perceived Future Perfect as providing these benefits or having the attributes (see percentages in table). Estee Lauder used its reputation for quality by associating the new product with its brand name, whereas Ultima II did not identify itself as the producer of Megadose.

The success of Future Perfect relative to Megadose reflects use of a strong and consistent set of quality signals. The willingness of Estee Lauder to invest heavily in image advertising, store displays and store location, and quality packaging and to proudly feature its reputable name provided the support needed to use a high price as a signal of quality. In fact, research indicates that increasing levels of advertising repetition, along with the use of color, prompt consumers to perceive additional manufacturer effort and cost. Such perceptions lead to the inference that the manufacturer is trustworthy and confident of the product's quality. On the other hand, Ultima II attempted to use a high price, but the remainder of its marketing mix was inconsistent with its attempt to convey high quality. Because quality is not readily revealed by the use of this product, the brand was unknown, and investments were not made for advertising, packaging, or store location and displays, consumers were skeptical about the product's quality and hesitant to purchase it. Successful quality signaling requires consistency in all aspects of the marketing mix.

Sources: Frank Alpert, Beth Wilson, and Michael T. Elliott, "Price Signaling: Does It Ever Work?" *Pricing Strategy & Practice 1*, no. 3 (1993), 20–30; Amna Kirmani, "Advertising Repetition as a Signal of Quality: If It's Advertised So Much, Something Must Be Wrong," *Journal of Advertising 26* (Fall 1997), 77–86.

Warranties and Guarantees

The seller might also offer a money-back guarantee if the buyer is not satisfied with the product or offer a warranty on the level of product performance. A *warranty* is a promise made by the seller that the product, or its performance-related attributes, is free from defects in materials and workmanship. Further, a warranty provides a commitment to correct problems if they occur during the warranty period. A *money-back guarantee* promises to return the buyer's purchase price if the product fails to satisfy the buyer during the period covered by the guarantee.

One important distinction between these two signals is time: A money-back guarantee normally should be available for a limited period of time after purchase and used with products whose quality-determining attributes are revealed quickly, whereas performance warranties should be used for products whose quality-determining attributes are revealed slowly and over periods of time. One of the interesting features of both money-back guarantees and warranties is that they permit the high-quality seller to receive a higher price for the product than it would otherwise. That is, rather than sacrificing profit margin to keep the low-quality seller out of the high-quality market, the high-quality seller uses the guarantee or warranty as a signaling cost. The guarantee or warranty reduces the buyers' perceived risks since they can get their money back (in the short term), receive a replacement product (also for a limited period of time), or receive free repairs during the life of the warranty.[5]

[5]Sridhar Moorthy and Kannan Srinivasan, "Signaling Quality with a Money-Back Guarantee: The Role of Transaction Costs," *Marketing Science 14*, no. 4 (1995), 442–66; Shiou Shieh, "Price and Money-Back Guarantees as Signals of Product Quality," *Journal of Economics & Management Strategy 5* (Fall 1996), 361–77.

Summary

Signals separate the overall market into high-quality and low-quality segments only if the cost of signaling is too high for the low-quality firm to profitably mimic it and if the promise of the high-quality firm is enforceable either by buyer action (such as refusing to remain loyal) or legal action. For example, a warranty offered by a fly-by-night firm would be difficult to enforce if the firm has ceased to be in business when the buyer seeks a remedy for the failure of the product to perform as warranted. Another important requirement for these signals is that buyers must be able to recognize that the firm has incurred unrecoverable costs, intentionally put its future revenues at risk, or made a firm commitment to honor its guarantees.

Moral Hazard

A moral hazard may occur when sellers can change the quality of their offerings without detection by buyers prior to purchase or trial. A moral hazard may also occur if sellers offer full-replacement warranties to signal quality but buyers do not provide proper care and maintenance for the product. Moral hazard problems such as these can be solved by offering incentives.

What can buyers do to ensure that the seller provides the level of quality implied by the quality signal? Written contracts can provide assurance, but they are not efficient. Contracts are often written ambiguously, are open to multiple interpretations, and usually are not able to cover every contingency. Instead, buyers can offer repeatedly to pay a higher price than normal for the level of quality desired. That is, the buyers provide a profit incentive through a willingness to pay a price premium with every purchase as long as quality remains at the desired level. In a survey, 149 senior purchasing executives indicated that they often paid a "price higher than normal" to ensure that the promised quality of a product was delivered.[6]

[6]Akshay R. Rao and Mark E. Bergen, "Price Premium Variations as a Consequence of Buyers' Lack of Information," *Journal of Consumer Research 19* (December 1992), 412–23; Akshay R. Rao, "The Price of Quality," *Pricing Strategy & Practice 1,* no. 2 (1993), 4–15.

Price Premiums

Under what conditions are we likely to see price premiums for high-quality products in the marketplace? Clearly, the more that buyers are concerned about quality for experience products and the larger the proportion of these quality-sensitive buyers in the market, the greater will be their willingness to pay price premiums. The more uninformed these quality-sensitive buyers are, the greater will be their willingness to pay price premiums. Also, buyers must be willing to remove the seller from their preferred list of suppliers if they do not receive the quality promised and to voice their reasons for this action to others. That is, buyers' willingness to pay a price premium coupled with their willingness and ability to punish the seller if quality is compromised provides incentives to solve this moral hazard problem.

An important implication of buyers' willingness to pay price premiums for quality is that as the firm invests in signals that it is providing quality, the magnitude of this unit price premium declines! That is, if the seller has invested nonsalvageable assets such as advertising or capital assets, established a reputation for quality, or offered a warranty or guarantee, it has an incentive not to compromise on quality. Indeed, the seller likely will increase its efforts to monitor quality to maintain its reputation and avoid incurring reductions in revenues or cost-increasing warranty compliance programs.[7] Thus prices likely will decline as the reputation for quality becomes well established in the market.

However, it should also be clear that this reduction in the price premium because of reputation does not imply that the seller will be less profitable. On the contrary, quality sells, and firms that are perceived to provide quality products and services tend to be market share leaders and enjoy above-average return on investment. Quality has been found to be positively and significantly related to profitability for almost all kinds of products and market situations: consumer and industrial, capital intensive and noncapital intensive. High-quality sellers usually receive premium prices. Typically, these firms can attain greater growth by combining premium quality with a moderate price premium relative to major competitors. When information asymmetry exists and moral hazard problems arise, quality conscious buyers need to

---

[7]Donald A. R. George, "The Price–Quality Relationship under Monopoly and Competition," *Scottish Journal of Political Economy 43* (February 1996), 99–112.

provide sellers with incentives to supply high-quality products and services as promised. Coupled with a commitment to provide repeat business, the buyer must be willing to pay a price premium to assure quality.

Product Warranties and Guarantees

Warranties can help solve and, at the same time, create moral hazard problems. First, the way buyers use and maintain products affects the performance of the products. To the extent that these behaviors are not observable by the seller, a moral hazard problem may occur if warranties and guarantees are present. For example, if the warranty provides for full replacement of the product if the product fails or if the buyer is dissatisfied with the product, then the buyer has little incentive to care for and maintain the product properly. Second, the actual quality of experience products is not observable to buyers. As we have seen earlier, in such a situation, the supplier of a high-quality product has an incentive to signal quality by providing a product warranty or a money-back guarantee. Moreover, providing a warranty or guarantee offers an incentive to the seller to maintain quality and thereby avoid or reduce the costs of the warranty and guarantee programs. Thus, the magnitude of the protection provided by the warranty or guarantee influences the behaviors of both buyers and sellers.

In most markets, buyers differ according to how they use a product and in the degree that they are risk averse. That is, some buyers normally will take proper care of the products and others will not exercise such diligence. In like manner, some buyers are quite risk averse and will desire the insurance protection of a full warranty or an unconditional guarantee. Recognizing this buyer heterogeneity in both use of the product and desire for protection, many sellers provide a base warranty covering those aspects of the product that are likely to fail within the warranty period due to product defects. They then offer separate extended warranties for longer periods of time and for those aspects of the product that are most vulnerable to use and lack of proper care. Generally, providing quality products and warranty protection may be used as substitutes for firms that face competitive disadvantages because of inherently higher costs of providing warranties. Such firms may choose to raise the level of quality to reduce the likelihood of product failure, thereby reducing the costs of and need for an extended warranty program.

Summary of Information Asymmetry

This section has discussed the situations that occur when neither buyer nor seller has perfect information about the market. Typically, the level of quality sellers provide varies. At the same time, the amount of quality buyers desire varies. In addition, the amount of information that buyers possess about prices and relative quality across sellers varies. As a result, buyers and sellers make decisions on the basis of observable product, service, seller, or buyer *characteristics* or *actual behaviors* of buyers and sellers. These behaviors convey information to the other parties in transactions. Moreover, price serves as more than just a rationing device—it is also an information cue and it affects behavior. Finally, quality depends on price and prices depend on quality.

When quality depends on price, markets may be characterized by demand that is unequal to supply and by multiple prices. Moreover, under reasonable circumstances, demand curves may not be downward sloping; that is, demand may increase as price increases! Given our observations in Chapter 3 about sellers operating on inappropriate beliefs about the behaviors of buyers and sellers in response to prices, we can begin to understand why good managers may not make good pricing decisions. However, the story is not yet complete. We now discuss how to manage competition using signals.

Competitive Signaling

Competitive signals are bits of information one seller provides to other competing sellers in the market. Such signals send information that the other sellers can use to make inferences about the behavior of the seller sending the signal. In essence, a competitive signal is a marketing activity that reveals insights into the unobservable motives for the seller's behavior or intended behavior.[8] Such a signal alerts others about the product quality, reputation, business intentions, previews of potential actions, or even forecasts concerning the expected business conditions in the market.

[8]Oliver P. Heil and Arlen W. Langvardt, "The Interface between Competitive Market Signaling and Antitrust Law," *Journal of Marketing 58* (July 1994), 81–96; Paul Herbig and John Milewicz, "Marketing Signals and Their Influence on Pricing Behavior," *Pricing Strategy & Practice 3,* no. 2 (1995), 25–33.

As with signals to buyers, signals to other sellers must be clear to avoid misinterpretation and consistent with other signals the seller uses. Moreover, when necessary, the signal must also have sufficient commitment so the receiving parties will perceive that the sender intends to follow certain actions. For these signals to be credible, the signaling firm must incur be some actual or potential cost or sacrifice revenues—revealing parts of its strategy may reduce competitors' response times, allow part of its product line to be cannibalized, or result in loss of face if it does not deliver as promised. Finally, signaling is a learning process. Based on the history of the sender, the receiver can adjust and then respond appropriately to the current signal, minimizing the possibility of interpretation error.

The perceived credibility of a market signal is an important factor affecting whether competitors who receive the signal are likely to respond. The receiver's assessment of the signal's credibility is influenced by the sender's reputation and the signal's potential reversibility. A firm's reputation for fulfilling its signals depends on its prior history of signaling. If it has consistently fulfilled past signals with a promised action, then its current signal likely will be perceived as legitimate. As with quality signals, if the firm has invested in tangible investments or made binding agreements with suppliers, dealers or customers, then its signals are more likely to be perceived as credible. Thus the more irreversible a signal appears, the more likely a competitor will respond.

One limitation of competitive signaling is that competitors tend to respond to signals with competitive behaviors rather than countersignals. That is, rather than responding with a signal of its own, a receiver of a competitive signal tends to respond with a behavior. A responding signal would be less expensive and an excellent opportunity to exchange information with the original sender, but it tends to be underutilized. Instead, firms often respond with a behavior, perhaps as an attempt to get the jump on the signaling competitor. This tendency to commit to a behavior rather than a countersignal can be more expensive, sometimes irreversible, and tactical rather than strategic. A behavioral signal is more convincing than a verbal signal as a credible signal commitment. But a rival firm can only react to a competitor's behavior after the act, making the behavior a less timely signal. (See Box 4.4 for an example of how

BUDWEISER SIGNALS "STOP!"   BOX 4.4

In 1989, the beer market in the United States was dominated by three firms: Anheuser-Busch (Budweiser), Miller Brewing Co., and Adolph Coors Co. Anheuser held a dominant market share and was reluctant to discount its prices too much or too often. Any price reduction required substantial increases in volume to be profitable. However, Miller and Coors were not as reluctant and in the summer of 1989 had engaged in price cutting by as much as 22 percent in some markets. Apparently Miller and Coors thought that they could take market share away from several weaker rivals through price cutting. Although Anheuser's sales were at a record 62.4 million barrels for the first nine months of the year, its sales growth had been below its goal. On October 25, the company announced that it would start matching the price discounts its competitors were offering in some markets. Anheuser also warned that its earnings growth would be lower than expected because of these pending price reductions. In a press release, the director of marketing said, "If price discounting continues as it has for the past 18 months, it could cause an erosion of our market share—unless we take action." August A. Busch III, CEO of the firm added, "We don't want to start a bloodbath, but whatever the competition wants to do, we'll do. Everyone understands that market share is key in a mature industry. We want 50% of the markets in the mid-1990s." Anheuser then selectively reduced prices in fewer than a third of their markets. Instead of starting a beer war, the rival companies quickly realized they could not match the marketing power of Anheuser and by December, prices had stabilized. One of Miller's wholesalers from San Diego indicated that the "war" was over by telling the press, "We are hoping the competition is looking at it the same way we are—that they want to back off, too."

Sources: Julia Flynn Siler, "A Warning Shot from the King of Beers," *Business Week* (December 18, 1989), 124; P. Sellers, "Busch Fights to Have It All," *Fortune 121*, no. 2 (1990), 81–88.

Budweiser successfully used verbal and behavior signals, along with a willingness to hurt its earnings, to prevent a price war from starting.)

When information is unavailable about one's intentions or reasons for a behavior, other sellers and buyers make attributions about motives and inferences about the likely consequences. In such cases, the competitive and somewhat adversarial environment that buyers and sellers operate in is more likely to lead to a conclusion that their own positions might be endangered or harmed. Such a conclusion may result in another seller's aggressive response or a customer's withdrawal of patronage. Quite often, making the reasons for particular pricing actions transparent is the most effective approach to avoid negative competitive reactions or negative buyer responses. Now let's see how we can use some of these prescriptions to avoid price wars.

Avoiding Price Wars

One of the frequently used metaphors for the "game" of business is that of a battle or a war. That is, rival firms battle for the patronage of the same customers, try to take business away from a rival, or seek to drive a competitor out of the market or even out of business. This perspective of business emphasizes the win–lose nature of competition. When a competitor seems to be gaining in these battles, often the first reaction is to retaliate. Because price is relatively easy to change and the effects of the price change are usually observable, firms frequently respond to the success of a competitor by reducing prices. Then, if the competitor responds with a price reduction, the firms are well on their way to a price war. The end result of such a price war is that this perceived win–lose game has been transformed into a lose–lose game!

Negative Effects of Price Wars

Price wars can lead to economic disaster and to psychological traumas for all involved parties. Everyone in business knows that price wars produce negative results, yet they occur regularly, and seemingly more savagely than people remember.[9] Let's briefly review some of these negative effects on business. First, it is difficult to increase profits by reducing prices. As we will develop in Chapter 11, depending on the firm's operating margin, sometimes substantial growth in sales volume is required to offset losses that occur as soon as price is reduced. For Coca-Cola, a 1 percent reduction in selling price could mean a $20 million reduction in operating profits annually.[10] *Operating profits are quite sensitive to even small price reductions.*

Compounding this difficulty of trying to generate a substantial growth in sales volume to offset a price reduction, any competitive advantage gained with a price reduction disappears quickly. Anytime a price reduction induces sales growth at the expense of competitors, they will respond

---

[9]Bill Saporito, "Why the Price Wars Never End," *Fortune* (March 23, 1992), 68–78; David R. Henderson, "What Are Price Wars Good For? *Absolutely Nothing*," *Fortune* (May 12, 1997), 156; Oliver P. Heil and Kristiaan Helsen, "Toward an Understanding of Price Wars: Their Nature and How They Erupt," *International Journal of Research in Marketing 18* (June 2001), 83–98.
[10]Betsy Morris, "Coke and Pepsi Step Up Bitter Price War," *The Wall Street Journal* (October 10, 1988), B1.

quickly, usually with a price reduction of their own. If competitors drop their price below that of the seller who initiated the first price reduction, a price war may erupt. A third negative effect is that dropping price to "encourage" a rival firm to leave the market rarely is successful. Losers do not leave—they are sometimes acquired by another organization, or they file for bankruptcy protection.

Price wars also affect the ways customers respond to price information. First, a price war may lower the price buyers use to judge the relative value of offerings in the market. If buyers' reference prices as to what is acceptable, fair, normal, or reasonable decline during a price war, then it will be difficult to return prices to their prewar normal levels. Moreover, a price war and the emphasis on lower or reduced prices reduces buyers' sensitivity to quality and benefits received. At the same time, their sensitivity to price differences increases and their willingness to pay prewar prices declines. The result is that buyers become loyal to price rather than to value.

Causes of Price Wars

Sometimes price wars start intentionally. That is, a firm strategically wants to enter a new market, increase its market share in its current markets, or change the way business is conducted in the market. For example, when Staples and Office Depot introduced office supply superstores, they changed the way office supply firms did business. Their emphasis on discounted prices, volume, and cash and carry opened office supply stores, which had previously primarily served business firms, to the general public. Individual consumers found that they could get their paper and home-office supplies conveniently in stores that offered many choices. In three years, these two firms changed the industry and substantially increased demand for office supply products.

Firms that improve their products and services by offering additional benefits to buyers often fail to seek a price increase commensurate with the increased value of the improved product. That is, firms may fail to seek price premiums for benefit advantages they offer to their buyers. As customers of other firms learn of the increased value in these products, they may shift their purchases to the improved product. The firms that are now losing sales and market share cannot quickly respond with product improvements, but they can reestablish a value equivalence by reducing the prices of their products. Hence a price war may start when either a new firm or a firm with an improved product fails to set a price that is commensurate with the value buyers receive.

Perhaps the most common reasons for price wars are that sellers either misread a competitor's intentions or misread changes in demand or market share. Typically, when one seller reduces its prices, the reaction of competitors is to not let it get away with that reduction. They may not realize that the competitor is simply reducing prices for a limited time to reduce some excess inventory or that there are very specific conditions on how a buyer may qualify for the price reduction, including a limit on the quantity that can be purchased at the lower price. Or the seller who has reduced price may have simultaneously reduced some level of benefits or service that previously was included with the product purchase.

If a firm expects demand in the market to grow by a given percentage, but it actually grows less than expected, it may infer that the smaller sales growth realized by the firm means its market share has declined. In actuality, its sales growth may be larger than that of competitors and its market share may have increased, yet it infers that it needs to reduce price to recapture a perceived loss in market share. Finally, sometimes firms overreact to a competitor's limited and focused price reduction with an across-the-board price reduction of their own. That is, they go to "war" when only a minor skirmish is necessary!

Staying Out of Price Wars

As implied by the review of some of the ways that price wars occur, the most important way of staying out of or getting out of price wars is to manage the pricing process strategically. This basic prescription means that firms must take a long-term perspective and anticipate the behavior of competitors and customers. Further, they must be able to look several moves ahead in the pricing game, with all of its moves and countermoves. (See Box 4.5 for how one firm succeeded when a price war occurred.)

One obvious way to avoid price wars is to not provoke one's competitors. It is important to avoid competitive and marketing actions that force competitors to respond with a price reduction. Instead, emphasis should be placed on understanding how value is provided from the customers' perspectives. Firms should also avoid pursuing strategies to gain market share that are aimed at a specific competitor. Indeed, firms should focus on selected market segments, not market share.

WINNING A PRICE WAR   BOX 4.5

The Quebec, Canada, grocery retailing market had been dominated by Steinberg for 30 years. Steinberg had followed a cost-squeezing, price-cutting strategy to achieve this position. However, in the mid-1980s the Quebec market had experienced some dramatic changes and Steinberg's market share had fallen to 20 percent, third place among the provincial grocery retailers. After a serious of mergers, Provigo had 31 percent and Metro-Richelieu's had 25 percent market shares respectively. The fourth largest grocery retailer, Hudon and Deudelin, had an 8.5 percent market share.

Virtually all industry observers believed that Steinberg needed to take strong action. Rumors began circulating that Steinberg would initiate major price reductions backed by heavy promotion. It had the resources to follow such a strategy. Indeed, Steinberg had taken this approach successfully in previous situations. Hudon and Deudelin knew they would have to respond to the expected competitive price and promotions by its three larger competitors, but it could not afford a prolonged price war. The firm commissioned a market experiment to test the effect of 20 percent price increases and 20 percent price decreases on two types of grocery products. Products that consumers can hold in inventory (stockup goods) showed an average price elasticity of -2.75 for the price reduction and -1.21 for the price increase (demand was price elastic). Products that consumers cannot easily hold in inventory (non-stock-up goods) showed an average price elasticity of -0.53 for the price reduction and -0.38 for the price decrease (demand was price inelastic). The results clearly indicated that in the event of a price war, reducing prices on stock-up products would be the preferred tactic.

Shortly thereafter Steinberg announced a new promotion offering a 5 percent rebate on every dollar spent in its stores. Moreover, the chain announced the hiring of several hundred new employees to give customers "even more special service." These moves reduced the chain's margins by 5 percent. This reduction in margin required a sales increase of 23 percent, or a market share of approximately 25 percent, to maintain profits at the prepromotion level. Although Steinberg executives expected that it would take competitors up to three weeks to initiate a response, it took Metro-Richelieu only two hours to announce that its cash register tapes could be saved and redeemed for 5 percent off future purchases. The next day Provigo offered a 6 percent cash discount on all items effective immediately. Like Steinberg, both of these chains lost about 5 percent of their margins through the promotions.

The day after Steinberg announced its promotion, Hudon and Deudelin reduced the price of about 500 stock-up items. They announced that their stores would be closed for Saturday to Monday to carry out the price reductions on the items involved. Hudon and Deudlin's margin fell by about 1.2 percent. It soon became clear that Steinberg would not be able to capture the necessary market share to break even on the promotion and the price war lasted only 14 weeks. Steinberg's market share had dropped to 19 percent whereas Provigo's market share had increased by 1 percent. However, while Hudon and Deaudelin had sacrificed only about 1.2 percent of its margin, compared to 5 percent or more for its competitors, its market share rose to 9.5 percent on a sales increase of over 10 percent. Recovering the profits lost by the price-cutting strategy actually required a sales increase of about five percent (see Chapter 11). To develop a price strategy to counter a price war, then, the firm had conducted careful pricing

continues

CONTINUED   **BOX 4.5**

research to determine the items that would be most responsive to price reductions (price elastic). By selectively reducing prices on these price-sensitive items, the firm not only withstood the price war, but actually improved its market and financial position in the process!

Source: Adapted from Roger J. Calantone, Cornelia Droge, David S. Litvack, and C. Anthony Di Benedetto, "Flanking in a Price War," *Interfaces 19* (March–April 1989), 1–12.

To avoid misreading the intentions of competitors, firms need to develop a complete understanding of their competitors.[11] It is important to understand all aspects of competitors' pricing, including a history of previous pricing moves for each competitor and an estimate of competitors' cost structure, capacity utilization, and actual pricing structure. It is important to know the actual transaction prices of competitors for all their relevant products; the list price is rarely what the seller receives.

To avoid competitors misreading a seller's pricing moves, it is important to use signals.[12] Using public media, firms should signal their estimates about the future growth of the market, their excess inventory, reasons for price changes, and any other information that will help competitors avoid misreading the firms' actions. Further, by determining a firm's sources and amount of customer benefit advantages, it can develop strategies and tactics to communicate value properly to customers. A separate advantage of properly communicating value to customers is that it also serves to signal competitors about the firm's competitive advantages and its commitment to maintain this value advantage.

As much as possible, the firm should strive to use price–market segmentation strategies. Recognizing that different buyers will have different degrees of sensitivity to price differences, price changes, and price levels means the firm should consider offering multiple products in each of its product lines. These products range from the basic model with no additional features to "fully loaded" models with

[11]Bruce H. Clark," Managing Competitive Interactions," *Marketing Management 7* (Fall/Winter 1998), 9–20.
[12]Akshay R. Rao, Mark E. Bergen, and Scott Davis, "How to Fight a Price War," *Harvard Business Review 78* (March–April 2000), 107–116.

much higher prices. The firm should also seek to use multiple distribution channels to reach customer segments with different degrees of price sensitivity. When price reductions are necessary, they should be focused to specific segments and not across-the-board price reductions. The firm should never discount its price per se, but instead offer buyers additional savings. Sometimes, these savings can be achieved through mutually beneficial long-term contracts or through more favorable terms. Moreover, changing the marketing emphasis to programs that reward customer loyalty rather than enticing buyers to switch from other sellers will help shift the firm and its customers' orientation towards benefits and value rather than price. Frequent purchasing programs help prevent price wars by offering the firm's regular customers greater value via loyalty awards but at the same item prices that nonloyal customers pay.

Rather than promote a "flexible" price policy, which really means that prices will be reduced whenever necessary, sellers should develop a flexible pricing structure that is transparent to buyers and competitors. That is, they can use bundled prices, with each of the bundle items priced individually; two-part prices that reward additional business rather than normal business (fixed price per unit for normal business and a lower per-unit price for incremental business); end-of-year rebates rather than quantity discounts; and functional discounts for activities performed rather than discounts for place within the distribution channel. Above all, the firm should maintain pricing integrity—it is fair to the firm and to its customers.

Finally, when necessary, sellers should respond to competitors' price moves directly and in kind ("tit-for-tat"). These responses should be precise and focused, and they should match the competitor's move. In addition, the seller must clearly communicate that it always intends to respond directly and in kind to pricing moves by competitors that impact the seller. When the competitor responds with a move toward more rational pricing, the seller should immediately support that move.

SUMMARY

Even though pricing managers are concerned about their competitors' pricing strategies and tactics, they usually do not have an ongoing competitive research program to develop a deep understanding of how the competitors think strategically. As a result, pricing managers tend to misread their customers and their competitors, which leads to the poor decisions that we have indicated routinely occur. One key to becoming a proactive pricing manager is to learn how to acquire, process, and utilize relevant and correct information about customers, competitors, and their environment.

To manage the pricing process successfully, managers must understand the pricing game. They have to be able to think strategically multiple moves ahead of the current decision. They need to think about how to make pricing a win–win game, rather than the lose–lose game that is so often found in the marketplace. Managers need to consider all players in this game: their firm, competitors, customers, suppliers, and complementary or supporting institutions such as banks and financial institutions. It is vital that managers learn to "step out of the box," think creatively, and seek to change the rules of the game.

Discussion Questions

1. What is meant by asymmetric information? Give some examples of the problems of adverse selection and moral hazard. How can these problems be solved?
2. What is a signal? What are the necessary conditions for signals to work? Give some examples of quality signals and competitive signals.
3. Under what conditions are we likely to see price premiums for high-quality products in the marketplace?
4. How do warranties and guarantees help solve and create moral hazard problems?
5. What are the roles of price in the marketplace?
6. Why do price wars occur? What are the effects of price wars? What are some strategies and tactics for avoiding or preventing price wars?

Suggested Readings

Clark, Bruce H: "Managing Competitive Interactions," *Marketing Management* 7 (Fall/Winter 1998), 9–20.

Erdem, Tulin, and Joffre Swait: "Brand Equity as a Signaling Phenomenon," *Journal of Consumer Psychology 7,* no. 2 (1998), 131–57.

Kirmani, Amna, and Akshay R. Rao: "No Pain, No Gain: A Critical Review of the Literature on Signaling Unobservable Quality," *Journal of Marketing 64* (April 2000), 66–79.

Rao, Akshay R.: "The Price of Quality," *Pricing Strategy & Practice 1,* no. 2 (1993), 4–15.

Rao, Akshay R., Mark E. Bergen, and Scott Davis: "How to Fight a Price War," *Harvard Business Review 78* (March–April 2000), 107–16.

Understanding Customer and Buyer Behavior

One of the most important factors in the price–demand relationship is how buyers use price in their purchase decision processes. As Chapters 5 through 7 demonstrate, the behavioral dimension of price is complex and different than either the traditional theory of price determination or the economics of information theory assumes. In this section, we will review some important research findings from behavioral price research and provide important implications for pricing management.

One of the prerequisites for using the proactive pricing approach developed in this book is an understanding of how customers perceive prices. Thus this section presents the behavioral theories about the perception, cognitive processing, and memory of price information, as well as important empirical findings. These theories and study results provide insights into how buyers respond to prices, price differences, and price changes. They also help us understand why buyers may not behave as either the economic theories presented in Section 2 or pricing managers assume.

An important extension of the material in Chapter 6 concerns how customers form value judgments given their price perceptions. Chapter 7 argues that these value judgments determine the willingness of customers to pay particular pricesfor the products and services they desire. As pointed out in Chapter 1, profitable pricing revolves around successful adaptation to the external factors affecting prices and profitability. A key aspect of this adaptation is the development of a value-oriented pricing strategy. Chapter 8 develops the concept of value analysis and techniques for transforming information on customers' value judgments into pricing strategies.

Finally, Chapter 9 reviews traditional and newer techniques for estimating price–volume relationships. Perhaps the most frequently asked question is, "What will happen to unit sales if prices change by X percent?" There are a number of ways to estimate both the historical and the prospective price-volume relationship, and these methods are presented in Chapter 9.

CHAPTER FIVE

Behavioral Foundations for Pricing Management

Low prices will beget contempt, neglect and disuse, and there is the end to trade.

Letter from Josiah Wedgwood to Thomas Bentley, April 14, 1773.

Do we know how price influences individual buyers in their purchase decisions? As discussed in Chapter 2, the downward-sloping demand curve has generally been assumed to illustrate decisions of what to buy and how much to buy. That is, as the price of a product increased, fewer buyers would decide to purchase it, and those buyers who still purchased the product would be disposed to purchase fewer units than before. In this case, price serves only as a measure of purchase cost (sacrifice) to the buyer. However, research and anecdotal evidence indicate that the role of price is more complex than that of a simple indicator of purchase cost to buyers. This chapter contrasts the traditionally assumed role of price as a determinant of buyer behavior with the empirical evidence of the complexity of price as an influence on purchase decisions.

As suggested in Chapter 1, a successful proactive pricer sets price to be consistent with customers' perceived value.

To understand how customers form value perceptions, the relative role of price must be recognized. However, as a first step, it is important to understand how people form perceptions. How do perceptual and cognitive processes influence perceptions of product, service quality, sacrifice, and value? We will first see how people form perceptions and then consider a conceptual model of the relationship among price, perceived quality, and perceived value. In Chapter 6, we will expand the model to consider how people evaluate both products or services and offers, such as price promotions.

Perception

Perception basically involves categorization—that is, we tend to place new experiences into existing classifications of familiar experiences. Thus when buyers are confronted by a price different from what they believe they have previously paid, they must decide whether the difference between the old and new prices is significant. If they perceive the price difference as insignificant, they may classify the two prices as similar and act as they have in the past. If buyers perceive the prices of two alternative products as comparable, although not identical, they may choose on bases other than price. On the other hand, if buyers perceive the price differences as significant, they may classify the products as different and make their choices on the basis of price. This price-based choice may favor the higher-priced alternative, a result that the traditional model described in Chapter 2, would not find likely.

During this process of perceptual categorization, buyers make heavy use of information cues or clues. A *cue* is defined broadly as any informational stimulus about or relating to the product, service, or purchase context. Some of these cues are price cues, which influence buyers' judgments of whether the price differences are significant. For example, buyers may utilize the actual price of a product or service as an informational stimulus that implies product quality. Marketing managers must identify the information cues buyers use so they can accurately judge buyers' perceptions of the products or services offered.

Traditional Model

The traditional model of buyer behavior that results in a downward-sloping demand curve assumes that the decisions of what to buy and how much to buy depend on (1) the prices of all goods, (2) the level of income or amount of purchasing power, and (3) the buyer's tastes and preferences. Assuming perfect information about prices, a fixed level of income (budget), and knowledge about tastes and preferences, the buyer maximizes satisfaction by minimizing the price paid for each good.

Criticism of the Model

The assumption of "rational behavior" implies

1. Perfect information about prices.

2. A buyer who is capable of perfectly processing information.

3. Prices that do not affect subjective wants or satisfactions.

4. Perfect information about tastes and preferences.

As noted in Chapters 1 and 3, assumptions 1, 2, and 4 do not hold true in real-life buying situations. The model also leads to the expectation that buyers' preferences or choices depend on how they evaluate the quality or benefits to be received from a product relative to the cost or sacrifice inherent in the price. Thus buyers' perceptions of value represent a mental trade-off between the quality or benefits they perceive in the product relative to the sacrifice they perceive by paying the price:

$$\text{Perceived value} = \frac{\text{perceived benefits (gain)}}{\text{perceived sacrifice (give)}} \quad \textbf{(5.1)}$$

where perceived benefits are a function of perceived quality, perceived quality is positively related to price, and perceived sacrifice is positively related to price.

The model in Figure 5.1 illustrates the role of price on buyers' perceptions of product quality, sacrifice, value, and willingness to buy. The model suggests that buyers may use price as an index of perceived product quality as well as an index of the perceived sacrifice that is made when purchasing a product or service. Perceived value represents a trade-off between buyers' perceptions of quality and sacrifice and is positive when perceptions of quality are greater than perceptions of sacrifice. The model posits a positive relationship between price and perceived quality, and price and perceived sacrifice. Willingness to buy is positively related to perceived value.

FIGURE 5.1 **Relationship of Price, Perceived Value, and Willingness to Buy**

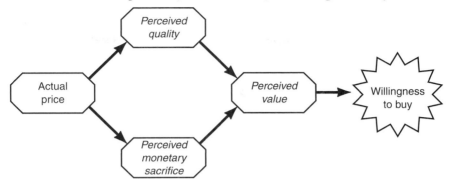

As Figure 5.1 shows, price may have both attracting and repelling attributes. For example, a new mustard was packaged in a crockery jar. Significant sales did not develop until the price was increased from $0.49 to $1.00 a jar. Moreover, as indicated in Chapter 3, evidence indicates that buyers generally are not able to assess perfectly a product's quality (the ability of the product to provide satisfaction). Rather, *perceived quality* is the relevant variable, and under appropriate conditions, the perceived quality in a product is positively related to price. Perceptions of value are directly related to buyers' preferences or choices; that is, the greater a buyer's perception of value, the more likely the buyer would be to express a willingness to buy or preference for the product. Box 5.1 gives another example of a price being too low.

Multidimensional Role of Price on Buyers' Perceptions

This dual, conflicting nature of price complicates the question of how price affects purchase decisions. It has been common to refer to these "irrational" effects of price on behavior as *psychological price phenomena*. The concepts of customary prices, price lines, and odd prices are among these effects. Theoretically, a buyer subject to psychological price factors would be perceptually sensitive to certain prices, and a slight departure from these prices in either direction would result in a decrease in demand.

Despite the apparent acceptance of these "psychological" phenomena, little substantive evidence supports this "magical" or "illusory" nature of prices. Some of these pricing

---

CAN A PRICE BE TOO GOOD? BOX 5.1

In 1980 Pathmark, a large, east coast supermarket chain, introduced its Premium All Purpose Cleaner. This product's chemical composition precisely duplicated the top-selling national brand, Fantastik. Furthermore, its packaging clearly mimicked the national brand's packaging. Finally, Premium was priced at $0.89, compared to $1.79 for Fantastik.

No matter how hard Pathmark tried to convince consumers that the product was as good as Fantastik, consumers declined to purchase it. Finally, in 1988, Pathmark took the product off the shelf. A spokesperson for the company said, "Clinically, it was an outstanding product in every respect. We believe the price was so low that it discredited the intrinsic value of the product." An executive of a market research firm added, "The farther the (price) distance from the national brand, the higher the credibility problem for consumers. Once you get outside the customer's comfort zone, the consumer psychology becomes, 'Gee, they must have taken it out in quality.'"

Source: Alix M. Freedman, "A Price That's Too Good May Be Bad," *The Wall Street Journal,* November 15, 1988, B1.

---

practices may have originated in traditional ways of retailing and of restraining salesclerks from pocketing money from sales transactions. Today, buyers accustomed to these pricing practices might be uncomfortable if products were not priced this way. Chapter 6 discusses how buyers perceive prices and the managerial errors that occur when such perceptions are not considered.

Odd price refers to a price ending in an odd number (e.g., 1, 3, 5, 7, 9), or to a price just under a round number (e.g., 99, 98). In perhaps the earliest behavioral pricing research, Ginzberg[1] imposed experimental patterns of odd and even prices ($.50 [.49], $.80 [.79], $1 [.98], $1.50 [1.49], $2, [1.98]) on selected items in a large mail-order catalog and could not find any generalizable purchasing pattern as a result. Later, Gabor and Granger[2] concluded that if sellers use odd pricing regularly, then some buyers will consider the odd price as the real or usual price and the round figure price as incorrect and respond in a negative way.

A study of pricing in the U.S. food industry revealed that retail food prices ending in 9 were most popular and prices ending in 5 were second most popular. More than 80 percent

---

[1]Eli Ginzberg, "Customary Prices," *American Economic Review 26* (June 1936), 296.
[2]Andre Gabor and Clive Granger, "Price Sensitivity of the Consumer," *Journal of Advertising Research 4* (December 1964), 40–44.

FIGURE 5.2
**Assumed Demand
Curve for Odd
Pricing**

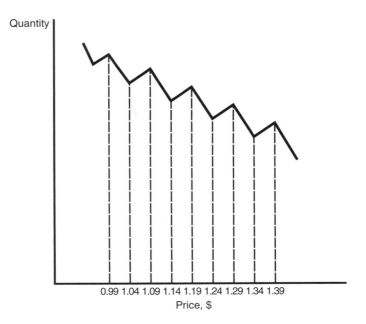

of the retail food prices ended in 9 or 5.[3] A study in Germany
showed that 91.7 percent of all prices ended in 9, while 8.3
percent ended in 8. Moreover, 63.5 percent of the tens digits
were also 9.[4] A survey of 1,415 advertisements from 43 Sunday newspapers showed that 30.7 percent of the rightmost
digit in these ads was a 9, and 27.2 percent of the rightmost
digits was a 0. The use of the digit 5 to end a price in these
advertisements occurred 18.5 percent of the time.[5] Finally,
another survey of 1,200 prices indicated that 56.8 percent of
actual retail prices ended in .99, 4.8 percent ended in .49,
and 2.1 percent ended in .29. Two other two-digit cents price
endings, .97 and .98, occurred 10.8 percent of the time. Only
40 prices ended in .00.[6]

[3]Lawrence Friedman, "Psychological Pricing in the Food Industry," in Almarin
Phillips and Oliver E. Williamson (eds.), *Prices: Issues in Theory, Practice, and
Public Policy* (Philadelphia: University of Pennsylvania Press, 1967), 187–201.
[4]Hermann Diller and Andreas Brielmaier, "The Impact of Rounding Up Odd
Prices: Results of a Field Experiment in German Drugstores," *Pricing Strategy &
Practice 3,* no. 4 (1995), 4–13.
[5]Robert M. Schindler and Patrick N. Kirby, "Patterns of Rightmost Digits Used in
Advertised Prices: Implications for Nine-Ending Effects," *Journal of Consumer
Research 24* (September 1997), 192–201.
[6]Robert M. Schindler, "Relative Price Level of 99-Ending Prices: Image versus
Reality," *Marketing Letters 12,* no. 3, (2001), 239–247.

Marketing people who use odd prices apparently assume a jagged demand curve as seen in Figure 5.2. Such an assumption implies that buyers will buy less as prices are increased until a *threshold price* is reached. In the vicinity of or at this threshold price point, buyers would purchase greater quantities. The demand curve in Figure 5.2 assumes an inverse relationship overall between price and quantity sold. For example, demand is greater at $0.99 than at $1.39. Yet, between prices of $1.04 and $1.09, demand increases, perhaps due to the "psychological" impact of the $1.05 and then the $1.09. Such a demand increase at these price points is an implied assumption of the practice of setting prices at these odd values, particularly those ending in either a 5 or a 9. Thus, two important questions emerge: Is there research evidence supporting the validity of this assumption? And what are the profit implications of this pricing practice? To be in a position to answer these two questions, we first need to explore how people process numerical and price information.

Psychophysics of Prices

Research has established that humans have upper and lower limits of responsiveness to physical stimuli such as sound and light. For example, those of us who have taken hearing tests are aware that some sounds are either too low or too high for us to hear. The low and high sounds that we can just barely hear are called our lower and upper *absolute* hearing *thresholds*. Much of the interest in thresholds originates in Weber's law, which suggests that small, equally perceptible changes in a response correspond to proportional changes in the stimulus:

$$\frac{\Delta S}{S} = k \qquad \textbf{(5.2)}$$

where

S = magnitude of the stimulus

ΔS = change in S corresponding to a defined change in response

K = constant

Weber's law applies to the perception of changes in a stimulus; that is, *to perceived differences between two intensities of a stimulus.* For example, Weber's law suggests that if the increase in a product's price from $10 to $12 is sufficient to deter us from buying the product, then the price of another product originally priced at $20 would have to be raised to $24 before we would become similarly uninterested. That is,

$$\frac{\$2}{\$10} = \frac{\$4}{\$20} = 0.20 = k \qquad \textbf{(5.3)}$$

(This example assumes that noticing a price increase is sufficient to change purchasing behavior. As pointed out later in our discussion on price elasticity, this connection between perceived price change and willingness to buy is more complex than the simple assumption made here to illustrate the concept.)   Later, Fechner reformulated Weber's law, and derived what is now known as the Weber-Fechner law:

$$R = k \log S + a \qquad \textbf{(5.4)}$$

where

$$R \;=\; \text{magnitude of response}$$

$$S \;=\; \text{magnitude of the stimulus}$$

$$k, a \;=\; \text{constants}$$

These two laws provide the basis for discussing how people perceive and process numerical information, which we present next. Later we will use these laws as the basis for discussing the behavioral issues underlying two pricing errors: (1) not recognizing the relationship between perceived value and price, and (2) not distinguishing between absolute price and relative price.

Processing of Prices as Numerical Information

We use numbers virtually everyday in our lives, for example, as a form of identification for ourselves or our possessions, to make a telephone call, to address a letter, or to pay a bill. However, the apparent ease with which we use numbers hides the fact that very complex cognitive processes are required to recognize numerical stimuli and to make simple numerical comparisons or calculations. In this section, we will review some of the current findings from numerical cognition research that have relevance for helping us understand the complexity of processing price information.

Numerical Cognition Processes

There are three different processes underlying the way people process numerical information.[7] First, number processing involves the ability to mentally manipulate sequences of words or symbols according to fixed rules (*number transcoding and calculation process*). This process occurs when a buyer is actually calculating the numerical difference between two prices, adding the surcharge of shipping and handling or tip to determine the total cost of the purchase, or determining the unit price of an offering.

The second *process of quantification or enumeration* enables people to determine the measurable quantity of a perceived set of items. This process includes three quantification processes: counting, subitizing (the process of enumeration when there are fewer than four items), and estimation. It does not appear that this particular process has serious implications for pricing.

It is the third *process of approximation and processing of quantities* that seems to be highly relevant to our understanding of how buyers process price information. "Tasks such as measurement, comparison of prices, or approximate calculations, solicit an 'approximate mode' in which we access and manipulate a mental model of approximate quantities similar to a mental 'number line' "[8] Approximation is the process by which Arabic or verbal numerals, for example, are first converted into an internal magnitude representation in our minds. The input mode, such as, dollars or ounces, is then ignored and the numerical quantities are represented and processed similarly to other physical magnitudes such as size or weight. In one study, subjects' judgments of quality, sacrifice, and value did not differ regardless of whether the numerical stimuli were presented in units of money or weight.[9] This encoding is automatic, fast, and independent of which particular number is encoded. These subjective numerical magnitudes appear to follow Weber's Law as well as Fechner's adaptation.

---

[7]Stanislas Dehaene, "Varieties of Numerical Abilities," in Stanislas Dehaene (ed.), *Numerical Cognition* (Cambridge, MA: Blackwell, 1993), 1–42.
[8]Ibid., 20.
[9]Rashmi Adaval and Kent B. Monroe, "Automatic Construction and Use of Contextual Information for Product and Price Evaluations," *Journal of Consumer Research 28* (March 2002), 572–88.

Complexity of Numerical Information

Numerical information can be presented visually in many ways. A number could be presented in words (e.g., "twenty-six"), or in Arabic numerals (e.g., "26"), or in Roman numerals (e.g., "XXVI"), or even symbolically (e.g., by displaying 26 dots). Numbers are sometimes used as arbitrary labels, such as telephone numbers, ZIP codes, and social security numbers. In these cases, the magnitude of the number (i.e., whether it is large or small) is irrelevant. Other times, numbers are used to denote amounts, such as prices, age, weight, and duration of time, and the magnitude of the number becomes meaningful.

A number may be encoded as a nominal representation, in which case the exact symbols are encoded and stored in memory. When numbers are used as arbitrary labels—that is, nominally—exact symbol identification is necessary for correct usage. Alternatively, the number may be encoded as a magnitude representation, and either the exact value or an approximation of the exact value of the number is encoded and represented in memory. For example, "26" may be represented as young (as in age), or light (as in weight), cold (as in temperature), or cheap (as in prices).

For price information to influence purchase decisions, normally buyers must encode it as a magnitude representation rather than a nominal representation. Given this encoding, we are interested in learning how people process price information when making price comparisons, (discriminating between two prices), whether the oddness of a price influences processing, and how a series of numbers that comprise a price may be remembered.

Comparing and Discriminating Numbers

The *distance effect* indicates that the time required to compare two numbers is an inverse function of the numerical distance between them. It takes longer to decide that 8 is larger than 6 than to decide that 8 is larger than 2.[10] Moreover, the *magnitude effect* indicates that, for equal numerical distance, it is easier to discriminate between small

---

[10]Daniel Algom, Amnon Dekel, and Ainat Pansky, "The Perception of Number from the Separability of the Stimulus: The Stroop Effect Revisited," *Memory & Cognition 24,* no. 5, (1996), 557–72.

numbers (e.g., 1 versus 2) than larger numbers (e.g., 8 versus 9).[11] These two effects indicate that numerical comparisons obey the Weber-Fechner Law. For example, the distance effect suggests that digits are not compared as numbers per se, but are initially compared as quantities.

The digit 5 has a special status in our numbering system. Initially, the digits 2, 3, and 4 are encoded as small, whereas 6, 7, and 8 are encoded as large. That is, the mental representation of numbers below 10 is divided into numbers above and below 5. Thus, in a price comparison task people first automatically encode the two prices independently and then classify the prices as "small" or "large."[12]

When judging which number in a pair is *larger*, people find the task easier when both numbers are large than when both are small (again the numeral 5 serves as the neutral point between small and large). The opposite is true when people have to decide which item is smaller. This effect is called the *semantic congruency effect* because it was initially observed in various semantic comparison tasks. The *size congruity effect* occurs when people are judging which of two numerals is larger. It is an easier task if the larger of the compared numerals is displayed in larger font size. Similar results occur when people are judging which of two numerals is smaller and the smaller numeral is displayed in smaller font size.

The above effects have been observed in tasks in which people are comparing or selecting from two presented numerals. In pricing, we are interested in whether these effects occur when the individual is comparing an observed price to an internal reference price. Research has concluded that two-digit numbers are compared holistically—the whole magnitudes the two numbers represent are compared.

Implications for Pricing Management

As suggested by the findings in number processing research, some types of price information processing may be more

[11]Stanislas Dehaene and Rokny Akhavein, "Attention, Automaticity, and Levels of Representation in Number Processing, *Journal of Experimental Psychology 21*, no. 2 (1995), 314–26; Stanislas Dehaene, "The Psychophysics of Numerical Comparison: A Reexamination of Apparently Incompatible Data," *Perception & Psychophysics 45,* no. 6 (1989). 557–66.

[12]Joseph Tzelgov, Joachim Meyer, and Avishai Henik, "Automatic and Intentional Processing of Numerical Information," *Journal of Experimental Psychology: Learning, Memory, and Cognition 18,* no. 1 (1992), 166–79.

automatic than others. Price comparisons in the lower-price range (smaller numbers involving fewer digits), which are more typical for most supermarket purchases, may be more likely to be processed automatically. Moreover, identifying whether a specific price is higher than another price will be processed faster when that price is indeed higher than the reference price.

Another issue is how to communicate price promotions. If a product's price is discounted 10 percent, do buyers perceive this reduction to be a "small" or a "large" discount? If it is perceived to be a small discount, but the advertisement or store sign presents the savings in a large font size, perhaps in a font size that is larger than the regular price (which numerically is larger than the amount of the discount) the semantic congruency effect suggests that buyers may have more difficulty in processing the promotion information. This difficulty in processing the information is enhanced because people often have only a few seconds to attend to, process, and interpret such information.

Analysis of the Effects of Odd Prices

The Odd Effect

Another potential issue in number processing is the distinction between even and odd numbers. For a variety of different tasks and judgments, even digits are processed faster and more accurately than odd digits.[13] A congruity effect also seems to occur when judging multiple-digit numbers—subjects were slower in making judgments about even numbers from 10 through 19 than from 0 through 9. That is, the odd-even status of the tens digit provides some interference with judging the ones digit.[14]

Perceptual and Cognitive Effects

Possible reasons for the assumed odd price effect on buyer behavior mentioned earlier can be categorized into two related types: effects of *price perception* (how people encode

---

[13]Terrence M. Hines, "An Odd Effect: Lengthened Reaction Times for Judgments about Odd Digits," *Memory & Cognition 18,* no. 1 (1990), 40–46.

[14]Stanislas Dehaene, Serge Bossini, and Pascal Giraux, "The Mental Representation of Parity and Number Magnitude," *Journal of Experimental Psychology: General 122,* no. 3 (1993), 371–96.

TABLE 5.1 **Effects of Odd-Price Endings**

Price Perception Effects	Price Cognition Effects
People encode prices as magnitudes.	People interpret odd prices as signals of inferior quality and round prices as signals of high quality.
People attend to prices from left to right.	People interpret odd prices as signals of reduced, discounted, or low prices.
People have limited ability to recall prices.	People interpret nonround prices as evidence that the prices have been precisely calculated and therefore are fair.

price information in their minds) and effects of *price cognition* (how people process the encoded price information) (Table 5.1).

In a delayed recall memory test, one study found that consumers had greater difficulty recalling prices ending with 98¢ or 99¢ than prices ending with 00¢. The respondents in this study had a tendency to underestimate prices ending in 98¢ and 99¢.[15] However, subsequent research failed to find any substantive underestimation of prices ending in 99¢ using an immediate recall memory test.[16] In the first study the number of digits in the 20 prices ranged between three and five, whereas for the second study, the number of digits in the three prices were four or five. Previous research has shown that the ability of people to remember accurately a series of numbers without explicit instructions to remember them exactly in sequence decreases as the length of the number in digits increases.

People process round (even) numbers more easily and are more likely to reproduce them when asked. One plausible implication of this evidence is that prices ending in 99¢ or 98¢ are more difficult for people to process, and as a result people may encode an approximation of the price rather than the precise price. Thus, a price of $23.99 might be encoded as approximately $20 and a price of $27.99 might be encoded as approximately $30. It is unlikely, however, that all nonround prices in the range of $20 to $29.99 would be encoded as approximately $20 on the assumption that buyers

[15]Robert M. Schindler and Alan R. Wiman, "Effect of Odd Pricing on Price Recall," *Journal of Business Research 19* (November 1989), 165–77.

[16]Robert M. Schindler and Thomas Kibarian, "Testing for Perceptual Underestimation of 9-Ending Prices," in Leigh McAlister and Michael L. Rothschild, eds., *Advances in Consumer Research*, vol. 20 (Provo, UT: Association for Consumer Research, 1993), 580–85.

only process the leftmost digits and encode an approximate lower round number ($20) for all prices in the range.

Another research study indicated that odd pricing seemingly communicates a low-price image *and a low-quality image*.[17] However, using three price levels ($29.95 versus $30.00, $79.95 versus $80.00, and $129.95 versus $130.00), a second study found no significant differences in consumers' perceptions of quality and perceptions of value for a branded consumer electronics product compared to a non-branded product.[18] An important difference in these two studies is that the first study used a 99¢ price ending whereas the second study used 95¢ price endings. A third study surveying 2,439 prices over 12 stores found that higher-priced stores used more round prices than low-priced stores. Also, higher-quality products within a product category and products for which quality is more difficult to detect prior to purchase tend to be priced using round numbers.[19] These latter results imply that when firms use price to signal quality, they are less likely to use odd prices.

The finding that perceived price has *meaning* that is distinct from its objective meaning in terms of perceived monetary sacrifice is important, and these results suggest that using an inappropriate price ending could have unwanted implications for the seller.[20] When a seller wishes to strategically communicate a low-price (or value) image to the market, using an odd-ending pricing tactic, such as a 99¢ ending, may also communicate that the products and services are of low quality. Thus, if customers infer a lower quality to products and services when sellers use certain odd prices, then using the incorrect odd price may lead to customers perceiving lower overall value than might be the case if the price ended in an even number.

[17]Robert M. Schindler and Thomas Kibarian, "The Image Effects of Odd Pricing," Working Paper, School of Business, Rutgers University, Camden, NJ, 1989; Robert M. Schindler, "Symbolic Meanings of a Price Ending," in Rebecca H. Holman and Michael R. Solomon, eds., *Advances in Consumer Research*, vol. 18 (Provo, UT: Association for Consumer Research, 1991), 794–801.

[18]William B. Dodds and Kent B. Monroe, "The Effect of Brand and Price Information on Subjective Product Evaluations," in Elizabeth C. Hirschman and Morris B. Holbrook, eds., *Advances in Consumer Research*, vol. 12 (Provo, UT: Association for Consumer Research, 1985), 85–90.

[19]Mark Stiving, "Price-Endings When Prices Signal Quality," *Management Science 46* (December 2000), 1617–29.

[20]Sandra Naipaul and H. G. Parsa, "Menu Price Endings That Communicate Value and Quality," *Cornell Hotel and Restaurant Administration Quarterly 42* (February 2001), 26–37.

Sales and Profit Implications

If the implied demand curve for odd pricing exists, then an abrupt change in demand would occur at specific price points. We call these specific price points where demand abruptly changes, either increasing or decreasing, *price thresholds*. For example, there might be a greater demand for a product priced at $99 than at either $95 or $100. Moreover, the increase in demand at $99 relative to $100 would be substantially greater than predicted by a 1 percent price reduction given the general price elasticity of demand for the product. That is, the demand curve for this product would not be decreasing for all prices as prices increase. Moreover, if this odd-price phenomenon exists for other reasonable odd prices in the product category, then we would expect greater demand at $89 than at either $90 or $85.

Figure 5.3 reproduces the sales response curve for Chiffon margarine, illustrating several shifts or changes in sales as prices increase. Note that there is a large decrease in sales as price increases from 49¢ to 51¢ to 53¢. Then, between 53¢ and 59¢ demand increases only to decrease again until the price is 64¢. Curiously, demand remains relatively flat between 64¢ and 69¢, but decreases again between 69¢ and 75¢. Thus, it would appear that there may be an odd-price effect leading to a sales increase (or an interruption in the downward trend of demand) between 53¢ and 59¢, between 64¢ and 69¢, and between 75¢ and 79¢. The price points at 59¢, 69¢, and 79¢ indicate that these are threshold prices and that demand resumes its downward trend when prices are increased beyond these points.

Two other studies have investigated the effect of odd prices on brand choice shares within a competitive context. For the products fly spray and a block of cheese, prices ending in 99¢ produced a significant increase in estimated utility relative to prices ending in either 95¢ or 00¢. However, for an electric kettle the odd-price effect occurred at 95¢.[21] It is possible that the difference in these results is due to a price-level effect—the electric kettle was priced around $50 while the other two products were priced under $10. Another study found that tuna fish lost choice shares as its price increased from 45¢, but the most significant share loss

---

[21]Philip Gendall, Michael F. Fox, and Priscilla Wilton, "Estimating the Effect of Odd Pricing," *Journal of Product & Brand Management Featuring Pricing Strategy & Practice 7*, no. 5 (1998), 421–32.

FIGURE 5.3   **Sales Response Function for Chiffon Margarine**

Source: Adapted from Kirthi Kalyanam and Thomas S. Shively, "Estimating Irregular Pricing Effects: A Stochastic Spline Regression Approach," *Journal of Marketing Research 35* (February 1998), 17.

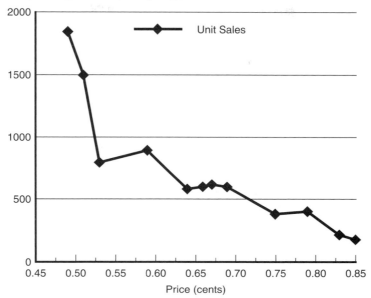

occurred when its price went from 48¢ to 49¢ and from 49¢ to 50¢, with little additional negative effect for prices above 50¢. However, yogurt actually increased choice share as its price increased from 48¢ to 49¢ and from 49¢ to 50¢. At 51¢ its choice shares fell substantially with little additional negative effect for prices above 51¢.[22]

Using a 169-item clearance sales catalog, a field experiment compared the sales effect of 99¢ price endings with 00¢ and 88¢ price endings.[23] The catalog with the 99¢ endings produced more purchasers and sales revenues than the other two catalogs. The differential was 8 percent more revenues compared to the catalog with 00¢ endings, for example. In Germany, researchers concluded that rounding odd prices up had no negative effect on unit sales or sales revenues for a drugstore chain. Rounding prices up, however, had a positive

[22]Mark Stiving and Russell S. Winer, "An Empirical Analysis of Price Endings with Scanner Data," *Journal of Consumer Research 24* (June 1997), 57–67.
[23]Robert M. Schindler and Thomas M. Kibarian, "Increased Consumer Sales Response through Use of 99-Ending Prices," *Journal of Retailing 72*, no. 2 (1996), 187–99.

effect on the image of the stores. The researchers estimated that the drugstore chain lost approximately $850,000 in profits per year by using odd prices.[24]

The way people respond to price information is considerably more complex than traditionally assumed in marketing and economics. These complexities make it more difficult to estimate demand response if prices are increased or decreased from their current levels. Depending on whether a price–image or price–quality perception exists for at least a segment of the market, setting price with a 9 ending could lead to a greater sales response than might be forecast using a general estimate of price elasticity. Yet, as some research has shown, setting price with a 5 ending or a 0 ending could lead to a relatively larger sales response.

As Box 5.2 illustrates, a price just below a round price may be effective when it can serve as a unique cue to consumers who may be uncertain about whether a specific price is a "bargain." If there are different market segments, such as a price-conscious segment and a quality-conscious segment, it is possible that there will be multiple price thresholds, and that some of these thresholds might exist at the 0 ending price rather than the 9 ending price.

Traditional pricing practices relying on odd-ending prices have not been consistently supported by existing research. Retailers have found that some pricing practices work better than others, thereby suggesting there are some buyer-perceptual phenomena underlying observed response patterns. However, as recent research on odd-even pricing illustrates, the opportunity for making strategic pricing errors apparently is enhanced when the price setter does not recognize the different roles that price plays in influencing buyers' perceptions and behavior.

Our discussion about the effect of odd prices has considered only a single price for a product or service, what might be called unidimensional price. However, offers often are made with multiple price attributes. For example, an automobile may be advertised with a price for the vehicle along with a combination of monthly payments, amount of down payment, and effective interest rate. Catalog and Internet offers typically quote selling prices and shipping and handling charges. When prices are multidimensional, additional computations are required to evaluate the offer, some of which

---

[24]Diller and Brielmaier, "The Impact of Rounding Up Odd Prices."

SETTING PRICES BELOW A ROUND PRICE: STRATEGIC OR TACTICAL? **BOX 5.2**

Two researchers convinced a national merchandiser of women's clothing to distribute three versions of its catalog randomly. These catalogs listed one item at $44, $49, or $54. Demand for the item at either the $44 or $54 price was almost identical. However, demand for the item priced at $49 was more than 50 percent greater. The researchers then increased the number of items with a 9-ending price in other catalogs to determine how effective this pricing tactic might be. They found that as the number of items in a catalog with a 9-ending price increased, the relative effectiveness of the 9-ending price diminished. The researchers concluded that if this tactic is used too frequently, it becomes less informative as a cue for a bargain. When the signaling aspect of a -9-ending price tactic is used as a pricing strategy, the so-called odd effect may disappear. The difference between pricing strategy and pricing tactics was discussed in Chapter 1 and will be revisited later in this chapter and in Box 6.1.

Source: "Why That Deal Is Only $9.99," *Business Week* (January 10, 2000), 36.

can be difficult. Also, some retail price promotions provide multiple discounts, for example, 40 percent off all merchandise with an extra 10 percent off if purchased at a certain time, and perhaps another 10 percent off for senior citizens. Offers that use odd-price endings or complicated prices, such as $23,977, for example, significantly affect buyers' abilities to evaluate prices to determine exactly what they will be paying for the item. The computational difficulty associated with multidimensional pricing is influenced by the price ending as well as the calculations to determine the price. Thus, consumers are less likely to form accurate perceptions of multidimensional prices.[25] It is also more difficult for the buyer to remember the price paid for items with multidimensional prices.

Price Awareness

Do buyers search for the lowest-priced alternatives and do they *know* the prices they pay? As pointed out in Chapters 2

[25]Hooman Estelami, "The Computational Effect of Price Endings in Multi-Dimensional Price Advertising," *Journal of Product & Brand Management Featuring Pricing Practice & Strategy 8,* no. 3 (1999), 244–56; Hooman Estelami, "Consumer Perceptions of Multi-Dimensional Prices," in *Advances in Consumer Research,* Merrie Brucks and Deborah J. MacInnis, eds., (Provo, UT: Association for Consumer Research, 1997), 392–99.

through 4, in traditional economic and marketing thought buyers are assumed to know the prices they pay. Furthermore, as discussed in Chapter 3, traditional theory also assumes that buyers are price sensitive and thus search for lower-priced choices. The term *price awareness* has been used to refer to the ability of buyers to recall prices paid.

Recent research has explored buyers' use of and memory for price information. These findings indicate that people who attempt to process price information because of their concern about prices, their involvement with the product, or the amount of attention they give to the selection are more likely to recall or recognize the prices paid. Although many buyers do not make explicit attempts to remember prices of items purchased, evidence at the market level indicates a general relationship between price and quantity sold.

Previous price awareness research has attempted to determine the extent that buyers do remember prices they have paid under the assumption that buyers are *consciously* involved in their purchasing behaviors and that product evaluations and choice decisions are a function of what information is accessible in memory. Information accessible in memory often is measured by what buyers *can consciously remember*. Buyers are assumed to make judgments that a particular item is "too expensive" or "a real bargain" based on some prices that they recall from past shopping experiences, and these recalled prices form a basis for the buyers' reference price.

Research attempting to measure buyers' ability to remember prices of recently purchased items, however, reports that a relatively low proportion of buyers can accurately recall prices of products they had recently purchased. Based on these data and other observational or survey evidence, it might be concluded that buyers do not consciously attend to price information when either considering or actually making purchase decisions. However, interviews often reveal that a shopper who does not recall the price of, say, the box of snack bars she just put into her cart may tell the interviewer that it is expensive. Thus, we must recognize that buyers may encode price information into memory in different representational forms.

Buyers may not only perceive and encode the numerical values of the prices (in actual or magnitude representations), they may also make comparisons (for example, that an item is priced higher than another item) and evaluative judgments (that it is expensive, or it must be better quality). Price comparisons involve some reference price and may result in buyers encoding a representation such as more or less than brand X, or more than last time. The buyer may also encode an evaluation of the price such as good/bad, favorable/unfavorable, expensive/inexpensive. Such evaluative judgments are also stored in memory.

Remembering versus Knowing

Research results provide evidence that *remembering* responses are closely related to conscious retrieval of information stored in memory, whereas *knowing* responses are based on a sense of familiarity that reflects the result of automatic or nonconscious processing. Thus the distinction between *remembering* and *knowing* contrasts the capacity for conscious recollection about the occurrence of facts and events to the capacity for nonconscious retrieval of the past event.

Buyers may make product evaluation and purchase decisions based on what they remember, or their decisions may be based on what they know. Remembering requires consciously recollecting having encountered a piece of information. For example, an individual may remember seeing an advertisement for a price promotion at a local store and decide several days later to check out the bargains. Conversely, knowing involves a sense of familiarity towards a previously encountered item, experienced without conscious recollection of the exposure event. This sense of familiarity may be the result of ease in retrieving the stimulus into memory when processing related information. A weekend shopper, for example, may be able to confirm that the store is conducting a special promotion on outdoor furniture and may seek out this store when deciding to shop for outdoor furniture. However, this buyer may not remember where the information about the promotion came from—billboards, newspaper, flyer, radio, TV, or a banner. Distinguishing between remembering versus knowing judgments helps us understand how price information may be processed and its impact on subsequent purchase decisions.

Consumers' daily purchase decisions typically are made under conditions of low involvement and time pressure. Indeed, most purchase decisions are made within five seconds, and when scanning the shelves, buyers may look at a specific product only about 1/25th to 1/50th of a second.[26]

---

[26]Phat X. Chiem, "Putting Shoppers on Cruise Control," *Chicago Tribune*, Section 5 (December 5, 1999), 1,7.

Often buyers rely on nonconscious, automatic processing when making purchase decisions, and these decisions often are based on what they know rather than what they remember.

Conscious versus Nonconscious Price Information Processing

Buyers process and retrieve price information either consciously or nonconsciously. When processing price information consciously, buyers pay attention to the price, make judgments regarding the value of the product using information that is either present in the external environment or retrieved from memory, and finally make a purchase decision. When buyers consciously process the actual price information, a magnitude representation of the price and their evaluative judgment may be transferred from working memory into long-term memory. If so, buyers would be more likely to recall the price of the product at a later time—they would demonstrate "price awareness."

Alternatively, it is possible that only buyers' comparative or evaluative judgments, not the actual price information, are transferred into long-term memory. In this case, the buyers would not be able to recall the actual price when asked to do so at a later point in time, and they would demonstrate "price unawareness." Yet, these buyers may be able to indicate that the product is "too expensive," "a bargain," or "priced reasonably." This scenario is consistent with the idea that an overall evaluation of a product may be more easily remembered than attribute information when the evaluation is formed at the time of exposure. Table 5.2 provides some alternate ways buyers may encode price information.

Conversely, when price information is processed at a nonconscious level, the buyer does not pay particular attention to the prices. Nonetheless, a judgment regarding the value of the product and a purchase decision may have been made. When such nonconscious processing of price information occurs, the buyer is more likely to demonstrate "price unawareness", and be unable to recall the price of the product at a later time. However, this same buyer who cannot recall the exact price like the buyers who have transferred only evaluative judgments into long-term memory, may still be able to indicate that the product is "too expensive," "a bargain," or "reasonably priced," suggesting that the price

TABLE 5.2 **Alternative Ways Buyers May Encode Price**

Price Use	Example of Encoded Price
Trade off price against benefits	*$120* was more than my need for a coat.
	The peppers *were expensive,* but I needed them.
	The estimated repair *cost of $100* was too much.
	The items were *on sale* and I *saved money.*
Price comparisons	The product was *40¢ more* but had an extra feature.
	I chose the rolls even though *they are higher.*
	Compared to other items, the *$7.95 entrée was lowest.*
	The 12-month membership involved *a discount.*
	I used the *unit prices* to compare the price.
	The new item was *$8 higher* than before.
Using price information	I *stored the price* for gas for future reference.
	I told my friend that my system cost *less than $500* two years ago.
	I checked to see if the *price was 85¢* before selecting the item.
	I checked the prices to see if they were *affordable.*
Judging prices	The additional $25 fee was an *unfair surcharge.*
	The *high price* for lettuce was due to poor weather.
Price as a signal	I wondered how good the play was given the *low admission price.*
	The price of shoes (nearly $100) *reflected quality.*
	The high price reflected the *exclusive image* of the store.

Source: Adapted with permission from Robert M. Schindler and Diana M. Bauer, "The Uses of Price Information: Implications for Encoding," in Gary Frazier et al., eds., *Efficiency and Effectiveness in Marketing* (Chicago: American Marketing Association, 1988), 68–73.

information has been processed and evaluated. Thus buyers are equally unlikely to demonstrate price awareness if they have processed the price information nonconsciously, or if they have processed the information consciously but only encoded the comparative or evaluative judgments into long-term memory.

Assessing Buyers' Processing of Price Information

As summarized earlier, current knowledge of how people process numerical information indicates that the process is more complex than commonly assumed. Research studying numerical comparative judgments, whether against a standard or between numbers, indicates that numerical quantities are not compared at a symbolic level, but are initially recoded and compared as quantities. When prices are processed as magnitudes or as relative quantities, even if buyers are actively evaluating the different alternatives in their choice set and consciously processing the price information, the actual prices may not be encoded or stored in memory. Under these circumstances, measures of price awareness such as recall of actual prices would give the erroneous conclusion that buyers do not process price information.

Commonly Used Measures of Price Awareness

Generally, researchers have equated buyers' price awareness with an ability to remember prices last paid. Indeed, the reference price concept as originally operationalized was the price the buyer had last paid for the particular item of concern. This approach assumed that buyers were able to remember the price last paid and that this particular price served as a reference point to compare the current price. Researchers have operationalized the concept of price awareness in three different ways: (1) buyers' ability to recall the exact prices paid, (2) buyers' ability to recall the relative price rank of alternative items in their choice set, or (3) buyers' ability to recognize the price paid for the item. Primarily, researchers have measured price awareness using a recall memory test and have judged recall accuracy either in terms of exact recall or the absolute difference between recalled price and the correct price expressed as a percentage of the correct price.

The ability of shoppers to recall the exact prices paid has varied between 8 percent and 61.3 percent. Such recall scores have led to inferences that buyers do not pay attention to prices they pay. However, this inference may be premature given the nature of the shopping tasks studied, how people process numbers (i.e., prices), and the differences between explicit and implicit memory tests.

Some researchers have measured price awareness as the absolute differences between recalled price and the correct price expressed as a percentage of the correct price. Average price recall error has ranged from 6 percent to 19.45 percent. This relatively small error percentage compared to the error percentage for recall of actual prices suggests a possible different conclusion about buyers' price awareness: Perhaps buyers do *know* the prices paid even if they cannot remember the exact prices.

Recognizing that buyers may not attempt to memorize exact prices, some researchers have also used a relative recall score. That is, buyers may know how brands rank against each other in terms of their prices. A relative price recall measure recognizes that buyers may compare multiple items before choosing. Indeed, one study reported that a number of buyers agreed that they encode price information this way.[27] If buyers do make comparisons at the point of choice, they will be more attentive to the price differentials than the actual prices; that is, it is more likely that price information will be encoded in a relative way than as exact prices. This attention to price differentials is likely to occur as long as the prices in the choice set remain within the buyers' acceptable price range.

Two studies have used recognition memory test to determine buyers' ability to remember price information. A recognition memory test provides additional cues to the respondents, because it presents the correct price along with incorrect prices. Respondents are asked to choose the correct price from the list provided. Two studies have found that subjects' price recognition performance was better than price recall performance.[28]

SUMMARY

Perception basically involves the process of categorization. That is, we tend to place new experiences into existing classifications of familiar experiences. Thus when buyers are confronted by a price different from what they believe they had previously paid, they must decide whether the difference between the new and old prices is significant to them. If the price difference is insignificant, they may classify the two prices as similar and act as they have in the past. However if they perceive the price difference as significant, they may classify the new price in a new price product category and change their purchase behavior.

During this process of categorization, buyers make heavy use of cues or clues. Some of these cues are price cues, which influence buyers' judgments of whether the price differences are significant. The review of some of the behavioral phenomena underlying this perceptual process has perhaps raised more questions than we currently can answer. However, as buyers we can become more sensitive to the

---

[27]Valarie Zeithaml, "Consumer Response to In-store Price Information Environments," *Journal of Consumer Research 8* (March 1982), 357–69.

[28]Christine P. Powell, "An Experimental Investigation of Recognition as a Measure of Price Awareness," Unpublished master's thesis, Department of Marketing, Virginia Polytechnic Institute and State University, Blacksburg, VA (1985); Tridib Mazumdar and Kent B. Monroe, "The Effects of Buyers' Intentions to Learn Price Information on Price Encoding," *Journal of Retailing 66* (Spring 1990), 15–32.

way price may influence our judgments about products that we are considering buying. At the same time, *to secure accurate perceptions of their offerings, price setters must be concerned with identifying buyer's cues.*

Discussion Questions

1. a. Listed below are two sets of prices. Without calculating the differences, which pair of prices, set A or set B, *appears* to be further apart?

A		B	
$83	$67	$87	$71

   b. In the next set of prices, which pair of prices, set A or set B, *appears* to be most different?

A		B	
$79	$93	$75	$89

   c. If you followed the directions and did not calculate the differences, what strategies or rules did you use?

2. a. Listed below are three sets of prices. Without performing any calculations, which set of prices *appears* to have the highest average?

A.	$87	$81	$75	$69
B.	$89	$79	$73	$71
C.	$84	$81	$75	$72

   b. Which set of prices *appears* to have the lowest average?

   c. What strategies or rules did you use to make your judgments?

3. A retail advertisement had the following claim: "50% off entire stock." It then went on to say "70% off original prices when you take an additional 50% off already reduced clearance prices." If an item was originally priced at $20.00, what would be the final price an individual would pay if purchased during this sale? Suppose the product was priced at $27.79, what would be the final price if purchased during this sale? What could the retailer do to make it easier for buyers to know the actual amount they would pay?

4. Look through the various price advertisements in a Sunday newspaper. How frequently are the different price endings used? Are there examples of multidimensional prices? Are there examples of price advertisements that make it difficult for buyers to determine the price they will actually pay?

Suggested Readings

Diller, Hermann, and Andreas Brielmaier: "The Impact of Rounding Up Odd Prices: Results of a Field Experiment in German Drugstores," *Pricing Strategy & Practice 3,* no. 4 (1995), 4–13.

Estelami, Hooman: "The Computational Effect of Price Endings in Multi-dimensional Price Advertising," *Journal of Product & Brand Management Featuring Pricing Strategy & Practice 8,* no. 3 (1999), 244–56.

Gendall, Philip, Michael F. Fox, and Priscilla Wilton: "Estimating the Effect of Odd Pricing," *Journal of Product & Brand Management Featuring Pricing Strategy & Practice 7,* no 5 (1998), 421–32.

Monroe, Kent B., and Angela Y. Lee: "Remembering versus Knowing: Issues in Buyers' Processing of Price Information," *Journal of the Academy of Marketing Science 27,* no. 2 (1999), 207–25.

Naipul, Sandra, and H. G. Parsa: "Menu Price Endings That Communicate Value and Quality," *Cornell Hotel and Restaurant Administration Quarterly 42* (February 2001), 26–37.

Schindler, Robert M., and Thomas M. Kibarian, "Increased Consumer Sales Response through Use of 99-Ending Prices," *Journal of Retailing 72,* no. 2 (1996), 187–99.

CHAPTER SIX

Pricing Practices That Endanger Profits

Irrationally held truths may be more harmful than reasoned errors.

Thomas H. Huxley

In this chapter, we continue to develop important information about how people perceive prices and price differences, stressing the second prescription for becoming a proactive pricer: *It is essential to understand how customers perceive prices, price changes, and price differences.* We first develop the important concept of reference price. Then, we discuss the concept of price thresholds, introduced during our discussion of odd prices in Chapter 5, more completely. Underlying the entire discussion of these two concepts is the key pricing principle: *Prices should be set so as to reflect customers' perceptions of value.* We also present behavioral research evidence that gives insight into how to overcome some critical pricing errors.

Reference Prices

A Brief Historical Perspective

In 1945, Scitovszky observed that consumers attribute two prices to every product: (1) a traditional past price ("normal" or "fair" price) that denotes its worth, and (2) the product's actual price.[1] Buyers contrast this normal or fair price to the actual price whenever they are different, and it is only when they are different that judgments of cheap or expensive occur. Scitovszky suggested that *cheap* was a synonym for inferior quality and *expensive* was a synonym for superior quality. He observed that sellers often use a comparative price framework to introduce a price indicating the product's worth, and a lower actual price indicating a bargain.

During the next 15 years, several French researchers made some important observations.[2] Stoetzel observed that buyers generally are uncertain about the quality of products available for purchase and therefore are uncertain about the "just" price to pay. However, depending on their income level and need for the product, consumers are willing to pay different prices for goods of different quality, and hence of different value. Thus buyers have a price band or *range of acceptable prices* that form a judgment scale to assess prices for a particular product category. They judge prices either as acceptable to pay or unacceptable. Unacceptable prices may be too low or too high relative to this acceptable price range. Adam followed this observation by suggesting that the width of this acceptable price range indicated a customer's degree of uncertainty as to what the price of the product should be. Shortly thereafter, Fouilhé discovered that familiar products had a narrower range of acceptability than unfamiliar products.

In the early 1960s, two English researchers observed that this acceptable price range would be influenced by the price last paid (or customarily paid), as well as the prevailing price structure of the different brands.[3] They concluded that where there are a multiplicity of competitive brands at different prices, consumers will compare the differences in prices with differences in imputed quality.

[1]Tibor Scitovszky, "Some Consequences of the Habit of Judging Quality by Price," *Review of Economic Studies 12,* no. 2 (1944–45), 100–105.

[2]Daniel Adam, *Les Reactions du Consommateur devant Le Prix* (Paris: Sedes, 1958); Pierre Fouilhé, "Evaluation Subjective des Prix," *Revue Francais de Sociologie 1* (1960), 163–72; Jean Stoetzel, "Psychological/Sociological Aspects of Price," from "Reflections (II): French Research: Consumer Studies" by Jean Stoetzel, Jacques Sauerwein, and Alain de Vulpian, in P. L. Reynaud, *La Psychologie Economique*, Lebraire Marcel Riviere et Cie, 183–88.

[3]Andre Gabor and C. W. J. Granger, "The Attitude of the Consumer to Prices," in Bernard Taylor and Gordon Wills, eds., *Pricing Strategy* (London: Staples Press, 1969), 132–51.

Thus from 1945 through 1970, researchers amassed observations and empirical evidence that consumers seem to evaluate prices of particular products by comparing actual prices to some price frame of reference. Moreover, the concept of an acceptable price range implies that this price frame of reference likely is not a reference price *point*, but rather some form of a subjective or psychological judgment scale. They suggested that this judgment scale would vary by income class, general price level of the product category, previous price(s) paid, the prevailing price structure, and the degree of buyer uncertainty, which was linked to product familiarity.

Theoretical Bases for Reference Prices

Around 1970 several researchers offered arguments for the existence of reference prices, acceptable price ranges, and a logarithmic psychological scale for price judgments.[4] These initial arguments were based on adaptation-level theory and assimilation-contrast theory (social judgment theory). Prospect theory also provides a basis for the reference price concept.

Adaptation-Level Theory

Adaptation-level theory is based on the assumption that people judge stimuli with respect to internal norms (*adaptation levels*) representing the combined effects of present and past experiences.[5] Therefore, all judgments are relative to an individual's existing adaptation level. The adaptation level denotes a *region* rather than a point on a continuum, and it changes from moment to moment.

An individual's behavior represents an adaptation to three classes of stimuli or cues: focal, contextual, and organic. *Focal cues* are the stimuli the individual is directly responding to, such as price. *Contextual* or *background cues* are other behaviorally based stimuli. *Organic cues* refer to the inner physiological and psychological processes affecting behavior. In this framework, purchase offers, including price, are the focal stimuli. Available monetary resources, purpose of

---

[4]Kent B. Monroe, "Measuring Price Thresholds by Psychophysics and Latitudes of Acceptance," *Journal of Marketing Research 8* (November 1971), 460–64; Kent B. Monroe, "Buyers' Subjective Perceptions of Price," *Journal of Marketing Research 10* (February 1973), 70–80.
[5]Harry Helson, *Adaptation-Level Theory* (New York: Harper & Row, 1964).

purchase, and the purchase environment—including other offers—are the contextual stimuli. Organic cues include the amount of cognitive resources a person has available to process the information about the product and offer. Thus, buyers' price perceptions depend on the actual price and their reference price or adaptation level (AL), which is influenced by these three classes of cues.

Every new price an individual encounters tends to move the adaptation-level price in its own direction (*anchoring effect*). New prices near the buyer's original adaptation level tend to have little effect on this change in adaptation level, and buyers typically judge them to be neutral, indifferent, equal, and medium relative to other prices. However, prices far above and below the original adaptation level not only displace the adaptation level in their direction, *but may also change the individual's perception of other prices in the series (contrast effect).* For example, assume an individual's reference price for a midsize automobile is "around $15,000." An article describing some of next year's midsize automobiles indicates that prices for these featured automobiles will be $22,000 and up. This new price information will shift the person's adaptation-level price for this category of automobiles upward, perhaps to "near $20,000." Previously, a midsize automobile priced at $14,500 would likely have been judged as an average price when the adaptation-level price was around $15,000. However, after the adaptation-level price shifts up to near $20,000, a $14,500 price would be perceived as "low," "not expensive," or perhaps "a good buy." Thus, a contrast effect has occurred as the judgment of the $14,500 price has shifted away from the neutral area of the judgment scale and away from the new adaptation-level price.

The concept of adaptation level or reference price indicates that *buyers judge or evaluate prices comparatively.* That is, buyers judge the acceptability of a price by comparison to another price. The comparative price is the buyer's reference price for that particular judgment. Failure to recognize this key point leads to the first pricing error, *not distinguishing between pricing strategies and pricing tactics.* In Box 6.1, a local tortilla producer tactically maintained price to be "competitive" on price with Frito-Lay, but ignored the important strategic issue of competing on perceived value (perceived quality to perceived sacrifice relationship—see Equation 5.1 on page 104.)

MAJOR ERROR #1: PRICING STRATEGY VERSUS PRICING TACTICS

BOX 6.1

The discussion in Chapter 5 laid some of the foundation for thinking about the relationship between price and perceived value. A local tortilla chip producer in the Phoenix market did not understand this relationship. The local tortilla chip enjoyed a competitive advantage until Frito-Lay upgraded its Tostitos chip. Instead of raising its price to continue to reflect a perceived quality–value relationship similar to that of Tostitos, the local producer reduced its quality and costs, but maintained price to protect its margin. Customers soon recognized that the local chip was now an inferior product, and they shifted their purchases to Frito-Lay.

Source: "Panelists Offer Pricing Strategy Advice for Consumer and Industrial Products," *Marketing News* (February 1, 1985), 1, 10–11.

Some important implications of adaptation-level theory for price perceptions are that[6]

1. Price perceptions are relative to other prices and to the product use.

2. There is a reference price for each discernible quality level for each product category, and this price influences judgments of other prices.

3. There is a region of indifference about a reference price such that changes in price within this region produce no change in perception.

4. The reference price may be some average of the range of prices for similar products and need not correspond to any actual price or to the price of the leading brand.

5. Buyers do not judge each price singly; rather they compare each price with the reference price and the other prices in the price range.

These principles of price perception stress the relativeness of buyers' perceptions of price. That is, judgments about prices are comparative and buyers apparently have some internal knowledge about the prices for different discernible quality levels for each product category. Although two prices may be different, consumers may not discriminate between them, that

[6]Fred E. Emery, "Some Psychological Aspects of Price," in Bernard Taylor and Gordon Wills (eds.), *Pricing Strategy,* 98–111.

is, they may not perceive them to be different. It is also possible that the price used for the comparative standard is an internal representation that may not correspond to any actual price at the time the comparative judgment is being made.

When considering how buyers perceive prices, bear in mind that perception is relative. That is, buyers compare a specific price to another price, or a reference price. Since consumers evaluate prices comparatively, their judgment of acceptability depends not only on their price expectations, but also on information in promotions or advertisements.

Assimilation-Contrast Theory

Similar to adaptation-level theory, the basic tenet of assimilation-contrast theory is that an individual compares new stimuli to a background of previous experience with the stimuli category.[7] This experience forms an individual's reference scale (sometimes referred to as a psychological scale). This reference scale changes when new stimuli are added or the total range of stimuli is shifted. The reference scale serves as a basis for an individual to compare and evaluate other subsequently encountered stimuli *perceived as related to* the reference scale stimuli.

New stimuli encountered for evaluation may also serve as anchors that result in changing the reference scale. Whether this changing or displacement of the reference scale toward the new stimulus produces an assimilation or a contrast effect depends on how other stimuli in the category are judged *after* the introduction of the new stimulus. For example, consider again the person interested in a midsize automobile. Assume that this individual has a reasonably well-established reference scale for the prices of midsize automobiles—$15,000–$17,000. Prices below this range of prices would be judged low (i.e., relatively lower), and prices above the reference range would be judged high (i.e., relatively higher). What happens when this person encounters a new automobile price for this category that is above this reference range, perhaps $20,000? As suggested by both adaptation-level theory and assimilation-contrast theory, the reference price range should move in the direction of this new price. However, as this reference price range moves toward the new price, the previously lower prices

---

[7]Muzafer Sherif and Carl I. Hovland, *Social Judgment* (New Haven, CT: Yale University Press, 1961).

become further away from the reference price scale. When judgments of these previously perceived low prices in the category do not change when a new price is encountered, an *assimilation effect* occurs because the new price is perceived as similar to the reference prices (i.e., closer to, or more similar).

However, when the new price displaces the reference price range by a sufficient margin, the original low prices will be perceived as lower than previously, and a *contrast effect* is said to occur. This contrast effect occurs because the new prices are perceived as different from the reference price (i.e., further away or not similar), but as still belonging to the same price category. With increased discrepancy between the reference scale and the new anchoring prices, the extent of the shift toward the anchor decreases, dwindling towards zero with the most remote price anchor. When the perceived differences between the new prices and the reference scale are extreme, they may not be perceived as belonging to the same product category, but rather as belonging to two entirely different categories. Thus, for assimilation or contrast effects to occur, the individual has to perceive that the new prices (anchors) belong to the same product category.

Prospect Theory and Transaction Utility

As with the above theories, prospect theory shows that an evaluation of an outcome is strongly influenced by a standard of comparison, reference point, or "zero" point.[8] This reference point determines whether outcomes are characterized as gains or losses; a shift in the reference point can change the comparative value of outcomes and thereby alter choice. As we will develop in Chapter 7, the value of an economic exchange can be decomposed into *acquisition value* (the perceived value of the economic good to the purchaser) and *transaction value* (the perceived value of the offer itself). If the price to be paid is less than an individual's reference price, transaction value is positive and enhances acquisition value to create additional perceived value.[9]

---

[8]Daniel Kahneman and Amos Tversky, "Prospect Theory: An Analysis of Decision Under Risk," *Econometrica 47* (March 1979), 263–91.

[9]Dhruv Grewal, Kent B. Monroe, and R. Krishnan, "The Effects of Price-Comparison Advertising on Buyers' Perceptions of Acquisition Value, Transaction Value, and Behavioral Intentions," *Journal of Marketing 62* (April 1998), 46–59.

As with the earlier theories presented, prospect theory recognizes that people judge or evaluate new stimuli relative to their current reference scale. When making comparative judgments, people judge new stimuli relative to their perceived difference from their internal reference scale.

Integrating the Theories

These theories lead to the conclusion that the *reference "point" is really a range of prices that are judged to be neutral or medium.* This internal reference range is *for prices within a specific product category or for a specific product in that category* and does not necessarily extend across all possible categories of an entity. For example, the product category automobiles is perceived to consist of several distinctive price categories.[10] Third, *the reference point or reference range is continuously changing as new prices are encountered.* These newly encountered prices serve as anchors, and if the reference range is displaced in a direction toward these new prices an assimilation effect is said to occur. Contrast effects occur when the new prices are perceived as different from the reference prices, but within the same category as the reference range. Fourth, *perceptions of prices equidistant from the reference price, but in opposite directions, are asymmetrical.* Prices above an individual's reference range are perceived as closer to the reference price than prices below the reference price, even though they may be an equal numerical distance from it. Thus, as with people's mental number line observed in Chapter 5 in our discussion on numerical cognition, buyers' psychological price ranges appear to follow some form of a logarithmic function rather than an arithmetic function.

An individual's reference range is continuously changing. The reference price changes as soon as new prices are encountered, whether in an experimental setting, an advertisement, or a purchase situation for another unit of the product. In addition, the particular structure of the price stimuli that the person is exposed to changes the reference range, as does the sequential order that these particular prices are available to the individual.

Many selling situations provide buyers with two prices: a *higher "regular" price* that may be compared to the current

---

[10]Paul M. Herr, "Priming Price: Prior Knowledge and Context Effects," *Journal of Consumer Research 16* (June 1989), 67–75.

lower selling price. We have adopted the convention of referring to the higher comparative price as an *external reference price*. It should be clear that the concept of a reference price scale is only an internal norm for such judgments and evaluations. New prices, such as an externally supplied comparative price, may serve as anchors that lead to shifts in the individual's internal reference price range. However, given these theoretical bases, the externally supplied comparative price is *not* a substitute for the internal reference price per se.

Implications for Pricing Strategies and Tactics

Thus buyers do form and use reference prices when evaluating prices, and buyers' internal reference prices do influence product evaluations, behavioral intentions, choice behavior, and quantity to purchase decisions. Quite importantly, the inability of buyers to accurately recall prices paid does not deflect from this conclusion. Pricing managers need to recognize that there are some important implications for distinguishing between pricing strategies and tactics (see Box 6.1).

Product-Line Pricing

In product-line pricing, the evidence suggests that the lowest and highest prices in the product line are more noticeable than those between and hence, *anchor* buyers' judgments. These end prices, along with the reference price, may accentuate the perceived value for a given product (a bargain) or may diminish the perceived value (too expensive), depending on where the product's price lies in the product line.[11] These same phenomena may occur when a single product is compared with a number of competitive products. If either or both end prices are outside the acceptable price range, a contrast effect may develop, and the products would be evaluated within a different context (see Chapter 15).

The perception of a sale price may depend on the position of the price in the price range. If the sale price is below other offerings, buyers may perceive a bargain (assimilation effect), or buyers may not believe that the sale price is a reduction from the advertised original price (contrasting

---

[11]Susan M. Petroshius and Kent B. Monroe, "Effect of Product-Line Characteristics on Product Evaluations," *Journal of Consumer Research 13* (March 1987), 511–19.

effect). For example, buyers might react more favorably if $600 television sets were on sale for $450 than if these sets were advertised as being on sale at $299.

If the price range is narrowed by shifting the end prices toward the middle of the range, or if there is little variation in prices, price becomes less dominant in purchase decisions. One reason for this result is that buyers will have greater difficulty discriminating among alternative choices leading to assimilation effects (no perceived price differences). Where there are few perceived price differences, buyers tend to base their choices on other factors, such as brand name.[12]

Order of Presenting Prices

The order in which buyers are exposed to alternative prices affects their perceptions. Buyers who initially see high prices will perceive subsequent lower prices as less expensive than they would if they initially see low prices.[13] Figure 6.1 illustrates the results from research testing the effect of the order of price presentation on buyers' judgments of the relative expensiveness of alternative prices. In the *descending price series*, people were asked to evaluate the prices for a product beginning with $23, and going successively to lower prices (i.e., $22, $21, . . . , $11, $10). In the *ascending price series*, people were asked to evaluate the prices for the same product beginning with $7, and then going successively to higher prices (i.e., $8, $9, . . . , $19, $20).

The common prices ($10 to $20) were judged to be significantly more expensive by the people evaluating them in the increasing order of magnitude—the ascending price series—than by the people judging these same prices in the decreasing order of magnitude—the descending series. When a reference or adaptation-level price is higher than the price being judged, then the perceptual phenomenon of contrast makes the lower price appear less than it is. Similarly, when the reference price is lower than the price being judged, then this contrast effect

[12]Kent B. Monroe, "The Influence of Price Differences and Brand Familiarity on Brand Preferences," *Journal of Consumer Research 3* (June 1976), 42–49.

[13]Albert J. Della Bitta and Kent B. Monroe, "The Influence of Adaptation Levels on Subjective Price Perceptions," in S. Ward and P. Wright (eds.), *Advances in Consumer Research,* vol. 1 (Boston: Association for Consumer Research, 1974), 359–69; Robert Slonim and Ellen Garbarino, "The Effect of Price History on Demand as Mediated by Perceived Price Expensiveness," *Journal of Business Research 45* (May 1999), 1–14.

FIGURE 6.1 **Effect of Order of Presentation on Price Perceptions**

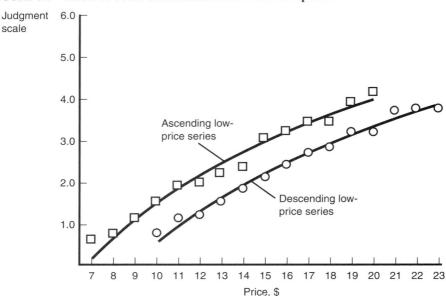

makes the price being judged appear to be more than it is. This perceptual effect helps explain why people, in general, are more sensitive to price increases than to price decreases.

Introductory Pricing Strategies and Tactics

Sellers commonly introduce new products with short-term "introductory low-price promotions." One of the objectives of this pricing tactic is to induce people to try the product to facilitate market penetration. However, available evidence indicates that this tactic of introducing a new product to the market using a short-term introductory low sale price produces lower long-run sales volume than if the product is introduced at its regular price.[14] Figure 6.2 and Table 6.1 illustrate this research result. In this research, a new brand was introduced at a low introductory price in one set of stores and at the normal selling price in a matched set of stores. After a short period of time the low introductory price was raised to the normal selling price and sales were monitored in both sets of stores during the entire period.

[14]Anthony Doob, J. Merrill Carlsmith, Jonathan L. Freedmen, Thomas K. Landauer, and Tom Soleng, "Effect of Initial Selling Price on Subsequent Sales," *Journal of Personality and Social Psychology 11* (1969), 345–50.

FIGURE 6.2

Sales Effect of an Introductory Price

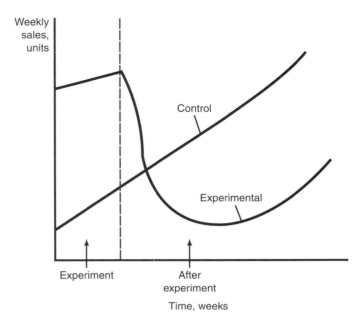

Table 6.2 summarizes the results of these experiments. In all five experiments the results are similar. The introductory low price produced more sales than in the control condition, but after the low price was raised to the normal selling price, sales were greater in the control condition. Although one might hastily conclude that the sales results in the experimental condition simply reflect a downward-sloping demand curve, the time series pattern of sales in the study belies this simple explanation. Whereas the control sales curve exhibits a steady growth in sales, the experimental sales curve drops and remains below the control sales curve after the prices are changed. Finally, the introductory low price tactic produced $3,364 less in contributions to profit than obtained from the control price conditions.

The implication of this study is that the tactic of an introductory low price to generate short-term sales actually may hinder the development of a favorable long-term sales pattern and may sacrifice contributions to profits. When a product is put on sale at a relatively lower price customers may tend to think of the value of the product in terms of the low price. When the price is increased subsequently to its regular price, these customers will tend to perceive it as overpriced, and will not be inclined to buy it at this much higher price. That is, the introductory low price serves as a reference price for evaluating a perceived price increase when the price is

TABLE 6.1   **Effect of Initial Selling Price on Subsequent Sales**

Product	Experimental Condition	Price, $	Length of Treatment, Weeks	Average Weekly Sales, Units*	
				During Experimental Price	After Experimental Price
Mouthwash	Experimental	0.25	1½	300	365
	Control	0.39	5	270	375
Toothpaste	Experimental	0.41	3	1,280	1,010
	Control	0.49	8	860	1,050
Aluminum foil	Experimental	0.59	3	4,110	3,275
	Control	0.64	8	2,950	3,395
Light bulbs	Experimental	0.26	1	7,350	5,270
	Control	0.32	4	5,100	5,285
Cookies	Experimental	0.24	2	21,925	22,590
	Control	0.29	6	21,725	23,225

*Not reported directly but estimated from graphical presentation of the data in Anthony Doob, J. Merrill Carlsmith, Jonathan L. Freedman, Thomas K. Landauer, and Tom Soleng, "Effect of Initial Selling Price on Subsequent Sales," *Journal of Personality and Social Psychology 11* (1969), 345–50.

raised to its normal price. And the contrast effect accentuates the price increase and makes it appear even greater than it is.

Consider the situation at the Singapore Sheraton in 1988. Management faced a very difficult pricing decision as they prepared to open the new Singapore Sheraton. The Ministry of Tourism had predicted that for the next several years, the number of business visitors and tourists was expected to remain at current levels and not grow as had been forecasted several years previously. Several other five-star hotels had either recently opened or were under construction, effectively doubling the number of hotel bed-nights available in Singapore within the next two years. Management expected that as the supply of hotel rooms increased relative to the flat demand for these rooms, five-star room prices would fall to four-star rates, with subsequent downward pressure on all hotel room prices. They did not want to reduce the reference value of their rooms by opening at lower listed prices than strategically desired. Thus, they purchased several credit card address lists worldwide and mailed a brochure and letter announcing the opening of the new Singapore Sheraton. Included in the brochure were pictures of the facilities and a room rate schedule. Finally, they offered coupons for up to five room-nights free within a defined time period. They gave away 20,000 room-nights, but by 1990, 80 percent of their business was repeat visits. Moreover, they maintained their five-star rates despite the flat demand for hotel rooms in Singapore during this period. Once the guests had tried the Singapore Sheraton, they recognized the value of the rooms at the regular room rates and returned on subsequent visits.

Price Thresholds

Absolute Price Thresholds

An important concept introduced in our discussion of reference price was the *acceptable price range*. This concept implies that buyers have a lower and upper price threshold. Furthermore, the existence of a lower price threshold implies that there are positive prices greater than $0, which are unacceptable because they are considered to be too low, perhaps because buyers are suspicious of the product's quality. Sometimes the upper price threshold is referred to as the buyer's *reservation price*. Regardless of the term used, it recognizes that at specific points in time there is a maximum price that buyers are willing to pay for a product or service. However, there is not just one acceptable price for a product or service; instead, there is some range of acceptable prices.

The acceptable price range has two dimensions that need to be considered. Individuals may differ not only in how *wide* a range of prices they may consider acceptable for a product category, but also in the price *level* around which this range is centered. For example, person A might consider it acceptable to pay $15,000 to $25,000 for an automobile while person B might be willing to pay $20,000 to $30,000. In this example, the width of their acceptable price range is identical—$10,000. But, for person A this acceptable price range is centered around $20,000 whereas for person B it is centered around $25,000.

Research has confirmed the existence of a range of prices buyers are willing to pay. As expected, it has been shown that the acceptable price range for a product shifts downward as buyers' income declines. Yet, as income falls, the upper price threshold drops less than the lower price threshold, implying that a low price is a more powerful deterrent to higher income groups than is a high price to lower income groups. These price limits are not constant, but shift as buyers obtain more information about the actual price range in the market or about the range of prices in a specific product line.

Variations in the level and width of buyers' acceptable price ranges are influenced by a number of factors. Research indicates that for a specific product category the upper price threshold is lower if buyers perceive that similar alternative offerings are available. However, if customer satisfaction increases or buyers become more loyal, then the upper threshold tends to be higher. Conversely, if customer satisfaction declines leading to lower buyer loyalty, buyers' upper price threshold would become lower. When buyers are relatively uncertain about prices for a product category—that is, when they are not knowledgeable—their acceptable price ranges tend to be relatively narrow and their lower and upper acceptable price limits tend to be lower than those of more knowledgeable buyers. Indeed, research indicates that as buyers become more knowledgeable, these lower and upper price limits tend to increase, with the upper price limit increasing more to produce wider acceptable price ranges. Moreover, we would expect that buyers' reference price (acceptable level) would increase as these buyers become more knowledgeable about market prices and variations in quality. This increase would also lead to wider acceptable price ranges as long as buyers' knowledge about the actual price and product quality relationship supports using price as an indicator of quality. Buyers who infer quality on the basis of price do tend to have higher acceptable price levels, higher upper acceptable price limits, and wider acceptable price ranges. On the other hand, buyers who are consciously concerned about prices tend to have lower acceptable price levels, lower upper acceptable price limits, and narrower acceptable price ranges.[15]

[15]Rashmi Adaval and Kent B. Monroe, "The Moderating Effects of Learning Goals and the Acquisition of Product Information on the Limits of Price Acceptability," in Frank R. Kardes and Mita Sujan, eds., *Advances in Consumer Research*, vol. 22 (Provo, UT: Association for Consumer Research, 1995), 225–29; Anthony D. Cox, "New Evidence Concerning Consumer Price Limits," in Richard J. Lutz, ed., *Advances in Consumer Research*, vol. 13 (Provo, UT: Association for Consumer Research, 1986), 268–71; Gurumurthy Kalyanaram and John D. C. Little, "An Empirical Analysis of Latitude of Price Acceptance in Consumer Package Goods," *Journal of Consumer Research 21* (December 1994), 408–18; Donald R. Lichtenstein, Peter H. Bloch, and William C. Black, "Correlates of Price Acceptability," *Journal of Consumer Research 15* (September 1988), 243–52; Kent B. Monroe, "Measuring Price Thresholds by Psychophysics and Latitudes of Acceptance," *Journal of Marketing Research 8* (November 1971), 460–64; Akshay R. Rao and Wanda Sieben, "The Effect of Prior Knowledge on Price Acceptability and the Type of Information Examined," *Journal of Consumer Research 19* (September 1992), 256–70.

MAJOR ERROR #2: PERCEIVED VALUE VERSUS PRICE (MICKEY GOOFED!)

BOX 6.2

Disneyland Paris, formerly known as Euro Disney, opened in April 1992 on the eastern outskirts of Paris. However, things did not go well in the 1992–1994 period. In fact, by winter 1993, five theme hotels were half-empty and a sixth hotel was closed. By 1994, losses were averaging $1 million a day.

Prior to Disneyland Paris's April 1995 opening, a market research survey determined that French consumers had a psychological threshold for theme park admission price of 200 French francs. That is, French people were unwilling to spend more than 200 francs for a single adult to enter the park. So Disneyland Paris reduced the 1995 admission price for a single adult from 250 francs to 195 francs. By setting the price below the 200-franc threshold, managers forecast an increase of 500,000 visitors to the park for 1995. That is, they projected about a 5.7 percent increase in the number of visitors in response to a 22 percent decrease in admission price. However, the number of visitors increased by approximately 23 percent in 1995 and, overall, by 33 percent by the end of the 1996 season. By 1996, 40 percent

of the visitors were French, half of them from the Paris area, and the park operated at a profit for the first time in 1995.

Apparently, managers at Disney did not understand that there are limits or absolute thresholds to the relationship between price, perceived quality, and perceived value. These limits to the relationship between price and perceived value were different for French people than they had been in earlier park openings for Americans or Japanese. Disney initially failed to recognize the important link between perceptions of quality and perceptions of value.

The reluctance of a French household to pay more than 200 francs for a single adult admission to Disneyland Paris in 1995 has disappeared. For the April through November 2000 season, the price for a single adult was 220 francs.

Sources: "Ticket Prices Drop at Disneyland Paris," *Chicago Tribune* (March 15, 1995), Section 3, 3; "Disney's Park Fools European Skeptics," *Chicago Tribune* (April 20, 1997), Section 3, 1.

Thus people apparently may refrain from purchasing a product not only when the price is considered to be too high, but also when the price is considered to be too low. Box 6.2 illustrates the pricing error made at Disneyland Paris, where French buyers were unwilling to pay more than a specific amount.

At a given time there can be an unexplained psychological barrier to price changes—an apparent reluctance to pay more than a certain amount. The candy bar example in Chapter 1 illustrates this point. Initially people were not willing to pay more than $1.00 for a multiple pack of candy bars. However, they eventually adapted to paying more than $1.00, and prices now reflect this acceptance. During the mid-1980s, cereal manufacturers found consumer resistance

BREAKING THE $1,000 BARRIER   BOX 6.3

On February 26, 1997, Compaq Computer Corp. introduced its $999 Presario 2000 personal computer. This computer was a sleek, black unit loaded with a 133-Mhz processor, CD-ROM drive, fast modem, stereo speakers, and 32 megabytes of memory. Although Packard Bell had actually entered the sub-$1,000 market six weeks earlier, experts believed that the market share leader's entry would make a difference. At that time, only 12 percent of households with incomes of less than $30,000 had a PC. Moreover, it was expected that households with higher levels of income would now be willing to add a second or third computer for other household members.

By early fall 1997, PCs selling for less than $1,000 accounted for 20 percent to 30 percent of PC sales through retail stores, up from 7 percent in January 1997. And by March 1998, 30 percent of all retail store PC sales were for sub-$1,000 machines, of which a third of these sales were to people who had never before purchased a PC. At that time, analysts were predicting that over 60 percent of U.S. homes would have a PC by 2002 and that 25 percent of U.S. homes would have multiple PCs in their homes by that time.

Sources: "Breaking the $1,000 Barrier," *Business Week*, (February 17, 1997), 75; Barbara Sullivan, "PC Bandwagon Lowering Fares," *Chicago Tribune*, (March 6, 1997), Section 3, 1, 2; "Uh-Oh, They're Going Like Hotcakes," *Business Week*, (October 13, 1997), 55–58; "Cheap PCs," *Business Week*, (March 23, 1998), 28–32.

to paying more than $3.00 for a box of dry cereal. As with the candy example, consumers adapted, and we now find dry cereal priced for more than $3.00 a box.

When IBM introduced its PC-jr personal computer in 1984, it was priced at about $1,200. In the first nine months following introduction, approximately 70,000 units were sold. Price was then reduced to under $900 and 200,000 additional units were sold in the next three months, primarily to the household market. At that time, consumers were reluctant to pay more than $1,000 for a home personal computer. However, IBM soon withdrew the PC-jr personal computer from the market, and it was about 10 years before computer manufacturers returned to the under-$1,000 market segment (see Box 6.3).

The acceptable price range concept is useful in understanding why buyers perceive that price is an indicator of quality. When buyers perceive that prices are relatively lower than they expect, then they may become suspicious of the product's quality. At such low prices, this low perceived quality may provide less satisfaction than the perceived sacrifice of the low price. Hence the mental trade-off illustrated in Figure 5.1, page 105, may lead to a negative perceived value. As with the findings about using odd pricing, an unacceptable low price may actually reduce the buyer's perceived value. At the other extreme, a perceived high price may lead to a perception of sacrifice that is greater than the perceived quality, also leading to a reduction in buyers' perceptions of value. Thus it is important that price setters not only consider the relationships among price, perceived quality, and perceived value, but also recognize that there are limits to these relationships.

Differential Price Thresholds

Usually a buyer has alternative choices available for a contemplated purchase and selects from among these choices. The prices of these alternative choices may provide cues (or information) that facilitate the decision process. However, even if numerical prices are different, it cannot be assumed that the prices are *perceived* to be different. Thus the problem becomes one of determining the effect of *perceived price differences* on buyer choice. Two concepts introduced in Chapter 2 are relevant when considering the issue of price differences: price elasticity and cross-price elasticity of demand.

Price Elasticity of Demand

Weber's law has often been cited as the basis for inferences concerning perceived price differences (see Equation 5.2). As Weber's law indicates, the perception of a price change or difference depends on the magnitude of the change. In addition, people are more sensitive to perceived price increases than to decreases, and the value of K in Equation 5.2 on page 108 varies for different products. The immediate implication is that buyers will be more sensitive to price changes for some products; that is, they will have lower differential price thresholds. But buyers may not perceive similar price changes for other products, thereby suggesting that these products have a relatively high K value.

As the example about pricing potato chips in Box 6.4 illustrates, relative price is a more important concept than absolute price. The concept of price elasticity (either own-price or cross-price elasticity) indicates how buyers perceive a price relative to another price, whether that price be the previous price paid, the price of the leading competitive offering, the highest or lowest price in the product line, or the expected price. In particular, price elasticity of demand, E_d, indicates the sensitivity of buyers to a price change for a particular product. Thus, if buyers *perceive* that the product's price is different from the last time they purchased it, then the issue is

MAJOR PRICING ERROR #3: ABSOLUTE VERSUS RELATIVE PRICE

BOX 6.4

The experience of a major snack food producer illustrates the *error of not recognizing the difference between absolute price and relative price*. Several years ago, the price of a specific size of this brand's potato chips was $1.59 whereas a comparable size of the local brand was $1.29, a difference of 30 cents. Over a period of time, the price of the national brand increased several times until it was being retailed at $1.89. In like manner, the local brand's price increased to $1.59. However, although the local brand was maintaining a 30-cent price differential, the national brand obtained a significant gain in market share. The problem was that buyers perceived a 30¢ price difference relative to $1.89 as less than a 30¢ price difference relative to $1.59. This example illustrates the notion of *differential price thresholds*, or the degree to which buyers are sensitive to relative price differences.

whether this perceived price difference makes a difference in their purchasing behavior. For example, a price reduction from $1.30 to $1.25 may not be sufficient to induce buyers to buy more of the product, whereas a price reduction to $1.15 might lead to an increase in demand. Conversely, a price increase from $1.30 to $1.35 might not be sufficient to deter some buyers from purchasing it, but an increase to $1.40 might lead to a noticeable decrease in demand.

Cross-Price Elasticity of Demand

The differential price issue is how the price of one product is perceived to differ from the price of another offering that buyers believe is an alternative choice to consider. These alternative products could be sold by different sellers competitively or they could be alternative models of the product sold by a single seller. For example, Kodak cameras compete with Minolta, Polaroid, and other brands as well as with different models within the Kodak camera line. From a managerial perspective, an important issue is how to price the different cameras within the product line as well as how to price the cameras relative to the competitors' cameras. Perhaps the most important strategic aspect of a pricing manager's job is to learn how to manage the price differentials within a product line as well as relative to competitors' products. Indeed, the idea of product positioning hinges directly on establishing price differentials relative to the pricing objectives for the product line.

CHOOSING AN EASY-TO-USE CAMERA

BOX 6.5

I. Assume you are interested in buying an inexpensive, easy-to-use camera. You are interested in a camera that is simple to use, has few options or buttons that you must learn how to use, is easy to load film, and takes very good pictures. So one day you go to a camera shop to get such a camera. At the camera shop, you settle on considering one manufacturer's line of cameras priced as shown below.

A	B	C	D	E
$35	$39	$59	$65	$99

Because you are interested in a low-price camera you are trying to decide between model A and model B. Model B is the same as model A except it has one extra feature: By pressing one button, you can take a close-up of your picture subject in addition to using the standard built-in focus that is available in both models. Which model would you choose, A or B? Why?

II. Now assume the same purchase objectives as in Part I, but with the prices of the five cameras as given below. You still are trying to choose between models A and B, and camera B is exactly as described above. Which camera would you choose now, A or B? Why?

A	B	C	D	E
$35	$45	$59	$75	$99

To illustrate this point consider the situation depicted in Box 6.5. Typically, when this illustration is used in training programs, virtually all of the participants choose camera model B in Part I, but a substantial number of them shift to camera A in Part II. Their reasoning for these choices is that the close-up feature is worth more than the $4 differential in Part I, but is not worth the $10 differential in Part II.

In Box 6.5, the range of prices in both sets is $35 to $99. However, in Part I, the prices for cameras A and B appear to be relatively close together, and the prices for cameras C and D also appear to be relatively close together. As a result, it appears that the manufacturer has cameras for three separate segments: a low-price segment (cameras A and B), a middle-price segment (cameras C and D), and a high-price segment (camera E). By building an extra feature in B, but pricing it perceptually close to A, and taking a similar approach for C and D, the manufacturer primarily sells cameras B and D. We can call this approach to pricing the product line the *trading-up pricing strategy* because buyers typically purchase the "better" camera in each price position.

The pricing in Part II, on the other hand, is the *segmented pricing strategy* because each price seems to stand by itself and it appears that there are five distinct cameras. The

A COMPETITOR LENDS A HELPING HAND

BOX 6.6

A producer of a consumer packaged good developed and marketed two versions of a product, A and B. The two versions were quite similar except that the label and packaging used for B gave it an image of being a better product. Initially A and B were the only two products in the market and the firm priced them as follows:

A	B
$14.95	$18.95

As would be expected, the lower-priced version, A, was the firm's best-selling product in this line. However, after a time, a competitor introduced its version of the product, C, positioning it as a high-price, high-quality product. Now the prices of the three products were:

A	B	C
$14.95	$18.95	$34.95

Interestingly, in a very short time, version B became the first firm's best-selling product in this product category! The product manager was mystified and sought help to figure out what had happened.

numerical difference between the prices in Part II increases as the prices get larger: $10, $14, $16, $24. These prices follow the psychophysical principle underlying our mental number line. Remember, as numbers get larger, the numerical difference between them is compressed in our minds. If we want the numbers to be perceived to be different in magnitude, we need to widen the difference between them as they increase in numerical value (Weber's law). Depending on our strategic pricing objectives for the product line, we can set prices to enhance the sale of one or more products in the line via some variation of the trading-up strategy, or we can set prices to permit each product to "sell itself" by using a variation of the segmentation strategy.

Understanding this basic psychophysical principle of - pricing has other important implications relative to how the overall price structure of competing offerings may influence demand. To illustrate this point further consider the true example in Box 6.6. Can you figure out why sales of B increased after a competitor introduced a much higher priced version?

To understand the psychological dynamics at work in this example first consider how buyers would evaluate B relative to A when they were the only two products in this category on the retail shelf. On a subjective scale of expensiveness, B would be judged as expensive, or perhaps high-priced.

However, after the competitor had introduced C, B would then be judged as not expensive, or perhaps moderately priced. Second, the $16 price difference between C and B made the $4 price difference between A and B perceptually smaller than previously. In effect, the perceptual effect of the competitor's pricing changed the perception of a product from expensive to not expensive. Third, it is a known human tendency to not choose extremes when there is a middle option. Indeed, a research study found that when buyers had multiple choices, their preferences tended to gravitate toward the "middle-priced" brands.[16] Thus, for these three reasons, consumers who had previously preferred A now purchased B. This example clearly indicates that when buyers cannot evaluate quality the strategic use of price information can influence preferences and choices.

Decomposing Price Elasticity

Price Increases versus Price Decreases

As indicated earlier, buyers, in general, are more sensitive to perceived price increases than to perceived price decreases. This result is consistent with behavioral research both on how people perceive gains and losses and on how buyers adapt to price changes. In practical terms, this difference in relative price elasticity between price increases and price decreases means it is easier to lose sales from current buyers by increasing price than it is to gain sales from new buyers by reducing price. (Later, when we introduce costs into the analysis in Chapter 11, this relative difference in elasticities becomes important in terms of determining the profitability of price changes.)

For local telephone calls, the price elasticity following a price decrease was estimated to be -0.022, whereas the price elasticity following a price increase was -0.215. In this case, the ratio of price-increase elasticity to price-decrease elasticity was 9.77. Other researchers have estimated this ratio to vary between 1.3 and 4.0 for different grocery products.[17]

---

[16]Kent B. Monroe and David M. Gardner, "An Experimental Inquiry into the Effect of Price on Brand Preference," *Proceedings*, Fall Conference (Chicago: American Marketing Association, 1976), 552–56.

[17]Miles O. Bidwell, Jr., Bruce X. Wang, and J. Douglas Zona, "An Analysis of Asymmetric Demand Response to Price Changes: The Case of Local Telephone Calls," *Journal of Regulatory Economics 8* (November 1995), 285–98.

Competitive Effects

Research also confirms that price elasticity of demand varies over brands within the same product category. In one product category, elasticity varied from -0.84 to -4.56.[18] Price elasticity also varies over market segments, but, interestingly seems to be independent of market share. However, price elasticity is not independent of the relative price level. The further a brand's price is from the product category's average price, in either direction, the lower will be its price elasticity.

If a brand's price is already at the extreme end of the price-market range, then a more substantial price change will be needed to produce a perceived price change. Extreme prices, high or low, become more price elastic as the prices are changed toward the market average or as competitors' pricing moves the brand's price toward the market average. Price elasticity will be relatively higher for products in the middle of a category because such a position increases the difficulty of establishing either a "low"-price or "high"-quality image.[19] Hence the perceived price difference between offerings seen as similar is a key aspect of a brand's price positioning. Box 6.7 shows how Pier 1 Imports got caught in a positioning dilemma by following a strategy of improving its price–quality image.

Asymmetric Competition

As we observed in Chapter 2, price elasticity of demand is affected most by the substitution effect. That is, the degree that demand for a product or brand is price elastic or inelastic depends on its cross-price elasticity relative to competing products. Moreover, as the Pier 1 Import example indicates (Box 6.7), a brand's price–quality positioning relative to its competitors influences its price elasticity. These competitive effects not only are asymmetric relative to price increases or decreases, but also relative to the price–quality positions of the competing products—price promotions by a higher-priced brand affect the market share of a lower-priced brand more than the reverse. Also, brands that are closer to each

---

[18]William T. Moran, "Insights from Pricing Research," in Earl L. Bailey, ed., *Pricing Practices and Strategies* (New York: The Conference Board, 1978), 7–13.
[19]Joel Huber, Morris B. Holbrook, and Barbara Kahn, "Effects of Competitive Context and of Additional Information on Price Sensitivity," *Journal of Marketing Research 23* (August 1986), 250–60.

PIER 1 IMPORTS LOSES ITS MOORINGS

BOX 6.7

Pier 1 Imports, Inc., is the largest retailer of decorative home furnishings and accessories in the United States. In its early days it sold inexpensive imported household goods in a bazaarlike setting. During the 1990s the firm upgraded the quality of its products and its image, and merchandise margins increased from 45 percent in 1985 to 56 percent in 1999. But as it upgraded its reputation from a seller of flimsy products to a seller of quality products, it became vulnerable to competitors at both ends of the price–quality spectrum. Specialty housewares retailers such as Pottery Barn and Crate & Barrel provided shoppers with more choices at the high-price end, and discounters such as Cost Plus, Inc., moved into the low end vacated by Pier 1. Pier 1 CEO Marvin J. Girouard commented, "We didn't have a whole lot of competition, so we kept upgrading and upgrading, and we thought 'there's no end to this.' Then all of a sudden there was an end to it."

What had happened was that as Pier 1 upgraded, its prices fell in the middle of the market, just where relative price elasticity is the highest. New competitors at either end of the price–quality spectrum effectively bracketed Pier 1 by appealing either to price-conscious buyers or quality-conscious buyers, leaving it in a middle market segment that was relatively more price sensitive. Pier 1 had priced itself out of the market for basic items and had not moved into the high-end furnishings market. "Pier 1 [is] lost in no-man's land right now," said a stock market analyst. For 2000, Pier 1 redefined its pricing strategy by lowering prices and using in-store promotion tactics. As a result, profits increased 46 percent over 1999 on a revenue increase of 15 percent.

Sources: Stephanie Anderson Forest, "At Pier 1, A Search for Lost Cachet," *Business Week* (November 1, 1999), 109–13; "A Pricing-Strategy Change Spurs Profit Jump to 46%," *The Wall Street Journal* (December 8, 2000), B6.

other in price have larger cross-price effects than brands that are priced further apart.[20]

To illustrate, consider this market situation. A household product category in the United Kingdom was dominated by three brands: A—the highest-priced brand that was advertised heavily; B—the middle-priced brand and market share leader; and C—the lowest-priced store brand. All three brands were sold in three versions and two sizes; B and C were also offered in a deluxe package. The largest price difference between the brands was between A and B; B and C were priced relatively closer. In one year all 30 different versions of the three brands in this category had 54 price

[20]Raj Sethuraman, V. Srinivasan, and Doyle Kim, "Asymmetric and Neighborhood Cross-Price Effects: Some Empirical Generalizations," *Marketing Science 18,* no. 1 (1999), 23–41; K. Sivakumar, "Price-Tier Competition: An Integrative Review," *Journal of Product and Brand Management Featuring Pricing Strategy & Practice 9,* no. 5 (2000), 276–90.

increases and 28 price decreases. Figure 6.3 shows the relative market share changes for the three brands for percentage price increases and decreases for the year.

As Figure 6.3 indicates, price changes of 2 percent in either direction did not seem to have much, if any, effect on market share of any of the brands. However, for price changes greater than 2 percent, the price elasticity relationships differed by brand relative to each brand's price position in the market. Moreover, for price reductions greater than 2 percent, brands A and B realized market share gains greater than those of the lowest-priced brand, C. For brand A, the loss in market share for a price increase exceeded the gain in share for the equivalent price decrease *if* the price change was 8 percent or less. For price changes greater than 8 percent, the loss in market share for price increases was less than the gain in share for the equivalent price decrease. For brand B, the effects on market share of price changes were the same as for A, except that the boundary for the asymmetric effect was for price changes of 10 percent or less. However, for brand C, the loss in market share for a price increase always exceeded the gain for the equivalent price decrease. This study further illustrates the important point that *price elasticities are not constant—they vary according to a brand's price position, the direction of a price change, and the magnitude of the price change.*[21]

The Effect of Price Thresholds

Both the absolute price threshold and the differential price threshold are important when estimating price elasticities. The example of Disneyland Paris (Box 6.2) indicates that the French people were quite price sensitive when the admission price exceeded 200 francs. However, an admission price of 195 francs was acceptable, and demand substantially increased relative to the earlier price of 250 francs. Thus it is likely that a price decrease of less than 50 francs would have resulted in little increase in demand.

When a price is at buyers' upper absolute price thresholds, we would expect a substantial reduction in demand if price is increased above the threshold. That is, demand would be very price elastic at this upper price point. Similarly, if some buyers are reluctant to pay less than a specific

[21]Jennifer George, Alan Mercer, and Helen Wilson, "Variations in Price Elasticities," *European Journal of Operational Research 88* (January 1996), 13–22.

FIGURE 6.3
Price-Response
Functions

Source: Adapted from Jennifer
George, Alan Mercer, and
Helen Wilson, "Variations in
Price Elasticities," *European
Journal of Operational
Research* 88 (January 1996),
13–22.

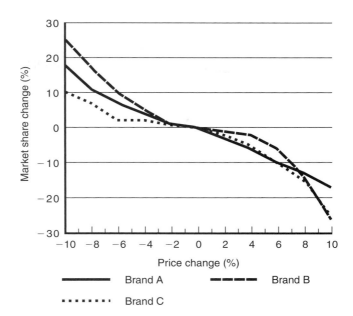

price because they would be suspicious of the product's quality, a price reduction below this lower absolute price threshold would result in a substantial reduction in demand rather than an increase. Again, demand would be very price elastic at this lower price point. A given buyer likely will have different price thresholds for different products, and different buyers will have different price thresholds for a given product. Box 6.8 illustrates how estimates of price elasticity must consider the absolute price threshold elasticity, the differential price threshold elasticity, the price elasticity for a specific price change from a particular price point, and the general price elasticity for a product category.

Other Influences on Price Elasticity

Besides these important characteristics affecting a product's price elasticity, several other influences on price elasticity should be considered. Sometimes a product may provide a *unique benefit* or have a *unique attribute* that buyers value. These unique benefits or attributes make the product less price sensitive. Regular buyers who believe that the product is of high quality tend to purchase more units than other buyers and to stay with the product longer even when price is increased. Thus, *improved perceptions of product and service quality* make the product less price sensitive. *How the*

EFFECT OF PRICE THRESHOLDS ON PRICE ELASTICITY

BOX 6.8

Consider the following distribution of prices and retail sales volume for a packaged product.

Prices	Proportion of Sales Volume	Cumulative Proportion
$0.99	0.15	0.15
1.09	0.12	0.27
1.19	0.14	0.41
1.29	0.15	0.56
1.39	0.12	0.68
1.49	0.28	0.96
1.59	0.04	1.00

Using historical figures for price changes and sales response, the overall price elasticity was estimated to be −1.10. The retailer who had been pricing the product at $0.99 thought that if his price was raised 10¢ (10 percent), he could withstand an 11 percent drop in volume. Indeed, with a gross margin of 40 percent he could afford to lose 20 percent of his volume before profits would decrease from the current price. However, his pricing consultant cautioned him that the data suggested that $0.99 was an absolute price threshold and that

he needed to consider the effect of losing the differential price advantage he enjoyed relative to the competitor who had set the price at $1.09. Research indicated that the absolute threshold effect would lead to an estimated sales decrease of 8 percent, and the differential price threshold effect would lead to an additional sales decrease of 4 percent. That is, increasing price from $0.99 to $1.09 would lead to a total sales decline of 23 percent, much more than the 11 percent estimated by considering only the overall category price elasticity.

product is used and the context it is used in may also influence its price sensitivity. One research study determined that buyers were willing to pay significantly more for a pair of pants to be worn to a symphony or cocktail party than for pants to be worn at a football game or rock concert.[22]

The *relative dollar magnitude of the purchase* may influence buyers' sensitivity to price differences. Consumers tend to be more price sensitive on their "big-ticket" purchases than on routine grocery purchases. Similarly, industrial firms may not be very sensitive to the price of routine supplies, but are quite sensitive to the price of a raw material that represents a significant portion of their production costs. Finally,

[22]Kent B. Monroe, Albert J. Della Bitta, and Susan L. Downey, "Contextual Influences on Subjective Price Perceptions," *Journal of Business Research 5* (December 1977), 277–91.

the *frequency of past price changes* can influence buyers' sensitivity to price changes. If prices have been changing relatively frequently, buyers may not have adjusted to the previous price change when a new change occurs. This phenomenon happens most often when inflationary pressures lead to frequent price increases. If buyers have not adjusted to the last price increase, then another price increase will be perceived as a larger increase than it actually is, making them more sensitive to it.

As our discussion on differential price thresholds implied, generally the perceived relative differences between prices influences buyers' use of price as an indicator of quality. In a similar way, relative perceived price differences between competing brands, different models in a product line, or a product's price levels at different points in time affect buyers' purchase decisions. *Price elasticities are not constant and they can be managed over products, brands, and time to a greater extent than previously recognized.* Managers need to pay attention to the nature of a price change, the characteristics of the targeted market segment, the magnitude of the price change, the direction of the price change, the duration of the price change, and the extent that the price change will be communicated or promoted to the market. Unfortunately, most business firms do not make sufficient efforts to track the sensitivity of demand for their products to price changes and to price differences over time.

Summary

As we saw in this chapter, ignoring the way buyers perceive prices can lead to major pricing errors, and placing primary emphasis on the cost aspects of setting prices is likely to enhance those errors. Finally, sellers' use and misuse of large discounts may have several undesirable results. Buyers may learn that the "true" or "usual" price is not the advertised regular price but the sale price, and they may develop their price perceptions and value judgments using the lower sale price. Another problem arises when retailers use fictitious "regular" prices to enhance buyers' value perceptions and thereby deceive buyers. Such practices will inevitably lead to public policy regulating these deceptive practices (issues discussed in Chapters 7 and 17). Buyers perceive and evaluate prices in very complex ways, and pricing decisions based on recognition of these price perceptions often are quite different from those that rely on traditional economic theory.

Discussion Questions

1. In Chapter 1, the pricing problem of two candy companies was considered. Assume you are the price administrator for the second company. Are there any behavioral implications of the alternative strategies you might consider for changing the price of your multipack candy? (Refer to your answer to Discussion Question 3 in Chapter 1.) In what way do you think the concept of a reference price (*AL*) applies to this decision problem?

2. *a.* Assume you are interested in purchasing a pair of pants (slacks) to go to a football game or a rock concert. In a store, you find five different pairs that are acceptable in term of style, fit, fabric, and color. The prices of these pants are $17, $19, $25, $31, and $39. Which price do you find most acceptable? Why? Are any of these prices unacceptable? Why?

   b. Suppose the prices were $27, $29, $35, $41, and $49. Which price do you find most acceptable? Why? Are any of these prices unacceptable? Why?

   c. Assume the purpose of your purchase is to buy a pair of pants to go to church, a cocktail party, or a symphony. Would your answer to *a* change? Why? Would your answer to *b* change? Why?

3. What are the different factors that influence the degree of price elasticity for a product? In what ways do price thresholds influence the degree of price elasticity?

4. Why are people, in general, more sensitive to price increases than to price decreases? What implications does this observation about people have for pricing managers?

5. Assume that there are three brands in a particular market. Brand A is the market share leader (40 percent) and is the highest-priced brand in the market. Brand B has about a 15 percent share of the market, and brand C has about a 10 percent market share. Both brands B and C are similarly priced, noticeably less than brand A. The remaining market share is divided among a number of small regional and local brands in the market.

   a. What do you think would happen to the market share of Brand A if it offered a temporary price promotion of 15 percent off and the prices of the other brands did not change? What would be the likely effect on brands B and C?

   b. Suppose instead that either brand B or C, but not both, offer a temporary price promotion of 15 percent off and the prices of the other brands remain the same. What do you think would happen to the market share of the brand that reduces price? What do you think might happen to the market share of brand A?

Suggested Readings

Anderson, Eugene W.: "Customer Satisfaction and Price Tolerance," *Marketing Letters 7,* no. 3 (1996), 265–74.

Biswas, Abhijit, Elizabeth J. Wilson, and Jane W. Licata: "Reference Pricing Studies in Marketing: A Synthesis of Research Results," *Journal of Business Research 27* (July 1993), 239–56.

Briesch, Richard A., Lakshman Krishnamurthi, Tridib Mazumdar, and S. P. Raj: "A Comparative Analysis of Reference Price Models," *Journal of Consumer Research 24* (September 1997), 202–14.

Kalyanaram, Gurumurthy, and Russell S. Winer: "Empirical Generalizations from Reference Price Research," Part 2 of 2, *Marketing Science 14,* no. 3 (1995), G161–G169.

Monroe, Kent B., and Jennifer L. Cox: "Pricing Practices That Endanger Profits," *Marketing Management 10* (September/October 2001), 42–46.

Sivakumar, K., "Price-Tier Competition: An Integrative Review," *Journal of Product and Brand Management Featuring Pricing Strategy & Practice 9,* no. 5 (2000), 276–90.

CHAPTER SEVEN

Price and Customers' Perceptions of Value

The size of sums of money appears to vary in a remarkable way according to whether they are being paid **out** or paid **in**.

Julian Huxley

As indicated in Chapter 5, behavioral research has provided explanations of how people form value judgments and make decisions when they do not have perfect information about alternatives. The common element in these explanations is that buyers judge prices comparatively; that is, a reference price anchors their judgments. A reference price may be an external price in an advertisement or the shelf price of another product; it may also be an internal price the buyer remembers from a previous purchase, an expected price, or some belief about the price of a product in the same market area.

Underlying the argument in this chapter is the important point made in Chapters 3 and 5: People seldom are good information processors. They often take short-cuts that may lead to errors in judgment and choice but that may also facilitate the choice process. For example, buyers who know that price and quality are positively related in a particular product category may use price as an indicator of product quality.

Price and Perceived Value

The model in Figure 5.1 illustrates the role of price on buyers' perceptions of product quality, sacrifice, value, and willingness to buy. This model suggests that buyers use price not only as a measure of sacrifice, but also as an indicator of product or service quality. As indicated by Equation 5.1, perceived value represents a trade-off between buyers' perceptions of quality and sacrifice. We will see that buyers' knowledge of the product and of actual price–quality relationships in the market moderates the extent to which price may be used to infer product quality. The significant price factor here is relative price rather than actual price. In comparing prices, buyers' judgments are influenced by the relative or perceived differences between the actual or offer price and the reference price. These points about price perception will help show how perceived price influences buyers' judgments of value, the second important aspect of proactive pricing.

Buyers' perceptions of a price derive from their interpretations of price differences (real or implied) *and* from their interpretations of focal and contextual cues in the offer. Thus two issues are of concern: (1) how buyers use price information and other cues to judge the value of the offer, and (2) the influence this evaluation has on their purchase decisions.

As we have discussed in Chapter 6, buyers usually have a set of acceptable prices. If an offered price is not acceptable, buyers are likely to refrain from purchasing the product and will either search for an acceptable offer or forgo any purchase. Since prices are evaluated comparatively, the judgment of acceptability depends not only on buyers' price expectations, but also on information provided in promotions or advertisements. The perception of savings conveyed by price advertising leads to positive or favorable behavioral responses.

The Price–Perceived Quality Relationship

Based on the research evidence concerning buyers' price awareness presented in Chapter 5, it is clear that buyers do not use price solely as a measure of cost (sacrifice). Buyers also use price as an indicator of product quality.

The early studies that investigated the price–perceived quality relationship considered situations in which the only differential information available to respondents was price. These studies found that perception of product quality was a function of price. Moreover, they found that buyers tend to prefer higher-priced products when price is the only information available, when there is a belief that the quality of available brands differs significantly, and when the price differences between choices are large.[1] Two reviews of this research clearly indicate that a positive price–perceived quality relationship exists.[2]

Buyers are assumed to assess product or service quality by the use of cues. Products, services, or stores can be conceptualized as consisting of an array of cues that may serve as indicators of quality. Buyers are likely to use these cues as long as the cues help them predict the actual quality of the product or service and as long as they have confidence that they can use and judge the cues accurately. Generally, buyers are likely to use cues that are high in predictive value and high in confidence value to assess quality. Cues can be further classified according to whether they are part of the product (e.g., ingredients) or not part of the product. *Extrinsic cues* are product-related attributes—price, brand name, packaging—but they are not part of the product. *Intrinsic cues* are also product-related attributes, but they cannot be changed without altering the physical properties of the product. Buyers rely on extrinsic cues and intrinsic cues when evaluating quality.

External cues such as store and brand name; product warranties and guarantees; a product's country of origin; and two moderating variables, perceived product and price *differences* and buyers' *familiarity* with the product or service, have been found to relate price and perceived quality.[3] Figure 7.1 shows

[1]Kent B. Monroe, "Buyers' Subjective Perceptions of Price," *Journal of Marketing Research 10* (February 1973), 70–80.

[2]Kent B. Monroe and R. Krishnan, "The Effect of Price on Subjective Product Evaluations," in Jacob Jacoby and Jerry Olson, eds., *Perceived Quality: How Consumers View Stores and Merchandise* (Lexington, MA: Lexington Books), 209–32; Akshay R. Rao and Kent B. Monroe, "The Effect of Price, Brand Name, and Store Name on Buyers' Perceptions of Product Quality: An Integrative Review," *Journal of Marketing Research 26* (August 1989), 351–57; Valarie A. Zeithaml, "Consumer Perceptions of Price, Quality, and Value: A Means-End Model and Synthesis of Evidence," *Journal of Marketing 52* (July 1988), 2–22.

[3]Akshay R. Rao and Kent B. Monroe, "The Moderating Effect of Prior Knowledge on Cue Utilization in Product Evaluations," *Journal of Consumer Research 15* (September 1988), 253–64; William B. Dodds, Kent B. Monroe, and Dhruv Grewal, "The Effect of Brand, Price and Store Information on Subjective Product Evaluations," *Journal of Marketing Research 28* (August 1991), 307–19; Paul S. Richardson, Alan S. Dick, and Arun K. Jain, "Extrinsic and Intrinsic Cue Effects on Perceptions of Store Brand Quality," *Journal of Marketing 58* (October 1994), 28–36; R. Kenneth Teas and Sanjeev Agarwal, "The Effects of Extrinsic Product Cues on Consumers' Perceptions of Quality, Sacrifice, and Value," *Journal of the Academy of Marketing Science 28*, no 2, (2000), 278–90; Merrie Brucks, Valarie A. Zeithaml, and Gillian Naylor, "Price and Brand Name as Indicators of Quality Dimensions for Consumer Durables," *Journal of the Academy of Marketing Science 28*, no. 3 (2000), 359–74.

FIGURE 7.1   **Price–Perceived Value Model**

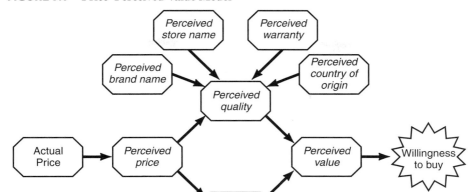

these extensions to the initial model in Figure 5.1. The basic notion of Figure 5.1, that perceptions of quality are compared or traded off with perceived monetary sacrifice to form perceptions of value, remains in the extended model. However, actual price has been replaced by perceived price because buyers may translate the actual price into different perceptions of the price (see Table 5.2). Perceived brand name, store name, country of origin, and product warranty are represented as other extrinsic cues.

As buyers become familiar with a product they are more likely to use intrinsic cues rather than price or other external cues as indicators of product quality. However, highly familiar buyers (experts) use either price or intrinsic cues as indicators of quality, depending on whether their knowledge includes information about the reliability of price as a quality indicator. That is, if buyers know that there is a positive price–quality relationship in the product market, they will probably use price as a quality indicator. However, if buyers know there is a weak price–quality relationship in the product market, they will be more likely to use intrinsic product cues to assess product quality. Thus, the use of price or other external cues, such as brand or store name, as indicators of product quality depends on the relative perceived differences between different cues and on the degree to which buyers know about the product and actual price–quality relationships.

Research has demonstrated that, generally, brand name is the most influential extrinsic cue for assessing quality. That is, the effect of brand name on quality perceptions has been larger than price, store name, or intrinsic ingredients or compositional characteristics. The relative ranking of the effect of extrinsic and intrinsic cues on quality perceptions indicates that price is second in relative size of effect, followed by physical characteristics or store name. This relative ranking of the different effects these cues have on quality perceptions seems to be relatively universal across multiple cultures.[4]

If certain countries are perceived to produce quality products in specific categories, then products in these categories identified as originating in such countries will be perceived to be of higher quality. For example, watches that come from Switzerland or consumer electronics from Japan would be perceived to be higher in quality than similar products originating from countries not noted for their expertise in the manufacture of these products.[5]

Chapter 4 explained that firms may use warranties as signals of quality when buyers are uncertain about quality. That is, to signal a high-quality product, a seller should provide a warranty that provides buyers better protection against product failure. A warranty accompanying a high-quality product would be broader in its scope of coverage and longer in duration than a warranty accompanying a low-quality product. Thus sellers offering extensive warranty coverage will attempt to provide high quality to avoid incurring high warranty costs.

The joint effect of multiple extrinsic cues seems to be stronger than the effects of individual cues. Indeed, although the effect of brand name on perceptions of quality generally is stronger than that of price, the effect of brand name on quality perceptions is stronger in the presence of price information. Conversely, the effect of price on quality perceptions is stronger in the presence of brand name. Similarly, research has found that price search increased when people had brand name information concerning product

[4]Niraj Dawar and Philip Parker, "Marketing Universals: Consumers' Use of Brand Name, Price, Physical Appearance, and Retailer Reputation as Signals of Product Quality," *Journal of Marketing 58* (April 1994), 81–95.
[5]Teas and Agarwal, "Extrinsic Product Cues"; Wai-Kwan Li, Kent B. Monroe, and Darius K-S Chan, "The Effects of Country of Origin, Brand, and Price Information: A Cognitive-Affective Model of Buying Intentions," in Deborah Roedder John and Chris T. Allen, eds. *Advances in Consumer Research*, vol. 21 (Provo, UT: Association for Consumer Research, 1994), 449–57.

JENNIFER CLEANS UP

Box 7.1

It took Jennifer Runyeon just six months to transform a financially troubled maker of windshield wipers into a successful firm. In 1988, Runyeon and a partner purchased the assets of the New Jersey firm Tripledge Wiper Corp. Renaming the firm Life-time Products, Inc., and relocating the business to Dallas, they saw wiper sales soar to $20 million compared to Tripledge's peak of $1 million in 1987.

Life-time's basic product is the Tripledge wiper, a multiedged wiper that is promoted as working better and lasting longer than the standard single-edged wipers. The company pursued the objective of obtaining a small portion of market share for wipers. Its direct-marketing strategy placed advertisements in monthly bills of gasoline credit card users, followed later by national advertising in selected publications and on syndicated television programs. After the wiper had become well known to attract national retailers, Life-time sold its distribution rights to another company for marketing to the large national retailers like Wal-Mart and Kmart. However, its most significant move was to double the wiper's price to $19.95, higher than most competitor's products.

How could a relatively unknown product experience a 10-fold increase in unit sales, while increasing its price 100 percent? Obviously the product had been underpriced, but why? The answer might be that the product is now promoted to be substantially better than competitive products in terms of performance and to last a "lifetime." Indeed, a warranty backs up the lifetime claim. The price of a product performing that much better than its rival products must be equivalent to the perceived value it claims to deliver. Thus the relevant pricing issue is not the price of competitive wipers, but the price consumers are willing to pay to get a wiper that is better than other alternatives. The price must be consistent with the relative quality level of the product that is being promoted in order to have a consistent marketing strategy.

Source: Suein L. Hwang, "Rescuers of Windshield-Wiper Manufacturer Clean Up," *The Wall Street Journal* (March 11, 1991), B2.

durability and performance. Box 7.1 illustrates the point that all signals of quality must be mutually consistent and credible if they are to be successful.

The Price–Perceived Monetary Sacrifice Relationship

Traditionally, price has been considered as a disincentive to purchase products and services—a negative product attribute. Price has also been assumed to be objective information and to be encoded, remembered, and later retrieved by buyers without error. And it has been assumed that one unit of money has the same utility to a person as any other. Given these assumptions, for any individual the disutility or pain of giving up an amount of money to acquire a product or service would not vary across situations, type of product, or service.

However, a buyer's perceptions of the sacrifice, "give up," or loss incurred by paying the monetary price for a product may vary according to a variety of situations and conditions. There is evidence that buyers may perceive equivalent prices as representing very different sacrifices. We now describe three conditions in which perceptions of sacrifice for the same amount of money will vary.

Begrudging Expenditures

The concept of *begrudging* refers to the idea that for some products or services, buyers would prefer not to make the expenditure. Thus the perceived sacrifice of paying a specific price for some products is psychologically more "painful" than for others, even though the monetary outlay may be equivalent. That is, buyers begrudge expenditures on some products but not others. For example, does a buyer perceive paying $50 for a dental cleaning to be an equivalent sacrifice to paying $50 for a ticket to a concert or sporting event? Thus the more that buyers are reluctant or hesitant to spend money on certain products, the more likely they are to search for bargains or lower prices. They will be more sensitive to price changes and to price differentials between alternative choices.

Perceived Price Fairness

An important point that we have developed in Chapters 5, 6, and this chapter is that buyers' price judgments are comparative. That is, to be able to judge whether a price is acceptable or fair, buyers must compare that price to a reference price. This reference price may be a previous price paid by the buyer, a previous price charged by the seller, a price paid by another buyer, or an expected price. In similar fashion, buyers make judgments of fairness by comparing an outcome to other possible outcomes. There are two types of transaction relationships that influence buyers' perceptions of price fairness.

First, when buyers believe that sellers have increased prices to take advantage of an increase in demand or a scarcity of supply, without a corresponding increase in costs, they perceive such price increases as unfair. That is, the sellers have increased their benefits of engaging in a transaction—their profits—without a corresponding increase in investment or effort, resulting in a net gain compared to previous transactions. On the other hand, buyers paying the higher price without a corresponding increase in benefits from the transaction have a resulting net loss relative to their previous position.[6]

Second, in situations when one category of buyers receives the benefit of a lower price for an equivalent product or service but another category of buyers does not, the price-disadvantaged buyers may perceive that the price they pay is unfair. Such situations typically arise when sellers provide discounts for buyers with certain characteristics, for example age or employment status. If there is no perceived discrepancy between the investment or effort that these favored buyers make to qualify for the lower price relative to the disadvantaged buyers, then they will be receiving the same benefits as the disadvantaged buyers but incurring a smaller monetary sacrifice.

Thus, whether considering buyers' judgments of price fairness in terms of their relationships with sellers or their lateral relationships with other buyers, a price judged as unfair can lead to lower perceptions of value and a reduction in willingness to pay. If there is no perceived difference in the quality or benefits received from acquiring a product or service whose price is judged as unfair, then this reduction in perceived value must result from an increase in perceptions of monetary sacrifice. That is, a perceived disadvantaged price inequity, or a loss, increases buyers' perceptions of sacrifice, thereby decreasing their perceptions of value and willingness to buy. Conversely, a perceived advantageous price inequity, or a gain, reduces buyers' perceptions of sacrifice, thereby increasing their perceptions of value and willingness to buy.

Fairness in pricing requires just and honest treatment of all parties in a transaction including those who are indirectly involved in the transaction, such as other buyers, for example. Developing and following pricing policies that promote a reputation for fair treatment will enhance customer goodwill and perceived product and service value (see Box 7.2). As an additional benefit, a price structure that is perceived to be fair is positively correlated to price acceptability. That is, when buyers perceive prices to be fair, their

---

[6]Margaret C. Campbell, "Perceptions of Price Unfairness: Antecedents and Consequences," *Journal of Marketing Research 36* (May 1999), 187–99; Jennifer Lyn Cox, "Can Differential Prices Be Fair?" *Journal of Product & Brand Management Featuring Pricing Strategy & Practice 10*, no. 5 (2001), 264–73.

AMAZON.COM CUSTOMERS SAY UNFAIR

Box 7.2

During the summer of 2000, an assistant professor of computer and information systems was doing research on the difference in DVD pricing between a retail environment with variable pricing, such as an auction house, and the presumably more stable pricing environment at Amazon.com. To his surprise, depending on the computer he used to access Amazon.com, prices could vary by at least 20 percent. For example, "The X-Files—The Complete Second Season" could cost between $80 and $100. Other regular customers were also finding that they paid more for an item if they were repeat purchasers. One customer paid $24.49 for his first DVD purchase and a week later found the price had increased to $26.24. When he stripped his computer of the electronic tags that identified him to Amazon as a regular customer, he was quoted a price of $22.74. Customers then began to compare their experiences in the DVDTalk.com chat room. As might be expected, they were quite upset that Amazon.com would adjust prices depending on a customer's purchase history with the company. The DVD Internet chat boards filled up with slams against Amazon for unfair pricing.

Amazon.com apologized to the customers, explaining that it was conducting an experiment. The company spokesperson said it would not happen again. "Dynamic pricing is stupid, because people will find out. Fortunately, it only took us two instances to see this."

Sources: Janet Adamy, "E-tailer Price Tailoring May Be Wave of the Future," *Chicago Tribune* (September 25, 2000), Section 4, p. 4; Joe Salkowski, "Amazon.com's Variable Pricing Draws Ire," *Chicago Tribune* (October 9, 2000), Section 4, p. 2; David Streitfeld, "On the Web, Price Tags Blur," *Washington Post* (September 27, 2000), www.washingtonpost.com, p. A01.

upper acceptable price threshold is higher than when prices are perceived to be unfair. Fair pricing policies should:[7]

1. Communicate the firm's overall pricing policies, as well as how specific prices were determined, to all customers.

2. Openly communicate precise information about qualifications or restrictions to receive more advantageous prices and terms to all parties. Whenever there is a deviation from a reference transaction, the reasons for it must be honestly and directly communicated to the parties affected by the deviation, including those who might not be eligible for the deviation.

[7]Sheryl E. Kimes, "Perceived Fairness of Yield Management," *The Cornell Hotel and Restaurant Administration Quarterly 35* (February 1994), 22–29; Jennifer L. Cox and Kent B. Monroe, "The Price May Be Right, But Is It Fair?" working paper, Department of Business Administration, University of Illinois, Champaign, IL (January 2002).

3. Inform customers of cost increases. Since buyers generally perceive cost-justified price increases as fair, it is good practice to keep customers aware of the seller's cost structure. This open policy about the firm's cost structure makes even more sense because research shows that buyers perceive it to be fair if a firm maintains prices when costs are declining.

4. Provide a reasonable period of time for customers to acquire existing inventory or products before a price increase goes into effect.

5. Move away from volume or other types of discounts toward some form of buyer reward program. A price discount program typically means that different customers pay different prices for equivalent purchases, increasing the potential for perceived unfair prices. A buyer reward program has the benefit of building customer loyalty rather than rewarding nonloyal buyers seeking low prices.

6. Consider reducing existing discounts before raising list prices. As we will demonstrate later in this chapter, people react more unfavorably to perceived losses than they react favorably to perceived gains. Thus, reductions in perceived gains—that is, reduced discounts—will be perceived less negatively than increased perceived losses—price increases.

7. Follow price increases unjustified by costs rather than leading such increases. Competitors who announce cost-unjustified price increases, or other types of price increases that are likely to lead to perceptions of unfairness or customer resistance, will bear the brunt of customer dissatisfaction. Even when a firm does follow the lead of a competitor in these situations, its prices will be perceived to be fairer than its competitor's.

8. When raising prices or imposing restrictions, seek ways to provide other benefits to customers or, at the very least, provide sufficient notice and rationale so customers can adapt their perceptions and behaviors before these new prices or restrictions become effective.

Brand Equity Effects

We observed earlier that brand name may serve as an indicator of quality. An implication of this brand-quality relationship is that brands that are perceived to provide high quality may also receive price premiums. Buyers likely would be willing to pay higher prices to acquire a product with a superior or highly favorable image than for competitive brands with a less favorable image. A second advantage of a perceived high-quality brand is that a monetary price that is equivalent to the competitive product may be perceived to require less of an outlay or sacrifice. That is, it may be perceived to be less painful to spend a specific amount of money on a perceived high-quality brand than to spend that amount of money on a perceived lower-quality brand. Thus, not only can brands with very favorable images receive above-average prices, it is also likely that these higher prices are not perceived to require as much monetary sacrifice as lower-priced brands that have less favorable images.

Integrating Price, Quality, and Sacrifice Information

As indicated in Figures 5.1 and 7.1, when buyers use price as an indicator of cost or sacrifice, increasing price has the effect of reducing perceived value for the product or service. On the other hand, if buyers use price as an indicator of quality or benefits, increasing price has the effect of increasing perceived value. Generally, buyers are not able to assess perfectly product or service quality (the ability of the product to provide satisfaction). Moreover, buyers' perceptions of monetary sacrifice for the same specific price may vary according to whether the price is perceived to be fair, the context in which the price is presented, the buyers' acceptable price range, and the extent to which they are concerned about price. Finally, perceived value represents a mental trade-off between buyers' perceptions of quality and sacrifice and is positive when perceptions of quality are greater than their perceptions of sacrifice.

A very important issue is how buyers are able to integrate these different bits of information to determine their overall perception of value. That is, information about the product or service attributes and benefits represents positive information (what the buyer gains from acquiring the product or service). Considering price as an indicator of cost represents negative information (what the buyer gives up or loses when acquiring the product or service). Attempting to integrate positive and negative information simultaneously to determine an overall value judgment is a difficult mental task for humans.

Complicating the task even further is the realization that price simultaneously may provide positive information relative to product quality (gain) and negative information relative to sacrifice (loss). In some situations, consumers may place relatively more weight on the positive information that price conveys, and in other situations, consumers may place relatively more weight on the negative information that price conveys. Rarely will they view price solely as a conveyor of positive or negative information. Research has attempted to determine both how buyers perform this mental calculation and when they may be more likely to rely on the price–perceived quality relationship and when they may be more likely to rely on the price–perceived sacrifice relationship. To understand how price influences value perceptions and purchase behavior requires understanding the various situations or contexts when these different roles of price are likely to be operating.

Modeling the Price–Quality and Price–Sacrifice Trade-offs

Recall that Equation 5.1 suggests that buyers determine perceived value by mentally trading off or comparing the perceived gains represented in their perceptions of quality or benefits to be received against the perceived loss represented in their perceptions of sacrifice required to acquire the product or service. Be careful not to view Equation 5.1 as a mathematical representation, but only as a way of suggesting that buyers make some type of mental comparison.

Implications of Price–Quality Trade-offs

When considering information integration, each piece of information about the product or service being evaluated is assumed to have some meaning, implication, or consequence for the buyer's value judgment. Second, each of these pieces of information has a relative degree of importance (or weight) to the buyer when making this judgment, and this relative importance may vary over products and purchase conditions. For example, a brand name provides some indication to the buyer about the relative quality of the product or service. Given this indication (signal) the buyer then may place more or less weight or attention on the brand name relative to other pieces of information, such as price, when making the value judgment.

The issue of whether buyers integrate price and other attribute information following a nonlinear (proportional) or subtractive process has important implications for doing price market research and for developing pricing strategy and tactics. In Chapter 8 we will discuss several ways of assessing the value buyers may perceive a product or service to provide. That is, conducting an attribute importance—performance analysis implicitly assumes that buyers average their assessment of the quality level of alternative product attributes and determine a performance/price ratio for each product being compared. For example, computers and industrial equipment are often compared on their relative performance/price ratios. Similarly, developing price–value maps assumes that perceived benefits or quality are compared proportionately to perceived or relative price.

On the other hand, economic value analysis assumes a subtractive model in which the relative economic value of a product is the customer's cost savings or revenue enhancement minus the product's price. Price market research using conjoint or multiple trade-off analysis assumes a linear model and that price as a negative attribute has disutility relative to positive utility derived from other product attributes.

How the customer actually processes the price and attribute information could lead to different choices. For example, assume that in a choice situation, product A's price is $20 and a competing product B's price is $27.50. Further, assume that the customer has quantified that the benefits of using A are equivalent to $60 per unit of A and $70 per unit of B. If a subtractive model is used, then the net value of A is $40 per unit and of B is $42.50 per unit. But if a ratio model is used, then the performance/price ratio for A is 3 and for B is 2.55. Thus, in the first approach B would be judged to provide more value, whereas in the other approach A apparently provides more value. Thus it is important to understand how customers perform this integration of price and other attribute information as well as the relative weight they place on these attributes. It is also important to determine the extent to which buyers use price as an indicator of quality as well as sacrifice.

Price–Quality Trade-offs: Price as a Negative Attribute

In some research on the price–quality trade-off, price has been considered only as a negative attribute, or disincentive to purchase. In general, two integration models have been investigated. First, as in Equation 5.1, to determine the perceived value of a specific product, buyers may combine price and quality information similar to a ratio or proportional model,

$$PV = \left[\frac{\sum\limits_{i=1}^{n} w_i Q_i}{\sum\limits_{i=1}^{n} w_i} \right] \div P \qquad \textbf{(7.1)}$$

where

Q_i = the buyer's subjective quality judgment of the ith product attribute

w_i = the relative importance weight the buyer places on the ith product attribute

Psychologically, this model assumes that buyers determine a quality rating per unit price. Note that if the relative importance weights are constrained to sum to 1.0, then Equation 7.1 becomes $PV = \Sigma w_i Q_i / P$, or essentially the model of Equation 5.1. Alternatively, buyers may subtract their subjective evaluations of the perceived sacrifice of paying the price from their overall perceptions of quality:

$$PV = \left[\frac{\sum\limits_{i=1}^{n} w_i Q_i}{\sum\limits_{i=1}^{n} w_i} \right] - P \qquad \textbf{(7.2)}$$

As before, if the importance weights are constrained to sum to 1.0, then Equation 7.2 becomes $PV = \Sigma w_i Q_i - P$. This representation assumes that buyers assess the positive quality information against the negative sacrifice information to determine their overall value judgment for the product. Both formulations assume that the attribute quality information is averaged to determine overall perceived quality and then compared to the perceived sacrifice represented by the product's price.

Early research implied that the subtractive model best represents the trade-offs made between perceived quality and perceived sacrifice.[8] In another study, subjects received information for two different purchases for hamburger. One purchase was described by price and quality (defined either as percentage fat or percentage lean); the second purchase was described only by price or only by quality. In the second purchase, subjects were asked to infer the appropriate price when only quality information was given, or the appropriate

---

[8]Michael R. Hagerty, "Model Testing Techniques and Price-Quality Tradeoffs," *Journal of Consumer Research 5* (December 1978), 194–205.

quality level when only price information was given. The researchers concluded that the subtraction model best represented buyers' processing of quality and price information.[9]

One important result from this second research study was the observation that the transformation of objective stimuli into subjective judgments can change as a function of the *context* in which judgments are made. That is, the quality of hamburger described as 80 percent lean was rated more favorably than hamburger described as 20 percent fat. This finding indicates that buyers may judge a $20 T-shirt as more expensive in a discount store than in a department store.

A second important result of the hamburger study was the finding that subjects had difficulty integrating two stimulus dimensions when high ratings of one dimension are favorable (e.g., high quality rating of product) and when high ratings of another dimension are unfavorable (e.g., high monetary sacrifice implied by a relatively high price). This result implies that when quality is uncertain and buyers use price as an indicator of the product's quality as well as an indicator of the monetary sacrifice, they face a difficult task of integrating the positive attribute quality information with price information that provides both negative information (sacrifice) and positive information (quality).

Price–quality Trade-offs: Price as a Multidimensional Attribute

A third research effort studying how subjects judged the risk of new products across the dimensions of warranty coverage, warrantor reputation, and price gives us insight into this difficult integration process.[10] Initially, subjects' perceived performance risk of a durable new product was a function of their perceived quality of the product given by the length of the warranty coverage and warrantor reputation. Prices provided both positive and negative risk information. It was expected that a positive price–perceived quality relationship would lead to a negative price–perceived performance risk relationship. That is, as perceived quality increased, perceived performance risk would decline. On the other hand, as with the price–perceived monetary sacrifice relationship, perceived financial risk would increase as price increased.

[9]Irwin P. Levin and Richard D. Johnson, "Estimating Price-Quality Tradeoffs Using Comparative Judgments," *Journal of Consumer Research 11* (June 1984), 593–600.

[10]J. Dennis White and Elise L. Truly, "Price-Quality Integration in Warranty Evaluation," *Journal of Business Research 19* (September 1989), 109–25.

However, subjects resolved this more difficult information integration task by not using price to assess performance risk. Instead they integrated the warranty coverage and reputation information to form their judgments of product quality. As expected, perceived performance risk was lower for the high reputation warrantor. Finally, perceived financial risk increased with increases in price and with decreases in warranty coverage and warrantor reputation.

After examining the individual subject data, the researchers concluded that buyer integration of price and quality information was not sufficiently represented by a simple subtraction process. Hence the researchers repeated the study using an expanded price by warranty coverage design. Contrary to the previous research, only 15 percent of the subjects used a subtractive integrative process.

This study clearly showed that only a minority of the subjects followed a strict subtractive integration process whereas a larger percent of subjects used some form of a nonlinear strategy for integrating price and quality information. Perhaps the most important implication of these results is that when making their judgments a majority of the subjects apparently relied heavily on either price information relative to the warranty quality information or the warranty quality information relative to the price information. Thus it is important to determine the conditions when buyers will be more likely to use price primarily either as an indicator of quality or as an indicator of sacrifice. When buyers are more likely to use price as an indicator of quality, we would expect them to be more quality conscious. Within limits, these buyers would be *less* sensitive to price differences. Conversely, buyers who use price primarily as an indicator of monetary sacrifice are likely to be *more* sensitive to price differences.

Summary

Although the current research has not been able to clarify the exact nature of this trade-off between perceived quality and sacrifice, what we do know has an important implication. The relative weights buyers attach to quality and sacrifice depend on the relative magnitude of the product's price. Generally, both quality and sacrifice are perceived to be low when price is perceived to be relatively low, and to be high when price is perceived to be relatively high.[11] When

---

[11]Gary M. Erickson and Johny K. Johansson, "The Role of Price in Multi-Attribute Product Evaluations," *Journal of Consumer Research 12* (September 1985), 195–99.

evaluating a low-priced product, buyers appear to weigh quality more heavily than sacrifice, thus judging the product as low in value. Yet, when judging a high-priced product, buyers tend to weigh sacrifice more heavily than quality, again judging the product as low in value. These generalizations assume that the buyers have sufficient motivation and cognitive resources to process the price and other attribute information to determine product value.

The Effect of Time Pressure on Buyers' Perceptions of Value

When conditions constrict or interfere with people's ability to process information, they tend to use simpler decision rules or heuristics when making judgments. Under these conditions, people are less likely to consider all product attributes and instead use judgmental heuristics to simplify their cognitive task (also see Chapter 3). Heuristics such as "high price means high quality" are necessary when a quick response based on less effort is required. When buyers are making decisions within limited amounts of time there is pressure to make the selection quickly. However, how time pressure influences buyers' level or amount of information processing depends also on their motivation to process information.

As we consider this issue, we need to remember that price information plays a dual role in buyer judgments of product value. In general, when buyers attempt to process all the available information, they are likely to place more emphasis on price as an indicator of sacrifice rather than on price as an indicator of quality. However, when information is processed heuristically, they are likely to place more emphasis on price as an indicator of product quality rather than on price as an indicator of sacrifice. *For a specific price*, when buyers place more emphasis on the price–quality inference, we would expect higher perceptions of value than when buyers place more emphasis on the price–sacrifice inference.

When buyers are motivated to process information, but the time available to make a decision decreases, price information is more likely to be processed heuristically, increasing the likelihood of price being used to infer quality. To investigate this prediction, researchers tested two products, each at a relatively high price and a relatively low price. For a relatively high price, subjects' perceptions of quality increased and perceptions of sacrifice decreased as the amount of time pressure increased, resulting in a continuous increase in perceived value. Conversely, for a relatively low price, subjects' perceptions of quality decreased and perceptions of sacrifice increased as the amount of time pressure increased, resulting in a continuous decrease in perceived value.[12]

Thus consumers who are motivated to process information, but are unable to process the information, are more likely to use a price–quality heuristic. For a relatively high-priced product, the perception of high quality leads to a relatively higher perception of value. But, for a relatively low-priced product, the perception of low quality leads to a relatively low perception of value. Moreover, under either price condition, perceptions of sacrifice change in the opposite direction of the changes in perceptions of quality, even though the price is the same across the different amounts of time pressure.

In the condition when motivation to process information was low, price information was processed heuristically at both low and high time pressure conditions, resulting in price being used more as an indicator of product quality. However, at a moderate level of time pressure, information was processed more completely and price was used more as an indicator of monetary sacrifice. Consequently, at a relatively high price, perceptions of value were relatively high at either the low or high pressure conditions, but lower at a moderate level of time pressure. Conversely, for a low price level, the perception of value was higher at the moderate level of time pressure. As when the motivation to process information was high, perceived value showed a reversal in the pattern of response depending on whether the product was priced relatively high or relatively low.

What this research shows is that the processing of price information depends both on the buyers' motivation to process the information and whether they have the cognitive resources for this processing. Further, at relatively low price levels, buyers are more likely to infer that a product is of low quality, and, because of the differential emphasis they place on this quality assessment, perceive that the product provides low value. Conversely, at relatively high prices, when they are using a price–quality heuristic, they put relatively

---

[12]Rajneesh Suri and Kent B. Monroe, "The Effects of Time Pressure on Consumers' Product Evaluations," working paper, Department of Business Administration, University of Illinois, Champaign, IL (May 2002).

more emphasis on the quality inference and perceived value is higher. But when buyers are likely to be processing the information, then they will place relatively more emphasis on price's sacrifice dimension and perceive higher-priced products as having less value.

Decomposing Perceived Product Value

One aspect of a buyer's purchase decision is whether the buyer believes that information about the offer is sufficient to support a choice. The overall perceived value of a product being considered for purchase is its (1) *acquisition value* (the expected benefit to be gained from acquiring the product less the net displeasure of paying for it) and (2) *transaction value* (the perceived merits or fairness of the offer).

Acquisition Value

As suggested earlier, buyers' perceptions of acquisition value represent a cognitive trade-off between the benefits they perceive in the product and the sacrifice they perceive to be required to acquire the product or service by paying the monetary price of the product:

$$\textit{Perceived acquisition value} = \frac{\textit{perceived quality or benefits}}{\textit{perceived sacrifice}}$$

(7.3)

In part, the perceived benefits of a product are related to the buyers' judgments about the product's quality. Lacking perfect information about the inherent quality of the product, many consumers tend to believe that there is a positive relationship between a product's price and its quality ("You get what you pay for"). Thus, other things remaining the same, a higher-priced product would be perceived to provide more benefits because of its higher perceived quality. However, at the same time, a higher price increases buyers' perceptions of their sacrifice. Thus, within some range of prices, the perceived benefits in the product will be larger than the perceived sacrifice, and buyers will perceive that there is positive acquisition value in the product. However, in addition to evaluating the product's value, buyers also evaluate the offer itself.

Transaction Value

Transaction value is defined as the buyers' perceived merits of the offer. Replacing the utility function of economics with a value function requires three key propositions:

1. The value function is based on *perceived* gains and losses relative to a reference point. (The premise that people respond to relative differences rather than absolute levels was discussed in Chapter 6 and is based on the psychophysics of prices as discussed in Chapter 5.)

2. As seen in Figure 7.2, the value function is assumed to be concave for gains and convex for losses, relative to the reference point.

3. People are more sensitive to the prospect of a loss than to the prospect of a gain.

In Figure 7.2, the gain of $10 is contrasted to a loss of $10. To provide a reference point, the current position is represented by the origin. Note that the concavity of the gain portion of the value function indicates that the function increases at a slower rate as gains become larger. However, the convexity of the loss portion of the value function at the smaller loss amounts indicates that the function increases at

FIGURE 7.2
Hypothetical Value Function

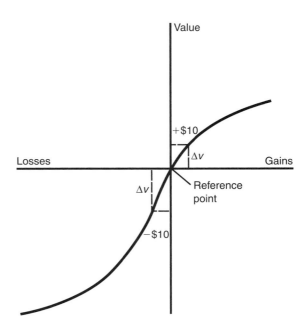

a faster rate initially and then later behaves like the gain function. In Figure 7.2, the decrease in perceived value for the $10 loss is greater than the increase in perceived value for the $10 gain.

Of concern here is how buyers evaluate a purchase situation in which the buyer gains a product but loses (gives up) the money paid for the product. Three price concepts explain the role of price in this process. The *perceived benefit* of the product is equivalent to the value inherent in the *maximum price* the buyer would be willing to pay for the product. The *acquisition value* of the product is the perceived benefits of the product at this maximum price compared to the actual selling price; that is $(p_{max} - p_{actual})$, which is equivalent to our initial perceived value concept. The *transaction value*, or the perceived merit of paying the actual price, is determined by comparing the buyer's reference price to the actual price, $(p_{ref} - p_{actual})$. Transaction value is positive if the actual price is less than the buyer's reference price, zero if they are equal, and negative otherwise.

When researchers were able to develop measures that clearly distinguished between acquisition value and transaction value, they discovered that when transaction value was present it enhanced acquisition value, but did not directly influence buyer behavior. Thus acquisition value was determined by the buyers' perceptions of quality or benefits to be received plus perceived transaction value, which represented the comparison of the selling price to the buyers' reference price.[13] Figure 7.3 shows the extension of this finding to the model of Figure 7.1.

One important implication of the finding that perceived transaction value enhances buyers' perceived acquisition value is that buyers need to feel confident that they can either determine quality prior to purchase or infer quality because the sellers' various signals of quality are appropriate indicators of quality.[14] The satisfaction of finding a lower price than expected will be more effective if consumers find the lower price believable and if they do not have reason to

[13]Dhruv Grewal, Kent B. Monroe, and R. Krishnan, "The Effects of Price-Comparison Advertising on Buyers' Perceptions of Acquisition Value, Transaction Value, and Behavioral Intentions," *Journal of Marketing 62* (April 1998), 46–59.
[14]Joel E. Urbany, William O. Bearden, Ajit Kaicker, and Melinda Smith-de-Borrero, "Transaction Utility Effects When Quality Is Uncertain," *Journal of the Academy of Marketing Science 25,* no. 1 (1997), 45–55.

FIGURE 7.3   Price, Perceived Transaction Value, Perceived Acquisition Value

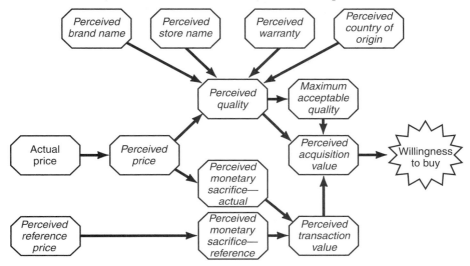

doubt that the quality level is commensurate with the higher reference price.

Enhancing Transaction Value

As indicated previously, the reference price may be a price internal to the buyer (an expected price, a believed fair or "just" price, or a remembered price) or it may be an external price in the purchase situation. The use of comparative price advertising or price tags to communicate the usual or regular price and a lower actual price is an attempt to provide buyers with a price frame of reference and to capitalize on transaction value. Coupons or rebates are also used to enhance transaction value, but the efforts expended to redeem coupons or qualify for rebates may increase perceived sacrifice.[15]

Transaction value can have a positive or negative effect on overall perceived acquisition value. Positive transaction value is the perceived reduction of a loss by a small gain (the original or reference price minus the savings perceived by a lower price). Framing the components of the offer in terms of a gain and a loss enhances the perceived acquisition value

[15]Kent B. Monroe and Joseph D. Chapman, "Framing Effects on Buyers' Subjective Product Evaluations," in Melanie Wallendorf and Paul Anderson, eds., *Advances in Consumer Research*, vol. 14 (Provo, UT: Association For Consumer Research, 1987), 193–97

FIGURE 7.4
Value Function

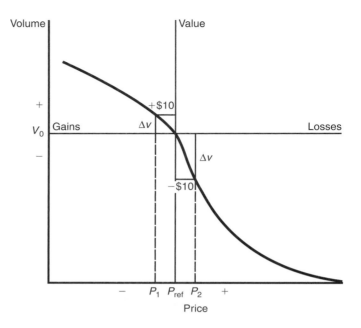

of the offer because positive transaction value augments acquisition value. Similarly, if a buyer perceives that a price has increased, this increase is perceived as a loss. The value function of Figure 7.2 can be redrawn as a demand curve, with the buyers' reference price shown as P_{ref} (Figure 7.4). A price increase viewed as a loss would be perceived to be larger than the same proportionate price decrease viewed as a gain. In Figure 7.4, a $10 price increase is perceived as a loss in that the buyer has to pay more than previously. Hence, the loss in perceived value at price P_2 is greater than the perceived gain from a $10 price reduction, P_1.

This explanation recognizes that people respond differently to perceived gains and perceived losses and suggests that buyers are more sensitive to price increases (perceived loss) than to price decreases (perceived gain). Figure 7.5 illustrates the implication of combining the behavioral theories we have developed in Chapters 5 through 7 on the demand curve for a product. The dashed portion of the demand curve within the range of acceptable prices (defined between the lowest acceptable price, P_L, and the highest acceptable price, P_{Max}) indicates that there is likely to be less change in demand in response to a perceived small price change relative to the buyer's reference price. However, once the buyer perceives the price difference ($p_{ref} - p$) to be

FIGURE 7.5
Value Function

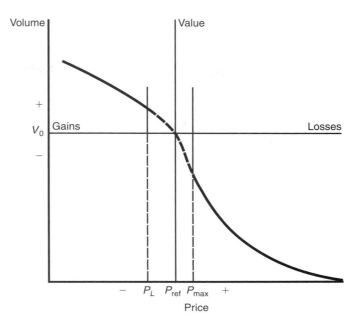

important, the change in demand is likely to be more noticeable (see also Figure 6.3). These price differences can occur because of either a price increase or decrease, or because of comparative price advertising in which the seller provides an external reference price for comparison. Thus, it is clear that small price differences, whether due to a price change or to differences between perceived similar offerings, are less likely to produce significant demand responses.

Framing Price Offers and Price Changes

Presenting a price offer or price change in different ways is similar to the framing of purchase decisions. A decision frame refers to a decision maker's perception of the behaviors, outcomes, and contingencies associated with a particular choice. It is often possible to frame a particular choice in more than one way. Moreover, shifts of reference points can change a perception of value and thereby change preferences. For example, including an external reference price in a purchase offer allows the seller to *frame* the buyers' choices. Comparative price advertising or point-of-purchase tags giving the usual or regular price and the lower asking price (sale price) provide buyers with a price frame of reference. Thus a price frame of reference enhances perceived acquisition value

TABLE 7.1 **Framing Price Changes**

a. Price Decreases

	Small Price Decrease	Large Price Decrease
Relative low price	Regular price and sale price, or regular price and percent off, or regular price, sale price, and percent off	Regular price and percent off
Relative high price	Regular price and sale price	Regular price, sale price and percent off

b. Price Increases

	Small Increase	Large Increase
Relative low price	Regular price, new price, and percent increase	Regular price and new price
Relative high price	Regular price and percent increase	Regular price and new price, or regular price and percent increase, or regular price, new price and percent increase

by increasing perceived transaction value (reducing the perceived sacrifice associated with the lower sale price).

Whether buyers process price information in an absolute or relative sense affects their perceptions of price changes. For example, buyers will perceive a $20 reduction on either a $100 jacket or a $400 television similarly if they process the price reduction information in an absolute way; that is, as a $20 savings. However, if they process the price reduction information in a relative way, then the savings on the jacket (20 percent) would be perceived as more favorable than the savings on the television (5 percent).[16] Thus, an offer of 50 percent off an item priced at $1.00 would be perceived more favorably than an offer of $0.50 off. On the other hand, an offer of $1,000 off a $20,000 automobile would be perceived more favorably than an offer of 5 percent off. Thus, the relative attractiveness of a price promotion depends not only on the absolute amount of the monetary savings but also on the price level of the promoted product. Similarly, the relative unattractiveness of a price increase depends on the absolute amount of the price increase as well as the price level of the

[16]Shih-Fen S. Chen, Kent B. Monroe and Yung-Chien Lou, "The Effects of Framing Price Promotion Messages on Consumers' Perceptions and Purchase Intentions," *Journal of Retailing 74,* no. 3 (1998), 353–72.

product. Table 7.1 presents alternative ways to frame price decreases and price increases depending on the relative price level and amount of price change.

The preceding discussion on price fairness suggested that when raising prices, sellers need to give buyers sufficient advance notice so that they can adjust their purchase behaviors. Further, it suggested that buyers be given an opportunity to purchase at the current lower prices before a price increase becomes effective. Utilizing this tactic gives the seller an opportunity to frame the current price as a lower price relative to the future higher price. Besides enhancing the perception of fairness, this tactic also produces a positive frame (gain today) rather than a negative frame (loss tomorrow). It also gives buyers time to adapt their internal reference prices upward toward the new higher prices.

Comparative Price Advertising

Effects of Plausible Reference Prices

One important issue connected with comparative-price advertising is the plausibility of externally supplied reference prices. Do buyers perceive them as believable? A comparative-price advertisement exposes the buyer to two prices: the higher usual or regular price and the lower sale price. To be able to judge the acquisition value inherent in the advertised offer, the buyer must be able to determine which price to use to help assess the product's relative quality or benefits. If the advertisement suggests that the product is usually or regularly sold at the higher price, and if buyers believe that the quoted higher price indeed is representative of the product's market value, then it is likely that the higher regular price will be used to assess the product's quality and benefits. But if buyers do not believe that the higher price is plausible, then they will likely substitute a price lower than the advertised regular price to make their assessments of product benefits. That is, they will substitute another price to use as a point of reference to make assessments of quality and benefits.

One of the possible ways that buyers judge whether the advertised reference price (usual or regular price) is plausible depends on their idea of a usual price for the product in question in the marketplace (that is, they have an internal reference price). Their price knowledge then forms the basis of their expectations about usual prices for the product in the marketplace. We will refer to this price expectation as an *internal reference price*. Buyers will probably compare this internal reference price to the advertised reference price to determine the plausibility of the advertised reference price. If they judge the advertised reference price as plausible or believable, then they are likely to use that price to assess the product's benefits and quality. But if they judge the advertised reference price as implausible or not believable, the buyers will either use their internal reference prices to judge product quality and benefits or they will search for more price information before judging the product.

Effects of Implausible Reference Prices

Do advertised reference prices affect buyers' internal reference prices? As suggested previously, buyers' internal reference prices are not static, but continuously move in the direction of new price information. That is, buyers adapt their notion of expected market price when they receive new price information. Thus if their internal reference price is below the advertiser's reference price, and if they judge the advertiser's reference price as implausible, their internal reference price is still likely to move toward the perceived implausible advertised reference price. As strange as this point may seem, the adapting process we described in our discussion on reference prices in Chapter 6 is automatic and proceeds without conscious thought. That is, even if the price is judged as implausible, it still has an influence in changing buyers' reference prices in its direction. Buyers will use this higher internal reference price to judge the product's quality and benefits. The net effect of an advertised reference price is to provide a higher comparison price for buyers to judge a product's acquisition value rather than using the lower sale price.

However, if buyers have no prior expectations about the usual price for the product being advertised, then they will probably determine the plausibility of the advertised reference price by the perceived difference between the advertised reference price and the advertised sale price. Other things remaining the same, the larger the perceived price difference, the more likely the advertised reference price will be judged as implausible. However, buyers may use the semantic cues (words used to convey that a price has been reduced, such as *regular, suggested list price, sale price*) to infer that the regular price is higher than the sale price. Thus buyers are more likely to form an internal reference price above the sale price but below the advertised reference price. As in the first situation, buyers will develop an internal reference price based on the available price information, including the perceived implausible advertised reference price. The perceived implausible price will serve as an anchor for their judgment, and the resultant new internal reference price will be affected by the magnitude of this implausible price. Again, buyers' internal reference prices for the advertised product will be displaced toward the advertised reference price.

In summary, when a product is featured in a comparative-price format, the higher advertised reference or regular price will be used either to directly assess the product's quality and benefits or to form a new internal reference price. If a new internal reference price is formed, buyers will use it to judge the product's quality and benefits. They will contrast this judgment to the perceived sacrifice of the sale price to determine the perceived acquisition value of the product.

Available Empirical Evidence

Research findings suggest that the acceptance of an advertised regular (reference) price depends on the size of the sales discount and whether or not a regular price is quoted. Buyers are more likely to accept any regular price provided in an advertisement—regardless of the ad's veracity. As the perception of value increases with the increase in the price discounts, the intent to search for alternatives is likely to decrease. Research also shows that the perception of value is greater for the sale price–regular price format (the comparative-price situation) than for the sale price–only format.

Advertisements that provide a high plausible reference price enhance perceptions of offer value in comparison to advertisements with no reference price. In one experiment, the presence of a reference price increased estimates of both the average market price and the advertiser's normal price, as well as increasing the perceptions of offer value. The strength of these effects increases with the size of the discount. Moreover, these effects occur even when the advertised discounts are well above normal expectations. Another study has shown that highly implausible reference prices lead to significantly higher value perceptions resulting in lower search intentions.[17]

---

[17]Joel E. Urbany, William O. Bearden, and Dan C. Weilbaker, "The Effect of Plausible and Exaggerated Reference Prices on Consumer Perceptions and Price Search," *Journal of Consumer Research 15* (June 1988), 95–110; Abhijit Biswas, Chris Pullig, Balaji C. Krishnan, and Scot Burton, "Consumer Evaluations of Reference Price Advertisements: Effects of Other Brands' Prices and Semantic Cues," *Journal of Public Policy & Marketing 18* (Spring 1999), 52–65.

Essentially, even if consumers perceive an exaggerated reference price as implausible, the extreme value can still influence offer value perceptions because buyers will have higher internal reference prices based on the exaggerated advertised reference prices. The effect of enhancing perceived transaction value through the use of advertised discounts reduces perceived benefits of search. As would be expected, the decreased perceived benefits from search increased the likelihood of acquiring the product from the advertiser. Even in the absence of knowledge about market prices, a reference price that is perceived as implausible may still influence market price estimates and perceptions of transaction value. Thus, given these findings, retailers may be tempted to exaggerate advertised regular prices leading to public policy concern with the practice of advertising reference prices.[18]

A study found support for the asymmetric price response to losses and gains as predicted. It also supported the notion of a price-insensitive region around the reference price, as suggested by the acceptable price range concept. Indeed, when the price change was greater than about 16 to 17 percent, consumers seemed to respond to the price increase or decrease. Finally, frequent price promotions seemed to erode the effectiveness of the promotions.[19] This result suggests that frequent price promotions may reduce buyers' reference price for the product, negating the perceived price difference in the offer.

Tensile Price Claims

Our discussion on the effect of advertised price comparisons focused on specific price cues such as regular price $X, sale price $Y, save $Z or ZZ percent. Sometimes sellers offer a range of merchandise at different amounts of price reductions and do not specify the exact monetary or percentage reduction for any specific product item. For example, the seller may advertise a range of potential savings ("Save 20 percent to 40 percent"), a minimum amount of price reduction ("Prices reduced 20 percent or more"), or a maximum amount of savings ("Save up to 70 percent"). A *tensile price claim* has a factual foundation but uses vague wording that

---

[18]Larry D. Compeau and Dhruv Grewal, "Comparative Price Advertising: An Integrative Review," *Journal of Public Policy & Marketing 17* (Fall 1998), 257–73.
[19]Gurumurthy Kalyanaram and John D. C. Little, "An Empirical Analysis of Latitude of Price Acceptance in Consumer Package Goods," *Journal of Consumer Research 21* (December 1994), 408–18.

increases ambiguity and reduces the specificity and concreteness of the information provided. Such promotions have two important elements: (1) the semantic cues that set the context of the offer, and (2) the factual information that specifies the magnitude of price reduction or savings in the offer. When buyers are confronted by such price promotions, two important issues are how they evaluate the ambiguous offer and how they form value judgments.

The available research on these issues suggests that when a price reduction range is provided (e.g., 20 percent to 40 percent off), buyers will tend to anchor on the minimum value (20 percent) and then make some adjustment upward to estimate the actual savings they might expect. However, if this range is relatively narrow (e.g., 20 percent to 30 percent off), then buyers are more likely to anchor their judgments on the lower value and not make an upward adjustment. For promotions that indicate only a potential maximum amount of saving (e.g., save up to 50 percent), buyers anchor on the maximum amount and make a downward adjustment to estimate the savings they might expect. When making adjustments from an anchor, people tend to be more heavily influenced by the anchor they are using. As a result, buyers' estimates of savings will be relatively less when promotions use a minimum amount of savings (save 20 percent or more), or a narrow range of possible savings.

When the range of savings is relatively wide or the promotion uses a maximum amount of possible savings, use of a higher anchor leads to relatively larger estimates of savings. Consequently, buyers' perceptions of savings and transaction value will depend on how the promotion is phrased even if the average amount of savings is equivalent across alternative promotions. While such promotions are more likely to be considered deceptive or unfair, sellers using them should promote the upper amounts of their tensile claims to achieve maximum benefit.[20]

[20]Mary Mobley, William O. Bearden, and Jesse E. Teel, "An Investigation of Individual Responses to Tensile Price Claims," *Journal of Consumer Research 15* (September 1988), 273–79; Abhijit Biswas and Scot Burton, "An Experimental Assessment of Effects Associated with Alternative Tensile Price Claims," *Journal of Business Research 29,* no. 1 (1994), 65–73.

Summary

Perception basically involves the process of categorization. That is, we tend to place new experiences into existing classifications of familiar experiences. Thus when buyers are confronted by a price different from what they believe they have previously paid, they must decide whether the difference between the new and old prices is significant to them. If the price difference is insignificant, they may classify the two prices as similar and act as they have in the past. However, if the price difference is perceived as significant, they may classify the new price in a new price or product category and change their purchase behavior.

During this process of categorization, buyers make heavy use of cues or clues. Some of these cues are price cues that influence buyers' judgments of whether the price differences are significant. Finally, the frequent and predominant use and misuse of deep discounting by retailers may have several undesirable results. Buyers may learn that the true or usual price is not the advertised regular price but the sale price; they may then develop their price perceptions and value judgments using the lower sale price. Another problem arises when retailers use fictitious "regular" prices to enhance buyers' value perceptions and thereby deceive buyers. These practices inevitably will lead to public policy regulating such deception. Perhaps, more than anything else, Chapters 5 through 7 have demonstrated that buyers frequently do not use price in ways commonly assumed.

Buyers may also use price as an indicator of quality and value. Proactive pricers must learn how their customers perceive price and how these perceptions influence their perceptions of value. Ultimately, it is the relationship between price and customers' perceptions of value that determines purchase decisions.

Discussion Questions

1. Carefully study the newspaper advertising for the retail stores in your area. What is the relative frequency use of a regular price–sale price format?

   a. What words (semantic cues) are used to convey the notion of a sale? Do these advertisements clearly tell the consumers how much they would save if they make the purchase? To what extent do these advertisements directly or indirectly attempt to enhance the consumers' perceptions of value? Are there any disclaimers or restrictions in the advertisements? What impact, if any, do you think these disclaimers or restrictions have on buyers' perceptions and value judgments?

b. Can you find any tensile price claims? How are they presented to consumers?

c. How easy will it be for consumers to determine the amount they would save in these advertisements? Can these calculations be done easily and accurately in a person's head?

2. Read Box 7.2 again. Can you think of ways that Amazon.com could have managed to improve customers' perceptions of price fairness? Could the company have provided some type of frequent buyer reward program that recognized the value of repeat customers?

3. Assume that you have been wanting to get a new backpack to carry your books and supplies back and forth to classes. One day in the bookstore you see a display of backpacks and decide to purchase one. You pay $75 for the backpack.

   a. When you get back to your room you discover that your roommate had also just purchased the same backpack at the bookstore. However, your roommate had used a $25-off coupon that had been in the store's advertisement in the campus newspaper that day. How do you feel? What are your feelings about the fairness of the price you paid? Do you think the price your roommate paid was fair? Why, or why not?

   b. Suppose the situation in *a* is the reverse in that you had the coupon and your roommate did not. Was the price you paid fair? Was the price your roommate paid fair?

   c. Returning to the initial scenario, suppose that on the way back to your room, you stopped to see one of your professors. While in the professor's office, you learn that she has just purchased the same backpack in the bookstore and had used the $25-off coupon. Was the price you paid fair? Was the price your professor paid fair?

   d. Now suppose that the situation in *c* is the reverse in that you had the coupon and your professor did not. Was the price you paid fair? Was the price your professor paid fair?

   e. Compare your answers and feelings in situations *a* and *b* to those in situations *c* and *d*. Are there differences in how you feel about these situations?

4 *a.* Assume you have gone to a store that is about 15 minutes away to purchase a calculator. You find one that meets your needs priced at $25. When you get to the checkout counter the clerk asks you if you have a $10-off coupon for the calculator that was in the morning's newspaper. You realize that you forgot to bring the coupon with you. Do you go back to your room to get the coupon, or do you decide to pay the $25?

b. Assume you have gone to a store that is about 15 minutes away to purchase a television. You find one that meets your needs priced at $250. When you get to the checkout counter the clerk asks you if you have a $10-off coupon for the television that was in the morning's newspaper. You realize that you forgot to bring the coupon with you. Do you go back to your room to get the coupon, or do you decide to pay the $250?

c. Compare your answers to *a* and *b.* In which situation are you more likely to go back and get the coupon? What seems to be the reason for this difference in the likelihood of going back to get the coupon?

Suggested Readings

Biswas, Abhijit, and Scot Burton: "Consumer Perceptions of Tensile Price Claims in Advertisements," *Journal of the Academy of Marketing Science 21,* no. 3 (1993), 217–29.

Boulding, William, and Amna Kirmani: "A Consumer-Side Experimental Examination of Signaling Theory: Do Consumers Perceive Warranties as Signals of Product Quality?" *Journal of Consumer Research 20* (June 1993), 111–23.

Campbell, Margaret C.: "'Why Did You Do That?' The Important Role of Inferred Motive in Perceptions of Price Fairness," *Journal of Product & Brand Management Featuring Pricing Strategy & Practice 8,* no. 2 (1999), 145–52.

Chen, Shih-Fen, Kent B. Monroe, and Yung-Chien Lou: "The Effects of Framing Price Promotion Messages on Consumers' Perceptions and Purchase Intentions," *Journal of Retailing 74,* no. 3 (1998), 353–72.

Compeau, Larry D., and Dhruv Grewal: "Comparative Price Advertising: An Integrative Review," *Journal of Public Policy & Marketing 17* (Fall 1998), 257–73.

Cox, Jennifer Lyn: "Are Differential Prices Fair?" *Journal of Product & Brand Management Featuring Pricing Strategy & Practice 10,* no. 5 (2001), 264–73.

Grewal, Dhruv, Kent B. Monroe, and R. Krishnan: "The Effects of Price-Comparison Advertising on Buyers' Perceptions of Acquisition Value, Transaction Value, and Behavioral Intentions," *Journal of Marketing 62* (April 1998), 46–59.

CHAPTER EIGHT

Customer Value Analysis

A cynic is a man who knows the price of everything, and the value of nothing.
Oscar Wilde

What we obtain too cheaply we esteem too lightly; it is dearness only that gives everything its value.
John Jakes, The Rebel

The quality is remembered long after the price is forgotten.
James E. Brill, ABA Journal *(September 1992), 85*

Value Analysis Management

Successful proactive pricers focus on the concept of *value*, not on the *current price*. Indeed, these two terms are often confused in current discussions on price; some writers even suggest that price is synonymous with value. However, as demonstrated in Chapters 5 through 7, buyers perceive value as a trade-off between perceived quality and benefits in the product or service on the one hand and perceived cost of acquiring and using the product or service on the other. Price is a component of the perceived cost, but price also plays a role in buyers' perceptions of product or service quality. Hence, price is not the same thing as value.

What sets the high-achieving firms apart is their commitment to providing the highest value possible to their customers. These firms have developed organizations that concentrate on understanding and meeting their customers' needs. Moreover, they have understood the difference between a value strategy and the use of tactics to create an impression that the firm is value oriented. For example, Hewlett-Packard committed to a strategy of delivering what customers value that focuses on (1) empowering employees to take ownership in solving customer problems, (2) organizing the corporate and business units around their customers, and (3) learning to listen, understand, and communicate what customers value throughout the organization.[1]

What these firms are discovering is that seeking to maximize customer satisfaction is not sufficient to achieve profit and market growth objectives. Indeed, they have discovered that aligning their businesses around what customers value is the leading indicator of profitable market share. Research clearly shows that customers' perception of value is the primary influence on purchase decisions. Moreover, value is the leading indicator of market share, revenue growth, profitability, and competitive advantage. Customer value management involves understanding all the experiences that customers have with the products and services the firm provides. Indeed, their experiences begin with the first encounter with a salesperson or with a marketing communication and continues through each encounter with the firm including ordering, receiving, billing, installing, using, supporting, and finally disposing. The goal of customer value management is to maximize the exchange of value between the firm and its customers so both the customers and the firm achieve the highest value possible from the exchange.

Value-oriented pricing is more difficult than cost-oriented pricing, but the profit potential for having a value-oriented pricing strategy that works is far greater than with any other pricing approach. Taking a value orientation means recognizing that customer preferences are not constant, but rather can be changed as we demonstrated in Chapters 5 through 7. A value orientation also means that pricing research goes beyond estimating price elasticity or sensitivity and focuses more on understanding customers' value drivers. Finally, a value orientation means that the firm's pricing is driven by

[1]Ross Goodwin and Brad Ball, "Closing the Loop on Loyalty," *Marketing Management 8,* no. 1 (1999), 25–34.

measurable value provided to customers and not by customers' expressed willingness to pay.

Value versus Price

As demonstrated in Chapters 5 through 7, there is a clear relationship between perceived quality and perceived value and successful firms recognize this relationship. Among the firms that have learned that product quality and value are related and that emphasis on maintaining and improving quality is profitable are Kodak, 3M, Caterpillar, Coca-Cola, John Deere, Proctor & Gamble, Hewlett-Packard, 3M, Motorola, Toyota, Honda, Sony, DuPont, and Whirlpool. These firms have developed significant experience-based or credence-based attributes in their products and services. The quality of a Kodak picture, a Caterpillar earth mover, a Honda car, or a Hewlett-Packard printer must be experienced by a customer to be fully understood and appreciated. By moving towards defining quality in terms of experience attributes of their products and services, these companies have created opportunities to receive above-average prices and profits from the market. These companies consistently strive to improve their products and service, and are willing to signal quality with strong warranties. The key to success using this approach, then, is offering products or services that deliver value to customers. As already demonstrated, the relationship between benefits received and the total cost of acquiring the product or service is important:

$$\text{Preceived acquisition value} = \frac{\text{perceived benefits or quality}}{\text{perceived total sacrifice}}$$

$$(8.1)$$

where perceived total sacrifice to the buyer equals purchase price plus start-up costs (acquisition costs, transportation, installation, order handling) plus post-purchase costs (repairs and maintenance, risk of failure or poor performance) and perceived benefits or quality equals some combination of physical attributes, service attributes, and technical support available in relation to the particular use of the product, as well as the purchase price, and other indicators of perceived quality.

Components of Perceived Acquisition Value

To use customer value analysis in pricing, it is useful to distinguish ways that customers may evaluate a product and service to assess its perceived acquisition value. Evaluation looks at several components:

1. Sacrifice—the sum of all costs and sacrifices that customers incur to acquire and use the product or service.

2. Equity—the perceived value of the brand, company, or store where the product is sold.

3. Aesthetics—the value that customers place on the properties or attractiveness of the product.

4. Relative use—the way a product is used.

5. Perceived transaction value—the perceived benefits or gain from taking advantage of the offer (see Chapter 7)

These first four components are briefly discussed next.

Sacrifice

Marketers must realize that price or purchase cost is not the only relevant cost of a product; cost actually has numerous components. Traditionally, costs include search, risk of nonperformance, service, maintenance, and any other life-cycle costs involved in the purchase and use of the product. For consumers, purchase costs include the price of the product or service as well as time and psychological costs involved in shopping or searching for the acquisition.[2] "Sticker price" is only one component of cost that purchasers consider in the buying decision. Equation 8.1 shows start-up costs and post-purchase costs are also important.

An important question to ask when conducting value analysis is how the firm affects the customers'costs. What sacrifices must customers make to do business with your company, and how can you eliminate these sacrifices and convert them to value?[3] The buyer's sacrifice in an exchange may include the less obvious costs related to order handling, materials handling, employee training and turnover, transportation costs, switching costs, inventory handling costs, risks of poor performance, product failure, or poor after-sales service. To understand what the buyer considers the total cost of acquiring and using a product, then, firms must consider buyers' perceptions of not only the monetary price,

---

[2]Wesley Bender, "Consumer Purchase Costs," *Journal of Retailing 40* (Spring 1964), 1–8, 52.
[3]Christopher W. Hart, "Sacrificial Offerings," *Marketing Management 8,* no. 3 (1999), 6–7.

ADDING VALUE BY REDUCING CUSTOMERS' SACRIFICES

BOX 8.1

Outside of Boston is a brake and tire shop, Direct Tire Sales, that understands the importance of providing added value to its customers. President Barry Steinberg offers a level of service so unique that customers welcome prices 10 percent to 12 percent higher than those of the competition. Customers are so satisfied that they not only pay the higher price once, but they return to Direct Tires Sales for all tire and brake repairs. In fact, on any given day nearly 75 percent of the customers have been to the shop before.

How does Barry Steinberg create value? He minimizes customer costs while providing added benefits. The shop's immaculate waiting room stocked with fresh coffee and a variety of magazines enables customers to wait in comfort, while the room's many windows overlooking the garage reduce the barriers between customers and technicians. If repairs extend beyond the shop's average one-hour service or if customers are unable to wait, Direct Tire Sales offers loaner cars, free of charge, until the repairs are finished. Uniformed employees, who are recruited through headhunter services, treat all customers with respect. Perhaps even more amazing is Steinberg's lifetime guarantee on all tires and service work.

Direct Tire Sales' additional services are costly. In order to ensure added value, Steinberg has implemented customized inventory software to maintain the shop's large collection of uncommon tires, updates the garage with the best equipment, and pays employees 15 percent to 25 percent more than the industry average. Although the cost of providing Direct Tire Sales' customers with added value averages more than $230,000 per year, the shop's 3 percent net margins are twice the industry average. Obviously Direct Tire Sales' unique approach to adding value has been well worth the cost!

Source: Paul B. Brown, "The Real Cost of Customer Service," *Inc 12* no. 9, (1990), 48–60.

but also relationship-specific investments: search efforts; psychic costs related to frustration, conflict, and anxiety; and perceived financial, performance, and social risks. By knowing what components of sacrifice customers perceive as important, sellers are in a better position to understand the buyers' value equations. Box 8.1 describes how one firm reduces its customers' perceived sacrifice, and earns premium prices and above-industry average profits.

Equity

This component refers to a number of market-related factors that influence perceptions of value. One important aspect of this component is the notion of brand equity—an image of excellence for products, brands, or service developed over time. The reputation of the firm or brand for quality products, additional efforts to provide prompt and reliable parts or service (e.g., Caterpillar's promise to deliver parts anywhere in the world within 24 hours), and trustworthy salespeople and customer service personnel all enhance perceptions of value by improving perceptions of quality or benefits provided. This image of excellence that companies like DuPont, Sony, and Caterpillar project fosters buyers' willingness to pay some premium to acquire their products or services. Since buyers usually are not able to evaluate a product or service prior to purchase and use, they may rely on the firm's or brand's reputation as a signal of quality and, therefore, value.

Aesthetics

Henry Ford was once quoted as saying that customers could have a car of any color as long as it was black. However, in contemporary marketing, it is clear that color, style, design, and interior furnishings all contribute to customers' perceptions of value of automobiles. In recent years, consumers generally have been willing to pay higher prices for color-toned appliances than for traditional white appliances. Similarly, product attributes such as hardness of a drill bit, softness of a fabric, or taste of a cola drink enhance the attractiveness of a product to prospective buyers and increase its perceived value. Although technical innovation remains the key value element of consumer electronics, style, design, and color are playing an increasingly important role in their sales.

Relative Use

How a product is used, along with its ability to reduce costs or improve gains through its use, enhance its perceived value. For example, a machine's value will increase with its life span or its reduced fuel consumption. A new machine that leads to labor or raw material savings or to increased output per hour over alternative machines will be perceived as delivering more value. Perceived value may also change relative to the way the product is used or its intended use.

The Concept of Benefits

In any purchase decision, the buyer is seeking to acquire benefits. To provide benefits a product or service must be able to (1) perform certain tasks or functions, (2) solve identified problems, or (3) provide specific pleasures. Thus, buyers do not purchase a product for its particular components, materials, or expertise per se, but rather for what the product or service does. For example, people do not buy quarter-inch drill bits; they buy the ability to make quarter-inch holes.

The drill bit has no extrinsic value except for the benefit of making the hole.

When thinking about benefits, it is helpful to consider how the triad of firms, products and services, and customers contribute to the level of benefits delivered. Benefits delivered must be consistent with the benefits desired by customers. The benefits customers or users want provide a key element to firms and the products or services they offer. Value is created when the benefits that products or services deliver match the benefits customers or users want. Customers or users have different behavioral characteristics that affect and determine the benefits they want as well as how the products or services satisfy their wants. The willingness of people to pay different prices for products that perform similar tasks or functions varies according to the projected use or purchase situation they are in when they purchase or use them. The critical variable may be the particular characteristics or attributes of a product, such as hardness of a drill bit. Buyers knowledgeable about these "intrinsic cues" may use them to evaluate the relative benefits and value of the product. Thus product characteristics or attributes are perceived to be important insofar as they deliver certain benefits to customers.

The benefit concept has certain implications for providers of goods and services. First, it is necessary to identify the benefits that the customers will perceive the product or service to offer. Second, it is necessary to determine the relative importance of those benefits that the customers place on the product or service. If customers perceive that an organization offers a better product, better technical advice, or better service, then that organization has a differential advantage.

Improving Perceived Acquisition Value

Essentially, perceived acquisition value can be improved by increasing the ability of the product or service to perform a function or task, solve a problem, or provide pleasure. Perceived value can also be improved by reducing the total sacrifice associated with acquiring and using the product; that is, by increasing perceived transaction value. Various combinations can be used to influence perceived acquisition value, some of which are favorable and some unfavorable. The most desirable combination is to provide more perceived benefits at less perceived sacrifice. The sacrifice in this relationship includes the selling price and all subsequent costs to the customer of acquiring, installing, maintaining, and using the product over its useful life (the concept of life-cycle

LEARNING TO BECOME VALUE ORIENTED

BOX 8.2

In 1987, PepsiCo began focusing on the value equation. Taco Bell led the fast food industry when it began offering its best-selling product—a taco priced at 59 cents, a reduction of 40 cents. At FritoLay, PepsiCo focused on increasing quality while reducing prices slightly. This shift in orientation at FritoLay came after a period of raising prices annually more than the rate of inflation, which had led to prices that were 15 percent to 20 percent more than the competition's.

In 1995, Audi began a comeback strategy by lowering prices and making the all-wheel drive Quattro feature available to more buyers. Previously the Quattro was available only in the highest-priced cars. Starting in 1995, Audi made Quattro available for $1,500, and in 1996 made it available with automatic transmission cars, not just in cars with five-speed manual transmissions. By offering more for less money, Audi U.S. sales surpassed previous levels by over 40 percent.

In these examples, companies found ways to deliver more value to their customers. In some cases, increasing value is accomplished by price reductions. In other cases, increased value is accomplished by offering more benefit-producing features. Increased value also occurs when customers have more options for selecting desired features. In other cases higher-priced products pay for themselves by reducing customers' life-cycle costs. Finally, products that provide more pleasurable experiences are perceived to provide more value, leading to a willingness to pay above-average prices.

Sources: Joseph B. White, "'Value Pricing' is Hot as Shrewd Consumers Seek Low-Cost Quality," *The Wall Street Journal* (March 12, 1991), A1, A6; "Chipping Away at Frito-Lay," *Business Week* (July 22, 1991), 26; "Value Marketing," *Business Week* (November 11, 1991), 132–40; "No Playing Catchup for PepsiCo," *Chicago Tribune* (August 30, 1993), Section 4, 6; "'Value Pricing' Pays Off," *Business Week* (November 1, 1993), 32–33; Jim Mateja, "Offering More For Less, Audi Grows," *Chicago Tribune* (February 5, 1996), Section 4, 6; William C. Symonds, "'Build a Better Mousetrap' is no Claptrap," *Business Week* (February 1, 1999), 47.

cost). Other favorable combinations include increasing perceived benefits while holding customer sacrifice constant, or holding perceived benefits constant while reducing customer sacrifice. Efforts to improve perceived acquisition value cannot concentrate only on the direct monetary costs of providing the product to customers. Box 8.2 describes how some firms have become value oriented.

The key to customer value management is to remember that customers want something done and someone pleased. Buyers want something enclosed, held, moved, separated, cleaned, heated, cooled, or whatever, under certain conditions, in certain situations, and within certain limits. Buyers also want a shape, color, aroma, texture, sound, feel, taste; a "precious" material; something to bring pleasure to themselves or to others they wish to please. That is, buyers purchase a product or service because of its ability to perform a certain task or function, solve a particular problem, or provide specific pleasures. It is what the product or service does and how well it does it that provides value.

The Five Steps of Value-Oriented Pricing

Current and prospective buyers, then, will make purchase decisions on the basis of perceived acquisition value. Since perceived acquisition value is a trade-off between perceived quality and benefits with the total perceived sacrifice, buyers do not determine a product's value solely on the basis of minimizing the price paid. Customers must be educated about the use and value of products and services. Finally, price must be consistent with customers' value perceptions. That is, a product perceived to be of higher value than competitive offerings will be granted the privilege of a premium price.

As discussed in Chapters 5 through 7, price is perceived differently by all types of buyers. For example, current clients or loyal buyers will perceive price and the price–value relationship differently than a periodic customer, and a prospective buyer will likely have another perception. For clients, it is apparent that the value received is perceived to be more than the price of the product or service. Indeed, it is likely that because of the perceived value received these buyers are not highly concerned with the price, at least within limits. Mercedes-Benz, Tiffany's, and Disneyland have successfully premium-priced their products because of the higher perceived quality or benefits (the premium value) of their offerings. The objective of value-oriented pricing is not simply pricing as high as feasible but rather pricing in relationship to the in-use benefits that buyers perceive they will gain from purchasing and using the product or service.

Step One: Conceptualize Customer Value

Customers ordinarily may not know how to translate product or service features and attributes into benefits that they receive from acquiring and using products and services. Moreover, they do not know how to quantify the benefits into monetary terms. This problem is particularly an issue for new buyers or for buyers of innovative products. As we discussed in Chapters 5 through 7, buyers do form or have reference price expectations as well as acceptable price ranges. Buyers who are uninformed about the benefits to be received from certain product attributes or features will tend to underestimate the value of innovations or products that are relatively unknown to them. As a result, their reference prices for these products or services will be relatively low and their acceptable price ranges will be low and narrow.

Consequently, it is important that the seller understand the ways the products may be used and the benefits that the product features and attributes will deliver to buyers. That is, the seller must translate the features and attributes into perceived benefits for prospective buyers. This prescription must also be filled for existing customers who do not fully understand the value of the product to them. To avoid the reply "We do not need this feature," the seller must anticipate skepticism and be prepared to demonstrate how the feature provides benefits. Moreover, it is important that the seller conceptualize how the services it provides along with the product offer benefits to customers. The seller must compare the relative benefits of its offering to the benefits of competitive offerings to establish the equivalent value. Finally, it is important to consider all sacrifices the seller will incur to acquire and use the product and services.

Step Two: Understand the Key Value Drivers for Customers

Although most companies regularly survey customers on issues concerning customer satisfaction, they rarely include measures or questions aimed at learning what customers actually perceive they gain by using the firm's products or services. Not all buyers benefit from the same attributes equally. An important feature to one buyer may be unimportant to another buyer. Similarly, buyers do not attach the same weights to the sacrifices required to obtain the product. Some buyers may place considerable weight on the transaction costs, whereas others may place more weight on life-cycle costs, and others may ignore risks. Thus it is important to develop a value profile of the firm's customers. An approach for developing and using these profiles will be developed below in the section on value mapping. However, a useful step in this process of developing customers' value profiles is to have members of the management and sales teams develop them from their own perceptions of what they believe their customers value. Then after the customers' actual profiles are developed it is revealing to compare what the firm's personnel think their customers value versus what the customers reveal themselves.

Step Three: Calculate Customer Value

The goal in this step is to develop the data required to build customers' value profiles. As these profiles are being developed, the seller needs to look for its sources of differentiation value; that is, where it has a competitive advantage in delivering value. Moreover, it needs to use the information from the research to determine customer value segments. To become expert "value sellers," firms must determine customer value segments and estimate the economic value they provide to these different segments.

For business-to-business marketing it is important that the firm determine how it influences customers' costs and revenues or cash flows. Sellers must identify and quantify how their customers can reduce or avoid costs. For this form of analysis, it may be necessary that the selling firm understand its customers' costs better than the customers themselves. The principles of activity-based costing and profitability analysis developed in Chapters 10 and 11 are relevant when attempting to understand customers' cost. An activity-based costing approach is required to learn what customer costs are actually incurred. When a customer uses a full-cost allocation system, costs will be attributed to activities based on arbitrary allocating rules and likely will not reflect actual cash costs incurred because of purchasing from the seller. When doing this analysis, it is helpful to determine what customer costs are a function of customers' requirements. It would also be useful to determine how competitors affect the customers' costs. Examples of cost-based sources of value include

- Salary and compensation savings.

- Productivity increases.

- Training/learning savings.

- Maintenance/set up savings.

- Hiring/turnover savings.

- Material handling savings.

One producer of roofing shingles discovered that it had lost an opportunity to improve its profitability by failing to realize how a change in its packaging of shingles reduced a large retailer customer's handling costs. The producer had substituted a shrink wrapping of bundles of shingles for the old way of wrapping the bundles with steel straps. When the producing firm's divisional officer visited the president of the retailing company, he learned that the new way of packaging had reduced the retailer's handling costs by 5 percent. The producer had only been concerned that the new packaging system reduced its own handling costs, so it had not considered the effect on the retailer's costs.

It is also important for sellers to identify and quantify how their customers may be able to increase their revenues or improve cash flows. Examples of revenue-based sources of value include

- Reducing customers' time to get their products to market.

- Helping customers gain a cost advantage in their markets.

- Helping customers gain new customers.

- Helping customers change to a more profitable customer mix.

- Helping customers increase their sales volume or market share.

- Helping customers improve or enhance the performance capability of their products.

Value Analysis and Value Engineering

Research needed to determine the buyers' perceived value of an offering includes value analysis and value engineering. Value analysis attempts to determine the relative value buyers place on the total product or service offering—their perceived benefits. It focuses on the process that customers use to determine the relative value of alternative product or service options. The focus of value analysis is on the customer and how customers determine the value of the product or service to them.

Value engineering is an organized effort to analyze the ability of products or services to perform desired functions, satisfy needs, or provide pleasure or satisfaction in the most profitable manner.[4] Value engineering focuses on determining essential product functions and characteristics and the cost of providing these functions and characteristics. The

[4]Jerry J. Kaufman and Ron F. Becker, *Value Engineering: An Executive Overview* (Houston, TX: Cooper Industries 1981); James C. Anderson, Dipak C. Jain, and Pradeep K. Chintagunta, "Customer Value Assessment in Business Markets: A State-of-Practice Study," *Journal of Business-to-Business Marketing 1,* no. 1 (1993), 3–29.

cost is determined by evaluating alternative concepts, designs, engineering procedures or processes, and raw materials. This method requires a detailed knowledge of how the firm's customers use the product. Typically, a firm makes assumptions about how tests conducted in the lab will generalize to customers' actual use of the product.

It is also important to consider the customers' cost of ownership over the normal life of the product. The disciplines of marketing, engineering and manufacturing, and other supporting disciplines work together to maintain a focus on the requirements, design, and cost from the customers' sense of value.

Value-in-Use Analysis

Value-in-use analysis can be used for pricing by considering the *perceived relative monetary value* of the product from the perspective of the customer. This approach recognizes that the maximum price that can be set is the price at which the customer disregards the difference between the product and the next best economic alternative (maximum acceptable price, or reservation price). As established in Chapter 2 and Figure 2.6, the difference between the maximum amount customers are willing to pay for a product and the amount they actually pay is called *consumers' surplus* (perceived acquisition value). This difference represents the customers' gain from making the purchase and is the sum of the money amounts of *value-in-use* minus *value-in-exchange*. Consumers' surplus represents the customers' net gain from the trade. Since buyers are seldom fully informed about products or prices, perceived acquisition value may be augmented by perceived transaction value (see Chapter 7).

To use the concept of value-in-use for pricing a product or service requires the determination of customers' *reference product*, customers' *life-cycle costs* using the reference product, and the *improvement value* of the product relative to the reference product. The reference product should be the customers' next-best alternative for meeting the same need as the current or proposed new product. This reference product may be the existing model about to be replaced or it may be the competing product being used by customers. In any case, the reference product must be the same reference product customers will use to make their comparisons.

Life-cycle costs represent all costs that a customer will incur over the product's useful life. These costs include the actual purchase price, start-up costs, and postpurchase costs

FIGURE 8.1 **Determining Maximum Acceptable Price to Customers**

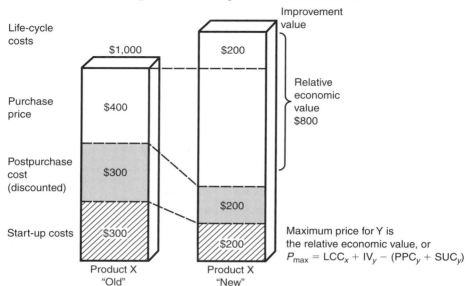

(Figure 8.1). Postpurchase costs include all costs the customer incurs once the product has been installed and is in use. For example, fuel, service contract, and other costs that will be incurred to keep the product functional are postpurchase costs. These costs, because they represent outlays over time, should be discounted back to the present time using an interest rate that reflects the customer's desired return on investment. Similarly, start-up costs include installation, training, and related costs that will be incurred prior to the product being fully operational. For consumer energy products, the concept of life-cycle cost could lead to substantial increases in perceived value if sellers attempted to help consumers understand this concept.

The improvement value of the product represents the potential incremental satisfaction or profits the customer can expect from this product over those of the reference product. This enhancement of customers' satisfaction or profit potential may occur because of attributes of the new product that improve productivity (reduce costs or increase output per unit of time), increase the value of the customers' output and, potentially, the output's price, or simply provide more pleasure.

The maximum price that could be set is the price that makes the customer ignore the monetary difference between the "new" product and the reference product (Figure 8.1). This maximum price is

$$P_{max\,y} = LCC_x + IV_y - (PPC_y + SUC_y) \qquad \textbf{(8.2)}$$

where

$$P_{max\,y} = \text{maximum acceptable price of product Y}$$

$$LCC_x = \text{life-cycle costs of the reference product}$$

$$IV_y = \text{improvement value for the "new" product}$$

$$PPC_y = \text{discounted postpurchase costs for the new product}$$

$$SUC_y = \text{start-up costs for the "new" product}$$

To illustrate this concept, assume that the old reference product has a current purchase price of $400, that its postpurchase costs (discounted) are $300, and that its start-up costs are $300. Therefore,

$$LCC_x = P_x + PPC_x + SUC_x \qquad \textbf{(8.3)}$$

or

$$LCC_x = \$400 + \$300 + \$300 = \$1,000 \qquad \textbf{(8.4)}$$

Now assume the "new" product, because of its efficiency in reducing material costs per unit of output and its ability to increase the number of units produced per hour, has an improvement value of $200. Further assume that the discounted postpurchase costs are $200 and the new product's start-up costs are $200. Therefore, the maximum acceptable purchase price is

$$P_{max} = \$1,000 + \$200 - (\$200 + \$200) \qquad \textbf{(8-5)}$$

or

$$P_{max} = \$800 \text{ (relative monetary value)} \qquad \textbf{(8-6)}$$

The maximum purchase price of $800 in Equation 8.6 may not be the price that "sells" to potential customers. If the price represents an economic indifference point, then some additional inducement may be necessary to convert customers to the "new" product. The seller must also consider internal pricing factors such as costs and objectives, as well as the degree of uncertainty that estimated life-cycle cost savings are less than expected. A second area of uncertainty that sellers must consider is whether the estimated internal direct variable costs might be higher than estimated for the analysis. Because of these two uncertainties, it would be appropriate to develop a feasible range or distribution of values for these critical estimates.[5] The seller's pricing discretion represents the difference between the maximum acceptable price in the marketplace and the direct variable costs associated with producing and selling the product. That is,

$$SPD = P_{max} - DVC \tag{8.7}$$

where

$$SPD = \text{seller's pricing discretion}$$

$$P_{max} = \text{customers' maximum acceptable price}$$

$$DVC = \text{direct variable costs of producing and selling the product}$$

For our illustration, assume the direct variable costs for producing and selling this "new" product initially are $400. Therefore,

$$SPD = \$800 - \$400 = \$400 \tag{8.8}$$

That is, the seller has a leeway of $400 for setting the actual price for the "new" product (Figure 8.2). The problem now is to determine how much of an inducement customers will need to switch to the product.

As we have discussed, the maximum acceptable price represents an economic indifference point to customers. At this price some customers might be willing to switch but others will have some degree of inertia. Therefore, to obtain the volume necessary to make the product a feasible alternative, a price less than $800 must be considered. Other subjective considerations that influence the outcome will include possible competitive reactions (e.g., price reductions on the reference product) and market entry with an imitative product. The firm may also need to consider the wisdom of generating a large sales volume quickly to reduce per-unit direct variable costs (this "experience curve" effect is discussed in Chapter 13). In any event, a price less than the maximum acceptable price represents the customers' surplus.

To complete the illustration, assume the new product's price is set at $600. This price will give the seller a $200

[5]Kenneth N. Thompson and Barbara J. Coe, "Gaining Sustainable Competitive Advantage through Strategic Pricing: Selecting a Perceived Value Price," *Pricing Strategy & Practice 5,* no. 2 (1997), 70–79.

FIGURE 8.2   **Determining Seller's Price**

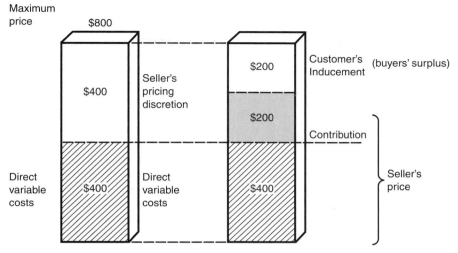

contribution per unit to fixed costs and profit while provid-ing a $200 inducement to customers. Once this decision has been made, the next step will be to develop a communication and sales strategy that reaches and convinces customers of the product's value to them. The example in Box 8.3 illus-trates a practical example of determining value in use.

One of the major difficulties of applying this value-in-use concept is estimating the relative improvement value of the product or service *as perceived by current and prospective buyers*. Indeed, in practice, firms often fail to do the field re-search necessary to complete step 3 above, and the completed value-in-use analysis represents the seller's perceptions. Sometimes the product offering is so new that it is difficult to accurately estimate its relative value to customers. Moreover, the improvement value may vary over time and over cus-tomers. In particular, the value of the product may be contin-gent upon the nature of the buyer, how the buyer uses the product, or variations in perceived benefits of the product by different buyers. Later in the chapter we will provide two ex-amples showing how estimates of the relative improvement value of new products can be developed.

Value Mapping

A value map illustrates the way customers in a value seg-ment trade off perceived benefits against perceived price. In

CONTACT LENSES ARE FOR THE BIRDS

BOX 8.3

There may have been stranger ideas, but none may be more unusual in the field of agriculture than contact lenses for chickens. Yes, Animalens—a small company in Massachusetts—is producing and marketing chicken-sized lenses in a rose color.

The objective of these lenses is to prevent laying hens, who habitually and literally establish a "pecking order," from harming and killing each other. Although scientists do not know why, chickens become positively mellow when they see the world through rose-tinted glasses. Red-eyed birds spend less time fighting and more time laying eggs. They also eat less grain.

Randall E. Wise, the owner of Animalens, has calculated that the tinted contact lens can reduce the mortality of laying hens due to fighting from 25 percent to less than 8 percent. Further, the hens lay more eggs when they are not tense due to fighting and actually eat less grain when they are not aggressive. Wise has calculated that the savings to a chicken farmer would be at least 50 cents per chicken, or 2.5 cents per dozen eggs. A single pair of lens will last a chicken's lifetime (about one year), and costs 5 to 10 cents a bird to install. Depending on the discount arrangements, the price for a pair of chicken contacts ranges from 15 to 20 cents. Thus by incurring a cost of 20 to 29 cents to acquire and install the lenses, a farmer will realize a savings of 50 cents or more per chicken per year. Even for a small chicken farm of 10,000 hens, a savings of $5,000 or more is not exactly chicken feed! For a large farm of 100,000 hens, the savings of $50,000 is quite impressive.

Source: "Chickens See the World through Rose-Tinted Lenses," *Roanoke Times & World News* (November 27, 1989), A1, A7.

Figure 8.3, the horizontal axis quantifies customers' perceptions of the relative benefits received from different sellers. The vertical axis shows their relative perceived price. If the market is stable, and if the pricing research has correctly measured customers' perceived benefits and perceived price, then competing sellers should fall along the diagonal line, or value equivalence line. Depending on the customers' desires for benefits relative to price, there would be a relatively clear and logical choice of preferred supplier.[6]

On the other hand, if market shares are still changing and competitors are changing their marketing mixes to improve their competitive positions, then we would expect those competitors who are losing market share to be positioned to the left of the value equivalence line (value disadvantage). Competitors who are gaining market share are likely positioned to the right of the value equivalence line (value advantage).

[6]Ralf Leszinski and Michael V. Marn, "Setting Value, Not Price," *The McKinsey Quarterly*, no. 1 (1997), 98–115.

FIGURE 8.3

Customers' Value Map

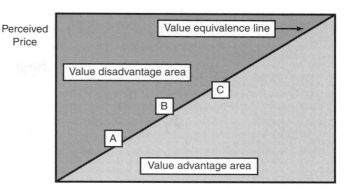

Perceived Price

Value equivalence line

Value disadvantage area

C

B

A

Value advantage area

Perceived Benefits

Value maps can be built by developing data on how customers perceive the firm's offerings relative to its competitors. Sellers can use customer interviews and focus groups to get the necessary information. (A useful beginning point is to conduct this research in-house using relevant managers and salespeople.) From these various interviews, the firm seeks to obtain a comprehensive listing of the features and attributes of the products and services that customers consider important when making purchase decisions. (If the respondents can think in terms of benefits received from these features or attributes, the exercise would be even more informative.) Customers should be asked to list all suppliers (competitors) that they consider when making the purchase decision and the features and attributes of the competitors' products and services that are relevant to their buying decisions. Repeating the task for competitors should reveal any different purchasing criteria that customers apply to competing sellers.

Once a listing of the competitors and the product and service features of the firm and its competitors has been determined, the customers should be asked to weight these features by importance. The sum of the weights assigned to the features should be forced to equal 100. (To keep this process manageable for the customer as well as the seller, weights should be assigned numerical values using no less than a 5 for any item, and the weight used should be rounded to the nearest 5 or 0. See Box 8.4 for an example of this initial exercise.

Customers should then be asked to evaluate each competitor's performance on each feature or benefit. Although it

ESTIMATING VALUE EQUIVALENCE

BOX 8.4

Sometimes it is not feasible for a company to do a complete customer analysis to determine the relative incremental value of a new product. However, it is still feasible for experienced product managers and salespeople to estimate the incremental perceived value of the product. The Sudbury Corporation faced such a situation, and this example illustrates the approach developed to solve the problem.

The Sudbury Corporation manufactured equipment for the application of adhesive materials in its customers' production and packaging operations. Although the company was the leading producer of such equipment with a nearly 40 percent market share, in recent years, it had lost its competitive edge, and although its products and services were still perceived to be superior, it no longer had the ability to set premium prices much above competitor prices. To regain its competitive edge and improve its profitability, it developed several new products that would be perceived to offer greater value to its customers than current products. As the first new product was ready to be introduced to the market, the company needed to estimate the premium price to charge for the new product relative to the current product's price. However, managers felt it was too late to do any type of actual market research.

The company brought together representatives of its research and development staff, product managers, and sales managers to discuss the problem. The research and development people outlined the five incremental benefits of the new equipment relative to the existing equipment, shown in Table 1. The product managers and salespeople had difficulty correlating the relative importance of these incremental benefits as estimated by the research and development staff to potential purchasers, so each benefit was given an equal relative weight of 0.2. Each improvement factor then was multiplied by its benefit weight and the products of the multiplication were summed to get an overall estimate of the product's relative improvement value. This estimate implied that a price premium of 14 percent might be feasible.

At this point considerable discussion took place. The marketing people questioned whether all potential buyers would perceive the new product as envisioned by the research and development staff. Another issue was that a 14 percent price premium would not lead to a recovery of the development costs in the planned time. Managers agreed that only the heavy users of equipment similar to the new product would be likely to consider the required investment feasible. Thus they repeated the analysis by considering only heavy user segment of prospective buyers.

As shown in Table 2, the dramatic increase in the material savings for the heavy users led to a substantial increase in the overall improvement value estimate. Moreover, because of the dollar savings a heavy user would realize by using less adhesive material, the relative importance of this benefit was believed to be much higher. Thus Sudbury decided to concentrate marketing efforts on the heavy user segment with a price premium over the existing "old" product of 22 percent. A price premium of 22 percent provided an opportunity to stay on the value equivalence line.

is common at this step to use a 7- or 10-point rating scale, it is more correct to ask the respondents to provide a ratio-level evaluation. Using one of the competing firms as a standard

TABLE 1

(1) Incremental Benefit	(2) Improvement Factor, %	(3) Benefit Weight	Weighted Factor, % (2) × (3)
Material savings	35	0.2	7.0
Output/hour	10	0.2	2.0
Adaptability	5	0.2	1.0
Quality of applications	10	0.2	2.0
Less maintenance	10	0.2	2.0
Total		1.00	14.0

TABLE 2

(1) Incremental Benefit	(2) Improvement Factor, %	(3) Benefit Weight	Weighted Factor, % (2) × (3)
Material savings	50	0.5	25.0
Output/hour	10	0.1	1.0
Adaptability	5	0.1	0.5
Quality of applications	10	0.2	2.0
Less maintenance	10	0.1	1.0
Total		1.00	29.5

of reference with a score of 100, the respondents should indicate first whether each other firm performs better or worse than the standard firm. Then, they should indicate how much different each firm's performance is from the standard firm. For example, if the firm being evaluated is judged to provide more benefits along a specific product or service feature than the standard firm, that judged firm should be given a score greater than 100. If the judgment is that the firm is 10 percent better, it would receive a score of 110. (See the discussion on magnitude scaling in Chapter 9.) The scores for each listed feature or attribute are then weighted by the customer's relative attribute weights and summed to produce a weighted score for each competitor. Averaging these weighted scores across responding customers for each competitor produces a quality index for each that can then be plotted as a point along the horizontal axis.

The next step is to ask the respondents to weight the relative importance of price and nonprice features for the purchase decision. For example, price might receive a weight of 40 percent and the nonprice features a weight of 60 percent. (The two weights should sum to 100 percent.) The final step in this data gathering activity is to ask the respondents to judge the relative prices of the competing sellers. The procedure is the same as above for judging the relative performances of the competitors. Select one competitor to be used as a standard and set its price equal to 100. Then ask each respondent to judge all other competitors' prices as either higher or lower than the standard competitor. If a specific competitor is judged to have prices 10 percent higher than the standard competitor, then it would receive a score of 110. As above, each competitor's price index can be plotted along the vertical axis. The slope of the value equivalence line is determined by the ratio of the purchase consideration weights (in the above example 40 percent/60 percent, or 0.67).

If a competitor is positioned to right of the value equivalence line, it is delivering more perceived benefits relative to perceived price. Any competitor to the left of the value equivalence line is delivering less perceived benefits relative to perceived price. Any competitor that is positioned horizontally to the right of another competitor has a perceived value advantage relative to that competitor.

Summary

An important benefit of a systematic attempt to calculate the perceived value delivered to customers is that the firm is forced to develop an understanding of what is important to customers. A second benefit of performing value-in-use analysis and value mapping is that the firm gains a stronger understanding of its competitors from the eyes and minds of customers. This deeper understanding of customers and competitors improves the likelihood of correctly predicting their likely reactions to price changes and product or service improvements by the firm. These analyses must be done periodically, at a minimum whenever market stability is interrupted.

Step Four: Communicate Value to Customers

Previously, Chapter 7 introduced the concept of framing and provided some perspective on how to communicate price increases or to present price promotions. In this section, we expand on those earlier suggestions to offer additional guidelines on communicating value to customers.

Following the previous steps of value-oriented pricing should have identified the different customer value segments that exist in the market. Moreover, the value-in-use and value mapping analyses should have provided information concerning the firm's perceived price relative to customers' perceptions of benefits received. By focusing on benefits and value provided, the firm can relate its price to customer usage and value received. Any price changes or product and service improvements necessary to enhance the firm's value position in the market should have been decided by this point. The communication principles provided here augment the principles given in Chapter 7:

1. Keep price structures understandable, flexible, and relatively easy to administer (see Chapter 16).

2. Consistently and clearly communicate price structure. Discounts, allowances, rebates, and rewards for loyalty should be aboveboard and clearly defined.

3. Provide complete and accurate information about each offer.

4. Provide appropriate reference price and actual selling price.

5. Avoid vague phrasing (e.g., "save up to 50 percent");

6. Minimize the amount of work and effort required for customers to take advantage of an offer.

7. Refrain from using "suggested list price" or similar phrases; buyers may distrust these phrases, and they may be considered deceptive.

8. Communicate the total savings in an offer; minimize the need for buyers to make calculations to determine savings.

9. Place a reference value on any "free" aspect of an offer.

10. For temporary price reductions, provide the specific ending date of the offer and the price in effect after the ending date.

11. For price increases, provide the beginning date of the new prices.

Step Five: Develop Ways to Capture Customer Value

One of the benefits of following this five-step approach to value-oriented pricing is that the seller becomes externally focused when managing prices. A second benefit is that the seller should become less tradition bound when managing the pricing function, leading to an ability and a willingness to "step out of the box." As a result, the pricing manager can learn to establish new pricing metrics that track value.

A second prescription for communicating value is to establish pricing rules or structure that force customers to acknowledge value received. The pricing structure should recognize customer loyalty rather than simply volume ordered in defined units of time. Value-added features or benefits should be unbundled and an equivalent-value price established for each feature or benefit. Thus if the firm offers a package of product and service features it can establish the overall value of the bundle by referring to the price list showing the individual item prices.

Being "value-oriented" involves not just satisfying customers, but *creating perceived value by framing the context of customer judgments and preference formation.* Profitable pricing depends not only on careful measurement of customer perceptions, but also on *developing effective strategies and tactics to manage those perceptions toward the true value of a firm's products and services.*

Contingency Value Pricing

Sometimes, particularly when the "new" product is comprised primarily of delivered services (as, for example, in an engineering consulting project), the buyer probably cannot calculate the value of the service before its delivery. Even though the provider of the service is sure that the service will provide value to the client, it would be difficult to determine its economic value. One way to develop a pricing solution for this problem is for the seller to share some of the risks of delivering this value to the buyer through a contingency pricing arrangement. There are several well-known forms of contingency pricing: money-back guarantees, real estate agents' commissions based on a percentage of the selling price, lawyers' or professional sports agents' fees based on a percentage of the damage award or contract negotiated. Another alternative to fixed prices is to let the customer decide the value-equivalent price (see Box 8.5). In the example below, the price is comprised of a fixed fee with a guarantee geared to the amount of the economic benefits the customer realized.

PAYING FOR WHAT YOU VALUE   BOX 8.5

The upscale restaurant Just Around the Corner opened in London in 1986 amidst heavy criticism that its owner was economically irresponsible, or perhaps worse, a lunatic. Michael Vasos, the owner, had decided not to put prices on the menu. Instead, the customers decide how much the meal and service is worth to them. Surprisingly, Mr. Vasos, who owns four other restaurants in London, says that he makes more money from this restaurant than any of the others. Generally, the people who patronize this restaurant overpay, averaging about 20 percent more than the price of the same meal at one of his other restaurants. If some customers seriously underpay, the waitress politely returns the payment saying: "We say thank you very much, you had a nice meal here and we don't want to spoil it." The embarrassed customers leave and do not return. Once four American businessmen left 600 pounds for a meal worth about 100 pounds. Mr. Vasos said "They asked if it was okay. I said, 'Of course.' If that's what they thought it was worth, then fine!"

Source: *The Wall Street Journal Interactive Edition* (December 11, 1998).

The EMS Company was an engineering services firm that suggested means of controlling and reducing energy use in large buildings.[7] EMS was one of three companies submitting a bid to a school district that was interested in reducing its expenditures for energy (heating oil, gas, and electricity). In the most recent year of operation, the school district had spent nearly $775,000 on energy, and the proposed budget for the coming year was $810,000. The school board was interested in a long-term solution to the energy use problem, that would enable the system to use less of its budget on energy and more on direct education expenses. EMS developed a proposal offering a computer-controlled system that monitored energy use and operated on/off valves for all energy-using systems. The proposal specified a five-year contract with a fixed price of $254,500 per year and a guarantee that the school district would save at least that amount of money each year or EMS would refund the difference. Included in the proposal was a carefully devised plan to take into account energy prices, hours the buildings were in use, and degree days so as to provide a basis of calculating the actual savings occurring. After five years the

[7]This example is adapted from Peter J. LaPlaca, "Pricing That Is Contingent on Value Delivered," presented at the First Annual Pricing Conference, The Pricing Institute, New York, December 3–4, 1987.

school district would own the system with the option of purchasing a management operating service for an annual fee of $50,000.

Although two other firms submitted multiyear bids of $190,000 and $215,000, annually, for three- and five-year contracts respectively, neither bid provided any guarantee for energy savings. Despite some questions about accepting the highest bid, the school board accepted the EMS proposal, because at worst the cost of the service was zero. During the first year, actual calculated savings exceeded $300,000. Interestingly, had the firm submitted a bid based on cost plus profit margin, the bid would have been about $130,000 per year. The use of contingency pricing by EMS removed the risk from the school board's decision and produced an additional $600,000 in profit contribution to EMS.

Summary

Value-oriented pricing can help prevent the error of setting a price that is too high relative to perceived or delivered value as well as that of setting a price too low relative to the value provided to and desired by customers. The Sudbury Company (see Box 8.4) probably would have set a price considerably higher than even the heavy-user segment would be willing to pay. Pricing from the viewpoint of satisfying internal profit needs only would have ruined the company's attempts to regain a competitive edge and to set prices above average market prices for its products. The EMS company developed a procedure for signaling the uncertain economic value to be delivered with a guarantee and successfully charged a premium price well above the cost-plus profit margin price. (See Chapter 3 for a discussion of signaling.)

As this chapter demonstrates, buyers seek to maximize the value received from purchasing products and services. Typically, they are not interested in what it costs the seller to provide the products or services but rather in the price–value relationship. Buyers are seeking benefits in the form of having certain functions performed, problems solved, or pleasures received. Value is created when the benefits the products or services deliver match the benefits customers, users, or clients want at a price consistent with this value. It is customers' perceptions that are important when developing a value-oriented pricing strategy. The market will enable product or service perceived to be of higher value than competitive offerings to obtain a premium price.

Discussion Questions

1. In Chapter 1 several examples indicated that even sellers of "commodity" products or services can set above-market average prices. What are some reasons that these sellers are able to set prices above market? List some products or services for which sellers set prices above market and some reasons why each of these products or services is higher priced.

2. Review the suggested relationship between price, perceived quality, and perceived value developed in Chapters 5 through 7. List some ways a firm can strategically increase its customers' perceptions of the value of its offerings. Do any of these ways have the potential of creating misperceptions and therefore deceiving customers? If so, how would you avoid such a situation?

3. In recent years, many retailers have chosen to become aggressive price promoters, routinely featuring sales offering 40, 50, and 60 percent off. Other retailers have been able to succeed without such extensive promotions. Why?

4. A company has developed an innovative product that has an incremental value of $200 over competitive products. The competitive products have, in general, a purchase price of $500, start-up costs of $100, and postpurchase costs of $300. The new product would have start-up costs of $50 and postpurchase costs of $250. What is the economic value of the new product to customers? If the company wanted to set the purchase price $25 below the competition, what would be the value of the customer inducements?

5. Recently a public social service agency that provides family counseling services decided to shift away from fee schedules based on clients' ability to pay. Instead, the agency asked clients who had completed the counseling program to pay what they thought the program was worth to them. (Payment schedules were arranged to fit the clients' income levels.) What do you think happened when they tried this approach? Why?

Suggested Readings

Anderson, James C., Dipak C. Jain, and Pradeep K. Chintagunta: "Customer Value Assessment in Business Markets: A State-of-Practice Study," *Journal of Business-to-Business Marketing 1,* no. 1 (1993), 3–29.

Chapman, Randall G.: "Equivalent-Value Pricing," *Pricing Strategy & Practice 2,* no. 2 (1994), 4–16.

Compeau, Larry D., and Dhruv Grewal: "Adding Value by Communicating Price Deals Effectively: Does It Matter

How You Phrase It?" *Pricing Strategy and Practice 2,* no. 2 (1994), 28–36.

Gale, Bradley T.: *Managing Customer Value* (New York: The Free Press, 1994).

Goodwin, Ross, and Brad Ball: "Closing the Loop on Loyalty," *Marketing Management 8,* no. 1 (1999), 25–34.

Hart, Christopher W.: "Uncovering Customer Value: Sacrificial Offerings," *Marketing Management 8,* no. 3 (1999), 6–7.

Higgins, Kevin T.: "The Value of Customer Value Analysis," *Marketing Research 10,* no. 4 (1999), 39–44.

Leszinski, Ralf, and Michael V. Marn: "Setting Value, Not Price," *The McKinsey Quarterly,* no. 1 (1997), 98–115.

Matanovich, Timothy, Gary Lilien, and Arvind Rangaswamy: "Engineering the Price-Value Relationship," *Marketing Management 8,* no. 1 (1999), 48–53.

CHAPTER NINE

Research Methods for Pricing Decisions

The past seven chapters have stressed the importance of demand in determining the price of a product or service. An implicit assumption has been that there are ways to determine the responsiveness of demand to alternative prices. If the concern is how volume sold of a product will change relative to a price change for that product, then the measure is price elasticity of demand. But if the concern is how volume sold for product A will change relative to a change in the price of another product B, then the concern is the cross-price elasticity of demand. Numerical estimates of the degree that demand for a product is sensitive to price differences can improve the ability of managers to set prices correctly, but serious pricing research must go beyond estimating price elasticity of demand. Indeed, learning how customers perceive prices and form value judgments is of greater importance than obtaining a global estimate of price elasticity.

Pricing Strategy and Pricing Research

Traditionally, business firms have not regularly used pricing research when developing pricing strategies. They rarely develop or maintain information systems that are up to date on market and competitive responses to price changes, price promotions, or product introductions and deletions. (See Box 9.1.) Yet pricing has a major impact on the profitability of an enterprise, and without information on the results of

| THE STRATEGY/PRICING RESEARCH MYTH | BOX 9.1 |

In the 1990s several studies were conducted investigating the extent that firms in North America do pricing research prior to setting or changing prices. One study found that only about 8 percent of the firms surveyed could be classified as conducting serious pricing research to support the development of a pricing strategy. On the other hand, 88 percent of the firms did little or no serious pricing research. McKinsey & Company's *Pricing Benchmark Survey* estimated that about 15 percent of the firms do serious pricing re-

search. In 1997, Coopers & Lybrand found that in the previous year 87 percent of the firms had changed prices, but only 13 percent of the price changes came as a result of scheduled reviews of pricing strategy. *It is a myth that most firms have a serious pricing strategy based on serious pricing research.*

Sources: Kevin J. Clancy and Robert S. Shulman, *The Marketing Revolution* (New York: Harper Business, 1991); Kevin J. Clancy and Robert S. Shulman, *Marketing Myths That Are Killing Business* (New York: McGraw-Hill, 1995).

past pricing decisions or on likely responses to contemplated pricing decisions, a firm cannot make informed pricing decisions. As discussed in Chapters 2 through 8, a well-developed pricing strategy begins with an understanding of how customers and competitors react to prices, their degree of sensitivity to specific prices or price levels and to price changes or price differences, as well as how they assess the value they receive.

Some Fundamental Questions

To estimate customers' and competitors' reactions to pricing decisions, some basic questions must be answered:

- Does the product or service perform a particular function, solve a problem, or provide pleasure for customers? Can these particular functions, problems, or pleasures be identified?

- To what degree do customers tend to associate product or service quality with price?

- How easy or difficult is it for buyers to determine the relative quality of the product or service before purchase? Do buyers tend to search for alternatives before purchase?

- What are the benefits that the product or service provides to different types of buyers?

- What is the size of the market for this product or service?

- What is the maximum amount that customers are willing to pay?

- What is the minimum amount that customers are willing to pay?

- What is the most acceptable set of prices for these customers?

- How much would these customers buy at these different prices?

- To what degree is the demand for the product or service sensitive to price differences?

- Are there different groups of customers with different levels of price sensitivity?

- How do customers purchase the product?

- Are customers aware of prices for this product category?

- Do customers perceive that substitute products or services are available?

- How are competitors likely to react to a particular price change, relative price difference, or pricing tactic?

- To what extent have competitors' pricing strategies and tactics affected the firm's sales volume in the past?

- To what extent have competitors' sales been responsive to their price changes? To the firm's price changes?

- Have competitors' past pricing moves been a surprise?

- Whom do customers perceive to be the firm's major competitors?

Several of these questions can be answered by maintaining an information system that tracks customer and competitor responses to economic conditions and to pricing changes. However, many of the questions need to be addressed by specific primary pricing research.

Three Basic Pricing Research Issues

Three important issues about the conduct of the research must be settled regardless of the technique.

First, will price sensitivity be tested for a single product or brand by itself or in the context of competing products? If there is no readily available reference product for customers, then initially testing the relative willingness to buy for the product in isolation is not too dissimilar from actual market conditions. However, when customers have viable alternatives, testing the effect of the price alternative in isolation implicitly assumes there will be no competitor reaction and buyers will be relatively unlikely to shift to a competitive offering.

Second, will customers' responses to the price be tested directly or indirectly? Often, a direct approach, (e.g., asking customers if they would be willing to pay a specific price for a product) increases buyers' concern for the price and, as a result, they may respond in a way they think is "rational" rather than according to their perceptions or beliefs. However, an indirect approach (such as asking respondents pricing questions within the context of questions about brand name or advertising) requires the researcher to assume that the underlying beliefs and perceptions have been measured, without strong evidence that this is so.

Finally, will each person be asked to respond to one price or to several prices? Obtaining people's responses to a single pricing situation makes it less likely that they will guess the underlying research question and try to provide "rational" responses. However, a single-price scenario makes it more difficult to determine each buyer's relative price sensitivity, and only aggregate measures can be obtained. Box 9.2 illustrates the issues involved when testing one price versus several prices with respondents.

General Pricing Research Approaches

Surveys

A frequently used method of estimating price sensitivity is the survey of brand preferences and purchase intentions. Surveying requires administering a questionnaire through personal interviews, telephone interviews, or the mail. Its basic objective is to elicit facts and opinions from respondents relating either to a prediction of the quantity they would be willing to buy at various prices or to their intent to buy in the near future.

Survey research to determine buyers' sensitivities to prices appears to be relatively easy to conduct and is one of the least costly research methods; nevertheless, it is possible to elicit unreliable responses unless the questions are developed carefully. One problem is that people tend to anticipate

EFFECTS OF PRICE PRESENTATION

BOX 9.2

One problem in conducting price research is how to get information from respondents about their willingness to purchase a product at different prices. Ideally, we would like to know how the individual would respond to different prices. However, once they realize that we are trying to estimate their demand curve individuals may provide answers that reflect their understanding of the traditional demand curve—that they buy more at lower prices and less or none at higher prices. The problem is that price is presented as a cost or sacrifice to potential buyers, not as an attribute. To present price as an attribute means that other product or service information must be presented to the respondents.

One research study looked at a range of prices, but the researchers varied whether only one price was presented to respondents or whether multiple prices were presented. In the multiple price situation, prices were presented sequentially, either high to low or low to high. As the graph indicates, substantial differences occurred in the estimates. Presenting multiple prices produced downward sloping demand curves, but a single price presentation revealed increasing estimated usage between $3 and $9, declining thereafter.

the answers the interviewer desires or to offer a socially desirable answer. Thus, when facing a direct question as to which of a set of prices would be preferred or acceptable, buyers often indicate the lowest price option because this would be a "rational" answer. Usually such questions overestimate the degree to which buyers are sensitive to price and lead to pricing decisions that do not reflect what buyers really are willing to pay.

A second problem is that surveys typically elicit responses from people when they are not very interested in making a purchase of that type of product. Thus they may not give much thought to their answer, and the answer may be considerably different than if they were seriously considering purchasing the product. In addition, unless nonbuyers are identified during the survey, the price elasticity estimates may be understated.[1] There is a likelihood that nonbuyers or buyers who are not interested in the product will be less price sensitive. Thus, questions related to previous purchase experience and interest in the product routinely should be included in the survey questionnaire or interview.

A third problem arises if respondents are required to respond to questions seeking their choices from alternatives at different prices. Unless these respondents can easily imagine the alternative products in their minds, it is likely that they will overstate price elasticity estimates. Thus, a pictorial representation of the products should be included in survey price research.[2]

Experimentation

Much of the research reported in the last four chapters on buyers' perceptions of prices resulted from controlled manipulations of prices. Indeed, many of the commercial techniques currently in use stem from the adaptation of the experimental techniques used to measure buyers' price perceptions. The advantage of the experimental approach is the opportunity it provides to isolate and control various market factors that may affect market demand and then to observe buyers' reactions to changes in one or more of these factors. However, in laboratory experimentation, the disadvantage is that the laboratory is not a natural shopping environment. Whether the findings from a laboratory study could be replicated in a natural environment is an important issue.

An alternative to laboratory experiments is to measure demand responsiveness to price and price changes in the marketplace by manipulating store prices in specific market areas and observing the effect on sales. Although such field experimentation is done in a natural shopping environment, the lack of control over other factors that affect sales—advertising, competition, weather—makes it difficult to know whether the changes in responses are the result of the price manipulations. Also, the passive observation of buyer behav-

---

[1]Malcolm Wright and Phil Gendall, "Making Survey-based Price Experiments More Accurate," *Journal of the Market Research Society 41* (April 1999), 245–49.

[2]Raymond R. Burke, Bari A. Harlam, Barbara E. Kahn, and Leonard M. Lodish, "Comparing Dynamic Consumer Choice in Real and Computer-Simulated Environments," *Journal of Consumer Research 19* (June 1992), 71–82.

ior does not provide information about whether buyers actually perceived differences in prices, either from a previous shopping opportunity or differences in alternative choices. If aggregate sales volume changes, the exact reason for the change is not known.

Perhaps the most serious problems associated with field experimentation are the time and expense required to change prices and monitor sales for the particular items. The availability of optical scanning equipment greatly increases both the speed and accuracy of obtaining sales volume data, but it still remains difficult to obtain estimates for more than a few products at a time. Careful application of experimental research designs, sampling methods, and statistical tests to evaluate the results will help control and measure the effects of extraneous factors.

Statistical Methods and Models

Several approaches rely on regression or econometric analyses of historical price–sales volume data to estimate price elasticity. An econometric approach develops a mathematical equation or equations relating demand to several variables, such as price, income, store location, and consumer density. Another recent modeling approach, neural networks, has developed from information technology. Neural networks are mathematical modeling techniques that emulate human trial-and-error learning to identify relationships in large databases. These approaches use statistical techniques to estimate the parameters of the equation(s) so as to derive an equation relating the independent variables to the dependent variable.

Among the advantages of using historical statistical analyses is that the researcher can test different scenarios in a form of "what if" simulations. Moreover, the data are based on actual price–volume data and allow the researcher to determine the best historical prices. Also, by including other relevant independent variables, the effect of the interaction of these other variables with price can be estimated.

However, this approach has some limitations. First, it essentially looks back at recent history and does not necessarily allow projections into the future unless two assumptions are made: that the market is stable and that the past is a mirror of the future. Furthermore, it does not provide information on whether other prices would have led to higher sales levels or whether such prices would be better in the future. Also, it may not be very useful for relatively new products.

Panels

In a consumer panel, the households that comprise the panel record their purchases by brand and price in a daily diary or their purchases are scanned at a store's checkout counter. The data are then aggregated across the panel on a weekly or biweekly basis. The advantage of these data is that observations accumulate quickly to establish an adequate database to develop and test models. Also, it is possible to identify purchases made with the use of coupons or at a special lower price. A disadvantage is that the panel is not likely to be representative of the general population and thus the ability to generalize from the data collected is limited. Another disadvantage is the possibility of errors because the respondent either forgets to record a purchase or makes an incorrect entry. Today, most research companies use scanner panel data recorded automatically at the time of store checkout. Panel members must identify themselves at the point of checkout for this procedure to work.

Some Specific Price Research Techniques

The set of fundamental questions posed at the beginning of this chapter reflects the behavioral points discussed in Chapters 2 through 8. That is, to estimate the maximum amount buyers are willing to pay one must determine their highest acceptable price, referred to as the upper price threshold. Questions about whether buyers infer product quality on the basis of price relate to buyers' unwillingness to pay low prices because of suspicions about quality. Thus the lowest acceptable price must be estimated.

An important issue in pricing products or services is determining what attributes or features of the product provide benefits that buyers perceive to be important. It is also important to determine whether buyers are aware of prices they pay and how sensitive they are to differences in prices either because of a price change or competitors' differential pricing.

As pointed out in Chapters 5 through 8, price judgments are comparative in nature. Thus simply asking people to respond to a hypothetical price without carefully providing a frame of reference forces the respondent to use his or her own reference point. The example in Box 9.3 illustrates how this error can lead to incorrect inferences about a firm's prices. *Pricing research must provide respondents a frame of reference that is consistent with the research question and*

THE TOP HAT RESTAURANT CHECKS ITS PRICES

BOX 9.3

A restaurant in a university conference center was experiencing some difficulty in generating sufficient revenues to break even. Explanations offered for this situation included that prices were too high and that the restaurant had the image of catering to conference attendees rather than offering a full-service menu. To determine how people in the local area perceived the restaurant, a consulting firm was hired to conduct a market survey. On the pricing issue, respondents were asked to agree or disagree with this statement: "Prices at the Top Hat restaurant are about right." As would be expected, a proportion of the respondents agreed with the statement and almost as many disagreed with it. The consulting firm conducted interviews with a sample of the respondents to determine why they answered as they did. Some respondents disagreed with the statement because they compared the restaurant to a fast-food operation and judged that the prices were too high; others disagreed with the statement because they compared the restaurant to a fancy restaurant and judged prices to be low. Respondents who agreed with the statement tended to compare the restaurant to another moderately priced restaurant in the area. Failure to provide respondents with a consistent frame of reference for answering the question could have led to a serious pricing error because management interpreted the majority of disagreements to mean the restaurant should reduce its prices, when in fact a majority of respondents did not perceive the prices to be too high.

across respondents, unless the research is explicitly studying the effect of varying the frame of reference on responses.

Estimating Price-Level Sensitivity (Absolute Price Thresholds)

The objective of determining buyers' upper and lower price thresholds is to identify the range of acceptable prices for the product or service. As suggested in Chapters 5 through 7, most buyers do not consider buying a product at only one specific price but instead are willing to buy within a range of prices. We also saw in Chapter 6 (Box 6.2) the problems Disneyland Paris encountered until price research indicated that they had set entry prices above potential French customers' upper price threshold.

Direct Question Approach

One approach to determining upper and lower price thresholds simply asks respondents two questions:[3]

[3]Jean Stoetzel, "Psychological/Sociological Aspects of Price," in Bernard Taylor and Gordon Wills, eds., *Pricing Strategy* (Princeton, NJ: Brandon/System Press, 1970), 70–74.

1. What is the *minimum price* you would be willing to pay for [product and/or brand specified]? (That is, below what price would you seriously doubt its quality?)

2. What is the *maximum price* you would be willing to pay for [product and/or brand specified]? (That is, beyond what price would you feel it would not be worth paying more?)

This procedure is simple and easy to implement, but it may put the idea into respondents' minds that there should be either a price that is too low or a price that is too high.

The analysis is also relatively easy. Excluding "don't know" answers, the proportions for each price are collected, beginning with the lowest price for those who would not buy because it is too low and ending with those who would not buy because it is too high. The cumulative proportion of those who find a price to be unacceptable because it is too low is labeled $L(P)$; the cumulative proportion of those who find a price to be unacceptable because it is too high is labeled $H(P)$. Subtracting $H(P)$ from $[1 - L(P)]$ at each price gives the proportion that would be willing to buy at each price, $[B(P)]$. Table 9.1 shows a sample set of data. To determine the lower and upper price limits for the product, usu-

TABLE 9.1 Determining Price Limits Using the Direct Question Approach

| | | Low | | | High | |
Price, $	Frequency, %	Unacceptable Cumulative $L(P)$	Acceptable Cumulative $[1 - L(P)]$	Frequency, %	Unacceptable Cumulative $H(P)$	Buy Price $B(P) = [1 - L(P)] - H(P)$
0.00	0.00	1.00	0.00	0.00	0.00	0.00
2.00	0.05	1.00	0.00	0.00	0.00	0.00
4.00	0.20	0.95	0.05	0.00	0.00	0.05
6.00	0.25	0.75	0.25	0.00	0.00	0.25
8.00	0.30	0.50	0.50	0.00	0.00	0.50
10.00	0.15	0.20	0.80	0.00	0.00	0.80
12.00	0.05	0.05	0.95	0.05	0.05	0.90
14.00	0.00	0.00	1.00	0.05	0.10	0.90
16.00	0.00	0.00	1.00	0.15	0.25	0.75
18.00	0.00	0.00	1.00	0.25	0.50	0.50
20.00	0.00	0.00	1.00	0.30	0.80	0.20
22.00	0.00	0.00	1.00	0.15	0.95	0.05
24.00	0.00	0.00	1.00	0.05	1.00	0.00
26.00	0.00	0.00	1.00	0.00	1.00	0.00
28.00	0.00	0.00	1.00	0.00	1.00	0.00

ally the median percentage for each distribution (50 percent in the cumulative distribution) is used. In Table 9.1, the low price limit is $8.00 and the high price limit is $18.00. Ninety percent of the respondents accepted prices of $12.00 and $14.00 and 75 percent of the respondents accepted a price of $16.00. Thus, it would appear that a price around $14.00 would have the highest acceptance in the market.

This approach is convenient but does not indicate whether the price that maximizes the percentage between the minimum and maximum acceptable price curves is the price that buyers find most acceptable. Moreover, each respondent provides only two prices, the lowest and highest acceptable prices. An easy extension is to give the respondents a price scale covering all the feasible market prices that might be charged for the product and ask them to indicate all the prices they would find acceptable. To determine whether the prices that have not been checked as acceptable are truly unacceptable, the respondents can be given a second scale and asked to indicate all unacceptable prices. Each respondent then can be asked to indicate the price that would be most acceptable for the product. Figure 9.1 illustrates how these questions may be posed.

The analysis of the data is similar to the direct question approach. Cumulative percentages of each price that is judged to be too low, too high, and most acceptable are developed and graphed. The median price that is too low is

FIGURE 9.1   **Scales for Determining Acceptable Prices**

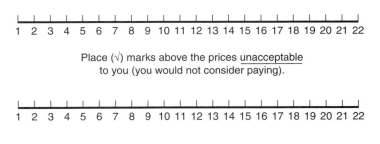

Product: Man's T-shirt (package of three, white)

Place X marks above the prices <u>acceptable</u> to you
(you would consider paying).

1 2 3 4 5 6 7 8 9 10 11 12 13 14 15 16 17 18 19 20 21 22

Place (√) marks above the prices <u>unacceptable</u>
to you (you would not consider paying).

1 2 3 4 5 6 7 8 9 10 11 12 13 14 15 16 17 18 19 20 21 22

Please indicate the price that would be <u>most acceptable</u>
to pay: $ _____

labeled the low-price limit, the median price that is too high is labeled the high-price limit, and the median most acceptable price is labeled the most acceptable price. The key advantage of this approach is that individuals' evaluations of each price are obtained with little additional effort.

Price Sensitivity Meter

The disadvantage of the direct question approach is that it forces a person to judge each price as acceptable or not. The price sensitivity meter (PSM) approach typically asks four questions:

1. At what price would you consider this [product and/or brand] to be so inexpensive that you would have doubts about its quality?

2. At what price would you still feel this product was inexpensive yet have no doubts as to its quality?

3. At what price would you begin to feel this product is expensive but still worth buying because of its quality?

4. At what price would you feel that the product is so expensive that regardless of its quality it is not worth buying?

These questions can be asked in an interview or as a part of a survey questionnaire. When used in a printed questionnaire, inclusion of a price scale such as the one in Figure 9.1 gives respondents an opportunity to recognize feasible prices for the product. Attempting to recall prices that might be feasible for a product without some retrieval cues makes the task difficult and introduces variation in individuals' responses.

The initial analysis is identical to that for the direct question approach. The cumulative frequency distributions for prices that are too low and too high are developed, and estimates of the lower and upper price limits are obtained using the median from each distribution (Table 9.2). As shown by the calculation of the buy response percentages, $B(P)$, the point of lowest buyer resistance is where $B(P)$ is the largest value, at about $10. This point of lowest resistance is also where the unacceptable-high and unacceptable-low curves intersect (Figure 9.2). Note that at this price the two acceptable cumulative curves also intersect, indicating, as would be expected, the price of highest receptivity. The point where the unacceptable-low and acceptable-low curves intersect is the point at which 50 percent of the respondents are

FIGURE 9.2   **Determining Price Limits: PSM Approach**

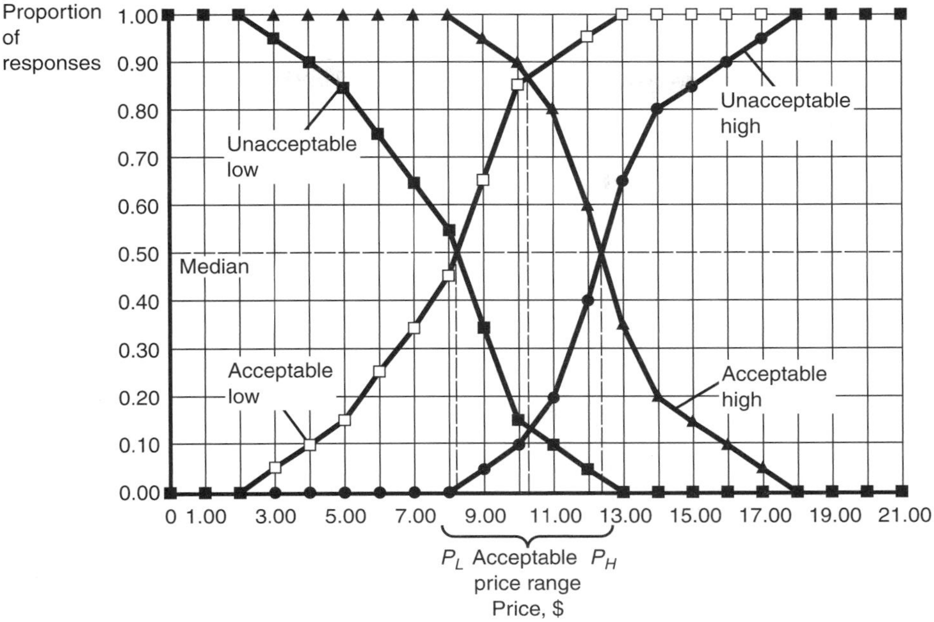

TABLE 9.2   **Determining Price Limits Using the PSM Approach**

		Low			High		
Price, $	Frequency, %	Unacceptable Cumulative $L(P)$	Acceptable Cumulative $[1 - L(P)]$	Frequency, %	Unacceptable Cumulative $H(P)$	Acceptable Cumulative $[1 - H(P)]$	Buy Price $B(P) = [1 - L(P)] - H(P)$
1.00	0.00	1.00	0.00	0.00	0.00	1.00	0.00
2.00	0.05	1.00	0.00	0.00	0.00	1.00	0.00
3.00	0.05	0.95	0.05	0.00	0.00	1.00	0.05
4.00	0.05	0.90	0.10	0.00	0.00	1.00	0.10
5.00	0.10	0.85	0.15	0.00	0.00	1.00	0.15
6.00	0.10	0.75	0.25	0.00	0.00	1.00	0.25
7.00	0.10	0.65	0.35	0.00	0.00	1.00	0.35
8.00	0.20	0.55	0.45	0.00	0.00	1.00	0.45
9.00	0.20	0.35	0.65	0.05	0.05	0.95	0.60
10.00	0.05	0.15	0.85	0.05	0.10	0.90	0.75
11.00	0.05	0.10	0.90	0.10	0.20	0.80	0.70
12.00	0.05	0.05	0.95	0.20	0.40	0.60	0.55
13.00	0.00	0.00	1.00	0.25	0.65	0.35	0.35
14.00	0.00	0.00	1.00	0.15	0.80	0.20	0.20
15.00	0.00	0.00	1.00	0.05	0.85	0.15	0.15
16.00	0.00	0.00	1.00	0.05	0.90	0.10	0.10
17.00	0.00	0.00	1.00	0.05	0.95	0.05	0.05
18.00	0.00	0.00	1.00	0.05	1.00	0.00	0.00
19.00	0.00	0.00	1.00	0.00	1.00	0.00	0.00
20.00	0.00	0.00	1.00	0.00	1.00	0.00	0.00
21.00	0.00	0.00	1.00	0.00	1.00	0.00	0.00

THE SOUTHWEST ALTERNATE
MEDIA PROJECT TESTS ITS
PRICES

BOX 9.4

The Southwest Alternate Media Project (SWAMP) tested pricing for its touring exhibition program with the Price Sensitivity Measurement (PSM) model. The exhibition, one of many film and video services that the Houston-based organization provides museums, community groups, and educational institutions, offered curatorial services to museums and community groups sponsoring film and video exhibitions. SWAMP surveyed potential clients to find the range of acceptable prices for its services. Using a price scale, prospects were asked to select four price points that represented their judgments of "expensive," "so expensive that it is beyond considering buying," "cheap," and "so cheap that you would question the quality." SWAMP was able to develop a value-based pricing schedule for its film series that would appeal to a wide variety of museums and community groups.

Source: J. B. Elmer, "Nonprofit Groups Can Profit from Commercial Techniques," *Marketing News 24,* no. 18 (1990), 16–17.

---

indifferent to the price because of quality concerns. Where the unacceptable-high and acceptable-high curves intersect is the price where 50 percent of the respondents are indifferent because of concerns of relative expensiveness. Between these low- and high-price limits is the acceptable price range. Box 9.4 briefly describes a successful use of this research technique. Perhaps because of its relative ease of use, many business firms choose this research technique.

Generally, most buyers are willing to go a little bit higher or a little bit lower before they completely refrain from a willingness to purchase. For this reason, it is useful to ask respondents to indicate those prices that are acceptable as well as those prices that are unacceptable. It would be useful to add a fifth question to this approach:

5. What price would be the *most acceptable* price to pay?

Price Categorization

Another approach to determining buyers' acceptable prices and price thresholds is to ask buyers to sort a set of prices for a product into smaller groups or categories according to how they perceive these prices to be similar or dissimilar to each other. This technique can be done by personal interviews, mail surveys, or experiments.

When respondents are interviewed in a setting that allows them to have some working space, the instructions given in

FIGURE 9.3   **Instructions For Price Categorization**

1. Developing Categories

In a general way, you have just been told what you are going to be doing in the next few minutes. Now let us explain the complete procedure. If, after reading the procedure, you have any questions, please raise your hand and the research assistant will come to you and answer them.

Imagine that you are in a store to buy a pair of semicasual shoes and that each slip of paper that you have in the envelope (handed to you) is a price tag on the shoes. Assume you can buy the color, size, and style, of your choice. Since price is the only basis for your decision, you carefully sort through the price tags.

Now take out the price tags in the envelope and sort them into any number of piles you choose. To help you start we are providing you with two category designations for your piles: (1) Too Cheap to Buy, and (2) Too Expensive to Buy. If you find any prices that you think are too cheap to buy, pile those tags on the left and mark this pile with the Category Identification Slip marked "Too Cheap to Buy." Similarly, if you find any prices that are way too high for you—that are simply prohibitive in price—pile them on your right and mark this pile "Too Expensive to Buy." *Remember that these two categories are provided as a starting point. You need not use these two categories if you do not find any prices (slips) that belong in these two categories.*

Decide on the piles on the basis of which prices (slips) seem to belong together. Do not be concerned about how many are in the piles or how many piles you create. If you change your mind, please feel free to rearrange things.

After you are finished placing prices in as many or as few piles as you like, raise your hand to indicate that you have completed this task. The research assistant will come to you and explain further procedures.

Are these instructions clear? If so, please proceed. If not, raise your hand and the research assistant will come and help you.

2. Labeling the Price Categories

Now you are provided with labels for naming the piles as categories. Use as many labels as you need. For naming the categories, follow these instructions:

1. On the one pile with the prices that are *most acceptable to you*, place the label "MOST ACCEPTABLE."
2. Place the "ACCEPTABLE" labels on any other pile or piles that are also acceptable. (Do not be concerned about how many piles you label "acceptable.")
3. Place the label "UNACCEPTABLE" on any pile or piles that are unacceptable to you.
4. On the piles labeled "UNACCEPTABLE" indicate, if you wish, any reason for their unacceptability.

Please return any unused labels to the research assistant. Please raise your hand to indicate that you have completed this part of the research study.

Thank you for your cooperation.

Figure 9.3 are used. If the research is being conducted by a mail survey, a response sheet similar to the one in Figure 9.4 is used. After the respondents sort the prices into categories, they should be asked to label any groups of prices that are unacceptable. If possible, they should indicate why the

FIGURE 9.4 **Price Categorization Response Sheet: Mail Survey**

PRODUCT:	Semicasual shoes
DIRECTIONS:	For this product, we have listed a series of prices below. First look at all the prices. Then place each price *anywhere* you feel is appropriate, in the column marked "price," to indicate your rating of that particular price for this product. You can indicate any number of prices at any spot.
ASSUME:	Your choices of style, color, and size are available.

PRICES:

$ 5	$ 6	$ 7	$ 8	$ 9	$10	$11	$12	$13
$14	$15	$16	$17	$18	$19	$20	$21	$22
$23	$24	$25	$26	$27	$28	$29	$30	$31
$32	$33	$34	$35	$36	$37	$38	$39	$40
$41	$42	$43	$44	$45	$46	$47	$48	$49

UNACCEPTABLE—TOO EXPENSIVE:
UNACCEPTABLE—EXPENSIVE:
ACCEPTABLE—HIGH:
MOST ACCEPTABLE:
ACCEPTABLE—LOW:
UNACCEPTABLE—INEXPENSIVE:
UNACCEPTABLE—TOO CHEAP:

prices in these groups are unacceptable. For the groups of prices that are acceptable, they should label the set of prices that is most acceptable to them. Generally, a wide range of prices, as many as 50, should be used. Experience has indicated that people will be able to group this many prices into five to seven categories.

The analysis proceeds as described for the direct question approach for each of the price categories identified: unacceptable-low, acceptable-low, most acceptable, acceptable-high, and unacceptable-high. If respondents are able to indicate the reasons for the unacceptable prices (e.g., too cheap or too expensive), then these labeled categories form additional categories. Respondents who label the unacceptable price categories provide information on why the prices are unacceptable. As before, using the median response, when 50 percent of the respondents indicate that a particular price might belong in a particular price category or the price category adjacent to it, then that price forms a category limit. Thus, the category limits are defined as the prices where the probability of a price being included in a designated category equals the probability of its being included in the immediately adjacent category.

The advantage of the categorization approach is that it does not implicitly assume there is only one definable set of acceptable prices in the market. In both the direct question and PSM approaches, an attempt is made to force the data onto one buy response curve or distribution. In the categorization approach, using a wide range of prices and explicit evaluations of prices enables the researcher to determine the acceptable price ranges for buyers who are more interested in relatively lower prices, buyers who will accept medium-level prices, and buyers who accept relatively higher prices. Also, asking buyers to indicate those prices that are most acceptable provides a means of determining whether there might be one price that clearly emerges as the best price for the product or service. Moreover, a judgment that a specific price is acceptable or unacceptable reflects an individual's subjective evaluation and is based on that person's set of purchase-influencing variables, an evaluative set of categories already established previously.[4]

Magnitude Scaling

With magnitude scaling, it is possible to elicit information about the intensity of respondents' judgments and how they make price–quality or price–value judgments. Underlying the approach is the fundamental belief that people can provide meaningful information about the magnitude of their sensory experiences.

This approach asks respondents to judge a product, service, or price relative to a reference product, service, or price. It can effectively be applied in face-to-face interviews, telephone interviews, or mail surveys. The most widely used form of magnitude scaling is *numeric estimation*, where respondents are instructed to assign numbers to the stimulus product or price relative to a standard number for the reference product or price. This approach is similar to the technique used to judge gymnasts or divers in competition, where the judging is on a 1 to 10 scale.

When measuring the price–value relationship for a product or service, the procedure would be as follows:

1. Respondents are asked to describe the current product or service that they are using. They should be encouraged to indicate the attributes and features of the product that

[4]See Kent B. Monroe, "Measuring Price Thresholds by Psychophysics and Latitudes of Acceptance," *Journal of Marketing Research 8* (November 1971), 460–64.

are important to them and the benefits that they receive from these attributes or features. Then they are asked to assign the current or reference product an index value of 100.

2. The product or service to be evaluated is described in terms of its attributes, features, and benefits delivered. Respondents are asked to judge the relative quality of the "new" product by assigning it a number above or below 100. That is, they are asked to compare the "new" product to the "old" or "current" product. They are instructed to give the "new" product a number greater than 100 if they believe it is of better quality than the "current" product or a number less than 100 if it is perceived to be inferior. For this step, the instructions on how to assign the number are very important. For example, "If you think that the 'new' product is about 10 percent better in quality, then assign it a 110; if you think it is two times better, give it a number of 200. But if you think the product has about 10 percent less quality, give it a number of 90; if you think it is half as good, give it a number of 50. Choose a number that reflects how you rate the new product relative to the 100 you assigned to the product you currently use."

3. Next, respondents are asked to give the price they currently are paying a number of 100. It is possible that a significant number of respondents may not be able to remember the price they paid for the reference product. However, this is not a serious problem, since the issue is how much more or less the person is willing to pay for the new product relative to the old one.

4. Then, the same instructions given in step 2 are used to ask the respondents to indicate the price that would be acceptable for the new product—how much more or less they would be willing to pay for it. Respondents do not have to remember the correct price for the current product; they only have to evaluate the new product relative to an index of 100 for the old product.

5. If several product–price combinations are being evaluated, the procedure is repeated by asking the respondent to evaluate the next "new" product against the original reference product.

By using several product–price combinations, a scale can be developed indicating the proportional perceived differences between price and different product attributes. The data can be analyzed using regression analysis. Taking logarithms of the numerical responses before doing the regression analysis provides for an estimated linear relationship between price and the different attributes used in the study.[5]

Determining Willingness to Buy

The Parker Pen Company applied magnitude scaling techniques along with attribute value analysis to determine the introductory price for a new pen, the Vector.[6] As the company entered the 1980s it believed it was necessary to enter the $1 to $3 pen market. One of the prototype pens was the Vector, a two-piece writing instrument with an initial target price of $2.98. To test market this new pen, the company followed a five-step process beginning with target market identification (10 to 45 year old people, particularly European students and white collar professionals).

In the second step, they identified the desirable pen attributes including writing smoothness, smear resistance, style, and dependability. Using external data from *Consumer Reports* they analyzed the different attributes, including price, of 50 competitive, inexpensive writing models. To explain retail price differences, a consumer panel indicated that the real differentiating characteristics in a pen were the "feel" of the pen and writing "control." Consequently, the research team described the attribute "feel" as a composite of weight, barrel size and shape, balance, and tactile impression. Similarly, "control" was measured by smoothness of pen movement across paper and the degree of fatigue experienced when writing. In the third

[5]For additional information and marketing applications, see Noel Mark Lavenka, "Measurement of Consumers' Perceptions of Product Quality, Brand Name, and Packaging: Candy Bar Comparisons by Magnitude Estimation," *Marketing Research 3* (June 1991), 38–46; Milton Lodge, *Magnitude Scaling: Quantitative Measurement of Opinions* (Beverly Hills, CA: Sage Publications, 1981); Bruno Neibecker, "The Validity of Computer-Controlled Magnitude Scaling to Measure Emotional Impact of Stimuli," *Journal of Marketing Research 21* (August 1984), 325–31; and Paul A. Scipone, "Perceived Value Gauged by Indexing Purchaser Response," *Marketing News 20* (April 11, 1986), 15.

[6]This section is based on Chuck Tomkovick and Kathryn E. Dobie, "Applying Hedonic Pricing Models and Factorial Surveys at Parker Pen to Enhance New Product Success," *Journal of Product and Innovation Management 12* (September 1995), 334–45.

step they estimated the "price" of each attribute in the following regression equation:

$$P = a + b_1W + b_2\text{Size} + b_3S + b_4B + b_5T + b_6R + b_7C$$

(9.1)

where

P = suggested retail price

W = weight

Size = circumference of the barrel

S = geometric shape of the barrel

B = whether the pen is balanced in the hand

T = tactile feel of the material

R = resistance—the amount of effort needed to write

C = consistency of the ink flow

The value of the coefficients, b_i, estimated from the model was then used to estimate the value that consumers attach to each attribute. Table 9.3 shows the equivalent estimated price or value for each attribute measure.

In step 4, a sample of consumers was given a pen to use as a standard of reference for the magnitude scaling exercise. This pen had the average weight and ink flow characteristics of a pen in the low-price pen category. Respondents were told that a panel of experts had assessed it to be worth $1.07. Compared to this reference pen, respondents were asked to evaluate a series of identical pens except with a variation. For example, to measure their response on the resistance measure of the attribute of control, they were asked: "If the baseline pen you were first given was worth $1.07 to you, how much more (less) would you be willing to spend on a similar pen that wrote 10 percent more smoothly? 20 percent? 30 percent? (10 percent less smoothly? 20 percent? 30 percent?). This pattern of questioning was continued until all key attribute measures had been considered.

From the responses obtained in step 4, the fifth step used regression analysis to calculate the respondents' willingness to pay more or less for any particular attribute. The test market customers indicated that there was demand for and a willingness to pay more for a pen that was somewhat heavier and wrote much more smoothly than the baseline pen. However, Parker managers concluded that the target con-

TABLE 9.3 Estimated Value Prices for Pen Attributes

Attribute	Measure	Regression Coefficient	Value Price
Feel	Weight	0.134	$0.15
	Size	0.102	$0.19
	Shape	0.164	$0.12
	Balance	0.103	$0.19
	Tactile	0.111	$0.18
Control	Resistance	0.201	$0.10
	Consistency	0.143	$0.14
Estimated Value Price			$1.07

sumers would be willing to pay substantially less than the original target price. So the Vector rollerball and fountain pens were launched at a lower price and became two of the best new product successes in the firm's history.

Estimating Sensitivity to Price Differences

The research techniques described thus far are used to determine the relative willingness of buyers to pay particular prices for a product or service. The primary objective of such research is to determine buyers' upper and lower acceptable price limits and the likelihood of several price-market segments for the product. If the respondents in the sample represent the targeted set of buyers, estimates of the relative size of these different price-market segments also can be obtained.

For established products, or when introducing a new model into an established product line, a second issue of price sensitivity concerns the degree that demand may be sensitive to price differences (differential price thresholds). As discussed in Chapter 6, sensitivity to price differences is important when deciding whether to change price for a product (demand price elasticity) or when attempting to establish a price differential for a product relative to comparable alternatives (cross-price elasticity). Strategically, it is an important issue when positioning products within a line or relative to competition.

Sequential Preferences: Two Brands

When the objective is to determine sensitivity to price differences for comparable brands, one approach is to ask respondents to indicate their brand preference as the price of a brand is changed. When comparing two brands, A and B (actual brand names would be used), it is important first to

FIGURE 9.5   **Response Sheet for Sequential Preferences: Two Brands**

DIRECTIONS: Below are some pairs of brands of spray cologne mist. For each pair please indicate your brand preference by circling the number that corresponds most closely with the description of your brand preference. Assume that you are interested in purchasing this product for yourself or a friend and that the pair represents the only choice available.

	Brand A				Brand B			
Price	Prefer A to B Strongly	Prefer A to B Moderately	Prefer A to B Slightly	No Preference	Prefer B to A Slightly	Prefer B to A Moderately	Prefer B to A Strongly	Price
$14.00	1	2	3	4	5	6	7	$14.00
14.00	1	2	3	4	5	6	7	14.25
14.00	1	2	3	4	5	6	7	14.50
14.00	1	2	3	4	5	6	7	14.75
14.00	1	2	3	4	5	6	7	15.00
14.00	1	2	3	4	5	6	7	15.25
14.00	1	2	3	4	5	6	7	15.50
14.00	1	2	3	4	5	6	7	15.75
14.00	1	2	3	4	5	6	7	16.00
14.00	1	2	3	4	5	6	7	16.25
14.00	1	2	3	4	5	6	7	16.50
14.00	1	2	3	4	5	6	7	13.75
14.00	1	2	3	4	5	6	7	13.50
14.00	1	2	3	4	5	6	7	13.25
14.00	1	2	3	4	5	6	7	13.00
14.00	1	2	3	4	5	6	7	12.75
14.00	1	2	3	4	5	6	7	12.50
14.00	1	2	3	4	5	6	7	12.25
14.00	1	2	3	4	5	6	7	12.00
14.00	1	2	3	4	5	6	7	11.75

establish each respondent's preference when prices are equal. Then, while holding the price constant for one of the brands, the price of the other brand is systematically changed by constant amounts, both increasing and decreasing from the original equal price point.

Respondents' reactions to these price differences can be obtained by asking them to indicate which brand they would prefer, A or B. This simple response method permits estimating the price difference necessary to induce a switch from the preferred brand, but it does not indicate the relative intensity of respondents' preferences. The rating sheet illustrated in Figure 9.5 permits recording not only of their preferences, but also whether these preferences are relatively strong or weak. These additional data may provide sufficient information to determine the relative size of a loyal segment versus a brand-switching segment. Moreover, allowing re-

FIGURE 9.6   **Sensitivity to Price Differences: Sequential Preferences Approach**

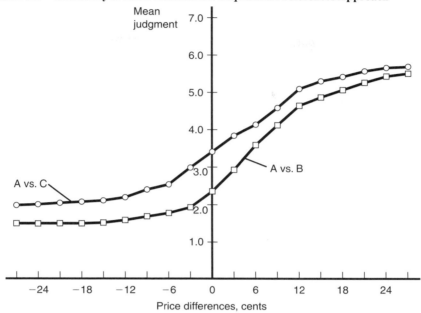

spondents to indicate an indifferent or no-preference response provides important information about the size of a
price difference necessary before a switch might occur. In effect, a no-preference response when there are price differences indicates the differential price premium that one of the
brands might successfully use in the market. To avoid potential order of presentation effects, the order of the brands, the
order of the price manipulations, and the reference brand
should be randomly varied over respondents. Standard statistical significance tests can be used to determine whether
there are significant differences in preferences across the
price difference conditions and at what specific price differences these results are significant.

The mean preferences for the various price differences
can also be graphed as Figure 9.6 shows. Negative price differences indicate a price advantage for the test brand, and
hence low mean judgments indicate preferences for the test
brand. The opposite situation exists for positive price differences (where a scale value of 4.0 represents a neutral or indifferent preference). In Figure 9.6, brand A exhibits a clear
preference strength over brand B at all price differences.
Note that until brand A has a 9¢ price premium over brand B,

it enjoys a stronger brand preference. However, while brand A has some preference strength relative to brand C, it is not as strong because at a price premium of 3¢ to 6¢ respondents are essentially indifferent in their preferences between brands A and C.

Trade-off Analysis

As Chapters 5 through 8 showed, buyers generally make trade-offs when evaluating alternative product offers. Indeed, the notion of acquisition value explicitly suggests that buyers compare the actual price of the item with the highest price that they would be willing to pay, P_{max}. The notion of transaction value suggests that buyers compare a reference price to the actual price. When we recognize that most product or service choices, for consumers or for organizational buyers, require not only comparing prices, as indicated earlier, but also comparing different attributes at varying levels, it is clear that some form of trade-off must occur. The need to make trade-offs while simultaneously evaluating multiple alternatives with multiple attributes occurs because no one alternative is likely to be perceived as superior on all evaluative dimensions. For example, buyers may have to trade off a higher price against higher perceived quality or a higher price against faster delivery.

In a general sense, trade-off analysis uses either what may be called a *limited-profile approach* or a *full-profile approach*. In a limited-profile approach, attributes comprising a subset that buyers perceive to be important are varied in alternative scenarios, usually in a limited number of levels. In a full-profile approach, called *conjoint analysis*, all of the important attributes are varied over as many levels as is reasonable for the respondents.

Conjoint analysis provides two important outcomes relative to pricing research. First, by providing a quantitative estimate of the contribution of each attribute to the purchase decision, it is possible to determine the relative importance of price compared to the other attributes. Second, by providing a measure of the sensitivity to each attribute, it is possible to estimate price elasticity. However, this elasticity estimate is limited because it is for the product category as a whole. As we have seen in Chapter 6, price elasticity varies by brand as well as over various types of situations.

To overcome this difficulty of obtaining a category estimate of price elasticity, researchers have shifted from using product profiles to market profiles. Now the respondents' task is to indicate which product they would buy—that is, emphasis shifts from measuring preferences to measuring choices. This approach allows measuring brand-specific price elasticities as well as brand cross-price elasticities. Own- and cross-price effects can be developed for each brand included in the study. Today *discrete choice modeling* involves developing choice sets that show product choices available in the market, along with their descriptions. Thus, this research technique represents a combination of conjoint scaling and brand–price trade-offs, but with the emphasis on choice rather than preferences. We begin with an example of limited-profile trade-off analysis.

DuPont managers were interested in determining the relative values of six important attributes of a specialty industrial product. They conducted a survey of decision makers in the market[7] that defined two levels of performance for each of six attributes and asked respondents to consider an offering with all the attributes at the high level. They were then told to assume that the selling company faced increasing costs and was considering sacrificing performance on one attribute by reducing it to the lower level rather than raising price (see Table 9.4). Each respondent was then given a pair of attributes (e.g., quality and retraining) and asked to indicate which attribute should be kept at the high level and the strength of this preference. Next, the respondent gave dollar values to the price difference that would be acceptable to retain the higher level of performance on each attribute. (A number of other paired comparisons were provided for a similar ranking and dollar assignment.) Finally, the respondents were asked to rate DuPont and its major competitor on their perceptions of how these two firms performed relative to the six attributes.

Based on the data and statistical analysis, a scale of relative dollar values for each attribute was constructed for each respondent. To determine the premium that a buyer would pay for the DuPont offering relative to its competitor, the relative dollar values for each attribute were weighted by the perceived performance differences between DuPont and the competitor.

Table 9.5 lists the calculated average contribution of each attribute to DuPont's price premium relative to its nearest

---

[7]This example is adapted from Irwin Gross, "Insights from Pricing Research," in Earl L. Bailey, ed., *Pricing Practices and Strategies* (New York: The Conference Board, 1978), 34–39.

TABLE 9.4 **Limited Profile Trade-Offs**

Attribute	High Level	Low Level
Quality	Impurities less than 1 part per million	Impurities less than 10 parts per million
Delivery	Within one week	Within two weeks
System	Supply total system	Supply chemical only
Innovation	High level of R&D support	Little R&D support
Retraining	Retrain on request	Train on initial purchase
Service	Available locally	Available from home office

Source: Adapted with permission from Irwin Gross, "Insights from Pricing Research," in Earl L. Bailey (ed.), *Pricing Practices and Strategies* (New York: The Conference Board, 1978), p. 37.

competitor. Although quality was the most important attribute to the buyers, because there were few perceived performance differences between DuPont and its competitor, it did not contribute as much to the price premium as did innovation. Thus not only did DuPont determine its relative price premium over a competitor, but it also was able to determine the relative contribution each attribute made to this premium.

Conjoint Analysis

To evaluate the volume effect of a change in price requires estimating buyers' sensitivity to the price change, likely competitive reaction to the price change, and the impact of competitors' pricing actions on sales volume. An individual's decision to purchase is a function of many individual

TABLE 9.5 **Relative Attribute Contribution to Price Premium**

Attribute	Premium
Quality	$1.70
Innovation	2.00
System	0.80
Service	0.25
Delivery	0.15
Retraining	0.40
Total	$5.30

Source: Adapted with permission from Irwin Gross, "Insights from Pricing Research," in Earl L. Bailey (ed.), *Pricing Practices and Strategies* (New York: The Conference Board, 1978), p. 39.

personal variables and many subtle buying influences that are a part of the perceived benefits of the product or service, the purchase situation, the use occasion, and associated perceptions and values. Conjoint analysis has been designed to explore these buying complexities to determine the relative perceived value in different product attributes including price.

To understand how conjoint analysis works, three terms commonly used when discussing conjoint analysis are important: factors, levels, and utility. *Factors* are the product or service attributes that provide the relative benefits buyers derive from acquiring and using the product. Table 9.6 lists such factors for a hotel. *Level* refers to the number of different options available for a particular factor. Although Table 9.6 considers two levels of hotel size, five levels of price, characterized as price ranges, will be studied. *Utility* refers to the quantified degree of preference a person has for a particular factor.

TABLE 9.6   Hotel Factor Description and Levels

Factor	Level	Factor	Level
Associated services		**Lounge/entertainment**	
Message service	2	Type of lounge	3
Limo to airport	2	Atmosphere	2
Laundry/valet	3		
Atmosphere/facilities		**Security/safety**	
Hotel size	2	Sprinkler system	3
Corridor/view	2	Smoke detector	2
Pool location	2	Security guard	3
Room		**Price range**	
Quality of decor	4	Very low price	5
Size	3	Low price	5
Bathroom amenities	3	Medium price	5
In-room TV/entertainment	3	High price	5
Recreation			
Game room	2		
Tennis courts	2		
Whirlpool/jacuzzi	2		
Sauna	2		

The underlying assumption of this approach is that buyers perceive a product option as a combination or bundle of features. Each feature has a separate utility that can be exchanged with any other feature that has the same utility value. Purchase decisions are made on the basis of these utilities. However, buyers are unaware of the utilities that they attach to different features. All that buyers can do is indicate their preferences for different combinations of features. Conjoint analysis is a technique for breaking down buyers' overall preferences into utilities for each feature.

To see how conjoint analysis works, assume a buyer is presented with a choice of two types of hotel and that the buyer has the utilities for the different features listed in Table 9.7. Hotel A is a small hotel with small rooms, an outdoor pool, and color TV with HBO; it is priced at $55 per night. Hotel B is a large hotel with standard-size rooms, indoor pool, whirlpool, sauna, and color TV with HBO; it is priced at $95 per night. For this buyer, Hotel A has a total utility of 4.7 (1.0 + 0.2 + 0.4 + 1.2 + 1.9); Hotel B has a total utility of 5.9 (0.8 + 0.6 + 1.0 + 0.8 + 1.2 + 1.5). Given this choice, the buyer would select Hotel B. For Hotel A to be successful with this buyer, it would have to increase the total utility by at least 1.2. One way to do that would be to enclose the pool and add a whirlpool and sauna, leading to an increase in utility of 1.4.

How are these utilities obtained? To determine the buyers' utilities, a researcher in consultation with the hotel manager decides on the particular combinations that are of interest to the buyers and develops presentation packages. Different "hotel packages," are offered to the buyers, who are asked to indicate their relative preference for each package. Possible hotel packages could include the following:

Small hotel, small room, outdoor pool, color TV with HBO, $55.

Small hotel, small room, indoor pool, color TV with HBO, $75.

Small hotel, medium room, outdoor pool, color TV with HBO, $75.

Large hotel, small room, outdoor pool, color TV with HBO, $75.

Large hotel, medium room, indoor pool, whirlpool, color TV with HBO, $95.

TABLE 9.7
Features and Utilities for a Hotel

Feature	Utility
Facilities (two levels)	
Small, two-story hotel, 100 rooms	1.0
Large, multistory hotel, 500+ rooms	0.8
Room (three levels)	
Standard-size room	0.6
Large room	0.8
Small room	0.2
Recreation/entertainment (four levels)	
Indoor pool	1.0
Outdoor pool	0.4
Color TV, HBO	1.2
Whirlpool, sauna	0.8
Price (single room) (three levels)	
$55	1.9
75	1.7
95	1.5

Some issues must be understood when considering using conjoint analysis. First, the underlying model of buyer behavior may not be appropriate. Instead of adding up each feature utility individually, buyers may prefer a particular bundle of features more than the simple sum of their parts. For example, some people may perceive that certain amenities of a hotel should come as a package rather than individual add-ons. Second, the same feature may have different utilities in different products. A security guard may have a higher utility for a city hotel than for a hotel in a suburban or rural location. Conjoint analysis assumes that a feature has the same utility across similar products.

A third problem occurs when different people interpret a particular attribute differently. For example, one person might interpret "large-size room" as a 20- by 20-foot room and another as a 14- by 14-foot room. It is likely, therefore, that utilities for the same descriptive feature may vary due to the respondents' interpretations as well as to reactions to a "large-size room." A fourth problem occurs when no attempt is made during analysis to determine whether distinct market segments exist for the product or service. A price–quality segment and a price-conscious segment could lead to average utilities for price that are incorrect.

HOUSTON GRAND OPERA'S EXPERIMENT WITH CONJOINT ANALYSIS

BOX 9.5

With the completion of the much anticipated Wortham Theatre in 1986, Houston Grand Opera's management expected season subscription sales to increase. However, the number of subscribed patrons remained the same as the previous year. An informal survey of current patrons led management to believe that ticket prices were excessive. As a result, management planned to reduce subscription prices with the goal of increasing sales. Management quickly reversed this decision upon learning from additional research that decreasing price would not increase the number of subscribers and would reduce revenues.

Conducting a conjoint analysis enabled management to divide current subscribers into two segments, price-sensitive and seat-sensitive. Each of these groups valued the opera experience differently and were willing to pay a price that equaled this perceived value. For example, seat-sensitive patrons displayed little sensitivity to a range of prices from $100 to $600 as long as they received their desired seats. Furthermore, the probability of subscription remained the same whether the price was reduced by 5 percent or 10 per-

cent, held static, or increased by 5 percent. This appearance of price inelasticity over the range of prices tested provided additional support to management's decision not to lower prices.

The Houston Grand Opera's experience with conjoint analysis reveals the benefits of understanding customer segments and the value each segment places on varying product or service options. If Houston Grand Opera's management had implemented its initial decision to reduce subscription prices, the opera would not have achieved its goal of increased sales and would have found itself with significantly lower revenues. Instead, management altered price to better match each segment's perceived value of the opera's seating. By selectively increasing the price of front seats and reducing the price for other areas within the theater, Houston Grand Opera surpassed sales goals for its subscription and single ticket sales by 11 percent!

Source: R.R. Batsell and John B. Elmer, "How to Use Market-Based Pricing to Forecast Consumer Purchase Decisions," *Journal of Pricing Management* (Spring 1990), 5–15.

Summary

As noted in Chapter 1, the prerequisites for taking a proactive approach to pricing include (1) knowing how prices work, and (2) understanding how customers perceive prices. As detailed in Chapters 2 through 8, the assumption that prices work exactly as prescribed in traditional economic theory, and that buyers simply use price as an indicator of their sacrifice or cost, leads to naive and often unprofitable pricing strategies and tactics. It should be clear that the role of price in buyers' decision making is complex and dynamic. Recognizing these complexities means that pricing decision makers must develop an information system that continuously provides information about markets, competitors, and current clients or customers as well as prospective buyers. The complexity of buyer behavior relative to price means that such an information system must be augmented with carefully designed and executed pricing research. Pricing research must be conducted with a working knowledge of how buyers behave relative to price.

To illustrate this last point, a major airline decided to determine the degree of price sensitivity of a one-way ticket between two cities. The price of a coach fare between the two cities had been $149 and was the price initially set by a discount-oriented competitor. The major airline set an experimental price for the one-way fare at $199 and quickly found out that a $50 price differential shifted traffic to the discount carrier. When asked how the airline had decided on a $50 price differential, management responded, "We pulled a nice round figure out of the air." Surprisingly, this major airline pulled an important aspect of pricing, determining the relative price premium to charge, out of the air! A more careful research effort would have developed a systematic approach by slowly raising the price of the fare, perhaps initially up to $155, to determine when travelers would believe that the trade-off between the perceived better airline service and the higher price made them indifferent between the two airlines. Several of the techniques described in this chapter could have been used to determine this price differential before executing the actual market experiment. As it was, the results of the $199 trial simply scared the airline away from doing additional and more carefully developed price-sensitivity research. We also saw in Chapter 6 that Disneyland Paris discovered after years of losses that they had priced admission to the park 25 percent higher than the maximum price the average French household was willing to pay.

In a more successful effort, a hospital introduced a program to establish overnight accommodations for their patients' families. After an analysis of costs and rates charged by nearby hotels, the hospital set a nightly rate of $55. However, after four months, the program had an average monthly use of only 2 to 8 guests instead of the projected 21 guests per night. Market research indicated that the hotels and motels within a mile of the hospital charged, on average, $38 per night, with a range of $27 to $54 per night, single occupancy. Respondents to a survey indicated that the maximum acceptable room rate was $35. After the price was reduced to $36, the occupancy rate increased from 114 nights to 243 nights in six months, with no additional marketing activity. What the hospital concluded was that "pricing a hospital product should be based on the market value instead of product cost."[8] Indeed, despite a price reduction of $19 per night, a net monthly revenue gain of $2,478 occurred.

These examples and the material presented in the last seven chapters indicate three important principles about price and the need to develop a careful research program to facilitate pricing decisions. First, it is clear that price is an important part of the marketing mix. To make pricing decisions primarily on the basis of internal financial considerations ignores this important principle. Second, customers buy on the basis of perceived value, not what it costs the seller to produce and have a product available for sale. Thus a buyer's perception of value is the important consideration in purchase decisions. Similarly, the third principle is that it is relative price, not absolute price, that is the key to understanding how pricing works in the marketplace. Buyers' determinations of perceived value depend on their perceptions of relative price differences, not absolute price level. A successful pricing research program must consider these principles of how price influences buyer behavior.

Discussion Questions

1. When doing research concerning how people respond to price, what specific differences about the price variable make it more difficult to ask people directly about their reactions?
2. Compare and contrast the different techniques for determining the maximum amount that buyers are willing to pay.
3. What are some specific conceptual differences between determining buyers' sensitivities to price levels as opposed to their sensitivities to price differences? What are the different types of pricing decisions relevant to each type of research issue?
4. As a project, develop an approach for determining the degree buyers can remember the prices that they have paid for different products and services.
5. For a particular product that would be of interest to your fellow students, develop a questionnaire to determine the degree they tend to associate product quality with price.

[8]Donna A. Newman and Terrance M. Tucker, "Research Shows Hospital Best Pricing Strategy," *Marketing News 22* (August 29, 1988), 16.

6. As an alternative project for the product considered in question 5, develop either a trade-off or conjoint analysis research project.
7. Discuss the relative importance for developing a pricing information system for pricing decisions. What would be the role of specific pricing marketing research projects in this information system?

Suggested Readings

Axelrod, Joel N., and Norman Frendberg: "Conjoint Analysis: Peering behind the Jargon," *Marketing Research 2* (June 1990), 28–35.

Green, Paul E., Abba M. Krieger, and Terry G. Vavra: "Evaluating New Products," *Marketing Research 9* (Winter 1997), 12–21.

Renken, Tim: "Disaggregate Discrete Choice," *Marketing Research 9* (Spring 1997), 18–22.

Tomkovick, Chuck, and Kathryn E. Dobie: "Applying Hedonic Pricing Models and Factorial Surveys at Parker Pen to Enhance New Product Success," *Journal of Product and Innovation Management 12* (September 1995), 334–45.

Profitability Analysis for Pricing Decisions

Perhaps the one topic in pricing that most concerns business executives is developing valid and useful cost information. The focus of the material in this section is on pricing decisions, not cost accounting theory.

Chapter 10 discusses cost concepts and classifications and the ways these different types of costs behave. The chapter introduces traditional break-even analysis, which is extended to a more dynamic method called profit analysis. Chapter 11 develops the key cost analysis methods and explores ways of using the data for analyzing pricing alternatives; it also discusses the effect of changing the underlying cost structure and develops a dynamic price–volume–profit analysis. An important problem when analyzing pricing alternatives is to estimate the effect on demand (volume) when prices are changed. Since the price setter cannot know prospective price elasticity of demand, the chapter develops a way to compute implied price elasticities for a given profit objective.

Chapter 11 extends profitability analysis to issues involving multiple products. Initially, we analyze the implications of the relative selling mix on profitability and then consider the issues that arise when common resources are used to produce or support sale of multiple products and services. An important issue occurs when an organization is operating at or near full capacity or when it operates on the basis of special orders. We will analyze these types of situations and develop the relevant decision criteria for making pricing decisions.

One of the least developed areas of costing is the analysis of the marketing effort and the determination of profit contribution by product line, customer account, order, sales territory, and salesperson. However, proper costs for pricing must include all costs that may change when activities are changed or redirected. Chapter 12 explores additional costing approaches to obtain data for analyzing the marketing effort. An important extension of the analysis is to understand customer profitability. Thus Chapter 12 also presents information about customer profitability analysis.

CHAPTER TEN

The Role of Costs in Pricing Decisions

Cost Fundamentals

As is well known, profits are the difference between revenues and costs. Price directly affects the quantity that can be sold in the marketplace, and Chapters 2 through 9 have analyzed the effect of price on demand. Given a firm's selling objectives, the demand variable provides an upper limit on its pricing discretion; this limit is the willingness of buyers to purchase at a stated price. The other variable directly affecting profits—costs—sets a floor to a firm's pricing discretion. If prices are too low in comparison with costs, volume may be high but profitless.

Correct cost data are essential for understanding the profit implications of alternative prices. Only by determining the difference between costs and the price under consideration and then balancing that margin against the capacity necessary to produce the estimated volume can the seller determine the value of the product in terms of its contribution to recovering the seller's initial investment.

To get maximum practical use from costs in pricing, three questions must be answered: (1) Whose costs? (2) Which costs? and (3) What is the role of costs? As to whose costs, four classes of costs are important: (1) those of prospective buyers, (2) those of existing and potential competitors, (3) those of suppliers, and (4) those of the seller. Cost should play a different role for each of these four, and the pertinent concept of cost will differ accordingly. A firm can enhance its profitability not only by understanding how it incurs costs, but also by understanding how its activities influence the costs incurred by its suppliers and its customers.

Buyers' Costs

The costs of prospective customers can be determined by applying the techniques of value analysis to find the price that will make the product or service attractive to buyers (see Chapter 8).

Competitors' Costs

Competitors' costs are usually the crucial estimate in appraisal of competitors' capabilities. For products already in the marketplace, the objectives are to estimate competitors' staying power and the floor of retaliation pricing. For the first objective, the pertinent cost concept is the competitors' long-run incremental costs. For the second, their short-run incremental costs are relevant.

Forecasts of competitors' costs for competing products that could affect a product's future can help assess the capability of competitors. These forecasts also provide an estimate of the effectiveness of a product pricing strategy to discourage entry. For this situation, the cost behavior to forecast is the relationship between unit direct costs and cumulative experience as the relevant products move through their life cycles (see Chapters 13 and 14). These cost forecasts should consider technological progress and should reflect the potential head-start cost advantages that one of the sellers might have.

Suppliers' Costs

Typically, a firm is only one part of a set of activities within a value chain. Suppliers not only deliver inputs the firm uses to create value for its customers, but also have an important impact on the firm's ability to develop and maintain a cost advantage in the product markets it serves. The firm must understand how its activities influence the costs of its suppliers because often the costs of the product that the firm incurs is determined by its linkages with its suppliers. Value analysis, similar to that conducted to understand how the firm helps its customers create value, must be conducted for the firm's suppliers as well.[1]

[1]John K. Shank and Vijay Govindarajan, *Strategic Cost Management* (New York: The Free Press, 1993).

Seller's Costs

The seller's costs play several roles in pricing a product or service. First, a new product must be prepriced provisionally early in the research and development (R&D) stage and then again periodically as it progresses toward market. Forecasts of production and marketing costs will influence the decision to continue product development and ultimately to commercialize. The concept of cost relevant for this analysis is a prediction of direct costs at a series of prospective volumes and corresponding technologies.

Second, the seller's cost is important in establishing a price floor that is also the threshold for maximizing return on the product investment over the long run. For both issues, the relevant concept is future costs, forecast over a range of volume, production technologies, and promotional outlays in the marketing plan. The production, marketing, and distribution costs that matter are the future costs over the long run that will be incurred by producing and selling this product.

Importance of Costs in Pricing

Customers seldom are concerned with what it costs the seller to be able to offer the product or service for sale. Thus to determine a "price that will sell," the seller's costs have relatively little importance. Indeed, cost is probably the least important factor to consider when setting product or service prices. This statement implies a relative ranking, and in no way suggests that costs can be or should be ignored when establishing prices. Moreover, the practice of adding a percentage (usually of some aspect of production or acquisition costs) to cover selling, marketing, distribution, and general administrative costs is an inadequate recognition of this point. Indeed, marketing and distribution costs are of the same importance as production and material costs.[2]

Despite this point, which will be developed throughout this section of the book, the most commonly used method to set prices is the cost-plus or full-cost method of pricing. Probably the two strongest reasons for the prevalence of this pricing approach is that traditionally it has been associated with the notion of the "just price," and that "objective" cost

---

[2]Herbert F. Taggart, "Distribution Costs," in Sidney Davidson and Roman L. Weil, eds., *Handbook of Modern Accounting,* 2nd ed. (New York: McGraw-Hill, 1977), 43-1–43-36.

data are easier to obtain from pricing research than are "subjective" price–volume estimates.

The full-cost approach, although seemingly objective, is neither objective nor logical. When considering the cost aspect of a pricing decision, the crucial question is what costs are relevant to the decision. When cost-plus methods of pricing are used and the cost portion of the formula is arbitrarily determined, the resultant price may be incorrect because the pricing formula does not allow for demand or competition.

It is important for the seller to know the determinants and behavior of product and service costs in order to know when to accelerate cost recovery, how to evaluate a change in selling price, how to profitably segment a market, and when to add or eliminate products from the product line. Cost information indicates whether the product can be made and sold profitably at any price, but it does not indicate the amount of markup or markdown on cost buyers will accept. Proper cost determination serves to guide management in the selection of a profitable product–service mix and the determination of how much cost can be incurred without sacrificing profit.

Costs for pricing must deal with the future. Current or past information probably will provide an adequate basis for profit projections only if the future is a perfect mirror of the past. Product costs must be based on expected costs of raw materials, labor wage rates, planned marketing expenditures, and other expenses to be incurred. In addition, information about research and market development and expected administration costs is needed. Information on product and service costs should be regularly developed to determine whether changes have occurred. It is planned costs that are important, not past costs, since profit planning necessarily deals with the future.

Cost Concepts and Classifications

Determining profit at any volume, price level, product mix, or time requires proper cost classification. Some costs vary directly with the rate of activity, whereas others do not. When these different costs are mixed together in a total unit cost, it is not possible to relate sales volume to costs or determine what costs will change due to pricing decisions. As a result, the pricing decision is likely to be reduced to a formula that can lead to serious errors. However, if the cost data are properly classified into their fixed and variable components and properly attributed to the activity causing the cost, the effect of volume or activity level becomes readily apparent and sources of profit are revealed.

It is important to emphasize the concept of *activity*. Commonly, costs that vary with production rate, such as labor or materials, have been classified as variable costs, and all other costs, including marketing and distribution costs, have been classified as fixed. However, such a classification scheme is inappropriate for proper cost classification. For example, the travel costs of supporting a salesperson vary directly with number of miles traveled. Also, when a salesperson is paid on commission, selling costs vary with sales. Therefore, it is important to recognize that the cost concepts presented here apply to marketing and distribution activities as well as production.

Cost Concepts

Direct Costs

Direct costs (also called *traceable* or *attributable* costs) are those costs incurred by and solely for a particular product, department, program, sales territory, or customer account. These costs may be fixed or variable. Material and labor costs can be traced to a unit of product. The administrative salaries, rent, and other office expenses can be traced to the district sales office and therefore are direct costs of the sales territory.

Indirect Traceable Costs

Indirect traceable costs can be objectively traced to a product, department, program, sales territory, or customer account if the costs can be identified with that unit. These costs, although not incurred solely for a product, may be objectively identified with the product. They may be fixed or variable. Materials used in the production of several products can be objectively traced to or identified by the rate of usage for the production of each different product. Classic examples include maintenance and repairs, heating, power, and lighting for plants and offices.

When cost allocations are used for pricing purposes, the sales volumes are usually estimates or forecasts, implying that several average unit cost figures must be developed, depending on the relative range of forecasted sales. When there are parallel or joint production or sales methods, the cost allocation process can become very complex and arbitrary, resulting in subjective cost estimates rather than the assumed objective estimates. Thus an indirect cost should be assigned only when there is a reasonably objective means of tracing it to the appropriate business segment for which it is incurred. Otherwise, it should be handled as a common cost as described below.

Common Costs

Common or general costs support a number of activities or profit segments. These costs cannot be objectively traced to a product or segment based on a direct physical relationship to that product or segment. The administrative costs of a sales district are common to all units of product sold in that district. A common or general cost does not change when one of the activities it supports is discontinued. Hence discontinuing a product in the line will not affect the administrative costs of the district or other general expenses such as market research or research and development.

Opportunity Costs

An opportunity cost is the marginal income forgone by choosing one alternative over another. Essentially, opportunity costs reflect the "cost" of not choosing the best alternative or opportunity. These costs are relevant when operating at or near full capacity or when resources are in scarce supply. If a decision is made not to produce a product with the largest contribution per resource unit consumed, then the difference between the income earned and the larger income that could have been earned is income forgone (opportunity cost). In a similar manner, when the organization is operating well below capacity, then sales volume becomes the limiting or scarce factor, and instead of maximizing contributions per scarce resource unit, the relevant decision criterion would be maximization of contribution per sales dollar. In these two situations, opportunity costs are relevant to price setting and must be included in the development of relevant costs for the decision.

Cash and Noncash Costs

Costs can lead to cash (or out-of-pocket) outlays or bookkeeping (depreciation or amortization) entries. The noncash costs do impact the cash flows but do not reflect actual monetary outlays in a particular accounting period. As Equation 10.1 shows, cash flow comprises net income (after all accounting expenses have been deducted) plus noncash accounting charges.

$$\text{Cash flow} = \text{net income} + \text{depreciation} + \text{depletion} + \text{amortization}$$

(10.1)

Consider, for example, depreciation expenses. There are very good reasons for charging depreciation, but the amount is calculated by an arbitrary formula and does not necessarily have to be set aside when the entry is made in the accounts. Depreciation as an allowable expense serves to reduce the organization's tax obligations, thereby enhancing the cash flow of the organization. However, it is not an actual cash or out-of-pocket expense and therefore is not a legitimate cost for setting prices. When analyzing the implications of particular price–expected volume combinations on profitability or financial status, these noncash costs become relevant. But they are not relevant for the determination of actual selling prices.

Cost Behavior

In addition to classifying costs according to ability to attribute a cost to a product or profit segment, it is also important to classify costs according to variation with the rate of activity. As noted previously, unless costs can be segmented into fixed and variable costs, it is not possible to trace the effects of changes in price, volume, or product selling mix on costs.

Direct Variable Costs

Costs that vary directly with an activity level are called direct variable costs. As production increases in a given time period, a proportionately higher amount of labor and materials is used. Assuming no changes in scale economies as the volume increases, these direct variable costs will be constant per additional unit produced. However, there usually is a point where unit direct variable costs change due either to economies of quantity raw-material purchases or to increased labor unit costs resulting from overtime or a second shift. Figure 10.1(a) illustrates direct variable costs.

In pricing, direct variable costs are also known as *out-of-pocket costs,* since these costs are incremental to the decision to make and sell and therefore require an outlay of immediate cash. One test of a unit variable cost is whether it is readily discontinued or whether it would not exist if a product were not made. Direct variable costs include those costs that the product incurs unit by unit and includes such costs as

FIGURE 10.1 Cost Behavior Patterns: (a) Variable Cost, (b) Semivariable Cost, and (c) Fixed Cost

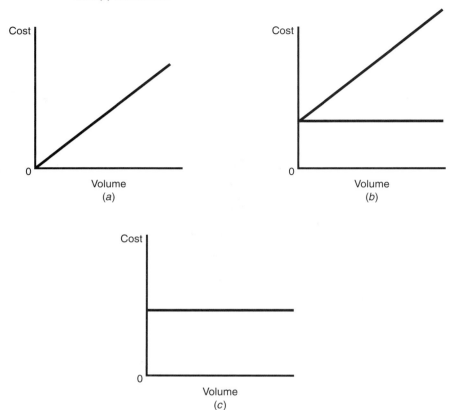

productive labor, energy required at production centers, raw material required, sales commissions, royalties, and shipping costs. The major criterion of a direct variable cost is that it be traceably and tangibly generated by, and identified with, the making and selling of a specific product.

Semivariable Costs

Some costs vary with activity rates but are not zero at a zero activity rate. Plant supplies are needed in some minimum amount to get activities started, and then additional quantities are required as the level of activity increases. Hence these semivariable costs consist of a base amount that is constant in relation to activity and a variable amount that varies directly with changes in the activity level. Figure 10.1(b) illustrates these costs.

Period Fixed Costs

Generally, fixed costs occur because of a legal, contractual, or moral obligation. Some of these costs, although fixed for the planning period are assigned to specific projects by management to fulfill company objectives. These *specific programmed costs* refer to costs used to generate additional revenues; they include opening a new sales district office or warehouse or a special advertising program for a specific product line. These direct fixed costs are separable because they can be charged to the product line or activity that is the recipient of the incurred cost.

Other costs are also fixed for the planning period, but they are incurred for the entire company and are common to the various products or activities. Examples of these *general programmed costs* are general and administrative salaries, research and development, and general marketing expenses. Other costs are neither separable nor inescapable during the planning period. These *constant costs* are common and are incurred as long as the firm is in business. Common costs support a number of activities or profit segments. These costs cannot be objectively traced to a particular type of service or product based on a direct physical relationship to that service or product. The administrative cost of a service facility is common to all units of service provided in that facility. A common or general cost does not change when one of the activities it supports is discontinued. Hence discontinuing a product or type of service provided will not affect the administrative costs of the facility or the general expenses such as market research or research and development. Included in these costs are depreciation, real estate taxes, rent, and interest payments on mortgages. In pricing, all the period fixed costs are referred to simply as fixed costs as long as the costs will be incurred in the planning period. These fixed costs are illustrated in Fig.10.1(c).

Table 10.1 summarizes the cost concepts and behavior discussed in this section. As the table indicates, some directly attributable costs vary directly with the activity level, and some costs, although fixed, are directly attributable to the activity level. For example, advertising expenses incurred for a specific product, even though fixed by contract for a period of time, are directly attributable to that product. It is important, then, to clarify specifically what is meant by

TABLE 10.1 Cost Classifications

Classified According to Variation with Activity Rate	Cost Component	Classified According to Ability to Trace or Attribute the Cost to a Product or Segment
Costs vary linearly with activity rate	Raw materials Utilities Shipping Royalties Sales commissions	Directly traceable or attributable
Costs vary with activity rate, but are not zero at zero activity level	Operating labor Direct supervision Maintenance Plant supplies	
Costs do not vary with activity level	Rent Insurance Taxes Depreciation	Directly traceable or attributable, but independent of activity level
	Payroll General plant overhead Storage facilities Medical and safety expenses	Indirectly traceable or attributable to a product or segment
	General administration Sales administration Market research Research and development	Common or general costs not easily traceable or attributable to a product or segment

Source: Adapted and reprinted with permission from Donald R. Woods, *Financial Decision Making in the Process Industry* (Englewood Cliffs, NJ: Prentice-Hall, 1975), p. 212.

the terms *direct* and *indirect. The directly traceable or attributable costs are those that we can readily determine as contributing to the product cost. However, whether a direct cost is variable, fixed, or semivariable depends on properly determining the source of that cost.*

Determinants of Cost Behavior

No cost is inherently fixed or variable. Furthermore, whether a cost is fixed or variable depends on whether that cost varies as the organization's activity level changes. Traditionally, it has been customary to consider variable costs as those costs that vary with production volume, usually measured in terms of product units. For example, material cost is usually considered a variable cost because it varies directly with changes in production activity.

However, when analyzing costs to set prices or justify price differences, it is important to recognize that there are other sets of activities in addition to production that incur costs. For example, a salesperson's travel expenses vary directly with the distance traveled (e.g., 35¢ per mile). A salaried salesperson's expenses in serving an account vary directly with the amount of time spent serving a customer account. The shipping department's cost of preparing an invoice may vary directly with the number of items on an invoice. For the U.S. Postal Service, the cost of providing a particular class of service varies with the number of pieces mailed, the weight, and the distance these pieces are mailed. In general, a cost is a variable cost if the cost changes because of a change in the activity causing that cost. The question is whether the cost changes as the relative level of activity changes per unit of activity, not whether the total cost of that activity changes on an annual basis irrespective of the total volume of the activity.

On the other hand, fixed costs are affected by long-range planning decisions. Some of these fixed costs are long-term lease commitments and depreciation costs, which remain constant over periods of time. These general programmed costs originate in capacity decisions, whereas specific programmed costs result from decisions on how to use that capacity. These specific programmed costs are planned expenditures to generate a sales volume or to handle a specified level of administrative work. Thus, managers can increase the specific programmed costs whenever they decide to do so.

Different decisions may produce different levels of fixed costs. For example, shut-down fixed costs are usually lower than operating fixed costs of a plant. Required power levels are lower and security and maintenance personnel are fewer when a plant is shut down than when it is running.

Fixed costs may also differ with the extent to which a fixed cost is traceable to a specific time period. Administrative salaries, lease payments, and taxes are direct costs of the time period in which they are paid. However, other fixed costs reflect a lump-sum payment that is apportioned over a series of future time periods. Depreciation, amortization, and depletion expenses are common costs apportioned over specific time periods and they vary according to the computational procedure employed. Because depreciation costs are subjective and reflect prior decisions, they are irrelevant for pricing and other planning decisions. Unfortunately, they are often lumped in with other fixed costs, unitized according to some estimate of projected volume, and become a part of the cost that price is expected to recover. *Depreciation, amortization, and depletion costs should be separated from other period expenses for the purpose of pricing.*

Although costs are not inherently fixed or variable, it is essential that an organization identify the behavior pattern that they follow. It is vitally important to know which costs vary with changes in activity levels and which costs remain constant. Box 10.1 illustrates how incorrect pricing decisions may result when an inappropriate cost system is used.

The Issue of Recovering Costs

One frequently offered reason for a full-cost pricing approach is that each product or activity should carry its "fair share of the burden." That is, the objective is to recover the costs incurred while performing the activities of the organization. On the other hand, pricing based on direct variable costs (sometimes referred to as marginal cost pricing) is criticized because the organization may end up "giving the product away." That is, the costs of performing the organization's activities will not be recovered. There is no disagreement that those costs incurred solely for and because of a particular business segment—direct variable and direct period costs—should be recovered. The question arises over the recovery of indirect and common period costs.

Direct period costs normally should be recovered in the period in which they are incurred and are relevant for pricing purposes. The recovery of indirect period costs, such as an investment in a production plant, generally depends on an arbitrary decision on how long the facility will last or be useful to the organization. Therefore, for pricing purposes, the amount to be recovered per period must be flexible and reflect the nature of the product-market fluctuations. The ultimate concern is whether the dollars invested in the facility or activity earn the desired rate of return over the useful life of the facility or activity. Thus, the appropriate concern is not whether the product recovers a fixed amount of the indirect period cost in a particular year or period but whether, over a reasonable number of periods, it makes a sufficient contribution to justify its continuance.

Determining the contribution each product or service should make to the recovery of indirect period costs and common period costs is a managerial decision that should

FINDING OUT HOW MUCH A BATCH REALLY COSTS

BOX 10.1

A liquid process manufacturer produced and sold the liquid in tanks, gallons, or drums. Material costs were 60 percent of sales and overhead costs were about 15 percent of sales. The company's traditional cost system assigned the costs of each batch setup for a new product or order regardless of the number of units (gallons) produced with a batch. The table shows the results of this cost system. Because product A had the largest gross margin (33 percent), the salespeople were urged to market the product aggressively. However,

the company continued to lose market share in virtually all product markets.

Switching to an activity-based costing system, the company recognized that there were more activities and costs associated with setting up and running each batch: inspection, order processing, material expediting, material handling, receiving, and shipping. As a result, products requiring more batches in small quantities received a greater portion of the batch-related activity costs on a per-gallon basis. The results are shown in the table.

	Products			
	A	**B**	**C**	**D**
Number of gallons	1	5	200	75,000
Number of batches	1	2	2	25
Traditional cost	$22.00	$19.00	$25.00	$7.50
ABC cost	$2,100.00	$600.00	$37.00	$6.50
Current price	$33.00	$27.55	$33.75	$9.38
Old gross margin	33%	31%	26%	20%
New gross margin	−6,200%	−2,000%	−10%	31%

Based on the old cost system, product D, which once held a 75 percent market share, had been priced considerably higher than the competitors' average price of $7.00 and its market share had fallen to 30 percent. Knowing that a more accurate per-gallon ABC cost was $6.50, the firm began to slowly reduce its price from $9.38 to a price closer to the competitors'

average price and became a strong competitor once again. For product A and similar products, prices were raised if price elasticity was low or if competitors' prices were high.

Source: Eileen Morrissey, "How to Use Activity-Based Costing as the Springboard for Pricing Decisions," *Journal of Pricing Management* 1, no. 4 (Fall 1990), 42–44, 48.

not be made using an inflexible and arbitrary allocation rule. Depending on the level of analysis, the following hierarchy of cost recovery can serve as a starting point:[3]

[3]Walter Georges and Robert W. McGee, *Analytical Contribution Accounting: The Interface of Cost Accounting and Pricing Policy* (New York: Quorum Books, 1987).

1. Direct product, customer, or sales territory costs.

2. Direct product, customer, or sales territory costs plus desired contribution to the costs of product group, customer group, or sales region.

3. Direct costs as in (1) and (2) plus desired contribution to division, cost center, or total organization.

To determine desired contributions, management must consider relative external factors such as competition, stage of the product's life cycle, demand, and general economic conditions. Although this approach is considerably more difficult than a cost-plus formula, it forces the price setter to actively consider the realities of the marketplace when determining prices. This is clearly an advantage because the important sources of profitability are external to the organization, and considering only the internal need to recover costs often leads to poor pricing decisions.

Pricing should not be perceived as a part of a cost recovery program; rather, pricing should be considered as a part of a revenue-generating program. Buyers generally are not concerned that the sellers have covered all their costs but rather with the perceived value of the product in relation to its price. Essentially, price must be acceptable to the market and above direct variable costs.

Elements of Profitability

Four basic elements affect the profitability of any multiproduct organization:

1. Price per unit of each product or service offering (P_i).

2. Costs: variable costs per unit of each offering (VC_i), and fixed costs per period (FC).

3. Volume produced and sold of each offering (Q_i).

4. Dollar sales mix of the offerings sold.

In profitability analysis, profit measures include contribution margin per unit, total contributions per period, profit-volume ratio, contribution per resource unit, net operating profit, net income (profit after taxes), and earnings per share. The actual data for the analysis may be in the form of (1) units and dollars or (2) dollars only. Preferably, the data should be in the form of units and dollars (price per unit, variable costs per unit, unit sales) because then the effect of each of these four elements of profitability can be calculated. A more limited analysis can be performed if the data are in dollars only (such as dollars of revenues or total variable costs).

Break-Even Analysis

Break-even analysis is a simple and easily understandable method of examining the relationship between fixed costs, variable costs, volume, and price. Detailed analysis of break-even data will show the effect of the following:

1. Decisions that convert costs from variable to fixed or vice versa.

2. Decisions that reduce or increase costs.

3. Decisions that increase sales volume and revenue.

4. Decisions to change selling prices.

To illustrate the concept of break-even analysis and its application to pricing decisions, consider a specialty retailer that buys T-shirts from a supplier at $16 each and sells them for $20 each. Assume that the fixed costs are $20,000 per year and that estimated sales volume is 10,000 shirts per year. The data in Table 10.2 summarize this situation. The data in the "one shirt" column suggest that the retailer earns $2 of profit per shirt sold. However, one difficulty with this conclusion is that profit per shirt is $2 *only if* 10,000 shirts are sold during the year. If fewer shirts are sold, average unit profit is less; if more shirts are sold, average unit profit is more. A second problem with the one shirt presentation in Table 10.2 is that it portrays fixed costs as though they vary with the number of units bought and sold. In this example, rent is fixed at a lump amount of $20,000, and it is illogical to develop an average fixed cost per unit. Indeed, *fixed costs should not be unitized.*

Each sale generates a contribution to fixed costs and profit of $4. The number of shirts that must be sold before the retailer breaks even is $20,000/$4.00 = 5,000 shirts. This figure is the retailer's break-even point: the level of sales volume that produces total contributions equal to the period fixed expenses. Only when the 5,001st shirt is sold will the retailer realize any profit for the year. The unit profit of $2 indicated above obviously is incorrect because no profits are realized until sales exceed 5,000 shirts.

TABLE 10.2

Planning Data for Retail Shirt Store

	One Shirt	10,000 Shirts per Year
Sales	$20.00	$200,000
Out-of-pocket costs	16.00	160,000
Fixed costs	2.00	20,000
Total costs	18.00	180,000
Profits	2.00	20,000

The break-even *point* is when sales revenue exactly covers all costs, that is, the level of sales revenue when profits are zero. Or, as illustrated, the break-even point is the amount of sales revenue that generates contributions equal to the period fixed costs.

Using the shirt example, the break-even formula is

$$BEQ = \frac{FC}{P-VC} \qquad \textbf{(10.2)}$$

where

$$BEQ = \text{break-even sales quantity (units)}$$
$$FC = \text{period fixed costs}$$
$$P = \text{selling price per unit}$$
$$VC = \text{direct variable costs per unit}$$

Applying the shirt data we obtain

$$BEQ = \frac{\$20,000}{\$20-\$16} = 5,000 \text{ shirts} \qquad \textbf{(10.3)}$$

Alternatively, the break-even formula can be expressed in terms of sales revenue:

$$BES = \frac{FC}{PV} \qquad \textbf{(10.4)}$$

where BES is the break-even sales revenue and PV is the profit-volume, or PV ratio, which indicates the proportion of sales dollars available to cover fixed costs after deducting variable costs:

$$PV = \frac{P-VC}{P} \qquad \textbf{(10.5)}$$

Applying the shirt data we obtain

$$PV = \frac{\$20-\$16}{\$20} = 0.20 \qquad \textbf{(10.6)}$$

and therefore

$$BES = \frac{\$20,000}{0.20} = \$100,000$$

Often it is desirable to picture the economic character of a business firm by showing the break-even analysis on a break-even chart. We normally plot the sales revenue on the *x* (horizontal) axis and the costs on the *y* (vertical) axis. Both are expressed in identical dollars on an identical scale. Thus, the 45-degree revenue line will indicate the same value whether referred to from either the cost or revenue scale. The point where the total-cost line intersects the revenue line is the sales volume where total costs equal total sales revenue. Figure 10.2 shows the break-even chart for the retail shirt store. Extending break-even analysis to include an analysis of the impact on profits follows.

Profit Analysis

Profit analysis attempts to determine the effect of costs, prices, and volume on profits in order to determine the best course of action. Accurate data about each product's contributions gives management a sound basis for determining how to allocate marketing efforts to products.

FIGURE 10.2
Break-Even Chart for the Retail Shirt Store

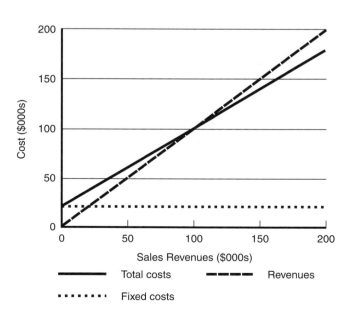

Perhaps the most important piece of data resulting from a profit analysis is *profit–volume ratio* (PV), which is the proportion of sales available to cover fixed costs and profits after deducting variable costs. Equation (10.5) gives the computational formula for PV on a unit basis. In the following data the contribution ratio or PV is the contribution of $3,500 ($10,000 − $6,500), divided by sales, or 35 percent. That is, PV can also be calculated using (total contribution dollars/total dollar sales). Thus, 35 cents out of each sales dollar contributes toward paying fixed costs and providing a profit.

Sales	$10,000
Variable costs	6,500
Fixed costs	2,500
Profit	$ 1,000

Once the PV has been calculated it is possible to determine the effects on profits of additional sales volume. If $1,000 of additional sales were generated, the additional profits would be $1,000 × 0.35, or $350. Since the fixed costs of $2,500 have already been covered by the original $10,000 of sales, additional volume contributes 35 cents of every sales dollar to profits. Thus, a 10 percent increase in sales produces a 35 percent increase in profits. A second increase in sales of 10 percent will produce a 28.5 percent increase in profits [($1,100 × 0.35)/($1,000 + $350)]. This analysis is possible only when all direct costs have been separated into their fixed and variable components.

In multiproduct firms emphasis should be on achieving the maximum amount of contribution revenue instead of attempting to maximize sales revenues. Each product faces different competition, has a different demand elasticity, and perhaps depends for its sales, at least in part, on the sales of the other products in the line. Table 10.3 shows the effect of changing product prices of a product line.[4] In the "before" situation, the firm subjectively set its prices at a uniform contribution level and ignored competition, demand elasticity, and product-line interdependence. However, after examining pricing decisions, management discovered that product A was price elastic, implying that a price reduction would

[4]This example is borrowed from Spencer A. Tucker, *Pricing for Higher Profit* (New York: McGraw-Hill, 1966), pp. 86–87.

TABLE 10.3   **Determining Contributions and Profits for a Product Line**

Item	Product A	Product B	Product C	Product D	Total
Unit variable cost	$ 9.00	$10.00	$11.00	$12.00	
Before					
Unit selling price	$ 15.00	$ 16.00	$ 17.00	$ 18.00	
Unit contribution	$ 6.00	$ 6.00	$ 6.00	$ 6.00	
Units sold (000s)	50	60	40	30	180
Total revenue	$750,000	$960,000	$680,000	$540,000	$2,930,000
Total contribution	$300,000	$360,000	$240,000	$180,000	$1,080,000
Less: Fixed costs					$1,000,000
Net profit					$ 80,000
After					
Unit selling price	$ 14.00	$ 19.00	$ 18.00	$ 20.00	
Unit contribution	$ 5.00	$ 9.00	$ 7.00	$ 8.00	
Units sold (000s)	70	40	40	25	170
Total revenue	$980,000	$760,000	$720,000	$500,000	$2,960,000
Total contribution	$350,000	$360,000	$280,000	$200,000	$1,190,000
Less: Fixed costs					$1,000,000
Net profit					$ 190,000

lead to a greater percent increase in sales volume. Product B was being priced below competition, and increasing its price to competitive levels would leave the total contribution unchanged although revenues would decrease. Products C and D were found to be demand inelastic; therefore, prices could be increased, leading to increases in revenues. As Table 10.3 indicates, the firm was able to earn twice the profit with lower unit sales and about the same revenue.

Extension of Break-Even Analysis

As we have seen, the break-even chart assumes that each dollar of revenue will have the same cost, the same profit–volume ratio, and eventually, the same profit. However, in the real world of business, operations are not so uniform. In fact, over time, we would expect changes in out-of-pocket (variable) costs, fixed expenses, and prices with resultant changes in profits.

In terms of the break-even chart, a decrease in unit variable costs with no change in fixed expenses decreases the slope of the total-cost line, leading to a lower break-even point. An increase in unit variable costs increases the slope of the total-cost line, leading to a higher break-even point. If prices are increased and the volume remains the same, contributions are increased because each sales dollar has less out-of-pocket cost content. Thus, the effect is to lower the slope of the total-cost line, producing a lower break-even point.

If only fixed costs are increased, the result is an increase in the break-even point, causing profits to start later, but at the same PV rate. Therefore, any changes in the price, volume, or cost variables can be shown on the break-even chart.

To illustrate some of the dynamics of the analysis, assume the data are as shown in Table 10.4. Now assume that the firm considers adding new equipment in the belief that it will reduce labor costs by $200,000 per period for the same volume level. However, acquiring the machinery will lead to a $100,000 increase in fixed expenses. As Table 10.5 and Figure 10.3 show, the break-even points are identical for the original and the proposed situations. However, the new situation would contribute 40 cents of profit per sales dollar above the break-even point, as compared to the original sit-

TABLE 10.4   Profitability Analysis Before Change in Cost Structure

1. Sales revenue (price = $10/unit)		$1,000,000
2. Direct material cost	$400,000	
3. Direct labor cost	400,000	
4. Total direct variable cost (2 + 3)	$800,000	
5. Fixed costs	100,000	
6. Total costs (4 + 5)		900,000
7. Contribution (1 − 4)		$ 200,000
8. Profit–volume ratio (7 ÷ 1)		0.20
9. Break-even sales (5 ÷ 8)		$ 500,000
10. Unit sales ($1,000,000 ÷ $10)		100,000
11. Unit contribution (7 ÷ 10)		$ 2.00
12. Break-even quantity (5 ÷ 11)		50,000

TABLE 10.5
Effect of Changing Cost Structure on Profitability

1. Sales revenue	$1,000,000
2. Variable costs	$ 600,000
3. Fixed costs	$ 200,000
4. Total costs (2 + 3)	$ 800,000
5. Contribution (1 − 2)	$ 400,000
6. Profit–volume ratio (5 ÷ 1)	0.40
7. Break-even sales (3 ÷ 6)	$ 500,000

FIGURE 10.3   **Effect of Changing the Cost Structure**

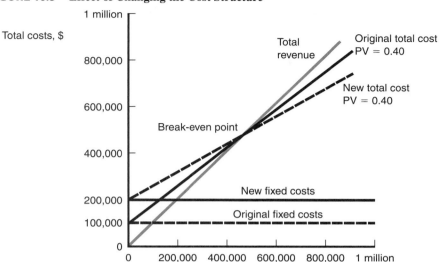

uation, which contributed only 20 cents of profit per sales dollar above the break-even point. This illustration provides an indication of the dynamics of break-even analysis.

Some Useful Guidelines for Break-Even Analysis

Let us return to the specialty retailer who buys shirts from a supplier at $16 each and sells them for $20 each. Fixed costs are $20,000 per year and estimated sales volume is 10,000 shirts per year. Recall that for this situation the break-even point is 5,000 shirts, or $100,000.

Now if fixed costs are increased to $30,000 per year, the break-even point becomes

$$\text{BES} = \frac{\$30,000}{0.20} = \$150,000$$

If price is raised to $22.00, the PV becomes 0.273 (i.e., $6/$22), and

$$\text{BES} = \frac{\$30,000}{0.273} = \$110,000$$

If fixed costs remain at $30,000, but the shirts are purchased for $14, the PV becomes 0.30 ($6/$20), and the break-even point is

$$\text{BES} = \frac{\$30,000}{0.30} = \$100,000$$

These three examples provide useful guidelines.

1. A change in fixed costs affects only the break-even point.

2. A change in the price and/or variable costs affects both the break-even point and the PV.

3. An increase in prices and/or a decrease in variable costs can offset an increase in fixed expenses (assuming volume remains unaffected).

We have seen that with fixed costs at $30,000, price at $20, and variable costs at $14, the break-even point is the same as in the original example. However, are profits the same? To answer this question we need an additional formula.

$$\text{Profit} = (\text{sales revenue} \times \text{PV}) - \text{fixed costs} \quad \textbf{(10.7)}$$

Applying this formula to the original situation for a sales level of $140,000 we get

$$\text{Profit} = (\$140,000 \times 0.20) - \$20,000 = \$8,000$$

And for the new situation

$$\text{Profit} = (\$140,000 \times 0.30) - \$30,000 = \$12,000$$

Thus, we have three additional guidelines:

4. Two products can have identical break-even points but will still earn profits or losses at their own PV rate.

5. Above or below the identical break-even points, the ratio of two products' profits or losses will be proportionate to the ratio of their PV rates, for example,

$$\frac{\$8,000}{\$12,000} = \frac{8}{12} = \frac{0.20}{0.30}$$

6. Above or below the break-even point, profits or losses are generated by the PV rate.

Suppose the retailer sets a target profit of $10,000 on target sales volume of $160,000. If variable costs are $17.00 per shirt and fixed costs are $30,000, what should be the price of the shirts? To answer this question we need two additional formulas. (Note that a profit objective is treated as a "fixed" expense in the analysis; we elaborate on this approach in Chapter 11.)

$$PV = \frac{\text{target profit} + \text{fixed expenses}}{\text{sales revenue}} \quad \textbf{(10.8)}$$

$$= \frac{\$10,000 + \$30,000}{\$160,000} = 0.25$$

$$\text{Price} = \frac{\text{variable costs}}{1 - PV} \quad \textbf{(10.9)}$$

$$= \frac{\$17}{(1 - 0.25)} = \$22.66$$

This example provides another guideline:

7. When the objective is to determine a price for a target PV, divide the appropriate variable costs by the complement of the target PV.

These seven guidelines provide a basis for examining the effect of changes in the product's or firm's underlying cost structure. Profit analysis is an extension of break-even analysis in that it is possible to use the methodology of break-even analysis to examine the effects on profits of changes in costs or prices. The concept that allows us to perform such analyses is the PV ratio. The key to the application of the PV ratio is the ability to classify relevant costs according to their behavior—fixed or variable—and according to their traceability to the business segment being analyzed.

Limitations of Break-Even Analysis

As the guidelines suggest, break-even analysis is useful for studying the relations among prices, costs, and volume. It is helpful for analyzing pricing alternatives, developing cost control programs, or making decisions about expanding production capacity. However, an inherent weakness of the technique is the assumption that variable costs remain proportional to volume at all output levels. Furthermore, it assumes that price is constant over the relevant volume levels. The assumption that variable costs remain proportional to volume will be relaxed in Chapter 13 when we discuss the experience curve phenomenon. One way to overcome the constant price assumption is to build different price–volume–cost scenarios into the analysis; Chapter 14 will develop this adaptation when discussing new-product pricing.

Another important limitation is that the costs used in the analysis may be relevant only over a limited range of volume.

That is, if volume is below or above certain capacity levels, the underlying variable and fixed costs may differ. For example, going to overtime or a second shift will raise the labor costs per hour and will increase the per-unit labor costs. Similarly, an additional quantity discount given for added materials purchases may reduce material costs per unit. Also, qualitative changes in the product or service may change the underlying cost structure and lead to different break-even points.

Used appropriately and with an understanding of its limitations, break-even analysis can be useful for a number of important business decisions. It can be used to analyze the profitability implications of alternative prices for a new product. It can be used to analyze the implications of changing the cost structure, such as shifting from a relatively high variable-cost to a relatively high fixed-cost structure. The key element in these decisions is the influence of volume changes on profitability when organizations have different relationships between fixed and variable costs. To understand these relationships we turn to the concept of leverage in Chapter 11.

Summary

Costs set a floor to a firm's pricing discretion. When considering the cost aspect of a pricing decision, however, the crucial problem is to determine what costs are relevant to the decision. It is also important to know the determinants and behavior of these costs in order to analyze the full impact of the pricing decision.

This chapter has discussed cost concepts and classifications, the different ways these different types of costs behave, and ways to identify patterns of cost behavior. Today, we have sufficient knowledge about generating and analyzing cost data. With the aid of information technology and statistical programs, the decision maker can know the relevant costs for pricing purposes. Thus, managers need to exert the will to develop detailed cost studies of their operations.

The seller must attribute the various types of costs to the products or facilities causing these costs. Direct costs that are identifiable with, and traceable to, a specific profit segment present no real difficulty. But the allocation of fixed or period costs requires using some basis for applying these costs to the different profit segments. Despite the inherent logic in some of the methods for applying overhead, they are still arbitrary. It is indefensible to believe there is one right allocation method. Generally, a product that is relatively labor-intensive has a greater chance of being assigned a relatively larger overhead burden despite the burden it places on manufacturing and marketing processes.

The attempt to unitize period costs distorts prices and can actually lead to profitless prices and volume despite the relative "security" of believing the prices cover full costs. Full costing distorts the information needed to analyze the product mix and the marketing mix. Full-cost pricing fails to recognize that in multiproduct companies, the products are in different stages of their life cycles and will not be equally profitable. Finally, full-cost pricing does not recognize the benefits of low-price-induced volume, which may lead to lower per-unit costs as volume increases.

Discussion Questions

1. *a.* Develop a list of the different types of costs that are incurred in the manufacturing process.
   b. Assuming a general situation, classify these costs as
      (1) Direct, indirect, or common costs.
      (2) Variable, semivariable, or fixed costs.
   c. What was your rationale in making these classifications?

2. *a.* Develop a list of the different types of costs incurred by a manufacturer in marketing and distributing its products.
   b. Assuming a general situation, classify these costs as
      (1) Direct, indirect, or common costs.
      (2) Variable, semivariable, or fixed costs.
   c. What was your rationale in making these classifications?

3. *a.* Develop a list of the different types of costs incurred by a retailer.
   b. Assuming a general situation, classify these costs as
      (1) Direct, indirect, or common costs.
      (2) Variable, semivariable, or fixed costs.
   c. What was your rationale in making these classifications?

4. *a.* Develop a list of the different types of costs incurred by a service organization, such as a bank, hospital, or tax consulting service.
   b. Assuming a general situation, classify these costs as
      (1) Direct, indirect, or common costs.
      (2) Variable, semivariable, or fixed costs.
   c. What was your rationale in making these classifications?

5. Review the different types and classes of costs identified in the four questions above. Are there any differences in the nature and behavior of the costs across these different types of organizations? What implications, if any, do these differences have for developing pricing strategies?

6. Discuss the role of cost in price decisions. How does the role of cost differ from that of demand?

7. Direct costing as applied to pricing has sometimes been called marginal pricing or incremental pricing. Opponents of marginal pricing contend that this method of pricing may lead the price setter to accidentally or intentionally ignore costs that do not vary with volume. If this possibility is correct, what safeguards would you propose to make sure the firm does not price its products unprofitably?

8. Most governmental regulatory agencies require a full-cost approach to rate setting. Why do you think they stress the full-cost approach? What are some arguments against the full-cost approach for regulating price? Can you think of a way to reconcile these differences in approaches?

9. Assume the specialty retailer discussed in this chapter determines that fixed costs have increased to $21,000 per year. Further, assume that the shirts can now be acquired for $18 and that the retailer raises the retail price of shirts to $24. Compute

   a. Contribution dollars per shirt.

   b. PV ratio.

   c. Break-even quantity.

   d. Break-even sales (dollars).

   e. Draw a break-even graph.

Suggested Readings

Cooper, Robin, and W. Bruce Chew: "Control Tomorrow's Costs through Today's Designs," *Harvard Business Review 74* (January–February 1996), 88–98.

Georges, Walter, and Robert W. McGee: *Analytical Contribution Accounting* (New York: Quorum Books, 1987).

Goebel, Daniel J., Greg W. Marshall, and William B. Locander: "Activity-Based Costing: Accounting for a Market Orientation," *Industrial Marketing Management 27* (November 1998), 497–510.

Kaplan, Robert S., and Robin Cooper: *Cost & Effect: Using Integrated Cost systems to Drive Profitability and Performance* (Boston: Harvard Business School Press, 1998).

Ness, Joseph A., and Thomas G. Cucuzza: "Tapping the Full Potential of ABC," *Harvard Business Review 73* (July–August 1995), 130–38.

Shank, John K., and Vijay Govindarajan: *Strategic Cost Management* (New York: The Free Press, 1993).

CHAPTER ELEVEN

Using Leverage for Developing Pricing Strategies

In the physical sciences, *leverage* is the application of a small amount of force to one end of a rigid mechanism balanced on a fulcrum to raise a heavy object at the other end. Similarly, when a relatively small change in sales volume leads to a larger change in operating profits (earnings before interest and taxes), leverage is at work. There are two types of leverage: operating leverage and financial leverage. Whenever a firm incurs a fixed operating cost (regardless of the level of its activities), it is using *operating leverage* to amplify the effect of sales volume on operating profits. *Financial leverage* is created by employing interest-bearing debt for capital formation (irrespective of its operating profit), which amplifies the effect of a change in operating profit on earnings per share.

In today's business environment it is essential to understand the concept of leverage, how it occurs, and how to use it to manage the firm's pricing function. It is through leverage that fluctuations in demand for the firm's products and services are amplified into its financial results (e.g., changes in operating profits or earnings per share). The financial health of a firm depends on marketing strategies because (1) marketing strategies directly influence profitability and (2) financial issues constrain marketing strategy options. Price influences the firm's financial position through its direct impact on revenues. Moreover, the impact of price on sales volumes influences costs and the development of marketing strategies. This chapter integrates the concepts of leverage

SOME EXAMPLES OF LEVERAGE **BOX 11.1**

1. In 1986 the Coca-Cola Co. formed Coca-Cola Enterprises Inc. (CCE) to gain greater control over the packaging and distribution of its sodas. It sold 51 percent of this new company to the public. Coca-Cola formed the separate company to keep the acquisition debt off of its own balance sheets and CCE carried the $3.1 billion debt on its own books. Unfortunately, the period of 1986 to 1989 was marked by a price war between soft drink bottlers trying to capture more shelf space. Net wholesale prices for CCE's products fell 2.5 percent in 1987, an additional 2.5 percent in 1988, and another 1 percent in 1989. As a result, CCE's operating profit margins fell to 8.1 percent in 1989 compared to 10 percent in 1987. Also, CCE's net income fell more than 40 percent in 1989.

   Recognizing that it had to change this financial trend, CCE introduced a 3 percent price increase in the latter half of 1989. CCE hoped that buyers would continue to buy even as prices increased because every 1 percent increase in wholesale price translated into a 20-cent increase in earnings per share.

2. In 1990 the drug company Warner-Lambert reported an earnings growth of 15.5 percent annually on a sales growth of less than half that rate.

3. In 1997 Kodak was trying to halt the competitive gains of Fuji. Fuji had been making large price reductions and had substantially increased its marketing efforts. However, Kodak was determined to not get into a price war, because every 1 percent drop in Kodak's film prices resulted in approximately a 1 percent decrease in earnings per share.

Sources: "Bottling is Hardly a Classic for Coke," *Business Week* (December 11, 1989), 130–35; "Warner-Lambert: Can R&D Take It To the Top Tier?" *Business Week* (September 24, 1990), 66–68; "Can George Fisher Fix Kodak?" *Business Week* (October 20, 1997), 116–28.

and marketing-oriented pricing strategies. It will show that firms with different degrees of operating and financial leverage that compete in the same product markets have different abilities to use price as a strategic variable. Box 11.1 illustrates applications of leverage that the chapter will develop. As these examples indicate, there is a direct relationship between price changes, sales volume changes, and changes in operating profits and financial performance, for example, earnings per share. Moreover, depending on how the firm is organized, operationally and financially, small percent price changes can lead to substantially larger percent changes in operating profits and earnings per share.

Operating Leverage

Operating leverage occurs when an organization has fixed operating costs that must be met regardless of sales volume.

The operating leverage of a firm is related to the ratio of total fixed costs to total variable costs. Firms with a higher proportion of total costs represented by fixed costs will have a higher operating leverage for a specific sales volume. The airlines are an example of firms with relatively high fixed costs. Once the break-even point in terms of passenger miles is reached, the revenues earned from each additional passenger contribute almost entirely to profits. To measure the effect of a change in sales volume on profits, we calculate

$$\text{Degree of operating leverage} = \frac{\text{Percentage change in operating profits}}{\text{Percentage change in sales volume}}$$

or

$$\text{DOL} = \frac{\triangle\text{OP}}{\text{OP}} \div \frac{\triangle Q}{Q} \tag{11.1}$$

where

DOL = degree of operating leverage

$\triangle\text{OP}$ = change in operating profits

OP = operating profits in the previous period (before interest and taxes)

$\triangle Q$ = change in sales volume (units)

Q = sales volume in the previous period

Note that Equation 11.1 is in essentially the same form as the price elasticity definition given in Chapter 2. Indeed, operating leverage is a measure of the degree to which operating profits are sensitive to changes in sales volume. Thus, if demand is sensitive to small price changes—that is, elastic—then increases in sales volume due to small price changes may lead to greater changes in operating profits if the DOL is greater than one.

For example, assume a firm had sales of 100,000 units last period with an operating profit of $50,000. In the current period, sales increased 20 percent to 120,000 units and operating profits increased 40 percent to $70,000. Thus DOL = 40 percent/20 percent = 2.0. Therefore, from the base sales level of 100,000 units, for every 1 percent change in sales, there will be a 2 percent change in operating profits *in the same direction as the sales change.* This magnification of changes in sales volume on profits occurs for either increases or decreases in sales so long as the cost structure (variable costs per unit and fixed costs) and price remain unchanged. We can compute DOL for any level of sales using

$$DOL = \frac{\text{Dollar contribution at sales volume Q}}{\text{Dollar operating profits at sales volume Q}}$$

(11.2)

Testing Pricing Alternatives

Whenever management considers changing prices it should consider the reactions of the market to the proposed changes. Moreover, the effect of any price change on volume, revenues, costs, contributions, and operating profits must be explicitly evaluated. A price change has several effects on revenues. The concept of demand price elasticity indicates that if demand is elastic, reducing prices will lead to increased revenues, and if demand is inelastic, increasing prices will lead to increased revenues. However, as discussed in Chapter 7, price elasticity is difficult to know prior to the price change, and the decision maker likely will not have sufficient information to decide whether to change price and, if so, in which direction.

Any change in revenues resulting from a price change is the result of two events that differ depending on whether price is decreased or increased. For a price decrease, the first event is that prior saleable units continue to be sold, but at a lower price and lower contribution margin. Thus, initially, losses in revenues and contributions occur. Then, because the price has been reduced, additional units are sold resulting in a gain in revenues and contributions. Only when the gain in revenues from selling additional units exceeds the loss in revenues incurred from reducing the price of saleable units can profits be greater than prior to the price reduction decision. Thus *price reductions immediately result in a loss of revenues and in profits* (assuming no change in the firm's cost structure [DOL]). The analytical question then is how many additional units need to be sold before the firm's profits will be equal to the level of profits prior to the price reduction decision.

Alternatively, for a price increase, an initial gain in revenues and in contributions occurs. Then, because the price has been increased, some previously saleable units will not be sold resulting in a loss in revenues and contributions. Only if the gain in revenues from selling the marked-up units exceeds the loss in revenues incurred from not selling higher-priced units can profits be greater than prior to the

TABLE 11.1 Analyzing Price Alternatives

	No Price Change	Decrease Price 6.2%	Increase Price 7%
Price per unit	$ 20.00	$ 18.76	$ 21.40
Variable costs per unit	$ 15.00	$ 15.00	$ 15.00
Contribution per unit	$ 5.00	$ 3.76	$ 6.40
PV	0.25	0.20	0.30
Fixed costs	$ 2,000,000	$ 2,000,000	$ 2,000,000
Desired profit	$10,000,000	$10,000,000	$10,000,000
Required sales revenue*	$48,000,000	$60,000,000	$40,000,000
Required unit volume#	2,400,000	3,200,000	1,870,000
		(+33%)	(−22%)

*Required sales revenue = (desired profit + fixed costs)/PV.
#Required unit volume = required sales revenue/price.

price increase decision. Thus *price increases immediately result in a gain of revenues and profits.* The analytical question then is how many units can the firm afford not to sell before profits become equal to the level of profits prior to the price increase decision.

Because the firm is unlikely to know the price elasticity of demand prior to making a price change decision, it cannot forecast the effect on sales or profits of a price change. Yet it is important to know the volume effect of a price change prior to making any price change decision. Using the concepts of operating leverage and the PV ratio, it is possible to analyze the implications of changing prices. To illustrate the analysis, the data in Table 11.1 show the result of evaluating three pricing alternatives: (1) keep price at $20.00 per unit; (2) decrease price by 6.2 percent to $18.76 per unit; (3) increase price by 7 percent to $21.40 per unit.

The data in Table 11.1 indicate that if the firm has a desired profit objective of $10 million, changing price requires different levels of volume and sales revenue because the PV changes. Thus if the price reduction alternative is being considered in order to penetrate a new market, the relevant research question is whether the price reduction can generate additional volume by 33 percent [(3,200,000 − 2,400,000)/2,400,000]. On the other hand, a contemplated price increase of 7 percent must not result in a decline in volume of more than 22 percent [(1,870,000 − 2,400,000)/2,400,000]. Obviously, if the price reduction results in a volume increase of more than 33 percent, the firm would be in a better profit position after the price reduction, if production capacity is available. Or, if the price increase leads to a volume decrease of less than 22 percent, the firm would be more profitable after the price increase.

Computing Necessary Volume Changes

The volume changes necessary to maintain a level of profitability for any given PV value can be determined. Tables 11.2 and 11.3 give the percent volume changes necessary to offset different percent price changes. For example, suppose that a firm is considering raising price by 7 percent and its current PV ratio is 0.30. Table 11.2 indicates that as long as volume does not decline more than 19 percent, the firm's profitability will be enhanced. Similarly, if the firm was considering a 9 percent price decrease, then Table 11.3 indicates that volume must increase at least by 43 percent to maintain the same level of profitability as before the price change.

In general, for a price decrease, the necessary volume increase before profitability is enhanced is given by

$$\text{Volume increase (\%)} = \left(\frac{x}{\text{PV}-x}\right)100 \qquad \textbf{(11.3)}$$

where x is the percentage price decrease expressed as a decimal.

Similarly, for a price increase, the permissible volume decrease before profitability is harmed is given by

$$\text{Volume decrease (\%)} = \left(\frac{x}{\text{PV}+x}\right)100 \qquad \textbf{(11.4)}$$

where x is the percentage price increase expressed as a decimal.

To illustrate these two formulas consider the volume changes necessary for a 9 percent price decrease, and then for a 9 percent price increase. Further, assume the current PV ratio is 0.30. From Equation 11.3, the percentage volume increase is

$$\text{Volume increase (\%)} = \left(\frac{0.09}{0.30 - 0.09}\right)100 =$$

$$\left(\frac{0.09}{0.21}\right)100 = 42.86\%$$

From Equation 11.4, the percentage volume decrease is

$$\text{Volume decrease (\%)} = \left(\frac{0.09}{0.30 + 0.09}\right)100 =$$

$$\left(\frac{0.09}{0.39}\right)100 = 23.08\%$$

TABLE 11.2   **Permissible Maximum Volume Decrease to Offset Price Increase**

Price Increase %	PV Ratio						
	.10	.15	.20	.25	.30	.35	.40
1	9.09	6.25	4.76	3.85	3.23	2.77	2.44
2	16.67	11.76	9.09	7.41	6.25	5.41	4.76
3	23.08	16.67	13.04	10.71	9.09	7.89	6.98
4	28.57	21.05	16.67	13.79	11.76	10.26	9.09
5	33.33	25.00	20.00	16.67	14.29	12.50	11.11
6	37.50	28.57	23.08	19.35	16.67	14.63	13.04
7	41.18	31.82	25.93	21.88	18.92	16.67	14.89
10	50.00	40.00	33.33	28.57	25.00	22.22	20.00
15	60.00	50.00	42.86	37.50	33.33	30.00	27.27
20	66.67	57.14	50.00	44.44	40.00	36.36	33.33
25	71.43	62.50	55.56	50.00	45.45	41.67	38.46
30	75.00	66.67	60.00	54.55	50.00	46.15	42.86
35			63.64	58.33	53.85	50.00	46.67
40			66.67	61.54	57.14	53.33	50.00
45				64.29	60.00	56.25	52.94
50				66.67	62.50	58.82	55.56

Price Increase %	PV Ratio						
	.45	.50	.55	.60	.65	.70	.75	.80
1	2.17	1.96	1.79	1.64	1.52	1.41	1.32	1.23
2	4.26	3.85	3.51	3.23	2.99	2.78	2.60	2.44
3	6.25	5.67	5.17	4.76	4.41	4.11	3.85	3.61
4	8.16	7.41	6.78	6.25	5.80	5.41	5.06	4.76
5	10.00	9.09	8.33	7.69	7.14	6.67	6.25	5.88
6	11.76	10.71	9.84	9.09	8.45	7.89	7.41	6.98
7	13.46	12.28	11.29	10.45	9.72	9.09	8.54	8.05
10	18.18	16.67	15.38	14.29	13.33	12.50	11.76	11.11
15	25.00	23.08	21.43	20.00	18.75	17.65	16.67	15.79
20	30.77	28.57	26.67	25.00	23.53	22.22	21.05	20.00
25	35.71	33.33	31.25	29.41	27.78	26.32	25.00	23.81
30	40.00	37.50	35.29	33.33	31.58	30.00	28.57	27.27
35	43.75	41.18	38.89	36.84	35.00	33.33	31.82	30.43
40	47.06	44.44	42.11	40.00	38.10	36.36	34.78	33.33
45	50.00	47.37	45.00	42.86	40.91	39.13	37.50	36.00
50	52.63	50.00	47.62	45.45	43.48	41.67	40.00	38.46

TABLE 11.3 Minimum Volume Increase Required for Price Decrease

Price Decrease %	PV Ratio .10	.15	.20	.25	.30	.35	.40
1	11.11	7.14	5.26	4.17	3.45	2.94	2.56
2	25.00	15.38	11.11	8.70	7.14	6.06	5.26
3	42.90	25.00	17.65	13.60	11.11	9.38	8.11
4	66.67	36.36	25.00	19.05	15.38	12.90	11.11
5	100.00	50.00	33.33	25.00	20.00	16.67	14.29
6	150.00	66.67	42.86	31.58	25.00	20.69	17.65
7	233.33	87.50	53.85	38.89	30.43	25.00	21.21
8	400.00	114.29	66.67	47.06	36.36	29.63	25.00
9	900.00	150.00	81.82	56.25	42.86	34.62	29.03
10	∞	200.00	100.00	66.67	50.00	40.00	33.33
15		∞	300.00	150.00	100.00	75.00	60.00
20			∞	400.00	200.00	133.33	100.00
25				∞	500.00	250.00	166.67
30					∞	600.00	300.00
35						∞	700.00
40							∞

Price Decrease %	PV Ratio .45	.50	.55	.60	.65	.70	.75	.80
1	2.27	2.04	1.85	1.69	1.56	1.45	1.35	1.27
2	4.65	4.17	3.77	3.45	3.17	2.94	2.74	2.56
3	7.14	6.38	5.77	5.26	4.84	4.48	4.17	3.90
4	9.76	8.70	7.84	7.14	6.56	6.06	5.63	5.26
5	12.50	11.11	10.00	9.09	8.33	7.69	7.14	6.67
6	15.38	13.64	12.24	11.11	10.17	9.38	8.70	8.11
7	18.42	16.28	14.58	13.21	12.07	11.11	10.29	9.59
8	21.62	19.05	17.02	15.38	14.04	12.90	11.94	11.11
9	25.00	21.95	19.57	17.65	16.07	14.75	13.64	12.68
10	28.57	25.00	22.22	20.00	18.18	16.67	15.38	12.50
15	50.00	42.86	37.50	33.33	30.00	27.27	25.00	23.08
20	80.00	66.67	57.14	50.00	44.44	40.00	36.36	33.33
25	125.00	100.00	83.33	71.43	62.50	55.56	50.00	45.45
30	200.00	150.00	120.00	100.00	85.71	75.00	66.67	60.00
35	350.00	233.33	175.00	140.00	116.67	100.00	87.50	77.77
40	800.00	400.00	266.67	200.00	160.00	133.33	114.29	100.00

Computing Required Price Elasticities

Once an alternative price proposal has been evaluated according to the volume changes necessary to enhance profitability, implied price elasticities can be computed. Recall that price elasticity of demand is defined as the percentage change in volume relative to a percentage change in price. From the example of Table 11.1, we have demonstrated that a proposed price decrease of 6.2 percent required a minimum volume increase of 33 percent before profits could be increased, if the current PV ratio is 0.25. This condition gives us the following required price elasticity of demand:

$$E_d = \frac{33\%}{-6.2\%} = -5.32$$

A price elasticity of demand of -5.32 indicates that demand must be quite elastic before the price reduction can be profitable. If management does not believe that demand is sufficiently price elastic, then the alternative of reducing price by 6.2 percent is not economically justified.

Similarly, the alternative of increasing price by 7 percent produces a required price elasticity of

$$E_d = \frac{-22\%}{7\%} = -3.14$$

When evaluating a price increase, it is important to remember that the estimated volume decrease is the maximum permissible if profits are to be enhanced. Hence, the actual price elasticity must be less elastic than the computed -3.14. For example, if management believes that price elasticity of demand is around -2, then the price increase of 7 percent will be profitable, but a price decrease of 6.2 percent will harm profits. Conversely, if management believes that price elasticity of demand is around -6, then the price decrease of 6.2 percent will enhance profits.

Financial Leverage

As defined previously, financial leverage refers to the use of debt in financing a firm. Interest on debt that is sold to obtain financing normally is a fixed financial charge that must be paid regardless of the level of the firm's earnings. The greater the use of debt, the greater the financial leverage and the more that fixed financial costs are added to fixed operating costs to enhance the impact of changes in sales volume. The degree of financial leverage (DFL) is defined as the ratio of the change in operating profits before interest and taxes relative to the change in operating profits before taxes:

$$DFL =$$

$$\frac{\%\ \text{change in operating profits before interest and tax}}{\%\ \text{change in operating profits before tax}}$$

or

$$DFL = \frac{\Delta OP}{OP} \div \frac{\Delta OPBT}{OPBT} \qquad \textbf{(11.5)}$$

where

ΔOP = change in operating profits before interest and taxes

OP = operating profits in the previous period (before interest and taxes)

$\Delta OPBT$ = change in operating profits before taxes (after interest)

$OPBT$ = operating profits before taxes (after interest) in the previous period

As with operating leverage it is also possible to compute DFL for any level of operating profits using

$$DFL = \frac{OP}{OP - iD} \qquad \textbf{(11-6)}$$

where

i = the interest rate on the debt

D = the amount of debt

Combined Leverage

When financial leverage is combined with operating leverage, the effect of a change in sales volume on earnings per share is magnified. Combining Equations 11.1 and 11.5 produces an expression for the degree of combined leverage DCL:

$$DCL = DOL \times DFL$$

or

$$DCL = \frac{(P - VC)Q}{OP} \times \frac{OP}{OP - iD}$$

giving

$$DCL = \frac{(P - VC)Q}{OP - iD} \qquad \textbf{(11. 7)}$$

Requirements for Successful Price Reduction Strategies

For a given cost structure and financial structure, reducing price to increase volume and profits may be quite difficult. Indeed, as shown in Table 11.3, a low contribution margin product (low PV ratio) must be capable of generating large increases in volume for even small price reductions. Thus two minimum requirements are necessary for a price reduction strategy to be profitable: (1) the product must have a relatively large contribution margin prior to the price reduction, and (2) the product-market must be in a growth situation. Essentially, this second requirement means that demand for the product or service must be price elastic to obtain proportionally larger increases in sales volume due to the price reduction and that the product should be in its growth stage of the product life cycle. For a price reduction strategy to be both profitable and competitively advantageous, a third requirement is that its combined leverage should be greater than its competitors'. Pricing decisions provide maximum leverage when they capitalize on existing competitive advantages.

Equal Profit Analysis

As we have indicated, pricing managers do not know the price elasticity of demand prior to deciding whether to change price. Moreover, we know price elasticity differs according to the direction of a price change—increase or decrease—and the magnitude of the price change. However, managers and salespeople usually have a general sense of the likely demand response to a proposed price change. Thus, we can extend the analysis developed above to consider multiple price changes, including increases and decreases simultaneously. In Table 11.4, we extend the analysis from Table 11.1 to seven pricing alternatives ranging from a 15 percent price increase to a 15 percent price decrease. Because we are assuming no change in the firm's operating structure, variable costs remain constant at $15 per unit and fixed costs remain at $2 million per period. Further, we

TABLE 11.4 **Equal Profit Analysis**

Price Change (%)	Unit Price	Unit Variable Cost	Unit Contribution	Required Volume (millions)	Total Contribution (millions)	Required Elasticity
15	$23	$15	$8	1.50	$12	−2.50
10	$22	$15	$7	1.71	$12	−2.88
5	$21	$15	$6	2.00	$12	−3.33
0	$20	$15	$5	2.40	$12	—
−5	$19	$15	$4	3.00	$12	−5.00
−10	$18	$15	$3	4.00	$12	−6.67
−15	$17	$15	$2	6.00	$12	−10.00

continue the assumption that desired profits equal $10 million. Therefore, total contributions remain constant at $12 million. Using Tables 11.2 and 11.3 or Equations 11.3 and 11.4, we can compute the required sales volume necessary to reach contributions of $12 million at any pricing alternative.

For any price change, the required sales volume is the minimum amount necessary to meet the contribution target. By comparing the sales volume change necessary (for price decreases) or permissible (for price increases) to the no price change alternative, the required price elasticity of demand can also be computed. In the example, for any price increase, demand can be elastic as long as it is not more elastic than shown for a specific price increase. However, for price decreases, price elasticity must not be less price elastic than the computed elasticities shown for a specific price decrease.[1] Thus the analysis gives the decision maker elasticity boundaries for the price change to at least leave the firm in a profit position that is no worse than if price were not changed.

The required volumes can be graphed against price to produce an equal profit curve as shown in Figure 11.1. This curve shows the minimum volumes necessary at each price to obtain the target profit, $10 million. For any price–volume point below this curve, actual profits will be less than the $10 million target. Now suppose that demand is either less or more elastic than the equal profit curve. That is, if demand

[1]Note that this analysis includes costs because the objective is to analyze the profit impact of a proposed price change. The conventional wisdom of raising price if demand is inelastic and reducing price if demand is elastic refers to the effect on revenues only. Therefore, this conventional wisdom may be misleading unless the analysis correctly confirms that profitability is affected similarly to revenues, which, as the example demonstrates, may not be true.

FIGURE 11.1
Equal Profit Curve

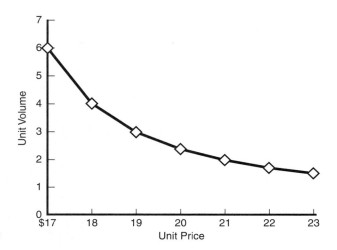

is less elastic than the equal profits curve, then profits change more for a given percentage change in price than does sales volume. When demand is less elastic than the equal profits curve, reducing price likely will lead to a sales volume that produces a profit level below the target. That is, sales likely will be less than required to maintain profitability. On the other hand, a price increase would likely lead to a sales decrease less than permissible and profits would be greater than the target. When demand is more elastic than the equal profits curve, reducing price likely would lead to profits greater than the target, and raising price would be less profitable than not changing price.

Figures 11.2 and 11.3 show two other possibilities with interesting implications. Figure 11.2 indicates that the demand curve lies above the equal profit curve at all prices except the current $20 price, suggesting that either a price increase or a price decrease would lead to a higher level of profits. Should the firm raise or lower its price? Actually, what the demand curve reflects is the likelihood that there are at least two different price segments—a low-price segment and a high-price segment. Thus, the firm should consider modifying the product to produce a line of two or three different models, each having different features and offering different levels of quality. Although not as attractive as the situation in Figure 11.2, the situation in Figure 11.3 also suggests that there are multiple price segments, but that the current product is not as attractive to either the low-price or

FIGURE 11.2
**Demand above Profit
Curve at All Prices**

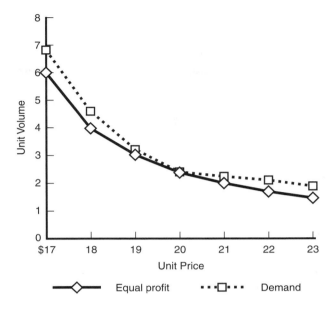

FIGURE 11.3
**Demand below Profit
Curve at All Prices**

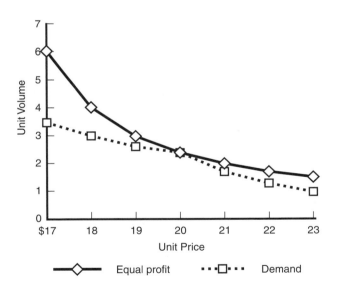

high-price segment. As before, appropriate adjustments to
the product to develop a more appealing low-price model
and a high-price model might overcome the current difficulty in which any price change is unprofitable.

Extensions to the Analysis

Up to this point in this chapter, we have been assuming that the firm produces and sells a single product. That is, the elements of profitability are the product's price, variable costs per unit, and fixed costs per period. We have also assumed that the firm's cost structure remains constant—that is, that there are no changes in unit variable costs or in fixed costs. Thus operating leverage does not change, and analysis can concentrate on the profit impact of a price-induced volume change. Now we will relax these assumptions to show how to adapt the analysis for these new situations.

Change in Unit Variable Costs

Assume that a volume increase due to a price reduction leads to a decline in unit variable costs. In our example from Table 11.1, let unit variable costs decline by $0.50 due to the 6.2 percent price reduction. As shown in Table 11.1, the price reduction leads to a decline in margin by $1.24. However, the 50-cent decline in unit variable costs effectively is an increase in margin. Therefore, the net change in margin is $-$0.74$. To determine the required volume increase to maintain the same level of profits, we use

$$\frac{-\text{net change in margin}}{(\text{original margin} + \text{net change in margin})}$$

$$\frac{-(-\$0.74)}{(\$5.00 - 0.74)} = 0.1737 \tag{11.8}$$

Therefore, if the volume increase reduces variable costs by $0.50 per unit, then sales volume must increase by 17.37 percent to overcome the reduction in the margin due to the price reduction.

Change in Fixed Costs

Assume fixed costs can be reduced by 50 percent to partially compensate for the margin loss due to the price decrease. The target profit plus fixed costs would become $11 million. As shown in Table 11.1, the new PV ratio is 0.20. Therefore, the required sales revenue is

$$\frac{\$11,000,000}{0.20} = \$55,000,000$$

The required unit sales volume is

$$\frac{\$55,000,000}{\$18.76} = 2,931,770$$

Finally, the required percentage sales volume increase is

$$\frac{2,931,770}{2,400,000} = 1.22$$

Thus, sales volume must increase by 22 percent to offset a 6.2 percent price decrease with a reduction in fixed costs of $1 million.

Responding to a Competitive Price Decrease

When a competitor reduces its price, a relevant question is how much of a sales decline can be accepted if we do not match the price reduction. To develop the analysis for this question assume that a competitor has decreased price by $0.80 on a product similar to ours. Further assume that our current contribution margin is $4.78. To determine how much we can afford to let sales volume decline before matching the price reduction, we use

$$\frac{\$ \text{ price change}}{\text{current margin}} = \frac{\$0.80}{\$4.78} = 0.167$$

If we expect sales volume to decline more than 16.7 percent, then we need to consider matching the competitor's price reduction. If sales are expected to decline less than 16.7 percent, then it is more profitable not to match the price reduction.

The Effect Of The Monetary Sales Mix

In a multiple product business, different products produce different profit volumes. Even the shirt store example in Chapter 10 could have a product mix. The retailer could sell ties with a PV of 0.10, shirts with a PV of 0.20, sweaters with a PV 0.40, and pants with a PV of 0.30. With a PV for ties of 0.10, the retailer would have to sell twice as many ties as shirts to gross the same contribution as shirts alone. But sales of only half as many sweaters as shirts would be required to generate the original contribution. Therefore, depending on the relative product sales mix, it would be possible to generate greater profits on fewer sales or smaller profits on more sales.

Within a multiproduct firm, each product has a different cost structure, including variable and fixed costs, different unit prices, different volume, and, of course, different revenues. These important factors not only are different, but they are changing. And as developed in Chapter 10, the conventional break-even chart is not dynamic and assumes a single-product situation. In multiproduct firms, it is important to emphasize achieving the maximum amount of contribution revenue for each product instead of attempting to maximize sales revenue. Each product offering faces different competition, has a different demand elasticity, and perhaps depends for its sales, at least in part, on the sales of the other products in the line.

The issue of managing the prices and profitability of the firm's product line is extremely important. Consider the prices of a major hotel chain. The same room in a given hotel can generate multiple rates: the regular rate (commonly referred to as the rack rate), a corporate rate that represents a discount for business travelers, a senior citizen rate, a weekend rate, single versus double rates, a group rate, and a conference rate, to name a few. Over time, the hotel's occupancy rate expressed as a percentage of rooms sold per night had increased from 68 percent to 75 percent. Yet despite increases in prices that more than covered the increases in costs, and increasing sales volume, profitability was declining.

After examining the problem, the hotel's management discovered that they were selling fewer and fewer rooms at the full rack rate while increasing sales, and therefore occupancy, of rooms at discounted rates that were as much as 50 percent off the full rack rate. As a result, the composite weighted PV ratio had significantly declined, indicating this decline in relative profitability. Furthermore, buyers' perceptions of prices were important: The price increases primarily had been at the full rack rate, creating a greater and more perceptible difference between, for example, the full rate and the corporate rate. More and more guests were noticing this widening price difference and were requesting and receiving the lower rates.

The analysis as developed thus far must now be modified to consider relative differences in cost structure, volume generated, and profit contribution by each product in the line. Each product has a different PV value and different expected monetary sales volume as a percentage of the line's total monetary volume. In multiple-product situations, the PV is determined by weighing the PV of each product by the percentage of the total monetary volume for all products in the line. To illustrate how we can adapt the PV analysis to the multiproduct firm, consider the data given in Table 11.5.

As the data show, each product has a different PV value and different planned volumes as a percentage of the firm's total volume. The problem now is to integrate these PVs and planned volumes to determine the appropriate PV for the analysis. In multiple-product problems the PV is determined by weighting the PV of each product by the percentage of the total monetary volume for all products. The appropriate calculations for this example are shown in Table 11.6.

The composite PV is used to determine the break-even point.

$$\text{BES} = \frac{\text{fixed costs}}{\text{PV}} = \frac{\$500,000}{0.25} = \$2,000,000$$

For a total sales volume of $4 million, operating profits are

$$\text{Profit} = (\text{sales} \times \text{PV}) - \text{fixed costs}$$

$$\text{Profit} = (\$4,000,000 \times 0.25) - \$500,000 = \$500,000$$

Note that because there are common fixed costs, we cannot determine the unique break-even point for each product. Rather, we can only determine the break-even point assuming the products are sold simultaneously.

What happens if the volume mix of the three products changes? To illustrate, assume the data of Table 11.5 change

TABLE 11.5
Initial Product Mix Data

Product	PV	Percentage of Total Monetary Volume (Revenue)
A	0.40	40
B	0.20	30
C	0.10	30

TABLE 11.6
Initial Product Mix PV Ratio

(1) Product	(2) PV	(3) Proportion of Total Monetary Volume	(4) Weighted PV (2) × (3)
A	0.40	0.40	0.16
B	0.20	0.20	0.06
C	0.10	0.30	0.03
Composite PV			0.25

to the relationships shown in Table 11.7. Table 11.8 shows the development of the composite PV. For a composite PV of 0.21, the new break-even point is

$$\text{BES} = \frac{\$500{,}000}{0.21} = \$2{,}380{,}950$$

For a total sales volume of $4,000,000, profits are

$$\text{Profit} = (\$4{,}000{,}000 \times 0.21) - \$500{,}000 = \$340{,}000$$

Thus, profits now are 68 percent of the original profit level.

To determine the new total sales volume required to return profits to $500,000, we compute

$$\text{Sales} = \frac{\text{desired profit} + \text{fixed costs}}{\text{PV}}$$

$$\text{Sales} = \frac{\$500{,}000 + \$500{,}000}{0.21} = \$4{,}761{,}905$$

Or, total sales must increase by 19 percent to regain the original profit level if the dollar sales volume mix shifts as indicated in Table 11.7.

When a shift in dollar sales mix results in a poorer PV, management frequently attempts to recover the profit level by an across-the-board increase in prices. Although the effect of this increase in prices helps to restore the original PV, this pricing reaction could lead to a further decline in profits. This deterioration of profits may occur because management has attempted to force the external factors of competition

TABLE 11.7
Revised Product Mix Data

Product	PV	Percentage of Total Monetary Volume (Revenue)
A	0.40	20
B	0.20	50
C	0.10	30

TABLE 11.8
Revised Product Mix PV Ratio

(1) Product	(2) PV	(3) Proportion of Total Monetary Volume	(4) Weighted PV (2) × (3)
A	0.40	0.20	0.08
B	0.20	0.50	0.10
C	0.10	0.30	0.03
Composite PV			0.21

TABLE 11.9 **Implications of Price Changes for Product Line**

Product	PV₁	PV₂	Implications
A	0.40	0.35	14.3 % volume gain needed
B	0.20	0.20	No change in volume
C	0.10	0.15	33.3% volume loss permissible

and demand to support the internal need for profit. When an across-the-board increase in prices leads to a substantial decrease in sales volume, it is quite possible that the remedy has aggravated the problem.

Instead of using an across-the-board price increase, suppose the price of product A is decreased by 5 percent and the price of C is raised by 5 percent. The data in Table 11.9 show the implications of these changes based on the profit volume Tables 11.2 and 11.3. Overcoming the price reduction for A requires an increase in sales volume of 14.3 percent, whereas C's profitability would not be harmed until sales volume declined by more than 33.3 percent. Thus, if sales of A increased by 20 percent and sales of C fell by 20 percent, overall profitability would have been improved with these selective price changes.

When there are differences in the PVs among products in a line, a revision in the product selling mix (the monetary sales mix) may be more effective than increasing prices. That is, by shifting emphasis to those products with relatively higher PVs, a firm has an opportunity to recover its profit position. Hence profit at any sales level is a function of prices, volume, costs, and the monetary sales mix. See Box 11.2 for another example of a multiple product situation.

Pricing with Scarce Resources

At various times, businesspeople have faced unexpected economic problems: shortages of critical materials, uncontrollable inflation even during a recession, and a lack of sufficient new capital to overcome material shortages. During 1973 and 1974 the world demand for materials overtook supply with sudden shortages of metals, wood products, and agricultural products.[2] "Typical of the problems faced by industry were those of Del Monte where the company faced

[2]"The 1970's: A Second Look," *Business Week* (September 14, 1974), 50–162.

SOURCES OF PROFITS FOR THEATER OWNERS

BOX 11.2

Movie theater owners don't make all of their profits from the dollars you pay at the box office. Indeed, over half of the money that they receive from admissions is returned to movie producers and distributors. In fact, without concession stands it would be difficult for theaters to remain in business. Let's see how movie theaters make their profits.

Popcorn accounts for about 40 percent of all concession revenues. Soft drinks bring in another 40 percent, and candy and other items garner the remaining revenues from concessions. Applying the concepts from profit analysis discussed in Chapter 11 for multiple products, we can get some feel for the relative profitability of concession sales. The direct variable costs of popcorn, oil, salt, and containers are about 10 percent of the selling price. That is the profit–volume ratio (PV ratio) for popcorn is 0.90 (90 percent of sales). For soft drinks the PV ratio is about 0.80, and for candy the PV ratio is about 0.60. Since popcorn accounts for about 40 percent of concession revenues (dollar sales), then the weighted PV ratio for popcorn is 0.36 (.90 × .40). For soda the weighted PV ratio is .80 × .40, or 0.32; for candy the weighted PV ratio is .60 x .20, or 0.12. Adding these three weighted PVs together we get the composite PV ratio for concessions to be 0.80 [0.36 + 0.32 + 0.12]. This value of 0.80 means that the movie theater is earning 80 cents of every concession sales dollar to help recover the fixed costs and then earn a profit.

Revenues from admissions sales comprise about 80 percent of the theaters' total revenues, while concessions comprise about 20 percent. On average, the theater owners keep about 45 percent of the admission revenues, with the other 55 percent going back to the producers and distributors. Thus, combining the percent of revenues earned by admission (80 percent) with the admissions PV ratio (0.45) produces a weighted PV ratio for admissions

of .36 (0.80 × 0.45). Finally, if we combine the weighted PV ratio for concessions with the percent of total revenues coming from concessions (0.80 × 0.20), the overall weighted PV ratio for concessions is 0.16. Thus, a weighted PV ratio of 0.36 for admissions and 0.16 for concessions produces an overall weighted profit–volume ratio for movie theaters of 0.52. Thus, on average, approximately 52 cents of each revenue dollar earned by the movie theater goes first to recover fixed costs and then to the theater's profits. The key point to note here is that the relatively large profit margin earned on concessions allows the theater owner to set a more modest profit margin, and, therefore, price on the admission. Yet, overall, a profit margin of 52 percent before paying salaries, rent, utilities, taxes, and other fixed expenses does not leave the theater owners with a very large profit margin. What we need to ask is what the market characteristics are that allow these differential profit margins on admissions versus concessions to exist?

Movie theaters can sell popcorn and soft drinks at such high markups because customers are truly a captive audience after buying their tickets. Movie fans will not choose to see a different film simply to get lower prices at the concession stand, but if the cost of admission increased dramatically, patrons might forgo snacking during the movie. Consequently, theater owners would like to keep ticket prices relatively stable while enticing as many customers as possible into visiting the concession stand. Consumers have many types of entertainment alternatives, including multiple movie theaters in most markets, which helps to explain why the profit margin on movie tickets is not high: If it were too high, people would simply opt for another alternative (such as renting films and watching them at home).

Source: "For Theater Owners, Many Flavors of Profit," The New York Times (November 5, 1983), 17.

shortages of fruits and vegetables, glass for jars, tinplate for cans, fibreboard for boxes, and labels for the jars and cans."[3] During the 1990s many firms faced shortages of productive capacity and skilled labor. In 2000, shortages of certain petroleum products occurred.

The problem of scarce resources has led some companies to prune their product lines by eliminating slow-moving and low-margin products. However, the elimination of products on the basis of the size of margin is primarily a defensive strategy that ignores the role of price. When a firm is operating at or near full capacity, or when key resources are scarce, the firm must determine how scarce resources can be allocated to its products so as to maximize contribution to fixed costs and profits.

The Problem of Common Resources[4]

The multiproduct firm typically manufactures various product lines using joint or common resources—the same plant and equipment, for instance, as well as research and development facilities. The same selling, administrative, and warehousing facilities may be used in the production and sale of the various products. Moreover, a critical or scarce resource may be used in production.

Because product prices must reflect the competitive situation and the reactions of buyers as well as costs and corporate objectives, not all products make the same use of resources per dollar of revenue or per dollar of out-of-pocket costs. However, when determining prices, the degree to which products (or special orders) use available facilities (capacity) and consume available resources is important. Otherwise, the firm may be short of the resources necessary to obtain the desired level of contribution.

Indeed, pricing special orders or composing the product line strictly on contribution (gross margin) may result in the exhaustion of available resources without obtaining the target contribution. Table 11.10A provides the basic price and cost data for a product line. Table 11.10B provides the demand forecasts, cost estimates, and required supply of a common resource material to meet the demand forecast. As

---

[3]"The Two-Way Squeeze on New Products," *Business Week* (August 10, 1974), 130–132.

[4]Material in this section is adopted from Kent B. Monroe and Andris A. Zoltners, "Pricing the Product Line during Periods of Scarcity," *Journal of Marketing 43* (Summer 1979), 49–59.

TABLE 11.10 **Product-Line Contribution Analysis**

	Product			
	A	B	C	Total
A. Unit Data				
1. Price	$ 2.20	$ 3.00	$ 4.00	
Variable costs:				
2. Direct labor	$ 1.20	$ 0.70	$ 0.60	
3. Direct materials	0.41	1.54	2.40	
4. Total	$ 1.61	$ 2.24	$ 3.00	
5. Contribution (1–4)	$ 0.59	$ 0.76	$ 1.00	
B. Data for planning period				
6. Demand (units)	6,200	8,100	5,000	
7. Revenue (1 × 6)	$13,640	$24,300	$20,000	$57,940
8. Direct labor (2 × 6)	$ 7,440	$ 5,670	$ 3,000	$16,110
9. Direct materials (3 × 6)	$ 2,542	$12,474	$12,000	$27,016
10. Contribution (5 × 6)	$ 3,658	$ 6,156	$ 5,000	$14,814
11. Tons of material required	500	2,500	2,400	5,400
12. Units per ton (6 ÷ 11)	12.4	3.24	2.083	
13. Tons per unit (11 ÷ 6)	0.081	0.309	0.480	

shown in Table 11.10A, product C contributes $1.00 per unit sold to cover fixed expenses and profits. This unit contribution by product C is $0.24 larger than B's unit contribution, and $0.41 larger than A's unit contribution. However, in Table 11.10B, because of total expected demand, the total dollar contribution is larger for product B, with product C ranked second, and product A ranked third.

In this illustration, two common resources—labor and material—are required to produce the three products. However, the mix of labor and material required to produce a unit of each product is quite different. Indeed, product A is a relatively labor-intensive product since 74.5 percent of its direct variable costs derive from labor. However, products B and C owe only 32.3 and 20 percent, respectively, of their direct costs to labor. Hence, products B and C require much more material input.

Now suppose that this common material resource currently is scarce and the firm has been advised that it can acquire no more than 3,000 tons during the planning period. Furthermore, the supply of this material is expected to be below demand for at least several years. The firm must now consider the alternatives of reducing the production of each product, eliminating a product and reducing the production of the other products, or some reasonable combination of these two choices. Clearly, the firm has a problem of allocating the scarce resource to its products in the product line.

Resource Allocation Criteria

A number of criteria have been used to make this decision. Some firms allocate the scarce resource according to the *unit contributions* (gross margin) of each product. Since product C has the largest unit contribution, the first 2,400 tons would be allocated to C and the remaining 600 tons to B. As Table 11.11 shows, the total contribution for the planning period would be $6,477, or $8,337 less than total contributions with no scarce resource.

Other firms make their allocations on the basis of *total contributions*. Since product B has the largest total contribution, product B would be allocated 2,500 tons. Product C would be allocated 500 tons because its total contribution is second in amount for the planning period. The total period contribution under this plan improves to $7,197, but still is $7,617 less than period contributions with no scarce resource. If the firm adopted either of these two plans, it would be necessary to eliminate product A from the line.

TABLE 11.11   Alternative Resource Allocations

Criterion	Resource Units	Units Produced	Total Contribution
Contribution per unit:			
A	0	0	$ –0–
B	600	1,944	$1,477
C	2,400	5,000	5,000
			$6,477
Total contribution:			
A	0	0	$ –0–
B	2,500	8,100	6,156
C	500	1,041	1,041
			$7,197
Proportion of resources required:			
A	270	3,348	$1,975
B	1,410	4,568	3,472
C	1,320	2,750	2,750
			$8,197

A third alternative would be to allocate the scarce material *proportionately on the basis of resource requirements.* Since product A requires 500/5,400 or 9 percent of the scarce resource if no constraints are present, it would be allocated 9 percent or 270 tons of material. The material would be allocated to B and C in similar fashion and total period contribution improves to $8,197.

As is apparent from Table 11.12, the contribution or margin criteria are inferior to the third allocation criterion. Moreover, contribution to overhead and profits is greater under the third alternative, and it is not necessary to eliminate a product from the line.

As demonstrated, pricing a product line strictly on gross contribution or margin may result in the exhaustion of available resources without the largest contribution to profits being obtained. Essentially, the margin approach does not consider how much of the scarce resource is consumed per unit of output. The data in Table 11.10 demonstrate that a ton of the resource material is necessary to produce 12.4 units of A, 3.24 units of B, and 2.083 units of C. As shown in Table 11.11, a resource allocation method that allocates less resources to C and B and more to A improves contribution. Hence a criterion that utilizes the information on how products consume scarce resources is necessary.

The Contribution per Resource Unit Criterion

As the data in Table 11.10B indicate, 0.081 ton of the scarce resource is required to produce a unit of product A, 0.309 ton to produce a unit of product B, and 0.48 ton to produce a unit of product C. At the current prices (Table 11.10A), each unit of A produces $0.59 contribution. Thus, 0.081 ton of scarce material helps produce a $0.59 contribution. Therefore, a ton of the material produces $0.59/0.081 or $7.28 contribution per ton. Similarly, for product B, the contribution per ton is $0.76/0.309, or $2.46. And for product C, the contribution

TABLE 11.12 Contribution per Resource Unit (CPRU)

	Product		
	A	**B**	**C**
1. Contribution	$3,658	$6,156	$5,000
2. Resource units	500	2,500	2,400
3. CPRU (1 ÷ 2)	$ 7.28	$ 2.46	$ 2.08

per ton is $1.00/0.48 or $2.08. These calculations, which can also be made using the period planning data from Table 11.10B, are shown in Table 11.12.

What the data of Table 11.12 indicate is that the first 500 tons of the scarce material should be allocated to product A since each ton used in A contributes more to profits and to covering fixed costs. This allocation is made because product A has the highest *contribution per resource unit* (ton). When the resource is in limited supply, the decision criterion is to allocate resources to the profit segments with the highest contribution per resource unit (CPRU). Using this decision criterion, Table 11.13 shows that product C, the highest-priced, largest unit margin product, is a candidate for elimination.

This illustration provides a fundamental principle: *When the volume of products that could be sold is greater than the resource capacity to produce them, the largest contribution (and profit) results from providing those products, services and orders that generate the greatest contribution per resource unit used.* The factors that cause the bottleneck could be machines, equipment, time, skilled labor, materials, or cash.

Pricing the Product Line Using CPRU

If the firm wishes to maintain the prices shown in Table 11.10, the best decision is to use the CPRU criterion and suspend production of product C. However, from a marketing viewpoint it may be desirable to keep product C in the line. For example, demand for product C may be expected to grow in the near future or the product may be necessary to complete the product line.

The firm should then consider repricing products C and B to increase their relative CPRUs. Initially, the analytical question is "What should the prices of C and B be so as to equalize contribution?" Table 11.14 shows that the price of C must be $6.49 and the price of B must be $4.49. However,

TABLE 11.13
Resource Allocation
Using CPRU

Product	Resource Units	Units Produced	Total Contribution
A	500	6,200	$3,658
B	2,500	8,100	6,156
C	0	0	–0–
			$9,814

it is unlikely that the original demand forecast will be valid at these prices. Hence a lower production volume would be required, which would reduce some of the firm's demand for the scarce material. A solution technique that incorporates price–volume relationships as well as cost–volume relationships is required.

It should be apparent that further pricing analysis requires the demand curve for each product in the line. One of the approaches described in Chapter 9 may be used to develop estimates of the price–volume relationships. Given the ability to obtain reasonable price–volume estimates for each product, the pricing problem becomes amenable to solution using a computerized technique.

However, management may feel that relatively large price increases are not desirable because of potential loss of customer goodwill, relative competitive prices, and potential government intervention. Such price increases may also dampen long-run demand, particularly if one or more of the products is in the growth stage of its life cycle. The firm may also wish to have wider price differentials to maintain perceptual differences in the product line (see Chapters 5 through 7, 15).

The effect of adjusting the prices may be assessed using the CPRU criterion with a different set of prices. For example, a firm may believe that the prices should be no higher than $5, $5, and $6 respectively; the product manager may feel that these prices are realistic and suitable for both the long-run objectives and environmental considerations of the firm. Total demand at these prices will exceed the firm's production capacity. The solution in Table 11.15 is the best product mix using the CPRU criterion relative to the prices

TABLE 11.14 **Pricing to Equalize CPRU**

	Product	
	B	**C**
1. Desired CPRU	$ 7.28	$ 7.28
2. Total resources required	2,500	2,400
3. Desired contribution (1 × 2)	$18,200	$17,472
4. Variable costs	$18,144	$15,000
5. Total revenue required (3 + 4)	$36,344	$32,472
6. Original demand forecast	8,100	5,000
7. New selling price (5 ÷ 6)	$ 4.49	$ 6.49

TABLE 11.15 **Optimum Price Solution: Resource and Price Constraints**

	Product		
	A	**B**	**C**
1. Price	$ 5.00	$ 5.00	$ 6.00
2. Variable cost	1.61	2.24	3.00
3. Contribution (1 − 2)	$ 3.39	$ 2.76	$ 3.00
4. Demand (units)	3,340	4,900	3,000
5. Units produced	3,400	4,900	2,528
6. Resources required (tons)	274.19	1,512.34	1,213.47
7. Contribution (3 × 5)	$11,526	$ 13,524	$ 7,584
8. CPRU (7 ÷ 6)	$ 42.04	$ 8.94	$ 6.25
Total contribution: $32,634			
Total resources required: 3,000 tons			

stated. In general, the CPRU criterion provides the best solution when there are resource constraints and price ceilings.

Summary

One of the most important lessons of this chapter is that the four elements of profitability—price, costs, volume, and monetary sales mix—are strategically interdependent. Moreover, the analytical techniques developed in this chapter make it clear that there are strategic trade-offs among these four elements. One of the most common trade-offs made is the price–volume relationship; that is, trading a price reduction for increasing volume or market share. However, the profitability analysis procedures developed in this chapter suggest that management should attempt to determine the relative worth of added market share in relation to forgoing short-term profits.

To analyze the trade-off between price and volume, operating leverage is an important concept. For example, Table 11.3 indicates that a firm with a PV ratio (contribution margin) of 0.20 requires a minimum volume increase of 33 percent to offset a 5 percent decrease in price. Another firm with a PV ratio of 0.60 would require only a 9 percent increase in volume to offset a 5 percent decrease in price. Clearly, the second firm gets greater leverage from volume gains than the first firm. A similar assessment should be applied to different products within a product line and across product lines. Different products and different product lines inherently have different cost structures and therefore different possibilities to leverage volume.

As noted, price–volume relationships vary over time. That is, in periods of tight capacity or resource bottlenecks, maximum profit leverage can be attained by emphasizing those products with the highest contribution per *resource unit*. Conversely, when there is excess capacity, maximum profit leverage can be attained by emphasizing those products with the highest contribution margin per *sales dollar*. Thus, pricing and marketing strategies and tactics should be developed to shift product dollar sales mix to preserve profitability in periods of slack capacity and to obtain maximum profit leverage in periods of tight capacity.

The concept of financial leverage indicates that competitive reaction to price reductions to gain volume and market share may differ due to the relative mix of debt to equity financing between competitors. Moreover, combining financial leverage with operating leverage suggests that differences in size, degrees of vertical integration, methods of distribution, and financing will make some competitors more sensitive than others to the price–volume trade-off. This stronger leverage position provides a price competitive advantage that makes a low-price strategy profitable, particularly for products with strong market growth. Clearly, the frequently implied principle that more market share (volume) is better is a pricing myth that needs to be recognized. As suggested in this chapter, specific conditions must be met before a price reduction strategy may be profitable. This chapter has developed the key cost analysis method useful for evaluating pricing alternatives. A contribution approach has the advantage of forcing an analysis of costs in terms of causal factors. Those activities that are directly related to the costs incurred in the production and sale of a product are included as relevant to the cost analysis.

Expanding break-even analysis to include the profit implications of alternative price decisions provides some dynamics to an otherwise static analytical method. This chapter demonstrates how use of the PV ratio can help determine necessary or permissible volume changes for considered price changes. Moreover, since it is difficult to estimate future or prospective price elasticities of demand, the chapter also shows how to compute implied price elasticities for necessary or permissible volume changes. Once management knows the conditions that must prevail before a price alternative will enhance profitability, it is in a position to make the best decision relative to the objectives of the firm and competitive factors.

This chapter has demonstrated the inadequacy of the gross margin criterion for product-mix and pricing decisions when the firm is operating at capacity due to resource constraints. We have shown that the contribution per resource unit is a superior criterion and that pricing decisions may be enhanced using this criterion. The contribution per resource unit criterion is best used when productive capacity is constrained by a bottleneck. Factors that may cause the bottleneck are machines, equipment, time, skilled labor, materials, or cash. Any industry or product line that depends heavily on a single resource would be particularly suited to the use of the CPRU criterion and the analysis outlined in this chapter.

Discussion Questions

1. An electronic equipment manufacturer has been producing 15,000 units of a special electronic component for one of its most important customers for the past three years of a five-year contract. The contract calls for delivery of these parts at $15 each. Direct labor and material costs are $10.50 per unit. Direct fixed costs are $20,000. At the beginning of the fourth year, a new customer requests a one-year contract to purchase 10,000 units of this part at a price of $11 per unit. The manufacturer's controller estimates that production costs at 25,000 units would be about $10.25 per unit, and that total fixed costs would increase to $30,000. Analyze this situation. Be sure to consider all implications of the situation. What action would you recommend?

2. The Justso Manufacturing Company produces and sells five models of an electric drill. The data provided below are for the current year. Common fixed costs are $100,000.

Model					
	A	B	C	D	E
Price per unit	$ 20.00	$22.50	$25.00	$30.00	$35.00
Variable costs per unit	$14.00	$15.00	$16.00	$18.00	$ 20.00
Sales per unit	15,000	20,000	40,000	30,000	20,000

a. Calculate the composite PV for the electric drill product line. Explain the meaning of the composite PV.

b. Assume that prices and variable costs remain the same, but sales for the next year are A, 20,000 units; B, 40,000 units; C, 30,000 units; D, 20,000 units; and E, 15,000 units. Compute a new composite PV ratio.

c. Compare the composite PV ratio for this year to the composite PV ratio for next year. What is the reason for the change? What might be some underlying causes for the situation at the end of next year?

d. The marketing research director has submitted a report to the vice-president of marketing that competitive prices for similar electric drill product lines range from $25 to $75. The report also indicates that customers perceive the Justso product line as lower quality when compared to competitive drills. The vice-president is perplexed because she knows that engineering and performance tests indicate that the Justso line is more durable and performs as well as competitive drills. Can you offer any possible explanation for the customers' perception?

e. Design a new pricing schedule for the electric drill product line. What factors influenced your solution? If the product-selling mix returns to the current-year relationship, what would be the composite PV for the product line? Explain the reasoning you used to set the price differentials between models in the line.

3. When a firm is faced with scarce resources or is operating at productive capacity, what pricing problems may result?

4. What problems are created by simply raising prices when the demand for a firm's output is greater than the firm can supply?

5. Why is the CPRU criterion superior to other criteria when a firm is operating with scarce resources?

6. *a.* When a common resource is used to produce multiple products, what problems result when a firm tries to reprice its product line?

b. Would these problems be similar if the firm added a new product to the line that was produced using a resource common to the product line?

c. Would your answer to part *b* differ if the common resource was not in scarce supply?

7. What information is necessary when repricing a product line under conditions of scarce common resources?

Suggested Readings

Cohen, Marcel: "Pricing Peculiarities of the UK Petrol Market," *Journal of Product & Brand Management Featuring Pricing Strategy & Practice 8*, no. 2 (1999), 153–62.

Dasgupta, Sudipto, and Sheridan Titman: "Pricing Strategy and Financial Policy," *The Review of Financial Studies 11* (Winter 1998), 705–37.

"Learning to Live with Leverage," *Business Week* (November 7, 1988), 138–56.

Mazumdar, Tridib, and Kent B. Monroe: "Using Leverage for Developing Pricing Strategies," *Proceedings,* Summer Educators' Conference, Chicago: American Marketing Association, 1986, 303–08.

Monroe, Kent B., and John T. Mentzer: "Some Necessary Conditions for When Price Reduction Strategies May Be Profitable," *Pricing Strategy & Practice 2,* no. 1 (1994), 11–20.

Monroe, Kent B., and Andris A. Zoltners: "Pricing the Product Line during Periods of Scarcity," *Journal of Marketing 43* (Summer 1979), 49–59.

Smith, Gerald E., and Thomas T. Nagle: "Financial Analysis for Profit-Driven Pricing," *Sloan Management Review 35* (Spring 1994), 71–84.

CHAPTER TWELVE

Marketing Profitability Analysis

One of the least developed areas in profitability analysis is determining the relative contributions of marketing and distribution to the overall profitability of the organization. Moreover, most firms have little understanding of the relative variations in profit contributions by product line, customer account, order, sales territory, or salesperson. Based on the size of most companies' advertising and sales promotion budgets, we might assume that management has information on the relative profitability of marketing expenditures. Because marketing and distribution costs may exceed 50 percent of manufacturers' cost of doing business, we might also expect that managers know the costs of marketing and distribution. Typically, this is not the case, and the marketing effort includes spending inefficiencies that are considered "unavoidable costs of marketing."[1] However, proper costs for pricing and profitability analysis must include all costs that may change when activities are changed or redirected.

Marketing costs may be classified as direct or indirect. As defined in Chapter 10, direct marketing and distribution costs are variable or fixed. Similarly, indirect marketing and distribution costs are variable or fixed. Although it is important to have a correct measure of profitability by product or product line, or by territory or channel, it is vital to

---

[1] See Jagdish N. Sheth and Rajendra S. Sisodia, "Feeling the Heat," *Marketing Management 4* (Fall 1995), 8–23.

understand customer profitability. A value orientation to pricing requires specific attention to managing the value relationship with customers. Indeed, customer profitability management provides the basis for designing marketing efforts to develop a successful customer loyalty program. Thus this chapter also explains customer profitability analysis.

Need for Marketing and Customer Cost Data

According to estimates, from 5 to 15 percent of marketing expenditures are losses. Indeed, in most businesses a small proportion of customers, products, territories, or orders is responsible for most of the profits. For example, the 20–80 rule indicates that about 20 percent of a firm's products generate about 80 percent of sales. Moreover, the 60–99 rule indicates that the highest-volume 60 percent of products generates 99 percent of sales (see Figure 12.1). Moreover, the most profitable 20 percent of products generate about 300 percent of profits (see Figure 12.2). There are many reasons for the misdirected efforts such figures indicate:

Attempts to achieve too high a market share.

Failure to adjust marketing efforts to variations in demand.

Failure to adjust national and international marketing strategies for product, customer, or market dissimilarities.

Data that are not reported in sufficient detail to permit profitability analysis by product, customer, market, or other meaningful profit segment.

Data that are incomplete or not presented on a comparative basis.

Product and distribution cost data that are averages or outdated standards, not reflecting current and future costs in serving a market or customer group.

Marketing managers who make little effort to define their information needs.

Poor communication between marketing, accounting, and systems personnel.

FIGURE 12.1
Cumulative Sales

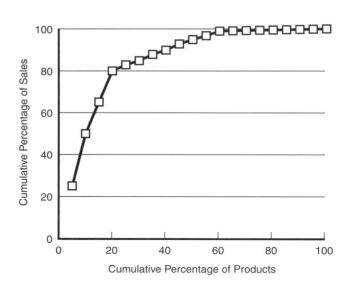

FIGURE 12.2
Cumulative Profitability

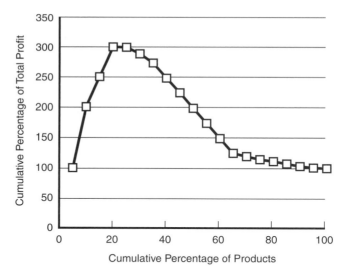

Responsibilities of Marketing and Distribution Management

Clearly, the major responsibilities for obtaining better marketing and distribution cost and profitability information lie within the realm of marketing management. Among these responsibilities is the need to define the types of decisions requiring better cost information. Management must also determine the value expected from better information. For

WEYERHAEUSER DOOR MANUFACTURER DISCOVERS CUSTOMER PROFITABILITY

BOX 12.1

For over 100 years, Weyerhaeuser Co. in Marshfield, Wisconsin, has led the door manufacturing industry. In 1995, the company faced increasing costs, declining sales, and diminishing employee morale. In fact, the factory operated at half capacity but incurred costs the equivalent of operating at full capacity. By 1999 Weyerhaeuser had experienced a drastic turnaround in which revenues grew 10 percent to 15 percent annually, complete and on-time deliveries rose from 40 percent to 97 percent, and U.S. market share climbed from 12 percent to 26 percent.

What was the source of Weyerhaeuser's astonishing comeback? DoorBuilder. This tracking software supports the company's efforts to build a communication network with its key distributors. The intranet has enabled Weyerhaeuser to offer customers faster turnaround times and often lower prices than those of the competition. But perhaps more important is DoorBuilder's ability to assist management in developing more accurate pricing strategies and tactics. For instance, before the tracking software management relied on ad hoc pricing

techniques derived from negotiations or favored relationships. DoorBuilder reversed these pricing behaviors by providing management with up-to-date costs and lead times for each customer order. Weyerhaeuser soon discovered the costs of maintaining each customer relationship and began to rank customers by their financial stability, price demands, average order size, and flexibility in meeting the company's new demands. High-cost, low-ranking customer orders were either refused or redirected to competitors.

Weyerhaeuser's implementation of Door-Builder and the software's ability to provide detailed cost and order information enabled the company to monitor customer relationships. Uncovering the costs of each customer order encouraged management to adopt customer profitability measures, which, in turn, doubled production to more than 800,000 doors annually and increased the factory's return on net assets from −2 percent to 27 percent!

Source: Marcia Stepanek, "How an Intranet Opened Up the Door to Profits," *Business Week E.Biz* (July 26, 1999), 32–38.

example, one company determined that a theoretical sales effort allocation plan suggested annual savings of $500,000 over the current practice. A limited test of the new plan revealed that it would cost $50,000 to install the necessary information system, but that the annual savings would approximate $400,000. Other companies have reviewed their procedures to determine how better information would be beneficial (see Box 12.1).

Benefits of Marketing and Distribution Cost Data

Today, the typical business firm, manufacturer, wholesaler, or retailer sells a relatively large number of products. Each of these products is in a different market and faces different degrees of competition. Consequently, to compete effectively, each product requires its own marketing mix. Moreover, these firms sell to different types and sizes of customers in different geographical locations. Essentially, then, marketing management is concerned with identifying and selecting alternative courses of action that lead to more profitable sales volumes. To identify profit opportunities, management needs to know how profit changes in response to sales volume shifts that occur when marketing expenditures change.

When analyzing alternative decisions, the proper information is the marginal or incremental profit contribution that covers fixed costs and profits after subtracting all direct and indirect traceable costs. By placing the accent on incremental profit opportunity and having relevant marketing and distribution cost data, the organization can

Determine the customer segments with highest profit opportunities.

Determine the level of selling effort to achieve profit objectives.

Decide when to accept new orders or introduce new products.

Determine the costs of different distribution patterns.

Determine the profitability of acquiring, retaining or losing customers.

Determine realistic prices.

Establish a basis for cost justification defenses against price discrimination complaints.

Design sales incentive plans.

Establish sales call patterns.

Set minimum order quantities.

Contributions to Pricing

Frequently, individual products, services and customers require a complex mix of marketing and distribution activities that are not profitable under current pricing and volume levels. Managers must understand the existence and sources of unprofitable business in order to take positive actions, such as

• Repricing products.

• Changing the product or customer mix.

- Developing substitute products or services.

- Redesigning products or sales territories.

- Changing processes, policies, strategies, or tactics.

- Eliminating products or customers.

Not only does the analysis estimate the profitability of various business segments at current and future prices, it also assesses when changes in pricing strategies and tactics are needed. It helps managers decide how to use pricing to (1) make certain distributors, customers, or order sizes profitable, (2) discourage growth of unprofitable business segments, and (3) encourage growth of profitable business segments. Such an analysis provides useful information that may offer a defense for differential pricing practices based on cost justification (see Chapter 18). Finally, the analysis should help to improve distribution support by increasing managers' understanding of their distributors' marketing and distribution costs. Given this understanding, pricing structures can be modified to enable distributors to improve their profitability.

Nature Of Marketing Profitability Analysis

Marketing profitability analysis involves a study of the organization's entire marketing and distribution function. The purpose of the analysis is to identify and measure marketing and distribution cost elements to determine the profitability of different market or sales segments, such as products, customers, territories, and sales order sizes, and to eliminate or reduce losses resulting from misdirected marketing efforts.

In its simplest form, this analysis can be made from five sets of data: (1) names and location of customers, (2) types of customer businesses, (3) number of each customer's orders in a given period, (4) total sales to each customer in the same period, and (5) total sales and gross profits on each product in the line.[2] Additional data frequently available include (6) number of shelf-stock and full-case orders, (7) number of deliveries, (8) method of delivery, (9) type of merchandise ordered, (10) method of payment, (11) nature and amount of discounts and allowances provided to

---

[2]Charles H. Sevin, *Analyzing Your Cost of Marketing,* Small Business Administration Management Aids No. 85, reprinted April 1971.

customers, and (12) amount of returns. These data can be collected from customer records.

Most firms' records will permit an extensive approach to analyzing marketing costs. Regardless of the sophistication of the firm's records, however, several common errors should be avoided. First, marketing costs should not be allocated to products, customers, or other profit segments on the basis of sales volume, since most marketing costs are not caused by sales. (Sales *result* from these activities and expenditures but do not cause the costs. An exception to this statement is a sales compensation plan formulated in part on commissions based on sales generated.) Second, general and administrative costs should not be arbitrarily allocated to profit segments. And, third, legitimate marketing costs should not be "lumped" into general cost categories such as manufacturing or general and administrative costs. As argued earlier, this lumping of marketing and distribution costs into general overhead not only is illogical but also precludes management from making informed pricing decisions.

Marketing Cost Classifications

Common fixed marketing costs are costs incurred in common for different profit segments and do not vary with the volume of sales or activities in any profit segment. For example, costs of institutional advertising of a company's name would not be allocated to individual segments.

Direct variable marketing costs vary with an activity and can be assigned to profit segments. Sales commissions, transportation costs, and some aspects of ordering and billing costs vary directly with sales volume, customer accounts, transportation rate or mode mix, and method of storing.

Separable fixed marketing costs are costs that can be assigned to specific profit/sales segments. Field supervision expenses and period warehousing costs are examples of fixed marketing costs that can be identified with specific segments.

Contribution Approach

The contribution approach essentially extends the contribution method of cost analysis developed in Chapter 11. To illustrate the approach, assume that a firm produces three types of lawn mower: X, a gasoline-powered mower; Y, an electric-powered mower; and Z, a gasoline-powered tractor

TABLE 12.1   **Marketing Profitability Analysis—Contribution by Territories**

| | Territory | | | | | | | |
	A		B		C		Total	
Sales revenues								
Product X	$300,000		$150,000		$120,000		$570,000	
Product Y	110,000		80,000		70,000		260,000	
Product Z	90,000	$500,000	120,000	$350,000	110,000	$300,000	320,000	$1,150,000
Variable costs								
Production	$350,000		$270,000		$180,000		$800,000	
Marketing— commission	35,000		23,000		20,000		78,000	
Marketing— transportation	9,000		7,000		6,000		22,000	
Marketing— ordering	6,000	400,000	5,000	305,000	4,000	210,000	15,000	915,000
Contribution		$100,000		$ 45,000		$ 90,000		$ 235,000
Direct fixed costs								
Rent	$ 2,000		$ 1,500		$ 2,500		$ 6,000	
Salaries	11,000		8,500		9,500		29,000	
Promotion	6,000	19,000	5,000	15,000	3,000	15,000	14,000	49,000
Territory contribution		$ 81,000		$ 30,000		$ 75,000		$ 186,000
Common fixed costs								25,000
Total contribution								$ 161,000

mower. Assume further that the company has three sales territories: A, B, and C. Production variable costs for each product, including materials and labor, are given in Table 12.1. Product X is sold at a price of $100; Y is priced at $150; and Z is priced at $450.

Tables 12.1 and 12.2 illustrate three types of direct variable marketing costs: commissions, transportation, and order processing costs. In Table 12.1 these variable marketing costs are directly assignable to the territories because they are directly related to the sales effort activity within each territory. In Table 12.2 these same variable costs are again assigned to the three products on the basis of a sales effort activity. It is also important to note that in Table 12.2 territory direct fixed costs are not assigned to the three products because there is no objective way to assign these common marketing costs to each product.

The main distinction between the contribution approach and the net profit approach (described later) is that the contribution method avoids arbitrary assignment of common, fixed marketing costs. As noted in Chapter 11, once the contribution of each product or profit segment is determined, a

TABLE 12.2 **Marketing Profitability Analysis—Contribution by Products**

Territory A

	Product			
	X	Y	Z	Total
Sales revenue	$300,000	$110,000	$90,000	$500,000
Variable costs				
Production	$210,000	$ 80,000	$60,000	$350,000
Marketing—commissions	25,000	6,000	4,000	35,000
Marketing—transportation	4,000	3,000	2,000	9,000
Marketing—ordering	3,500	1,500	1,000	6,000
Total variable costs	$242,500	$ 90,500	$67,000	$400,000
Product contribution	$ 57,500	$ 19,500	$23,000	$100,000
Territory direct fixed costs				
Rent				$ 2,000
Salaries				11,000
Promotion				6,000
				$ 19,000
Territory contribution				$ 81,000

PV ratio can be computed and alternative prices for each product can be analyzed exactly. For example, the PV ratio for product X in territory A is $57,500/$300,000, or 0.19. If the firm is considering raising the price of gasoline-powered lawn mowers in territory A to $110—a 10 percent price increase—then using the formula from Equation 11.4, volume in territory A can fall no more than 34.5 percent if the territory's profit contribution from product X is to be enhanced.

Net Profit Approach

This approach, primarily of use to manufacturers and wholesalers, is adaptable for use by retailers as well. In general, it makes reference to profit segments, which should be understood as individual products, product lines, customer types, specific customer accounts, sales territories, or alternative channels of distribution.

The net profit approach attempts to assign all indirect costs among the profit segments. Essentially, this approach is similar to the full-costing method and has the same disadvantages. Indeed, the contribution method avoids arbitrary allocation of common, fixed marketing costs. However, the Federal Trade Commission requires a full-cost allocation approach for justifying cost differences under the Robinson-Patman Act. Perhaps more appropriately, short-run decisions would be concerned more with the profit contribution made by specific segments. Thus either the contribution approach or the net profit approach may be appropriate, depending on the purpose of the analysis.

The net profit approach has two analytical steps:

1. Marketing expenditures of a business are reclassified from a *natural-expense* basis into *activity-cost* groups. The activity-cost groups comprise all the costs associated with each marketing activity (function) performed by the business.

2. Activity-cost groups are assigned to profit segments on the basis of *measurable factors* that exhibit causal relationships to the activity costs.

A natural-expense item refers to the usual way expenses of a business, such as rent or wages, are classified for accounting purposes. However, a natural expense such as wages may *functionally* be related to direct selling, selling supervision, order assembly, order billing, and credit. Each of these activities is a part of a separate marketing function, and the natural-expense item, such as salespeople's salaries, must be assigned to several activity-cost groups. This concept of functionality follows directly from the idea of classifying costs as variable or fixed, according to activity, as developed in Chapter 10.

To classify marketing and distribution costs according to functions requires a study of the business's marketing activities. The assignment of natural-expense items to activity-cost groups often is accomplished by means of work-measurement studies, space measurements, managerial estimates, and statistical techniques. It is important to establish a cause-effect relationship between various marketing costs and the corresponding activity-cost grouping. Table 12.3 gives examples of activity-cost groups and bases of assignment.

As Table 12.3 indicates, certain types of data are required before marketing costs can be assigned to products. Essentially, the data needed are

1. The average inventory value of finished goods.

TABLE 12.3 Activity-Cost Groups and Bases of Assignment

Activity-Cost Group	To Products	To Customers	To Sales Territories
1. Selling—direct costs: personal calls by salespeople and supervisors on accounts and prospects; sales salaries, incentive compensation, travel, and other expenses	Selling time devoted to each product, as shown by sales-call reports or other studies	Number of sales calls times average time per call, as shown by sales-call reports or other studies	Direct
2. Selling—indirect costs: field supervision, field sales-administration expense, sales-personnel training, sales management; market research, new-product development, sales statistics, tabulating services, sales accounting	In proportion to direct selling time or time records by projects	In proportion to direct selling time or time records by projects	Equal charge for each salesperson
3. Advertising: media costs such as TV, radio, billboards, newspapers, magazines; advertising production costs; advertising department salaries	Direct, or analysis of space and time by media; other costs in proportion to media costs	Equal charge to each account; or number of ultimate and consumers prospects in each account's trading area	Direct analysis of media circulation records
4. Sales promotion: consumer promotions such as coupons, premiums; trade promotions such as price allowances, point-of-purchase displays, cooperative advertising	Direct, or analysis of source records	Direct, or analysis of source records	Direct, or analysis of source records
5. Transportation: railroad, truck, barge; payments to carriers for delivery on finished goods from plants to warehouses and to customers; traffic department costs	Applicable rates times tonnages	Analysis of bills of lading	Applicable rates times tonnages
6. Storage and shipping: storage of finished goods inventories in warehouses; rent, public warehouse charges, insurance and taxes on inventories, physical handling; labor, equipment, space and material costs	Warehouse space occupied by average inventory; number of shipping units	Number of shipping units	Number of shipping units
7. Order processing: checking and processing of orders from customers, checking prices, weights, and carload accumulation, shipping dates, coordination with operations, preparation of customer invoices; credit and collection; provision for bad debts; salaries, supplies, space, and equipment costs	Number of order lines	Number of invoice lines	Number of invoice lines

2. The amount of storage space required for these finished goods.

3. The frequency with which the product is ordered (number of invoice lines).

4. The number of "packs" of the product sold (gross, cases, dozen).

5. The weight or number of units shipped.

6. The proportion of selling time spent on the product.

7. Direct advertising and promotion costs.

The data required for assigning marketing costs to customers (costs to serve) are

1. The total number of invoice lines for the period.

2. The total weight or number of units shipped.

3. The number of sales calls and "selling time" per call.

4. Any direct advertising, promotion costs, or allowances.

5. The number of customer orders.

6. The average amount of accounts receivable.

7. The number of invoices posted to accounts receivable.

8. The amount of returns.

9. Amount of presales support (marketing, technical, sales).

10. Amount of postsales support (installation, training, warranty, field support).

The analysis of marketing costs by territory generally is simpler than the analysis either by products or by customers. When a firm's marketing activities are organized along well-defined geographical boundaries, a large proportion of marketing expenses is directly traceable to the territories. Hence, assigning indirect marketing expenses to territories is less burdensome than it is for products or customer accounts. Once functional expenses have been assigned to the marketing profit segments, a profit and loss statement is prepared for each segment.

TABLE 12.4 Classifying Natural Expenses into Functional Expenses

	Natural Accounts	Selling	Advertising and Promotion	Order Processing	Storage and Shipping
Rent	$ 2,000	$ –0–	$ –0–	$1,000	$1,000
Salaries	11,000	4,000	3,000	2,000	2,000
Promotion	6,000	–0–	6,000	–0–	–0–
	$19,000	$4,000	$9,000	$3,000	$3,000

TABLE 12.5 Bases for Assigning Functional Expenses to Products

Product	Selling: Proportion of Selling Time	Advertising and Promotion: Number of Advertisements	Order Processing: Number of Orders	Storage and Shipping: Number of Units Shipped
X	0.50	40	300	1,000
Y	0.30	40	75	733
Z	0.10	20	50	200
Totals	1.0	100	425	1,933
Functional expenses	$4,000	$9,000	$3,000	$3,000
Allocation Formula	Direct proportion of selling time	Cost per advertisement: $\frac{\$9,000}{100} = \$90$	Cost per order $\frac{\$3,000}{425} = \$7.06$	Cost per unit $\frac{\$3,000}{1,933} = \$1.55$

To illustrate some of the problems with the application of the net profit approach, assume that the lawn mower manufacturer wishes to assign the rent, salaries, and promotion expenses of territory A to products X, Y, and Z. As indicated, the first step is to reclassify these natural-expense items into activity marketing cost groups. The relevant marketing cost groups for territory A are selling, advertising and promotion, order processing, and storage and shipping. The reclassification of the natural indirect expenses into activity costs is shown in Table 12.4. Table 12.5 shows the basis for assigning the functional expenses to each product, which is the second step in the net profit approach.

In Table 12.4, the rent is divided evenly by the order processing, storage, and shipping activities because salespeople work away from the territory office and an advertising agency handles the advertising and promotion activity. The district sales supervisor, who also sells and coordinates the territory's advertising and promotion activities, spends about 57 percent of the time in selling. Therefore, the supervisor's salary is divided proportionately between (1) selling and (2) advertising and promotion. The remaining $4,000 of salaries is divided between (1) order processing and (2) storage and shipping.

Once the natural expenses have been classified into activity expenses, the task is to assign each activity expense to the three products. Table 12.5 shows the assignment formulas and the data necessary to complete this task. The sales reports filed by the supervisor indicate that 50 percent of the selling time is devoted to product X, the gasoline-powered lawn mower. Hence, 50 percent of the $4,000 fixed selling expense is assigned to product X, as seen in Table 12.6. Advertising and promotion expenses are assigned on the basis of the number of advertisements and the average cost per advertisement. Since product X was featured in 40 local advertisements, $3,600 ($90 × 40) is assigned to product X. Similarly, the remaining marketing costs are assigned to the three products on the basis of average cost per order processed and average shipping cost per unit shipped.

As shown in Table 12.6, the last step is to calculate the net profit for each product. Thus, an accounting profit or loss

TABLE 12.6   Territory A: Profit and Loss by Product

	Product			
	X	Y	Z	Total
Sales revenue	$300,000	$110,000	$90,000	$500,000
Variable costs	242,500	90,500	67,000	400,000
Product contribution	$ 57,500	$ 19,500	$23,000	$100,000
Fixed costs				
Selling	$ 2,000	$ 1,200	$ 800	$ 4,000
Advertising and promotion	3,600	3,600	1,800	9,000
Order processing	2,118	529	353	3,000
Storage and shipping	1,550	1,140	310	3,000
Total expenses	$ 9,268	$ 6,469	$ 3,263	$ 19,000
Net profit	$ 48,232	$ 13,031	$19,737	$ 81,000

can be computed for the profit segments, which in this example are products.

Customer Profitability Analysis

Overall, profitability is the ultimate measure of value created. The desired objective of marketing is to acquire, satisfy, and retain customers profitably. Recognizing this fundamental point requires shifting from a focus on product profitability to customer profitability. What is needed is an approach for measuring how well a firm creates value for its customers and how well it leverages that value to create profitability.[3]

The justification for customer profitability analysis is simply the fact that each dollar of revenues does not contribute equally to net income. Differences in customer profitability can occur either because of variation in revenues received across customers or because of differences in the cost to serve. A McKinsey study showed that managers often are unaware of the actual net price they receive from customers.[4] Every discount, rebate, or allowance results in a reduction of revenue from a customer. Often these discounts and allowances are managed by different people in the firm and are not accumulated by customer or order. Included in these reductions from invoice price are early payment (cash) discounts, annual volume bonus, cooperative advertising allowances, freight allowances, and off-invoice promotions. When these additional reductions from invoice were included in the analysis, the actual transaction price varied between 16 percent to 29 percent off the invoice price for the firms studied.

Clearly, firms that use invoice price as their price performance metric likely are overreporting the effectiveness of their pricing management. Because of the variability of these off-invoice discounts and allowances across customers, no product sells for exactly the same transaction price. The McKinsey study found variations between the lowest to the highest transaction unit price across customers for different firms to vary up to 500 percent! Customers who are perceived by managers to be very profitable often end up be-

[3]Timothy Matanovich, "Value Measures in the Executive Suite," *Marketing Management 9* (Spring 2000), 35–40.
[4]Michael V. Marn and Robert L. Rosiello, "Managing Price, Gaining Profit," *Harvard Business Review 70* (September–October 1992), 84–94.

FIGURE 12.3   **Cumulative Customer Profitability**

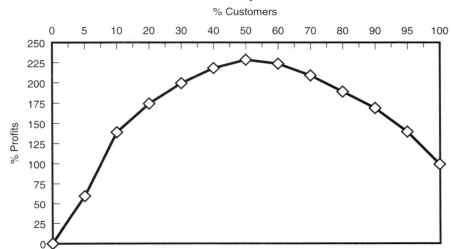

ing unprofitable and other customers perceived to be unprofitable may actually be profitable. Indeed, large customers tend to be either the most profitable or the least profitable of a firm's customer base.[5] Figure 12.3 illustrates the possibility that a relatively small proportion of customers are very profitable while another proportion are not profitable. In Figure 12.3, 50 percent of the customers contribute 225 percent of the firm's profits.

The Concept of Customer Profitability

Customers can be viewed as the main source of profits for the business firm. Customer behavior not only leads to product sales (revenues), but also generates costs for the selling firm. Measuring customer profit requires identifying the customer, measuring the net revenue received (transaction price $\times$ volume) and actual costs incurred while serving the customer, and combining these elements into an estimate of profitability for each customer. Today, firms can easily identify customers who are profitable and who have profit improvement potential (see Boxes 12.2 and 12.3). Once the

[5]Robert S. Kaplan and Robin Cooper, *Cost & Effect: Using Integrated Cost Systems to Drive Profitability and Performance* (Boston: Harvard Business School Press, 1998).

FIRMS THAT USE CUSTOMER PROFITABILITY ANALYSIS — BOX 12.2

1. Federal Express Corporation rates customers based upon their profitability to the company and designs its marketing and customer service policies to meet the needs of each customer segment. High-spending, low-maintenance customers receive superior service, whereas expensive customers who require extensive and costly customer service encounter higher shipping prices. FedEx no longer directly targets customers who spend little, in terms of both dollars and patronage.

2. U S West has an extensive database that records as many as 200 observations of each customer's calling behaviors. Using this information along with customer profiles, the company identifies and separates consumers based on their current and future profitability status. Further, U S West measures the percentage of telecom expenditures that each customer spends with the company. U S West then takes all of this information and determines a marketing expenditure limit for each individual customer.

3. A profitability survey conducted by Standard Life Assurance (Europe's largest mutual life-insurance company) revealed that the insurer's customer base comprised mostly unprofitable customers. Standard Life's direct-mail campaign had attracted senior couples and stay-at-home mothers, encouraging them to register for costly home visits that reduced the insurer's margins.

4. Each month Bank of America reviews the profits of more than 75 million accounts and analyzes the cost to the bank of maintaining each of these accounts. This process enables the bank to monitor the most profitable households. Any changes in a customer's banking transactions are noted, and changes that indicate a highly profitable customer may defect immediately prompt customer service calls and heightened customer service.

Source: Paul. C. Judge, "What've You Done for Us Lately?" *Business Week* (September 14, 1998), 140–44.

customer is identified data must be collected on the relevant revenue-generating behaviors.

Second, when estimating the costs associated with each customer, it is important to distinguish between costs related to customer acquisition and customer retention. Generally, it is more expensive to acquire customers than it is to serve existing customers. Moreover, loyal customers tend to purchase more, are easier to serve, and less costly to serve than new customers. Indeed, relatively new customers are less likely to be profitable in the short run than existing customers. Loyal customers

- Stay longer.

- Cost less to serve.

BANKS ASSESS CUSTOMER PROFITABILITY

BOX 12.3

The days when all bank customers receive equal treatment in terms of basic services are nearing an end as banks seek to improve profitability. According to estimates, 20 percent of a bank's consumer customers yield 140 percent to 150 percent of overall income, but the bottom 20 percent of customers drain as much as 50 percent from profits! Using specialized tracking software, banks now can measure customer profitability and design products and services based upon each customer's value to the bank.

Current technology that automatically signals a customer's profitability rating to tellers during a bank visit enables tellers to differentiate the level of service they provide each customer. Banks may waive the fees of profitable customers whereas several banks now charge fees to unprofitable customers for a variety of services. In 1995, First Chicago Corp., now Bank One Corp., was one of the first banks to implement a customer profitability initiative and announce that it would, under certain circumstances, charge customers $3 per teller visit. This move resulted in public disapproval of the new policy, but the bank insisted that the fee was initiated to motivate customers to use less costly automated teller machines. More recently, Bank One Corp. announced its plans to drop unprofitable corporate clients, claiming that the bank's relationship with its clients is in the form of a partnership. Quite simply, those unprofitable corporate customers who wish to continue doing business with the bank will either increase their usage of more profitable products and services or be denied service. Bank One Corp. estimates that approximately 15 percent (1,800) of the bank's corporate customers will no longer be serviced.

Although banks' use of customer profitability analysis has received negative public opinion, they will most likely continue with and improve the practice of measuring customer value. Customer analysis enables banks to better segment customers based upon their profitability, design new value services, and implement incentives to encourage more profitable relationships.

Sources: Melissa Wahl, "Sizing up Customers," *Chicago Tribune* (Sunday, November 8, 1998), Section 5, pp. 1, 6–7; Melissa Allison, "Bank One Showing Some Clients the Door," *Chicago Tribune* (Sunday, May 13, 2001), Section 5, p. 2.

- Provide higher margins.
- Purchase from more product lines.
- Purchase more.
- Tend to resist competitors' efforts.
- Tend to be less price sensitive.[6]

Costs to serve analysis identify actual and assignable costs of the resources used and activities required to provide

[6]Ross Goodwin and Brad Ball, "Closing the Loop on Loyalty," *Marketing Management 8* (Spring 1999), 25–34.

ROHM AND HAAS FINDS REWARDS IN CUSTOMER PROFITABILITY ANALYSIS

BOX 12.4

During the early 1990s the Polymers and Resins (P and R) division of Rohm and Haas faced increasing price pressures from customers and demands for a higher rate of return to corporate shareholders. At the same time the number of competitors within the emulsions market where P and R competes increased. The entrance of high-volume, low-price retailers, including Wal-Mart and Home Depot, restricted Rohm and Haas's previous practice of passing price increases to customers who then forwarded the higher prices to end-consumers. In fact, prices for Rohm and Haas's polymer emulsions products remained stable over a five-year period. This inability to raise prices, combined with the company's policy of providing various costly services to all customers, resulted in rapidly narrowing profit margins.

In 1995 management implemented a redesign initiative and discovered that P and R had served over 4,000 customers in two years. They then segmented customers as follows: (1) partners or potential partners, (2) strategically important customers, (3) important customers, and (4) other customers. Partners or potential partners comprised 2 percent of P and R's total customers but were responsible for 59 percent of the division's sales volume. The other customers group had 3,200 customers accounting for only 4 percent of sales volume!

Rohm and Haas's management then identified the valued services and needs for each segment and changed its business model to accommodate these findings. Instead of offering uniform services for all segments, they offered tailored service packages to each segment. For example, expensive, specialized services were offered solely to partners and potential partners, and customers pertaining to the most unprofitable segment were turned over to an extensive distribution network. Rohm and Haas's efforts to improve customer profitability not only reduced administrative and distribution costs but also enabled the firm to focus on improving relations with key customer groups.

Source: Anthony J. D'Allessandro and Alok Baveja, "Divide and Conquer: Rohm and Haas's Response to a Changing Specialty Chemicals Market," *Interfaces 30* (November–December 2000), 1–16.

the product and/or service to the customer. The cost to serve a given customer varies according to the resources used by the customer. A visit by a salesperson costs more than a telephone or computer contact.

The third step is to combine the revenues and costs associated with each customer into an estimated profitability for each customer. This calculation of customer profitability should reflect both historical and prospective profitability profiles.[7] Box 12.4 illustrates Rohm and Haas's successful

[7]Fred A. Jacobs, Wesley Johnston, and Natalia Kotchetova, "Customer Profitability: Prospective vs. Retrospective Approaches in a Business-to-Business Setting," *Industrial Marketing Management 30* (May 2001), 353–63.

customer profitability analysis. As this example indicates, it is important to examine any a priori segmentation model that is based on product or use criteria. In many cases such segmentation criteria may not be consistent with customer needs and requirements. Simply because different customers purchase the same products or have similar uses does not make them homogeneous in their requirements and demands for the intensity of service, relationships, or interactions.[8]

Enhancing Customer Profitability

Analyzing the historical profitability of customers is an important beginning because management can then assess (1) the relative success of marketing strategies, (2) the relationship between customer-related costs and customer-based revenues, and (3) the relationship between customer profitability and financial performance (shareholder value). However, the real benefit from customer profitability analysis is that it provides a basis for developing a customer profitability management program. Thus, it is important to develop a proactive strategy that maximizes the future value of the firm's customer base. Indeed, a necessary prerequisite for the efficient utilization of resources requires directing marketing efforts toward enhancing the profit potential of customer relationships.

Customer profits can be increased by (1) acquiring new customers, (2) increasing the profitability of existing customers, and (3) maintaining customer relationships over longer periods of time (loyalty). In general, companies serve only a fraction of their target customers and neither receive the maximum margin possible nor the maximum available business from existing customers. In addition, a relatively large proportion of customer relationships do not last as long as they should. To determine the gap between the current level of customer profitability and the potential requires a careful analysis of both existing customers and target customers not currently served by the firm.

Although the cost of customer acquisition normally is higher than customer retention, viewing customer acquisition costs as an investment to be recovered over multiple years provides a basis for analyzing the feasibility of investing in

[8]Joan O. Fredericks, Ronald R. Hurd, and James M. Salter II, "Connecting Customer Loyalty to Financial Results," *Marketing Management 10* (Spring 2001), 26–32.

customer and market development activities. One grocery store chain determined that expanding its customer base by 2 percent with primary shoppers (those who give the store 80 percent or more of their business) would increase the store's profitability by 45 percent.[9] Thus seeking to expand the customer base by understanding the value drivers of the unserved target customers and then finding ways to deliver a value relationship to these potential customers must be one aspect of the profit-enhancing strategy. New customers should be sought only if the potential profit increase is sufficient to justify the required investment.

To determine the profit potential of existing customers, a firm must understand how and why they currently behave. The potential of these customers can be addressed by determining the firm's share of each customer's total expenditures in the product categories the firm provides. This question requires examining not only the firm's sales share, but also the customer's profit margin (net transaction price or the cost to serve). Do any of these customers provide opportunities for the firm to acquire new customers either through referrals or through the customer's reputation of buying only from quality suppliers? Sometimes new customers are positively influenced by information in the marketplace stemming from the experiences of a satisfied current customer.

The profit impact of customer retention, via customer loyalty, derives not only from future revenues and future revenue increases, but also from decreases in future costs. Customer loyalty enhances revenue growth through repeat purchases and referrals, reduces costs associated with acquiring and establishing relationships with new customers and replacing defecting customers, and reduces employee turnover costs while enhancing employee productivity. It has been estimated that increasing customer retention rate by 5 percent can increase profitability by 25 to 100 percent.[10]

To take advantage of customer profitability analysis and develop a customer profitability management strategy requires firms to identify and analyze their target customer segments in great detail. Such an analysis requires going

[9]Allan W. H. Grant and Leonard A. Schlesinger, "Realize Your Customers' Full Profit Potential," *Harvard Business Review 73* (September–October 1995), 59–72.
[10]Frederick F. Reichheld, *The Loyalty Effect,* (Boston, MA: Harvard Business School Press, 1996).

TABLE 12.7   Solutions for Unprofitable Customers

1. Reassign marketing and selling resources to profitable customers
   - Establish call frequencies for profitable versus unprofitable customers
   - Encourage mail, telephone, or electronic orders for unprofitable customers
   - Unbundle services and make them available on a fee basis
   - Change channel of distribution
2. On small orders:
   - Require customers to pick up orders or arrange for delivery
   - Charge for delivery
   - Establish a minimum order size
       Include a surcharge for orders below a minimum size
       Require cash on orders below a minimum size
       Eliminate small orders
3. Establish a price structure
   - Use volume discounts
   - Establish surcharges for small orders
   - Provide end-of-year patronage discounts (rewards)
4. Establish a credit policy
   - Establish credit lines
   - Include cash discounts (early payment rewards) in price structure

beyond knowing who buys what and in what quantities to knowing exactly how the customer's behavior affects profits. The company must know the customer's share of business; the costs of serving the customer (credit, warranty, pre- and postsale service); the transaction price paid (all discounts, allowances, and purchase or loyalty rewards); and referrals (direct by customer or indirect via customer's reputation and expressed satisfaction). With this information, managers can then identify segments with the highest profit potential and develop strategies to deliver value to these segments.

Solutions for Unprofitable Customers

As we have discussed, customer profitability analysis often reveals a substantial percentage of unprofitable customers. Should the business fire or threaten to fire these customers as illustrated in Box 12.2? Before considering such a drastic move, the firm should consider a number of potential solutions to the problem of unprofitable customers. Some of these solutions have the objective of reducing the costs to serve these customers and others have the objective of increasing the revenues received from them. Table 12.7 summarizes alternative solutions to unprofitable customers.

TACO BELL INCREASES PROFITS USING CUSTOMER PROFITABILITY ANALYSIS   **BOX 12.5**

During the late 1980s Taco Bell transformed its mass marketing strategy into a strategy based on meeting the needs of the company's most profitable market segments. Specifically, Taco Bell's strategy distinctly divided the company's customer base into three key market segments—weekly patrons, monthly patrons, and consumers who avoid Taco Bell because of their dislike for Mexican food.

Further analysis revealed two highly profitable consumer groups that formed less than 30 percent of Taco Bell's customer base but over 70 percent of the company's volume. The first group, "penny pinchers," comprised consumers between the ages of 18 and 24 who frequently purchase low-priced menu items. The second group, "speed freaks," characterized as active, two-income couples or parents, frequented Taco Bell less than the "penny pinchers" but concerned themselves more with convenience than price.

Once Taco Bell better understood its most profitable customer segments, the company reformed its business practices to improve its relationships with both "penny pinchers" and "speed freaks." For example, an inventory-based approach was adopted into the production model to improve speed, and a reduction in the prices of Taco Bell's core menu items attracted the price-conscious consumers. In fact, Taco Bell's value pricing initiative resulted in 1988 prices that were 25 percent below those in 1982.

Taco Bell's efforts to uncover the most profitable customer segments and to direct the company's marketing strategy towards meeting the needs of these specific segments greatly improved profits. By 1994, earnings had risen to $273 million from $82 million in 1988! Taco Bell continues to use customer profitability analysis to better identify and serve existing and potential high-profit segments.

Sources: Allan W. H. Grant and Leonard A. Schlesinger, "Realize Your Customers' Full Profit Potential," *Harvard Business Review 73* (September–October, 1995), 59–72; Bloomberg Business News, "No Playing Catchup for PepsiCo," *Chicago Tribune* (August 30, 1993), Section 4, 6.

One cost-reducing solution is to reassign marketing effort and resources away from unprofitable customers to more profitable customers. One firm changed its sales call policy from a minimum of one customer visit per month to one per quarter or even less for the unprofitable customers while increasing the call frequency for the profitable customers. One caution with this solution is to make sure that the change does more than just reassign costs from the unprofitable customers to the profitable customers. Assigning additional resources to profitable customers should lead to increased revenues and profits even though the costs to serve them have increased. Similarly, shifting the unprofitable customers to distributors may reduce selling costs but will the reduction in costs to serve be overcome by the necessary margin to the distributors?

Several price-related solutions to the unprofitable customer problem can be used. To motivate customers who frequently place small orders to change their behavior the firm could impose a service charge on each invoice below a stated minimum order size. Alternatively, the firm could raise prices and then offer a discount for all orders above a minimum order quantity. Or the firm could charge for delivery for orders below a certain size. Another approach would be to sell to slow-paying customers on a cash basis only to eliminate the cost of capital due to accounts receivable or bad debts.

Improving Retail Management with Better Cost Information

Just like manufacturers, retailers traditionally have lumped a large proportion of their operating costs into overhead categories and then allocated these costs using arbitrary formulas. Historically, the yardstick for measuring profits was sales. That is, as long as sales increase, profits should increase. In the 1960s retailers recognized that a valuable asset was the amount of store space devoted to displaying and selling merchandise. Hence, measures of profitability were developed using sales per square foot as the criterion. Refinements of these profitability concepts have continued, leading to other indicators of profitability such as gross margin, gross margin per square foot, or gross margin return on investment.

As discussed in earlier chapters, these gross measures do not provide accurate information about the relative profitability of each and every product sold in the store. By lumping such costs as the salaries of buyers, inventory, shipping, and marking into an overhead category, it is not possible to determine the profit contribution of individual selling items. Operating managers cannot control these nonmerchandise costs and items that appear to be profitable may not generate the return that the store requires.

For example, suppose the store's buyer of intimate apparel contracts to buy 144 black lace camisoles at $15 each with an expected retail price of $35. This contract seems to provide for a gross margin of $20, or 57 percent. However, shipping costs are $150 and the unmarked items will require 10 hours of labor to receive, check, mark, and distribute to the floor at a direct cost of $100. If all 144 camisoles are sold at $35 and there are no other direct costs, the profit margin is now 52.2 percent. However, suppose that after three weeks, 50 camisoles remain unsold and the store reduces the price by 20 percent and advertises the sale in local media as well with point-of-purchase signs and a special display. The costs of the advertising, promotion activities, and display are $500. If the remaining 50 are sold during the sale, the actual profit contribution realized will be $1,100 below the original gross margin projected by the buyer.

As this simple example demonstrates, lumping nonmerchandise costs into selling and general and administrative overhead precludes a proper identification of the relative attributable costs and profit contribution of merchandise lines. Operating managers have no way of understanding the impact of their decisions on the eventual profits earned.

The types of costs that can be identified and classified according to their behavior and attributability are distribution costs, selling costs, and inventory costs. Distribution costs include all costs incurred in bringing the merchandise to the selling floor: shipping, receiving, checking, marking, and setting up on shelves or displays. Selling costs include commissions, base salaries of salespeople, packaging (bags, boxes, wrapping paper), and credit costs. Inventory carrying costs vary according to how long it takes to turn the merchandise and the costs of financing inventory. Depending on these two variables, inventory carrying costs can be a significant proportion of the merchandise costs. The benefit of a detailed marketing and distribution analysis for a retail organization is that the firm will be in a position to make better buying decisions, pricing and promotion decisions, and operating decisions related to store size and layout, department space allocations, and inventory management.

Is such a detailed analysis for a store with thousands of items worthwhile? Neiman-Marcus implemented a profit contribution plan even though it has over 200 departments. Management developed standard costs for identified variable costs and was able to make decisions leading to improved performance. Neiman-Marcus has over 9 million transactions per year; with an improvement of just 20 cents per transaction, the bottom line improves by $2 million per year.[11]

Furthermore, not accounting for the fact that some categories of merchandise are more important than others in consumers' patronage decisions will understate the marketing

---

[11]Alan L. Gilman, "The Benefits of Looking below Gross Margin," *Retailing Issues Letter 1* (November 1988), 1–4.

profits for these categories.[12] For example, assume that a segment of consumers shops in a grocery store because members of this group perceive that it offers high-quality fresh produce. While getting their fresh vegetables and fruits, these consumers also purchase meat and dairy products. Thus in assessing the profitability of the produce department, it is important to account for the extra profits generated in the meat and dairy departments because of the drawing power of the produce department. Thus, even if the gross margins are relatively low in the produce department, these cross-selling effects mean that the produce department is more profitable than traditional merchandising accounting would indicate.

Starting a Profitability Analysis Program

Perhaps the comment managers hear most frequently when they discuss details of a marketing profitability analysis program is: "We have so many products and customers; how can we even begin such an effort?" The way to begin is to work with the major products in the firm's offerings. As indicated earlier, a relatively small number of products or product lines contribute a substantial amount of both sales and profits to the organization. By concentrating initially on these products, the details of the program can be developed and the incremental performance improvements maximized.

A second recommendation is to group profitability segments together to simplify the analysis and reduce the costs of developing and implementing the program. For example, Neiman-Marcus determined that items within departments exhibited similar cost patterns. That is, individual departments seemed to emphasize common merchandise sources and marked merchandise in similar ways, and the inventory turns of merchandise within a department fell within a narrow time frame. A cosmetics firm might develop product groupings according to lipsticks, nail polish, and facial creams and distribution groupings such as drug stores, department stores, and supermarkets. As shown in Box 12.3, Rohm and Haas found it very helpful to segment customers into meaningful groups.

---

[12]Yuxin Chen, James D. Hess, Ronald T. Wilcox, Z. John Zhang, "Accounting Profits versus Marketing Profits: A Relevant Metric for Category Management," *Marketing Science 18,* no. 3 (1999), 208–29.

When establishing groups for profitability analysis, several important points should be observed:

1. The groups should provide management with relevant information on sales, costs, and profits, not with arbitrarily allocated information.

2. Within a group, sales, costs, and profits should behave in a similar manner (i.e., the items within a group should be relatively homogeneous).

3. Data should be provided in an accurate and timely manner.

4. Revenues and costs should be separated out. Cost data should be separated into variable and fixed categories.

5. Groups should be mutually exclusive and collectively exhaustive.

6. Large-volume products or product lines or other large-volume segments should be analyzed separately and not grouped with low-volume categories.

7. Measures should be developed for assessing the importance of cross-selling effects across product categories, and marketing profits as well as accounting profits should be calculated.

Regardless of the level of aggregation, performance can be enhanced when firms retreat from the illogical lumping of nonproduction costs (for manufacturers) or nonmerchandise costs (for retailers) into general overhead categories. Performance enhancement occurs because these organizations learn how costs behave and why they are incurred, as well as how and why revenues occur. This information also provides insights into the development of more profitable pricing strategies and tactics. For example, learning which products, customers, and channels are not profitable may lead to pricing decisions about imposing service charges on low-volume orders, establishing volume discount price breaks, increasing prices, negotiating with distributors about terms of trade, or managing the selling effort of salespeople.

Regardless of the changes that are implemented, improving the productivity of the marketing and distribution function is the last frontier for establishing or maintaining a competitive advantage for many organizations. By emphasizing the profit contributions of these activities, the firm will be able to develop a decision support system that increases the effectiveness of its managers' decisions because they will understand what is under their control.

Summary

As discussed in Chapter 10, the role of costs for pricing decisions, although limited, is very important. However, there is a great tendency to lump marketing and distribution costs into a general cost category, often called administrative, selling, and general overhead. Such a classification of costs is a gross error. Marketing and distribution costs, like production costs, can be classified into direct traceable, indirect traceable, and common fixed costs. By so classifying these costs, management is in a position to know the effects of price changes on volume and on production, marketing, and distribution costs. Thus, given a precise measure of marketing and distribution costs, all relevant costs for pricing will be known.

Such a measure also places the firm in a position to estimate the profitability of various sales/profit segments at past prices and at alternative future prices. By knowing which products, territories, or customer accounts are not profitable, price changes can be analyzed to discourage growth of unprofitable segments and to encourage growth of profitable ones. This approach enhances control of marketing and distribution costs and provides a method of reassigning marketing efforts to more profitable segments. Finally, as illustrated in this chapter, marketing and distribution cost analysis provides a means of justifying price differentials.

Discussion Questions

1. A wholesaler of office supplies conducted a marketing cost study. At the conclusion of the study, the main results were summarized for the manager as seen in the accompanying table.

   a. Identify the marketing cost approach probably used by the company.

   b. What are some of the possible causes of class A accounts being unprofitable?

   c. Refer back to the "Definition of Price" discussion in Chapter 1. What are some ways that price can be used to enhance the profitability of serving class A accounts?

   d. Can you think of any other alternative solutions to enhance the profitability of serving class A accounts?

   e. On what basis do you think the wholesaler allocated the four types of expenses to the account classes? Can you think of other ways to allocate these expenses?

f. Consider your answers to parts *c* and *d*. If the wholesaler implemented your solutions, what changes might occur in the expense accounting? What assumptions did you make to arrive at these changes in the expense accounting?

	Account Classification				
	A	B	C	D	E
Number of accounts	500	400	300	200	100
Average order	$ 100	$ 300	$ 500	$ 900	$ 1,200
Annual sales	$500,000	$1,500,000	$2,250,000	$2,000,000	$1,800,000
Contribution	$150,000	$ 450,000	$ 675,000	$ 600,000	$ 540,000
Selling expense	$ 60,000	$ 50,000	$ 45,000	$ 25,000	$ 20,000
Delivery expense	50,000	50,000	45,000	30,000	20,000
Credit and collection expense	40,000	20,000	15,000	10,000	5,000
Order processing expense	30,000	30,000	25,000	20,000	15,000
Total expenses	$180,000	$ 150,000	$ 130,000	$ 85,000	$ 60,000
Profit (loss)	$(30,000)	$ 300,000	$ 545,000	$ 515,000	$ 480,000

2. A small electric appliance company made two products: a food blender and a food mixer. The company sold in two territories, A and B. The cost and revenue figures for last year appear in the accompanying table.

	Blender	Mixer
Selling price per unit	$40.00	$ 20.00
Sales volume in units		
Territory A	6,000	8,000
Territory B	4,000	13,000
Direct variable manufacturing costs per unit	$20.00	$ 9.00
Variable selling costs per unit	$ 2.00	$ 1.50
Variable distribution costs per unit	$ 4.00	$ 0.50
Promotion expenses per year	$2,500	$ 2,000

Fixed costs for territory A were $5,000 and for territory B were $5,400. Other fixed expenses for the firm amounted to $12,000.

a. Perform a contribution analysis by products.

b. Perform a contribution analysis by territories.

c. The firm is considering an across-the-board price increase of 10 percent. What is the maximum permissible volume decrease before profitability is harmed?

d. What additional information would you want before deciding to raise prices? Why?

Suggested Readings

Fredericks, Joan O., Ronald R. Hurd, and James M. Salter II: "Connecting Customer Loyalty to Financial Results," *Marketing Management 10* (Spring 2001), 26–32.

Grant, Alan W. H., and Leonard A. Schlesinger: "Realize Your Customers' Full Profit Potential," *Harvard Business Review 73* (September–October 1995), 59–72.

Jacobs, Fred A., Wesley Johnston, and Natalia Kotchetova, "Customer Profitability: Prospective vs. Retrospective Approaches in a Business-to-Business Setting," *Industrial Marketing Management 30* (May 2001), 353–63.

Lemon, Katherine N., Roland T. Rust, and Valarie A. Zeithaml: "What Drives Customer Equity," *Marketing Management 10* (Spring 2001), 20–25.

Marn, Michael V., and Robert L. Rosiello: "Managing Price, Gaining Profit," *Harvard Business Review 70* (September–October 1992), 84–94.

Matanovich, Timothy, "Value Measures in the Executive Suite," *Marketing Management 9* (Spring 2000), 35–40.

Goodwin, Ross, and Brad Ball, "Closing the Loop on Loyalty," *Marketing Management 8* (Spring 1999), 25–34.

Developing Pricing Strategies

Chapters 13 to 15 use the concepts and analyses presented in Chapters 2 through 12 to discuss approaches to determining prices. In many pricing decision contexts it is important to forecast trends in market prices, particularly because competitive prices constrain a firm's pricing discretion. Because price forecasting is also important for pricing products over their life cycles, Chapter 13 provides a transition from the demand and cost analysis given in Chapters 2 through 12 to the determination of pricing decisions. The experience curve phenomenon often has been used to justify the objective of increasing market share. Chapter 13 illustrates how the experience curve may be used in pricing. Because many companies attempt to develop pricing strategies using the experience curve as a strategy rather than an analytical technique, this chapter also develops the requirements for when a pricing strategy using the experience curve might be successful.

Chapter 14 focuses on the different pricing problems and solution approaches as the product matures through the life cycle. The chapter stresses analysis and planning for pricing strategy. We discuss behavioral and market implications, and apply costing and price forecasting techniques. Most firms produce and sell many products that are demand related and sometimes also cost related. From a market perspective, such firms have discovered that there are specific price-market segments for their products and that determining prices that differentiate these products is a complex process.

Whether to add a midpriced product or reduce or increase the number of price offerings depends not only on the potential number of price market segments, but also on clearly differentiating the products in the minds of buyers. Chapter 15 develops a behavioral approach to determining ways to position products in a line according to price. This chapter will also explore the tactic of price bundling, a practice that has been widely used in recent years. Finally, Chapter 15 presents yield management, a technique for maximizing revenue by adjusting prices relative to differences in buyers' sensitivity to prices.

CHAPTER THIRTEEN

Experience Curve Pricing

In many pricing decisions in which competitive prices constrain the firm's pricing discretion, it is common practice to forecast prices. Price forecasts are used in decisions about marketing strategy, new investments, budgeting, and materials purchasing. However, even though profitability depends on prices, costs, and sales volume, much effort has been expended on forecasting costs and sales volume, but little on forecasting prices. Indeed, many corporate plans forecast period sales volume, estimate the costs to reach the forecasted sales volume, and deduce the price "necessary" to achieve the profit objective.

This chapter develops the specific technique of forecasting using the experience curve. The objective of increasing market share continues to be a focal topic for business managers. A common approach has been to decrease prices faster than the competition to generate greater market share. The experience curve phenomenon is often cited as an explanation for this price–volume–market share relationship. Thus firms utilizing the experience curve have a positive basis for developing a product's price over its life cycle.

What separates the winners from the losers in the use of the experience curve is an understanding of how the experience curve may be used to gain competitive advantage and how to monitor the company's and competitors' progress down the experience curve. The experience curve is a tool to be used in developing pricing strategies; it is not a strategy per se. Thus correct use of this tool can be beneficial to a firm developing its pricing strategy. However, incorrect use of the experience curve—or simply assuming its existence—can lead to disastrous results.

The Phenomenon of the Experience Curve

It has been shown that costs decline by some characteristic amount each time accumulated volume is doubled. Accordingly, because of the competitive nature of most products, prices tend to decline along a similar pattern as long as competitive relationships are stable. Given these long-term, predictable cost and price behavior patterns, it should be relatively easy to forecast costs and prices. Indeed, many companies have developed successful marketing and production strategies utilizing this relationship among costs, prices, and accumulated experience.

From a planning viewpoint, given the experience relationship, it is clear that a firm's costs can be projected. It is also clear that competitors' costs can be estimated given some basic market information. However, this cost–price relationship to accumulated experience does not occur by accident, and a strict utilization of this phenomenon has some disadvantages.

It is important to distinguish two approaches to this volume growth–cost reduction relationship. The *learning curve* (sometimes called the start-up function or progress function) shows that *manufacturing costs* (primarily labor) fall as volume increases. Typical examples include air frames, industrial chemicals, and cameras. The *experience curve* shows that total unit costs of a product line decline over time as volume increases. Hence the experience curve considers a broader range of costs, including material, marketing, and distribution costs. Gas ranges, facial tissues, motorcycles, television receivers, and digital technology products are typical examples.

Empirical data show that prices and costs tend to decline when reported on a *constant dollar* basis. This experience phenomenon is not automatic; it does not just happen. Rather, management effort is needed to ensure that it occurs, and its use as a technique in developing pricing strategies requires careful consideration. Management must know its direct and indirect product costs, understand the sources of cost savings attributed to the experience, and estimate the actual experience curve that applies to its operation. Management must also understand the particular circumstances when the experience curve can be used to its advantage. One industrial company had been manufacturing small electric motors for nearly 20 years when it decided to reduce its prices, increase sales volume, and utilize the cost savings from sliding down its experience curve to improve profits. However, the firm lost substantial amounts of money because the experience effects were not available for a very mature product such as small motors. Like many other firms, this company assumed the experience curve automatically operated any time sales volume increased.

Costs and Experience

As noted, data show that costs tend to decline by a predictable amount each time accumulated experience doubles. This phenomenon makes it possible to forecast not only one's own costs, but also competitors' costs and industry average costs and prices. Generally, this decline in costs ranges between 10 and 30 percent, with a usual decline of between 20 and 30 percent each time accumulated volume is doubled. In *constant dollars* this decline continues as long as demand for a product is growing. If demand is not growing, then the rate of cost decline slows approaching zero because the doubling of accumulated volume now takes a long time. Figure 13.1 is an example of a cost–price experience on a linear scale.

When accumulated volume of a product is increasing at a constant percentage rate, each year of product experience produces about the same percentage effect on cost. When plotted on log-log paper percentage change is shown as a constant distance between two points (Fig. 13.2). A straight line means that a percentage change in one factor (accumulated volume) results in a predictable corresponding change

FIGURE 13.1
Cost/Price Experience Relationship

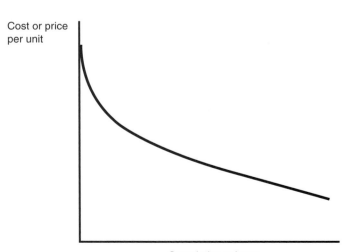

Cost or price per unit

Cumulative volume

FIGURE 13.2
Cost/Price Experience Relationship

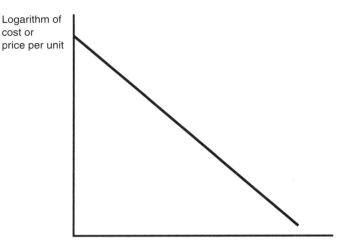

Logarithm of cost or price per unit

Logarithm of cumulative volume

in the other factor (costs, price). The slope of the line reveals the nature of the relationship and can be read directly from the graph.

Three key points must be understood about the cost–price experience phenomenon. First, note that we are talking about *accumulated experience* (volume) over time and not about doubling the production or sales rate between two points in time. Table 13.1 illustrates this point. Assuming a constant market growth of 10 percent per year, column 2 shows the yearly sales index. For example, if sales in year 1 were 100,000 units, then sales in year 2 would be 110,000 units, and in year 3 sales would be 121,000 units. For the experience curve analysis, we are interested in the total production and sales from the beginning. Thus, at the end of year 2, accumulated experience would be the sum of sales of years 1 and 2, or 210,000 units. Analytically, we are interested in the amount of time that accumulated experience doubles. Thus, accumulated experience doubles during the second year relative to the first year's experience of 100,000 units. It doubles again during the fourth year (going from 200,000 units to 400,000 units), during the seventh year, and the twelfth year. Thus, during the second, fourth, seventh, and twelfth years, unit costs will have declined by a constant percentage.

The second point is that costs are measured in *constant dollars*. Hence, cost data must be deflated through the use of an appropriate economic deflator. Because inflation primarily

TABLE 13.1
Accumulated
Experience

Year	Yearly Growth (10.0%)	Accumulated Experience	Periods of Doubling Experience, %
1	1.00	1.00 ⎫	110.0
2	1.10	2.10 ⎭	
3	1.21	3.31 ⎫	121.0
4	1.33	4.64 ⎭	
5	1.46	6.10 ⎫	
6	1.61	7.71 ⎬	104.3
7	1.77	9.48 ⎭	
8	1.95	11.43 ⎫	
9	2.14	13.57	
10	2.36	15.93 ⎬	125.6
11	2.60	18.53	
12	2.86	21.39 ⎭	

serves to mask the true price or cost effect of production or marketing improvements, price and cost data should always be developed on a constant dollar basis to enable management to determine actual cost or price effects due to volume changes. Whenever inflation is a significant factor, a test of the sensitivity of analysis to the inflation corrective factor should also be made.

Third, as noted in Chapters 10 through 12, management must be careful about what costs are included in the analysis. As much as possible, costs that vary with activity levels should be considered, since any arbitrary cost allocations will tend to hide the real changes in costs. Hence, the emphasis should be on the controllable costs associated with value-added activities. That is, the relevant costs are the out-of-pocket or cash costs. In addition, variations in accounting practices between companies, and in the same company over time, will distort the cost–price trend line because of the distortions in reported costs.

Prices and Experience

Available data show that prices, in constant dollars, generally tend to decline by some given amount each time accumulated experience is doubled. In very competitive, rapid growth, technological industries prices tend to parallel costs over time, as seen in Figure 13.3. If prices do not parallel costs in early periods, then a kink in the price pattern may result, as seen in Figure 13.4. During the introductory period, price may be set below cost to gain a foothold in the market (phase A) and in anticipation of lower costs in the future. In phase B, the initial seller and any entering sellers hold a price close to its initial level to recover operating losses incurred in the introductory period and to provide funds for rapid growth in capacity, working capital, research and development, and market development. Such a pricing strategy also encourages high-cost producers to enter the market. Eventually, growth slows, late entrants cut prices to gain a foothold in the market, and the market leader reduces price to stem the erosion of market share. Thus, phase C, the shakeout period, prevails, and severe price competition forces prices to decline faster than costs.[1] Finally, in phase D, stability emerges as the price–cost relationship stabilizes. In phase D, the effect of experience on actual costs and prices becomes less noticeable and may actually disappear. Figure 13.5 shows the recent price and cumulative sales volume history of DVD players. As the figure indicates, average prices have fallen quickly as cumulative sales volume has increased.

The implications of such price–cost relationships are profound. The experience curve relates costs, prices, volume, and profit margins over time, providing a powerful tool for evaluating alternative price and marketing strategies. The

FIGURE 13.3
A Stable Cost–Price Experience Relationship

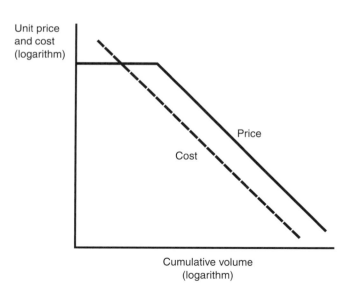

Unit price and cost (logarithm)

Price

Cost

Cumulative volume (logarithm)

[1]George S. Day and David B. Montgomery, "Diagnosing the Experience Curve," *Journal of Marketing 47* (Spring 1983), 44–58.

ability to predict prices better than one's competition is a major strategic advantage over the long term. Finally, the price experience curve concept suggests the need to develop marketing plans over the product life cycle.

To be able to utilize the experience curve, it is necessary to understand how to obtain the estimates of the parameters of the curve. The appendix to this chapter outlines an estimating procedure.

FIGURE 13.4

An Unstable Cost–Price Experience Relationship

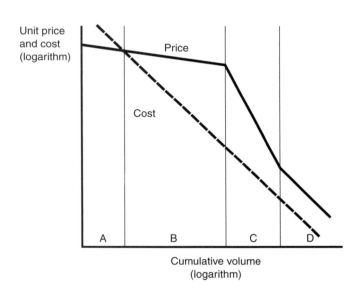

FIGURE 13.5

Price Experience Curve—DVD Players (1997–2000)

Data source: Rick Bentley, "I Want My DVD," *The News-Gazette* (March 26, 2001), D-1-2.

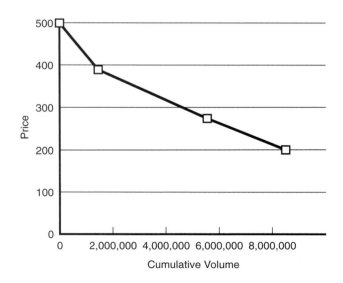

Managing the Experience Effect

Although considerable empirical evidence supporting the experience curve phenomenon is available, its value can be realized only by careful management. There usually is not one but several experience curves for a product category for a firm, one occurring at every stage of the value-added process. That is, experience effects may be observed in research and development, procurement, fabrication and assembly, marketing, and distribution.

There are three major sources of the experience effect in each of these value-added stages. *Learning* occurs whenever people develop skills that allow them to be more efficient. These skills result from repetitive practice, the use of ingenuity and increased dexterity. Discovering better ways to do the work, improving the work process, and dividing the tasks to permit specialization and standardization of the tasks leads to increased productivity per worker. Learning may occur at all levels—production, marketing, and distribution—however, most learning effects tend to occur early in a product's history.

Technological improvements are a second source of the experience effect. As volume increases, opportunities occur to improve the product and the production, marketing, and distribution processes. Changing from a labor-dominated production process to an automated one, substituting materials in the production process, and better management of the product–sales mix all result from increasing volume. Also, layout changes, improved ways of handling and storing materials and finished products, better maintenance procedures, and better distribution methods all provide the opportunity for reducing costs. However, these changes and activities also must be management directed; they do not just occur.

Economies of scale resulting from increased efficiencies due to size also contribute to the experience effect. Economies of scale can affect most value-adding activities, and many factors combine to produce a downward trend in the cost curve as cumulative volume increases. The dominant factors influencing scale economies include improved technology for production, long production runs, integrating several manufacturing processes, sharing corporate resources across products, access to volume discounts in purchases, and shipping in full carload or truckload lots.

Types of Experience Curves

There are three important experience curves for strategic planning. The *firm's cost experience curve* relates changes in the firm's costs to changes in cumulative volume. This curve generally is the easiest to estimate for it relies on internal cost and volume data. However, it is important to have appropriate data on direct and indirect traceable costs, including marketing and distribution. These costs must be deflated costs and reflect only those costs representing a direct cash outlay. Thus depreciation charges and general overhead are inappropriate for the analysis.

Competitor cost experience curves show the current costs of all direct competitors relative to their cumulative volume experience. These curves are more difficult to estimate because it is unlikely that competitors' costs can be known precisely. However, it is important not to assume that all competitors have essentially the same cost curve or to assume that the first entrant and firm leading in market share has the cost advantage because of greater experience. Indeed, firms entering later may be able to operate on a steeper cost curve than the initial entering firm. Moreover, it is likely that they will be able to enter at a lower per-unit cost than the first entrant because of technology transfer and because suppliers have learned by serving the initial entrant. They may be able to enter with more current technology, a larger scale of operations, or distribution already in place. Furthermore, over time cost differentials tend to narrow between competitors.

Industry cost and price experience curves relate industry average costs and prices to cumulative volume. These curves are the hardest to establish because it is difficult to determine average industry cost figures and actual selling prices. List prices are inaccurate because of discounts, rebates, and other allowances. Moreover, list prices will not be comparable for several models with disparate features and accessories or for different firms with different product and marketing mixes. Customers buy because they perceive value in use, and this perceived value can be changed by changing perceived benefits and services provided without directly changing the monetary price.

The Insatiable Appetite of Market Growth

As we saw in Chapter 11, price reduction strategies may be profitable when contribution margins and market growth are relatively high. Firms often develop price reduction strategies to "take advantage of the experience curve" because of some dramatic cost and price reductions that have been reported for other products or industries. Table 13.2 illustrates that this phenomenon not only requires growth but actually feeds on growth. Table 13.2 provides a per-unit cost index for

TABLE 13.2 Indexed Cost Reductions: Constant Market Growth

	Annual Market Growth			
End of Year	5%	10%	15%	20%
A. 90% Experience Curve				
1	1.00	1.00	1.00	1.00
2	0.90	0.89	0.89	0.89
3	0.84	0.83	0.83	0.82
4	0.80	0.79	0.78	0.77
5	0.77	0.76	0.75	0.74
6	0.75	0.73	0.72	0.71
7	0.73	0.71	0.69	0.68
8	0.71	0.69	0.67	0.65
9	0.69	0.67	0.65	0.63
10	0.68	0.66	0.63	0.61
B. 80% Experience Curve				
1	1.00	1.00	1.00	1.00
2	0.79	0.79	0.78	0.78
3	0.69	0.68	0.67	0.66
4	0.62	0.61	0.60	0.58
5	0.58	0.56	0.54	0.52
6	0.54	0.52	0.50	0.48
7	0.51	0.48	0.46	0.44
8	0.48	0.46	0.43	0.41
9	0.46	0.43	0.40	0.38
10	0.44	0.41	0.38	0.35
C. 70% Experience Curve				
1	1.00	1.00	1.00	1.00
2	0.69	0.68	0.67	0.67
3	0.55	0.54	0.53	0.51
4	0.47	0.45	0.44	0.42
5	0.41	0.39	0.37	0.36
6	0.37	0.35	0.33	0.31
7	0.34	0.31	0.29	0.27
8	0.31	0.29	0.26	0.24
9	0.29	0.26	0.23	0.21
10	0.27	0.24	0.21	0.19

three experience curves—90, 80, and 70 percent—and for four levels of constant market growth—5, 10, 15, and 20 percent. It is apparent from Table 13.2 that differences for a particular experience curve are few whether the market is growing at a constant 5 or 20 percent. For a 90 percent experience curve, the per-unit costs at the end of year 5 will range from 77 to 74 percent of the costs at the end of the year 1. For an 80 percent experience curve, the cost at the end of the year 5 will range from 58 to 52 percent of the year 1 costs, whereas for a 70 percent experience curve this range will be from 41 to 36 percent of the year 1 costs. Thus although there is some interaction between the experience phenomenon and market growth, there are few differences across market growth rates if they are constant over time. The lesson is clear: The use of price reductions to increase profits requires not only market growth but large increments of growth.

Using Price to Increase Market Share

Although using price reductions to increase market share is a popular strategy, it is clear that the firm must view this strategy as an investment. Moreover, without substantial growth in sales volume, accompanied by significant reductions in unit costs, such a strategy is not likely to enhance profitability.

Box 13.1 illustrates how the pursuit of market share via price reductions in a mature industry can lead to a price war. Essentially, the big six tire makers were attempting to capture additional market share to reduce unit operating costs. Their folly was to expect demand for their products to grow substantially faster than the 1 to 2 percent growth in demand for tires. For example, as Table 11.3 indicates, with a PV ratio of 0.50, a 5 percent price reduction requires a sales increase of 11.1 percent. Because no tire maker was willing to give up market share, aggressive pricing led to price wars even though the industry was operating at 90 percent of capacity. As we saw in Chapter 3, in a situation where demand was beginning to exceed supply, price wars were occurring, another price anomaly. Moreover, as competing firms increased capacity faster than demand growth, additional pressure to sell capacity further aggravated the situation.

Ordinarily, when selling in mature markets, using price reductions to increase market share should not be considered if (1) current profit margins are low or negative, (2) competitors

TIRE MAKERS SPIN THEIR WHEELS

BOX 13.1

Between 1986 and 1990, foreign competitors bought six U.S. tire makers to enhance their ability to compete on a global basis. By 1990, six producers controlled 80 percent of the non-communist world's tire production. However, U.S. tire prices, although increasing since 1987, remained at 1985 levels. In addition, in their efforts to gain market share producers were increasing capacity at a rate of 5 percent per year even though demand was growing at the rate of only 1 to 2 percent annually.

In 1989, recognizing that U.S. tire plants were operating at 90 percent capacity, Goodyear, then the market share leader, raised wholesale prices and reduced discounts. Its market share fell 2 percent to 28 percent. Other tire makers held their prices, but General Tire priced aggressively. However, General experienced production problems and could not produce enough tires to meet demand. Meanwhile, U.S. Cooper Tire & Rubber made record profits of $58 million on sales of $867 million. This company's strategy was to sell through independent dealers. Even though Cooper is about 1/10th the size of Goodyear or Bridgestone, by concentrating on profitability

it succeeded despite the tire price wars that broke out.

In 1990, in an effort to regain its lost market share, Goodyear introduced a low-priced tire to appeal to price conscious buyers. Under the new price structure, a typical size would range in price between $28.95 and 36.95, compared to the previous lowest Goodyear price of $45.85. Finally, in 1990, Michelin reached its goal to become the world's number 1 tire maker. In October 1990, it forecast a $460 million loss for the year. In Europe, Michelin had followed an aggressive pricing strategy, with prices to automakers falling 40 percent over the previous three years. It was believed that Michelin's price cutting was to signal Japanese tire makers to be careful about attempting to take some of its 35 percent European market share.

Sources: Zachary Schiller, "Why Tiremakers Are Still Spinning Their Wheels," *Business Week* (February 26, 1990), 62–63; "After a Year of Spinning Its Wheels, Goodyear Bets a Retread," *Business Week* (March 26, 1990), 56–58; "Michelin: The High Cost of Being a Big Wheel," *Business Week* (November 5, 1990), 66.

likely will follow price reductions, and (3) there are no significant secondary advantages. In essence, the tire makers were following an unprofitable "kamikaze" pricing strategy.[2]

Summary

This chapter has reviewed issues relative to applying the experience curve to cost and price estimating. The key point of this chapter is that costs, prices, volume, and profit margins are related. And if analysis can objectively relate these four concepts to each other, a powerful tool exists for evaluating alternative pricing strategies. Moreover, the ability to predict

[2]William W. Alberts, "The Experience Curve Doctrine Reconsidered," *Journal of Marketing 53* (July 1989), 36–49; Reed K. Holden and Thomas T. Nagle, "Kamikaze Pricing," *Marketing Management 7* (Summer 1998), 31–39.

FOLLOWING THE EXPERIENCE CURVE WHEN PRICING THE AFTERMARKET

BOX 13.2

In Chapter 2, we suggested that using a low price to achieve objectives when there was a strong aftermarket could be appropriate (see also Chapter 14). Traditional examples of this strategy would be pricing cameras relatively low, or even below assignable costs, to create a market for film and other camera accessories. The classic example of razors and razor blades also applies. Interestingly, the revolution spawned by digital technology has widened the application of this pricing strategy. The technology paradox is that businesses can survive as long as exponential growth of their markets is faster than the exponential decline of their prices.

One important result of this paradox is the recognition that value must be redefined from product benefits, per se, to the value of a long-term relationship with a customer (see Chapter 12). Thus pricing the new base product low, or perhaps giving it away, to establish the aftermarket becomes strategically important. For example, Nintendo priced its video game consoles very low to boost sales of software. Its profits came from sales, license fees, and manufacturing fees on the game software. In some cases, products are most valuable to firms when low prices generate larger volumes of other products in the product line.

Source: Neil Gross and Peter Coy, "The Technology Paradox: How Companies Thrive as Prices Dive," *Business Week* (March 6, 1995), 76–84.

prices over time is a strategic advantage for purchasing, production planning, demand estimation, and capital planning.

The cost–price experience curve provides a method for objectively relating costs, prices, volume, and profit margins. However, simply knowing how to use this tool will not in itself allow a firm to realize its benefits. Underlying the successful application of experience curves is a management philosophy that seeks every possible way to reduce costs while recognizing that a truly profitable product is one that satisfies customers' needs. Hence, managers must remain market oriented and exhibit a will to innovate, sustain an environment that facilitates creativity, and focus on strategic cost management.

Finally, cost, price, and volume analysis is a powerful conceptual and analytical tool. As shown in previous chapters, analytical techniques are not panaceas, nor do they simplify decision making. They do, however, provide a means for understanding the factors that cause certain predictable patterns to exist. Moreover, careful attention to trends and their underlying causes may help eliminate unsound pricing practices. The experience curve can be a useful analytical tool for forecasting costs and prices. In particular, using the experience curve to forecast the cost of a new product over its estimated life cycle can be helpful in planning the product's price during different life cycle stages.

Discussion Questions

1. Distinguish between a learning curve and an experience curve.
2. What is the role of cost estimating in developing a product's price?
3. Explain what is meant by the following concepts within the context of the experience curve:
   a. Accumulated experience
   b. Constant dollars
   c. Cash flows
4. Complete Table 13.1. In what year will accumulated experience double again?
5. The experience curve is often construed to reflect economies of scale due to mass production. Can you provide examples of economies of scale resulting from marketing?

Appendix 1:

Applying the Experience Curve

Opportunities to apply the experience curve are to be found in procurement, production, marketing, and finance. In purchasing, the experience curve may be used to negotiate a price, or to analyze the make-or-buy decision. In cost estimation, decisions related to bidding, pricing, and capital investments may be based on the experience curve. Often contract negotiations are reopened after the experience of time and cost are known for the prototype unit. Indeed, aerospace firms follow this practice with the U.S. Air Force.

The experience curve may be defined if the total direct costs required to complete the first unit are established and if the improvement rate due to experience

is specified. Alternatively, the experience curve can be defined if direct costs for a later unit and the experience curve rate are estimated.

The concept of constant reduction of cost (or time) between doubled accumulated volumes can be expressed as

$$TC_x = KX^{1-b} \qquad \textbf{(13.1)}$$

where

TC_X = cumulative total direct cost

X = number of units

K = cost estimate, for the first unit

b = slope parameter or a function of the experience (improvement) rate, $0 < b < 1$

The cumulative average cost, AC_x, is

$$AC_x = KX^{-b} \qquad (13.2)$$

The experience curve is usually plotted on double logarithmic paper. The plot of Equation 13.2 will result in a straight line on log-log paper. Thus, the function can be plotted knowing either two points or one point and the slope, for example, cost of the first unit and the percentage improvement (experience rate, e.g., 20 percent cost reduction every time cumulative volume doubles).

Relationship Between b and the Experience Rate

To facilitate the estimation, the relationship between a, the experience rate, and b is given by

$$b = \frac{\log 100 - \log a}{\log 2} \qquad (13.3)$$

Table 13.3 shows this relationship for a values ranging from 50 to 100.

Cost Estimation with Cost of First Unit Known

When both the cost of the first unit, AC, and the experience rate, a, are known, the cost of X units can be calculated directly. If cost of the first unit is $1,800 and the experience rate is 80 percent, the total costs for eight units are

$$TC_8 = \$1,800\,(8)^{1-0.322} =$$

$$\$1,800\,(8)^{0.678} = \$1,800\,(4.095)$$

$$= \$7,371.70$$

and the average cost for the eight units is

$$AC_8 = \frac{\$7,371.70}{8} = \$921.46.$$

TABLE 13.3

Relationship between a (percent experience) and b

a	b	a	b
50	1.000	75	0.415
51	0.971	76	0.396
52	0.943	77	0.377
53	0.916	78	0.358
54	0.889	79	0.340
55	0.863	80	0.322
56	0.837	81	0.304
57	0.811	82	0.286
58	0.786	83	0.269
59	0.761	84	0.252
60	0.737	85	0.234
61	0.713	86	0.218
62	0.690	87	0.201
63	0.667	88	0.184
64	0.644	89	0.168
65	0.621	90	0.152
66	0.599	91	0.136
67	0.578	92	0.120
68	0.556	93	0.105
69	0.535	94	0.089
70	0.515	95	0.074
71	0.494	96	0.056
72	0.474	97	0.044
73	0.454	98	0.029
74	0.434	99	0.015
		100	0.000

Source: Adapted with permission from C. Carl Pegels, "Start Up or Learning Curves—Some New Approaches," *Decision Sciences 7* (October 1976), 711.

Alternatively, the average cost for the eight units could be calculated using

$$AC_8 = \$1,800(8)^{-0.322} =$$

$$\frac{\$1,800}{(8)^{-0.322}} = \frac{\$1,800}{1.953} = \$921.66$$

where the differences are due to rounding.

Finding the Experience Curve from Two Points

Suppose a company audited the 20th and 40th production units and found that the production costs were $700 and $635, respectively. The firm now wants to estimate the costs of producing the 80th unit. From Equation 13.2, the average costs are

$$AC_{20} = K(20)^{-b} = \$700$$

$$AC_{40} = K(40)^{-b} = \$635$$

Taking logarithms,

$$\log 700 = \log K - b \log 20 \quad \text{(A)}$$

$$\log 635 = \log K - b \log 40 \quad \text{(B)}$$

Subtracting (B) from (A):

$$\log 700 - \log 635 = b\,(\log 40 - \log 20)$$

$$b = \frac{\log 700 - \log 635}{\log 40 - \log 20}$$

$$= \frac{2.8451 - 2.8028}{1.6021 - 1.3010}$$

$$= \frac{0.0423}{0.3011} = 0.140$$

Looking at Table 13.4, we note that a b of 0.140 lies between $a = 91$ percent and $a = 90$ percent. Interpolating, we obtain an estimated value for a of 90.8 percent.

Using the data for the 20th unit,

$$\log 700 = \log K - 0.14 \log 20$$

$$\log K = \log \$700 + 0.14 \log 20$$

$$= 2.8451 + 0.14\,(1.3010)$$

$$= 3.02724$$

$$K = \$1.065$$

Therefore, the experience curve is

$$AC_x = \$1,065\,(X)^{-0.14}$$

Finally, for the 80th unit, average costs are

$$AC_{80} = \$1,065\,(80)^{-0.14} =$$

$$\frac{\$1,065}{(80)^{0.14}} = \frac{\$1,065}{1.845} = \$577$$

Developing Cost Estimates with *a* Unknown

Although a firm may be able to determine the cost of the prototype unit, it may be uncertain what experience rate will prevail. In such a situation, the firm may wish to determine alternative cost–experience patterns, using different values of a. In this way, the decision maker would be able to develop alternative cost schedules to assist in developing the new product's price.

Consider the situation where the cost of the first unit, AC, is $1,800, but the firm does not have a reasonable estimate of a. Assume that with previous new products the experience rate ranged between 70 and 90 percent. Table 13.4 shows the alternative experience–cost schedules for a values of 70, 80, and 90 percent. These cost schedules reveal the dramatic differences in feasible prices, depending on the actual experience curve that prevails. Indeed, if the 70 percent experience rate is attained, price is likely to be set lower, other things remaining the same. Figure 13.6 illustrates those same three experience curves.

TABLE 13.4
Alternative Experience–Cost Schedules

Number of Units	Cumulative Average Cost When *a* is		
	70%	**80%**	**90%**
1	$1,800	$1,800	$1,800
2	1,259	1,440	1,620
4	882	1,154	1,459
8	617	922	1,312
16	432	738	1,181
32	302	590	1,063
64	211	471	956
128	148	377	861
256	104	302	775
512	72	241	697

FIGURE 13.6   **Alternative Experience–Cost Schedules**

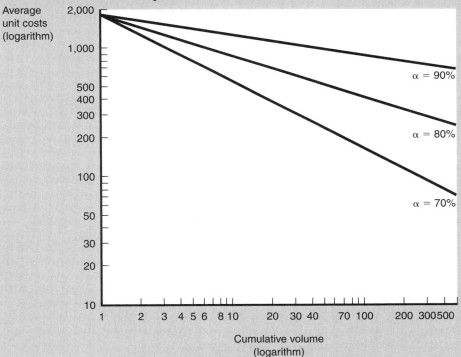

Discussion Questions

1. If costs of the first unit are $1,200 and the experience rate is 90 percent, find
   a. The total costs for 10 units.
   b. The average costs for 10 units.
   c. The average costs for 100 units.
2. A company audited its 50th and 100th production units and determined that the production costs were $900 and $800, respectively.
   a. Determine the experience curve for this firm.
   b. Estimate the average costs for the 200th production unit.
3. a. Develop an experience–cost schedule for the situation where the average cost for the first unit is $1,800 and the assumed experience rate is 85 percent. Develop the schedule for the first 131,072 units.
   b. What conclusions do you draw about the appropriate cost to use when determining price?
4. The Springer Manufacturing Corporation is considering producing and delivering 40 units of an industrial plating machine to a new customer.

The customer has indicated that the maximum feasible price for each plating machine is $5,000. The average cost of building the first unit is estimated by research and development to be $8,000. In the past, the company has usually operated along an experience rate of 85 percent.
   a. Several executives believe the potential price of $5,000 is too low. Prepare an analysis that answers their concern. In your analysis show
   (1) The average and total costs for the following units: 1, 2, 4, 8, 16, 32, 40.
   (2) The total revenues received for 1, 2, 4, 8, 16, 32, and 40 units.
   b. After the first 40 units have been delivered, the customer offers to purchase 100 more units at $2,000 each. Prepare another analysis exactly like the one in part a, except show the average and total costs and total revenue for 1, 2, 4, 8, 16, 32, 64, and 100 units. (Hint: The cost of the 40th unit in part a is the beginning cost for this problem.)

Suggested Readings

Alberts, William W.: "The Experience Curve Doctrine Reconsidered," *Journal of Marketing 53* (July 1989), 36–49.

Day, George S., and David B. Montgomery: "Diagnosing the Experience Curve," *Journal of Marketing 47* (Spring 1983), 44–58.

Ghemawat, Panky: "Building Strategy on the Experience Curve," *Harvard Business Review 63* (March–April 1985), 143–49.

Holden, Reed K., and Thomas T. Nagle: "Kamikaze Pricing," *Marketing Management 7* (Summer 1998), 31–39.

CHAPTER FOURTEEN

Pricing over the Product Life Cycle

As noted in Chapter 1, recent environmental changes in the markets for goods and services have renewed interest in pricing. Yet many of the changes in pricing practices lack a clear-cut conceptual framework and often provoke unanticipated consequences. The previous chapters outlined cost and demand approaches to obtaining relevant information for pricing decisions. Chapters 14 and 15 explore some important pricing decisions and ways the analytical framework developed in previous chapters can be utilized.

One thesis of this book is that the management of a multiproduct firm should be concerned with managing products over their products' life cycles. Management, therefore, must develop plans that consider the life cycles of sales, total contribution, separable fixed costs, and separable assets for the different products. Moreover, management must control production and marketing costs as well as the level of common costs and common assets employed. Indeed, the experience-curve evidence suggests that, as product sales grow, costs and prices decline, although this process is not automatic. The purposes of this chapter are to review the conceptual product life cycle model and to present methods for developing pricing strategies during different stages of the product life cycle.

Product Life Cycles—The Conceptual Model

Although the product life cycle is most frequently pictured in terms of a sales trend, there are actually several relevant life cycles. As Figure 14.1 shows, the cash flow life cycle has direct relevance to payback and profitability. Indeed, Figure 14.1 indicates that an earlier life cycle stage—development—is relevant to the pricing decision.

Development Stage

In the development stage, the product concept is engineered from the idea to the actual design. During this stage no revenues are generated, only costs represented by direct cash outflows. Once the product idea is engineered, market tests are conducted to determine market acceptance and preparations are made for producing the product. Thus, the accumulated cash investment is substantial before the product is introduced for sale.

FIGURE 14.1   **Investment Life Cycle**

Source: Adapted and reprinted with permission from John Sizer, "Accountants, Product Managers and Selling Price Decisions in Multi-Consumer Product Firms," *Journal of Business Finance 4* (Spring 1972), 76.

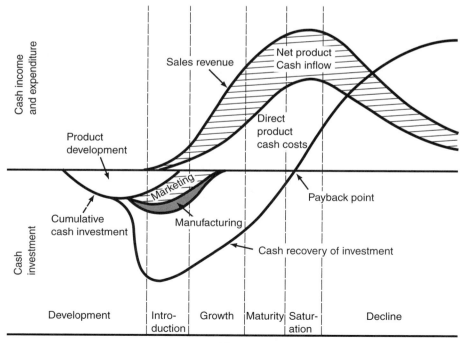

Introduction

When a new product is introduced, initial market awareness is minimal and market acceptance slow. If the firm is the only seller of the product, even though there may be functional substitutes, competition will also be minimal. The firm's marketing efforts are geared to stimulating *primary demand* (demand for the product itself), and there may be some difficulty in gaining widespread distribution. The introduction stage is the period of initial success or failure for new products.

Growth

The product begins to make rapid sales gains as the rate of market acceptance accelerates. It becomes easier to obtain distributors, and competition increases as imitators introduce their versions of the product. Competitors' marketing strategies focus on stimulating *secondary demand* with emphasis on product differentiation. Market volume expands and new market segments are opened up. Unit costs (in constant dollars) may decline as sales volume grows, facilitating still lower prices.

FIGURE 14.2   **Product Life Cycle Stages and Industry Price Experience Curve**

Reprinted with permission from George S. Day and David B. Montgomery, "Diagnosing the Experience Curve," *Journal of Marketing 47* (Spring 1983), 51.

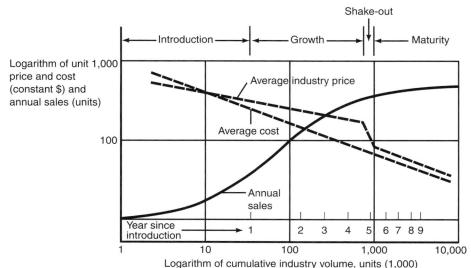

Maturity

Eventually the rate of market acceptance decreases as the number of new potential customers diminishes. Pressures of excess capacity lead to some price competition, and further price competition comes from private-label versions. Replacement sales constitute an increasing proportion of demand. Marketing strategies are designed to create customer preference and loyalty, and continued growth requires an increase in market share.

Saturation

At this stage, products and production methods have become standardized, and buyers generally are well aware of similarities and differences between products. The market is crowded by competitors, and competition for market share intensifies. Replacement demand is the major source of demand, and there may be extensive private labeling. Brand switching takes place, encouraged by pricing strategies that involve offering specials, better credit terms, more services, and increased discounts. Inefficient producers begin to leave the market.

Shakeout

It is during the later stages of the maturity phase and into the saturation stage that the shakeout phase occurs. At this point prices tend to decline faster than do costs. As noted in our discussion of the experience curve phenomenon in Chapter 13, this shakeout phase is marked by competitive turbulence, and the high-cost sellers tend to be forced out of the market. Figure 14.2 illustrates this relationship between the experience curve and the product life cycle at the industry level.

Decline

Sales begin to diminish as customers turn to new or better products. Private labels take an increasing share of the market and profits tend to be minimal. However, through product improvements and isolation of small but profitable market segments, some firms are able to maintain a continuing and profitable product offering.

Price Elasticity over the Product Life Cycle

This brief description of the stages of the product life cycle has alluded to possible differences in the degree that buyers are sensitive to prices, price changes, or price differences over the life cycle. Indeed, this issue of whether differences in price elasticity exist for the various stages in the product life cycle has led to several speculations and some limited empirical research. A recent study covering 17 consumer product categories found that generally price elasticities are dynamic over the life cycle. The direction of price elasticities varies across categories. For some, such as television receivers, price elasticity decreased over time. For others, such as bed covers, price elasticity increased over time. In other product categories, elasticities either increased and then decreased (e.g., refrigerators), or decreased and then increased (e.g., freezers) over their life cycles. As products become necessities, elasticities generally fall over the life cycle.

What can we conclude from this evidence? As we discuss later in this chapter, there are two broad strategies for pricing new products: skimming, (setting relatively high prices) or penetration, (setting relatively low prices). The decision to set initial prices high or low is based on special circumstances. If the initial price is set high because some buyers are not price sensitive (those who have a relatively high reservation or maximum acceptable price), and if experience factors combine with product quality improvements and increasing competitive pressure from entering firms to lead to a declining price trend, then we would expect to see increases in price elasticity. However, if the initial price is set low to penetrate the market quickly because buyers are sensitive to prices and there is the possibility of early competitive entries, then the price trend is likely to be increasing over time. If the product does provide benefits and value to buyers, then even as the prices edge upward, we are not likely to see evidence of increased price sensitivity, at least until maturity.

Thus it is difficult to make unequivocal statements about how price elasticity may change over the stages of the product life cycle. Simply, it depends on how the product is initially priced (which should reflect buyers' initial sensitivity to price differences), whether the product's price follows a decreasing or increasing trend over time (which is partly a reflection of the introductory pricing strategy), the degree to which sellers make quality improvements over time, and the degree that buyers perceive real benefits and therefore value-in-use in the product. As we discussed in Chapter 7, each product will have its own unique pricing history, and the dynamics of price elasticity over the product's life cycle have to be monitored for each product.

Because of the different patterns in the time path of price elasticity over time, managers need to monitor price elasticity continuously. Price can influence the rate of adoption and diffusion not only of relatively high-priced products, but also the rate of diffusion of relatively low-priced products. Late adopters are not necessarily more price sensitive than early purchasers. Thus managers should not assume that large price reductions later in the life cycle will lead automatically to significant increases in the category-level (primary) demand. Often, quality improvements will lead to an increase in perceived benefits, producing increases in perceived value and a decline in price elasticity. Only during the decline stage do price elasticities tend to increase, providing an opportunity to use price reductions strategically. However, if a product category demonstrates decreasing price elasticity during the decline stage, then profitability could be enhanced by price increases.

Managers must not assume that price elasticity is constant over products, markets, or time. If price elasticity is likely to decline for a new product category, then price reductions aimed at increasing overall demand will have their strongest effects early in the product's life.[1] Moreover, category sales are less likely to be affected by price changes near and in the mature stage of the life cycle. On the other hand, if price elasticity increases over the life cycle, then price reductions to increase demand will have less effect early but an increasing effect as the product matures.

Strategy Implications

The intuitive appeal of the product life cycle, its theoretical foundation in the adoption process, and empirical tests suggest that the model does have strategic implications. Yet there is no fixed time length for a cycle or for the lengths of the various stages within the cycle. Although advances in technology are believed to have shortened the typical life cycle, research also suggests that any acceleration of new product diffusion is a function of broad macroeconomic and demographic forces as well as product characteristics.[2]

---

[1] Philip M. Parker and Ramya Neelamegham, "Price Elasticity Dynamics over the Product Life Cycle," *Marketing Letters 8* (April 1997), 205–16.

[2] There is some contrary evidence to this commonly held belief. An analysis of the personal computer industry showed that product technology and product model lifetimes have not accelerated. However, as would be expected, products of late entering firms using previously existing technology do tend to have shorter lifetimes. See Barry L. Bayus, "An Analysis of Product Lifetimes in a Technologically Dynamic Industry," *Management Science 44* (June 1998), 763–75.

Indeed, both the level of the introductory price and the rate of price reductions during the introductory stage have an important influence on the length of the introductory stage. Generally, low-priced innovative products had shorter introductory stages, and on average, price at takeoff (beginning of the growth stage) is 70 percent of the introductory price. Moreover, for consumer durables, takeoffs often occur at specific price points. Of the 31 product categories studied, 16 took off around either the nominal prices of $1,000, $500, or $100.[3] These data imply that there may be specific upper price thresholds above which buyers find prices for new products unacceptable (see Chapter 6). Thus it is important to recognize that pricing strategy is vitally important at each stage of the life cycle.

Basic Pricing Decisions

The pricing decisions for a modern business organization are complex and important. Today, business firms are encountering competitors with more efficient methods of production and generally lower labor costs. As a result, more and more firms are rediscovering price as an active determinant of demand and are actively making pricing decisions.

As Table 14.1 shows, a firm must make many kinds of pricing decisions. It must decide on a specific price to charge for each product or service marketed. But the specific price to charge depends on the type of customer to whom the product or service is sold. If different customers purchase in varying quantities, should the seller offer volume discounts? If the firm markets through a mixed distribution channel, what prices should it charge wholesalers who in turn distribute the products to their retail customers, and what prices should it charge retailers who buy direct from the manufacturer?

The firm must also decide whether to offer discounts for early payment. If the firm decides on a cash discount policy it must then determine when a customer is eligible for a cash discount and how much to allow for early payment. Should the firm attempt to suggest retail prices or should it price to the immediate customer only?

---

[3] Peter N. Golder and Gerard J. Tellis, "Will It Ever Fly? Modeling the Takeoff of Really New Consumer Durables," *Marketing Science 16* no. 3 (1997), 256–70; Christophe Van den Bulte, "New Product Diffusion Acceleration: Measurement and Analysis," *Marketing Science 19* no. 4 (2000), 366–80.

TABLE 14.1 Basic Pricing Decisions

1. What to charge for the different products and services produced by the firm
2. What to charge different types of customers
3. Whether to charge different types of distributors the same price
4. Whether to give discounts for cash and how quickly payment should be required to earn them
5. Whether to suggest resale prices or only set the price charged one's own customers
6. Whether to price all items in the product line as if they were separate or to price them as a "team"
7. How many different price offerings of each item to have
8. Whether to base prices on the geographical location of buyers (i.e., whether to charge for transportation)
9. For established products, whether to change prices (e.g., short-term price promotions; long-term changes)

Most firms sell many products, and it must answer the pricing questions just posed for each product. Additionally, the need to determine the number of price offerings per product and the price relationships between the products offered make the pricing problem more complex. For example, should a camera manufacturer produce and sell only one camera model or several models? Usually, the decision to sell several models of a product means the seller is attempting to appeal to several market segments. Once it decides to offer a number of differently priced models, the seller must decide on the price of the least expensive model and on price differentials between each alternative offering.

Today's difficult pricing decisions require careful managerial planning. Because the traditional practice of pricing has been to imitate the pricing practices of others, it is likely that many managers will seek to follow the pricing prescriptions found in the contemporary literature. However, each firm should carefully analyze its markets, competitors, and costs before developing a pricing strategy.

New-Product Pricing

One of the most challenging decision problems is determining the price of a new product. New-product pricing decisions are usually made with very little information about demand, costs, competition, and other variables that may affect the chances of success. Given the rate of new-product introductions and the rate of failures, the importance of the new-product price decision is apparent.

Many new products fail because they do not possess the benefits buyers desired or because they are not available at the right time and place. Others fail because they have been wrongly priced, and the error can as easily be in pricing the product too low as in pricing it too high. One reason for new-product pricing errors is the lack of knowledge about how pricing decisions should be made. Thus the decision maker often relies on intuition, and experience does not appear to measurably improve chances of success.

The most difficult new-product pricing problem occurs when the product is unique—that is, functionally dissimilar to any other product. If the product is a major innovation in the market, uncertainty surrounds the pricing decision. Essentially, the market is undefined—demand is unknown—and not all potential uses of the product are known. There are no comparable market experiences regarding channels of distribution, markups, or production and marketing costs. Potential customers will be uncertain about the product's function, reliability, or durability. They may be concerned about whether improvements will be made and the effects of these improvements on the product. Customers may also wonder whether prices will be reduced later when more sellers are distributing the product and when mass production techniques lower production costs. Pricing decisions usually have to be made with little knowledge and with wide margins of error in the forecasts of demand, cost, and competitors' capabilities. Today, many new high-technology products and services have very low incremental production costs and both sellers and buyers are uncertain about the benefits the product or service may provide.

Factors to Consider When Pricing New Products

As developed in Chapter 1, five essential factors must be considered when setting price. Demand considerations provide a ceiling or maximum price that can be charged. The determination of this maximum price depends on the customers' perceptions of value in the seller's product or service offering. On the other hand, costs provide a floor, or minimum possible price. For a new product, the relevant costs are the future expected direct costs over the product's life cycle.

Loading irrelevant costs onto a new product's burden may simply push the price floor beyond the price ceiling, leading to a decision to set the product's price too high. Recently, a medical equipment producer, a supplies manufacturer, and an

TABLE 14.2 Systematic Approach to New-Product Pricing

Step	Activity
1	Estimate demand at different prices over expected life cycle
2	Estimate costs over expected life cycle
3	Estimate price–volume–profit relationship
4	Determine likely competitors
5	Determine competitors' entry capabilities
6	Estimate competitors' likely entry dates
7	Determine a marketing strategy
8	Estimate marketing requirements over product's life cycle
9	Select a specific price

industrial machinery producer all experienced new-product failures when they set their introductory price too high. Their pricing error occurred because of the felt need to recover their investment in product development too quickly.

A product that is new to the world passes through distinctive competitive stages in its life cycle. The appropriate pricing policy is likely to be different for each stage. As new competitors enter the field and innovations narrow the gap of distinctiveness between the product and its substitutes, pricing discretion narrows. The distinctive "specialty" product becomes a "commodity" that is little differentiated from other rival products.

The core of new-product pricing takes into account the price sensitivity of demand and the seller's incremental promotional and production costs. What the product is worth to the buyer, not what it costs the seller, is the controlling consideration. When developing a new product's price, the relationship between the buyers' perceived benefits in the new product and the total acquisition cost is important. One approach for assessing buyers' perceived value is to conduct a value analysis as developed in Chapter 8.

As Table 14.2 indicates, a systematic approach to new-product pricing emphasizes the development of a "true" marketing plan. Instead of viewing pricing as an isolated problem, the systematic planning approach considers price as one of the variables that interacts to determine product success. The pricing decision, therefore, is only one of several interrelated decisions.

Estimating Demand for a New Product

The first step in new-product pricing is to estimate demand in the selected market targets. How can demand for new products be estimated? How can the range of prices that people will consider acceptable for a new product be estimated?

The demand estimation problem can be separated into a series of research problems: (1) Will the product fill a need or want and, therefore, sell if the price is right? (2) At what range of prices will the product be acceptable to potential buyers? (3) What is the expected sales volumes at feasible price points in the acceptable price range? (4) What is the extent of potential competitive response?

The research methods presented in Chapter 9 for estimating buyers' ranges of acceptable prices can be used to estimate the acceptable price range for a new product. Two basic kinds of information must be generated from potential users of the product: (1) the highest and lowest prices they would consider paying for the product and (2) the price last paid for the nearest comparable product or service. The first piece of information provides estimates of the acceptable price range and can be translated into a frequency distribution called a *buy-response curve* (see Figure 9.4). The midpoint price of the buy-response curve provides an estimate of the price that potential buyers are likely to judge most acceptable, as well as an estimate of the proportion of buyers likely to consider buying the product at that price.

For industrial products, an easy way to find this acceptable range is to ask professionals experienced in looking at comparative product performance in terms of buyers' costs and requirements—for example, distributors, prime contractors, consulting engineers, and engineers of prospect companies.

For consumer goods, another approach may be used. In estimating the price range of new products, the concept of barter equivalent may be useful. For example, a manufacturer of paper specialties tested a new product this way: A variety of consumer products totally unlike the new product were spread out on a big table. Consumers selected the products they would swap for the new product.

The second piece of information, price last paid for a comparable product or service, indicates a reference point buyers may use when contemplating the purchase of the new product. A comparison of the midpoint of the buy-response curve with the midpoint of the price-last-paid curve will indicate the degree of discretion available in pricing the new product. For example, if the midpoint of the buy-response curve is at a higher price than the midpoint of the price-last-paid curve, then a price higher than the price last paid may have a degree of buyer acceptance. A limitation to this research approach occurs if the product is such a major innovation that buyers have no concept either of the product or of comparable alternatives.

The example given in Box 6.2 concerning the pricing error made when opening Disneyland Paris and the research data showing the relation between introductory price and the length of an innovative product's introductory period make it clear that careful pricing research must be conducted prior to setting the initial price. Moreover, given that introductory price has a direct influence on the length of time before the growth stage occurs and that the length of the introductory stage has been reduced by 50 percent, there is less opportunity to correct new pricing errors.

Selecting Probable Prices

The buyers' viewpoint should control pricing. For every new product there are alternatives. Buyers' best alternatives are usually products already tested in the marketplace. The new product will, presumably, supply a superior solution for some categories of buyers, but the degree of superiority of any new product over its substitutes may differ widely in different buyers' viewpoints.

Buyers' Alternatives

The prospective buyer of any new product does have alternatives. These indirectly competitive products provide the reference for appraising a new product's price–performance package and determine its relative attractiveness to potential buyers. Such an analysis of demand can be made in the following steps:

1. Determine the major uses for the new product. For each application, determine the product's performance characteristics.

2. For each major use, specify the products that are the buyers' best alternatives to the new product. Determine the performance characteristics and requirements that buyers view as crucial in determining their product selection.

3. For each major use, determine how well the product's performance characteristics meet the requirements of customers compared with the performance of these buyers' alternative products.

4. Forecast the prices of alternative products in terms of transaction prices, adjusted for the impact of the new product and translated into units of use. Estimate from the prices of these reference substitutes the alternative costs to the buyer per unit of the new product. Real transaction prices (after all discounts), rather than list prices, should be used to reflect marketplace realities. Price after the introduction of the new product should be predicted to reflect probable competitive adaptation to the new product. Where eventual displacement of existing substitutes appears likely, short-run incremental cost can forecast rivals' pricing retaliation.

5. Estimate the superiority premium; that is, price the performance differential in terms of the value buyers place on the superior solution the new product supplies.

6. Determine a "parity price" for the product relative to the buyer's best alternative product in each use for major categories of customers. Parity is a price that encompasses the premium a customer would be willing to pay for comparative superiority in performance characteristics.

Pricing the Superiority Differential

Determining the price premium that the new product's superiority will most profitably warrant is the most intricate and challenging problem of new-product pricing. The value to the customer of the superiority of the new product is surrounded by uncertainties: whether the product will work, whether it will attain its designed superiorities, what its reliability and durability performance will be, and how soon it, in turn, will become obsolete. These uncertainties influence the price customers would pay and the promotional outlay that would be required to persuade them to buy. Thus, customers' uncertainties will cost the seller something, either in price or promotion. It is also important to remember that buyers may use price as a signal of product performance (see Chapter 4).

In essence, the superiority premium requires translation of differential performance characteristics into dollars, based on value analysis from the buyer's viewpoint. The premium will differ among uses, among alternative products, and among categories of customers. What matters is superiority as buyers value it, not superiority as calibrated by technicians' measurements or by sellers' costs.

Estimating Costs

Perhaps the most common error managers make in pricing new products is to follow an inside-out approach. That is, they delay the pricing decision until near the end of the development process when the production and marketing costs can be reasonably estimated. Then target margins and required distributor margins are added to get the market price. However, a value-oriented approach to pricing new products begins with establishing what the target market would be willing to pay for the projected performance level of the new product. Once the target price has been established, it is the task of the development process to design a product that will have a target cost that provides sufficient profit margins to the firm as well as to distributors.[4]

A second common error is to attempt to recover the investment in a new product as quickly as possible. An acceptable price for a new product is one that will attract both resellers and ultimate users. A high price requiring substantial selling effort to overcome buyer resistance will not receive enthusiastic support from distributors.

A third error is to base initial prices on the wrong cost data. Including development costs and high initial unit production costs in the new product's costs is likely to result in a price that will repel both distributors and final customers and effectively kill the product. Development costs must be considered as an investment to be recovered over the life of the product. The appropriate unit direct costs are those costs expected when the product reaches its growth stage, or when steady production and sales rates are achieved.

As outlined in Chapter 10, to get maximum practical use from costs in new product pricing, three questions must be answered: (1) Whose cost? (2) Which cost? and (3) What role? As to whose cost, three classes of costs are important: (1) those of prospective buyers, (2) those of existing and potential competitors, and (3) those of the producer of the new product. Cost should play a different role for each of the three, and the pertinent concept of cost will differ accordingly.

---

[4] Stephan A. Butscher and Michael Laker, "Market-Driven Product Development," *Marketing Management 9* (Summer 2000), 48–53; Robin Cooper and W. Bruce Chew, "Control Tomorrow's Costs through Today's Designs," *Harvard Business Review 73* (July–August), 88–98; Ogenyi Ejye Omar, "Target Pricing: A Marketing Management Tool for Pricing New Cars," *Pricing Strategy & Practice 5* no 2 (1997), 61–69.

Buyers' Costs

The costs of prospective customers can be determined by applying value analysis techniques discussed in Chapter 8 to prices and performance of alternative products to find the superiority premium that will make the new product attractive to buyers.

Competitors' Costs

Competitors' costs are usually the crucial estimate in appraisal of competitors' capabilities. For products already in the marketplace, the objectives are to estimate their staying power, and the floor of retaliation pricing. For the first objective, the pertinent cost concept is the competitor's long-run incremental cost. For the second, the short-run incremental cost is relevant.

Forecasts of competitors' costs for unborn competing products that could blight a new product's future or eventually displace it can help assess the capability of prospective competitors. It also provides an estimate of the effectiveness of a new-product pricing strategy to discourage entry. For this situation, the cost behavior to forecast is the relationship between unit direct costs and cumulative experience as the new producer and rivals move from pilot plant to large-scale mass production. These cost forecasts should consider technological progress and should reflect the potential head-start cost advantages. When defining one's competitors, it is necessary to think globally. That is, future competitors may come from international companies in other parts of the world.

Seller's Costs

The cost of the producer plays several roles in pricing a new product. First, a new product must be prepriced provisionally early in the R&D stage and then again periodically as it progresses toward market. Forecasts of production and marketing costs will influence the decision to continue product development and ultimately to commercialize. The concept of cost relevant for this analysis is a prediction of direct costs at a series of prospective volumes and corresponding technologies, and it includes imputed cost of capital on intangible as well as tangible investment.

The production and distribution costs that matter are the future costs over the long run that will be added by making this product versus not making it. The added investment necessary to manufacture and distribute the new product including intangibles such as R&D, promotion, launching outlays, and increased working capital, should be estimated. Then the added costs of manufacturing, promoting and selling the product at various sales volumes should be estimated. It is important to calculate total costs with and without the new product. The difference can then be assigned to the new product. Present overhead that will be the same whether or not the product is added to the line should be ignored; future additions to overhead caused by the new product are the only relevant overhead considerations in pricing. Two sets of cost and investment figures must be built up—one showing the situation without the new product and the other showing the situation with the new product added to the line—at several possible volumes. High costs of pilot-plant production and of early small-scale production plants should be viewed as intangible capital investment rather than current operating costs. The losses of a break-in period are a part of the investment on which a satisfactory return should be made.

Estimating the Price–Volume–Profit Relationship

The effect of the new product's price upon its sales volume is the most important and most difficult estimate in pricing. The best way to predict the effect of price on sales volume for a new product is by controlled experiments: offering it at several different prices in comparable test markets under realistic sales conditions. When test marketing is not feasible, another method is to broaden the study of the cost of buyers' alternatives and include forecasts of the sales volume of substitutes. Ideally, the analysis and planning for pricing a new product begins at the start of the product development stage. The investment analysis requires estimate of revenues and expenditures over time for each alternative under consideration. The analysis must project estimated cash flows over the entire investment life cycle (see Figure 14.1). Therefore, some preliminary price–volume estimates for the different stages of the product life cycle are necessary at the outset.

Then, for each price-volume estimate, direct production and marketing costs must be estimated. Again, it is important to emphasize the need to consider realistic costs (costs that are comparable to costs to be incurred during the product's growth stage). It is also important to avoid the temptation to apportion common costs to the product because, as Chapter 11 showed, any apportionment is essentially arbitrary.

Alternative Strategies for Pricing a New Product

Two alternatives have been generally assumed for pricing a new product: "skimming" pricing, which calls for a relatively high price, and "penetration" pricing, which calls for a relatively low price. There are intermediate positions, but the issues are made clearer by comparing the two extremes.

Skimming Pricing

Some products represent drastic improvements upon accepted ways of performing a service or filling a demand. For these new products a strategy of relatively high prices with large promotional expenditures during market development (and lower prices at later stages) has frequently proved successful. A "skimming-price" strategy may be appropriate for new products when

1. Sales of the product are likely to be less sensitive to price in the early stages than when the product is "full-grown" and competitive imitations have appeared. That is, price elasticity of demand is expected to increase over the product's life cycle.

2. Launching a new product with a high price is an efficient device for breaking the market up into segments that differ in price elasticity of demand. The initial high price serves to skim the cream of the market that is relatively insensitive to price.

3. A skimming policy is safer, in that facing unknown elasticity of demand, a high initial price serves as a "refusal" price during the stage of exploration. How much costs can be reduced as the market expands and as value engineering improves production efficiency is difficult to predict.

4. High prices may produce greater sales revenue during market development than low initial prices. If so, skimming pricing will provide funds to finance expansion into the larger-volume sectors of a market.

5. A lower volume is less demanding on capacity and financial resources.

6. The product or service offers realistic (perceived) value.

7. A high introductory price provides room for future price decreases.

8. A high introductory price may be used to signal quality when customers are uncertain about the product's benefits and quality is revealed slowly over time.

9. A high introductory price may be used to signal customers and competitors that the firm expects to have a relatively low experience effect on costs.

Skimming is not always appropriate in these situations, and it does have its disadvantages. A skimming strategy is less likely to induce buyers to enter the market, and it does not encourage rapid adoption or diffusion of the product. Moreover, if skimming results in relatively high profit margins, competitors may be attracted into the market. One research study found that a skimming pricing strategy led to more competitors in the market during the product's growth stage than did a penetration pricing strategy.[5]

Penetration Pricing

Despite its many advantages, a skimming-price policy is not appropriate for all new products and services. Using low prices as a wedge to get into mass markets early may be appropriate when

1. Sales volume of the product is very sensitive to price, even in the early stages of introduction.

2. Buyers can determine product quality and benefits quickly after trial and use.

3. Substantial economies in unit cost of manufacturing and distributing the product can be achieved through fast growth of accumulated volume.

4. A product faces threats of strong potential competition very soon after introduction.

5. No segment of buyers is willing to pay a higher price to obtain the product.

6. Available capacity in production and distribution is high.

7. A low introductory price may be used to signal customers and competitors that the firm expects to have a relatively large experience effect on costs.

While a penetration pricing policy can be adopted at any stage in the product's life cycle, this pricing strategy should always be examined before a new product is marketed at all. Its possibility should be explored again as soon as the product has established an elite market. To avoid the disadvantages of skimming and penetration, some firms employ both alternatives. They pursue a skimming strategy after the

---

[5] William H. Redmond, "Effects of New Product Pricing on the Evolution of Market Structure," *Journal of Product Innovation Management 6* (1989), 99–108.

product has been introduced—typically until competitors enter the market. Then they switch to a penetration strategy by lowering prices to hold market share and build volume. Sometimes a product can be rescued from premature death by adoption of a penetration price after the market has been skimmed.

Skimming versus Penetration

One important consideration in the choice between skimming and penetration pricing at the time a new product is introduced is the ease and speed with which competitors can bring out substitute products. If the initial price is set low enough, large competitors may not feel it worthwhile to make a big investment for slim profit margins.

Another important consideration is customers' and competitors' expectations about the ability of the firm to realize cost reductions due to the experience phenomenon. If customers expect that the firm will experience greater cost savings due to experience than the firm actually will realize, they may delay purchases in anticipation of price reductions. These customers may anticipate that the price reductions will occur relatively sooner and be larger than the firm is capable of providing. These expectations may prompt buyers to delay purchasing until the price reductions occur. If so, sales for the new product may be lower than the firm had forecast based on its market research. Moreover, if competitors have similar expectations, then they might be less inclined to enter the market fearing a cost disadvantage relative to the firm.

As developed in Chapter 4, then, we have a condition of information asymmetry and the firm may use price and other publicly available information to signal customers and competitors about the likely future price path for the new product.[6] A relatively high introductory price can be used to signal that the firm expects to realize slow experience cost savings and that prices will be slow to decline due to experience-induced cost savings. On the other hand, a relatively low

---

[6] Subramanian Balachander and Kannan Srinivasan, "Modifying Customer Expectations of Price Decreases for a Durable Product," *Management Science 44* (June 1998), 776–86; Eileen Bridges, Chi Kin (Bennett) Yim, and Richard Briesch, "A High-Tech Product Market Share Model with Customer Expectations," *Marketing Science 14* (Winter 1995), 61–81; Peter Doyle and John Saunders, "The Lead Effect of Marketing Decisions," *Journal of Marketing Research 22* (February 1985), 54–65.

introductory price can be used to signal that the firm expects to be on a more rapid experience curve and that to realize the benefits of such a curve quickly, it is pricing to build volume and capture as much of the potential market as possible before competitors can enter.

Understanding and addressing customers' price expectations is strategically important. If a price is noticeably below customers' expectations, it may have a negative effect on sales because customers infer a quality issue. Or customers may infer that the firm is about to introduce a new and improved version and will decide to wait for the new, better-performing version. On the other hand, if the price is noticeably above customers' expectations, it likely will also have a negative effect on sales.

IBM's PS/2 Model 70 personal computer in 1990 met customers' expectations for both technology and price. As a result, its market share was over five times the average market share for personal computers. However, IBM did not change this model's price or technology in 1991 as did some of its competitors, and actual relative market share fell over 35 percent. According to estimates, 11 percent of this decrease was due to the relative price increase of this model compared with competitors' reduced price, 22 percent of the decrease was due to overall poorer performance of the IBM brand name, and 67 percent of the decrease was due to price that was noticeably above customers' expectations, as they had expected 1991 prices to be lower than 1990 prices. [7]

The factors mentioned above may suggest an overall pricing strategy for a new product. However, *these two alternative strategies should not be viewed as either/or alternatives*. Rather, they merely reflect two opposite strategy extremes. Considerable latitude, therefore, exists in choosing the specific price level for a new product.

Summary

The important determinants in pricing product innovations are complex, interrelated, and hard to forecast. Experienced judgment is required in pricing and repricing the product to fit its changing competitive environment. This judgment may be improved by these guidelines:

1. Corporate goals must be clearly defined.

---

[7] Bridges, Yim, and Briesch, "A High-Tech Market Share Model."

2. Pricing a new product should begin during its development stage.

3. Pricing a new product should be a continuing process of successive approximations. Rough estimates of the relevant concepts are preferable to precise knowledge of historical irrelevancies.

4. Costs can supply useful guidance in new-product pricing, but not by cost-plus pricing. Three categories of costs are pertinent: those of the buyer, those of the seller, and those of the seller's rivals.

5. The role of cost is to set a reference base for picking the most profitable price. For this job the only costs that are pertinent to pricing a new product are incremental costs—the added costs of going ahead at different plant scales. Costs of R&D and of market testing are sunk and hence irrelevant.

6. The pricing implications of the changing economic status and competitive environment of a product must be recognized as it passes through its life cycle.

7. The product should be seen through the eyes of the customer and priced just low enough to make it an irresistible investment in view of available alternatives.

8. Customers' rate of return should be the main consideration in pricing novel capital goods. Buyers' cost savings (or revenues gained), expressed as a return on their investment in the new product, is the key to predicting the price sensitivity of demand and to pricing profitably.

9. The strategic choice between skimming and penetration pricing should be based on a careful analysis of the market.

Gillette's New Product Pricing

Box 14.1 summarizes the pricing and results of Gillette's three recent introductions of new razor systems. In each of these introductions, analysts have strongly criticized the company. In the introduction of Sensor, Gillette seemingly did not understand how successful the new razor would be, and it could not meet retailer's demand for the razors or the refill cartridges. Despite its inability to meet early demand the product became very successful. Given the principles of new-product pricing that have just been outlined, it would

GILLETTE SETS NEW STANDARDS FOR RAZORS

BOX 14.1

In the late 1980s, the blade and razor market in the United States and Europe was rapidly becoming a commodity market with increased consumption of disposable razors. To avoid competing on price and to revamp shaving systems that were losing share to disposable razors, Gillette focused on its core strength, the development of high-quality permanent razors and disposable cartridges.

Sensor, launched in 1989, served as Gillette's first response to the disposable razor. As the company's first new product in over 13 years, Sensor had been the most expensive project in Gillette's history—expenses totaled over $300 million. At that time, Gillette's gross profits on disposable razors equaled 8¢ to 10¢; the firm earned 25¢ to 30¢ in gross profits per Atra and Trac II cartridge. Gillette introduced Sensor with a price of $3.75 for the basic razor, which was about 35 percent lower than the price of its Atra and Trac II razors. However, given a strong aftermarket for cartridges and blades, Sensor's cartridges sold for $3.79 per five-pack, which was 25 percent more than for Gillette's old systems.

The higher price for Sensor's cartridges did not appear to "scare off" consumers. Following a $3 million television advertisement during the 1990 Super Bowl, demand for the new razor system far exceeded supply. Gillette shipped nearly 4.5 million razors throughout the month of January and still found itself not meeting demand! Sensor helped Gillette's razor and blades division expand sales to $2 billion in 1991 versus $1.2 billion in 1989, a 67 percent increase.

Then in 1998, Gillette introduced the Mach3 triple edge razor system for men. Including the marketing launch budget of $300 million, this new shaving system represented a $1 billion investment. The razor was priced at 35 percent over the Sensor and the refill cartridges were priced at $1.50 each compared to $1 for the Sensor cartridges. To help mitigate direct price comparisons with the Sensor cartridges, the Mach3 refills were sold in packages of 4 and 8 cartridges whereas the Sensor refills were sold in packages of 5 and 10 cartridges. Although critics questioned this price premium, Gillette executives said a 45 percent price premium had been tested and met little consumer resistance. Because the new blade edge was three times stronger, it was expected to lead to about a 10 percent decline in consumption of cartridge refills. Mach3 boosted division sales from 1997 to 1999 by 14 percent to $3.3 billion. In 2000 Mach3 sales were $1 billion. The president of the division said that Gillette sold 60 percent more razors in two and a half years with Mach3 than in a similar time frame with the Sensor launch.

Hoping to capture a similar success in the women's shaving market, in March 2001 Gillette launched Venus, a triple-blade razor specifically designed for women. Priced at $8 for a razor, two cartridges, and a storage compact, it became the most expensive women's razor on the market. A package of four refill cartridges was also priced at $8. By comparison, other women's razors ranged in price from less than $1 to $6 or $7 for other cartridge models. Again, analysts questioned Gillette's pricing.

Sources: Laurence D. Ackerman, "No Guts, No Glory: Product Strategy for Europe," *Management Review* (September 1991), 29–32.; Keith H. Hammonds, "How a $4 Razor Ends Up Costing $300 Million," *Business Week* (January 29, 1990), 62–63.; Keith H. Hammonds, "It's One Sharp Ad Campaign, But Where's the Blade?" *Business Week* (March 5, 1990), 30; David Shook, "Gillette Needs Venus to Woo Investors," *Business Week Online* (January 26, 2001); William C. Symonds, "Would You Spend $1.50 for a Razor Blade?" *Business Week* (April 27, 1998), 46; Heesun Wee, "Venus Envy for Gillette's Rivals," *Business Week Online* (February 14, 2001).

seem that Gillette set the Sensor's introductory price too low because early demand greatly exceeded its capacity resources. However, despite serious management misgivings, one objective of the Sensor strategy was to stop the loss of market share to the disposable razor and its low profit margin. Thus pricing the Sensor below the Atra and Trac II razors increased the comparative value of the Sensor, which provided a smoother and closer shave than these other two systems.

However, when introducing the Mach3, with its revolutionary three-blade system and the claim of a much better shave than with the Sensor, Gillette had to set a premium price above the Sensor. Critics suggest that the Sensor had a proportionately greater impact on the division's sales in the first year after launch than Mach3, but the pricing strategies were quite different. The Sensor was priced relatively low to achieve penetration quickly and to curtail the inroads of the disposable razor. On the other hand, Mach3 was priced relatively high, although apparently not as high as the market might have accepted.

As with Mach3, Venus has been launched at a relatively high price. However, to back its claim of providing a superior shaving experience for women, the price must be higher than competing alternatives. Time will tell how successful Gillette will be with Venus, because the disposable razor market is apparently stronger for women than men.

Pricing during Growth

If the new product survives the introductory period, the nature of contribution analysis changes. Usually, a number of competitors are producing and selling a similar product, and an average market price emerges. Normally, a relatively wide range of market prices is found early in the growth stage, but this market price range narrows as the product approaches maturity.

Three essential points for pricing during the growth stage should be noted: (1) the range of feasible prices has narrowed since the introductory stage; (2) unit variable costs have decreased due to the experience factor; and (3) fixed expenses have increased because of increased capitalization and period marketing costs. The pricing decision during the growth stage is to select a price that, subject to competitive conditions, will help generate a sales volume that enables the firm to realize its target contribution.

As the product's sales growth slows, two important issues arise. First, what should the firm do when it faces new competition from lower-priced competitive offerings? Second, what can the firm do to prolong the growth stage and delay the onset of maturity and decline?

Sometimes the firm may have a period of time during the growth stage when it either has protection from competition via patents or by the nature of the innovation. If so, the firm may realize substantial profits because of this protected position. However, such profits will lead to entry of competitors either as the patent expires or as soon as they have duplicated the innovation. Typically, these new entrants will introduce lower-priced versions of the original product.

Rather than waiting for the lower-priced entries to erode its sales of the profitable higher-priced version, the firm should consider introducing one or more lower-priced versions itself.[8] Although such a move will reduce sales of the higher-priced product, it will have the effect of preventing a competitor from enjoying early-mover advantage in the low-price market segment, and it may stimulate additional overall sales growth. Moreover, such a move provides a signal to future competitors that the firm will defend its current market position.[9] If the firm is concerned that introducing a low-priced version will provide conflicting price–quality signals, it may use a different brand name for the low-price version. Making such a product-line move puts the firm into a product-line pricing situation, which we discuss in Chapter 15.

Pricing during Maturity

As a product moves into the maturity and saturation stages, it is necessary to review past pricing decisions and determine the desirability of a price change. Replacement sales now constitute the major demand, and manufacturers also incur competition from private-label products. Market conditions do not appear to warrant a price increase, and the pricing decision usually is to reduce price or stand pat.

To price appropriately for later stages in the life cycle, it is important to know when a product is approaching matu-

---

[8] Klaus Hilleke and Stephan A. Butscher, "How to Use a Two-Product Strategy against Low-Price Competition," *Pricing Strategy & Practice 5* no. 3, (1997), 108–15.

[9] Louis A. Thomas, "Incumbent Firms' Response to Entry: Price, Advertising, and New Product Introduction," *International Journal of Industrial Organization 17* (1999), 527–55.

rity. When the new product is about to slip into the commodity category, it is sometimes desirable to reduce real prices promptly as soon as symptoms of deterioration appear. Some of the symptoms of degeneration of competitive status toward the commodity level are

1. Weakening in brand preference, evidenced by a higher cross-price elasticity of demand among leading products because the leading brand cannot continue demanding as large a price premium as it did initially without losing position.

2. Narrowing physical variation among products as the best designs are developed and standardized. This effect has been dramatically demonstrated in automobiles and in personal computers.

3. The entry of private-label or low-price substitutes.

4. Market saturation. The ratio of replacement sales to new-equipment sales serves as an indicator of the competitive degeneration of durable goods.

5. The stabilization of production methods, indicated by slow rate of technological advance, high average age of equipment, and great uniformity among competitors' introduction technology.

When is a price reduction profitable? We know that when demand is price elastic it is profitable to reduce prices if costs do not rise above the increase in revenues. But because competitors can be expected to follow any price decrease, it is also necessary that the *market demand* curve be elastic within the range of the price reduction. Moreover, as demonstrated in Chapters 11 and 13, the requirements for a profitable price reduction strategy include beginning with a relatively high contribution margin, opportunity for accelerating growth, a favorable combined leverage position, and a price-elastic demand. When a product has reached the maturity stage of its life cycle, it is most likely that these conditions will not exist (see Box 13.1).

Because of the number of close substitutes, a firm's demand curve will probably be elastic. But if all sellers match the price reduction, the firm's market share will remain relatively constant, and any increase in the firm's demand will result from an increase in market demand. Therefore, to reduce price for a mature product, market demand must be elastic, the firm's demand must be elastic, and the marginal revenues associated with the increased volume must be greater than the marginal costs of producing and selling the additional volume.

At the maturity stage of the life cycle, the firm probably should attempt to maximize short-run direct product contribution to profits. Hence the pricing objective is to choose the price alternative leading to maximum contribution. If competition reduces prices, the firm may, however reluctantly, match the price reduction. On the other hand, it may try to reduce costs by using cheaper materials, eliminating several labor operations, or reducing period marketing costs. Any or all of these actions may allow the firm to match competitively lower prices and still maintain target contributions to profit.

Pricing a Declining Product

During the declining phase of a product's life, direct costs are very important to the pricing decision. Normally, competition has driven the price down close to direct costs. Only those sellers who were able to maintain or reduce direct costs during the saturation stage are likely to have remained. If the decline is not due to an overall cyclical decline in business but to shifts in buyer preferences, then the primary objective is to obtain as much contribution to profits as possible.

As long as the firm has excess capacity and revenues exceed all direct costs, the firm probably should consider remaining in the market. Generally, most firms eliminate all period marketing costs (or as many of these costs as possible) and remain in the market as long as price exceeds direct variable costs. As noted in Chapters 10 and 11, the direct variable costs are the minimally acceptable prices to the seller. Thus, with excess capacity, any market price above direct variable costs would generate contributions to profit. Indeed, as suggested in Chapter 11, the relevant decision criterion is to maximize contributions per sales dollar generated. In fact, it might be beneficial to raise the price of a declining product to increase the contributions per sales dollar (see Box 14.2).

Focused Price Reductions

As discussed above and in Chapters 11 and 13, the stringent requirements for price reduction strategies to be profitable

| COMPETING IN A DECLINING MARKET | BOX 14.2 |

Often reductions in demand go unnoticed by managers who focus more attention on revenues than unit volumes. When the end of a product life cycle occurs, firms experience declining profit margins resulting from lower sales and excess capacity. A decline in sales growth may occur as a result of a number of situations, including changing demographics and lifestyles, evolving technology, and introduction of substitute and competing products. Managers must recognize the reasons behind the lack of growth in sales and understand the impending maturity of their products by phasing out product lines that are no longer profitable to the company as a whole.

Not every firm can remain in a declining market; however, the last firm standing may remain profitable as it serves continued demand. To signal a firm's intention to continue competing in a particular industry, managers should continue to invest in the market and should purchase rivals' assets to reduce the competition's exit barriers while preventing costly price wars.

When should a firm follow a strategy that positions it as one of the last remaining firms within a market? A firm should increase investment in a declining market when (1) sufficient demand exists for the product; (2) the costs associated with repositioning the current marketing strategy to address the "last" customers may be recovered quickly, and (3) very few competitors can meet the needs of the smaller customer segments as well as the firm.

How should a firm competing in a declining market structure its pricing strategy? As mentioned previously, firms in the later stages of a product's life cycle should avoid price wars. However, reducing prices may enable the firm to maintain sales volume while firms that are not able to compete in a declining market exit.

Source: Kathryn R. Harrigan, "Will You Be 'the Last Iceman'?" *Sales & Marketing Management* (January 1990), 62–67.

make it questionable to ever consider across-the-board price cuts. Yet, over the product life cycle, competitive pressures or price-sensitive buyers in the market may require a firm to consider reducing prices. Thus if the firm can selectively reduce price to specific market segments, then focused price reductions may be profitable. To pursue focused price reductions, the firm must know both the different degrees of price sensitivity across price-market segments *and* the relative costs of serving these segments. We next describe some different ways that focused price reductions can be implemented.

Base Product versus Option Prices

Often, by selling the basic product without add-on features and options, the seller can appeal to a price-sensitive market, those who want only the basic product, and other buyers who are not price sensitive. Many customers will make their purchase decision using the base price alone and become less price sensitive to the additional options or accessories that can be purchased separately. The discussion in Chapters 5 through 8 on how buyers form value judgments suggests that this segregation of perceived losses with differential gains (the features) may lead to positive value perceptions. Some examples of this practice include bank practices of separating interest rates and fees, movie theaters separating seat tickets from concessions, automobile buying, and service contracts on consumer appliances.

Channel Specific Pricing

The success of off-price retailers and factory outlets suggest this approach. High-price designer clothing can frequently be purchased in these types of retail stores at a fraction of the price that it is successfully sold in the upscale stores. Although the assortment available and amenities and services provided may differ somewhat, fashion clothing can be purchased at relatively lower prices in these stores. The objective of using this strategy is to identify distribution channels that serve price sensitive customers and offer lower prices through these channels only.

Pricing According to Customers' Perceived Values

The relative success of airlines and hotels in offering similar services to customers at different prices (see the discussion on yield management in Chapter 15) supports the use of this approach. Offering lower prices for demand that occurs during off-peak hours—for example, long distance telephone or midnight to 5:00 A.M. utility rates—is a price reduction strategy that not only shifts demand, but enhances volume from price sensitive segments.

Price Bundling

Price bundling is the practice of offering two or more products or services at a price that usually is lower than the sum of the individual prices. Price bundling is pervasive today, and like any price reduction strategy, it can only be successfully used in particular circumstances. We will discuss this price reduction strategy in Chapter 15.

Product Redesign

This strategy is a variation of unbundling the base product from the options. The difference is that the product is changed in some way (fewer features, lower grade material, different brand name) and sold as a separate, lower-priced product. Again, the objective is to appeal to price sensitive customers who would normally not buy the original product at its regular price.

Summary

This chapter has developed techniques for establishing prices over a product's life cycle. Contribution analysis is important for developing prices over the life cycle. Because a pricing strategy should be developed during the development stage, both price <u>and</u> cost forecasting are important to the analysis.

To avoid the common mistake of basing a new product's price on unrealistic introductory production and marketing costs, the experience curve can be utilized to obtain more realistic cost estimates. Furthermore, developing an experience curve for a product permits recognizing when volume increases due to price reductions will also lead to unit cost decreases.

Finally, it is important that the price setter has the proper accounting and financial data. Accountants who prepare data for pricing administrators should tailor their analyses to the life-cycle stage for each product. Product profit–volume charts can provide a good understanding of the implications of each pricing alternative.

This chapter has also demonstrated that price reduction strategies for mature products are likely to also reduce profitability. The need to consider specific focused price reductions instead of across-the-board price reductions was briefly outlined.

Discussion Questions

1. Describe the pricing environment for each stage of the product life cycle.

   a. What are the possible pricing objectives?

   b. What are the general pricing strategies for each of these objectives?

   c. As a product progresses through the different life-cycle stages, how do these objectives and general pricing strategies change? Why?

   d. Carefully discuss the role of competition on the objectives and strategies you have developed in parts *a* and *b*.

2. The Scientific Corporation is in the final stages of developing a new product. Preliminary market tests show that potential customers like the product. Based on these market tests and customer surveys, the market research staff has provided the following sales estimates for the first three years of the product's life:

Price	Year 1	Year 2	Year 3
$12	20,000 units	40,000 units	60,000 units
$14	15,000 units	25,000 units	45,000 units
$16	12,000 units	22,000 units	40,000 units
$18	10,000 units	20,000 units	35,000 units
$20	8,500 units	18,000 units	30,000 units

After reviewing the marketing, production, and financial plans for the new product, the controller estimates that direct variable costs will average $8.00 for the first 25,000 units produced, $7.00 after the first 25,000 units produced, $6.50 after the first 50,000 units produced, and $5.00 after the first 100,000 units produced. Period fixed costs are expected to be $50,000, $100,000, and $150,000 for the first three years, respectively. In addition, the Malloy Corporation is expected to be able to market a similar product by the beginning of the second year and to have a cost experience similar to that of the Scientific Corporation.

Develop a pricing strategy for the first three years of Scientific Corporation. Support your strategy with the necessary exhibits and analyses. What is the rationale of your strategy?

Suggested Readings

Butscher, Stephan A. and Michael Laker: "Market-Driven Product Development," *Marketing Management 9* (Summer 2000), 48–53.

Monroe, Kent B., Akshay R. Rao, and Joseph D. Chapman: "Towards a Theory of New Product Pricing," in *Contemporary Views on Marketing Practice,* eds. J. Sheth and G. Frazier (Lexington, MA: Lexington Books, 1987), 201–13.

Parker, Philip M., and Ramya Neelameghan: "Price Elasticity Dynamics over the Product Life Cycle: A Study of Consumer Durables," *Marketing Letters 8* (April 1997), 205–16.

Shipley, David, and David Jobber: "Integrative Pricing via the Pricing Wheel," *Industrial Marketing Management 30* (April 2001), 301–14.

Simon, Hermann: "Pricing Opportunities—And How to Exploit Them," *Sloan Management Review 33* (Winter 1992), 55–65.

CHAPTER FIFTEEN

Product-Line Pricing

A fundamental marketing decision problem is the determination of price for a product or service. Among the factors that complicate pricing decisions are cost per unit, competitor and buyer sensitivity to price, objectives of the firm, legal constraints, potential entry or exit of competing sellers, and the total product/service offering of the firm. Each of these factors, with the exception of the total product/service offering of the firm, has been discussed in some detail in the pricing literature. Because few firms today offer single products, we need to consider the issue of setting prices for multiple products or services.

From a market perspective, many firms have discovered that there are specific price/market segments for their products and that determining prices to differentiate these products is a complex process. Whether to add a midpriced product or change the number of price offerings depends not only on the number of price/market segments but also on whether the objective is to differentiate the products in the minds of buyers (segmentation strategy) or to encourage buyers to trade up to a higher-priced product (trading-up strategy). This chapter develops a behavioral approach to determine ways to position products in a product line according to price. Many of the important costing issues relative to multiple product offerings were discussed in Chapter 11 (for example the sales dollar mix and the use of common resources to produce, market, or distribute products or services).

Nature of the Decision Problem

Most firms sell a variety of products or services that require different marketing strategies. Generally, a firm has several product lines—groups of products that are closely related because they are used together, they satisfy the same general needs, or they are marketed together. Within a product line, some products are usually substitutes for one another and some complement the demand for other products in the line. Because of the demand interrelationships and cost interrelationships inherent to such a product line, and because there are usually several price-market targets, product-line pricing is one of the major challenges that a marketing executive faces.

Although an organization may wish to pursue a pricing policy of high prices only (or low prices only), it still must decide how high (or low) its prices should be and the differentials between different products in the line. In addition, it must decide on the lowest (or highest) price that helps to maintain a consistent price policy. Thus three types of pricing decisions are required:

1. Determining the lowest-priced product and its price *(low-end product).*

2. Determining the highest-priced product and its price *(high-end product).*

3. Setting the price differentials for all intermediate products.

The pricing problem is compounded because complementarity may exist even if the products in the product line or assortment are functionally substitutable. Demand for a product or service is complementary if it changes in the same direction when demand for another product changes. For example, as demand for DVD players increases so does the demand for DVD titles. By adding new items or reducing certain prices, a firm may increase demand for already existing products. Finally, the lowest- and highest-priced products are more frequently remembered and noticed, implying a further complementarity. This issue of pricing multiple products to maximize contributions to profits extends to retail firms and to service providers.[1]

[1]John D.C. Little and Jeremy F. Shapiro, "A Theory for Pricing Nonfeatured Products in Supermarkets," *Journal of Business 53* (July 1980), S199–209; David J. Reibstein and Hubert Gatignon, "Optimal Product Line Pricing: The Influence of Elasticities and Cross-Elasticities, *Journal of Marketing Research 21* (August 1984), 259–67; Steven M. Shugan and Ramaro Desiraju, "Retail Product-Line Pricing Strategy When Costs and Products Change," *Journal of Retailing 77* (Winter 2001), 17–38.

The low-end price usually is the most frequently remembered one and probably has considerable influence on the marginal buyer (the buyer who is doubtful but still seriously considering buying). Hence, the lowest-priced product is often used as a traffic builder. On the other hand, the highest-priced product is also highly visible and, through quality connotations, may also stimulate demand.

Many of the behavioral pricing principles discussed in Chapters 5 through 8 provide the price setter with operational guidelines for solving these complex pricing problems. The notion of the acceptable price range may help the firm establish the boundaries of different price/market segments and help determine the prices of the low-end and high-end products in the line.

In addition to the inherent complementary relationships within a product line, products that are functionally complementary present a pricing problem. For example, the pricing of cameras and film or razors and razor blades introduces further problems. Clearly, the sale of cameras or razors enhances demand for film or razor blades. Should the firm intentionally set the price of razors and cameras relatively low in order to increase demand for blades and film?

Finally, some buyers may be willing to purchase several products in the line, yet the individual prices for some of the products may exceed the maximum price they are willing to pay for those products. The practice of price bundling (offering several products or services at one price) has been used to overcome this particular problem. We will discuss this pricing practice later in the chapter and offer guidelines for its use.

Conceptual Framework

Generally, a firm produces and distributes multiple products because (1) the demands for the various products are interrelated, (2) the costs of production and distribution are interrelated, (3) both costs and demands are interrelated, or (4) multiple products enable the firm to appeal simultaneously to several diverse market segments (that is, the products are neither demand nor cost related, but instead they permit the firm to pursue expansion or diversification objectives).

Products are demand related if a change in the price of a product, Q_1, induces the buyer to change the quantity of his or her purchases of other products ($Q_2, \ldots, Q_n$), along with changing purchases of Q_1. Similarly, products are related by production and distribution if a change in the quantity produced and distributed of a product, Q_1, results in a change in the unit costs of other products, $Q_2, \ldots, Q_n$. If the firm's products are related by both demand and costs, the quantity it produces and sells of any particular product affects both the revenues and costs of other products that a firm sells. Thus adjusting the price of a particular product to increase net profit for that product may or may not increase profits for the entire firm. In such situations, if the firm is interested in *maximizing contributions to profits*, it must consider not only the effect on revenues and costs of adjusting price for a particular product, but also the changes in revenues and costs for all other related products.

Theoretically, the optimal solution for a firm producing multiple products is to equate the adjusted incremental revenue for each product with the adjusted incremental cost for each product. The adjustment required depends on the impact of the product's price and volume changes on the revenues and costs of the other products in the line. The reason for specifying adjusted incremental revenues and costs is that the level of sales and costs for any one item in the product line may change in response to a price-induced volume change of another product in the line. Thus changing price for any given product may or may not produce the desired result unless prices of the other products in the line are also adjusted.

Note that a decrease in price for a complementary product that leads to increased demand for that product also will increase demand for the product it complements. The reduced price for the complementary product also leads to a lower incremental revenue for that product. Therefore, the adjustment in the incremental revenue for this product is downward. On the other hand, for substitute products in the line, adjustments to incremental revenues and price are upward.

Complicating the application of the theoretical solution is the firm's inability to obtain sufficient data concerning the demand and cost interdependencies of the products in the line. A further complication arises when the issues of price perception are considered. Research on buyer reactions to price indicates that the lowest-priced product in the product line may affect the quantity sold of all products in the line to a greater degree than the price of any other products.[2] These reactions appear

[2]Kent B. Monroe, "The Information Content of Prices: A Preliminary Model for Estimating Buyer Response," *Management Science 17* (April 1971), B519–B532.

to be related to a principle of Gestalt psychology called *out-standingness:* Some objects have certain special qualities that make one's perception of them easier and more lasting than a perception based merely on their physical attributes. Applying this principle and these observations leads to the suggestion that the price of the lowest-priced product is the price most frequently noticed and most frequently remembered. The principle of outstandingness also suggests that the price of the highest-priced product in a product line also is relatively more visible to potential buyers than are prices spaced between the lowest and highest prices (the end prices).

If the end prices of a product line are relatively more visible to buyers than are other prices in the line, then these end prices may influence sales of all products in the line. That is, end prices may have information content for potential buyers, and these buyers may then transfer their interpretation of this information to the entire product line, forming a bargain versus a quality interpretation. Because end prices can affect demand for all products within a product line, the firm must determine the optimum end prices that will enhance the sale of products in the product line as well as the optimum price for each individual product.

Product-Line Examples

The discussion thus far has illustrated the concept of a product line with reference to cameras and photographic accessories and to razors and razor blades. In both examples one type of product is a complement to the other type. Sometimes, however, it is convenient to consider only a line of cameras or a line of hand razors. For example, as a manufacturer expands its line of cameras from the simplest camera to the sophisticated camera used by professionals, each camera appeals to a different market segment, and these segments value each differential feature differently. The pricing problem is to decide on a set of prices that corresponds to what each market segment is willing to pay.

Moreover, the price differentials between camera models must correspond to perceived differences in the separate cameras (see Box 6.5). For example, if the simplest camera, model A, is priced at $45 and model B, which includes a telescopic lens, is priced at $49, buyers will perceive that $4 is or is not too much to pay for this added feature. But if buyers are willing to pay up to $55 for model B, then a pricing error has been made *unless* it is the seller's intent to "trade buyers up" to model B.

The pricing of hotel or motel rooms is a product-line pricing problem. A hotel or motel may be viewed as offering a product line consisting of different types of rooms and different types of occupancy, usually single or double. Also, motels or hotels often have different-sized rooms and rooms with a desirable location such as a pool or park and others with less desirable location such as a parking lot or a busy highway. Management must determine a single and a double rate for each type of room. If suites are available, an additional pricing decision must be made. Most hotels derive a large part of their room business from repeat transients, who are sometimes thought of as satisfied guests. Hotel guests are willing to pay a reasonable room rate provided they perceive that they have received a fair value for that rate. For example, if a guest is given a $75 room when he or she expected to pay $50, that individual will probably not be dissatisfied if the $75 room is *noticeably worth $25 more than the $50 room of a previous visit*. Thus the pricing problem is to price each room correctly in relation to other rooms *and* to match the number of rooms at each rate to the demand for rooms at each rate.

Product lines are also prevalent in the industrial sector of the economy. For example, a company selling in the copier market normally sells plate makers, offset duplicators, plate materials, chemicals, and parts and offers service/maintenance contracts. Moreover, the company may have several models of plate makers and several models of offset duplicators, each with different features.

Determining End Prices and Price Differentials

End-Price Concept

The concept of end prices was briefly introduced at the beginning of this chapter. We suggested that buyers are likely to have a range of acceptable prices for a product, and that if the desired product is priced within this price range, the buyer probably would be favorably disposed to complete the purchase. Extending the concept of a price range to a product line provides the concept of an acceptable range of product-line prices.

In effect, then, the existence of high and low price limits represents a price-decision constraint. That is, if a product is priced too low or too high for a particular buyer, he or she will be less likely to purchase the item unless the parameters of the decision change. Similarly, if some products are priced outside the acceptable price range and others are priced within this range, a buyer is less likely to buy any product than if all the products in the line were priced within the acceptable price range. In such a situation, the price setter would want to constrain his or her pricing flexibility to those prices within the price range with the highest probability of being accepted.

One study revealed that the price characteristics of the product line influence consumer product evaluations.[3] Specifically, the research indicated that the range of prices in the product line influenced consumers' judgments of a particular model in the line. This influence depends on the acceptability of the highest price in the line and the relative position of the specific model being evaluated. Products positioned at the higher end of the product line's prices were evaluated as of higher quality but lesser value than products positioned at the lower end of the line's prices. This result is consistent with the price–perceived quality–perceived value model developed in Chapter 7. That is, both perceived quality and perceived monetary sacrifice increase as price increases, but at least for this study and the prices considered, perceptions of sacrifice increased faster than perceptions of quality. Thus when adding or deleting a model from a line of products, it is necessary to consider where the model's price lies in relation to the other models' prices. Above all else, this research highlights the need for relationship pricing when pricing a product line.

When extending the analysis to include all potential buyers within a market segment, a firm must consider expected variation among individual buyers because buyers are not expected to have identical threshold prices. A given market target would have a distribution of high- and low-threshold prices. The mean and variance of this distribution can be identified when the decision objective is to determine the end prices of the product line.[4] Knowing the mean and variance of the distribution in turn enables the firm to determine the distribution of either the low-end price or the high-end price, depending on whether relatively low or high prices

---

[3]Susan M. Petroshius and Kent B. Monroe, "Effect of Product-Line Pricing Characteristics on Product Evaluations," *Journal of Consumer Research 13* (March 1987), 511–19.
[4]Monroe, "The Information Content of Prices."

were used to stimulate the market responses. As described in Chapter 9, selecting either the mean or median price in these two distributions would provide the end prices for the product line.

Determining Price Differentials

Chapter 5 presented the Weber-Fechner law, which represents the relation between the measured magnitude of a stimulus and the measured magnitude of response,

$$R = k(\log S) + a \qquad \text{(15.1)}$$

This law justifies the use of the logarithmic relationship between a price and a market response as well as the use of the lognormal distribution when the market response is probabilistic. When determining price differentials the concept of a constant proportion between just-noticeably different (JND) stimuli is important. Stating the situation in reverse, the prices of two products should not be different unless the products themselves are perceived as different by buyers.

Beginning with the lowest price in the product line, P_{min}, the price of the next product would be determined by adding a constant rate, k, to the P_{min}. Continuing in this manner by adding a constant rate, k, to the previously determined price until each product has been priced results in a set of prices reflecting noticeable differences among products.

The basic assumption of this approach is that the subjective price scale of the buyer resembles a ratio (logarithmic) scale rather than a natural scale (see Chapter 5). *That is, the differences in prices between products should reflect relative differences rather than absolute differences.* For example, it is often the practice of clothing retailers to carry three price lines of merchandise, with the price difference between lines being a constant amount of dollars. But if the low line is priced at $30 and the medium line is priced at $45, the high line should be priced around $65, not $60, to provide an approximate 50 percent difference in price at each level. This prescription corrects the error of not recognizing the difference between relative and absolute price differences that was discussed in Chapter 6 (see Box 6.4).

Assuming the products in the product line have been ranked in ascending order (that is, the product designated the lowest-priced product is ranked 1, the product designated as the next-to-lowest-priced product is ranked 2, and so on, until the highest-priced product is ranked n), then any product can be priced once the P_{min} has been set. The price of the jth ordered product is given as

$$P_j = P_{min}k^{j-1}$$ **(15.2)**

where k is the constant rate, $k > 1$, and j is the jth ordered product.

Because we assume that there is a given number of products in the line and that the low and high end prices have been determined, the constant rate k is easily determined using the relationship

$$\log k = \frac{1}{n-1}(\log P_{max} - \log P_{min})$$ **(15.3)**

or

$$k = (P_{max}/P_{min})^{1/n-1}$$

If P_{min} and k are known, the price of any product in the line can be set, thereby determining the price differentials among products. For the example shown in Table 15.1, a firm had six products in a line and decided that the low-end product should be priced at $25 and the high-end product at $150. As the table indicates, by using the three values P_{max}, P_{min}, and n, a constant multiplier of $k = 1.431$ was determined. Applying this constant multiplier to each price beginning with the low price of $25 produced the "theoretical prices" shown. The firm wanted all of its prices at round values, so each price was adjusted to the actual prices shown. This procedure does require perceptible differences in the benefits buyers received from each product. The next section discusses how to communicate these quality or benefit differences between products in the product line.

Managing Quality Cues

Many product lines consist of different models or versions of the basic product, each with different performance capability and differing prices, called price–quality tiers. The previous section discussed how to set price differentials according to the organization's selling objectives. However, the way the seller presents these different choice options can influence the way that buyers make judgments about the differences in quality and therefore value across the choices in the product line. Some sellers use descriptive labels as well as price to distinguish among the quality variants. For example, a gasoline retailer might label its three grades of gasoline as

TABLE 15.1
Price Differential Example

	Price, $	
Model	**Theoretical**	**Actual**
A	25.00	25.00
B	35.78	36.00
C	51.19	55.00
D	73.25	79.00
E	104.82	109.00
F	150.00	150.00

$P_{min} = \$25.00;\ P_{max} = \$150.00;\ n = 6$

$$\text{Log}k = \frac{1}{5}(\log 150 - \log 25)$$

$$= \frac{1}{5}(2.1761 - 1.3979)$$

$$= \frac{1}{5}(0.7782) = 0.1556$$

$k\quad = 1.431$
$P_B = \$25.00\,(1.431) = \$\ 35.78$
$P_C = 35.78\,(1.431) = \quad51.19$
$P_D = 51.19\,(1.431) = \quad73.25$
$P_E = 73.25\,(1.431) = \quad104.82$

"regular," "super," and "supreme." This retailer might also provide some numerical cues such as the octane levels 87, 89, and 92. Nonprice indicators of quality within a product line are of three types:

- Purely descriptive—"good, better, best"

- Cues based on ratios—ranking (such as one to five), octane ratings

- Actual numerical information—proportion of fat in ground beef

As we discussed in Chapters 5 through 7, buyers face the difficult mental activity of integrating both positive and negative information about the product and the offer when judging overall value. Moreover, judging value becomes more difficult if some of the information to be integrated is numerical; we have discussed the difficulties of processing numerical information. Price is one cue that can be used to infer quality, but how does the buyer infer actual quality across multiple choices in the product line with different prices, different qualitative cues or labels about quality variation, and different numerical cues about quality variation? If buyers are trying to determine the choice that represents the best value for them, they face a difficult information integration task.

Research indicates that the use of ratio-scaled quality cues along with price differentials helps buyers make quality–price tradeoffs, that is, value assessments.[5] When buyers are attempting to make their choice on the basis of perceived value, a clear and direct relationship between price and quality allows buyers to choose according to whether they are quality conscious or price conscious. However, often the other quality cues are not clear. Labels such as "premium" or "supreme" indicate the seller's ranking but do not help the buyer determine the actual quality difference relative to the price difference between choices. Thus to help buyers make more accurate value assessments, ratio-scale numerical quality information should be provided along with price information. For example, instead of a line of trash bags being described by different magnitudes of thickness—0.85 ml., 1.0 ml., 1.15 ml.—the manufacturer could describe the two thicker bags as 17 percent and 34 percent stronger than the first bag. If the prices of the two stronger bags are 15 percent and 30 percent more than the first bag, the buyer then can make price–quality tradeoffs. Regardless, in this example the quality information must not only be clear but also communicate the actual benefit the product's attribute provides. In the trash bag example, the thickness feature is translated into the benefit of bag strength. As we pointed out in Chapter 8, when communicating value, sellers need to find ways to translate features into benefits for their customers.

Guidelines for Setting Price Differentials

Once the two end prices are determined, a range of prices can be set for the product line. Given the price range and the number of products in the line, price differences among the products are obtained by adding a constant proportion to the previously determined price to get the next price in the line.

The correct pricing of a product or service line for a *segmented pricing strategy* should follow these principles:

[5]Joseph P. Guiltinan, "Managing Quality Cues for Product-Line Pricing," *Journal of Product & Brand Management Featuring Pricing Strategy & Practice 9* no. 3 (2000), 150–61.

1. Each product or service should be priced correctly in relation to all other products in the line. Specifically, noticeable differences in the offerings should be equivalent to perceived value differences.

2. The highest and lowest prices in the product line have a special complementary relation to other offerings in the line and should be priced to encourage desired buyer perceptions.

3. Price differentials between products in the product line should get wider as price increases over the product line. This principle follows the behavioral finding that price perception follows a logarithmic scale rather than an arithmetic or linear scale.

If the organization wishes to use a *trading-up strategy* when pricing the product line, it must first decide which products or services are to be designed and priced to be similar to each other. Then the higher-priced product should have an observable benefit that buyers would perceive as valuable, but the incremental price for this extra feature or benefit should be less than its perceived value. In this situation, instead of a wider price differential between these two products, a smaller price differential should be set. That is, the price differential should be perceived as less than the incremental value obtained by trading up to the higher-priced product.

Some Applications of Differential Pricing in a Product Line

Segmenting the Candy Market [6]

In 1987, the market for boxed chocolate candies in Israel was comprised of three companies with about 75 percent market share and another five to seven smaller firms. The firms offered about 80 products. To analyze the prices of these offerings, the prices for 1987 and 1988 were grouped into price ranges so that the boundaries between adjoining ranges were clear and the differentials between the highest price in the low-price range were quite distinct from the lowest price in the high-price range. As Table 15.2 indicates,

[6]This example is based on Yehoshua Liebermann, "Behavioral Aspects of Product Line Pricing: An Actual Marketplace Perspective," *Pricing Strategy & Practice 3* no. 1 (1995), 14–20.

TABLE 15.2   Chocolate Candy Price Segments, 1987 and 1988

	1987			1988		
Segment	Price range[a]	Number of items	Market share of segment (percent)	Price range[a]	Number of items	Market share of segment (percent)
1	2.99-4.82	21	16.73	3.07-4.60	17	15.73
2	5.11-6.61	12	15.05	5.11-6.60	15	15.50
3	7.82-9.20	12	20.63	7.06-9.20	18	21.20
4	9.69-13.80	19	34.40	9.70-13.80	25	24.14
5.	15.05-15.82	2	2.33	15.33-16.60	2	13.48
6	17.25-18.90	8	5.78	17.25-19.60	7	5.37
7	19.50-21.31	4	4.40	20.31-21.90	2	0.67
8	23.53-25.97	3	0.65	23.53-25.97	2	0.71

[a]All prices are nominal New Israeli Shekel (NIS). Currently, $1 exchanges for approximately NIS3.

Source: Reprinted with permission from Yehoshua Liebermann, "Behavioral Aspects of Product Line Pricing: An Actual Marketplace Perspective," *Pricing Strategy & Practice 3* no. 1 (1995), 16.

about 75 to 85 percent of sales came from the three lowest-price segments. The question was whether making a systematic change in prices would lead to increased sales of the higher-margin, higher-priced products. If so, such a change in the product selling mix would enhance profitability. Another problem with the current pricing that became apparent was that generally the price differences between different offerings were too small to indicate any corresponding quality differences.

Applying the theoretical approach outlined above led to a new pricing scheme by the leading firm in 1989. Table 15.3 compares the results for 1989 to 1988. As can be seen, revenues in segments 1 and 2 declined, but revenues in segments 4 and 6 increased substantially. Even though the total number of units remained essentially the same, total revenues increased by 23.4 percent. Adjusting for inflation, the firm attributed a 2.7 percent real increase in revenues to the price differentiation schedule. A second benefit from this analysis and the price changes was a 20.2 percent reduction in the number of different candy items, leading to a reduction in production, handling, and distribution costs. Moreover, consumer confusion over the previously unorganized price and quality levels was reduced.

TABLE 15.3   Price and Candy Units Sold, 1988 and 1989

Segment	1988 Mean price	1988 Units sold	1988 Revenue ($K)	1989 Mean price	1989 Units sold	1989 Revenue ($K)
1	3.84	124,267	477.2	3.93	64,227	252.4
2	5.86	122,450	717.6	5.87	84,609	496.7
3	8.13	167,480	1,361.6	8.59	166,532	1,430.5
4	11.75	190,760	2,240.8	11.75	249,956	2,937.0
5	15.97	106,492	1,700.6	15.55	86,347	1,342.7
6	18.43	42,432	781.9	18.70	121,818	2,278.0
7	21.11	5,293	111.7	23.95	16,590	397.3
8	2.48	5,609	13.9	-	-	-
Total	-	789,000	7,405.3	-	790,000	9,134.6

Note: computed by segment share x overall number of units sold.

Source: Reprinted with permission from Yehoshua Liebermann, "Behavioral Aspects of Product Line Pricing: An Actual Marketplace Perspective," *Pricing Strategy & Practice 3* no. 1 (1995), 19.

Ford Enhances Profitability by Managing the Selling Mix[7]

In 1999, Ford Motor Co. earned an auto industry record $7.2 billion in profits. Yet, between 1995 and 1999, its market share fell from 25.7 percent to 23.8 percent! To accomplish this performance, beginning in 1995, Ford did extensive market research to determine what features customers wanted and were willing to pay for in their vehicles. They then designed option packages, for example more comfortable supercabs on trucks, that matched these wants. Given this information, they repriced their vehicles to encourage customers to trade up to high-profit vehicles. For example, prices of low-margin vehicles such as Escort and Aspire were increased while prices of high-margin vehicles such as Crown Victoria and Explorer were reduced. As a result, Ford sold 420,000 fewer low-margin vehicles but 600,000 more high-margin vehicles. Ford's ability to make substantially more profits without making many more vehicles was attributed primarily to product-mix improvement. In this case, Ford followed the essentials of a trading-up pricing strategy to move customers up to option-laden models that have bigger profit margins. Prior to 1995, Ford's pricing could be characterized

[7]Material for this example is drawn from Peter Coy, "The Power of Smart Pricing," *Business Week* (April 10, 2000), 160–64; Scott Leibs, "Ford Heeds the Profits," *CFO* (August 2000).

FIGURE 15.1   **Logarithmic Price Segments of American Cars—1993**

Source: Reprinted with permission from E. M. Monroe, R. L. Silver, and H. E. Cook, "Value versus Price Segmentation of Family Automobiles," *SAE Technical Paper Series*, #970765, Society of Automotive Engineers (1997), 53–61.

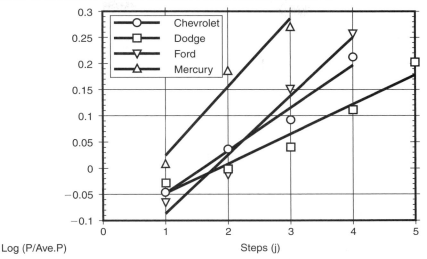

primarily as a price segmentation strategy. Figure 15.1 shows that Ford was primarily pricing in three segments, whereas Dodge had five price segments. Moreover, consistent with the meaning of *j* as described in Equation 15.2, Ford's price segments were equally spaced when considered logarithmically, further attesting to the strategy of pricing to keep auto markets perceptually separate.

Price Bundling

In marketing, one widespread type of product-line pricing is the practice of selling products or services in packages, or bundles. Such bundles can be as simple as a restaurant menu offering dinners and the same items a la carte or as complex as a ski package that includes travel, lodging, lift and ski rentals, and lessons. Additional examples of price bundling include the following:

Maintenance contracts sold with appliances or technical equipment.

Vacation packages combining travel, lodging, and tours at special rates.

Health clubs offering membership packages that include access to individual programs.

Cable TV plans that include premium channels in a special "package rate."

Bedroom and living room suites offered by furniture stores.

Option packages offered by automobile manufacturers.

Hardware and software packages offered by computer companies.

"Value meals" that include a sandwich, soft drink, and fries or chips offered by restaurants.

Essentially, bundling is a segmentation strategy based on the theory that different customer segments value different combinations of products or services differently. Unless the firm's managers understand customer segmentation, it is unlikely that they will develop a successful strategy. Some customers find a one-stop purchasing source desirable. Full-service banks attempt to capture such customers by offering full financial services at one institution. However, other customers want a simple checking and saving service only. If the bank forced all customers to pay for full financial services that they neither need nor want, or if the bank priced each service separately, neither customer segment would be satisfied. In either situation, the bank would be treating very different customers in a similar manner.

Types of Price Bundling

In practice, bundling may occur in a variety of ways. Of course, products and services can be sold separately without being included in a bundle. In *pure bundling* only a bundle of items is offered for sale; buyers do not have the option of buying the individual items. Microsoft's bundling of its Internet Explorer software with its Windows operating system was a major area of contention in the Microsoft antitrust case. One legal issue was whether such bundling was an illegal attempt to create a monopoly.

In *mixed bundling*, on the other hand, the customer can purchase products or services individually or as a package. Normally there is a price incentive for the customer to purchase the package rather than acquiring the items in the bundle individually. In *mixed-leader bundling,* the price of one product is discounted if another product is purchased at full price. For example, if cable TV customers buy the first premium channel at full price, they may be able to acquire a second premium channel at a reduced monthly rate. Assuming that premium channels A and B are individually priced at $10 per month each, then B might be offered for $7.50 if A is acquired at its regular rate. In *mixed-joint bundling,* a single price is set for the combined group of services. In this situation, the two premium channels would be offered together for one price, such as $17.50 per month. If customers base their decision only on the total price, $17.50, then the question is whether it matters if mixed-leader or mixed-joint bundling is used. As we will show, even though the net outlay for the customer buying either bundle is the same, the question remains whether customers perceive two lower prices ($10, $7.50) as equivalent to one higher price ($17.50). Thus the seller must weigh several factors in deciding which type of mixed bundle to offer.

Another common marketing tactic is to offer *tie-in sales.* A tie-in-sale requires the buyer to purchase a main product (tying product) and then one or more complementary products (tied products) that are necessary to use the tying product. For example, dealers of photocopying equipment may stipulate that the purchaser or leasee of the equipment purchase and use paper and other supplies from them. Although such requirements have received considerable legal scrutiny under the antitrust laws, the courts have held that the seller may minimally stipulate the quality of the supplies that should be used even if purchased from an alternate supplier. A variation of this tactic is *add-on bundling*. Purchasing a full tank of gasoline may qualify buyers for a discount if they have their cars washed and waxed. However, this discount for the wash and wax is available only if added on to the gasoline purchase.

Rationale for Price Bundling

As observed in Chapter 11, many businesses are characterized by a relatively high ratio of fixed to total variable costs. Moreover, several products or services usually can be offered using the same facilities, equipment, and personnel. Thus the direct variable cost of a particular offering is usually relatively low, meaning that it has a relatively high PV ratio. The incremental costs of selling additional units therefore are low relative to the firm's total costs.

In addition, many of the products or services most organizations offer are interdependent in terms of demand, either being substitutes for each other or complementing the sales of another offering. To maximize the benefits customers or clients receive, relationship pricing, or pricing based on the inherent demand relationships among products and services, is appropriate. *The objective of price bundling is to stimulate demand for the firm's product line in a way that achieves cost economies for the operations as a whole while increasing net contributions to profits.*

Economics of Price Bundling

Underlying the notion of bundling is the recognition that different customers have different perceived values for the various products and services offered. That is, these customers are willing to pay different maximum amounts for the products or services. For some customers, the price of the product is less than this maximum acceptable price (upper price threshold), resulting in some consumer surplus. However, for these customers, the price of a second product or service may be greater than they are willing to pay, so they do not acquire it. If the firm, by price bundling, can shift some of the consumer surplus from the highly valued offering to the less valued offering, then there is an opportunity to increase the total contributions these offerings make to the firm's profitability. The seller's objective is to influence the sales of the items in the product line so as to enhance the product line's contributions to profits.

The ability to transfer consumer surplus from one offering to another depends on the complementarity of demand for these products or services. Products may complement each other because the joint purchase reduces the search costs of acquiring them separately. It is economical to have both savings and checking accounts in the same bank to reduce the costs of having to go to more than one bank for such services. Services may complement each other because acquiring one may increase the satisfaction of acquiring the other. For the novice skier, ski lessons will enhance the satisfaction of skiing and increase the demand to rent skis. Finally, a full-service seller may be perceived to be a better organization than a limited-service seller, thereby enhancing the perceived value of all services offered.

As noted in Chapters 3 and 6, demand is likely to be more price elastic for products and services that can be evaluated on the basis of search attributes than for those that can be evaluated only after receipt of the service or not at all. Thus products or services to consider for a bundling strategy should have search-based salient attributes because one requirement for profitable bundling is that at least one of the products or services be price elastic.

Developing a Price-Bundling Strategy

In this section we present four basic steps for developing a price-bundling strategy:

Step 1: Define Customer Segment Targets

A two-product situation has four basic customer segments: 1 and 2 buy only one of the products under consideration for bundling (they buy A only or B only); 3 buys both products (A and B); and 4 buys neither A nor B. Each of these segments has a different buy response curve (see Chapter 9) for the products as well as different distributions of the maximum price they would be willing to pay for the products or services. Thus it is necessary to determine the price distributions for these different segments using one of the research methods outlined in Chapter 9.

Step 2: Determine the Bundling Objectives

There are three basic bundling objectives. First, the firm could target either segment 1 or segment 2 and attempt to cross-sell. That is, the firm could attempt to convince buyers of A only to also buy B or buyers of B only to also buy A, or it could try to convince both types of buyers to buy the other product. Thus *cross-selling* is the attempt to persuade buyers to buy another product on the basis of the product they are currently buying. For example, if male customers of a clothing store typically do not buy shirts when purchasing suits, the store might offer shirts at a reduced price when a suit is purchased.

A second objective would be to target customer segment 4, that is, to acquire new customers for A and B. This objective is much more difficult to achieve simply because the seller must first determine the reasons these customers do not buy product A or B. Thus sellers first must make some effort to determine who these nonbuyers are and why they either do not buy or buy from a competitor. Then the seller would be in a position to determine whether price bundling might be an effective strategy.

The third objective, price bundling to retain current customers who buy both A and B, is least likely to be used. If the seller adopts the cross-selling or retention objective, the benefits will be available to current buyers of A and B. Thus, reducing price to cross-sell or to acquire new customers will lead to a reduction in revenues from current buyers who take advantage of the offer.

Step 3: Determine Demand Requirements for Each Objective

When cross-selling is the primary objective, the focus is on buyers of A only or B only. To decide whether to use mixed-leader bundling or mixed-joint bundling, the relative unbundled demand for each product is an important consideration. If unit sales volume of one of the products is substantially greater than the other, then *mixed-leader bundling* should be used. The product with the higher sales volume should be used as the leader. For example, assume A is currently priced at $20 and has a unit sales volume of 10,000. Product B is priced at $10 and has a unit sales volume of 5,000. These two products produce unbundled revenues of $250,000 ($200,000 + $50,000). If the firm offers to sell A at $15 when customers buy B at the regular $10 price, and if all customers take advantage of the offer, the maximum revenues are 15,000 x $15 plus 15,000 x $10, or $375,000. Note that there is more to gain by reducing the price of A to those who buy B at regular price than the reverse. Potentially, 10,000 customers can be induced to buy B, but only 5,000 can be cross-sold A.

However, if the unit volume sold of A is approximately equal to that for B, then the appropriate strategy to use is *mixed-joint bundling*. Continuing with the example, assume that both A and B have unbundled unit sales volume of 7,500. Unbundled revenues are $225,000 (7,500 x $20 + 7,500 x $10). If the seller offers to sell both A and B for $25, and if all customers take advantage of the offer, the maximum revenues will be $375,000 (15,000 x $25). Because the unbundled sales volumes are equal, there is no relative advantage to using one of the products as a leader.

If the objective is to acquire new customers (customers not now buying either A or B), there is no way to define a leader. We simply do not have sales data for this customer segment. In this case the key is to determine the relative price sensitivity of these customers for the products in question. Price research as described in Chapter 9 would provide valuable information for this objective. We can also use the notions from economics described earlier to gain some insights as to which products to use in the bundling strategy and how they might be used. Remembering that products or services with attributes that are relatively easy to evaluate are likely to be more price elastic, we might select a product that has these types of attributes as the lead product. Thus, we would use a mixed-leader strategy. The second product must complement the lead product for this strategy to be successful. For example, offering a set of microwave dishes at a reduced price when a microwave oven is purchased would fit these prescriptions. Use of a mixed-joint strategy requires products with attributes that are easy to evaluate, are price elastic, and complement each other.

Step 4: Determine the Profitability of Alternative Strategies

When examining the relative profitability of bundling strategies, it is important to remember that the bundling offer will be available to current customers. This means that the seller will receive less contribution from sales to profits from customers who previously bought both A and B. In addition, there will be fewer customers who buy A only or B only (although these customers who buy only A or B will provide the same contribution margin as before). If the unit contribution margins of A and B are different, then the firm's profitability will be enhanced if the larger increase in bundled sales comes from those customers who previously purchased only the lower margin product.

Criteria for Selecting Products to Bundle

Developing a bundling strategy, then, requires careful thought and analysis of the consequences of reducing price to enhance volume. Since the objective is to increase the overall sales level of the firm, the products or services selected for price bundling should be relatively small in unbundled sales volume, which will minimize the effects of cannibalization. For mixed-leader bundling, the lead product or service, A, must be price elastic, must have attributes that are easy to evaluate before purchase, must be the higher volume product or service in the bundle, and should be the lower margin offering. The lead product should be customers' most preferred product in the bundle because consumer surplus may not transfer if customers do not want the lead product.[8] When using mixed-leader bundling, the objective is to use a price reduction for A to generate an increase in its volume, which "pulls" an increase in demand for a lower volume–higher contribution margin offering, B. The increase in B's volume will contribute more to profits than the reduced contributions of the lead product.

For mixed-joint bundling, the contribution margins of the products in the bundle should be about equal, their unbundled sales volumes should be about equal, their demand should be price elastic, and each should functionally complement the other product. Moreover, customer preferences for the products should be similar across the products. In any case, these products or services individually should not be high sales volume offerings.

Products selected for a bundle should be functionally related to each other and of equivalent quality. Research has shown that when evaluating a bundle, buyers tend to first evaluate the main or lead item in the bundle. Then, anchoring on this lead product they will adjust their initial evaluation of the bundle by successively evaluating the contribution that the other items make to the bundle's perceived value. If the additional products in the bundle are perceived to be of lower quality than the main or first item evaluated, then buyers will adjust their judgments downward.[9] Other research has demonstrated that buyers tend to evaluate bundles of related products higher than those of unrelated products.[10]

Presenting the Bundle Offer

The economic rationale for bundling assumes that the manner in which the bundle offer is presented will not influence buyers' judgments and choices. However, as indicated in Chapters 5 through 7, buyers may not perceive a mixed-leader bundle as they do a mixed-joint bundle even if the amount of savings from the sum of individual prices is

---

[8]Manjit S. Yadav, "Bundle Evaluation in Different Market Segments: The Effect of Discount Framing and Buyers' Preference Heterogeneity," *Journal of the Academy of Marketing Science 23* no. 3 (1995), 206–15.

[9]Manjit S. Yadav and Kent B. Monroe, "How Buyers Perceive Savings in a Bundle Price: An Examination of a Bundle's Transaction Value," *Journal of Marketing Research 30* (August 1993), 350–58; Manjit S. Yadav, "How Buyers Evaluate Product Bundles: A Model of Anchoring and Adjustment," *Journal of Consumer Research 21* (September 1994), 342–53.

[10]Gary J. Gaeth, Irwin P. Levin, Goutam Chakraborty, and Aron M. Levin, "Consumer Evaluation of Multi-Product Bundles: An Information Integration Analysis," *Marketing Letters 2* (January 1991), 47–58.

equivalent. For example, assume that a luggage retailer lists a garment bag at $120 and a duffel bag at $60. If the two bags are bought at regular prices the total cost would be $180. However, the retailer decides to bundle the two bags at a lower bundled price. One way to present the bundle would be to offer the two bags for a combined price of $150; that is, a savings of $30 (mixed-joint bundle). Saving $30 on a $180 combined purchase is a discount of 16.7 percent. A second way would be to reduce the price of one of the bags by $30 when the other bag is purchased at regular price (mixed-leader bundle). For example, the offer might indicate that a duffel bag would cost $30 when a person purchases a garment bag at its listed price. Moreover, this particular offer could be promoted by indicating that the duffel bag is 50 percent off regular price when purchased with a garment bag (see our discussion in Chapter 7 on framing price offers). Alternatively, the offer could indicate that the garment bag would be discounted $30 when purchased with a duffel bag at regular price. However, note that offering $30 off a $120 item would be a 25 percent reduction in the price of the garment bag. Even though the economics of these alternative ways of presenting the offers are equivalent, the underlying psychological processes will differ, leading to different levels of buyer responses.

Previous research has consistently shown that mixed bundling leads to higher profits than either separately pricing the items in the product line or pure bundling. Recall that mixed bundling entails offering the bundle and the bundle's individual items at separate prices. Through mixed bundling, firms have experienced profit improvements between 10 and 40 percent.[11] This superiority of mixed bundling over pure bundling would generally be expected to hold unless a product bundle purchase is normal or logical (e.g., car options, furniture suites).

Because of the difficulty of integrating multiple pieces of information, including positive information about the products, perceived gains due to the price reduction for the bundle, and the negative information concerning the monetary

---

[11]Hermann Simon and Georg Wuebker, "Bundling—A Powerful Method to Better Exploit Profit Potential," in Ralph Fuerderer, Andreas Herrmann, and Georg Wuebker, eds., *Optimal Bundling: Marketing Strategies for Improving Economic Performance,* New York: Springer–Verlag, (1999) 7–28; see also Stefan Stremersch and Gerard J. Tellis, "Strategic Bundling of Products and Prices: A New Synthesis for Marketing," *Journal of Marketing 66* (January 2002), 55–72.

sacrifice, bundles generally should not be larger than five items. In one study comparing three, five, and seven related items in a bundle, the researchers found that the most favorable evaluations occurred for the five related bundled items option.[12]

As discussed in Chapter 7, one explanation for possible success of price bundling is that buyers perceive transaction value in the bundled offer. That is, not only do bundles offer additional acquisition value via the combination of products in the bundle, but also the price reduction induces perceptions of transaction value. As pointed out in Chapter 7, enhancing perceived transaction value augments perceived acquisition value and thereby increased willingness to buy. Research has shown that price reductions of at least 20 percent usually are required to sufficiently enhance transaction value and willingness to buy.

Price reductions on individual items improve perceptions of savings not only for the individual items but also for the bundle offer. Thus instead of offering one large savings on the bundle alone (e.g., $40 for the two luggage items in the bundle), dividing up that savings between the items (e.g., $10 off each item) and an additional $20 off for the bundle as a whole may simultaneously attract two segments of buyers: (1) those interested in buying only the individual items and (2) those wishing to buy the bundle. That is, such a presentation enables the seller to reach the A-only and B-only segments as well as the A plus B segment.[13]

Note that the perceived value of a price bundle would be enhanced if the price reduction for the combination of products and services were unbundled. That is, dividing the bundle's price reduction among the bundle's individual items and the additional reduction if the entire bundle is purchased enhances overall perceived transaction value, which in turn enhances perceived acquisition value. Sometimes sellers routinely offer "full service" that effectively bundles multi-

---

[12]Andreas Herrmann, Frank Huber, and Robin Higie Coulter, "Product and Service Bundling Decisions and Their Effects of Purchase Intentions," *Pricing Strategy & Practice 5* no. 3 (1997), 99–107.

[13]Yadav and Monroe, "How Buyers Perceive Savings in a Bundle Price"; Rajneesh Suri and Kent B. Monroe, "Consumers Prior Purchase Intentions and Their Evaluation of Savings on Product Bundles," in Fuerderer et al., *Optimal Bundling: Marketing Strategies for Improving Economic Performance,* 177–194; Michael D. Johnson, Andreas Herrmann, and Hans H. Bauer, "The Effects of Price Bundling on Consumer Evaluations of Product Offerings," *International Journal of Research in Marketing 16* (1999), 129–42.

ple products and services with a single price. Especially in business-to-business marketing, as the product category reaches maturity and pressure to reduce prices increases, these sellers often lament that customers do not understand the value their "full service" offering provides. One solution to this problem, and perhaps one that should have been routinely applied before this maturity problem occurred is to unbundle the bundle and list each product and service at its full price and at the reduced price when the customers purchase the "full service" bundle. In essence, this solution is another example of the advantage of making both prices and value transparent (see the initial discussion of price and value transparency in Chapter 4).

Summary

These principles suggest that firms should not pursue price-bundling strategies simply because others are doing it. Bundling can be an effective pricing strategy, but it should be applied only after a careful analysis of the nature of the products or services offered and an understanding of customers' perceptions of the value of these offerings. Box 15.1 provides some background for an analysis of an attempt by McDonald's to change from a mixed-joint bundle to a mixed-leader bundle for one of their "value meals."

As Box 15.1 reveals, McDonald's Campaign 55 offered a Big Mac for 55 cents on the condition that customers purchase french fries and a drink, a mixed-leader bundle that would cost the customer about $2.55. Previously, the Extra Value Meal was a mixed-joint bundle with an order of a Big Mac, french fries, and drink costing the customer about $3.00. Campaign 55 in effect offered a combination meal for a price reduction of about 45 cents, or 15 percent. On average, fast-food companies earn profits on fries and drinks of 80 to 90 percent, while margins for hamburgers equal just 10 to 15 percent or less. Thus, we can estimate that the margin for the Extra Value Meal priced at $3.00 would be about $1.15, with a PV ratio of 0.38. For Campaign 55 to be a profitable bundle, using Equation 11.3, sales of the combination meal would have to increase by 65 percent (0.15/[0.38 - 0.15]), not an easy task.

A second difficulty emerged in the way McDonald's promoted the 55 campaign. Because it placed so much emphasis on the 55 cent price for a Big Mac, customers didn't understand the condition that they needed to buy a drink and an order of french fries to receive the low price. Hence

MCDONALD'S TRIES A NEW BUNDLE

BOX 15.1

To combat a decline in same-store sales and increased competition within the fast food industry, McDonald's announced a new sandwich promotion on February 26, 1997 (later dubbed "Hamburger Wednesday"). The deal, which lowered the price of a Big Mac to 55 cents only with the purchase of fries and drink, reduced the price of a combination meal (sandwich, fries, and drink) from around $3 to $2.50.

Unfortunately, the 55-cent campaign was not as successful as management had anticipated. First, the company's strategy of lowering price to thwart competitors reminded Wall Street of Marlboro Friday in 1993, when Philip Morris's premium cigarettes were reduced in price by 40 percent, leaving smaller competitors scrambling to make a profit. Share prices for the fast-food industry as a whole declined, reflecting investors' concern about price wars within the industry. In addition to declining share prices McDonald's encountered negative reaction from franchisees who claimed

that the 55-cent sandwich deal not only barely covered costs but also confused customers. Customers arrived expecting a 55-cent Big Mac and became confused when they discovered that the Big Mac was 55 cents only with the purchase of fries and drink. When customers were charged the total amount for their meal, it was much more than their reference price of 55 cents.

The company stopped the promotion after six weeks. A spokesperson explained: "Customer response over the first six weeks of the value initiative was not up to our expectations."

Sources: Greg Burns, "McDonald's: Now, It's Just Another Burger Joint," *Business Week* (March 17, 1997), 38.; Jim Kirk, "McDonald's Marketing Message Appears Muddled," *Chicago Tribune* (June 5, 1997), Section 3, 1, 12.; Jim Kirk, "McDonald's Dumps Discounts," *Chicago Tribune* (June 4, 1997), Section 3, 1, 4.; Nancy Millman, "55-Cent Burgers to Debut in April," *Chicago Tribune* (March 1, 1997), Section 3, 3; Glenn Collins, "Egg McMuffins, Priced to Move," *New York Times* (March 3, 1997), C1.

customers showed up expecting to order one or more Big Macs for 55 cents each. This problem highlights the importance of carefully presenting price bundles to customers. The purchase requirements to qualify for the bundle price must be as transparent as the promoted bundle price. This need to be transparent about both the price of the bundle and the purchase requirements is necessary to prevent customers from forming reference prices that are lower than the bundle price. Otherwise, confusion, anger, and perceptions of unfairness may occur, making it that much more difficult to reach the sales and profit goals of the promotion.

Yield Management and Differential Pricing

A form of segmentation pricing that the airlines developed after deregulation is called yield management. Like price bundling, yield management operates on the principle that different segments of the market have different degrees of price sensitivity. Therefore, seats on airline flights are priced differently depending on the time of the flight, day of the week, length of stay in the destination city, when the ticket is purchased, and certain other conditions or restrictions. Researchers seeking to generalize this particular inventory management and pricing problem refer to it as perishable-asset revenue management. Managing perishable assets through price segmentation can be applied outside the lodging and travel industries to spectator events (e.g., theater, sports), electric utilities, services (e.g., photo studio, hair salon, auto repair), transportation, high-technology products, and advertising.[14] Also, banks, savings and loans, and telephone companies have used yield management to increase sales revenues through differential pricing. Retail firms can also use yield management to determine when to mark down slow-moving merchandise and when to schedule sales (see Box 15.2).

The Nature of the Airline Pricing Problem

Using super computers, the airlines make fare changes daily to reflect changes in demand, changes in seat capacity available between any two cities, and shifts in traffic. The objective is to fill seats with the highest possible revenue generated per seat-mile flown. However, realization of this objective is complicated by (1) the existence of a multitude of prices with varying amounts of restrictions that limit the availability of all but the highest-priced seat; (2) numerous flights operated by several airlines over different routings, any one of which could be used by passengers to get to their destinations; and (3) varying degrees of demand for the seats on an airline's flight segment over time.

Thus airlines must determine the best mix of passengers and prices for a particular flight. There are two elements to solving the problem.[15] One is to maintain a reservation-monitoring system that keeps track of what seats are sold

[14]Samuel E. Bodily and Larry R. Weatherford, "Perishable-Asset Revenue Management: Generic and Multiple-Price Yield Management with Diversion," *Omega, International Journal of Management Science 23* no. 2 (1995), 173–85; Ramarao Desiraju and Steven M. Shugan, "Strategic Service Pricing and Yield Management," *Journal of Marketing 63* (January 1999), 44–56; Anil Lahoti, "Revenue Management," *OR/MS TODAY 29* (February 2002), 34–37.
[15]Fred Glover, Randy Glover, Joe Lorenzo, and Claude McMillan, "The Passenger-Mix Problem in the Scheduled Airlines," *Interfaces 12* (June 1982), 73–79.

THE GROWING POPULARITY OF YIELD MANAGEMENT

BOX 15.2

Yield management enables firms to capture the rewards of meeting supply and demand by predetermining prices that meet several demand requirements. That is, yield management recognizes that revenues can be maximized by establishing prices for the different market segments that desire the product and are willing to pay different prices.

Before the airline industry was deregulated in 1978, government officials determined airline fares based upon the length of the flight and required all airlines to charge the same price per flight length. The end of deregulation marked the beginning of yield management as airlines discovered the rewards of offering a variety of ticket prices for essentially the same product and service. Today, airline ticket prices vary continuously depending upon whether an individual travels for business or personal pleasure, the date and time of departure, and the duration of the business engagement or vacation.

The airlines' success with yield management, combined with increasingly sophisticated computer technology, has encouraged others (i.e., hotels, car rental companies, and cruise lines) to adopt the practice of charging different prices for the same product or service. Although yield management may enable a firm to maximize its revenue potential, firms must keep in mind issues of pricing fairness and competitor reactions. For example, last-minute airfare discounts may anger passengers who have already purchased a ticket at a higher price. In addition, a strong focus on offering discounted prices may signal to competitors that a firm may initiate a price war. When ITT Sheraton Corp. announced its decision to use yield management techniques to lower prices for certain categories, competing hotel chains reacted strongly, chastising the company for potentially creating a price war.

Sources: Robert L. Crandall, "How Airline Pricing Works," *American Way*, (May 1, 1998), 10, 12.; James C. Makens, "Yield Management: Pricing Strategy of the '90s?" *Marriott's Portfolio* (November/December 1989), 14, 17–18.; Steven Morris, "Hotels Try to Mix Business, Pleasure," *Chicago Tribune* (May 11, 1992), Section 4, 1, 4.

and at what prices. Generally, a small number of seats are designated as discount or special fare seats, and these seats usually sell first. However, as the actual time of the scheduled flight approaches, more discount seats may be made available if a large number of seats remain unfilled. For each flight, the airlines have data on the usual number of seats that are likely to be bought just a few days before departure, and if unfilled seats seem likely, then additional low-price seats will be made available. However, if demand for seats on that flight is greater than usual, the airline will stay with the full-fare ticket and not offer additional discount seats. The objective is to sell as many full-fare seats as possible while minimizing the number of empty seats. Because a seat is a perishable asset, any revenue above the relatively low direct variable cost of filling that seat is a positive contribution to the operations.

The second element in airline pricing is to evaluate different price–route scenarios to determine the most profitable price/passenger ratio. The profitability of a passenger depends on the length of the trip and the fare class the passenger travels. Although revenue per mile is usually less for passengers traveling long versus short distances, the total revenue to the airline is greater for these passengers. Associated with each passenger on a given flight segment is the opportunity cost that the passenger occupies a seat that could have been sold at a higher price. An empty seat generates no revenues, and the objective is to sell the seat from its original point to its final point. An interesting complication of this revenue management problem occurs when airlines form alliances and code share. For example, a Chicago to Sydney round trip might involve American Airlines (Chicago to Los Angeles round trip) and Qantas (Los Angeles to Sydney round trip). Now the alliance revenue management problem not only seeks to maximize the combined revenues of the alliance partners, but also to determine a fair distribution of the revenues between the airlines.

The General Perishable-Asset Revenue Management Problem

For a particular selling occasion (airline flight, theater seats, rooms or cars to rent per day, short retail selling season), the seller has a fixed number of units (capacity), q_{cap}, to sell at or by a certain date in the future. If the units are not sold during this selling occasion, they cannot be sold at any price later. In the simplest two price segments situation, some portion of potential buyers will have a higher maximum acceptable price than the other potential buyers. However, the total number of actual buyers with the high maximum acceptable price for this selling occasion will be lower than the available capacity. If only a single high price is set, then an unknown portion of the units will not be sold ($q_{cap} - q_{low}$), where q_{low} is the number of units that could be sold to low-price buyers. However, if the seller chooses to sell q_{low} units at a discounted price, p_{low}, then revenues would be increased.

The decision problems are to choose q_{low}, the number of units to offer at a discount, the discount price, p_{low}, and the full price, p_{high} to maximize total revenues for the selling occasion. In the simplest case, all of the demand for the discounted units will occur before the high-price units are sold. Thus, given the nature of demand that occurs for the discounted units, the seller must decide when, and whether, to stop selling the discounted units and offer only the high-price units for the remainder of the selling period. The decision problem of deciding how many units to offer at a discount is similar to an electric utility deciding how much power to sell wholesale on contract, a hotel deciding how many rooms to set aside for a convention at a reduced rate, an airline determining the number of nonrefundable discounted seats to sell, or a car rental agency determining how many cars in each category to provide at special rates.

As developed in Chapter 11, the appropriate decision criterion is to seek to maximize contributions per selling occasion. Because of a relatively high fixed costs to total costs operating structure, so long as p_{low} is greater than the unit direct variable costs of the product or service, revenues will be greater than if only (q_{cap} - q_{low}) units are sold at p_{high}. Hence, maximizing revenues will maximize total contributions.

$$\text{Total revenues} =$$
$$\begin{cases} q_{low}p_{low} + Xp_{high} & \text{if } q_{low} + X{<}q_{cap} \\ q_{low}p_{low} + (q_{cap} - q_{low})p_{high} & \text{if } q_{low} + X{\geq}q_{cap} \end{cases}$$

$$(15.4)$$

where X = the number of seats sold at the full price p_{high}.

Adding one more unit to q_{low} provides additional revenue of p_{low}. So long as there is sufficient capacity to meet demand X at p_{high}, no other effects occur. However, if (q_{low} + X) exceeds capacity, the firm's revenue is lower than what otherwise could have occurred by the amount (p_{high} - p_{low}). It can be shown that the firm should add an additional discount customer if the probability that

$$(q_{low} + X){<}q_{cap} > \frac{p_{high} - p_{low}}{p_{high}} \qquad (15.5)$$

For example, if the discount price is 50 percent of the high price, the firm should continue to add discounted units for sale as long as the probability that the total demand (q_{low} + X) will be less than capacity is greater than 0.5. If the discount price is 70 percent of the high price, then the firm should continue to add discounted units for sale as long as the probability that total demand will be less than capacity is greater than 0.3.

An important issue is to develop ways to separate the high-price segment from the low-price segment. The airlines have accomplished this by establishing purchase conditions to qualify for the low-price ticket. Such conditions as 14-day nonrefundable advance purchase with Saturday stayover has served to separate the less price-sensitive business traveler from the more price-sensitive leisure traveler. However, as the price differential between the full price and discounted price has widened, some firms are insisting that their employees make extra efforts to acquire discounted air tickets. In 1999, business travelers were paying about 63 percent of the unrestricted fare, down from 74 percent in early 1996.[16]

This problem of the presumed nonprice-sensitive business travelers purchasing more of the restricted low-price fares is known as *diversion*. Diversion occurs when buyers from a high-price segment are able and willing to shift their purchases, to the low-price offering. To understand why buyers in the high-price segment might divert their purchases, we can use the basic value model we introduced in Section 3. First, the restrictions and conditions placed on buyers purchasing the low-price tickets effectively raise the overall sacrifice these buyers incur (see Chapter 7). For example, the stay-over Saturday night may require an extra night in a hotel, meals, and additional monetary outlays, as well as paying for the ticket 14 to 30 days in advance. These additional elements of the sacrifice must be balanced against the monetary savings obtained by paying the lower price. Now if the business travelers increase their willingness to accept these additional sacrifices in order to obtain a low-price ticket, the airline faces the possibility that the original targeted low-price leisure customer may not obtain a ticket because the inventory of allocated discount seats has been sold. The airline either must open up additional discounted seats or face the possibility that a number of full-price seats will remain unsold. In either situation, revenues will be lower than before these diversions occurred. However, if these diverting passengers can be encouraged to upgrade to high-price seats, then more discounted seats will be available for price-sensitive passengers. Thus the airlines allow members of their frequent flyer programs to use some of their frequent-flyer miles to upgrade to business class or first class if seats are available.

---

[16]David Leonhardt, "Revolt of the Executive Class," *Business Week* (February 1, 1999), 68–71.

Conditions for Using Yield Management

Although the airlines have been most associated with the use of yield management, it has been applied in a wide variety of situations, sometimes with dramatic success, other times not. As with any sophisticated analytical technique, a number of conditions should exist for an organization to adopt yield management and practice differential pricing. These conditions are summarized in Table 15.4.

The first four conditions are necessary for organizations to attempt to use perishable-asset management techniques. Having a fixed capacity such as a given number of seats in an airline, stadium, or theater; a specific number of vehicles or rooms to rent; or a fixed number of fashionable or very

TABLE 15.4   **Conditions for Using Yield Management**

Enabling Condition	Requirement
1. Fixed capacity	Capacity is relatively fixed (capacity change costs are high)
2. Perishable inventory	Merchandise sold or services provided cannot be sold after the selling occasion
3. Fluctuating demand	Demand across segments varies randomly, sometimes creating stockouts and sometimes leading to unused capacity
4. Fixed costs	The ratio of fixed costs to total costs are high, i.e., operating leverage is relatively high
5. Segmentable markets	Price sensitivity varies across customers; price-sensitive customers can be identified and separated from less price-sensitive customers
6. Arbitrage can be prevented	Customers who purchase at a low price ahead of the use occasion cannot resell to less price-sensitive customers
7. Advance or early purchase feasible	Customers are willing and able to purchase items early or in advance of use occasion
8. Historical sales databases	Existing information technology makes it feasible to monitor sales response to price and other marketing mix changes
9. Accurate sales forecasts	Segment by segment accurate demand forecasts facilitate selective discounting to improve capacity utilization and improve revenues
10. Sophisticated information systems	The more sophisticated the information system, the easier it will be to utilize yield management

Source: Adapted with permission from Frederick H. deB. Harris and Peter Peacock, "'Hold My Place, Please,'" *Marketing Management 4* (Fall 1995), 34–46.

seasonal items available for sale (see Box 15.3). In each of these examples, when the purchase or use occasion ends, the unsold inventory of seats, vehicles, rooms, or merchandise is no longer available or feasible for future sale and the seller loses any opportunity to gain revenue contributions to fixed costs and profits. Typically, to be in business, the organization has incurred a relatively high ratio of fixed costs to total operating costs. Because of this high operating leverage, any monetary sales above direct variable unit costs will make positive contributions. However, because of demand fluctuations, sometimes most of the inventory could be sold at a relatively high price, whereas during slack demand periods a relatively large portion of inventory must be sold at low prices. Indeed, if demand is known with certainty, following a fixed price policy would be near optimal.[17]

Conditions 5–7 make it feasible for the organization to use yield management techniques. As we will develop further in Chapter 17, for price segmentation to be successful, the seller must be able to identify the distinguishable characteristics of customers in the different segments, and customers must be separable into different price–quality segments. Finally, conditions 8–10 outline the necessary resources and capabilities for managers to effectively apply yield management techniques. Sophisticated information systems make it feasible to develop high-quality sales databases, and from them, accurate demand forecasts.[18] Indeed, the Internet has made yield management feasible in a wider range of applications in such areas as broadcasting, retailing, and manufacturing. For example, as businesses sell excess

---

[17]Guillermo Gallego and Garrett van Ryzin, "Optimal Dynamic Pricing of Inventories with Stochastic Demand over Finite Horizons," *Management Science 40* (August 1994), 999–1020; Wen Zhao and Yu-Sheng Zheng, "Optimal Dynamic Pricing for Perishable Assets with Nonhomogeneous Demand," *Management Science 46* (March 2000), 375–88;Youyi Feng and Baichun Xiao, "A Continuous-Time Yield Management Model with Multiple Prices and Reversible Price Changes," *Management Science 46* (May 2000), 644–57; Youyi Feng and Guillermo Gallego, "Perishable Asset Revenue Management with Markovian Time Dependent Demand Intensities," *Management Science 46* (July 2000), 941–56.

[18]Barry C. Smith, John F. Leimkuhler, and Ross M. Darrow, "Yield Management at American Airlines," *Interfaces 22* (January–February 1992), 8–31; M. K. Geraghty and Ernest Johnson, "Revenue Management Saves National Car Rental, *Interfaces 27* (January–February 1997), 107–27; Barry C. Smith, Dirk P. Gunther, B. Venkateshwara Rao, and Richard M. Ratliff, "E-Commerce and Operations Research in Airline Planning, Marketing, and Distribution," *Interfaces 31* (March–April 2001), 37–55.

CAN YIELD MANAGEMENT TECHNIQUES BE APPLIED TO RETAILING?

BOX 15.3

In Chapter 3 we observed that sellers sometimes reduce prices when either demand or buying activity increases. We called this phenomenon a pricing anomaly because traditional economic theory would predict that when demand increases while supply remains constant, prices should increase. As discussed in Chapter 3, prices were lower both during Thanksgiving weekend, when holiday shoppers fill the stores and malls doing Christmas gift shopping, and the pre-Christmas period compared to the week following Christmas. Physical products that are primarily sold during this one time of the year, such as toys, or seasonal specialty products, such as gift wrap, commonly are promoted at large discounts during the last days of the Christmas buying season. The normal reason for these discounts is that the retailers are trying to shed their leftover inventory rather than either holding unsold products until the next Christmas selling season or salvaging them. However, note that as the opportunity to find an appropriate gift or needed gift wrap before Christmas declines for those people who have yet to make these purchases, their sensitivity to price declines, especially in comparison to those who were shopping right after Thanksgiving. Note that this trend in price elasticity is the same for airlines in that the most price-insensitive buyers are those who buy tickets shortly before flight.

We can contrast this situation with that of a fashion goods retailer that also sharply discounts remaining inventory as the selling season ends. However, since the value of the fashion item seemingly is enhanced the longer the buyer has and uses the product, we would expect that its price elasticity increases as the end of the selling season approaches. Thus retailers seem to follow the same basic pricing model even though the trends in price elasticity over the selling season for these types of products are quite different. Both cases involve the problem of how to price a perishable-

asset inventory within a limited time period so as to maximize revenues.

Although traditional yield management techniques could be applied to seasonal goods that are used, or given, at the end of the selling season, it is less apparent that yield management could be applied by fashion goods retailers because price elasticity increases as the selling season progresses. Yet, both situations involve developing prices over a discrete time period in which the prices are a function of the inventory and time left in the selling season.

Given the different nature of the trend in price elasticities, we would expect that the discounts for end-of-period use products— gifts and related one-time use products— would occur early in the selling season (Thanksgiving weekend) and disappear as the time left declines. However, retailers often panic if Christmas sales develop slowly, and they continue to mark down their merchandise even as price sensitivity declines, which, of course rewards those who wait to the last minute to do their shopping. One solution to this dilemma would be to announce that early discounts in the Christmas season will be effective only for a defined time during the season. Note that this suggestion is very similar to our earlier discussion on introductory pricing tactics (Chapter 6), and to guidelines for communicating value (Chapter 8).

But, for seasonal goods that are used throughout the selling season, we would expect the discounts to occur later in the selling season. Indeed, this type of behavior is regularly observed.

Sources: Keith S. Coulter, "The Application of Airline Yield Management Techniques to a Holiday Retail Shopping Setting," *Journal of Product & Brand Management featuring Pricing Strategy & Practice* 8 no. 1 (1999), 61–72; Gabriel R. Bitran and Susana V. Mondshein, "Periodic Pricing of Seasonal Products in Retailing," *Management Science 43* (January 1997), 64–79.

inventory through Internet auctions, yield management is being extended to dynamic pricing and focused price reductions to individuals for airline tickets, home mortgages, new car sales, long-distance calling, and even groceries. Revenue management processes and systems utilize complex forecasting and optimization models, and fully implementing a system takes several years and millions of dollars. Companies should take a phased approach, concentrating first on developing the historical sales databases and the demand forecasting models. Then the optimization models should be developed to align pricing with the variations in demand across segments and products.

Benefits of a Revenue Management Pricing Program

One unique benefit to a company of a revenue management pricing program is continuous monitoring of demand for products. Anticipated changes in demand are reflected in proactive price changes. If the product is not selling fast enough, then price reductions can be initiated to stimulate sales. Because of a relatively high fixed costs to total variable costs cost structure, these focused price reductions offer leverage for increasing operating profits by their effect on sales volume. As we saw in Chapter 9, with relatively high contribution margins (high PV ratios), small price reductions can be profitable without large increases in volume.

Because of the initial emphasis on operations and inventory management, organizations using yield management often had separate pricing and yield management departments. Today more firms are recognizing the wisdom of integrating their pricing and yield management departments into a single revenue management unit. Moreover, information technology has made it feasible to develop decision support systems to enhance demand forecasting and to facilitate proactive dynamic pricing. Finally, industries in which negotiated or contract pricing is important (e.g., electric utilities, broadcasting, custom or job shop manufacturing, package delivery, transportation services) are using adapted yield management techniques when preparing bids. Perhaps one of the most important implications of yield management is that focusing on revenue management shifts performance measures from averages to contributions per unit of resource, whether that resource be a measure of capacity, product unit, or customer. As we pointed out in Chapter 11, these performance measures are more logical because they are

Coulter: "Product and Service Bundling Decisions and Their Effects on Purchase Intention," *Pricing Strategy & Practice 5,* no. 3 (1997), 99–107.

Yadav, Manjit S., and Kent B. Monroe: "How Buyers Perceive Savings in a Bundle Price: An Examination of a Bundle's Transaction Value," *Journal of Marketing Research 30* (August 1993), 350–58.

directly related to profitability. It has been estimated that firms using revenue management techniques have seen revenues increase 3 to 7 percent without significant new capital expenditures, resulting in 50 to 100 percent increase in profits.[19]

Summary

This chapter has applied some of the concepts developed in Chapters 3 through 11 to pricing a product line. Chapter 15 has also placed more emphasis on aspects of price determination other than cost. A firm that produces several products sells products that are distinguishable in terms of the products' life cycles, extent of competition, and buyer acceptance of the products and their prices. Hence basing prices on a full-costing formula is arbitrary and does not consider market factors. Finally, a more careful consideration of how price affects buyer perceptions of a firm's product offerings can isolate new pricing alternatives. Development of pricing

Managing the Pricing Function

Perhaps the most difficult aspect of the pricing decision is developing procedures and policies for administering prices. Up to this point, our emphasis has been on setting base or list prices. However, as we pointed out in Chapter 12, the list price is rarely the actual price customers pay. Discounting from list price for volume purchases or early payment, extending credit, charging for transportation—all effectively change the price paid. In this section, we consider such decisions within the analytical framework developed in Chapters 2 through 12. Chapters 16 and 17 review the problems of managing the pricing function, and Chapter 18 reviews the various legal issues involved in pricing strategies and tactics.

The implementation of pricing strategies and tactics affect dealer or distributor cooperation and motivation as well as salespeople's morale and effort. Although it is difficult to control prices legally through the distribution channel, it is possible to elicit cooperation and provide motivation to adhere to company-determined pricing policies. Because price directly affects distributors' revenues and salespeople's commissions, it can be used to foster desired behaviors by channel members and salespeople. Finally, feedback is essential for a firm in today's dynamic economy. Chapter 17 discusses these management problems and offers approaches to solving them.

One of the most complex and frustrating problems of pricing is justification of price differentials. The need to justify price differentials may arise from litigation initiated by a customer, a competitor, or the government. Or it may come about because customers often request—or demand—justification for price increases. Because it has been traditional to use cost-plus pricing, which incorporates arbitrary overhead allocations, the cost defense has rarely been successful in a legal proceeding. Moreover, many firms are hard-pressed to justify price increases to their customers. In fact, the firms' sales personnel are often the least satisfied by such justification attempts. Chapter 18 reviews the major legislation concerning price discrimination and provides guidelines for justifying price differentials.

CHAPTER SIXTEEN

Developing a Price Structure

We now consider the problem of managing base or list prices throughout the distribution system and the markets in which the products are sold. Pricing management deals with organizing the organizational unit responsible for pricing, establishing, and implementing the tactics to use when adjusting prices or determining price schedules that establish price differentials for sales made under different conditions, such as sales made

In different quantities.

To different types of distributors performing different functions.

To buyers in different geographic locations.

With different credit and collection policies.

At different times of the day, month, season, or year.

Managing Transactions

The discussion of pricing thus far has been oriented toward determining what may be called a base or list price. This price, or some reasonable deviation therefrom, represents the strategic aspect of pricing. As we discussed in Chapter 1, this list or base price that is communicated in price lists, advertisements, catalogs, websites, and other publicly available outlets provides customers and competitors with the firm's value statement. Chapters 1 and 12 indicated that the actual amount of revenues received for the same product or service varies over time for the same customers and, of course, across customers. Chapter 12 also showed that differences in customer profitability can occur either because of these variations in revenues received from customers, or because of differences in the costs to serve these customers. Every discount, rebate, or allowance results in a reduction in revenues. As a result, most managers are unaware of the actual net price they receive from different customers.[1]

In many firms, different people or organizational units play a role in price adjustments, such as various discounts, loyalty refunds, advertising allowances, trade deals, price promotions, freight allowances and other forms of "giveaways." Thus, it is important to distinguish between the

- List price—published or generally quoted unit price.

- Invoice price—price after usual volume, trade, and cash discounts.

- Pocket price—price after all other allowances, refunds, and discounts.

Although managers focus on the strategic aspects of determining price levels for their products and services, they often do not recognize that there is another vital dimension to prices, called price structure. Price structures provide the foundation for prices by determining

1. The time and conditions of payment.

2. The nature of discounts.

3. Where and when buyers will take title.

4. Who pays for the transportation of the goods and how these charges are determined.

Essentially, price structure decisions define how differential characteristics of the product or service will be priced. These price structure decisions are of strategic importance to manufacturers, distributors or dealers, and retailers. Establishing a price structure offers many opportunities to antagonize distributors and even incur legal liability. While using the price structure to achieve the desired profit objectives, these dangers must be avoided.

---

[1] K. K. S. Davey, Andy Childs, and Stephen J. Carlotti, Jr., "Why Your Price Band Is Wider Than It Should Be," *The McKinsey Quarterly*, no. 3 (1998), 116–27.

In earlier chapters we noted that the definition of price includes the buyer's required monetary outlay as well as such complexities as terms of agreement, terms of payment, freight charges, warranty, timing of delivery, and volume of the order. Moreover, offering different products or services in the product line with different features or benefits at different prices gives sellers the opportunity to develop prices for buyers who have different degrees of sensitivity to price levels and price differences. Moving from a simple one-price-for-all structure to a more complex pricing structure permits pricing flexibility through price variations based on specific product and service characteristics as well as buyer or market differences. Moreover, a more complex price structure enhances the ability of firms to respond to competitor, buyer, or market changes.

Price structures can be relatively simple, as in offering one fixed price per product regardless of quantity or other conditions of purchase. Complex price structures provide flexibility because they allow for price variations based on variations in product or service attributes, customer characteristics, customer behavior, or changing competitive conditions. Moreover, although complex price structures provide opportunities to shield some aspects of the firm's pricing strategy from competitors, or even customers, there is a danger that complex price structures can become inconsistent and incomprehensible to customers. As indicated in Chapters 4 and 7, clear and consistent price signals can reduce the likelihood of price wars and provide important quality information to uncertain buyers. Moreover, when buyers understand how prices they pay are determined, they are more likely to perceive pricing procedures as fair and thus accept the prices. Box 16.1 illustrates the difficulties of making a price structure or schedule too complex.

Pricing strategy can be linked to overall marketing strategy through price structure, a valuable aspect of both pricing and marketing strategy. The decision makers must determine how prices should vary across customers, products, territories, and purchase occasions to meet corporate objectives. To accomplish this goal of differential pricing requires identifying the key factors that differentiate price-market segments. Then the elements of the price structure that reflect these factors can be developed. When devising the price structure, conflicts inevitably will necessitate accepting trade-offs to achieve the best overall profitable sales mix.

DO THE PRICES ADD UP? BOX 16.1

Special promotions and discounts for various consumer groups have led to unstable pricing. What one individual pays for an airline ticket may be vastly different from what the passenger sitting next to him or her paid. Hotels offer a multitude of pricing schedules based on a person's affiliation with a certain customer segment or even the length and time of the visit. Differential pricing may result in confusion for both the seller and the buyer.

In the spring of 1998, Ameritech announced that it intended to raise the price of local toll calls for Chicago customers by 40 percent. The increase and new calling plans were designed not only to meet varying consumer needs but also to support the cost of unprofitable consumer segments. For example, Ameritech's Simpli-Five plan charged customers a nickel for each local call and a nickel a minute for calls more than eight miles away. But, for calls 8 to 15 miles away, the rates for calls increased from nearly 4 cents for the first minute and less than 2 cents for each extra minute. A customer could also choose a basic plan in lieu of Simpli-Five, which would result in a rate of 7 cents per minute for calls to places 15 miles or further away. Ameritech's different calling plans (Simpli-Five and the basic) confused customers so much that the Chicago-based Citizens Utilities Board created a 20-page booklet to assist Illinois customers with understanding their monthly Ameritech bills!

Whereas Ameritech focused on offering a variety of prices, Procter & Gamble (P&G) sought to simplify its business practices in an effort to lessen consumer confusion. By reducing product proliferation and marketing expenses by standardizing formulas and packaging, selling off marginal brands, eliminating inefficient promotions, and limiting new product launches, P&G increased sales through lower prices and achieved higher margins. In fact, P&G's goal of communicating clearly to the consumer directed the company towards a strategy that favored lower list prices instead of supermarket specials. By eliminating costly trade deals that lead to weekly changes in price and train customers to shop for price in place of perceived brand quality, P&G reduced confusion for both consumers and supermarkets and also prevented surges in demand as retailers stocked up at the sale price.

The lesson from both Ameritech and P&G is that although differential pricing provides firms with a method to charge different prices based on varying customer needs and value perceptions, a multitude of pricing plans may create customer confusion and even frustration. P&G's efforts to eliminate varying prices resulting from marketing initiatives such as trade deals and special promotions reduced confusion while increasing corporate sales, suggesting that there is value in keeping things simple.

Sources: Scott Burns, "Prices Nowadays Are Unknowable, Ubiquitous." *The News-Gazette* (August 30, 1998); Jon Van, "Toll Call Price Hike Triggers Criticism," *Chicago Tribune* (March 7, 1998), Section 1, 1, 9; Zachary Schiller, "Make It Simple: That's P&G's New Marketing Mantra—and It's Spreading," *Business Week* (September 9, 1996), 96–104.

An Overview of Discount Decisions

A product's list price is the product's price to final buyers. Throughout the distribution system, manufacturers grant intermediaries *discounts*, or deductions from the list price.

These price concessions from producers may be seen as payment to intermediaries for performing the distribution function and for providing time and place utilities. The difference between the list price and the amount that the original producer receives represents the total discounts provided to channel members. Channel members themselves employ discounts in various ways. Wholesalers pass on discounts to retailers just as manufacturers pass along discounts to wholesalers. Retailers may offer promotional discounts to consumers in the form of sweepstakes, contests, and free samples. Some sellers offer quantity and cash discounts to regular customers. They may even pass seasonal discounts along—for example, to reduce inventory of Halloween candy or Christmas cards.

Trade or Functional Discounts

Firms typically offer independent wholesalers and retailers discounts from list price to motivate them to perform needed marketing activities. *Trade discounts* are based on a distributor's place in the distributive sequence. *Functional discounts* represent payment for performance of certain marketing functions that the manufacturer would otherwise perform. Although we are accustomed to think of price as a single number, price is usually quoted to distributors as a series of numbers, for example: "30, 10, 5 and 2/10 net 30" or "30, 20, 5, and 2/10 net EOM [end of month]." The first three numbers represent successive discounts from the list or base price. The list price designates the approximate or suggested final selling price of a product and is the price usually referred to when discussing the methods of price determination. However, the list price is used to quote and figure the discounts.

In the first quote above, if the list price was $10.00, then the price the dealer pays is $10.00 − 0.30($10.00) = $7.00; then $7.00 − 0.10($7.00) = $6.30; and $6.30 − 0.05($6.30) = $5.98. The 2/10 net 30 part of the quotation states that an additional 2 percent discount is allowed if payment is made within 10 days, and in any event the full $5.98 is due within 30 days. If the 30, 10, 5 part of the quotation is for a specific dealer, the 30 refers to the trade discount for the position the dealer occupies within the distribution channel; the 10 and 5 refer to discounts allowed for promotional expenses the dealer might incur or other functions performed for the manufacturer.

The justification for trade and functional discounts is that different distributors perform different functions within the distribution channel and should be compensated accordingly. For example, some wholesalers provide storage facilities for the manufacturer, help the retailer set up displays, extend credit to the retailer, and perform personal selling services for the manufacturer. Often it is difficult to fully identify the various functions the distributors perform and therefore to determine a trade and functional discount structure that reflects the services performed. Much of this difficulty is due to the fact that some distributors combine the functions of wholesalers and retailers. It also results from the existence of so many different kinds of wholesalers and retailers.

Promotional Discounts

A promotional discount is an allowance for distributors' efforts to promote the manufacturer's product through local advertising, special displays, or other promotions. These allowances may take the form of a percentage reduction in the price paid or additional merchandise (for example, a free case for every dozen cases ordered), or they may be an outright cash payment either to the distributor or to the promotional vehicle, (such as a local newspaper). In recent years, sales promotions in the form of special deals to distributors have increased in frequency and magnitude. In many situations, the dollars budgeted for sales promotions now exceed the amount budgeted for advertising expenditures.

Cash Discounts

A cash discount is a reward for the payment of an invoice or account within a specified period of time. At the start of the section, we saw that the terms 2/10 net 30 referred to the cash discount, 2 percent, that could be taken if payment is made within 10 days. The net 30 provides information concerning the length of the credit period the seller is willing to grant—that is, if the buyer does not pay within 10 days and take the cash discount, then the entire invoice or account must be paid in full within 30 days.

Advance-Purchase Discounts

In Chapter 15, we pointed out that airlines and other firms using yield management may provide lower prices (discounts) when buyers make reservations a period of time before flying or using the product. One outcome of this practice is that buyers with lower price sensitivity—for example, those who decide to make a trip with very short notice—pay more for the same service relative to those who purchase (commit to use) the service ahead of usage. The concept of *advance-purchase discounts* extends to other types of business operations as well. Firms that experience seasonal demand for their products use advance-purchase or advance-order discounts to encourage buyers to commit to their purchases before they actually need the product. For example, chemical firms making fertilizers, heavy-construction equipment companies, and toy manufacturers all experience demand for their products that follows typical seasonal patterns. To utilize their capacities more consistently, however, they desire to produce their products at a reasonably even rate throughout the year. By offering advance-purchase discounts, firms reduce the uncertainty of demand at peak periods and reduce the costs of underutilized capacity during the slow selling periods. Advance-purchase discounts also give these manufacturing firms an opportunity to plan their purchases to reduce acquisition costs and, if payment is received in advance of the buyers' receipts of the goods or services, to have use of the cash while producing the products instead of borrowing money.

Peak-Load Pricing

Peak-load pricing was originally developed for public utility, regulated monopolies. Applied to public utilities such as electricity firms, it considers the pricing issue that arises when demand for a good or service is periodic and subject to fluctuations. To be able to handle periods of high demand (peak load), firms have to install capacity that is underutilized in periods of normal or low demand. If prices were uniform over time, the quantity demanded would rise and fall periodically. However, if prices were higher during periods of peak demand, thereby shifting some demand to off-peak periods when prices are lower, less capacity would be needed, reducing capacity costs. Applications of peak-load pricing can be found when electric utilities or telecommunications firms use time-of-day pricing.[2] In such applications, prices per unit of electricity or time are lower in periods of low demand, such as 11:00 P.M. to 5:00 A.M. for electricity, or 7:00 P.M. to 6:00 A.M. for telephone calls. Another

[2]Michael A. Crew, Chitru S. Fernando, and Paul R. Kleindorfer, "The Theory of Peak-Load Pricing: A Survey," *Journal of Regulatory Economics 8* (November 1995), 215–48.

application of peak-load pricing is ski resorts' lower ski lift and accommodation prices for early season (e.g., until December 10) and for late season (e.g., after March 21) skiing. Some resorts also have lower prices for midweek skiing than for weekend skiing.

Service-differentiated pricing provides an important application of peak-load pricing. Priority service pricing, in which speed of service is the basis of different prices, is an example. The postal service, by delaying processing certain classes of mail, can more effectively handle the peak periods of mail processing, for example, the 6:00 P.M. to 12:00 A.M. period reserved primarily for priority and first class mail. Indeed, bulk mail and other classes of mail can be held for several days before they must be processed.

Quantity Discounts

Perhaps the most common type of discount is the quantity discount. Such a discount is granted for volume purchases (measured in dollars or units), either in a single purchase (noncumulative) or over a specified period of time (cumulative, deferred, or patronage discount). The discount schedule may specify a single product or a limited number of products, or the discount may allow for a complete mix of products.

Noncumulative quantity discounts as in the example that follows, serve to encourage large orders, which leads to fewer orders over a given time period. This ordering policy benefits sellers in that they have fewer orders to process, ship, and invoice, thereby reducing total costs for these activities. Cumulative discounts do not have these benefits, but they do tend to tie a buyer to a seller over the discount period if the buyer is eager to obtain the discount. However, the nature of a product sometimes makes it advantageous to place small orders, as is the case with perishable products, large consumer durables, or heavy equipment and machinery. For these kinds of products, buying in small quantities is practical, and a cumulative discount schedule is beneficial to both parties.

An Example

To illustrate the nature of these discounts assume that the Stepup Ladder Company produces and sells a line of ladders for commercial and household use. The company produces five different types of ladders that vary in the materials used and ladder length. The suggested list prices of these ladders

TABLE 16.1

Applying Discounts

A. The Hardware Distributing Company Order	
10 ladders @ $ 30	$ 300
6 ladders @ $ 50	300
10 ladders @ $ 90	900
5 ladders @ $120	600
4 ladders @ $150	600
Total	$2,700

B. Applying the quantity discounts	
Total order amount	$2,700
Discounts, $2,700 × 0.05	135
Net order amount	$2,565

C. Applying the trade discounts	
Net order amount	$2,565.00
Less: 40% discount	1,026.00
	$1,539.00
Less: 10% discount	153.90
	$1,385.10
Less: 5% discount	69.26
Amount due manufacturer	$1,315.84

D. Applying the cash discount	
Amount due manufacturer	$1,315.84
Less: 3% discount	39.48
Net remittance	$1,276.36

are $30, $50, $90, $120, and $150. These ladders are sold through hardware distributors to discount department stores and hardware stores. Typical trade discounts are 40, 10, 5. Further, the company quotes a cash discount of 3/10 net 30, and it allows an additional 5 percent discount to distributors for orders of $1,000 or more at list prices.

The Hardware Distributing Company places the order in Table 16.1. As the table shows, the total order amounted to $2,700 using list prices. Since the order exceeds $1,000, the quantity discount of 5 percent applied, making the net amount of the order $2,565. The trade discounts are then applied successively in the order shown in Table 16.1C. The total amount of the trade discounts is $1,249.16 ($1,026 + 153.90 + 69.26). Finally, if the order is paid within 10 days of delivery, an additional discount of 3 percent is allowed. Thus, if all discounts are applied, the manufacturer receives $1,276.36 from an order that amounted to $2,700 at list prices.

Quantity Discount Structures

Quantity discounts are offered for several reasons. One obvious reason is that sellers can reduce costs in several ways by convincing buyers to place larger orders. First, assuming a constant level of demand, fewer orders have to be processed and shipped and fewer sales calls are necessary to generate these large orders. Second, longer production runs may be possible and the manufacturer may now qualify for quantity discounts on raw materials purchases. Third, by shifting to the buyers the cost of carrying finished goods inventory, the seller further reduces operation costs. Fourth, assuming that payment for the goods is prompt, the money available can be reinvested sooner. Fifth, quantity discounts can be viewed as a form of profit sharing between channel members, leading to channel cooperation.[3] When deciding whether to offer quantity discounts and the type of discount structure to use, the behavioral objectives underlying the policy must be considered. That is, what type of buyer purchasing and ordering behavior will enhance the profit position of the firm, and what form of price inducement is necessary to achieve such buyer behavior?

Nonlinear Pricing

The above examples clearly indicate that the actual price per unit declines when some form of a quantity or volume discount is available and buyers take it. However, as shown in Table 16.2, there are a number of ways to structure quantity discounts. Figure 16.1 illustrates the revenue and unit price implications for these different discount structures. *Nonlinear pricing* refers to situations when a price structure leads to a decline in per-unit price as volume sold (ordered) increases.[4] The decisions that must be made when setting up a noncumulative quantity discount structure include

[3]Abel P. Jeuland and Steven M. Shugan, "Managing Channel Profits," *Marketing Science 2* (Summer 1983), 239–72.
[4]Robert B. Wilson, *Nonlinear Pricing* (New York: Oxford University Press, 1993); Farid Gasmi, Michael Moreau, and William Sharkey, "Strategic Nonlinear Pricing," *Journal of Economics 71,* no. 2 (2000), 109–31.

TABLE 16.2   **Types of Price Discount Structures**

Types of Discount Structures	Pricing Decisions	Number of Decisions
Fixed (uniform) price	Price	1
All units quantity discount	Price	2 or more
	Break points	1 or more
Two-part prices	Fixed price	1
	Variable price	1
Two-block prices	Fixed prices	2 or more
	Variable prices	2 or more
Price points	Prices	2 or more
Multiperson pricing	Prices	2 or more

1. The minimum quantity to be purchased before any discount is applied.

2. The number of breaks or additional discounts for larger purchases.

3. The maximum quantity qualifying for any additional discount.

4. The amount of discount to offer at each quantity level.

As a base of comparison, Figure 16.1a shows a fixed or uniform price situation. Since price remains constant or fixed over all units, revenues increase at a constant rate as the quantity sold increases. Since price is constant per unit, it is a horizontal line in the figure.

The *all units quantity discount* structure shown in Figure 16.1b represents the situation where a quantity discount applies for all ordered units after the minimum quantity level has been reached. Total revenue increases as the number of units ordered increases from zero to the quantity break point. For example, the quantity discount schedule specifies that the price is $100 per unit for the first 99 units ordered. However, for all orders of 100 units or more, the price is $95 per unit *for all units*. Thus, for an order of 99 units, total revenues would be $9,900. If 100 units are ordered, then total revenues would be $9,500. Hence, at the price break point of 100 units, total revenues decline rela-

FIGURE 16.1   **Alternative Price Discount Structures**

a.

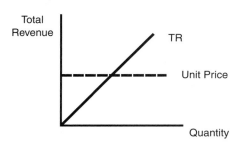

b.

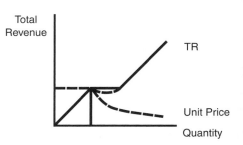

c.

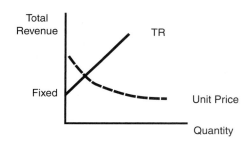

d.

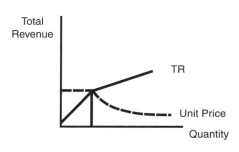

e.

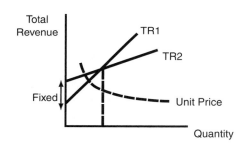

f.

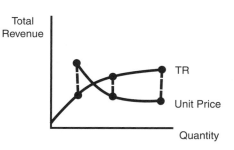

tive to an order of 99 units (see dash portion of the total revenue line). When order size is 105 or more units, revenues would exceed $9,900 and would then increase with additional quantity at the rate of $95 per unit.

Uniform two-part pricing, shown in Figure 16.1c, features a fixed price for the service regardless of whether any units are used. Once the customer uses the product or ser-

CHANGING CUSTOMER BEHAVIOR WITH A PRICE STRUCTURE CHANGE

BOX 16.2

A company that provided information search and chemical analysis for clients initially charged a specific price per request. However, an analysis of a recent history of requests revealed that over a defined period, many clients made a relatively large number of service requests. However, each request contained one or a very few unique search and analysis requests. A cost analysis of this service activity showed that each time a client submitted a request, the firm incurred a relatively large setup and handling cost, whereas the actual cost of conducting the search and analysis for a request was consistent with the price per request currently charged.

To change this activity from a money-losing operation, the firm instituted a new price struc-

ture. Each time a client made a request for information search and analysis, a fixed price (fee), *a*, was applied. However, for each separate search and analysis contained within the request, the firm charged an additional separate price, *p*, that was actually lower than the variable cost of providing this service. The objective of this two-part pricing structure was to encourage customers to bundle their requests and make multiple service requests on any occasion, increasing the profitability of the service.

Source: This example is based on the author's consulting experience.

vice, a uniform per-unit price is applied. This structure is similar to telephone companies, which charge a monthly connect fee and then charge an additional amount per unit of time the phone is used. Various forms of clubs similarly have an annual membership fee and then charge a fee per visit (health clubs) or for goods purchased (buying clubs). As the customer increases usage of the phone or club, the fixed price is spread over more units, leading to a declining price per unit purchased.

A way to represent a uniform two-part price structure is $(a + pq)$. Each buyer pays a fixed price, *a*, for the right to purchase any quantity, *q*, of the product or service at price *p*. Depending on the magnitude of the fixed price, *a*, the price per unit, *p*, could be above or below the variable cost of providing a unit of *q*. For example, an amusement park that charges an entrance fee, but does not charge for any of the park's rides has a two-part uniform price with $p = 0.$[5]

[5]Steven P. Cassou and John C. Hause, "Uniform Two-Part Tariffs and below Marginal Costs Prices: Disneyland Revisited," *Economic Inquiry 37* (January 1999), 74–85.

Box 16.2 illustrates how a company changed from a uniform fixed price structure to a two-part price structure.

In Figure 16.1d, *two-block prices*, a fixed price per unit is charged until the quantity price break point is reached. Then the quantity discount is applied to all units purchased *after* the break point. Thus, instead of applying the price discount to all units purchased once the quantity price break point was reached, as shown in Figure 16.1b, the lower price per unit applies only to the quantity beyond the quantity price break point. Thus, if the first 99 units are priced at $100 and 100 or more units are priced at $95 each, revenue continues to grow after the break point, but at a slower rate.

Figure 16.1e shows a more complex price structure. This situation has two blocks of prices, each at a different unit price. However, each block also has a fixed fee as well as a variable price per unit used or purchased. In this price structure, the customer has two options: (1) to pay a relatively low annual fee (fixed) and higher per-unit usage price (variable); or (2) to pay a relatively high annual fee and a lower per-unit usage price. Option 1 becomes the uniform fixed price structure when the annual fee is $0.

Figure 16.1f shows an extended two-block price situation. Here, the firm would have multiple quantity price breaks and reduce the per-unit price at each. Thus, the first 99 units would be priced at $100 each, then 100–149 units at $95 each, 150–199 units at $90 each, and so on depending on the number of quantity price breaks the structure includes. This price structure is similar to the situation in which the first person in a group pays "full" price, and then each succeeding member of the group pays a progressively lower price. The airline promotion that offers the spouse or child of a full-fare adult passenger a half-price fare is a variation of this structure.

"All You Can Eat" Pricing

Some businesses have tried to simplify their pricing structures by using only flat-rate pricing regardless of levels of volume or other characteristics of service for which costs vary with some measure of usage. Box 16.3 describes America Online's (AOL) flat-rate pricing attempt. The demand for AOL connect time greatly exceeded its ability to supply it to subscribers. In this case, AOL did not recognize an important condition for flat-rate pricing: There must be some natural barrier limiting the level of demand or demand may be

AOL TRIES "ALL YOU CAN EAT PRICING"

BOX 16.3

In December 1996, America Online (AOL) eliminated its various pricing schedules to implement a flat-rate pricing structure. Instead of basing price upon the amount of time a customer stayed online, AOL offered customers a $19.95 monthly rate for unlimited monthly access. AOL's primary goal of initiating flat-rate pricing was to increase advertising revenues through a larger membership. AOL did vastly increase its membership (to 8 million subscribers), but the company's upgrades and modems were unable to meet the surge of members, both existing and new. Whereas the varied pricing schedule encouraged customers to limit their time online, the flat-rate pricing for unlimited monthly access placed no restrictions on AOL members, resulting in longer usage periods. In fact, the amount an average customer stayed online after the announced monthly rate increased 100 percent! By 1998, the average monthly use per customer increased from 7 to 23 hours.

AOL's flat-rate pricing initiative led to customer complaints. AOL admitted its inability to provide for existing members, reduced advertising in an effort to limit new membership, and promised to add new equipment. Furthermore, AOL refunded $20 million to those customers who were unable to access the Internet due to the company's inability to meet the demand surge.

AOL's first experience with flat-rate pricing did not dissuade the company from maintaining a flat monthly rate for unlimited access. Critics of such moves towards flat-rate pricing schedules argue that flat rates should be reserved for products or services for which there is a natural demand and where these flat rates do not attract less price sensitive consumers.

Sources: Amy Barrett, Paul Eng, and Kathy Rebello, "For $19.95 a Month, Unlimited Headaches for AOL," *Business Week* (January 27, 1997), 35; Peter Coy, "Are Flat Rates Good Business?" *Business Week* (February 10, 1997), 108; Jon Van, "AOL Kicks Flat Rate Up 10 Percent," *Chicago Tribune* (February 10, 1998), Section 3, 1–2.

much greater than the firm's capability to supply. Thus, restaurants that offer "all you can eat" buffets rely on the fact that humans will become satiated and will not continuously eat. Placing a time limit on the "all you can eat" buffet, for example, 5:00 P.M. to 8:00 P.M., operationalizes this need to place a reasonable limit on demand. Amusement park operators who utilize one admission price for the day for all rides similarly specify time of operation to limit the demand for a single admission fee.

A Simple Quantity Discount Model

As we discussed in Chapter 1, ultimately the overall objective of pricing decisions is to influence the purchasing behavior of buyers. That is, the objective of setting a specific price, changing a price, or establishing price differentials is to enhance the opportunity of obtaining profitable sales. Thus, one purpose of a quantity discount schedule is to enhance demand while reducing the costs of meeting that level of demand. Viewing the quantity discount as a price reduction decision suggests that the elasticity of demand with respect to the percentage discount should be a decision consideration. However, this demand elasticity depends on the relative costs to buyers of balancing their ordering costs with their inventory carrying costs. That is, increasing the size of their orders results in fewer orders being placed within a given time period, but it also results in buyers carrying a higher level of average inventory over the same time period. Hence a quantity discount schedule should recognize the potential change in buyers' inventory costs if they change the size of their orders.

The seller must consider the cost of obtaining an order as a function of order size. For example, if customers were to place and pay for their entire sets of orders on the first day of the planning period, this purchasing behavior would represent a gain to the seller, who could immediately reinvest these revenues. Moreover, the seller's total cost of filling orders decreases as the number of orders decreases, that is, as the volume per order increases (see Chapter 12).

To see the relative trade-offs between the increase in buyers' costs and the reduction in the seller's costs consider the following model for determining these two costs: *the change in buyers' inventory costs as quantity purchased increases and the change in the seller's costs as the purchase order size increases.* The buyers' cost function is given as

$$\text{TEK}_B = (Ad)/q + (qki)/2 \qquad \textbf{(16.1)}$$

where

TEK = total expected inventory costs

A = the cost of placing a single order

d = number of units required during the planning period

q = number of units ordered at one time

k = price of one unit

i = cost of carrying one unit of inventory per period expressed as a fraction of the unit's value

Using differential calculus to find the minimum value for TEK_B as q varies and then solving for q produces the equation for the economic purchase quantity:

$$q_o = \{(2Ad)/(\text{ki})\}^{1/2} \qquad \textbf{(16.2)}$$

The seller's cost function is

$$\text{TEK}_S = (Ad)/q - (pkiq)/2 \qquad \textbf{(16.3)}$$

where p is the percentage gross margin on an item.

Both the seller's and buyer's optimal annual ordering and inventory costs can be determined before any discount is offered. Then for any larger quantity ordered, it would be possible to determine

1. The increased cost to the buyer.

2. The decreased cost to the seller.

3. The net decrease in total cost to both parties (the change in their joint costs).

By splitting the decrease in cost to the seller between both parties, the amount of the possible discount can be determined. The exact proportional split can be determined according to the seller's perceived relative worth of inducing the buyer to purchase in larger quantities.

To be nondiscriminatory, the seller must offer the discount structure to all buyers. Therefore, customers must be classified according to historical average order size, and then the seller may select the order classification to develop the foregoing analysis. The seller then can determine whether more or fewer price breaks would allow a broader appeal to other order-size buyer classifications. The primary advantage of such an approach is that the seller is forced to consider customers and their needs and to balance these needs against the seller's own pecuniary objectives.

This process of determining the optimal quantity discount schedule requires negotiations between buyer and seller. That is, as a quid pro quo, the seller and buyer could negotiate the minimum joint cost function between them rather than each seeking unilaterally to optimize the operations. Dolan has developed a quantity discount model that demonstrates that this joint cost function can be reduced by introducing several price breaks. That is, the more complex the price discount structure, the more effective the seller can be in gaining the buyer's cooperation.[6]

[6]Robert J. Dolan, "A Normative Model of Industrial Buyer Response to Quantity Discounts," *Proceedings of the 1978 AMA Educators' Conference*, Chicago: American Marketing Association, 121–25.

Some Additional Managerial Issues

The discussion thus far has presented a method and thought process for developing a rational quantity discount schedule. However, once a discount schedule has been developed, there is a tendency to retain it although conditions in the marketplace change. It is imperative that any pricing policy be modified as market and internal conditions change. For example, many discount schedules are based on the dollar volume purchased. Yet as prices are increased without a corresponding change in the discount schedule, more buyers qualify for a discount or for additional price breaks, leading to additional discounts being offered even if there is no change in the size of purchases.

A second problem may occur when two buyers merge either in terms of actual ownership or by forming a buying group. In either situation, the seller may again give more discounts than previously even though there is no increase in purchase volume. Third, as industrial buyers become more proficient using the Internet to track and use different vendor discount structures, they are able to selectively vary volume purchases across vendors.

Finally, another issue concerns the possibility that buyers will find it profitable to buy in very large quantities at a relatively low per-unit cost and then ship the goods to other markets for resale (see Chapter 20). For example, cameras produced in Japan and shipped overseas to other countries have been reshipped to Japan and sold profitably to Japanese consumers at prices lower than those of cameras shipped directly from the Japanese producer to the Japanese retailer. This particular issue illustrates a classic example of price discrimination failing when buyers paying a lower price can ship the product back to the higher-priced market. In devising a quantity discount price schedule, the seller must periodically examine the discount structure to determine whether any of these flaws exist.[7]

Pricing Special Orders

The contribution per resource unit (CPRU) criterion developed in Chapter 11 can be used even when a firm is not operating at capacity or is faced with the shortage of critical

---

[7]James B. Wilcox, Roy D. Howell, Paul Kuzdrall, and Robert Britney, "Price Quantity Discounts: Some Implications for Buyers and Sellers," *Journal of Marketing 51* (July 1987), 60–70.

resources. Essentially, use of the CPRU when establishing prices provides a means of maintaining consistency over customers, product lines, or special orders. A special order is defined as an order placed by an established customer for a quantity different from the normal one, a one-time-only order for a substantial quantity placed by a nonregular customer, or an order placed for a product not usually produced by the firm but which the firm has capacity to produce. In each of these situations, the firm must establish a price that is consistent with prices for regular products and customers and is acceptable to the originator of the special order. The CPRU criterion is useful in pricing such a special order.

To illustrate the application of the CPRU to pricing special orders, assume that the firm normally sells a product in a standard order of 500 units. The basic cost and contribution data for a standard order are given in Table 16.3A. On a standard order of 500 units, the firm spends 10 hours to set up the production equipment to make the production run. Labor costs per hour for a production setup are $14. The standard hourly rate for the machines used in the process is $9, and five units can be produced per hour. Therefore, an order of 500 units requires 100 hours of machine time. A standard order of 500 units currently is priced at $20 per unit or $10,000 per order.

Suppose a nonregular customer approaches the firm with an offer for a one-time-only order for 1,000 units. This potential customer is aware that a standard order is 500 units at a price of $20 each. However, the customer asks for a price quotation. Obviously, the customer is seeking a lower price than $20 per unit. The firm has the capacity to handle this special order but wishes to be consistent in its price quotation to be able to justify such a lower price to regular customers should they object.

The data in Table 16.3A indicate that the CPRU per production hour is $54.18 for a standard production run (order) of 500 units. The data in Table 16.3B show the calculations for determining the selling price that meets the two objectives of (1) a lower per-unit price and (2) maintaining the CPRU. The price that satisfies these objectives is $19.32 per unit for an order size of 1,000 units.

It is important to note that this price will not necessarily be attractive to the buyer. Nor does the price of $19.32 imply that the seller could not get more from the customer for a 1,000-unit order. But the price does provide management information on the costs and the necessary markup to achieve

TABLE 16.3 CPRU Pricing of a Special Order

A. Data for Standard Order (500 Units)		
1. Revenue at $20 selling price		$10,000
2. Variable costs		
Setup cost (10 hours @ $14/hour)	$ 140	
Machine cost (100 hours @ $9/hour)	900	
Materials ($6 per unit)	3,000	
Total		4,040
3. Contribution		$ 5,960
4. Total hours (10 hours + 100 hours)		110
5. CPRU per hour (3 ÷ 4)		$ 54.18

B. Data for 1,000-Unit Orders		
1. Desired CPRU per hour	$ 54.18	
Time required (hours):		
Setup	10	
Machine (100 x 2)	200	
2. Total hours	210	
3. Required order contribution (1 x 2)		$11,377.80
4. Variable costs		
Setup cost (10 hours @ $14/hour)	$ 140	
Machine cost (200 hours @ $9/hour)	1,800	
Materials ($6 per unit)	6,000	
Total		7,940.00
5. Required sales volume for 1,000 units (3 + 4)		$19,317.80
6. Unit selling price (5 ÷ 1,000)		$ 19.32

a specific profit objective. Alternative selling prices can be developed that take into consideration specific demand, competition, and other market factors. Essentially, the CPRU criterion as applied to the pricing of special orders gives management a specific price alternative for a given profit contribution objective. Developing a CPRU pricing mechanism with time as the critical resource is common for many types of professional service firms including consulting, lawyers, plumbers, car repairs, cleaning and janitorial firms, and other types of "special order" sellers (see Chapter 20).

Legal Considerations

Quantity discounts have been regularly scrutinized by the Federal Trade Commission for possible Robinson-Patman Act violations. It is the responsibility of the seller to prove that the noncumulative discount schedule has been offered to all competing buyers on the same basis and can be justified because of demonstrable cost savings. However, in the past, primarily due to inadequate cost data, the cost defense has had little success. Hence there are strong reasons for removing intuition and arbitrary decision rules from such pricing decisions. The more rational approach to developing quantity discount decisions illustrated here would provide a stronger economic defense of a discount schedule.

Cumulative quantity discounts are difficult to justify because they invariably favor large-volume purchasers and are therefore discriminatory to small purchasers. However, this price discrimination is unlawful only if potential or real injury to competition can be shown (providing there are measurable cost savings involved).

Cash Discounts and Credit Decisions

As observed previously, a cash discount is a reward for the payment of an invoice or account within a specified amount of time. For example, assume that after the trade and promotional discounts have been applied, the invoice indicates that the amount due is $456. The invoice also indicates that the credit policy of the seller is 2/10 net 30. If the buyer pays within 10 days, the correct remittance is $446.88 (98 percent of $456). If the cash discount is not taken because payment was not made within 10 days, then the full amount, $456, must be paid within 30 days. From a decision perspective, the seller must determine

1. The amount of cash discount (2 percent in the above example).

2. The length of the credit period (the total time the bill is outstanding, which equals 30 days in the example).

3. The amount to spend on attempting to collect overdue accounts.

4. The customers to whom to offer credit terms.

5. The magnitude of the line of credit.

Cash discounts and credit decisions traditionally have been considered the purview of finance, and this viewpoint has persisted. Closer analysis of the elements of credit policy decisions suggests that demand is affected by these decisions and therefore that a more active decision approach can have positive effects on a firm's demand. Moreover, terms of trade have been recognized as an important factor influencing the degree of channel cooperation or conflict. [8]

An active approach to determining credit policy requires analyzing the relationship between demand and (1) the credit period, (2) the amount of the cash discount, and (3) collection expenditures. Other things remaining the same, we would expect demand to increase with a lengthening of the credit period. That is, for a given list price, a movement away from an "all sales cash" policy to allowing purchases on account would result in an increase in demand that would grow with the number of days an account is allowed to be outstanding. In addition, increasing the amount of the cash discount or lengthening the time period that the discount applies will normally result in increases in demand. In either decision the key information is the elasticity of demand with respect to changes in these variables.

Reasons for Cash Discounts

Among the reasons cited for using cash discounts are the following:

1. To encourage prompt payment of invoices, thereby providing for more rapid turnover in the seller's cash flow. Cash is an asset and the more times it is turned over (used successively), the better the firm's pricing flexibility.

2. To reduce credit risks and the cost of collecting overdue accounts. Since buyers are rewarded for prompt payment, in theory there will be fewer overdue invoices.

3. To follow industry or historical practice. One manufacturer in the clothing industry was puzzled over the custom of offering a cash discount of 8/10 net EOM. An examination of sales records revealed that the firm had granted about $500,000 in cash discounts on $7 million in sales. It simply had been following the same discount policy established many years earlier. (As suggested previously and amplified later, cash discount and credit policies should be reviewed periodically to determine their appropriateness for current and future market conditions.)

---

[8]Michael Levy and Dwight Grant, "Financial Terms of Sale and Control of Marketing Channel Conflict," *Journal of Marketing Research 17* (November 1980), 524–30.

Problems with Cash Discounts

Buyers tend to take cash discounts regularly because of the amount of savings involved. In the example of the clothing manufacturer mentioned above, if we assume that the cash discount is taken by the 10th day of the month, then the seller has the use of the money 20 days sooner than if payment was made by the end of the month. In essence, the clothing manufacturer was willing to pay the retail buyers an interest rate of 144 percent on an annual basis for the privilege of using the money 20 days earlier. (In a 360-day year, there are 18 periods of 20 days. Thus, (360/20)8 percent = 144 percent.) Clearly, it may be more economical for a firm to borrow money on a short-term basis than to offer cash discounts.

A second problem occurs when large buyers take the cash discount as a matter of routine, even though payment is not made within the discount period. In such circumstances, many sellers are reluctant to press the issue and the effective interest rate they are granting these buyers is even higher. Thus the problem of equitably policing the discount policy is often a difficult one. Moreover, permitting such variances in the cash discount policy is unlawful. Cash discounts are legal under the Robinson-Patman Act so long as they are offered under the same terms to all competing buyers.

Third, during periods of inflation many customers pay bills more slowly. Apparently, higher interest rates and inflationary pressures lengthen the payment period. By forgoing the cash discounts, customers are using suppliers' funds as a source of capital. Unless the seller is indifferent to this change in payment practices, the lengthening of the payment period could lead to a conflict within the marketing channel. Some wholesalers believe that sales terms are among the most important aspects of customer service and affect purchase behavior.

Communicating the Value of a Cash Discount

If it is assumed that the motive for extending a cash discount is to increase the number of buyers making prompt payments, the method of relating the policy to customers should be considered. Research suggests that people seek out positive alternatives; choosing among negatives seems like no choice at all. As discussed in Chapter 7, people value perceived gains differently than perceived losses. Consider one way the cash discount and credit policy may be framed on an invoice:

Terms: 2/10; net 30. Invoices outstanding after 30 days will be assessed a service fee of 10 percent.

On a bill for $100, the buyer is faced with paying $98 in 10 days, $100 within 30 days, or $110 later. That is, the buyer is offered a *reward* (gain) of $2 for early payment and threatened with a *penalty* (loss) of $10 for late payment.

Now suppose the invoice states that the charge is $110 but offers the buyer a $12 reward (gain) if payment is made in 10 days or a $10 reward (gain) if payment is made between the 10th and 30th days. In this case, the buyer is offered a choice between two positive alternatives—paying early and gaining $12 or paying a little later and gaining $10. In the original statement, the buyer was offered a choice among a positive alternative (gain $2 if paying early), a neutral alternative (paying within 30 days), or a negative alternative (paying a penalty of $10 if paying late).

Apart from the economic reason for making early payment—savings—the idea of presenting a cash discount and credit policy to the buyer in terms of positive choices may increase the chance of early payments. Developing positive feelings on the part of buyers will increase their desire or willingness to respond favorably to the cash discount and credit policy. Early payment is the behavioral objective of a cash discount and communicating rewards or gains as opposed to penalties or losses creates a more favorable attitude and behavioral tendency. Moreover, to take advantage of a positive frame of reference, the seller may wish to present the actual dollar alternatives on the invoice. That is, the invoice could indicate that the buyer gains $12 if paying within 10 days. This procedure is similar to the notion of transaction value induced by a sales promotion (discussed in Chapter 7). Given computerized billing systems, such a communication procedure is very feasible. Indeed, one of the critical ingredients of implementing a price structure is the communication of the structure to buyers in a way that fosters the desired buyer behavior.

Geographical Pricing Decisions

One of the most significant costs in marketing arises from the transportation of goods from points of origin to points of destination. We normally think of marketing as primarily related to the stimulation of demand. However, a necessary corollary activity is to supply the various markets with the demanded products. The costs of performing this supply activity range well into billions of dollars annually for transportation alone. The way that sellers solve the transportation problem affects their marketing programs by influencing the range of geographic market areas they serve, the degree to which they may be vulnerable to price competition in some markets, their profit margins, their ability to control resale prices, and the effectiveness of their personal salespeople.

From a pricing perspective, part of the decision problem revolves around whether sellers wish to account for their shipping costs in their price structure. If they do, there are two general methods they can use: the F.O.B. origin pricing method and the delivered pricing method. A second aspect of the decision problem is to determine relative competitive advantage considering both list price and transportation costs in various geographic markets. These two issues will be discussed in this section.

F.O.B. Origin Pricing

F.O.B. origin pricing means that the seller quotes prices from the point of shipment. **Free on b**oard (F.O.B.) means it is the buyer's responsibility to select the mode of transportation, choose the specific carrier, handle any damage claims, and pay all shipping charges. Thus, the net return to the seller is the same for all buyers purchasing in the same quantities and with the same trade status, regardless of their locations. The seller's freedom from responsibility for transportation and provision of the same net return for every similar sale are the primary advantages of the F.O.B. origin method.

However, unless all sellers are located in geographical proximity, product demand is relatively inelastic, and there is a degree of product differentiation, sale of a product becomes increasingly difficult the further away a market is located. Also, because the cost to distributors varies with their distance from the seller, it becomes increasingly difficult to control and maintain resale prices. Finally, the seller's salespeople will find it increasingly difficult to quote an accurate cost to customers because the costs will vary with distance and with the transportation method(s) selected by the buyer.

Delivered Pricing

In *delivered pricing*, the price quoted by the manufacturer includes both the list price and transportation costs. In such cases, the prices are quoted as *F.O.B. destination*, meaning the manufacturer bears the responsibility of selecting and paying for the method of transporting the product. In general, delivered pricing systems allow firms to compete effectively over larger geographical areas than would be possible under F.O.B. pricing.[9]

Single-Zone Pricing

In single-zone pricing, the seller receives a different net return (delivered price minus transportation costs) when transportation costs for customers vary. That is, the seller quotes one list price plus transportation costs to all buyers regardless of their location. On the other hand, buyers pay a uniform delivered price regardless of their location relative to the seller. In essence, then, all buyers pay the same "average transportation cost."

Multiple-zone pricing

In a multiple-zone pricing system, delivered prices are uniform within two or more zones. Most retail mail-order catalogs use a multiple-zone pricing system. That is, buyers must determine which concentric circle (zone) around the catalog's distribution center they are in to determine the shipping costs per pound for their order. The differences in price between zones depend on distance from the shipping point, competition, and demand in geographic market segments.

Zone systems generally make it easier to sell in distance markets, since prices are determined by "average" transportation costs. Within any zone, therefore, it is easier to control resale prices and increase the ability of salespeople to quote prices. Indeed, the simplicity of zone pricing permits a substantial reduction in accounting costs, which may be used to bolster the firm's sales presentations.[10] Using multiple zones enables the seller to geographically segment markets if there are varying price elasticities and thus to determine several satisfactory prices. Multiple-zone systems also facilitate dealing with variations in strength and type of competition. That is, a seller can lower prices in zones where it faces strong price competition, but set higher prices in zones where price competition is weak.

[9]Mingxia Zhang and Richard J. Sexton, "FOB or Uniform Delivered Prices: Strategic Choice and Welfare Effects," *The Journal of Industrial Economics 49* (June 2001), 197–221.

[10]Dominique Peeters and Jacques-Francois Thisse, "Zone Pricing," *Journal of Regional Science 36,* no. 2 (1996), 291–301.

But there are some drawbacks. The seller does not receive the same net return per sale because the net return varies with the actual shipping costs. Moreover, the demand center for the firm may shift geographically, leading to, for example, more shipments going to more distant buyers than before. However, a properly designed information system can monitor these market shifts and alert the firm to change its pricing structure. Within any zone, some buyers are paying more and some are paying less than the actual cost of transportation, because the cost is averaged for any zone. Moreover, buyers located on the boundaries of zones may pay more than nearby buyers because they have arbitrarily been positioned in a different price zone. One result of closely situated buyers paying different prices is that the firm may not be able to prevent resales from customers paying lower prices in one zone to customers residing in the adjacent, higher-priced zone. This problem occurs frequently in international pricing where pricing zones are related to national boundaries, which will be discussed more completely in Chapter 20. Finally, zone-pricing methods require the seller to choose the mode of transportation, select the carrier, handle the damage claims, and pay the freight bills. Each of these responsibilities may become an increased burden to the selling firm.

F.O.B. with Freight Allowed

Another form of delivered pricing is F.O.B. with freight allowed. The buyer arranges and pays for the transportation but deducts these transportation costs from the invoice total and remits the net amount. Thus, by arranging cheaper transportation methods, such as using a private fleet of trucks, the buyer pays a lower total price. However, the seller receives varying net returns and the resale prices may also vary.

Basing-Point Pricing

In another variation of delivered pricing, the delivered price is the product's list price plus transportation costs from a basing point to the buyer. The basing point is a designated city where the product is produced. But in basing-point pricing the product may actually be shipped from a city other than the basing point. Firms or plants at the basing points receive the same net returns, whereas firms or plants not at the basing point receive different net returns from different sales. This variation in net returns is due to the difference between actual shipping costs and the transportation factor used in the price quotation.

Figure 16.2 illustrates the principle of basing-point pricing. All three mills, X, Y, and Z, quote the same delivered price to customer A, $120, which is determined by adding the $100 base price at mill X to the freight charge of $20 from mill X to customer A. To quote the $120 delivered price, mill Y must absorb $10 of freight charges (called freight absorption), whereas mill Z collects $10 of phantom freight.

One or more basing points can be used for any transaction, depending on whether the pricing method used is a *single basing-point system* or a *multiple basing-point system*. The system may be a company system used by a firm with several geographically dispersed production plants or an industrywide system used by most firms in the industry. An industrywide system may develop as a result of an industry tradition of using particular basing points, or it may evolve from a practice of price leadership in which firms follow the basing-point pricing practices of the price leader.

FIGURE 16.2   **Basing-Point Pricing System**

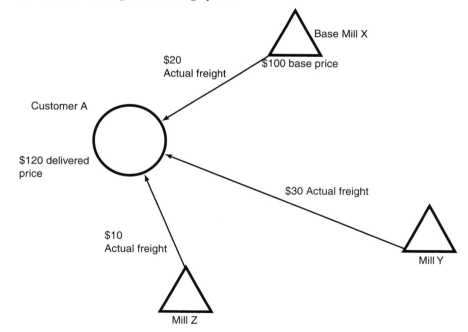

An industrywide system may also be the result of collusion by the firms involved.

In a multiple basing-point system, several locations are designated as basing points. On a given sale, the basing point chosen is the point that yields the lowest delivered cost to the buyer. With a multiple basing-point system, both the basing-point plant or firm and the plants or firms not located at a basing point receive varying net returns from different sales.

Both types of multiple basing-point systems have advantages and disadvantages. The advantages of a company-wide basing-point system are

1. It eliminates price competition between the firm's different production facilities. The buyer pays the same price no matter where he or she is located or what the origin of the shipment is.

2. It allows the firm to balance shipments from the different plants and thus ensure that plants receive enough shipments to keep them operating at a desirable level of capacity.

3. It simplifies price quotations in that a schedule of delivered prices need be prepared only for the basing points and not for every production facility.

The disadvantages of a companywide basing-point system are

1. Customers who discover they pay more for transportation than the actual costs will be unhappy. This unhappiness will be more pronounced when they discover that other customers pay less than the actual costs of transportation.

2. It may result in a large amount of freight absorption.

3. The return to the seller varies on each sale.

4. The price discrimination features of companywide basing-point pricing may produce legal difficulties.

The advantages of an industrywide basing-point pricing system are

1. Price competition based on differences in transportation costs is eliminated.

2. It permits a firm to secure greater volume because large transportation costs do not prevent the firm from expanding its geographic market area.

3. Any firm or plant can sell in a larger geographic area because transportation costs are not a factor in buyers' purchasing decisions.

Among the disadvantages of an industrywide basing-point system are

1. Buyers who find they are paying for transportation costs from producing plants that do not originate the shipment will be dissatisfied.

2. Buyers may object to the lack of price competition in transportation costs.

3. Because the delivered price is the same regardless of shipping point, there is less incentive to use the least costly transportation.

4. The reduced basis for price competition may lead to higher and less flexible prices.

5. It may lead to excessive freight absorption, varying sales returns, and legal difficulties for the seller.

Legal Considerations

A long history of legal questions surrounds geographical pricing practices. F.O.B. origin pricing is legal. But zone-pricing systems have an inherent element of price discrimination because some buyers pay more than the cost of transportation while other buyers pay less. Sellers who practice single-zone pricing have not been prevented from maintaining a uniform delivered price. Apparently, because there are no price differences at the point of *destination* with this system, the Federal Trade Commission and the federal courts have not viewed the system as discriminatory.

Multiple-zone systems have had difficulty only when all firms have had similar zone-pricing systems. Indeed, the Federal Trade Commission has taken the position that when competing firms establish zone systems with identical boundaries and price differentials, collusion is likely to be present.

Basing-point pricing has had considerable difficulty under the Robinson-Patman Act and the Federal Trade Commission Act. These difficulties stem primarily from the fact that different firms or plants receive varying net returns from different sales under similar circumstances without real cost justifications. Although such sales are generally held to be price discriminatory, unless there appears to be clear-cut evidence of conspiracy, it is relatively unlikely that the Federal Trade Commission will initiate proceedings against delivered pricing systems.

Despite the position of the Federal Trade Commission, basing-point pricing is patently unfair to at least some customers. The unfairness of the system can eventually lead to customer dissatisfaction (see Chapter 7). In a competitive environment, dissatisfied customers will seek out alternative sources of supply from competing sellers.

Using Price Structure to Gain Competitive Advantage

This chapter emphasizes that the development of a more complex price structure provides for pricing flexibility and enhances a firm's ability to respond to competitor, buyer, or market changes. Indeed, the discussion on quantity and cash discounts has suggested that developing more complex discount structures may offer profit opportunities. The purpose of this section is to illustrate the opportunities of using price structure to either gain competitive advantage or to diminish a competitive disadvantage. The problem of handling freight costs will be used to develop the example.

As should be apparent from the preceding discussion on geographical pricing, the relative distances from competing sellers to a customer may play a role in the customer's purchase decision, particularly if the products sold by the two sellers are perceived to be similar. Indeed, if the buyer perceives that there is relatively little difference in the products offered by the two sellers, then the purchase decision is likely to be determined by the relative costs of buying from each seller. Thus the buyer will assess the total cost of acquiring the product from each seller.

For the moment assume that one seller (A) enjoys a manufacturing cost advantage over another seller (B) and that this translates into a list price of $15 per ton less than B's price. However, assume B is located closer to the buyer and enjoys a relative advantage in terms of freight costs. In Table 16.4A, the price advantage of A is assumed to be $15 at all feasible order sizes. But the freight disadvantage A encounters declines per ton as the feasible order size increases through economies of larger shipments. As Table 16.4A indicates, seller A has a relative advantage at all order sizes except the smallest one. Moreover, this relative advantage increases as order size increases. Thus if the customer is small in terms of usual order size, it is more likely to place its orders with seller B. However, at all order sizes above five tons, the buyer is likely to order from seller A.

In Table 16.4B, seller A faces a price disadvantage relative to a third seller (C), but being closer to the buyer enjoys a relative freight cost advantage. Further contributing to the price disadvantage is the fact that seller C offers a quantity discount of $1 per ton at each of the larger order sizes, thereby increasing seller A's relative price disadvantage. Thus, seller A would enjoy a competitive advantage at the lowest feasible order size but would be at a disadvantage at all other order sizes. If seller A decided to match the quantity discount schedule of seller C, then its relative disadvantage would be the same as depicted in Table 16.4A for seller B.

This simple illustration shows that when a price structure is kept simple, it is relatively more difficult to take advantage of differential characteristics that may lead to a competitive advantage, or it is more difficult to diminish or remove a competitive disadvantage. However, by using distance between seller and buyer and by understanding the buyers' relative costs of carrying inventory and costs of capital, a seller can develop a price structure that affords an opportunity for differential pricing that reflects buyer, market, and product

TABLE 16.4   Evaluating Relative Competitive Advantage: Price and Freight Costs

Order Size (tons)	Price Advantage $/Ton	Freight Advantage $/Ton	Net Disadvantage $/Ton	Relative Advantage $/Order
A. **Seller A vs. Seller B**				
5	15	−16	−1	−5
10	15	−14	+1	+10
15	15	−12	+3	+45
20	15	−10	+5	+100
25	15	−9	+6	+150
2. **Seller A vs. Seller C**				
5	−15	+16	+1	+5
10	−16	+14	−2	−20
15	−17	+12	−5	−75
20	−18	+10	−8	−160
25	−19	+9	−10	−250

or service characteristics. Moreover, such a price structure provides additional flexibility when responding to market, buyer, or competitor changes.

Summary

This chapter introduced the problem of administering the prices of products and services. This problem usually begins with a decision on the price to offer buyers. The price setter must also consider adjusting prices for sales made in different quantities, sales made to different types of buyers located in different markets, sales made with different credit and collection terms, and sales made at different times.

This chapter considered the decision problems connected with developing a quantity discount schedule and with setting cash discount and credit policies. Generally, quantity and cash discount decisions have been made on the basis of convenience and tradition. One consequence of such decision making has been the inability to defend such pricing decisions when faced with legal or buyer scrutiny. However, if the motive for offering quantity and cash discounts is to influence the behavior of buyers—to order more at a time or to pay early—then analysis underlying these decisions must begin with buyers. For both types of decisions, the problem is determining what "price breaks" will motivate buyers to behave in a manner favorable to the firm. The seller must then balance these price breaks against the costs of providing them. When a firm sells to many different types of buyers, it must set the price breaks or rewards to avoid discrimination on the basis of price. Hence price administration is fraught with legal complications.

Geographical pricing involves large dollar amounts, and sellers tend not to understand its difficulties and importance. As with quantity and cash discounts, the determination of a geographical pricing policy should begin with a consideration of the buyers. Transportation charges vary with many factors, including weight and distance. Geographical pricing practices are concerned primarily with the effect shipping distances have on delivered prices. Again, developing a geographical pricing policy solely on the basis of convenience and tradition will ignore real differences in buyers and in the costs of serving them. Dissatisfied customers are no basis for long-run profitability.

Discussion Questions

1. Briefly discuss the different types of decision problems in price administration.
2. Explain what is meant by
    a. Price structure.
    b. Base or list price.
    c. Functional discount.
3. Explain the difference between a cumulative quantity discount and a noncumulative quantity discount.
4. Explain and illustrate the decision problems encountered when developing a quantity discount schedule.
5. Explain and illustrate the decision problems encountered when establishing a cash discount and credit policy.
6. What are the behavioral objectives involved in establishing trade discount, quantity discount, and cash discount policies? What can a pricing manager do to reach these behavioral objectives?
7. Explain and illustrate the decision problems encountered when establishing a geographical pricing policy.
8. Explain what is meant by
    a. Free on board origin.
    b. Free on board destination.
    c. Delivered pricing.
    d. Zone pricing.
    e. Basing-point pricing.
    f. Phantom freight.
    g. Free on board with freight allowed.
9. If the list price is $600 and the seller quotes a chain discount of 30, 10, 5, with a cash discount of 3/10 net 30, what is
    a. The total trade and promotional discount amount?
    b. The cash discount amount?
    c. The correct remittance if all discounts are taken?
10. Discuss the legal implications of determining a geographical pricing policy.

Suggested Readings

Davey, K. K. S., Andy Childs, and Stephen J. Carlotti, Jr: "Why Your Price Band Is Wider Than It Should Be," *The McKinsey Quarterly,* no. 3 (1998), 116–27.

Dolan, Robert J.: "Quantity Discounts: Managerial Issues and Research Opportunities," *Marketing Science 6* (Winter 1987), 1–22.

Garda, Robert A.: "Use Tactical Pricing to Uncover Hidden Profits," *The Journal of Business Strategy* (September/October 1991), 17–23.

Potter, Donald V.: "Discovering Hidden Pricing Power," *Business Horizons* (November–December 2000), 41–48.

Stern, Andrew A.: "The Strategic Value of Price Structure," *Journal of Business Strategy 7* (Fall 1986), 22–31.

Wilcox, James B., Roy D. Howell, Paul Kuzdrall, and Robert Britney: "Price Quantity Discounts: Some Implications for Buyers and Sellers," *Journal of Marketing 51* (July 1987), 60–70.

CHAPTER SEVENTEEN

Pricing to and through the Channel

In Chapters 5 through 8 we saw how prices influence buyers' perceptions of value. We suggested that certain prices anchor, or frame, buyers' responses, for example, the end prices of a product line, the price of the brand last purchased, and the price of the leading brand. We also pointed out that the price differences between products in a product line, as well as those between national and private brands, between different national or private brands, or following price changes influence buyers' perceptions. In addition, for some products and under certain conditions a positive price–perceived quality relationship exists. Thus, because prices and price differences may affect the ultimate buyers' perceptions and purchase behavior, the manufacturer is naturally concerned about how to present prices to buyers.

Part of the problem of controlling price through the channel lies in setting a discount policy for distributors. Where rival sellers are competing for distributor support, the price paid for distributor cooperation must reflect not only the marketing functions distributors perform but also the competitive environment. That is, the manufacturer must consider not only competition from other manufacturers but also the competition the distributors face at each level in the channel. For example, if competition at the distributors' level has pared the distributors' margins, then to gain the distributors' support for the manufacturer's policies, it may be necessary to increase the trade or functional discount.

Pricing decisions and the policies that are derived from these decisions impact dealer cooperation and motivation as well as sales force morale and effort. Although it is legally difficult to control prices through the distribution channel, it is possible to motivate people to adhere to company-determined pricing policies. Because price directly affects the revenues of the trade and salespeoples' commissions, it can be used to foster desired behaviors by channel members and salespeople.

To use price as a means of influencing channel members, the seller may offer trade discounts or special price promotions and deals. As defined in Chapter 16, a trade or functional discount is offered to members of the distribution channel because they provide certain marketing services (functions) for the seller. Although offering a functional discount may seem easy, in fact this discount decision is fraught with managerial and legal difficulties. Similarly, price promotion tactics and short-term price deals are more complex than is apparent. This chapter discusses these managerial problems and suggests approaches for their solutions.

Trade and Functional Discounts

As pointed out in Chapter 16, trade or functional discounts traditionally have been based on a distributor's place in the distributive sequence and represent payment for performing certain marketing functions. The justification for these discounts has been that different distributors perform different functions within the distribution channel and should be compensated accordingly. For example, some wholesalers provide storage facilities for the manufacturer, help the retailer set up displays, extend credit to retailers, and perform personal selling services for the manufacturer. Often it is difficult to fully identify the various functions the intermediaries perform, and therefore it is difficult to determine a trade or functional discount structure that reflects those services. Much of this difficulty arises because some distributors are wholesalers as well as retailers and because there are many different kinds of wholesalers and retailers.

Legal Status of Functional Discounts

Since the Robinson-Patman Act (see Chapter 18) fails to specifically mention functional discounts, the validity of these discounts is determined by case law under Section 2(a), which makes it unlawful to discriminate in price when the effect may be to lessen or injure competition. The legal test is whether the price difference due to a functional discount has an adverse competitive effect. Thus *the validity of a functional discount derives solely from the doctrines and facts of competitive effect, not from any general principles governing functional discounts.*[1]

Traditionally, wholesalers receive larger trade discounts than retailers because these two types of distributors are on different trade levels. Economically, distributors positioned higher up the distribution channel, such as wholesalers, have a need to buy at lower prices than direct-buying retailers in order to survive. This trade discount is valid if it does not lessen the ability of the direct-buying retailers to compete with the wholesalers' retail customers. Although direct-buying retailers are, in effect, performing all or most of the wholesaler's function, it would probably be construed that competition might be harmed if they set lower prices because of a more favorable discount afforded them.

Dual-Function Discounts

The preceding observations refer to *single-function buyers*; that is, buyers who perform essentially the same marketing services irrespective of the level or position in the distribution channel. However, the validity of a functional discount for a particular service (function) performed by one buyer is questionable when that buyer and its competitors perform other functions for which no one receives a discount. Buyers who perform more functions than their competitors and who receive a discount for these additional functions are referred to as *dual-function buyers*.

To illustrate the nature of a dual-function discount system, consider the Purolator case.[2] Figure 17.1 is a flow chart of the distribution system used by Purolator, a manufacturer of automotive filters in the replacement parts market. Purolator sold only to warehouse distributors, of which there were two types: type I distributors, which had only a single warehouse location, and type II distributors, which had either branch warehouse locations or affiliated jobbers. The type II distrib-

---

[1]William E. Beringer, "The Validity of Discounts Granted to Dual Function Buyers under the Robinson-Patman Act," *The Business Lawyer 31* (January 1976), 783–800.

[2]Purolator Products, Inc., 65 F.T.C. 8, CCH Trade Reg. Rep. P 16, 877 (1964), *affirmed*, 352 F.2d 874 (7th Circuit, 1965).

FIGURE 17.1
Purolator's
Distribution System
for Automotive
Filters

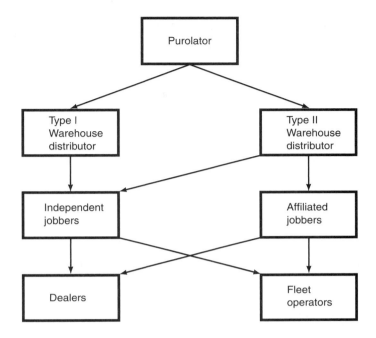

utors sold either to independent jobbers or to their affiliated jobbers. Type I distributors sold only to independent jobbers. All jobbers sold to dealers and fleet operators.

The amount of functional discount Purolator gave to its warehouse distributors depended on (1) whether or not the distributor had either branch locations or affiliated jobbers and (2) the type of customer, dealer, or fleet operator to whom the filters were resold. Purolator offered a 4 percent discount to the type II distributors. The type II distributors performed an additional distribution function that the type I distributors did not perform.

The Federal Trade Commission held that the additional 4 percent discount to the type II distributors injured competition because it subsidized their internal operation. Purolator had offered evidence that the reshipping operations of the type II distributors (from their central warehouse to the affiliated branches) increased the operational costs of these distributors, and the discount was granted to offset these costs. The commission noted that the affiliated warehouse distributors had selected their method of operation and that customers' internal costs could not justify a price difference. Thus Purolator's additional discount to the type II distributors was illegal.

FIGURE 17.2   Types of Channel Structures

Source: Reprinted with permission from Mark T. Spriggs and John R. Nevin, "The Legal Status of Trade and Functional Price Discounts," *Journal of Public Policy & Marketing 13* (Spring, 1994), 63.

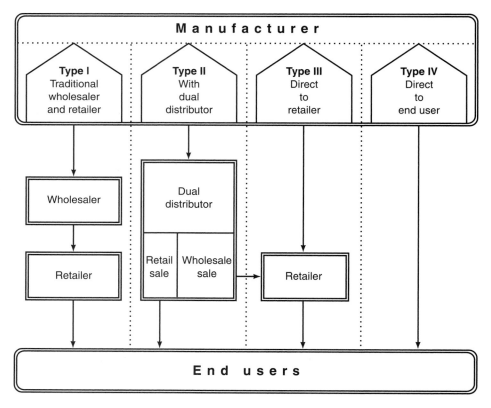

Guidelines for Setting Functional Discount Policy

The policy of offering price concessions to members of the distribution channel can be cumbersome and legally complex. Marketing channels have become quite complex as well. The emergence of multiple channel arrangements, along with electronic commercial selling, has blurred traditional distinctions between retailers and wholesalers. Figure 17.2 illustrates some of this increasing complexity.

Figure 17.2 shows four different channel structures. Type I represents the traditional channel of manufacturer, wholesaler, and retailer. Type II shows a dual-function distributor who sells directly to end users (acts as a retailer) and also performs as a wholesaler to other retailers. Note that this distributor competes with its retail customers. A manufacturer who operates in a Type I channel can also sell directly through retailers to end users (Type III) as well as directly to end users via catalog sales or the Internet (Type IV). Following a multichannel distribution strategy provides for potential competitive advantages by enabling a firm to reach previously unreached markets. Such new market segments may enhance profitability through higher sales volume and lower distribution and transaction costs.[3] Multiple channels can lead to conflicts between channels when a firm's supplier is also one of its competitors. Multiple channels can also lead to charges of illegal price discrimination if competing buyers receive different discounts and the buyer receiving the larger discount gains a competitive advantage. With the additional complexities of multiple-channel distribution systems, sellers must carefully analyze trade and functional discount policies.

When establishing a channel-based discount pricing structure, the seller should determine

1. The functions the distributors should perform for the seller.

2. The costs to the distributors for performing these functions.

3. The relative costs of selling to different types of distributors.

4. The trade status of each buyer; that is, the buyer's position in the distribution sequence.

5. The extent of competition among buyers at all levels in the distribution sequence.

6. The savings in costs of serving the various distributors.

In essence, the seller should establish a resale verification program and analyze the pass-through price effects. For combination wholesaler–retailer buyers, the seller should determine the sales that are wholesale and the sales that are retail.

Trade discounts (a discount because of an intermediary's place in the channel) should be used only if competing channel members can easily be categorized as wholesaler or retailer. Functional discounts should be based on justified cost savings to the seller and should not exceed the cost of that

[3]Mark T. Spriggs and John R. Nevin, "The Legal Status of Trade and Functional Price Discounts," *Journal of Public Policy & Marketing 13* (Spring 1994), 61–75.

part of the function the buyer actually performs. All discounts should be made available on proportionately equal terms to all other customers competing in distribution. *In a multiple-channel system, any preferential discount (a discount available only to selected resellers) on sales made in competition with a firm's own customer-dealers is illegal.* This point about preferential discounts is true regardless of the value to the manufacturer of the service performed by a dual distributor, no matter how efficient it may be to integrate functions within a single distributor, and no matter how valuable and efficient the arrangement may be to the customer.

Price Promotions and Deals

Advertising and personal selling have received considerable attention as methods of stimulating demand for products and services. Until recently, price promotions have not been as well studied, yet they represent an important aspect of marketing. Major forms of price promotion include cents-off deals, buy X and receive Y free, free samples, coupons, refunds, and rebates. Price promotions are tactics designed to achieve specific objectives in a limited time in a target market and are directed at two primary audiences: consumers and the trade.

Some of the benefits of price promotions are that they

1. Generate new interest in an old product.

2. Accelerate demand for products or flush out old merchandise to make room for new merchandise.

3. Introduce a new product (Often, introductory lower prices, coupons, or rebates may be used to introduce a new product. By stimulating trial of new products, promotions reduce some of the retailers' risk in stocking new brands. See Chapter 6.)

4. Meet specific competitive situations in different geographic locations, for limited time periods, for specific products or services.

5. Help sellers adjust to fluctuations in supply and demand without changing list prices.

6. Help small sellers compete against national brands with large advertising budgets. (Normally promotion costs are variable with sales and therefore occur as the sales are

made, whereas advertising requires a fixed cash commitment. Small sellers without the cash resources for a large advertising budget may use variable promotional costs to compete more effectively.)

7. Enhance advertising by conveying some message about the product's features and benefits as well as the price and deal information.

8. Facilitates consumer decision making by
   - Increasing consumer choice over time.
   - Enhancing consumer information about product benefits.
   - Increasing price awareness and knowledge.

However, at the same time price promotions have several disadvantages. They

1. May decrease brand loyalty.

2. May increase buyers' price sensitivity.

3. May have a negative effect on perceived quality.

4. May lower buyers' reference prices.

5. Focuses management on short-term results.

Incidence of Price Promotions

In recent years, manufacturers and retailers have made increasing use of coupons, rebates and refunds, short-term price reductions, and free samples to stimulate short-term demand for their products and services.[4] However, despite the popularity of these price deals, it is not at all clear that a majority of these deals are profitable.[5] If the short-term price reduction can be focused to appeal to a market segment that didn't previously buy the product while maintaining full-price sales to most previous buyers, then the incremental sales resulting from the price deal may enhance profits.

Simply offering a coupon, rebate, or price-off deal to current buyers in the hope of stimulating a substantial increase in unit sales is likely to reduce profits unless mostly new

[4]Kusum L. Ailawadi, Scott A. Neslin, and Karen Gedenk, "Pursuing the Value-Conscious Consumer: Store Brands versus National Brand Promotions," *Journal of Marketing 65* (January 2001), 71–89; Jack Neff, "Trade Promotion Rises," *Advertising Age 71* (April 3, 2000), 24.
[5]K. J. Cheong, "Observations: Are Cents-Off Coupons Effective?" *Journal of Advertising Research 33* (March/April 1993), 73–78.

buyers take advantage of the deal. Thus, *the underlying objective of a price promotion to final customers should be to focus on a price-market segment that is more price sensitive or deal responsive than existing buyers.*

Effect of Price Promotions on Buyers' Perceptions

Discounting through price promotions has become quite important in the marketplace because consumers view it as an acceptable method of reducing price. Because the objective of a price discount is to enhance unit sales of the product or, if used to increase store traffic, to enhance total sales of the store, the trade-off between lower unit margin and increased sales volume determines whether the promotion will have a positive impact on profits. If buyers do not perceive that there is a "deal" or an enhancement in value, the discount strategy may not have the desired impact on revenues. Thus an incorrect price discount decision can be detrimental in terms of lost sales and profits.

Price Promotion as Price Discrimination

Not all buyers of a product on price promotion take advantage of the promotion. Redemption rates for coupons and rebates indicate that many buyers do not redeem coupons or follow through and take the rebate that is offered. In 1981, of the 102.4 billion coupons distributed, 4.1 billion were redeemed. In 1986, of the 202.6 billion coupons distributed, 5.5 billion were redeemed. And in 2000, of the 330 billion coupons distributed, fewer than 4.5 billion were redeemed (less than 2 percent). In 2000, the average face value of the coupons distributed was 71 cents, and the total value of the redeemed coupons was $3.6 billion (80 cents per coupon). One obvious reason for this lack of redemption, or follow through, is that the perceived cost of redeeming coupons or qualifying for the rebate is higher than the perceived value of the coupon or rebate. Because buyers who do not take advantage of the price promotion pay the regular price, a coupon or rebate offer effectively segments the market into two price segments.

This practice of charging different prices for the same product to different segments is price discrimination. However, if a coupon or rebate is available to all buyers—and some buyers choose not to take advantage of it—this price discrimination is passive and the seller is not legally culpable. For this type of segmented pricing to be profitable, some additional conditions must prevail. First, the segments must be separable to some degree. This separation must either be due to some natural separation, such as geographic region or location, time of purchase, or category of buyer (business buyer versus consumer, for example). Second, these segments must have different degrees of price sensitivity or different variable purchasing costs. Third, the variable costs of selling to these segments must not be so different that the effect of the lower price is canceled by increased selling costs.

Price Promotion Decision Variables

To understand the complexity of developing a price promotion policy, it is useful to review the types of decisions that must be made before a promotion can be implemented. Despite the fact that promotional expenditures have been growing to become the major expenditure category of the marketing budget for many companies, little attention has been placed on designing the best price promotion policy for a seller. The following questions indicate the extent of planning that price promotions require.

1. Should a price promotion be offered? The first question is simply whether the seller should offer a coupon, rebate, cents-off deal, or promotional discount. This decision cannot be made without considering the following decision issues.

2. To whom should the deal be offered, dealers or final customers? Offering a price promotion to dealers or distributors in anticipation that they will pass it along to final customers is not the same as offering it directly to final customers. Dealers may choose to reduce their prices the full amount, less, or not at all. Further, they may buy excess amounts of the deal merchandise, relative to actual demand, and sell some units at full price after the deal period is over. This activity is known as *forward buying*.

3. When should the promotion be offered? This question refers not only to the specific time of the year but also to questions such as whether to offer the deal during peak or slack selling seasons and when to respond to competitors' price promotions. For example, should ketchup manufacturers offer price promotions during the peak outdoor cooking season (May–September) or during the winter months? (See the discussion on price anomalies in Chapter 3.)

4. How frequently should a promotion be run? If a product is offered frequently on some form of price deal, customers may come to expect the deal and buy only on deal. The effect is that the product is rarely sold at full list price, and the advantage of price segmentation is lost.

5. How long should the promotion be run? This decision is related to the issue of promotion frequency, peak versus slack selling periods, and the length of buyers' repurchase periods. Consumer coupons that have no expiration date extend the promotion period indefinitely and make it difficult to measure the effectiveness of the coupon promotion.

6. How many units should the promotion cover? When deals are offered to the trade, they often restrict the amount that a dealer can order on deal. This restriction may be some proportion of the dealer's usual order size for the length of the promotion period. Some manufacturers may produce a specific type of product especially for the promotion. For example, one luggage company produced a special overnight bag solely for its winter luggage sales promotion and offered it at a "special" price.

7. What products or sizes should be promoted? Should a coffee producer offer a coupon on all package sizes of coffee or on the 13-ounce size only? Should a luggage manufacturer feature all of its luggage or only certain models in the promotion?

8. How much should the price be reduced? What should the amount of the rebate be? What should the value of the coupon be? As discussed in Chapters 5 through 7, the degree of buyer sensitivity to the price reduction, or the degree to which buyers perceive additional transaction value, will have an impact on the success of the promotion. The important issue is how much of a price difference is necessary to induce buyers to take advantage of the offer—to perceive additional value in the offer.

As should be apparent from the foregoing list and brief commentary, a variety of issues must be considered before developing and implementing a price promotion. In the sections that follow, we will discuss this complex and important decision problem.

Who Responds to Price Promotions?

The basic attractiveness of the price deal is that it can stimulate sales by appealing to buyers' bargain-consciousness or to their satisfaction from being careful and smart shoppers. However, although price deals have been widely used by manufacturers and retailers, there is little conclusive evidence available on the characteristics of deal-prone buyers or their reasons for using these deals.

Coupons are documents that entitle the holder to a reduced price, or to x cents off the actual purchase price of a product or service. For years, coupons have played a substantial role in the promotion and purchasing of products. Yet, while the incidence of couponing increased, there has been an overall decline in the rate of coupon redemption.

Because of this increasing and widespread use of promotions and emphasis on price reductions, the profitability of price promotions is an important managerial issue. Some evidence suggests that there is a group of heavy coupon users that accounts for a large proportion of total coupon redemptions. Box 17.1 summarizes information concerning coupon redemption. Box 17.2 summarizes some of the issues related to coupons.

The Tactics of Price Promotions

The popularity of price promotions has led to questions of when is it best to offer a price deal, how many price deals a product should have in a given time period, and what the optimal duration of a price deal is. Consumer advocates have expressed some alarm at the possible fraudulent use of price deals. However, temporary price reductions remain a legitimate price tactic. Among the shortcomings of price deals are these:

1. Off-season price reductions are more profitable.

2. Too-frequent price promotions may make consumers more price conscious.

3. Deals are not very effective in countering new competitive brands, nor are they necessarily more effective when accompanied by product or package innovations.

4. Price deals are more effective for new brands (see Chapters 4 and 6).

5. Price deals are not cures for generally "sick" products.

WHO REDEEMS COUPONS   BOX 17.1

1. A higher percentage of coupon redemptions are by nonloyal buyers and by buyers of low-share brands. Apparently, loyal buyers of high-share brands are less likely to redeem coupons. Thus, distributing coupons in a product category characterized by a large proportion of brand-loyal buyers is less likely to be productive.

2. Higher coupon values are more likely to be redeemed by nonbuyers than lower values. The lower coupon values are more likely to be redeemed by loyal and semiloyal buyers. Thus, unless the objective is to gain new triers, offering a higher coupon value is not likely to be profitable.

3. Direct mail approaches produce more redemptions by nonbuyers.

4. There is a lower incidence of female heads of households employed full time in the heavy coupon user group. Also, heavy coupon users are more likely to be nonloyal or semiloyal buyers (brand switchers).

The above findings indicate that heavy coupon users tend to be low in both brand and store loyalty. They tend to be better educated, have higher incomes, and live in urban areas. This segment of coupon users would appear to have a relatively high response elasticity to coupons, and would likely be responsive even for low-value coupons. However, the light coupon users tend to be store and brand loyal; they are older, less educated, have lower incomes, and are located in nonurban areas. Because they do not respond well to normal coupon offerings, it is likely that coupons with higher face values, free samples, or in-store promotions would be more effective promotion vehicles.

Sources: Steve Kingsbury, "Study Provides Overview of Who's Redeeming Coupons—and Why," *Marketing News 21* (January 2, 1987), 56; Kapil Bawa and Robert W. Shoemaker, "The Coupon-Prone Consumer: Some Findings Based on Purchase Behavior across Product Categories," *Journal of Marketing 51* (October 1987), 99–110; Kapil Bawa and Robert W. Shoemaker, "Analyzing Incremental Sales from a Direct Mail Coupon Promotion," *Journal of Marketing 53* (July 1989), 66–78.

The evidence on price deals suggests that many sellers misuse this pricing tactic. Some sellers run price deals during the peak selling season, thereby providing a price discount at a time *when demand is heavy* and relatively less price sensitive (see Chapter 3). Other sellers run frequent price deals and find it difficult to sell the product at its "regular" price because buyers have either stocked up or are waiting for the next deal.

Other problems in developing and implementing price promotion tactics include the following:

1. Approximately 25 percent of the coupons redeemed do not have a corresponding purchase, costing manufacturers approximately $250 million per year (see Box 17.3).

2. Refunding and coupon clipping have become a hobby. Today, many bulletins and newsletters alert members to all

COUPONS—THE GOOD AND THE BAD

BOX 17.2

Since 1970, the number of coupons distributed experienced double-digit annual growth until 1993. As the number of coupons distributed increased, the average face value offered also increased from 20 cents in 1981 to 71 cents in 2000. However, the coupon redemption rate has declined continuously from an average 4 percent in 1981 to less than 2 percent in 2000.

Couponing is one of the basic promotion tools manufacturers and retailers use to spur trial, generate incremental sales, and reward loyal consumers. In economic downturns, use of coupons can be a deal for both manufacturers and consumers. For example, during the economic downturn in 1990, coupon distribution increased by 16.7 percent over that of 1989 and consumers saved $3.52 billion through the use of coupons, a 6.4 percent increase over 1989 coupon savings.

However, with rising popularity, many of the negative aspects of coupons show up. Although nearly 80 percent of U.S. households use coupons, about 31 percent of the households make over 72 percent of the redemptions. Coupon distribution cost marketers roughly $8 billion in 1995, while the redemption rate dropped to 2 percent. Lack of targeting, soaring distribution costs, and a declining redemption rate led manufacturers to question the efficiency of coupons. In 1996, Proctor & Gamble ceased coupon distribution in a test market, switching to offer savings by lowering regular prices. Surprisingly, sentiment for coupons was so strong that 23,000 residents in the test markets signed a petition and sent it to the company asking for a return of the coupons.

Sources: George Lazarus, "Manufacturers Clip Coupon Distribution," *Chicago Tribune* (January 7, 1994), section 3, 2; *Progressive Grocer 63*, 66, 67; Mati Otsmaa, Charles M. Greenberg, "Relationships Offer Lifetime Value, Not Just One-time Trial," *Marketing News 23* (September 25, 1989), 16; "Coupon Use Low among Young, Working Women," *Marketing News 21* (April 10, 1987), 24; Zachary Schiller, "First, Green Stamps, Now, Coupons?" *Business Week* (April 22, 1996), 68; "Deal Reached in Clipped No-Coupon Test," *Chicago Tribune*, (September 11, 1997).

the new offers currently available, provide for an exchange of coupons and labels or other proofs of purchases, and offer information on the latest trends. Couponing groups even hold conventions for their members. A spokesperson for a consumer products company said that coupons meant to be used in one part of the country show up in other areas and ruin test markets.

3. Competitors often react quickly to counter an offer or even offer a more attractive deal.

4. Many deals require changing the retail prices. At one chain store, price deals required changing prices on 44 different brands of products on the same day.

5. The distributor often is offered an insufficient allowance to justify price changes or special promotional efforts. One deal offered the retailer 60 cents per dozen on a slow-moving item if each retailer would set up a special

COUPON FRAUD   BOX 17.3

Have you ever received a Sunday newspaper without the free-standing inserts (FSIs) that your neighbors got? Do you throw away the package for the product you just used? The missing FSIs and package proof of purchase, which may mean nothing to you, mean everything to some people who live on coupon fraud. Some people search garbage for packages that could be used as proof of purchase to get rebates. Others pay newspaper truck drivers to steal FSIs and pay people to clip the coupons. The coupons are then sold to local retailers for a fraction of face value or go to rented "stores" that are drop points for coupon redemption checks. Experienced frauds crank out phony coupons or proofs of purchase to get even more "free money."

Coupon fraud is not small business. Reports in 1989 detailed how one individual built a $12 million empire out of fraudulent coupons in four years. Fraudulent coupon redemptions are estimated at $1 billion or more a year. Manufacturers used to pay little attention to these frauds because of limited resources or simply because they thought it was not important. Some manufacturers paid reimbursements if retailers complained, even after the coupon clearinghouse warned them of fraudulent coupons. However, recently marketers have been making efforts to spot frauds. They are experimenting with new software, new checkout scanning technology, coupon clearing technology, an identification system for retailers, and shortening coupon lifetimes to detect fraudulent coupon redemption more effectively. For example, Quaker Oats Co. computerized its coupon redemption center to serve several purposes, including to help foil coupon fraud. Quaker checked 100 percent of the coupons to ensure no fraudulent coupon was paid. Yet, most manufacturers use a sample by weight payment method and randomly survey only 5 percent of the coupons presented for redemption.

Sources: Lynn G. Coleman, "Cons to Explain Pros of Coupon Security," *Marketing News 23* (April 24, 1989), 2; Art Harris, "Prison Term Doesn't Clip Coupon Queen's Passion," *Roanoke Times & World News* (May 4, 1990), A12; Christopher Power, "Coupon Scams Are Clipping Companies," *Business Week* (June 15, 1992), 110; "Computers Help Foil Coupon Fraud," *Marketing News 20* (August 15, 1986), 1, 22.

display and reflect the allowance in a lower retail price. The retailers did not believe that 5 cents per item was a sufficient inducement, and the deal allowance failed.

6. Many offers create confusion among retailers and distributors. One instant coffee producer offered an allowance of $2.40 per case, encouraging retailers to change the retail price from $3.35 to $3.15. However, before this deal expired, the producer offered a larger size jar containing 2 ounces of coffee "free" at the regular retail price of $3.35. Distributors did not know whether to reprice the original deal back to $3.35 or continue to offer the regular jar at $3.15 and simultaneously the "2-ounce free" jar at $3.35, with resulting confusion for consumers. Such confusion

leads to mistrust and wariness by consumers about the truthfulness of special deals. Moreover, distributors become less accepting of such deal opportunities.

7. In the past few years, regulations have come into force to counter potential and actual deception in the use of price deals. Price deals often had been used to camouflage price increases. To counteract such difficulties, the Federal Trade Commission has published guidelines and regulations governing "cents-off," "economy-size," and other savings representations. Moreover, many states have prosecuted firms for deceptive comparative price advertising. In one case, Maryland charged a local department store chain with falsely advertising mattresses for sale at prices drastically reduced from "regular" prices that never existed. For example, according to the state the store offered a nationally branded mattress in a newspaper advertisement as reduced from a "regular price" of $420 to $188.99. The state's lawsuit contended that the mattress had been offered at prices between $188.99 and $209.99 during 36 of the previous 40 weeks. The mattress had never been sold at the $420 price. Although the store admitted no wrongdoing, it agreed to pay a $500,000 penalty to settle the lawsuit. In a similar type of lawsuit, a department store chain in New York agreed to a $250,000 penalty after the state contended that it had falsely advertised sale prices of up to 50 percent off "regular prices" when the items, in fact, had never been sold at those regular, higher prices.[6]

8. For many manufacturers and retailers, sales, deals, coupons, rebates, and other forms of promotions have become almost the normal way of doing business. As a result of the almost constant promotions, buyers have been conditioned to wait for a sale or deal before buying. Indeed, one of the negative consequences of this frequent discounting by sellers is that buyers' reference prices are established at the lower deal prices and they resist buying when prices return to regular levels (see Chapters 5 through 7).

[6]"Hecht's to Pay $500,000 Settlement," *The Baltimore Evening Sun*, July 28, 1988; "Sibley's $225G Payment Settles Ad Investigation," *Syracuse Post-Standard*, April 28, 1989; Patrick J. Kaufman, N. Craig Smith, and Gwendolyn K. Ortmeyer, "Deception in Retailer High-Low Pricing: A 'Rule of Reason' Approach, *Journal of Retailing 70,* no. 2 (1994), 115–38; Dhruv Grewal, Diana S. Grewal, and Larry D. Compeau, "States' Crackdown on Deceptive Price Advertising: Retail and Public Policy Implications," *Pricing Practice & Strategy: An International Journal 1,* no. 2 (1993), 33–40.

One negative result is that buyers have become conditioned to look for the deal (transaction value; see Chapter 7) rather than the product's benefits (acquisition value). Another negative result is that sellers become tempted to use the deceptive practices illustrated here.

Some Perspectives on Price Promotions

As we noted earlier, promotions comprise a significant portion of the marketing communications budget. With this increased managerial importance of price promotions has come considerable research on how promotions affect sales. However, much of this research information is quite recent and the evidence on how promotions affect sales is still emerging. In this section, we will summarize some of this emerging information in three different time frames:[7] (1) the week or weeks in which the promotion occurs (immediate); (2) the weeks or months following the promotion (intermediate); and (3) the months or years following the implementation of several promotions (long term).

Immediate Effects of Price Promotions

There is a significant impact on brand sales. Promotions seem to have a substantial immediate impact on brand sales. As Figure 17.3 shows, price reductions are accompanied by immediate increases in brand and category sales.[8] When such price promotions are coordinated with special point-of-purchase displays and local feature advertising, sales might increase as much as 10 times normal sales levels. Because of such immediate observable sales impact, many brands of packaged consumer goods are frequently promoted.

Brand switchers account for most of the sales increase. As Box 17.1 indicates, a large proportion of this immediate increase in sales is due to nonloyal buyers (brand switchers). For example, one study showed that 84 percent of the increase in coffee brand sales generated by promotions came

---

[7]Robert C. Blattberg and Scott A. Neslin, "Sales Promotion: The Long and Short of It," *Marketing Letters 1* (December 1989), 81–97.

[8]Robert C. Blattberg, Richard Briesch, and Scott A. Neslin, "How Promotions Work," *Marketing Science 14*, no. 3, Part 2 (1995), G122–G132; Praveen K. Kopalle, Carl F. Mela, and Lawrence Marsh, "The Dynamic Effect of Discounting on Sales: Empirical Analysis and Normative Pricing Implications," *Marketing Science 18*, no. 3 (1999), 317–32.

FIGURE 17.3   **Sales and Price of a Promoted Item**

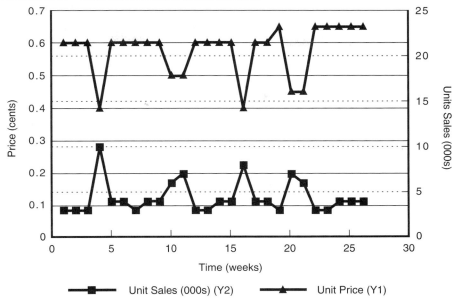

from brand-switching consumers.[9] However, not all brands have the same capability of inducing consumers to switch brands with a promotional activity.

The brand switching effect differs across brands. The effect of brand A's promotions on brand B's sales likely is different than the effect of brand B's promotions on brand A's sales. This asymmetry of the promotion cross-elasticities is a very important managerial finding (see Chapter 6). That is, a strong brand, say brand A, may be more successful inducing buyers of brand B to switch to brand A with a promotion, than would the weaker brand B using a similar promotion be able to induce buyers of brand A to switch to brand B. This finding implies that when there are simultaneous promotions by both brands, brand A likely will experience a more positive sales impact than will brand B.

[9]Sunil Gupta, "Impact of Sales Promotions on When, What, and How Much to Buy," *Journal of Marketing Research 25* (November 1988), 342–55; David R. Bell, Jeongwen Chiang, and V. Padmanabhan, "The Decomposition of Promotional Response: An Empirical Generalization," *Marketing Science 18*, no. 4 (1999), 504–26.

Different forms of promotion have different effects on sales. Another important finding is that different forms of price promotions have separate effects on sales. When several forms are used together the total impact may be greater than the sum of the effects due to each form. For example, a display-only promotion (with no discount) might increase sales by 13 percent, a 10 percent price discount only might increase sales by 77 percent, whereas both a display and a 10 percent price discount might increase sales by 101 percent.

Intermediate Effects of Price Promotions

Usually, promotions have been considered short-term tactics to provide for an immediate increase in sales. However, much like advertising, effects occur even after a particular promotion campaign has expired. For example, if a consumer purchases brand A for the first time when A is being promoted, will that consumer buy brand A on the next purchase occasion (repeat purchase)? Or, will the consumer develop a loyalty to the "deal" and look for another promoted brand on the next purchase? The managerial implications of a promotion extend beyond the immediate sales effect of that promotion.

Whether promotions lead to repeat purchases is unclear. Although there has been considerable research on whether brand purchasing enhances repeat brand purchases, the problem is that such research provides conflicting results. There is some evidence that a prior brand purchase may increase the likelihood of buying that brand again. However, given the increasing use of promotions, other research shows no evidence that promotions enhance repeat brand purchases.

One reason for the possibility that promotions do not enhance repeat brand purchases is the question of why consumers may decide to buy the brand initially. Some consumer behavior research has suggested that people may attribute their purchase to the deal that was available and not to finding the brand itself attractive.[10] If consumers attribute a negative reason to a purchase decision, there is less likelihood that the experience will be a positive learning experience relative to the brand itself. If a brand is promoted quite

---

[10]Carol A. Scott and Richard F. Yalch, "Consumer Response to Initial Trial: A Bayesian Analysis, "*Journal of Consumer Research 7* (June 1980), 32–41; Karen Gedenk and Scott A. Neslin, "The Role of Retail Promotion in Determining Future Brand Loyalty: Its Effect on Purchase Event Feedback," *Journal of Retailing 75*, no. 1 (1999), 33–57.

frequently, then the learning to buy the brand occurs because of the reward of the deal, not the positive experience of using the brand itself.

The immediate sales effect is due to purchase acceleration. *Purchase acceleration* occurs either because loyal consumers buy larger quantities when the brand is promoted or purchase the brand sooner than normal. The issue of purchase acceleration is very important when we try to determine whether a promotion has been profitable. Indeed, if buyers do not change their rate of consumption of the product, then larger purchase quantities or earlier purchases mean that there will be fewer sales later at the regular price. Purchasing a product earlier than normal is called *forward buying* and is illustrated in Figure 17.4. However, for some product categories, such as some food categories, increased inventory due to purchase acceleration may lead to increased consumption, thereby dampening the negative effect of forward buying.[11] Finally, it appears that consumers do not manage their inventory levels optimally and do not make up for their accelerated purchases until weeks or even months after the promotion. Thus, the postpromotion dip may dissipate over time and may not be observed in the immediate postpromotion period.[12]

Increased price promotions can reduce baseline sales. Postpromotion sales may be less than prepromotion sales if discounting hurts brand equity. The reduction in brand equity leads to reduced sales at regular prices. Increased price promotions may reduce repeat purchase rates, also leading to reduced sales at regular prices. Moreover, consumers may learn to wait for deals, decreasing baseline sales. Finally, price promotions may reduce consumers' reference prices, making regular prices less attractive and dampening future sales.[13]

Long-Term Effects of Price Promotions

In the long run, the relevant issue concerns the ability of the brand to develop a loyal following among its customers. The important objective is to develop favorable brand attitudes

---

[11]Kusum L. Ailawadi and Scott A. Neslin, "The Effect of Promotion on Consumption: Buying More and Consuming It Faster," *Journal of Marketing Research 35* (August 1998), 390–98.

[12]Scott A. Neslin and Linda G. Schneider Stone, "Consumer Inventory Sensitivity and the Postpromotion Dip," *Marketing Letters 7,* no. 1 (1996), 77–94.

[13]Carl F. Mela, Sunil Gupta, and Donald R. Lehmann, "The Long-Term Impact of Promotion and Advertising on Consumer Brand Choice," *Journal of Marketing Research 34* (May 1997), 248–61.

FIGURE 17.4 **Charting the Effectiveness of a Promotion**

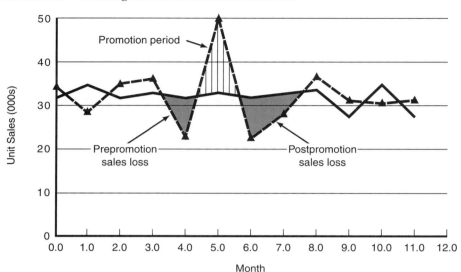

among customers so they request that the retailer carry the brand and are unwilling to buy a substitute. However, if buyers come to expect that the brand will often be on some form of a deal, they will not be willing to pay a regular price.

A second problem develops if consumers begin to associate a frequently promoted brand with lower product quality. That is, if consumers believe that higher-priced products are also of higher quality, then a brand that is frequently sold at a reduced price may become associated with a lower perceived quality level. Thus the result may be that buyers form a lower reference price for the product.

Overall, the strong short-term effects of price promotions weaken over time and rarely result in permanent shifts in category demand. It appears that diverting resources to enhance price promotion efforts do not enhance a brand's long-run market position. An increased use of price promotions by a brand reduces its baseline sales, increases price sensitivity, and diminishes its ability to use promotions to take market share from competitors.[14]

[14]Vincent R. Nijs, Marnik G. Dekimpe, Jan-Benedict E.M. Steenkamp, and Dominique M. Hanssens, "The Category-Demand Effects of Price Promotions," *Marketing Science 20* (Winter 2001), 1–22.

Summary

Considerable evidence from a variety of sources indicates that consumers adapt their purchasing to the contexts in which they shop. First, frequent price promotions do increase buyers' price sensitivity by lowering their reference prices, making it more difficult to sustain postpromotion price increases. Second, promotions lead to accelerated purchases and higher consumer inventories of the promoted products. The long-term effect of higher inventories due to promotions is lower baseline sales in subsequent nonpromoted periods. Third, as the frequency of promotions increases, they become less effective, making it necessary to offer larger discounts in future promotions. Fourth, consumers learn to wait for the next deal, leading to reduced quantity purchased in any nonpromotion period, but increased quantity when buying on promotion. This volatility of demand increases the difficulty of managing inventories and increases costs. These effects combine to diminish category profits.

Estimating the Profitability of Price Promotions

As indicated, sellers have become trapped into offering more and more price deals at larger and larger amounts off. One reason for this entrapment is that sellers have attempted to create more perceived value by offering price discounts. Yet, as observed in earlier chapters, price reductions have limited capability to enhance profits. The analytical tools provided in earlier chapters offer ways to establish the relative profitability of price promotions.

Coupon Profitability

The issues and problems of couponing and dealing reviewed thus far lead to some important questions about when couponing might be a profitable activity. Assume that the brand for which a coupon will be distributed is A, and that all other competing brands are C. The first question that needs to be answered is, How many customers who usually buy A will redeem the coupon? The coupon is a reduction in price for these buyers and a loss in revenue for this firm. The proportion of loyal buyers who redeem the coupon is difficult to estimate because it is likely that unless the coupon has a relatively short fixed expiration date, the redeeming household will not immediately redeem it. One study found that 70 percent of the redeeming households did not redeem the coupon on their first purchase opportunity.[15]

Second, how many customers who usually buy C redeem A's coupon? Customers who switch to A because of the coupon represent a gain in revenues for the firm. However, the evidence reviewed previously indicates that loyal buyers are least likely to redeem coupons of nonpreferred brands. Hence, if the market is comprised of a large proportion of brand-loyal buyers there will be little gain from this loyal segment of brand C buyers.

The third question is, How many nonloyal buyers will redeem the coupon? Again, nonloyal buyers who switch to A because of the coupon represent a gain in revenues. The fourth question is, How many of the C-loyal and nonloyal buyers will repeat purchase brand A and how many repeats will occur? This question addresses the issue of whether the coupon promotion is able to sustain an increase in market share once nonloyal A buyers try A because of the coupon. If the promotion attracts a proportionately larger number of switchers, these buyers are not likely to continue purchasing the brand after the deal, thereby lowering the observed repeat purchase rate.[16]

Given that the firm decides to issue a coupon for brand A, the last question is, What will be the value of the coupon, the percentage off the regular price expressed in dollars and cents? If there is a large segment of brand C loyal buyers, then a coupon with a value that is relatively high compared to other coupon values is more likely to bring in new users but not repeat purchasers. If there is a large segment of switchers, then a low-value coupon (e.g., 25 cents) may be sufficient to attract new customers but again not many repeat purchasers. Also, a low-value coupon is likely to attract some current customers, but at a lower margin. We now develop a framework for determining whether to use coupons as a promotional tool and, if used, the actual value of the coupon. As expected, the incremental gain in revenues must be compared to the additional costs associated with the development, distribution, and redemption of the coupons.

[15]Kapil Bawa and Robert W. Shoemaker, "The Effects of a Direct Mail Coupon on Brand Choice Behavior," *Journal of Marketing Research 24* (November 1987), 370–76.
[16]Scott Neslin and Robert W. Shoemaker, "An Alternative Explanation for Lower Repeat Rates after Promotion Purchases," *Journal of Marketing Research 26* (May 1989), 205–13.

To illustrate the issues in determining profitability, consider the example developed in Table 17.1. Assume we wish to examine the potential profitability of a coupon promotion for a brand of coffee. We will need to look at the increase in costs due to the promotion (incremental costs) as well as the increase in revenues due to the incremental increase in sales in order to estimate the relative profitability of the coupon promotion. Assume that we plan to distribute 30 million coupons at a cost of $10 per thousand, or $300,000. The second major cost to be incurred occurs when consumers redeem the coupons. For our example, assume that each coupon will have a face value of 50 cents and that 5 percent of the coupons will be redeemed (cost is $750,000). We also need to pay the grocery stores and distributors for giving the 50 cent allowance to consumers and for processing the coupons that are collected. We will assume the processing cost is 7 cents per coupon redeemed (cost is $105,000). Thus, the total incremental costs of the coupon promotion will be an estimated $1,155,000.

Now we need to develop an estimate of the incremental sales the promotion needs to generate. However, this estimate is quite difficult to make before the coupon promotion runs. One way to handle this question is to ask ourselves what the incremental sales level must be if we were to break even on the coupon promotion. That is, what incremental sales must be generated for the new profit contribution from these sales to equal the incremental costs we have identified above? As Table 17.1 shows, if our price is $2.50 per unit and we have a 30 percent margin, we make a 75-cent profit contribution per coupon redemption sale. Then our final question is, How many new additional sales per redemption are necessary for us to generate the contributions to recover the costs of the promotion? As we saw in Chapter 10, we can calculate a breakeven point by dividing the relevant fixed costs by the relevant contribution margin. In this example, we see in Table 17.1 that this calculation produces the result that 1.027 new units need to be sold per coupon redeemed. Note that this result means that new sales above and beyond the sales occurring when the coupons are redeemed would be about 1,540,000.

Although this increase in sales volume may seem to be quite large, remember our discussion in Chapter 9 about what occurs when we reduce prices. In this example, we have a margin of 75 cents per unit, but with a 50-cent coupon we give up two-thirds of that margin for each sale

TABLE 17.1
Profitability of a
Coupon Promotion

Incremental Promotion Costs:	
(1) Coupon distribution	
30,000,000 coupons × $10/thousand	$300,000
(2) Redemption of coupons	
30,000,000 × 5% redemption means	
1,500,000 coupons redeemed	
(a) 1,500,000 × 50¢ face value	750,000
(b) 1,500,000 × 7¢ processing cost	105,000
Total incremental costs	$1,155,000

Incremental Unit Sales Required:

Assume a unit price of $2.50 and a 30% margin.
Therefore, profit contribution per unit is 75¢.
The profit contribution of the coupon promotion is
1,500,000 redemption sales × 75¢ × incremental
sales, or $1,125,000 × incremental sales.

The breakeven incremental unit sales per redemption is

$$\frac{\text{Total incremental costs}}{\text{Total incremental profit}} = \frac{\$1,155,000}{\$1,125,000} = 1.027$$

Thus, to break even on the promotion, 1.027 new sales
must be generated per coupon redemption sale.

with a coupon. Hence to recover that lost margin does require net new sales.

To understand what our assumption of 5 percent coupon redemption means, Figure 17.5 shows the relationship between breakeven incremental sales and coupon redemption rate for this particular example. Note that as the redemption rate increases, the breakeven incremental new sales approaches 0.85 per redemption as a necessary requirement *before the coupon promotion can be profitable*. That is, at a minimum, sales that would otherwise not have occurred must occur at the rate of 0.85 per coupon redeemed. This analysis tells us that we need to have carefully developed objectives to evaluate the success of the campaign. Moreover, if profitability is our only criterion, then it is likely, as many consumer product manufacturers know, that many promotions fail.[17] It is not easy to generate the necessary incremental sales to overcome the profit margins sacrificed when using a price promotion.

[17]Magid M. Abraham and Leonard M. Lodish, "Getting the Most Out of Advertising and Promotion," *Harvard Business Review 68* (May–June 1990), 50–60.

FIGURE 17.5   **Incremental Sales Required to Break Even on a Coupon Promotion**

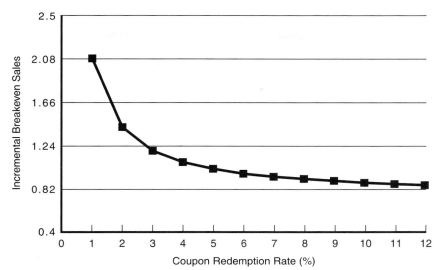

Requirements for Segmented Pricing

There are two specific requirements for segmented pricing to be effective. First, the market segments must be separable. That is, different market segments must exhibit different degrees of sensitivity to price differences, and different channels of distribution must be available to reach these different market segments (see the discussion on focused price reductions in Chapter 14). The objective of separating the market segments with different degrees of price sensitivity is to minimize leakage and diversion. For example, targeting the price-sensitive market segment with direct-mail coupons or promotions allows for both market separation and lower variable promotion costs. Another way of separating the markets according to price sensitivities would be to impose restrictions or conditions on the offer, such that only the price-sensitive buyers expend the effort to qualify for the price reductions. Second, different market segments must have different price sensitivities, and/or the firm must incur different variable costs of serving the segments. It makes little sense to reduce price to a price sensitive market segment if the variable costs of serving that segment are greater than serving the less price sensitive segment.

Summary

To estimate the profitability of a price promotion, managers need to know:

1. The variable costs of serving each market segment.

2. The price-quantity relationships for each market segment.

3. The degree that leakage might occur.

4. The cost of separating the market segments:
   - Printing and distributing coupons or rebate certificates.
   - Cost of redemptions.
   - Control and monitoring promotions.
   - Implementing trade promotions.

Trade Promotions

The practice of manufacturers offering retailers short-term incentives to increase their purchases of the manufacturers' products is quite prevalent and has been increasing. Indeed, this practice may be becoming more prominent than advertising in the promotions budget of many firms.[18] As the incidence of trade promotions increase, there have been increasing complaints that these tactics of price discounts and allowances erode brand equity and confuse consumers. Another criticism of trade promotions is they may involve reducing list prices in return for the retailer purchasing a larger quantity than normal, a cost increasing activity for the manufacturers. These subsequent swings in sales, inventories, and production lead to increased production and distribution costs. Moreover, the manufacturers lose margin on the product that the retailers buy on deal but do not sell at reduced prices. Trade promotion inefficiency has become the most important sales and marketing issue among manufacturers.

In response to these observed problems with trade promotions, Procter & Gamble in 1991–92 adopted a "value pricing" strategy. It reduced the number of deep discounts on wholesale prices on 40 percent of its products while reducing wholesale list prices between 10 and 25 percent. The price adjustments left the total costs to retailers about the

---

[18]F.J. Arcelus, Nita H. Shah, and G. Srinivasan, "Retailers' Response to Special Sales: Price Discount vs. Trade Credit," *Omega: The International Journal of Management Science 29* (October 2001), 417–428.

same. At the same time P&G increased its advertising in an effort to strengthen brand equity. In 1996 P&G began experimenting with cutting out the use of coupons.[19] While P&G has kept quiet about the overall effectiveness of this change in advertising and pricing strategy and tactics, researchers have estimated that it lost about 18 percent of its market share across 24 categories due primarily to a net increase in price (because of the reductions in deals and coupons) and increased competitor promotions. However, despite the increase in fixed costs due to advertising, researchers also estimated that P&G was able to increase its profits by more than a billion dollars in the 1990–1996 period they studied.[20] Nevertheless, the issue of everyday pricing versus high-low pricing remains a controversial issue and is discussed next.

Everyday Pricing versus High-Low Pricing

In the late 1980s, a number of retailers and nonretailers attempted to move away from frequent price promotions to more consistent prices over periods of time. The tactic of frequent price promotions has been called *high-low pricing.* When using a high-low pricing approach the seller sets relatively higher prices on a regular or everyday basis, but offers frequent price promotions in which prices on selected items are reduced by as much as 30 to 50 percent. *Everyday pricing (EDP)*, sometimes referred to as everyday low pricing (EDLP), or everyday fair pricing (EDFP), is when the seller sets a constant, everyday price with no (or very infrequent) temporary price promotions. Typically, but not always, the EDP is somewhere between the high-low price extremes (see Figure 17.6).

Several advantages of everyday pricing have been suggested as reasons for its use. First, everyday pricing should make it easier to communicate to customers and to establish a particular price image. A second advantage is that everyday pricing may help reduce operating costs. Lower operating costs may be achieved by (1) reduced inventory and handling costs due to steady and more predictable demand,

[19]Zachary Schiller, "A Rash Decision? Why P&G Cut Its Diaper Prices," *Business Week* (April 26, 1993), 36; P&G to Experiment with Ending Coupons," *Marketing News 30* (February 12, 1996), 11.

[20]Kusum L. Ailawadi, Donald R. Lehmann, and Scott A. Neslin, "Market Response to a Major Policy Change in the Marketing Mix: Learning from Procter & Gamble's Value Pricing Strategy," *Journal of Marketing 65* (January 2001), 44–61.

FIGURE 17.6 **EDLP versus High-Low Pricing**

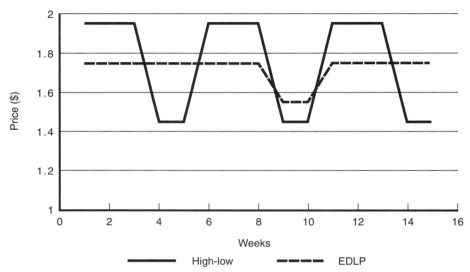

and (2) reduced labor costs related to less frequent temporary price reductions. Each temporary price reduction requires re-marking merchandise before and after the price promotion, printing and distributing new price lists, and other specific promotion-related costs. Third, everyday pricing reduces promotional costs and other forms of trade spending. Overall, it has been presumed that these cost reductions, coupled with steady demand, would lead to increased profits and, perhaps, even lower prices.

In practice, everyday pricing seems to work for some firms. However, for others, such as Sears Roebuck, the evidence is not as positive (see Box 17.4). Typically, firms that have adopted everyday pricing have pursued it as EDLP and have implemented across-the-board price reductions. As Chapter 11 explained, a profitable price reduction strategy requires a relatively high contribution margin or PV ratio to begin with and the ability to achieve substantial sales growth. For example, as shown in Table 11.4, a 10 percent price reduction would require a sales growth of 66.67 percent if the PV ratio is 0.25 to break even on the change to EDLP. In most mature market situations, such sales growth would be unlikely. On the other hand, a firm with a PV ratio of 0.25 in which sales increase 5 percent when prices are

WHY EVERYDAY LOW PRICING FAILED FOR SEARS BUT WORKS FOR WAL-MART

BOX 17.4

Sears introduced EDLP in February 1989. The pricing strategy did not help—the company lost $6.9 million in the third quarter of 1989 and in 1990, one year after implementing EDLP, Sears' retail operating income fell 63 percent to $73 million. An *Advertising Age*/Gallup organization poll found that Sears' EDLP had failed to convince consumers its price or merchandise selection was better than its rivals'. A high-low pricing retailer in the past, Sears did not take time to reeducate consumers. Consumers still perceived Sears as a high-low pricing retailer, and Sears' "special sales" confused them.

Sears faced a serious identity crisis. Its prices generally were not competitive, even though it marked down 50,000 items, the markdown was not sufficient to achieve credibility as an EDLP retailer. Only 16 percent of consumers indicated that they shop at Sears for price in any case, so consumers were not motivated to shop there. Sears also failed to improve its cost position. Overhead at Sears at the beginning of 1989 was about 32 percent of sales, whereas it is only about 17 percent of sales at Wal-Mart.

In Wal-Mart's case, 60 percent of its customers shop regularly at its stores. As an innovator of EDLP, Wal-Mart has a pricing strategy that does not confuse customers. In addition, Wal-Mart's EDLP works well because frequently purchased products and nonfashionable merchandise make up 85 percent to 90 percent of its assortment, unlike at Sears, where infrequently purchased products make up more of its inventory. Wal-Mart is able to achieve credible price comparisons because its merchandise is generally medium or low priced. Wal-Mart also manages costs much better.

Sources: Gwen Ortmeyer, John A. Quelch, Walter Salmon, "Restoring Credibility to Retail Pricing," *Sloan Management Review 32* (Fall 1991), 55–66; Michael J. McDermott, "Can the Big Store Be Fixed?" *Adweek's Marketing Week* (October 30, 1989), 2; Kate Fitzgerald, "Sears Plan On the Ropes," *Advertising Age* (January 8, 1990), 1.

reduced will need to substantially reduce its operating costs in order to break even when moving to EDLP pricing.

One study comparing EDLP to high-low pricing estimated that EDLP reduced profits by 18 percent, and high-low pricing increased profits by 15 percent. The researchers also tested a policy of frequent, shallow price promotions for 18 grocery categories and found that this policy led to an average 3.2 percent increase in sales and a 4.1 percent increase in profits.[21]

The choice of everyday pricing versus high-low pricing is an aspect of a firm's positioning strategy. That is, firms that pursue either of these pricing formats must also choose a

[21]Stephen J. Hoch, Xavier Dreze, and Mary E. Purk, "EDLP, Hi-Lo, and Margin Arithmetic," *Journal of Marketing 58* (October 1994), 16–27.

unique combination of advertising, pricing, and service. The EDLP firm advertises the price of a bundle, generally prices its products midway between the high-low firms' regular and promoted prices, and offers a lower level of service. In contrast, the high-low firm advertises the prices of promoted products in some fashion over the broad categories of products, and offers a higher level of service.[22]

The greater degree of pricing fluctuations in high-low firms provides consumers with greater flexibility in their shopping. That is, consumers can stock up when items are on promotion and defer purchases when prices are at higher regular levels. Thus, high-low pricing encourages price-sensitive consumers to visit high-low stores more often than everyday pricing stores, but spend less per shopping trip.

Price-Matching Guarantees

"We will match any competitor's price!" "We will never be undersold." "Low(er, est) Price Guaranteed." "Refund 150 percent of price difference." These claims are variations of price-matching guarantees or a price-matching policy, a pricing tactic that has become quite popular. A *price-matching guarantee* is a seller's policy of actively matching a lower price offered by other sellers on an identical or similar item and refunding the price difference for a period of time after the sale has been made.

Effect on Competition and Market Prices

Price-matching guarantees have been considered in theory as a device to facilitate tacit price collusion among competitors, resulting in less competition and higher market prices.[23] The reason behind this argument is that rival competitors have no incentive to undercut the price-matching seller's price because any price difference will be matched anyway. Thus, the market price remains at a level that is higher than it would be in a competitive pricing situation.

Though it is widely accepted that price-matching policies decrease sellers' incentive to undercut competitors' prices, not all researchers agree that the final result would be higher market prices and less competition. They argue that besides

[22]Rajiv Lal and Ram Rao, "Supermarket Competition: The Case of Every Day Low Pricing," *Marketing Science 16,* no. 1 (1997), 60–80.
[23]Z. John Zhang, "Price-Matching Policy and the Principle of Minimum Differentiation," *The Journal of Industrial Economics 43* (September 1995), 287–99.

the competition dampening effect, there is also a competition enhancing effect. That is, if price-matching only dampens competition, there should be no price disparity among sellers where price-matching prevails, and there should be no incentive for sellers to offer price promotions. However, the prevalence of price promotions co-existing with price-matching, along with the existence of price differences, seems to question the competition dampening theory.

How Do Sellers Apply Price-Matching Guarantees?

Why do sellers adopt price-matching policies? Are they consciously trying to achieve price collusion, or using it as a competitive tactic? The following factors may prompt sellers to adopt price matching:

- *Proximity of sellers*. Clusters of stores result in more competition, make it easier for customers to search for price differences, and make the price-matching offer more credible to customers.

- *Standardization of products*. The more comparable the products are, the more likely that sellers adopt price matching.

- *Customer's price sensitivity*. Since price sensitivity varies with product characteristics as well as with customer characteristics, price-matching guarantees are more likely if price is a major factor in purchase decisions.

- *Price level and price variability*. The higher the price level and the more that prices vary across sellers, the more time and effort customers spend on searching for price differences, with or without the presence of price matching. This point explains why a price difference refund is applied most often to big-ticket items, such as home appliances, whereas grocery stores typically announce a general price-matching policy. Because few customers actively search for price differences for grocery items, a price difference refund policy would be less credible to customers.

Table 17.2 summarizes the decisions a seller must make when adopting a price-matching policy. As more sellers adopt price matching, the terms are becoming more aggressive. The most obvious is the percentage price difference refunded to customers: 110 percent even 150 percent, are

TABLE 17.2 **Decisions for Pricing-Matching Guarantee Policies**

Decision	Range of options
Amount of money refunded	Actual difference; more than actual difference
Time limitation	14 days; 30 days
Geographical limitation	"Any local store"; metropolitan area
Mode of refund	Immediate cash/credit; check from headquarters; vouchers
Items covered	Identical item; similar items
Prices covered	Sale prices; advertised prices; verifiable prices
Burden of proof	Customer must bring ad or offer; the retailer will verify

Source: Used with permission from K. Sivakumar and Robert E. Weigand, "Price Match Guarantees: Rationale, Implementation, and Consumer Response," *Pricing Strategy & Practice 4,* no. 4 (1996) 4–13.

common now, with some retailers announcing 200 to 300 percent refunds for a verified price difference. Another aggressive approach is that sellers promptly respond to a price change, rather than asking customers to provide proof. American TV and Appliance claimed that its "patent pending Price Check Network" would initiate price changes twice a day, according to the competitors' prices collected from in-store shopping and competitive ads. "As a result every sale price available in the market from our competitors is on our floor every day!"[24]

Customer Perceptions and Response to Price-Matching Guarantees

Some studies have showed that in the presence of price-matching, buyers' perceptions of market prices are not significantly affected. However, they do tend to believe that the price-matching store has lower prices than competitors. This result helps to explain why a price-matching guarantee may be effective in attracting customers to a specific store, especially when the proportion of stores adopting price-matching in a particular market is not very high.

How does price-matching affect the search effort of customers? Signaling theory (see Chapters 3 and 4) suggests that when search costs are low, price-matching would be more credible because sellers would expect more customers to search and get refunds if there is a price difference. When search costs are high, price-matching would be less credible because sellers would expect fewer customers to ask for

[24]From American TV's website www.americantv.com/pricecheck.html.

refunds. Thus when search costs are low, search effort should be less because the signal that the store has the lowest price would be more credible. However, one study showed that when search costs were low, more customers tended to search in the presence of price-matching. When search costs were high, customers searched less and took the price-matching guarantee at its face value.[25]

Another study has found that price-matching guarantees consisting of modest refund offers, such as refunding the difference between the price paid and a competitor's lower price, enhance buyers' perceptions of credibility. Buyers view more aggressive policies, such as the price difference plus 20 percent of the difference, with skepticism. Buyers also perceive that price-matching guarantees that do not restrict the competitive area provide more value, leading to more positive attitudes toward the seller and perceptions that the seller is competitive on price. Respondents were more likely to patronize retailers perceived to provide more value while maintaining competitive prices.[26]

Development and the Future of Price-Matching Guarantees

Using a price-matching policy is not restricted to retailing. Many other firms are using price-matching in less traditional ways with the assistance of computer technology. The prevalence of the Internet and wide adoption of procurement software enables firms to create an online market where price comparisons are much easier. Thus price-matching has almost no hassle cost to consumers. In such situations, suppliers in the market will have no incentive to undercut competitor's prices, and thus higher market prices may result.

Guidelines for Enhancing Distributor Performance

As indicated earlier, one way to gain distributor cooperation and motivation to improve the sales performance for the manufacturer's products is the offer of trade or functional

[25]Joydeep Srivastava and Nicholas Lurie, "A Consumer Perspective on Price-Matching Refund Policies: Effect on Price Perceptions and Search Behavior," *Journal of Consumer Research 28* (September 2001), 296–307.
[26]Monika Kukar-Kinney and Rockney G. Walters, "Measuring How Consumers Respond to Different Types of Retail Price-Matching Guarantees," unpublished working paper, Kelley School of Business, Indiana University, Bloomington, IN (July 2001).

discounts and promotional discounts or allowances. Other types of incentive programs involve the compensation plans of the manufacturer's sales force as well as incentive plans for the distributing firm or its sales force. Unfortunately, the discount plans or incentive plans are often offered as short-term efforts to improve sales performance and are not part of an overall strategic marketing and pricing plan. This section offers some guidelines for using price to gain a strategic advantage in the distribution network.

Earlier chapters stressed that sellers need to offer superior value to their customers in order to gain competitive advantage. In like manner, manufacturers need to provide their distributors with the opportunity to gain superior value with the resale of the manufacturers' products. Manufacturers who are able to gain a channel position advantage by offering distributors superior value are more likely to gain eventual competitive advantage in the final selling markets. Thus manufacturers must not only seek to provide superior value to their final customers but also, through the use of discounts, dealer support, and incentive programs, develop a long-term partnership with their distributors.

The guidelines outlined below extend some basic principles that were developed in earlier chapters as well as offering some principles directly related to channel management. For effective distributor performance, manufacturers need to[27]

1. Recognize the strategic importance of (perceived) product quality and brand reputation (see Chapters 3 through 8).

2. Recognize the strategic importance of financial terms of trade (see Chapter 16 and this chapter); the emphasis when doing so should be on encouraging the distributor to set prices that improve total channel profits while maintaining adequate product availability and merchandising support.

3. Link manufacturer price to distributor price (any discount is related to the price paid by the distributors' customers, not quantity purchased or sold).

[27]James A. Narus and James C. Anderson, "Strengthen Distributor Performance through Channel Positioning," *Sloan Management Review 29* (Winter 1988), 31–40; Nirmalya Kumar, "The Power of Trust in Manufacturer-Retailer Relationships," *Harvard Business Review 74* (November–December 1996), 92–106.

4. Recognize that incentive programs must be an integral part of the price-channel strategy; such incentive programs should

 a. Be institutionalized with a few well-understood major annual efforts aimed at improving distributor performance.

 b. Be simple and easy to implement.

 c. Be tied to "real" sales increases, not to building distributor inventories.

 d. Encourage activities that have long-term benefits, such as sales training programs.

 e. Help distributors improve their own financial performance.

 f. Direct the incentive programs to the distributor firm and not to the distributors' sales force (enhances distributor management control without interference from the manufacturer).

Thus the seller's focus is on ways to enhance the total value to its dealers and distributors. When the seller meets the overall goal of increasing profits for the dealer or distributor, it gains cooperation and a share in those profits.

Sales Compensation Plans

Not only must the manufacturer be concerned with getting the cooperation of distributors, but also of the sales force. Many companies have indicated that they must be more careful explaining changes in prices or price policy to the sales force than to customers.

As Chapter 1 explained, many firms' recent pricing changes have reduced the flexibility of the sales force and have increased sales force dissatisfaction. Moreover, the increased emphasis on profit margins and on dropping products and services requires management to develop compensation plans that reward rather than penalize the sales force.

By using the profitability analysis techniques developed in earlier chapters, management can develop a sales compensation plan that rewards salespeople in terms of their contributions to profit. Helping salespeople increase sales profitability requires a careful analysis of the various ways profits are earned: product sales mix, customer mix, sales territory, and salespeople. The product profitability analysis developed in Chapter 11 and the segment and customer profitability analysis developed in Chapter 12 can help determine which products, customers, territories and salespeople are profitable and which are not. Then training programs can help salespeople understand how selling more products with high contribution margins to customers who can be served at low cost, while maintaining the integrity of prices will benefit both the company and the sales force. Salespeople must be trained and compensated for taking a value-oriented selling approach rather than selling mainly on the basis of price and features (see Chapter 8).

Companies are increasingly turning to compensation plans based on contribution to profits. Such plans reward salespeople to the degree that they help the firm reach its profit goal, and they discourage salespeople from putting their effort into easy-to-sell, low-margin products. Moreover, when companies move away from a varying-price policy to a one-price policy, such a compensation plan gives the salesperson incentive to avoid shading or reducing prices as a means of soliciting sales. Finally, a compensation plan based on profit contributions will influence salespersons to restrict selling expenses, which will improve their sales performance.

A compensation plan that properly motivates the sales force can be effective in managing the product-sales mix. If significant compensation is attached to improving profits, motivated salespeople will find ways to achieve the desired results. Thus sales compensation plans offer another example of how pricing policy is intricately related to all parts of the marketing management function.

Summary

This chapter has shown the relationship of pricing management to three major marketing decision variables: distribution and channel decisions, promotion management, and sales force management. Previously, Chapters 14 and 15 linked the pricing decision to product management and Chapter 16 discussed the relationship between pricing and transportation decisions.

Chapter 1 defined price as a ratio of the quantity of goods and services provided by the seller to the quantity of goods and services given up by the buyer. Many options are available to the seller when price must be changed. The seller can change the product's performance or attached services, the discount structure, the methods of distribution, or the price and sales promotion methods. Thus price, as the only revenue-generating marketing variable, is intimately linked to the other marketing variables, which provides many alternatives when making either short-term or permanent price changes.

The ultimate objective of a pricing decision is to influence buyer behavior. Thus the pricing decision should be based less on traditional practice than on an analysis of what pricing alternatives will positively influence buyers. This chapter has demonstrated that the underlying rationale for pricing decisions is also useful when making distribution, promotion, or sales management decisions.

Discussion Questions

1. a. Discuss the problem of controlling prices through the distribution channel.
   b. What are some legal ways of developing price controls?
   c. Why would a manufacturer be concerned with controlling price through the channel?

2. a. Distinguish between single-function and dual-function buyers.
   b. Why is this distinction important?

3. What should a manufacturer do to establish a legally valid functional discount pricing structure?

4. a. Why would a firm reduce prices temporarily?
   b. What are some alternative ways to temporarily reduce prices?
   c. What are some of the problems of establishing a special price promotion?

5. If a manufacturer paid close attention to the behavioral aspects of price as discussed in Chapters 5 through 7, what behavioral principles would you suggest be used when developing a price promotion strategy?

6. a. What are some ways that a seller might use price promotions deceptively?
   b. Can you formulate any prescriptions for avoiding such deceptions?

7. a. Look through several general circulation magazines. List the number of different types of deals—coupons, refunds, and premiums—that you find.
   b. Look through several Sunday newspapers and the Wednesday or Thursday food section of your newspaper.

List the number of different types of deals—coupons, refunds, and premiums—that you find.

c. If you took advantage of all the coupons you found, how much would you save?

d. Compare the weekly advertisements of several grocery stores in your area for at least a month. Are any national brands featured as specials by rival supermarkets? Are they the same brands?

e. Why do you suppose rival supermarkets would feature the same national brands as price specials?

Suggested Readings

Ailawadi, Kusum, Paul Farris, and Ervin Shames: "Trade Promotion: Essential to Selling through Resellers," *Sloan Management Review 40* (Fall 1999), 83–92.

Blattberg, Robert C., Richard Briesch, and Scott A. Neslin: "How Promotions Work," *Marketing Science 14*, no. 3, Part 2 (1995), G122–G132.

Narus, James A., and James C. Anderson: "Strengthen Distributor Performance through Channel Positioning," *Sloan Management Review 29* (Winter 1988), 31– 40.

Sivakumar, K., and Robert E. Weigand: "Price Match Guarantees: Rationale, Implementation, and Consumer Response," *Pricing Strategy & Practice 4*, no. 4 (1996), 4–13.

Spriggs, Mark T., and John R. Nevin: "The Legal Status of Trade and Functional Price Discounts," *Journal of Public Policy & Marketing 13* (Spring 1994), 61–75.

Tang, Christopher S., David R. Bell, and Teck–Hua Ho: "Store Choice and Shopping Behavior: How Price Format Works," *California Management Review 43* (Winter 2001), 56–74.

CHAPTER EIGHTEEN

Legal Aspects of Pricing Strategy

As the two previous chapters have made apparent, developing a price structure to implement a pricing strategy not only is a difficult and complex task, but also is fraught with the potential of violating federal and state laws. Some of the legal implications of pricing were briefly discussed in Chapters 7 (comparative price advertising), 12 (justifying price differentials), 16 (quantity and cash discounts and geographical pricing), and 17 (functional discounts and price promotions). In fact, the legal aspects of pricing strategy comprise one of the most difficult parts of marketing strategy and have left many businesspeople vulnerable to legal action because of their pricing activities.

Firms should name a pricing administrator or manager to coordinate the many facets of pricing products and product lines as well as the interrelationships of price to advertising and promotion, channel management, and sales management. One of the important advantages of a price administrator is that he or she can oversee the legal implications of various pricing strategies and tactics.

This chapter offers a broad view of U. S. federal laws affecting pricing management. First, we survey the main federal laws affecting pricing in the United States. For the most part, the discussion will be brief, without examination of major landmark cases. Our objective is not to provide an opinion on what constitutes legal or illegal pricing decisions or actions; this is a function of legal counsel. Rather, this chapter emphasizes the need to be attentive to the legal aspects of pricing decisions because most people involved in pricing at various firms have had neither formal training in pricing nor exposure to the real complexities of the legal environment for pricing. Consequently, many of these people come dangerously close to violating federal and state statutes on a regular basis. At the same time, many pricing behaviors in firms and industries have become more or less traditional, so little attention is given to the possibility of illegal pricing strategies and tactics.

One of the most complex and frustrating areas of pricing is the justification of price differentials. This problem may arise (1) when a customer believes that he or she has been illegally charged a price higher than the price charged to other customers for the same product; (2) when a competitor believes that a rival's prices are lower in markets where they both compete than in markets where they do not compete; (3) when the government believes that competing customers of a seller are charged different prices; and (4) when price changes must be justified to customers, the sales force, or a price control board. Conditions 1, 2, and 3 generally arise as a result of legal proceedings after a charge of illegal price discrimination. The fourth condition prevails more frequently during inflationary periods.

A second major purpose of this chapter is to illustrate how price differentials may be justified when a firm is faced with either litigation or disgruntled customers and sales force. Although other legally defensible approaches will be discussed, cost justification of price differentials seems to have wider application than the other approaches. A cost justification study for differential prices can be used to prevent further litigation, soothe disgruntled customers, or develop a sound price structure. Other legal defenses are suitable primarily within the legal arena.

An Overview of Major Federal Laws Affecting Pricing

Many firms attempting to gain volume or market share often resort to price reductions. Other competing firms often feel compelled to follow these price reductions, and often undercut the original price-reducing firm. Pressure, real or perceived, sometimes prompts firms to grant certain buyers a favored status by giving them additional discounts. To counteract these pressures to reduce prices and to stabilize profits, some businesses have attempted, either by overt or covert actions, to stabilize prices and market share. In other situations, a larger firm has intentionally reduced prices in one market area, or to a specific set of customers, in order to reduce competition or to drive a competitor out of business.

Each of these possible strategies or tactics is covered by some form of federal legislation and regulation. In fact, there are laws concerning *price-fixing* amongst competitors, *exchanging price information or price signaling* to competitors, pricing similarly to competitors (*parallel pricing*), *predatory pricing*, and *price discrimination*. In this section we provide a brief overview of the laws that cover these types of activities. Although our attention will be on the U. S. federal statutes, many of the individual states have patterned their laws after the federal laws. Moreover, since the United States was a forerunner in the development of anti-trust laws and laws to preserve competition, the laws of many countries also are broadly patterned after the U. S. statutes. Box 18.1 provides a brief summary of some recent legal cases involving pricing issues.

Collusion: Fixing Prices, Rivals, and Rules[1]

A premise of antitrust law is that collusion among business rivals inevitably leads to a monopoly outcome, typically higher prices and profits that the colluding organizations share. The classic case of collusion is collective action to raise prices through direct control of prices, by restricting output, or by dividing the market into competition-free sub-markets, each of which is controlled by a member of the cartel.

A second form of collusion involves attempts to disadvantage rivals who are not a part of the collusion. Colluding firms can reduce rivals' revenues through boycotts or predatory pricing. If these practices cause the rivals to leave the market or reduce their competitive behaviors, the colluding firms, perhaps through prior agreement, are able to raise prices. Colluding firms also can take actions that raise their rivals' costs, necessitating price increases to remain profitable.

A third form of collusion, instead of attempting to influence market outcomes, imposes rules of competition on the members of the cartel. The goal of such rules of conduct is to lessen price competition among the members of the cartel. Typically, the rules attempt to take advantage of the fact that consumers lack full information about prices and product or service features available from competing firms (see Chapter 4). Included in such efforts are agreements to limit

[1]Robert H. Lande and Howard P. Marvel, "The Three Types of Collusion: Fixing Prices, Rivals, and Rules," *Wisconsin Law Review* (2000), 941–99.

A SAMPLING OF SOME RECENT LEGAL ACTIONS CONCERNING PRICING   BOX 18.1

1. January 1989—Panasonic agreed to pay $16 million to consumers who were allegedly victims of a pricing scheme between Panasonic and numerous retailers. Panasonic had pushed retailers not to set prices below minimum levels, threatening not to supply stores that did not comply.

2. The Antitrust Amendments Act of 1990 increased the maximum penalties for price-fixing from $1 million to $10 million.

3. December 1990—Coca-Cola and Pepsi-Cola bottling companies proposed a $1 million settlement for price-fixing. (Pepsi executives were given immunity for cooperating.)

4. May 1990—D.F. May was found guilty of artificially raising "original" or "regular" prices, then promoting discounts from those prices to create the illusion of offering bargains.

5. June 1994, Washington, D.C.—Kanzaki Specialty Papers and Mitsubishi agreed to settle a price-fixing charge on fax paper for a total of $6.5 million. Kanzaki also settled with the Canadian government for US$687,895.

6. October 1994—Caremark International, Inc., and 26 other drug firms were sued for alleged price discrimination. Under pressure from mail-order drug companies, HMOs, and other managed-care facilities, the drug firms provided discounts that were not made available to community pharmacies. February 1996—two drug companies agreed to pay $52 million over three years to about 40,000 retail pharmacies. September 1998, Chicago—A U.S. District Judge approved a $342 million payment by four drug manufacturers to settle these federal price-fixing lawsuits.

7. 1995, Baltimore—Mattress Discounters paid a $50,000 fine and agreed to stop inflating regular prices when advertising a sale. In 1988, Hecht's (a D.F. May Co.) paid a $500,000 penalty for a similar practice. In Boston, Mattress Discounters paid a $950,000 fine for deceptive practices in the selling of mattresses.

8. May 1995, Washington, D.C.—Reebok paid a $9.5 million penalty for dictating retail prices of shoes (vertical price fixing).

9. August 1995, Washington, D.C.—ICI Explosives USA Inc. paid a record of $10 million criminal fine for price fixing. A senior vice president pled guilty and paid a criminal fine of $50,000.

10. December 1995, Oxford, Mississippi—Conagra Inc. and Hormel Foods Corp. agreed to pay $21.1 million to settle a lawsuit that they conspired to fix prices on processed catfish. The third co-conspirator, Delta Pride Catfish, Inc. agreed to pay "several million dollars."

11. February 1996, Orlando, Florida—Four major carbon dioxide suppliers (Liquid Carbonic Industries Corp., Liquid Air Corp., BOC Group, Inc., and Archer Daniels Midland) agreed to pay more than $55 million to settle a price-fixing lawsuit. Liquid Carbonic agreed to pay $23 million and an undisclosed additional amount to other companies including PepsiCo, Coca-Cola, Anheuser-Busch, and Kraft Foods.

12. April 1996, Chicago—Archer Daniels Midland Co. (ADM) and two Japanese companies agreed to settle a class-action antitrust case for $45 million. The case, brought to court by lysine purchasers, accused ADM of fixing prices within the lysine market. October 1996—ADM was

found guilty of criminal price fixing in the global lysine market and fined a then-record $100 million penalty. In addition, two ADM executives were convicted of conspiring to fix prices and received jail time of two years. However, in June of 2000, this jail time was extended and the European Union fined ADM $45 million for its part in the global price-fixing cartel for lysine.

13. April 1998, Washington, D.C.—UCAR International Inc. pleaded guilty and accepted a fine of $110 million for fixing prices of its graphite electrodes and dividing market share with competitors.

14. September 2000, New York—Art buyers and sellers will receive $512 million after a deal was reached with the two auction houses, Sotheby's and Christie's, for years of fixing fees.

15. May 2001, Washington—Mitsubishi Corp., convicted for its part in helping an international cartel fix the price of graphite electrodes, was fined $134 million. Six other members of the cartel were also convicted and fined over $300 million total.

advertising, including posting prices, making it difficult for consumers to search or acquire information by restricting hours of operation, preventing third parties from providing comparative price information, or preventing the discussion of fees for consulting services until the project has been fully outlined with the client. Another form of collusion related to pricing involves agreements to not offer discounts to certain classes of customers, to not offer "double refunds" on manufacturers' coupons, or to agree on the discounts to offer certain customers. Drug companies that offer discounts to large-scale purchasers such as health maintenance organizations (HMOs) and not to "corner drug stores" illustrate one form of agreement on the offering of discounts.

Price-Fixing

The Sherman Anti-Trust Act (1890) specifically addresses issues related to price-fixing, exchanging price information, and price signaling. It also has an effect on the issue of predatory pricing. Section 1 of the act prohibits all agreements in restraint of trade. Generally, violations of this section are divided into per se violations or rule of reason violations. *Per se violations* are automatic. That is, if a defendant has been found to have agreed to fix prices, restrict output, divide markets by agreement, or otherwise act to restrict the forces of competition, he or she is automatically in violation of the law and subject to criminal and civil penalties. There is no review of the substance of the situation—whether there was in fact an effect on competition. In contrast, *rule of reason doctrine* calls for an inquiry into the circumstances, intent, and results of the defendants' actions. That is, the courts will examine the substantive facts of the case including the history, the reasons for the actions, and the effects on competition and the particular market. The general attitude of federal and state agencies and courts is that price fixing is a per se violation and that criminal sanctions should be applied to the guilty persons as well as the companies involved. Box 18.2 summarizes one person's personal consequences of being found guilty of conspiring to fix prices. However, as explained below, a recent Supreme Court decision removed a form of vertical price-fixing from the per se category.

In two previous Supreme Court decisions, the abhorrent view of price fixing was extended to the attempt to control *maximum prices* that may be charged. The Maricopa County Medical Society and its physician members agreed to establish a maximum fee schedule for health services. The Court, in 1982, declared that agreements to fix maximum prices were as repugnant to the Sherman Act as agreements to set minimum prices. Also, in 1982, the Court declared that a chiropractic association's attempt to control prices through a peer review committee was in violation of the Sherman Act. Thus the attempt of a professional association to set prices is an illegal pricing practice. In effect, all overt interferences with the independence of the pricing mechanism were prohibited.

However, a 1997 Supreme Court decision concerning setting maximum prices that may be charged within a channel of distribution now qualifies that interpretation. In 1968, the Supreme Court, in *Albrecht* v. *Herald*, made vertically imposed maximum resale prices illegal per se. But, in its 1997 *State Oil* v. *Khan* decision, the Supreme Court unanimously overruled the *Albrecht* decision. The Court's decision returned the antitrust treatment of maximum resale price restraints to the rule of reason. That is, suppliers who set maximum prices for their products do not automatically violate federal antitrust laws.

Khan had operated a gasoline station in Addison, Illinois. He bought all of his gasoline from State Oil Co, which set a

THE PRICE OF FIXING PRICES   BOX 18.2

In 1974, Armand Gravely was hired by Pepsi-Cola Bottling Company of Fresno, California, as a route salesman. Three years later he was promoted to specialty sales representative with responsibility for training new drivers. In August 1981, Allegheny Pepsi offered him a job as area sales manager in Baltimore. In January 1983, he was appointed division manager in Richmond, Virginia.

In late spring 1983, Gravely received a call from his colleague Stan Fabian, Allegheny's Norfolk division manager. Fabian said that their boss, vice president of sales Jerry Pollino, wanted Gravely to come to Norfolk to meet with Randy Allen, the Virginia division manager of Mid-Atlantic Coke. So, on the morning of June 6, 1983, the three men met with Randy Allen at a restaurant in Norfolk.

Jerry Pollino indicated that he was concerned with the problems that had been occurring due to deep promotional discounts. After a short discussion, the men agreed to set minimum prices at $5.50 a case for cans and $0.95 per unit on two-liter bottles. The desired price levels were set at $6.25 to $6.00 on cans and $1.15 on a two-liter. The agreement covered only cola beverages.

In spring 1984, the manager of a motel in Virginia Beach tried to set a price for the beverages he would be purchasing during the summer season. The sales representative of Mid-Atlantic Coke set the price at $5.50 per case, and refused to negotiate a lower price. When the manager hinted he would try to get a lower price from Pepsi, the Mid-Atlantic sales person said he would be unlikely to get a lower price since they had an agreement with the Pepsi company. The motel's manager contacted the FBI, which notified the Antitrust Division of the Justice Department.

Once the Antitrust Division believes a conspiracy exists, they perform an orderly investigation: Documents are subpoenaed and low-level employees of the companies under suspicion are interviewed. Generally, the government must offer immunity from prosecution to several participants in a price-fixing scheme to gather sufficient evidence for a conviction. The goal is to avoid immunizing high-level participants by obtaining evidence from lower-ranking employees.

In fall 1984, the Norfolk division of Allegheny Pepsi was served with a subpoena for documents. On January 15, 1985, Gravely was informed that the Richmond division was also under investigation. Fabian was offered immunity and he accepted. Gravely, however, refused to cooperate. To build a sufficient case, prosecutors went above Gravely and offered immunity to Pollino, who cooperated.

The first person to be indicted was Armand Gravely, who went on trial in January 1987. The prosecution's star witnesses were Jerry Pollino and Stan Fabian. The jury convicted him of price-fixing and obstruction of justice. Noting that "hundreds of thousands of dollars were removed from the public and put into the coffers of Allegheny Pepsi" by Gravely's actions, the judge sentenced Gravely to three years in jail, suspended except for 120 days, fined him $15,000, and required him to perform 16 hours of community service per month for three years. Gravely, who had been fired by Allegheny on the day of his conviction, indicated that he did not have the funds to pay the fine.

A Justice Department prosecutor says that the government tends to seek jail sentences in price-fixing cases. "Individuals in business . . . are typically willing to pay whatever fine we insist on if they can avoid going to jail."

Source: Andrew Galvin, "The Price of Fixing Prices," *Journal of Pricing Management 1* (Summer 1990), 46–51. The article originally appeared in *Beverage World,* January 1990.

"suggested" retail price. Although Khan was not prohibited from setting a higher price, all revenues earned from exceeding the suggested price had to be returned to State Oil. Within a year Khan was broke and State Oil evicted him. He sued under the auspices of the *Albrecht* decision, and the case eventually made its way to the Supreme Court. This ruling does not mean that suppliers can always fix maximum resale prices. Now judges and juries must weigh the evidence to determine whether, on a case by case basis, a particular practice of setting a maximum resale price amounts to an unreasonable restraint of trade. An important distinction between this case of vertical maximum price-setting and the Maricopa and chiropractic association attempts to set maximum prices is that the latter were attempts to fix prices horizontally between competitors. Horizontal price-fixing remains a per se antitrust violation.[2] As might be expected, manufacturers and retailers had opposite views of the *Khan* decision.

Section 2 of the act prohibits the act of monopolizing, that is the wrongful attempt to acquire monopoly power. Thus, having a monopoly is not illegal, but the deliberate attempt to become a monopoly is illegal. The issue here has been not whether a firm had acquired a monopoly per se, but the methods of achieving such market power. Thus the courts have become increasingly aware of a firm's need to develop a strong competitive position in the markets it serves and that a strong competitive position may translate into a dominant market share. However, if a dominant market share leads to above-average market prices, some form of legal or regulatory action may take place (for example, the dominance of some airlines in hub cities recently has been questioned). This issue of how Microsoft had achieved alleged monopoly power was a primary focus of the *U.S. et al.* v. *Microsoft* case.

---

[2]Roger D. Blair and Francine Lafontaine, "Will *Khan* Foster or Hinder Franchising? An Economic Analysis of Maximum Resale Price Maintenance," *Journal of Public Policy & Marketing 18* (Spring 1999), 25–36; Richard M. Steuer, "*Khan* and the Issue of Dealer Power—Overview," *Antitrust Law Journal 66*, no. 3 (1998), 531–36; Roger D. Blair and John E. Lopatka, "*Albrecht* Overruled—At Last," *Antitrust Law Journal 66*, no. 3 (1998), 537–66; Warren S. Grimes, "Making Sense of *State Oil Co. v. Khan*: Vertical Maximum Price Fixing under a Rule of Reason," *Antitrust Law Journal 66*, no. 3 (1998), 567–611; Mark E. Roszkowski, "*State Oil Company v. Khan* and the Rule of Reason: The End of Intrabrand Competition?" *Antitrust Law Journal 66*, no. 3 (1998), 613–40.

Exchanging Price Information

Many trade associations collect price information from and disseminate it to their members. A legal issue arises when there is an apparent agreement to set prices based on the exchanged price information. Moreover, if members discuss prices and production levels at meetings and if prices tend to be uniform across sellers, then it is likely that the exchange of information led to some form of price fixing. Again, the legal issue is whether the exchange of price information seems to have the effect of suppressing or limiting competition, which is a violation of section 1 of the Sherman Act.

The exchange of price information may be lawful when it can be shown that the price information is about past prices, not future prices, where individual firms are not identified, where the data are publicly available to nonmembers of the trade association, and where meetings did not include discussions of price and production policies. Competing sellers must take care about exchanging price information as the trend in litigations has been to make it more difficult to prove that such exchanges do not violate section 1.

Parallel Pricing and Price Signaling

In many industries and markets, one firm may emerge as a price leader. That is, the firm often is the first to announce price changes, and most rival sellers soon follow the price changes made by the leader. At other times, another firm may initiate the price changes, but if the price leader does not introduce similar price changes, the other firms as well as the initial firm adjust their prices to correspond to the price leader's prices. The legal question here is whether these somewhat concerted price changes constitute a tacit, informal, and illegal agreement in violation of section 1.

Recent court actions seem to indicate that parallel pricing per se is insufficient to prove a violation. Rather, parallel pricing *plus* evidence that the defendants acted in a concerted way and that they communicated in some way to achieve a common understanding over prices must be present.

The ramifications of price signaling from a legal perspective remain to be determined either by legislative action, litigation, or further debate.

Predatory Pricing

Predatory pricing is cutting prices to unreasonably low or unprofitable levels so as to drive competitors from the market.

If this price cutting is successful in driving out competitors, then the price cutter may have acquired a monopoly position via unfair means of competition, a violation of section 2 of the Sherman Act.

There is considerable controversy about predatory pricing, particularly how to measure the effect of a low-price strategy on the firm's profits, on competitors, and eventually on consumers. Predatory pricing occurs whenever the price is so low that an equally efficient competitor with fewer resources is forced from the market or is discouraged from entering it. The primary effect on the smaller seller is a drain on cash resources, not profits per se. As argued in Chapter 12, if the cash inflow from the sale of products or services does not exceed the cash outflow, the firm cannot recover its investment in the product. Moreover, if the cash inflow does not cover the firm's cash outflow, then the cash drain prohibits it from investing in new products and other types of business activity. Thus, one aspect of the controversy concerns determining the proper set of costs to be used when assessing the relative profitability of the predator's actions.

Previously, the courts seem to have adopted the rule that predatory pricing exists if the price does not cover the seller's average variable or marginal costs. However, the intent of the seller remains an important consideration in any case.[3] For example, in 1976, the Federal Trade Commission issued a complaint that General Foods had sold its regular blend Maxwell House coffee at unreasonably low prices, sometimes below cost (predatory pricing), and that it had engaged in discriminatory pricing as well as promotional and advertising practices. At the time, Maxwell House enjoyed market shares of 45 to 50 percent in the Eastern United States. In January 1982, an administrative law judge for the FTC ruled that General Foods' actions were legitimately defensive. Essentially, the judge recognized that coffee consumption had been declining, that a major competitor, Proctor & Gamble had entered the eastern market with a nationally recognized brand, Folgers, and that for a mature product like coffee, sales growth would only occur if market share was taken from rival sellers. Thus, General Foods had

---

[3]Gregory T. Gundlach, "Price Predation: Legal Limits and Antitrust Considerations," *Journal of Public Policy & Marketing 14* (Fall 1995), 278–89; Joseph P. Guiltinan and Gregory T. Gundlach, "Aggressive and Predatory Pricing: A Framework for Analysis," *Journal of Marketing 60* (July 1996), 87–102.

a legitimate defense: It had engaged in these activities to prevent losing market share to Proctor & Gamble by letting them enter this regional market. Thus there seemed to be greater opportunity for competitors to be more aggressive in their pricing decisions.[4]

Then, in the 1993 *Brooke Group Ltd.* v. *Brown & Williamson Tobacco Corp.* case, another important standard for assessing predatory pricing complaints was established. The essence of this standard is that the predator must have a reasonable probability of recouping the predatory losses through higher prices later on. The attention of the courts on this recoupment test has led to a basic premise that plaintiffs find very difficult to overcome: Predatory pricing is rarely successful in recovering losses due to predatory pricing, and, consequently, rational decision makers would not intentionally incur losses to drive out a competitor or to prevent competitor entry into a market. Essentially, plaintiffs must bear the burden to show that in the relevant market the defendant has a dominant market share (minimally above 30 percent), that there are significant barriers to entry such that new competitors are unlikely to enter if the prey is forced from the market, and that other current competitors in the market lack the capability to increase output in the short run. That is, the plaintiff must show that there is a reasonable probability that the alleged predator could recover the predatory losses, not an easy task.[5]

Along with the *Khan* case, the courts appear to be moving away from a strict use of neoclassical microeconomic theory in antitrust cases. Indeed, in some cases the courts have recognized information asymmetries in markets that require considering the current realities of the marketplace when looking at behaviors that allegedly violate norms of competitive behavior. Table 18.1 provides some indicators of when price reductions or promotional pricing might be considered predatory. Although it has become increasingly difficult for a plaintiff to win a case of alleged predatory pricing, such cases continue to be filed, especially in state courts and civil litigation proceedings. Table 18.2 provides some guidelines for avoiding such litigation.

---

[4]Susan S. Samuelson and Thomas A. Balmer, "Antitrust Revisited—Implications for Competitive Strategy," *Sloan Management Review 30* (Fall 1988), 79–87.
[5]C. Scott Hemphill, "The Role of Recoupment in Predatory Analysis," *Stanford Law Review 53* (July 2001), 1581–612.

TABLE 18.1 Factors That Might Make Price Reductions Predatory

Factor	Indicator
Cost	Price is below average variable cost (to determine average variable cost look at all activities in production, marketing, and distribution).
Barriers to entry	If barriers to entry are high, then price cutting is more likely to be considered predatory.
Intent	The issue is whether the intent is to meet rather than destroy or harm competition.
Market share	A large company (market share greater than 30 percent) reducing prices against one or more small companies may be viewed as predatory.

Other Important Laws

The Clayton Act (1914) was passed to correct certain defects and omissions of the Sherman Act. It prohibits anticompetitive mergers, tying arrangements, exclusive dealing agreements, interlocking directorates, and the acquisition of stock in competitor companies. Certain mergers, interlocking boards of directors, and the buying of a competitor's stock were thought to lead to dangerous oligopolies and the control of market prices. Section 2 of the act also prohibited predatory price discriminations.

As noted earlier, except for the per se violations, the Sherman Act is not violated unless substantial adverse effects on competition can be proved. With the Clayton Act an action that has the *potential* of substantially lessening competition may be illegal. Thus the Clayton Act provided an important distinction between actual harm to competition and the potential for such harm to occur.

TABLE 18.2 Guidelines for Avoiding Predatory Pricing Litigation

1. Do not target action against a smaller competitor.
   Broaden price and promotional activities across product and geographical markets.
2. Avoid targeted, excessive promotional spending.
3. Do not create plans or other documents that permit an inference of a targeted strategy.
   For example, different profit objectives in various product and geographical markets may illustrate intent.
4. Avoid across-the-board price reductions *below* a defendable measure of variable cost.
   Exceptions:
   Liquidation of excess inventory.
   Excess industry capacity.
   Matching competitor's lawful price (beware of historical price differentials).

The Federal Trade Commission Act (1914) established the Federal Trade Commission, and prohibited "unfair methods of competition in commerce, and unfair or deceptive acts or practices in commerce" (section 5). Unfair methods of competition include acts or behaviors that violate the Sherman or Clayton Acts. However, if for a technical reason an action is beyond the scope of either of these two acts, the FTC may invoke section 5 if there are indications that the action has had or has potential to have substantial anticompetitive effects.

Congress created the FTC to protect the competitive structure from monopoly tendencies and to protect businesses from unfair methods of competition. In 1938, Congress passed the Wheeler-Lea Act as an amendment to the Federal Trade Commission Act, broadening the FTC's purpose to include protection of the public from deceptive business practices. The amendment also prohibited false and misleading advertising and provided more stringent penalties and enforcement procedures. In 1950, Section 15 of the Federal Trade Commission Act was amended to strengthen the FTC cease and desist order by providing that a separate violation could be found for each day the violation of a final order continued. The penalty for each such violation could be up to $5,000. Thus the FTC has the authority to eliminate deception and to provide consumers with information that will help them make intelligent purchase decisions.

The Nature of Price Discrimination

Both the Clayton Act and the Robinson-Patman Act prohibit illegal price discrimination, but neither prohibits price differences, as is often believed. In fact, price discrimination can be found in many markets. Although price discrimination in selling to ultimate consumers is assumed by the Federal Trade Commission, the courts, lawyers, and marketers to be legal, many cases of permissible and accepted price discrimination involve ultimate consumers. As we pointed out in Chapter 17, whenever some buyers are willing to pay a higher price or do not take advantage of the opportunity to buy at a lower price, there is some form of price discrimination. But, some recognized acceptable price differences for the same product or service also reflect either differential price sensitivity or ability to pay. For example, it is readily accepted that many retirees, with limited fixed incomes, should be offered discounts or other opportunities to pay less for some products or services. There are also discounts for professional association members that are benefits of membership, for students and educators, and for the time that the purchase is made, for example, matinee performances. Moreover, when businesses sell to businesses, the Robinson-Patman Act indicates certain situations in which it is lawful to discriminate on the basis of price.

Economically, price discrimination occurs whenever price differences for the same product or service sold by a single seller are not justified by cost differences or changes in the level of demand. Price discrimination also occurs when two or more buyers of the same product or service are charged the same price despite differences in the cost of serving these buyers.[6] Thus, to know whether price discrimination exists between two or more buyers in the economic sense, it is necessary to know both the price and the total relevant costs applicable in each instance of possible discrimination.

As the definition of price in Chapter 1 indicates, price discrimination may arise in a variety of ways. The product sold to some buyers may be physically different or of different quality. There may be differences in services that accompany the products, for example, delivery, storage, credit extension, and sales force efforts. Some buyers may qualify for volume, cash, or trade discounts. Hence, whether there is price discrimination in the economic sense depends on analyzing the factual detail surrounding the transactions.

The legal basis for price discrimination, however, goes beyond these economic tests. Indeed, the Robinson-Patman Act sets out conditions beyond cost differences in which price discrimination may legally exist. We turn now to an overview of the Robinson-Patman Act.

Provisions of the Robinson-Patman Act

Section 2 of the Clayton Act sought to prevent sellers from reducing prices in areas where strong competition existed while maintaining higher prices in areas with little or no competition. Essentially, the act was aimed at preventing local price cutting. However, section 2 was also interpreted as applying to price discrimination among competing buyers.

---

[6] *The Attorney General's National Committee to Study the Antitrust Laws* (Washington, D.C.: Office of the *Federal Register*, National Archives and Records Service, 1955), 333–36.

During the 20 years following passage of the Clayton Act in 1914, chain stores grew rapidly and increased their buying power. As the chains' buying power increased, some chain buyers began coercing price concessions to their advantage. This type of price discrimination behavior was thought to threaten the survival of independent wholesalers and retailers, and section 2 was insufficient to protect these independent distributors. Hence, in 1936, Congress passed the Robinson-Patman Act as an amendment to the Clayton Act. This act prohibits certain discriminatory pricing and promotion practices relative to the sale and distribution of products in the United States.

Section 2 of the Robinson-Patman Act, which is divided into six parts, amends section 2 of the Clayton Act. Section 2 of the Robinson-Patman Act contains civil prohibitions and section 3 lists criminal prohibitions.

Section 2(a) is the backbone of the act. It prohibits sellers from charging different prices to different buyers for similar products where the effect might be to injure, destroy, or prevent competition in either the buyers' or sellers' market. It also provides a defense when the seller can cost-justify a price discrimination, and it offers other limited defenses and exceptions.

Section 2(b) places the burden of proof on the person charged with a price discrimination violation under 2(a). Section 2(b) also provides a defense if the seller can prove that the lower price was made to equal a lawful low price of a competitor.

Section 2(c) prohibits the seller from paying and the buyer from receiving any brokerage fee, commission, or other form of compensation for a transaction. It has also been construed to prohibit commercial bribery.

Section 2(d) prohibits a seller from granting discriminatory allowances and section 2(e) prohibits discrimination in services and facilities, unless such allowances or services are available on proportionately equal terms to all competing customers.

Section 2(f) makes it unlawful for a buyer knowingly to induce or receive an illegal discriminatory price.

Section 3 prohibits a seller from providing secret allowances to a favored buyer. The section also forbids territorial price reductions or sales at unreasonably low prices for the purpose of destroying competition or eliminating a competitor. Section 3 is a criminal statute in that it makes it a crime for any person to be a party to its prohibition.

Maximum penalties include a $5,000 fine and imprisonment for a year. However, the U.S. Supreme Court has held that Section 3 is not an antitrust statute and therefore does not provide for liability for treble damages by private litigants if a conviction occurs.

As we shall see, the act does not cover all aspects of pricing within a distribution system. In some instances, benefits provided loyal resellers may not lead to violations of the act. For example, quicker delivery times, preferential product allocations, exclusive distribution of specific products to some resellers, differences in credit terms that reflect legitimate business reasons, making or guaranteeing loans at prevailing interest rates, or preferential bid quotes where the disadvantaged bidder is not otherwise a customer of the seller do not constitute violations of the act.[7]

As in Chapters 16 and 17, an important aspect of selling to and through distributors or resellers is providing discounts and allowances to encourage additional purchases of the seller's products. Whether these discounts are conventional volume or quantity discounts, share of current or future business discounts, or increased advertising or merchandising funds, the way these price structures or promotion programs are managed makes it possible that different customers or resellers will receive different discounts or promotion allowances. The extent to which competing sellers and disadvantaged customers can claim illegal price discrimination within the confines of the Robinson-Patman Act will be briefly outlined next.

Jurisdictional Defenses—Section 2(a)[8]

Unlike economic price discrimination, a price differential is not illegal price discrimination per se; certain requirements specified in section 2(a) must be met. In any price discrimination litigation, the seller first may attempt to prove that the act does not apply to the price differences at issue. Primarily, a *jurisdictional issue* is a legal matter and does not include

---

[7]Barbara O. Bruckmann, "Discounts, Discrimination, and Exclusive Dealing: Issues under the Robinson-Patman Act," *Antitrust Law Journal 68*, no. 2 (2000), 253–95.

[8]In the commentary that follows, specific court cases will not be cited. Excellent overviews of the Robinson-Patman Act that include case citations are Earl W. Kinter, *A Robinson-Patman Primer* (New York: Macmillan, 1970); Paul H. LaRue, "Meeting Competition and other Defenses under the Robinson-Patman Act," *The Business Lawyer 25* (April 1970), 1037–51; and Bruckmann, "Discounts, Discrimination, and Exclusive Dealing."

JURISDICTIONAL REQUIREMENTS OF SECTION 2(A) OF THE ROBINSON-PATMAN ACT

BOX 18.3

Before a violation of Section 2(a) can be demonstrated, it must be shown that

1. The same seller

2. Charged different prices

3. To two or more different purchasers

4. For use, consumption, or resale within the United States or any territory.

Furthermore, it must be shown that

5. There were two or more sales

6. Reasonably close in time

7. Involving commodities

8. Of like grade, quality, and quantity

9. And that at least one sale was "in commerce."

the actual issue of the price differentials. Box 18.3 lists the jurisdictional requirements for a violation of section 2(a). Each of these jurisdictional requirements will be discussed in turn.

The Same Seller

Although this requirement seems uncomplicated, it has presented some thorny problems. Primarily the problems occur when parent corporations sell through independent subsidiaries or distributors and when at least one of the purchasers bought directly from the parent, while unfavored customers bought from an independent distributor or subsidiary.

Legally, it must be shown that the distributor or subsidiary possesses sufficient autonomy insofar as distribution policies are concerned. That is, the issue is not ownership per se but rather whether there is sufficient managerial autonomy in the subsidiary or distributor's marketing activities. There are no specific guidelines on how a firm can determine whether sufficient marketing control resides with the distributor or subsidiary to legally define the parent and the distributor or subsidiary as separate sellers. However, if legal autonomy is proved, then the alleged discrimination did not result *from sales by the same seller* and illegal price discrimination is not present.

An offer to sell or a bid that is not accepted does not result in a discriminatory price. Moreover, refusal to sell ordinarily is not a violation of the Robinson-Patman Act. Either an unaccepted offer to sell or a refusal to sell does not result in two sales and a resulting price difference between purchasers.

A Price Difference

Within the legal setting, price has been defined simply as what the buyer has actually paid the seller as consideration; that is, what the seller gives up to acquire the goods and services. The U.S. Supreme Court has held that a difference in price is *prima-facie* (at face value) evidence of price discrimination. Thus if the seller has one price for all customers and they pay transportation expenses, there is no violation of Section 2(a).

Because price discrimination legally is equivalent to price differentiation, equal prices are not unlawful. As Chapter 17 indicated, a firm may sell at the same price to wholesalers, retailers, and consumers. However, when there are differing terms or conditions of sale, an illegal, indirect price discrimination may occur.

The pricing activity under examination for a possible violation must be something other than a reasonable policy of price flexibility. An important issue is whether the price difference and the amount of goods sold at different prices are substantial enough to have a serious anticompetitive effect to the detriment of the public interest. As we observed in our definition of price in Chapter 1 and discussed in Chapters 16 and 17, price can be differentiated in many ways besides the direct dollar quotation. Promotional, trade, cash, and quantity discounts, rebates, premiums, or free goods, guarantees, provision of delivery, warehousing, or credit all affect how much the buyer actually receives. Differences in these terms and conditions of sale have been held to result in indirect price discrimination within the domain of section 2(a). Moreover, under sections 2(d) and 2(e), these terms and conditions of sale must be available to all competing customers on proportionately equal terms.

Two or More Purchasers

Similar to the requirement that there be a single seller, it must also be shown that the alleged price discrimination was between two or more purchasers. Again, this issue arises when a manufacturer uses more than one channel of distribution. That is, the manufacturer may sell direct to some customers and through distributors or subsidiaries to other customers who compete on the same level as the direct-buying customers.

In some cases in which the manufacturer also deals directly with the distributor's or subsidiary's customers, courts have held that these customers are also *indirect purchasers* of the manufacturer in the eyes of the law, and they may therefore pay a higher, discriminatory price than competing direct-buying customers. As in the situation of the same seller, this legal issue revolves on the question of managerial control. Although a subsidiary or distributor may be legally autonomous within the purview of the same-seller requirement, however, it is possible that the manufacturer may have sufficient contact with the indirect customers to establish the requirement of two or more purchasers. Indeed, this was one of the legal issues prevailing against Purolator as discussed in Chapter 17.

Perhaps the safest approach is to have no contact between a manufacturer and its distributor's customers. Such an approach would rule out the use of missionary salespeople who arrange store displays, check retailer's inventory, and occasionally take orders. Furthermore, this "hands off" approach would prevent controlling wholesalers' or retailers' selling prices. The legal precedents in this area are inconclusive, and at this time, raise additional questions about what is legally acceptable distribution control.

Geographical Requirement.

Section 2(a) cannot be applied to sales made for use, consumption, or resale in a foreign country. That is, export sales are exempt but import sales are not exempt from the provisions of section 2(a). However, sections 2(c), 2(d), and 2(e) have been applied to export sales.

Two or More Sales

The different-purchasers requirement has been interpreted to mean that both sets of transactions consist of sales. Consignments, then, are not "sales" for the application of the Act. The issuance of a loan, the making of a gift, and terms of leases are not "sales." Furthermore, refusing to sell is not, per se, an unlawful price discrimination. Hence price discrimination that involves nonsale transfers of property or refusal to sell is not prima-facie evidence of unlawful price discrimination.

Contemporaneous Sales

Because discrimination occurs when there is a price differential for similar transactions under comparable conditions, then the act is operative only if sales are reasonably close in time. The courts have ruled that price differences must be reasonably close in time and must involve delivery of the products also reasonably close in time. Thus two contracts for future delivery at different times will not necessarily be in violation because delivery does not occur at the time of the contract agreement.

Section 2(a) also permits "price changes from time to time . . . in response to changing [market] conditions." Included in such price changes are obsolescence of seasonal goods, perishable products, going-out-of-business sales, closing-out-a-line sales, and court-sanctioned distress sales.

Tangible Commodities

Courts have consistently found that section 2(a) applies only to tangible products and does not encompass price differences for real estate, services, technology licenses, lease of facilities, or contract rights or privileges. Thus the courts have said that the word *commodity* is restricted only to products, merchandise, or other tangible goods.

Products of Like Grade and Quality

Jurisdiction is not present when it is demonstrated that the products involved are of different grade and quality. Basically, the defendant must show that there are substantial physical differences affecting consumer preference or marketability. However, brand differences alone are not a sufficient defense.

The courts seemingly have applied some current marketing thinking and have considered customer preferences for the products in question. Thus, if there is substantial customer preference for a variation in design and if the customer is willing to pay a higher price for the product, then the two products are not of like grade and quality. These design variations should not be decorative features that have no demonstrable effect on consumer demand.

The effect of using different labels or brand names was argued in the landmark Borden case. The Borden Company had been producing private-label evaporated milk for about 20 years when the FTC issued a complaint on April 22, 1958. Borden was charged with price discrimination by selling milk of "like grade and quality" to different purchasers at higher prices than to the private label purchasers. Borden readily admitted that there were no physical differences between the Borden brand and the private brands of evaporated milk. However, Borden contended that the Borden brand commanded a higher market price because of consumer acceptance. Hence the Borden brand of evaporated milk was a different product than the private brands.

The hearing examiner, the full Federal Trade Commission, and the U.S. Supreme Court all concluded that Borden's evaporated milk and the private brands that Borden produced were of like grade and quality. However, the U.S. Supreme Court remanded the case back to the Appeals Court to make a final determination of the issues of injury to competition and cost justification.

The Fifth Circuit Court of Appeals rendered the final decision on July 4, 1967. The Court's opinion was that Borden's policy of selling private-brand milk did not result in injury to competition, and the case was resolved in favor of Borden. The Court did not take a position on the cost justification issue.

Thus the court recognized that when the buyer perceives a difference between two branded products, then there is a valid difference, so long as the "price difference is reasonable." What constitutes a reasonable price difference has not been established.

One Sale in Commerce

Section 2(a) provides "that it shall be unlawful for any person engaged in *commerce*, in the course of such *commerce* . . . to discriminate in price . . . where either or any of the purchasers . . . are in *commerce*." (italics added.) Thus one jurisdictional defense is that the alleged discrimination did not involve a sale "in commerce." Generally, the courts have held that for a sale to be "in commerce" the product must cross a state line. Legally, a firm is not engaged in commerce if it sells its products only in the state where they are produced. So the use of local plants selling their products only in the producing state has become a recognized way of avoiding the prohibitions of section 2(a). However, individual states may have statutes that parallel the Robinson-Patman Act, and illegal price discrimination may be found at the state level.

In 1983, the Supreme Court extended the coverage of the Robinson-Patman Act to include governmental agencies that are not purchasing goods for "traditional" purposes. Sales to governmental agencies cannot be made at lower prices than sales to buyers in the private sector if the agencies are reselling the products at prices lower than private firms. This extension of the Robinson-Patman Act to governmental agencies raises questions about universities that buy personal computers at low prices for resale to their students. Moreover, an agency that bargains for such low prices may be charged with knowingly inducing price discrimination in violation of section 2(f).

The "No Statutory Injury" Defense

Section 2(a) provides another jurisdictional defense in that price discrimination is illegal if the effect is to injure, destroy, or prevent competition. As pointed out in the discussion on the Borden case, the Appeals Court determined that no competitive injury had resulted from the price differentials. As with Borden, many Robinson-Patman defendants have prevailed by showing no injury to competition. Injury to competition can occur at different levels within a distribution system. Competitive harm can occur (1) between the discriminating seller and its competitors (*primary-line injury*), (2) between favored and disfavored customers (*secondary-line injury*), or (3) between the customers of the disfavored customers (*tertiary-line injury*). The standard for establishing primary-line injury differs in important ways from the standard for either secondary-line or tertiary-line injuries.

The "Guidelines for Setting Functional Discount Policy" in Chapter 17 included a recommendation for knowing the buyer's position in the distribution sequence, which enables the seller to know whether differential prices to different channel members would have the effect of injuring competition. For example, suppose manufacturer M sells to two distributors, D_1 and D_2. D_1 in turn sells to retailer R_1, and D_2 also sells to retailer R_2, which sells to final consumers in a separate market area. Figure 18.1*a* illustrates this possibility.

If M charges D_1 and D_2 the same price, there is no discrimination at the distributor level and no competitive injury. However, because D_2 competes with R_1, it is possible that D_2 could sell to consumers in market A at a price lower than R_1's price. If the price advantage harms the competitive position of R_1, (tertiary-line injury), then illegal price discrimination exists.

If the price to D_1 is lower than the price to D_2, then there is no illegal price discrimination because D_1 and D_2 do not compete for the same customers. However, if the lower price to D_1 permits R_1 to sell in market A at a price lower than D_2's price, *and* if D_2's competitive position is harmed (secondary-line injury), then there is illegal price discrimination by the manufacturer. If prices to R_1 and R_2 differ because of the manufacturer's pricing policy, however there is no illegal price discrimination to these two retailers, because R_1 and R_2 do not compete with each other.

FIGURE 18.1
Hypothetical Distribution Systems

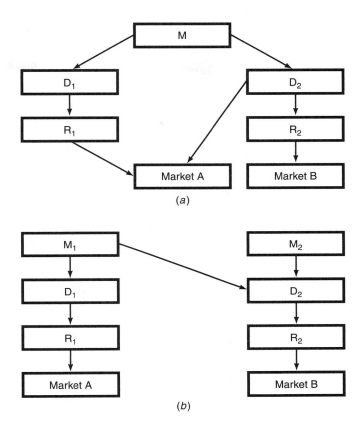

In each of the foregoing situations, a possible competitive injury due to a manufacturer's pricing policy occurs somewhere in the distributive sequence. For either secondary-line injury or tertiary-line injury to occur at some level of distribution, competing buyers must purchase the same product at different prices and the disadvantaged buyer's competitive position must be injured. The important issue here is whether competition has been injured.

Now, consider the situation depicted by Figure 18.1*b*. M_1 competes with M_2 for the purchases of D_2. There is no other competition at lower levels of the distribution system. Suppose M_1's price to D_2 is lower than the price to D_1. Since M_2 does not sell to D_1, it is possible that M_2's competitive position can be harmed. Indeed, it is not necessary that M_1's price to D_2 be lower than M_2's price to D_2 for a possible finding of competitive injury to prevail. This second example is a *primary-line injury case*. Primary-line cases usually involve area price reductions at the seller's level of competition. Normally, injury may be shown whenever predatory intent can be proved or inferred. The Supreme Court's decision in *Brooke Group Ltd.* v. *Brown & Williamson Tobacco Corp.* indicated that a competitor must prove that (1) the defendant's prices were below an appropriate measure of cost, and (2) the defendant had a reasonable likelihood of recouping the investment in below-cost prices (see the section on predatory pricing above). However, because the provisions of the Robinson-Patman Act relative to predatory pricing are broader than the Sherman Act, the requirement of showing that the defendant has market power, or that it is reasonable to infer it may acquire such power, does not require indication of a monopoly position. In primary-line cases, excessive concentration and the possibility of price coordination may be sufficient to show injury to competition under the act.

The burden on a primary-line injury plaintiff to prove competitive injury is substantial. It would appear that unless the seller-defendant has sold the discounted product below a relevant measure of cost and has or likely will obtain sufficient market power to raise prices and recoup the investment in prices below cost, various short-term price promotions or discount structures will not be deemed discriminatory at the primary level of injury.

Customers' price discrimination claims (secondary-line claims) are not subject to the same burden of proof of competitive injury as primary-line claims. Proof of injury may be shown by demonstrating lost sales or profits. Moreover, competitive injury may be inferred if the challenged price difference was substantial and persisted over time. However, a secondary-line injury price discrimination claim will not survive if the plaintiff cannot show that the discount was not available to it. The issue of whether the discount was available to the plaintiff is a matter of fact. The availability of the discount may depend on customers' financial resources, warehousing capabilities, and ability to comply with the seller's conditions. When most customers can purchase at the volume required to get the lowest price, the discount would be considered available. If the buyer's decision not to participate in the discount program, or to qualify for the lowest price in the discount structure is within the buyer's control, the courts have not been willing to find illegal price discrimination. Secret concessions to one buyer, or "flexible" discount policies (such as retroactive quantity adjustments) that essentially favor one or a few customers, are not likely to meet the availability requirements and likely would be found to constitute illegal price discrimination.

Even if one or more of the nine jurisdictional requirements discussed in the previous section is present for a determination of price discrimination, the defendant may prevail by proving no competitive injury. As we have discussed, injurious price discrimination can occur at the seller's level (primary-line injury) or at a lower level in the distribution sequence (secondary-line injury). Furthermore, a seller's attempt to match a lower competitive price in one market area while maintaining higher prices elsewhere may lead to an inference of predatory intent to harm competition. Clearly, the legal complexities of establishing the presence of price discrimination within the domain of section 2(a) makes pricing a difficult managerial task.

The Affirmative Defenses

Even when an alleged price discrimination charge has withstood the jurisdictional defenses just outlined, the seller may still show justification using one of three affirmative defenses: meeting competition, changing market conditions, or cost justification. These defenses may be utilized when it has been established that the price differences constitute price discrimination under the Robinson-Patman Act. Because the act has jurisdiction over the price differences, there is a prima facie case of price discrimination—the seller is guilty until proven innocent.

Defense of Meeting Competition

A seller may reduce prices in a good-faith attempt to meet an equally low and lawful price of a competitor. Meeting competition is a complete defense under section 2(b), but there are strict rules for when such a defense should be used.

First, the defense is not available if the defendant knew, or should have known, that the competitor's price was unlawful. The seller must show that there was reason to believe that the competitor's price was lawful.

Second, the seller's price discrimination must have been temporary, not part of a permanent price schedule. That is, the seller may reduce a price to hold a customer or gain a new customer, but this new, lower price must be temporary and not part of a plan to systematically charge higher prices to some customers.

Third, "an equally low price of a competitor" must be for a given quantity. The competitor's product need not be of like grade and quality, but the products in question must be competitive, and the prices must be for similar quantity.

Fourth, the seller's lower price must be available to specific customers. That is, the price concession must be limited to those specific customers to whom a competitor has offered the lower price.

Fifth, the statute expressly permits reducing prices to *meet* a competitor's lower price, but the competitor's price cannot be bettered. That is, the seller's price cannot be reduced below the competitor's price. As simple as this condition seems, it becomes complicated when the products are premium and nonpremium products, for example beer or gasoline. Where historically there has been an established range of price differences between a premium and a nonpremium product, meeting competition means preserving the established price differentials.

For a seller facing a price discrimination charge, the evidence necessary for a successful meeting-competition defense includes

1. Existing market conditions and foreknowledge of competitors' low prices.

2. A good-faith effort to verify the competitors' low prices.

3. Facts indicating it was reasonable to believe the reports of competitors' low prices to be true.

4. A belief that the business would be lost without the price reduction.

Changing Conditions Defense

Section 2(a) provides that prices may be changed to reflect changing market conditions or changes in the marketability of the product. The section also lists a number of applicable examples: "actual or imminent deterioration of perishable goods, obsolescence of seasonal goods, distress sales under court process, or sales in good faith in discontinuance of business in the goods concerned."

Few defendants have attempted to use this defense. As with the meeting-competition defense, there are strict rules for using the changing conditions defense:

1. The specific market change or change in marketability must be a departure or variation from usual market

conditions. These market changes must not result from behavioral changes by a competitor or by the defendant.

2. The market must resemble the provisions of the statute; that is, the defense is confined to sales of products whose marketability has been affected by obsolescence or by changes in buyer preferences.

Cost Justification Defense

Earlier in this chapter, we observed that price differences not warranted by cost differences constituted economic price discrimination. Section 2(a) provides for a complete defense if the price differentials "make only due allowance for differences in the cost of manufacture, sale, or delivery resulting from the differing methods or quantities in which such commodities are to such purchasers sold or delivered." Thus, the Robinson-Patman Act provides for a defense based on economic principles.

Despite congressional intent, it has not been easy for a seller to justify price differentials on the basis of cost differences. Cost defenses have been successful, and many investigations by the Federal Trade Commission have been closed upon showings of cost justification. Yet the cost justification defense has been used infrequently relative to the total number of cases litigated under the act.

The cost justification defense has had limited use for a number of reasons. First, areas of business operations that provide recognizable cost savings for serving particular customers are limited. If a manufacturer produces to maintain inventory and sells from inventory, there are no demonstrable savings due to manufacturing. Because it is impossible to causally relate any order, large or small, to the manufacturing process, volume discounts cannot be justified because of "production economies of scale." Only if the seller produces to fill specific orders can manufacturing costs be a part of the cost justification.

Second, the Federal Trade Commission has consistently accepted actual costs only. Incremental or marginal costs have been unacceptable, as have investment and opportunity costs.

Third, officially sanctioned accounting standards for performing a cost justification study are lacking. As noted above, manufacturing costs usually cannot be used as cost justification of price differences. Thus, the primary area of study is marketing and distribution. However, as shown in Chapter 12, little attention has been devoted to developing and utilizing standards for marketing and distribution cost analysis.

Fourth, a cost justification defense is usually expensive and, because of the inexactness of marketing and distribution cost analysis, unpredictable. Moreover, since the cost studies used as a defense invariably follow the discrimination citation, lack of good faith in setting price differentials based on cost differences is obvious.

As we pointed out in Chapter 12, determining the relative cost to serve different customers when doing customer profitability analysis can identify opportunities for using price to enhance profitability. Moreover, developing activity cost tracking systems will make it much easier to identify costs associated with production scheduling, ordering processing, materials handling, warehousing, small and frequent ordering patterns, and shipping. When it can be shown that the seller avoids or reduces these costs based on the purchasing and ordering behavior of customers, then a cost justification of a price structure that features discounts should be considered.

Guidelines for Justifying Price Differentials

As the above summary indicates, price differentials can be successfully defended in a number of ways. However, a careful reading of the litigation history of the Robinson-Patman Act reveals a woeful lack of attention to the pricing function by many firms. Most defenses to a price discrimination charge have relied on hastily developed studies that, when subjected to cross-examination, have failed to justify the price differentials.

Despite its relative lack of use, the cost justification defense remains one of the most viable defenses available. However, firms must develop cost accounting techniques for analyzing marketing expenditures and refrain from lumping marketing and distribution costs into general overhead categories such as selling, general, and administrative. Chapter 12 outlined the basic approach to marketing cost accounting.

Any seller who, in the normal course of business, charges different customers different prices should not leave compliance with the Robinson-Patman Act to chance. From a policy perspective, the firm must have clearly defined policies and procedures.

Administrative Guidelines[9]

Minimally, these policies and procedures should

1. Provide a published price list that includes the price breaks and discount eligibility criteria.

2. Establish all discount schedules on a cost-justified basis.

3. Communicate to all sales personnel the policy of adhering to the established price lists and discount schedules.

4. Provide for specific procedures when departing from the established prices and discount schedules.

5. Develop a program for cost-justifying discount schedules and other sources of price differentials.

6. Instruct sales personnel to obtain, whenever possible,

   a. Copies of the competitor's offers, price lists, discount schedules, and invoices from customers.

   b. Signed statements from customers about competitors' price concessions.

   c. Memoranda of conversations with customers who report competitive offers.

Salespeople should also list customers lost because of lower competitive offers. The firm should use all this information for a periodic review of all price concessions granted to meet competition.

Cost Justification Guidelines

To cost-justify price differences, the seller should develop a marketing and distribution cost accounting system. Such an accounting system should be able to prepare reports showing the cost and price differences of serving different types of customers. Marketing and distribution costs should not be averaged, but should be traced objectively and directly to the activities that give rise to these costs.

Cost justification studies should

1. Be made before price lists and discount schedules are established.

---

[9]These guidelines are adopted from Ronald M. Copeland, "The Art of Self-Defense in Price Discrimination," *Business Horizons 9* (Winter 1966), 71–76; LaRue, "Meeting Competition and other Defenses"; and John E. Martin, "Justifying Price Differentials," *Management Accounting 47* (November 1965), 56–62.

2. Be periodically reviewed to determine effects of cost changes.

3. Analyze only those costs that vary among customers.

4. Include marketing, accounting, and legal personnel.

5. Include only the seller's costs.

6. Group customers according to similarities of marketing to them and according to similarities of their purchasing behavior. (The average cost of dealing with the group should be a valid indicator of the cost of dealing with any specific group member.)

7. Classify relevant costs into their variable and fixed components.

8. Compare cost differences to the price lists and discount schedules to determine the legal basis of the price differentials.

In addition to providing for legal defense to a price discrimination charge, these administrative and cost justification guidelines provide management with useful knowledge for making pricing decisions. The value of good intelligence reports from salespeople and the value of marketing and distribution cost studies is that they provide useful guidance for developing overall marketing strategies.

Resale Price Maintenance

As we discussed in Chapter 17, a concern of suppliers, particularly manufacturers, is that the price to the final buyer be in accord with the suppliers' overall marketing strategies. Resale price maintenance is the supplier's specification of the prices below or above which channel members may not sell the supplier's products. This issue revolves around the extent that manufacturers may control prices at which their prices are resold. Prior to the passage of the Consumer Goods Pricing Act of 1975, the Miller-Tydings Act of 1937 exempted the practice of fixing prices vertically in the channel from antitrust laws. In effect, prior to 1975, state laws permitting resale price maintenance contracts ("fair trade") were exempt from the federal antitrust laws. Manufacturers had legal permission to use coercive power to control prices in their channels of distribution. In 1975, Congress repealed this exemption to price fixing from antitrust violations.

As noted previously, with the exemption of maximum price setting, price fixing is illegal per se. Thus whether the price agreement is horizontal—between rival sellers—or vertical—between a manufacturer and members of the distribution channel—it is illegal. Attempts to enforce prices at points of resale through any form of coercive act or threat is illegal per se. For example, Panasonic agreed to a large financial settlement with the attorneys general of the states of New York and Maryland after attempting to coerce retailers to agree not to discount their consumer electronic products. The alleged coercive attempts included refusals to sell and "backroom persuasion."

The current environment surrounding the status of resale price maintenance is somewhat murky. Congress has attempted to pass some form of a resale price maintenance bill, typically labeled as a "fair trade" bill. The courts have not fully established a set of consistent legal precedents about when a supplier may have a legally defensible resale price maintenance program. However, it does seem clear that if the resale price maintenance program involves a conspiracy or combination to fix prices, involves written agreements, and uses implied or actual coercion to enforce the maintenance program, it is likely a per se violation of the Sherman Act.

Perhaps the most important point of a resale price maintenance program is that the supplier act unilaterally.[10] There can be no attempt to force dealers to register complaints or enact boycotts if rival dealers do not conform to the pricing policy. Nor can there be any form of coercion, such as nonrenewable contracts for nonconforming pricing behavior or termination and then reinstatement of discounting dealers. Legal means of obtaining dealer cooperation about prices include establishing a "partnership" as discussed in Chapter 17, printing the retail price on the product or package, advertising the suggested retail price, announcing suggested retail prices in catalogs or sales brochures, and supporting the advertising efforts of dealers who feature the suggested retail prices.[11] However, it must be abundantly clear that the dealers are free to deviate from the printed or suggested prices should they feel it in their best interests to do so. Dealers

---

[10]Mary Jane Sheffet and Debra L. Scammon, "Resale Price Maintenance: Is It Safe to Suggest Retail Prices?" *Journal of Marketing 49* (Fall 1985), 82–91.
[11]Virginia G. Maurer and Michael Ursic, "Resale Price Maintenance: A Legal Review," *Journal of Public Policy & Marketing 6* (1987), 171–80.

cannot be compelled to follow a specific recommended price of the supplier.

Deceptive Price Promotions

The Wheeler-Lea Amendment to the Federal Trade Commission Act gave the FTC jurisdiction over business practices that tend to mislead and deceive consumers. Chapters 5 through 8 explained the various ways consumers perceive prices and the effects of these perceptions on value judgments and purchase behaviors, and Chapter 17 discussed how use of fraudulent advertised regular prices may influence consumers' formation of reference prices for making price comparisons. Thus, given the complex and important role that price plays in purchasing decisions, the advertising and promotion of "special" prices, cents-off deals, sales, and other forms of price promotions have the capacity to attract buyers to the store to purchase the items being price promoted. Indeed, a number of European countries, Canada, and Australia have established regulations to check the deceptive effects of price promotions.

Normally, promotion prices either explicitly or implicitly claim or imply that the seller's price is lower than some comparative price for the item being promoted. The comparison may be to a previous or former price, a manufacturer's suggested selling price, a usual price in the market area, or, as in an introductory offer, to a future price. Because consumers vary greatly in their knowledge of usual or regular prices (see Chapter 5), and in their search for product and price information (see Chapter 3), they often have no knowledgeable basis for determining the truthfulness of such claims.

Price promotion offers can be viewed as a healthy aspect of price competition that directly or indirectly help buyers save money. But when such offers are false or misleading, they become an unfair practice that is detrimental to both competition and consumers. And when they have the capacity to confuse or mislead consumers, they are simply undesirable. One survey taken in Norway, Sweden, Denmark, and Finland indicated that comparison price promotions tended to confuse significant numbers of consumers.[12] This capacity to confuse and mislead consumers has led to increased

---

[12]*Bargain Price Offers and Similar Marketing Practices*, Report by the Committee on Consumer Policy (Paris: Organization for Economic Co-operation and Development, 1979).

concern about the widespread use of sales and price promotions by businesses.

The Competition Act of Great Britain

In March 2000, Great Britain's tough Competition Act went into effect. This act gives regulators strong powers to prosecute business cartels and a variety of unfair pricing practices. The act gives the Office of Fair Trading the power to enter premises and seize documents without warning. Firms convicted of monopolistic practices can receive fines of 10 percent of total sales, which can be tripled in some cases. Although U.S. antitrust laws were used as an example, the act is almost a verbatim copy of the European Union competition law.

Summary

The chapter has provided an overview of the legal environment for managing the pricing function. Litigation history yields few clear guidelines for developing lawful price structures but clearly suggests that such guidelines are necessary. Those firms that have prevailed against price discrimination charges often could demonstrate an underlying analytical foundation for their pricing practices. At the very least, price analysis of a firm's pricing practices is a good-faith attempt to comply with the requirements of the Robinson-Patman Act.

This chapter has also integrated material from Chapters 3 through 8, 11, 12, 16, and 17 and shown the importance of knowing both the direct and traceable costs of manufacturing and marketing activities. Arbitrary allocation of marketing costs with no clear understanding of how these costs vary when serving different types of customers usually fails to justify price differentials. In Chapters 16 and 17, we repeatedly argued against tradition as a basis for establishing discount policies. Given the dynamic nature of our economy, the guidelines in this chapter also stress a planned, periodic review of all prices and underlying analyses. Regardless of the legal benefits of such control, reviews are simply sound management practice.

Another benefit of an analytical base for making pricing decisions is that it facilitates explanation of the necessity for price changes to sales personnel, customers, or a price control board. During periods of inflation, price increases generally are expected, but the frequency and amount of these increases often exceed the expectations of salespeople, distributors, and customers. To help these people adapt to the price increases, a reasoned justification is useful. Chapter 22 gives additional prescriptions for pricing management.

Discussion Questions

1. Contrast the meaning of price discrimination from the economic point of view with the legal view represented in the Robinson-Patman Act.
2. Develop additional examples of permissible price discrimination; that is, when it is legal and/or acceptable for buyers to pay different prices for essentially the same product or service. Do you feel that these forms of price discrimination are justifiable?
3. What is a jurisdictional defense? What are the nine jurisdictional requirements for price discrimination as set forth in the Robinson-Patman Act?
4. What is a primary-line injury case? What is a secondary-line injury case?
5. Explain the meaning of the "no statutory injury" jurisdictional defense.
6. What are the affirmative defenses to a charge of price discrimination?
7. Describe the necessary conditions for the following defenses to a charge of price discrimination:
   a. Meeting competition.
   b. Changing conditions.
   c. Cost justification.
8. What is the rationale for the proposed administrative and cost justification guidelines given in the chapter? How do these guidelines help a pricing administrator manage the pricing function?

Suggested Readings

Bruckmann, Barbara O.: "Discounts, Discrimination, and Exclusive Dealing: Issues under the Robinson-Patman Act," *Antitrust Law Journal 68*, no. 2 (2000), 253–95.

Guiltinan, Joseph P., and Gregory T. Gundlach: "Aggressive and Predatory Pricing: A Framework for Analysis," *Journal of Marketing 60* (July 1996), 87–102.

Gundlach, Gregory T.: "Price Predation: Legal Limits and Antitrust Considerations," *Journal of Public Policy & Marketing 14* (Fall 1995), 278–89.

Hemphill, C. Scott: "The Role of Recoupment in Predatory Pricing," *Stanford Law Review 53* (July 2001), 1581–612.

Kaufman, Patrick J., N. Craig Smith, and Gwendolyn K. Ortmeyer: "Deception in Retailer High-Low Pricing: A 'Rule of Reason' Approach," *Journal of Retailing 70*, no. 2 (1994), 115–38.

Kelley, Craig A.: "US Antitrust Issues and Pricing Strategy," *Pricing Strategy & Practice 2*, no. 2 (1994), 17–24.

Maurer, Virginia G., and Michael Uric: "Resale Price Maintenance: A Legal Review," *Journal of Public Policy & Marketing 6* (1987), 171–80.

Special Topics on Pricing

Chapters 19 to 21 discuss some specific aspects of pricing. Chapter 19 presents an overview of auctions and the problem of developing competitive bids to meet special orders for products or services. The chapter provides applications of costing and discusses specific considerations of competitive strategy. Chapter 20 reviews some of the particular problems of developing prices for services and provides an introduction to setting prices in international markets.

Chapter 21 discusses the more recent phenomenon and issues of pricing on the Internet. Although we have made reference to issues related to the Internet in earlier chapters, given the rapid growth of electronic commerce some additional information on this new technology and its impact on pricing is required.

CHAPTER NINETEEN

Auctions and Competitive Bidding

In business-to-business marketing and in selling to the government, firms may compete by submitting bids that detail the services and product specifications to be offered at a stated price. Sealed or closed bidding takes place when two or more bidders submit independent bids for the rights to property or to render a service. In a broad sense, this form of competitive bidding is a form of an auction. Auctions have become increasingly popular with the advent of the Internet and are used in business-to-business marketing, business-to-consumer marketing, and even consumer-to-consumer marketing.

This chapter presents an overview of the problem of developing fixed-price bids either for providing products or services on an order basis, for purchasing products, either singly or in lots, or for accepting purchase offers from others for items that are available for sale. We will review the various types of auctions, whether for scarce objects or for multiple items as variations of closed bidding. After discussing a procedure for determining whether to submit a bid, the chapter considers cost estimation, determining the probability of winning the contract, and determining the best bid. The chapter concludes by introducing important variations to the basic fixed-price competitive bidding model.

Auctions

Auctions have been a means for determining price and transferring ownership since the earliest days of civilization. The volume of goods sold by auction, whether in auction houses

TABLE 19.1   **Characteristics of Different Auction Forms**

Types	Characteristics	Winning Bid
English auction	Most common form; price is successively raised until only one bidder remains	The highest bid
Dutch auction	Auctioneer calls an initial high price, and then lowers the price until one bidder accepts the current price	The highest bid, but the winner pays the lowest winning price
First-price sealed bid auction	Competitors submit bids secretly, or sealed.	The highest bid when competing for goods; the lowest bid when competing to offer a service
Second-price sealed bid auction	Competitors submit bids secretly, or sealed	The highest bidder, but pays the price of the second-highest bidder
Reserve-price auction	A reserve price is set by the seller	The highest bidder, if above the seller's reserve price
Reverse-price auction	The price declines at a regular interval	The first bid during the price decline

or via the Internet, and the publicity of auction sales, has exploded in recent years. Auction houses have facilitated this growth by building prestigious images, expanding their offerings to include memorabilia and collectibles, and publicizing lifestyles associated with unique or scarce goods. However, the popularity of auctions conducted on the Internet in all types of marketing forums has brought the concept of an auction to the attention of a wide range of businesses and consumers. Table 19.1 provides a summary of the characteristics of different types of auctions.

Types of Auctions

There are many different forms of auctions. The most common form, the English auction, is one in which the highest bidder among potential buyers, or the lowest bidder among potential sellers, is the winner. (The distinction between situations in which bidders are buying or are selling is relatively unimportant.)[1] Auctions can be open or closed. In open auctions, prices are publicly announced and bidders are able to

[1]Michael H. Rothkopf and Ronald M. Harstad, "Modeling Competitive Bidding: A Critical Essay," *Management Science 40* (March 1994), 364–84.

indicate their willingness to transact at specific prices. In closed auctions, bidders submit offers simultaneously, and the bid-taker evaluates the offers. The most common closed auction is the standard sealed bid (often referred to as competitive bidding).

Open auctions can be progressive in that the auctioneer solicits successively better bids until no bidder offers a better bid (English auction). Alternatively, auctions can be conducted by the auctioneer (or an electronic device) starting with a high price and successively announcing a lower price until a bidder bids and wins the lot for sale (Dutch auction). The English auction generates more receipts on average than the Dutch/sealed bid auction, and it is more efficient relative to information gathering and bid preparation activities and costs.[2]

In an English auction, it is best for bidders to reveal their valuation of the item and to bid accordingly. In such situations, the person with the highest valuation wins the item and pays a price equivalent to the valuation of the second highest valuation (by the next highest bidder). In a Dutch auction, the winning bidders must pay their bid. Thus they will shade their bid and bid below their valuation of the item. In a sense, an English auction is truth revealing, whereas a Dutch auction requires strategic behavior.[3]

Among the disadvantages of English auctions is that they require the bidders be present, which may limit the number of bidders at a specific auction. When conducted over the Internet, obviously this restriction is greatly reduced. Another disadvantage of English auctions is they are susceptible to *rings of bidders*. A ring is a group of bidders who agree to reauction the item among themselves when one of them successfully wins the item at auction. In this way they do not compete during the bidding and usually are able to secure the item at a lower price than otherwise. When the threat of rings is large, the auctioneer likely will favor a sealed-bid auction to avoid this possibility.

Elements of Auctions

Auctions are complex, being made up of a composite of elements. Understanding the elements of auctions helps us un-

---

[2]Paul Milgrom, "Auctions and Bidding: A Primer," *Journal of Economic Perspectives 3* (Summer 1989), 3–22.

[3]Gerard J. van den Berg, Jan C. van Ours, and Menno P. Pradhan, "The Declining Price Anomaly in Dutch Dutch Rose Auctions," *American Economic Review 91* (September 2001), 1055–62.

derstand how and why auctions work. The basic elements of an auction are the participants, the object(s) or services(s) available for bidding, and the type of auction or set of rules used to determine the price and the buyer (or seller).

Participants

Auctions require the actions of two parties, and often a third. A seller (buyer) offers a right or an object to prospective buyers (sellers) who are invited to bid. Bidders gather together, or in the case of the Internet, watch via their computers, to participate in the auction. Often a third player, the auctioneer or auction house, actually conducts the auction and receives a commission from the seller based on the price paid. Increasingly, the auction house also receives a buyer's commission paid by the winning bidder (often referred to as a "buyer's premium"). For example, assume an object has sold for $1,000. The winning bidder might pay the auction house $1,150 and the auction house in turn remits $850 to the previous owner of the object. Although various differences in personalities and other external elements influence the dynamics of each auction, every auction requires a seller and one or more bidders competing over a common object or service.

Scarcity

Typically, limited quantities of the object (often only one) are available for sale. Auctions provide an opportunity to determine the value of these scarce objects, in contrast to mass-produced and mass-merchandised goods and services that are offered for sale at a fixed price. Selling a unique item at auction allows the seller to determine the market value of an object at any point in time. The item is sold to the bidder with the highest value. Scarcity is the element that makes this method of sale feasible.

Why Auctions Work

Auctions and bidding are used widely: in financial markets; in harvest sales of grain, meat and fish, fruit, seeds and bulbs, leather, and tobacco; in settlements of bankruptcies and repossessions, in procurement and subcontracting; in selling unique assets such as book manuscripts, free-agent athletes, and works of art; and in the sale of rights such as mineral or oil exploration. Auctions are just one way that society can transfer assets. Fixed or posted pricing is common in retail sales and in a broad range of transactions.

As we have seen, to set a fixed price, the seller must know or have a reasonable estimate of the value that buyers may place on the item. Not knowing what price to post, or the value that buyers may place on an asset, is a reason for holding an auction or engaging in negotiation or haggling. Another reason for holding an auction is that the formality of the procedure provides a perception of legitimacy that may not be obtained in other forms of asset transfer. Bidding is usually viewed as fair, especially in situations that are subject to possible political interference.

Fixed or posted prices work well for commonly used and standardized products and services. The product can be offered widely and sold depending on the specific needs and demands of buyers. However, when products are not standardized or when market prices are not stable, fixed prices do not work well and auctions become a viable alternative. For example, at a horse auction, each animal to be sold will vary along many dimensions and it will be difficult to set a single price to cover these variations. An auction allows prices to vary depending on how the buyers value these variations in the horses to be sold.

The amount of information that each participant in an auction has is an important issue. The available information forms the basis for understanding the item to be auctioned, determining a value and bidding strategy, and ultimately determining the price that will be paid. Some information will be public, but other information is known only to the individual participants.[4] For example, the participants will conceal their actual value of the item being auctioned. Thus auctions resemble the asymmetry of information market situation described in Chapters 3 and 4.

The sellers know their value of the item offered for auction. They may have some estimate of what price the auction will provide. However, the sellers do not know who will attend and bid in the auction, or what each bidder's value and price limit is for the object. Thus, the sellers do not know what will be the highest bid and who will make that bid.

On the other hand, the potential buyers have established their value for the item, and have determined the maximum price they would be willing to pay to acquire the item (called a *cap* in auction terminology). The bidders do not know if the seller has set a reserve price (minimum acceptable price)

---

[4] R. Preston McAfee and John McMillan, "Auctions and Bidding," *Journal of Economic Literature 25* (June 1987), 699–738.

that reflects the seller's value for the item. Each bidder does not know what the competitor bidders have set as their caps for the item. Thus each bidder is uncertain whether his or her best offer will be too low to win the item or if a lower bid would have been successful.

Finally, the auction house also operates in this imperfect information environment. Yet its goal is to produce the most beneficial conditions for the sale to occur. Research has shown that as the number of bidders becomes larger, the auction price becomes a better estimate of the true value of the item.[5] To encourage attendance and participation, auction houses group and consolidate items and aggressively advertise and promote the auction. By providing catalogs that include estimates of the high and low prices of what the item will bring, the auction houses seek to remove some of this information uncertainty. Such information alleviates some of the risk and encourages more aggressive bidding by low bidders, thereby escalating the bids of other bidders. Auction houses are most successful when they can find the largest number of bidders who value the objects to be auctioned more than other bidders.

Fixed-Price Competitive Bidding

Competitive bidding is a fascinating, challenging, and difficult job involving judgmental assessment of customers and competitors as well as scientific analysis. The theory of fixed-price competitive bidding covers such situations as (1) deciding what price to bid when the number of competitor bidders is known and when the identity of competitors is known, (2) deciding what price to bid when the number and identity of competitors are unknown, (3) deciding whether to submit a bid at all, and (4) deciding how many contracts to bid on simultaneously when a company cannot afford to win them all.

Normally, when all other factors such as quality and service are equal, the low bidder is awarded the contract. Thus the decision problem is to submit a bid that will help the firm achieve its objectives and be lower than the competing bids. What to bid depends largely on the objectives of the firm.

The basic decision models generally assume that the firm is interested in achieving immediate profits. Such models

---

[5]Orley Ashenfelter, "How Auctions Work for Wine and Art," *Journal of Economic Perspectives 3* (Summer 1989), 23–36.

also assume that the lowest bid gets the award, so the chances of the firm winning the bid decrease as the bid price increases. Yet if the firm does not get the bid its profits are zero. Thus the amount of profits to be earned from any particular bid is uncertain, and probability theory is used to determine the optimal bid. The theory of competitive bidding assumes the bidder's objective is to maximize expected profits.

An example can help make this point clearer. Suppose a firm determines that its costs for fulfilling a particular contract would amount to $50,000. Further assume that the probability of being awarded the contract is 0.70 if the bid is $60,000 but only 0.40 if the bid is $90,000. Which bid should the firm submit if it wishes to maximize expected immediate profits? As shown in Table 19.2 if a bid of $60,000 is submitted, expected immediate profits are $7,000 [0.70 × ($60,000 − $50,000)]. If a bid of $90,000 is submitted, expected immediate profits are $16,000 [0.40 × ($90,000 − $50,000)]. Thus in this simple example, the firm should bid $90,000 on the contract.

In practice, the greatest difficulty in competitive bidding is to develop the required information to estimate the probabilities of winning the contract at various prices. Usually a firm has some idea of the costs that it will incur if the bid is awarded. In addition, it must estimate the number of bidders submitting a bid because the probability of winning a bid is also a function of this number. The firm must also estimate what competitors are likely to bid since competitors will keep their intentions secret. Assuming that bids decrease with decreasing cost estimates, the low bidder wins only when he or she has one of the lowest cost estimates. However, if the low bidder underestimates the actual costs incurred while fulfilling the contract, then this bidder may suffer from what has been called the "winner's curse," winning the item or contract, but making below normal or negative profits.[6]

In some respects, the nature of a fixed-price competitive bidding situation resembles that of some auctions in which the basic roles of buyers and sellers are reversed. In an auction, the seller, or bid-taker, must develop a strategy that allows him or her to maximize expected revenue from the auction. This revenue depends on how the bidders bid, and

---

[6]Douglas Dyer and John H. Kagel, "Bidding in Common Value Auctions: How the Commercial Construction Industry Corrects for the Winner's Curse," *Management Science 42* (October 1996), 1463–75.

TABLE 19.2   Competitive Bidding Example

Bid (B)	Cost (C)	Immediate Profits (B − C)	Probability of Contract (P)	Expected Immediate Profits [P × (B − C)]
$ 30,000	$50,000	$−20,000	1.00	$−20,000
40,000	50,000	−10,000	0.90	−9,000
50,000	50,000	0	0.80	0
60,000	50,000	10,000	0.70	7,000
70,000	50,000	20,000	0.60	12,000
80,000	50,000	30,000	0.50	15,000
90,000	50,000	40,000	0.40	16,000
100,000	50,000	50,000	0.30	15,000
110,000	50,000	60,000	0.20	12,000
120,000	50,000	70,000	0.10	7,000
130,000	50,000	80,000	0	0

their bidding behavior depends on a variety of factors. For example, the bid-taker announces auction rules that specify how the bidding will be conducted and how the bidding determines who pays how much and to whom. These rules may affect the number of bidders in the auction. Other important factors affecting the auction outcome include the amount and type of information that each bidder has about the underlying situation, the bidders' perceived value in acquiring the object or services being auctioned, and whether the auction is single bid or multiple bid.

Prebid Analysis

When offered a contract opportunity, a firm should first perform an analysis to determine whether to prepare a bid. By being selective in its bidding, a company can save time and money that would be spent on bid activities such as cost estimation, engineering proposals, purchasing (there will be fewer requests for subcontract quotes), and printing the bids. Some companies use a screening committee to evaluate bid opportunities in terms of potential growth, engineering capability and facilities needed, and potential competition.

Determine Bid Objectives

Whether to bid and what to bid depend largely on the firm's objectives. As already indicated, the objective may be the typical economic objective of profit maximization, either in terms of return on investment or absolute profits, or it may be to keep labor busy, gain an entree into a new business, or overcome a survival crisis. A bidder should define objectives carefully before evaluating bid opportunities. Whenever possible, the objectives of potential competitive bidders should also be analyzed. This information will be useful in assessing the chances of winning the contract.

Develop Evaluation Criteria

To evaluate a bid opportunity the firm needs benchmarks or criteria.

The firm must determine whether it has the *necessary labor skills and engineering capability* to complete the bid project as specified. If major extensions of skills are required, the firm must consider the cost of acquiring these capabilities.

Available plant capacity is an important factor. To bid on a contract requiring 20 percent of a firm's capacity when the firm is already operating at 90 percent would usually be inappropriate. A company operating at 60 percent capacity, however, would probably be quite interested in the bid opportunity.

The firm should also consider whether it has capacity for future business that might result from winning the contract. For example, if the firm's business has been growing normally, it might not be able to accommodate this growth in the next few years if current slack capacity is devoted to the contract.

Many bid opportunities provide the possibility of *follow-up orders* after the first contract has been fulfilled. Winning a federal government contract to develop a new defense system, for example, gives the winning bidder expertise that would be important in future bids to supply more components for the defense system. Moreover, winning a contract may make other potential buyers aware of the firm's expertise and capability.

Jobs with low *design content* may not fully utilize a company's design engineering talent. A precision, design-oriented company would want to keep its engineers occupied developing new processes or special materials and would be less interested in jobs requiring little design effort.

To determine the chances of winning a bid, the firm must consider the number and identity of *probable competitors* for the contract. In general, the more profitable a bid opportunity seems to be, the greater the number of competitive bids that will be submitted.

In high-technology fields, the *degree of familiarity* the firm has with the bid project is significant. Often, the firm's degree of competency is an important factor in winning an award. Some companies prepare for future bids by adding skills and experience in advance.

A fundamental factor in awarding contracts is whether a bidder can *deliver the project on time*. Indeed, the federal government will invalidate a bid if it appears that the bidder may not be able to deliver as specified. The firm must also consider the effects on permanent customers if an awarded contract is given priority in production.

Finally, the firm should consider whether the quantity of items specified in the bid will allow a cost savings due to the *experience curve* (see Chapter 13). For example, if the contract results in doubling cumulative production volume, then the cost savings will extend to all similar products. Hence the contract could make the firm more cost competitive in its traditional markets.

Develop a Screening Procedure

A firm must analyze the eight criteria outlined above to measure the value of a bid opportunity. One procedure would be to assign a weight to each of these factors according to its relative importance to the firm. Then, for a particular bid, the relative merits of each factor could be assigned a rating of high, medium, or low. These ratings might then be assigned quantitative values, for example, 10, 5, and 0, so that a project using existing labor skills would get a rating of 10. The product of each factor's weight and rating could be summed to give an overall score that the firm can compare to previous bids or to a predetermined minimum acceptable value. If the bid opportunity passes this prebid analysis, then the firm would proceed to develop a bid.

Cost Estimation

Cost estimation involves the familiar procedures for costing discussed in Chapters 10 through 12. As discussed earlier, the direct-cost data set a price floor below which the firm will not want to make a bid. A firm operating well below capacity may choose to bid less than full cost, whereas, when operating near capacity, it may choose to submit a full-cost-plus-profit bid. In any event, the firm should avoid arbitrary cost-estimating formulas and instead prepare careful cost estimates based on realistic activity levels.

Estimating the Probability of Winning

As indicated earlier in this chapter, the theory of competitive bidding relies on the use of probabilistic models. A key factor in submitting a bid is to estimate the chances of winning the contract. Assuming that the lowest bid will win the contract, as is true in most governmental bidding situations, the problem is predicting how competitors will bid. Probabilistic bidding models assist a firm in determining a bid price that optimizes the combination of probability of winning and profit if it does win.

A number of approaches can estimate the chances of winning. The *winning bid approach* simply uses the history of competitors' winning bids. The *average-opponent approach* uses the history of competitors' winning and losing bids to represent the bidding behavior of an average opponent. The *specific-opponent approach* uses the past bidding behavior of specific competitors.

Problem of Determining Reasons for a Winning Bid

The structure of the above fixed-price competitive bidding in essence assumes that the lowest bid in competitive bidding or the highest bid in an auction is selected. However, as Chapters 5 through 8 explained, buyers and sellers often have complex reasons for making purchase decisions, or in the case of an auction, selling decisions. That is, the bid-taker may be attempting to maximize the perceived value of the decision by trading off price with other product or service attributes. For example, in evaluating the bidding situation for performing off-shore oil drilling, the Western Oceanic contract drilling company found out that the safety record of the bidding company's rigs was an important consideration for the oil companies.[7] Superstar athletes sometimes turn down better financial offers to accept the offer of a team in a preferred geographical location.

As Chapter 9 argued, a firm bidding for contracts or participating in auctions must undertake pricing market research and develop a continuing price information system. It is often difficult to know the extent to which loss of a bid was due to price, other factors, or some combination of factors. In business marketing, the salespeople involved with the buying company should try to determine reasons why the

---

[7]Gabriel M. Gelb, "Conjoint Analysis Helps Explain the Bid Process," *Marketing News 22* (March 14, 1988), 1, 31.

bid was lost. However, this particular method of feedback depends on an honest report to the salesperson from the customer and an accurate report back from the salesperson to the bidding management team.

Another research approach for postbid analysis is to conduct interviews with clients to elicit information about the bid selection and the reasons for selecting the winning bid. However, like the salespeople asking for feedback, the customer may attempt to rationalize the selection.

The techniques of trade-off or conjoint analysis described in Chapter 9 are better for getting information on the bidding process. As mentioned earlier, the Western Oceanic drilling company conducted a conjoint analysis to determine the important factors for oil companies awarding drilling contracts. A small interview sample of drilling superintendents and purchasing agents ranked various combinations of price, safety, and other important performance factors. Based on the conjoint analysis, a number of important decisions were made about what bids should be made and when. As a result of these decisions, the utilization rate for Western Oceanic's drilling rigs went from 39 to 93 percent.[8]

Determining the Best Bid

Probabilistic bidding models assist the firm in determining a bid price that optimizes the combination of the probability of winning and of making a profit if the bid wins. The optimal bid is the bid that offers the highest expected contribution to profit and overhead. The expected contribution of a bid $E(B)$ is determined by multiplying the probability of winning with a bid, $P(B)$, by the difference between the bid price and the estimated direct costs $(B - C)$:

$$E(B) = (B - C) \times P(B) \qquad \textbf{(19.1)}$$

Table 19.3 and Fig. 19.1 illustrate the relationship between the probability of winning and expected contribution. The maximum expected profit occurs with a bid of 115. The expectation curve in Fig. 19.1 shows the expected profit contribution corresponding to each bid. The optimal bid is 115, or 15 percent above the direct cost. Zero expectation will always occur at a bid equal to direct cost. A bid below direct costs will always have a negative expectation and bids above direct costs will range upward from zero to an upper value,

[8]Ibid.

TABLE 19.3   Expected Contributions in Relation to Size of Bid

Bid as a Percentage of Direct Cost (B)	Probability of Bid Winning [P(B)]	Contribution Margin, % (B − C)	Expected Contribution from Bid, % [E(B)]
80	1.00	−20	−20
85	1.00	−15	−15
90	1.00	−10	−10
95	1.00	−5	−5
100	0.88	0	0
105	0.73	5	3.65
110	0.60	10	6.00
115	0.42	15	6.30
120	0.24	20	4.80
125	0.07	25	1.75
130	0.01	30	0.30
135	0	35	0
140	0	40	0

and then taper off, reaching zero again for bids far above direct costs.

Sometimes a firm may wish to maximize expected contributions, but only with some minimum probability of winning the bid. For example, assume that a firm wishes to have at least a probability of 0.60 of winning the contract. The firm is in need of some work, has sufficient short-term financial resources, and does not feel the need to maximize its expected contributions. As Table 19.3 shows, a bid of 110 is the best bid because the expected contribution of 6 percent is the best under the probability-of-winning constraint.

On the other hand, the firm may already be operating near capacity and will only consider new business if it has higher than usual contributions. If, for example, the firm decides that a contribution of 20 percent is the lowest it will accept, then a bid of 120 maximizes the expected contribution subject to the contribution margin constraint.

As these examples indicate, frequently a firm will change its bidding objectives depending on the overall bidding situation. Regardless of the objective selected, the firm ultimately must trade off the chances of winning against maximizing expected contributions to select the best bid. The procedures outlined above allow management to consider the firm's objectives, its market and financial positions, current and future competition, and current and future opportunities to select the

FIGURE 19.1   **Relation between Probability of Winning and Expected Contribution**

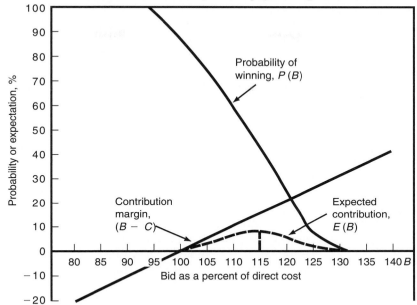

best bidding strategy. Moreover, these procedures also allow management to *subjectively* change the data to reflect current perceptions of the bidding situation.

Contingent Contracts

Often, neither the bidding firm nor the bid-taking organization has complete information about the costs of performing the service or developing and providing the product or the value to be derived from receiving the service or using the product. As illustrated by the EMS example in Chapter 8, the cost of providing the service and the value of the service cannot be determined exactly at the time the contract is bid and awarded. Thus contingency contracts are used when these types of uncertainties are present in the contractual relationship to share the risks. Another aspect of the risks involved in these situations is that the parties involved have different amounts of information available when making the decision. Presumably, the performing organization has more and better information about its capabilities and costs, and the purchasing organization has better information about the relative value of the product or service to it.

One form of contingency contract is a cost-plus contract. This type of contract addresses the issue of determining the amount of "guaranteed" profit for the performing organization. However, the purchasing organization faces considerably more risk under such a contract because it offers no incentives to prevent cost overruns. Instead it gives the performing firm a guarantee for a certain level of profit. (The government has been beset by such contracts in recent years.) An incentive or risk-sharing contract would provide some relief from a cost-plus contract. For example, the performing firm might agree to pay for 20 percent of any cost overrun. Another example of a contingency contract is the EMS contract (see the example in Chapter 8) in which the engineering firm guaranteed the school system energy savings at the risk of forfeiting its fee.

In a contingency-value contract, the bidding firm uses the amount of the incentive it builds into the bid as a signal of its performance capabilities. That is, other things remaining the same, the more of the cost overrun the firm is willing to share, the greater is the likelihood that its cost estimates will be correct. Thus the bidding firm's contingency terms help the bid-taking organization to screen bids that have been submitted.[9]

Bidding with Capacity Constraints

A firm may be offered the opportunity to bid on a project when it is operating near full capacity. In such a situation, the contribution margin criterion is insufficient to help the firm set its bidding strategy. When operating at or near full capacity, the firm is in a position to allocate its resources to *maximize contributions per resource unit*. Chapter 11 developed this criterion and showed its application to product-line pricing. When capacity constraints exist, the bidding firm should substitute the contribution per resource unit criterion for contribution margin in the analytical procedures developed in this chapter, and then proceed as usual.

Summary

This chapter has presented an overview of the problem of developing bids for providing products or services on an order basis. It has explored applications of direct costing and

[9]William Samuelson, "Bidding for Contracts," *Management Science 32* (December 1986), 1533–50.

considerations of competitive strategy and capacity constraints. The most serious limitation of a probabilistically developed bidding strategy is the assumption that competitors will follow the same bidding behavior in the future that they followed in the past. There is no guarantee that this assumption will prevail. Hence it is important that any analytical procedure allow management to change the data based on subjective criteria that reflect its perceptions. Competitive bidding models provide management with useful and objective procedures for developing appropriate pricing strategies.

Discussion Questions

1. Compare fixed pricing to price setting by using auctions. What conditions favor using auctions to set price?
2. What are the advantages and disadvantages of the types of auctions listed in Table 19.1? Find some real examples of these types of auctions.
3. What is the most difficult part of preparing a competitive bid? Why?
4. Why should a firm perform an analysis to determine whether to prepare a bid?

Suggested Readings

Ashenfelter, Orley: "How Auctions Work for Wine and Art," *Journal of Economic Perspectives 3* (Summer 1989), 23–36.

Bandyopadhyay, Subir, GuangBo Lin, and Yan Zhong: "Under the Gavel: Smart Marketers Are Sold on Online Auctions," *Marketing Management 10,* no. 4 (2001), 24–28.

McAfee, R. Preston, and John McMillan: "Auctions and Bidding," *Journal of Economic Literature 25* (June 1987), 699–738.

Milgrom, Paul: Auctions and Bidding: A Primer," *Journal of Economic Perspectives 3* (Summer 1989), 3–22.

Rothkopf, Michael, and Ronald M. Harstad: "Modeling Competitive Bidding: A Critical Essay," *Management Science 40* (March 1994), 364–84.

Samuelson, William: "Bidding for Contracts," *Management Science 32* (December 1986), 1533–550.

CHAPTER TWENTY

Extending the Concepts of Strategic Pricing

As mentioned in Chapter 1, the developed economies around the globe have increasingly been shifting from their product-based history to a service base. In part, this change has resulted from a level of income for a majority of people that allows for more leisure activities. But this shift also reflects some important changes in life styles and values. There has been an increasing emphasis on education, health and personal care, private and publicly funded care and assistance programs, entertainment and travel, financial and insurance services, and various types of advising and counseling services, to name some wide-ranging examples.

Another trend noted in Chapter 1 is the "globalization" of markets, the increasing foreign competition in domestic and foreign markets. The development of trade agreements that expand regional economic areas, the unification of the Western European economy, the continuing industrialization of the developing countries and the Pacific Rim countries, as well as the use of the Internet for sourcing supplies on a global basis, have increased the pressure on pricing products and services.

Over time, service marketing has spawned a lengthy list of terms that euphemistically replace the term *price*. For example, we pay a postage *rate* to the United States Postal Service. *Fees* are paid to doctors and dentists. We pay *premiums* for insurance coverage, *rent* for apartments, *tuition* for education, and *fares* for taxis, buses, and airlines. Also, we pay *tolls* to cross a bridge and *admission* to go to a sporting event, concert, movie, or museum. Banks may have *user fees* for credit charges, *minimum required balances* for a checking account service, *rents* for safety deposit boxes, and *fees* or *interest charges* for automatic teller machine (ATM) use or cash advances. Moreover, in international marketing *tariffs* and *duties* are paid to import goods into another country.

As we wade through this variety of terms, we often fail to recognize that the setting of a rent, interest rate, premium, fee, admission charge, or toll is a pricing decision exactly like the price of a product purchased in a store. Moreover, most organizations that set these fees, rates, and the like must also develop a price structure. That is, for all the services offered, decisions related to discounts, terms of payment, different types of client, and the like must be made exactly as discussed in Chapters 16 and 17. Moreover, a proactive pricing approach is a strategic necessity, and just as for products, the price setter must understand how pricing works, how customers perceive price, and how customers develop perceptions of value.

Another important prescription for service marketing is that the price setter must understand the behavioral objectives of the price decision. That is, whether the financial goal is make a profit or to break even (say for the U.S. Postal Service or the YMCA), the price setter must understand how price is used to influence buyers' behavior so the financial goal can be achieved. For example, the athletic department of a major university recognized that it needed to increase revenues from revenue-producing sporting events to help defray the increasing costs of running the athletic program. Recognizing that several football games were usually sold out and that others barely sold 50 percent of the seating capacity, the marketing manager developed several different season ticket plans as well as a differential per-game admission fee to reflect the differential perceived value of the various football games. Average attendance increased from 60 percent of capacity to 78 percent of capacity in the first year, and increased to 86 percent in the second year. Net revenues for the admission fee plan substantially increased from previous years.

Pricing Services

One important characteristic of most services is that they are primarily of the retailing type. That is, the seller or provider of the service deals directly with the final buyer or user. In fact, in many cases, the work or performance of the seller *is* the service. The final buyer may be a business firm, a government agency, an institution, or an individual. Unlike retailers of tangible goods, service retailers generally cannot rely on a manufacturer to produce the offering or to assist in determining the service's price. In effect, service retailers produce and distribute the service to purchasers or users.

Services are distinct in that relevant costs for profitability analysis are determined by an approach different from the usual standard costing systems. As Chapters 10 through 12 explained, relevant costs for pricing purposes are identified by focusing on the activity or function being performed rather than thinking in terms of production variable costs such as materials and direct labor. Because many service organizations have little or no direct material costs, and some, such as the airlines or hotels and restaurants, have proportionately fewer direct labor costs, it becomes very important to focus on those costs that are attributable to the provision and sale of the particular service activity.[1]

Another unusual characteristic of services is that most consumers are unable to assess the price–quality relationship prior to purchase, and often they cannot assess even after purchase and use.[2] Moreover, consumers do not appear to learn the prices of many commonly used services.[3] As indicated in Chapters 2 through 7, the more people know about the relative relationship between price and quality, the more likely they are to be sensitive to price differences. Moreover, for some services, such as medical and legal counsel (that is, credence good; see Chapters 3 and 4), the inability to evaluate the service even after acquisition makes service buying more risky. In such situations, it is more likely that buyers will be less sensitive to price and will ascribe quality on the basis of the price charged. However, these characteristics of services make it even more imperative that service marketers make every effort to understand how their customers use and benefit from the services the organization offers. Customers are often confused about the prices they pay and are

---

[1]John Dearden, "Cost Accounting Comes to Service Industries," *Harvard Business Review 56* (September–October 1978), 132–40.

[2]Joseph P. Guiltinan, "A Conceptual Framework for Pricing Consumer Services," *Designing a Winning Service Strategy*, eds. Mary Jo Bitner and Lawrence A. Crosby (Chicago: American Marketing Association, 1989), 11–15.

[3]L. W. Turley and Roy F. Cabaniss, "Price Knowledge for Services: An Empirical Investigation," *Journal of Professional Services 12,* no. 1 (1995), 39–52.

uncertain whether they have received the best value available. This confusion may lead to mistrust and requests for government intervention and regulation.

The prescriptions for communicating value and for making prices transparent to customers presented earlier in this book (see especially Chapter 8) apply particularly to services. The complexity and often risk in buying many services underscore the need to be open and straightforward when establishing pricing strategies and tactics for services. As our discussion on price fairness in Chapter 7 indicated, prices are more likely to be perceived as fair when customers understand how they are determined and that they are receiving value comparable to other buyers. Several broad approaches to service pricing can be used independently or jointly to achieve an effective pricing approach.[4]

To alleviate customers' uncertainty about the quality of services that might be provided, the service provider can offer a guarantee for the service. That is, as discussed in Chapter 4, the provider could offer a refund or a reduction in the amount paid if customers are dissatisfied with the service. Offering a guarantee provides a signal of the provider's commitment to provide quality service and confidence that it will provide the level of service quality desired by its customers. To be effective, such signals of the provider's commitment must also reveal either a cost already incurred or a future cost that would be incurred if the service is below the level of quality guaranteed.

As Chapter 8 pointed out, understanding the benefits that the service provides customers is an important characteristic of value pricing. When customers can relate the prices or charges to the benefits they receive, they are more likely to be able to judge that the value received is commensurate to the price paid.

Sometimes engaging a service firm means that the price to be paid for the service will not be known until the service has been completely rendered. For example, the cost of legal services may depend on the amount of time the lawyers and other personnel spend on the various aspects of the case. While the billing rate per hour may be predetermined, the number of hours that will be billed cannot be determined in advance. One approach to handle this uncertainty is for the service provider to establish a flat-rate price for the service.

[4]Leonard L. Berry and Manjit S. Yadav, "Capture and Communicate Value in the Pricing of Services," *Sloan Management Review 37* (Summer 1996), 41–51.

For example, a tax accountant might charge $100 per tax return completed, regardless of the complexity of any specific return.

Pricing Financial Services

Customers of financial services pay not only in "hard" money such as coins and currency, checks, drafts, and credit cards, but also indirectly in the forms of balances that are kept on deposit. If customers are required to leave non-interest-bearing balances on deposit, or balances that earn less than market rate of interest (the rate of interest they could get elsewhere), then the customers give value to the institution because it can invest these balances to earn additional revenues. This concept of *fees and balances* is unique to financial institutions and is fundamental to pricing financial services.

Whether to charge explicit fees for financial services or require balances on deposit should be considered from the perspective of a bank's customers. As Table 20.1 indicates, the argument for fees versus balances depends on how customers perceive the relative differences between these two ways of pricing financial services. Point 3 stems from the 1980 Depository Institutions Deregulation and Monetary Control Act, which requires a bank to hold in its vault or at a Federal Reserve Bank up to 12 percent of its total deposits as a reserve. These funds cannot be invested by the bank and therefore are not available to accrue interest for customers.

To determine the appropriate relationship between a balance pricing system and a fee pricing system, a financial institution must evaluate four interrelated components: (1) the price or fee, (2) the annual equivalent of a monthly fee, (3) the earnings credit rate (what the institution would need to pay to obtain the deposit balance in the market), and (4) adjustments for nonearning assets (that is, the ratio

TABLE 20.1
Arguments for Fees versus Balances—Customer's Point of View

Fees	Balances
1. Customer earns a return on money rather than paying for services	Customer is unable or not inclined to earn a market return on money
2. Customer can apply fees against tax obligation	Customer cannot apply fees against tax obligation
3. Fractional reserve system requires a percentage of deposits held	Financial institution does not have a large reserve requirement

of nonearning assets to earning assets, for example, reserve requirements).[5]

Determining the relationship between a required balance and a fee represents only one aspect of the development of a pricing structure for an interest-bearing checking account. Many other pricing decisions must be made:

1. Should there be a charge for each draft or check written, and if so, what should it be?

2. How much should be charged for each deposit transaction?

3. How many checks or drafts may be written before a charge or fee is applied?

4. How much should be charged for "excessive check" usage?

5. What should be charged for returned canceled checks?

6. What should a stop-payment order cost?

7. How much should be charged for insufficient funds?

8. What should personalized checks cost?

9. Should a customer pay for help in balancing a checkbook, and if so, how much?

10. What should be the minimum account balance, below which no interest will be paid to the depositor?

As with product pricing, these decisions must weigh the institution's costs and revenues for the service against the benefits customers perceive and value. Depending on the actual figures for these components and the behavioral objectives for the bank, the alternative fee versus balance relationship can be adjusted. For example, if the bank wants more people to leave larger balances in their transaction or demand-deposit accounts, then reducing the monthly fee while increasing the required average deposit balance to qualify for reduced-cost or free checking will help to achieve this objective. People who qualify for the perceived "free" service will have increased perceptions of value (see Chapter 8). This decision will also depend on the type of competition that the financial institution faces.

---

[5]G. Michael Moebs and Eva Moebs, *Pricing Financial Services* (Homewood, IL: Dow Jones-Irwin, 1986).

Automated teller machines (ATMs) have become widespread, and many banks use them to increase their service hours while minimizing the demand on tellers for many routine transactions. The typical pricing approaches have been to charge nothing for the service, to charge by transaction, to charge a monthly or annual card fee, or some combination of these elements. Indeed, the most typical pricing approach when introducing an ATM was to offer it "free." Later, when attempting to recover some of the costs associated with the ATM, banks began charging a fee of some sort. However, the issue now becomes one of determining the relative perceived value to the customers of having an ATM card versus standing in line for a teller during normal banking hours. Box 20.1 illustrates the way such fees have become an important part of banks' revenues.

Pricing Bank Card Services

Another popular service that banks and other financial institutions provide is the extension of credit through Mastercard, Visa, or similar credit and debit cards. To develop a pricing structure for this service, the price setter must balance the costs of providing the service against the benefits provided to the cardholders and the merchants who accept the card in lieu of money. The bank provides two services to the cardholder: (1) a transaction service—that is, a mechanism to complete a purchase without using money—and (2) a credit service—the extension of a short-term line of credit before paying for the transactions. For the merchants, the bank provides a transaction service and a collection service.

From the banks' perspective, offering credit cards involves a fixed cost of maintaining each active card account, a variable cost for each transaction (that is, the number of entries or transactions), and a cost of extending credit to the cardholder. Costs also include establishing the account and periodically issuing a card to the cardholder. The pricing issue is how to develop a pricing structure that offers customers enough perceived value from the benefits received to encourage them to use the cards while allowing the bank to recover its costs of offering the service and earning a reasonable profit for it.

Selecting the appropriate pricing structure depends on understanding how customers value the credit card service, how they use the card, and the financial institution's behavioral objective for pricing the card service. If the institution

INCREASING BANKING FEES   BOX 20.1

During the 1990s, U.S. banks introduced a number of fees for their services. According to the *Fee Income Report,* there were more than 250 different types of bank fees in 1996 compared with 96 in 1990, and the average annual cost of an account rose from $155.30 in 1990 to $184.16 in 1993, an increase nearly twice the rate of inflation.

Why did banks begin to charge fees for services that used to be free? A major reason was that after deregulation in 1981, banks competed with many competitors, such as mutual funds, brokerages, credit-card issuers, credit unions and even check cashing firms. The banks' share of the financial services market eroded dramatically. From 1975 to 1995, the portion of U.S. household financial assets held in bank deposits fell from 25.8 percent to 13.7 percent. Facing severe competition, banks began to rely more on fees as a source of income because the revenue from lending and investing was shrinking. In 1994, fees produced 34 percent of the industry's $44.7 billion in profits.

Banks increased fees either by charging more for services such as money orders and bounced checks, or by adding new services, such as charging $0.50 to $1.50 for an ATM transaction, $2 to $3 for using a teller for transactions that could be done through an ATM, or even for part of the cost of protection provided by the Federal Deposit Insurance Corp.

Banks have insisted that the fees are justified and honest. Some banks said that fees were used to modify customer behaviors, such as encouraging them to use the ATM instead of human teller, to reduce costs, and eventually to benefit customers. However, the resistance from customers and even politicians was strong. According to a senior partner at Andersen Consulting in 1995, "A large proportion of the population believes they have a constitutional right to free banking service." Consumers in some states pushed for legislation to control bank fees, though with little success.

Banks were facing a difficult situation. On one hand, they found it necessary to increase fees as a revenue source. On the other hand, they ran the risk of alienating and losing customers by establishing new fees. Some banks found out that communicating with customers was critical in getting their understanding and maintaining customer loyalty. For example, First National Bank of Chicago (now Bank One) became the target of jokes throughout the industry and was skewered on national television after it announced plans to scrap its traditional checking and savings account offerings. The bank replaced these traditional accounts with a new account offering customers a choice of paying a fee to see a teller for some transactions or maintaining a minimum balance to see a teller for free. In spite of the tide of criticism, the bank did several things to obtain customers' understanding. They sent letters to customers explaining the new policy, placed full-page advertisements in the local media promoting the benefit of the new policy, installed hotlines for customers to call in and get information, and made some adjustments to the plan to provide more value to their customers. According to the bank, the number of accounts with the bank remained the same two months after announcing the new policy and though "Banking has never been in the news the way it was with the $3 teller fee, we won that chess game."

Sources: "Dare to be Different," *ABA Banking Journal* (September 1995), 65–66; John Schmeltzer, "First National Charges Ahead with Teller Fees," *Chicago Tribune* (June, 1, 1995), C1, 3; John Schmeltzer, "Banks Waging Fee Wars and Winning," *Chicago Tribune* (March 18, 1996), Section 4, 2; Alison Rea, "Why Rising Bank Fees Are Backfiring," *Business Week* (August 19, 1996), 66; Amy Dunkin, "Getting Soaked by Soaring Bank Fees?" *Business Week* (September 20, 1993), 108.

CUSTOMER PROFITABILITY ANALYSIS AND THE PRICING OF CREDIT CARDS

BOX 20.2

As Box 12.3 indicated, customer profitability analysis is important for the success of financial institutions. Banks and other financial institutions offer a variety of complicated products and services that affect pricing. However, thanks to customer tracking techniques, it is a lot easier to assess the profitability of even an individual customer. This same analysis is influencing the pricing of credit cards.

In 1996, GE Capital decided to charge a $25 annual fee to its members who paid their balances in full each month, while simultaneously lowering the interest rate from 17.1 percent to 11.9 percent. The reason behind this decision was that customers who paid their balances in full were actually not profitable for credit card issuers. Finance charges produce 76 percent of card issuers' revenues, and these "good" customers do not contribute to such revenues. The simultaneous interest rate reduction was designed to attract more profitable customers who would delay their payment and thus provide interest income to GE Capital. The firm was not concerned that the new policy might drive away 20 percent of its users because those who would be driven away were not profitable.

Despite GE's move to a lower interest rate, other bank cards began to charge higher interest rates, hoping to stop an increase in debt delinquencies. In 1996, the average interest rate reached 18 percent, yet a majority of American cardholders did not pay off their credit card balance, resulting in an average balance of $3,900 per cardholder. Knowing that risky customers would be very costly to serve, issuers asked for higher rates and began targeting specific high-risk customers.

Sources: "Dunned If You Do, Dunned If You Don't," *Business Week* (September 23, 1996), 130–31; Mitchell Schnurman, "Credit Firms Say Stricter Penalties, Higher Fees Needed," *The News-Gazette* (November 28, 1996), B-6; Sanford Rose, "The ATM Is Not a 'Profit Center,'" *Journal of Retail Banking* 16 (Winter 1994–95), 5–6; William T. Gregor and Jonathan M. Sandler, "The Outlook for Consumer Payment Services," *The Bankers Magazine* (January/February 1995), 18–23.

would like to change customers from a credit card to a debit card (which deducts the amount of the purchase from the person's bank account), then it also must understand customers' purchase and payment behaviors and devise pricing strategies that reflect this understanding. To simply offer a credit card service for free, or to suddenly establish an annual or monthly fee schedule without understanding the consumers who use the cards, would be a mistake.[6] Moreover, establishing a means for analyzing different types of consumers who use credit cards would lead to a better understanding of which customers use the service without paying for it—which customers' service costs are greater than the

[6]Robert W. Johnson, "Pricing of Bank Card Services," *Journal of Retail Banking* 1 (June 1979), 16–22.

revenues the bank generates for providing the service. Box 20.2 provides information on how credit card companies are using profitability analysis in their pricing decisions.

Pricing Online Information Services

The ability to retrieve information from databases for personal or business use has grown at a dramatic rate. However, for information service providers to become proactive pricers, they must understand how pricing works and how customers perceive prices and price changes.

Understanding pricing and customers' perceptions in the context of online services requires determining what buyers are purchasing when they query an online service and why they want the "product." People buy online services because they need information to solve a problem or make a decision. The information has little intrinsic value by itself; its value is relative to the nature of the problem or decision that an individual or organization is facing. In this context, information has value only when it reduces the uncertainty or risk of making a decision or pursuing a course of action without that information. (In some situations, finding through an online search that no other information exists also has value. For example, a researcher whose bibliographic search finds no articles on a specific topic has learned that no one else has published research on this topic, thereby indicating that the researcher is involved in pioneering work.)

As Chapters 5 through 8 argued, perceived value represents a trade-off between customers' perceptions of benefits to be received by using the information relative to the perceived costs of acquiring the information. Although the online service user may know the pricing structure of the distributor or vendor, the buyer rarely knows prior to search what the information to be received will actually cost.[7] For example, if the pricing structure is a fixed charge per hour of connect time plus a print charge, the buyer does not know a priori either the amount of time the search will take or how much information will be printed out. Similarly, the buyer has no way of anticipating the benefit of the information to be acquired until after it has been received.

A basic pricing approach consists of two types of charges: (1) a fixed fee per inquiry or specific activity, and

---

[7]Arnold A. J. Jansen, "Towards a New Pricing Structure for Online Databases," *Journal of Information Science 10* (1985), 125–30.

(2) a variable price per unit of information received by the searcher. (Depending on the mechanism used to provide the information to the searcher, such as online printing, a fixed and variable rate structure is also required to represent the costs to the provider and the value to the searcher of receiving the information via an online print.) The fixed fee component of the pricing mechanism enables the provider to recover the costs incurred of having the service available regardless of the length of the search in terms of time or amount of information provided. The variable portion of the charges relates to the variable cost of providing the connection over the time period and the relative value to the searcher of the information received. Moreover, assessing a fixed charge and a charge for the portion of the fee that relates to the variable cost of providing the connection is a way to collect revenues even when the search uncovers no information. As indicated earlier, such a result does have value to the client. Box 20.3 shows how a two-part pricing structure can work in practice.

The pricing mechanism can also be changed to develop a variable pricing structure offering subscription rates (with clearly defined rules of membership), volume discounts, and peak-load and off-peak-load prices. A variable pricing structure can take into account different perceived values by setting differential rates based on the type of file queried, the type of search utilized (e.g., bibliographic versus factual database), and perhaps the nature or type of organization doing the search (e.g., university versus business firm).[8] The markets for these types of services are not homogeneous, and a differential pricing structure can be developed that recognizes differences in buyers' sensitivities to prices due to differences in the perceived value of the information to be received. Developing a pricing structure that reflects an understanding of how buyers perceive the value of information and that encourages buyers to utilize the online service to acquire valuable information should be the pricing goal of online service organizations and distributors.

Pricing Professional Services

Doctors, lawyers, architects, marketing researchers, and consultants typically are highly educated and trained in their

[8]Frances H. Barker, "Pricing of Information Products," *Aslib Proceedings 36* (July/August 1984), 289–97.

REUTERS MOVES TOWARD A BENEFIT-ORIENTED PRICING STRUCTURE BOX 20.3

In January 1995, Reuters, a financial information and news provider, introduced a new pricing structure to the U.K. market as part of its move toward standardized global pricing. The new pricing structure had two key components. First, Reuters provided a new price list for its products and services. Rather than changing prices for a single service, the pricing structure increased prices for a combination of two or more services. The second component was a shift away from a flat-rate access price to a per-user pricing structure (actually a change in Reuter's two-part pricing structure).

Before the pricing change, users paid a relatively high monthly charge for access and a low per-user charge based on the amount of data monitored simultaneously. This new pricing structure meant that larger users, who previously were able to spread the high monthly access charge over many workstations, now faced an increase in the per-user (variable) price for access to the data. On the other hand, smaller users would now pay a much lower monthly fee and a lower total price for data access because of the small number of users. For example, the monthly fee for one of the products, Selectfeed, went from £5,000 a month to £1,100. The revised cost of the monthly service was more in line with the actual benefits users, small and large, received from subscribing to this information service.

Source: Sharona Talmor, "The Price of Change," *The Banker* (December 1994), 73–75.

specific fields of practice. Although there is a common belief that professionals charge too much for their services, most professionals complain that they are unable to make a reasonable profit.

Some professions, such as architecture, once had an industry ethical code preventing professionals from price competition to "protect the ethical integrity and quality of the work." However, with the antitrust movement in the 1960s and 1970s, the Sherman Act began to cover professions, and the practice of industrywide price protection was ruled illegal price fixing.[9] This ruling led to more competition among professionals on the basis of price. For example, beginning in 1971, architects were allowed to submit competitive bids and provide discounts or even free services.

The most common pricing method for professional services today is billing clients on an hourly basis.[10] Even those

[9]Elizabeth Harrison Kubany and Charles D. Linn, "Why Architects Don't Charge Enough," *Architectural Record 187* (October 1999), 110–21.
[10]Victoria Arnold, "Believe It or Not, Most Professionals Don't Charge Enough," *Journal of Pricing Management 1* (Spring 1990), 57–59.

professionals who set prices on a project basis usually do so by estimating hours performed by each individual assigned to that project. The widely used "rule of three" is to bill at an hourly rate that is three times the hourly wage of the individual(s) performing the service. Ideally, one-third goes to salary, one-third covers overhead, and the rest is gross profit. However, there are two problems with this method. One is that firms often underestimate the actual cost of their overhead, which has been increasing in recent years. For example, the overhead cost in law firms has been estimated at 45 percent of the total project cost instead of the 33 percent assumed in the "rule of three." The old rule leaves the firms with only 20 percent gross profit, rather than the expected 33 percent. Another more fundamental problem is that billing by hour is conceptually wrong because it suggests that professional firms are selling time, not the talent and knowledge of professionals (see our earlier comment about the flaw in this practice when pricing information services). To move to value-oriented pricing, professional firms must educate their clients to understand the value created by professional services, not just the time spent by professionals.

The following principles can help improve the pricing and profitability of professional firms:

1. *Communicate value.* Base the price on the value created by the service. For example, a personal financial advisor should be rewarded by the additional value created by his or her financial suggestions and marketing service companies can be rewarded by the effectiveness of their marketing campaigns, ad designs, and promotions. Although it is difficult to estimate the monetary value of services in some professions, there are some creative ways to measure value. HLW International, an architect firm, measured value delivered by evaluating the difference in satisfaction of its clients before and after moving into a new building.[11]

2. *Understand costs.* As just mentioned, professional firms do not understand overhead costs very well and tend to underestimate them. Chapters 10 and 11 explained that professional firms must trace the activities performed for specific clients, such as transportation, office supply, and secretarial services. Outsourcing some duties, such as preparing documents and arranging conferences, will reduce the time service professionals spend on non-revenue-generating activities.

[11]Elizabeth Harrison Kubany and Charles D. Linn, "How to Increase Your Fees in a Tough Market," *Architectural Record 187* (November 1999), 60–67, 198.

3. *Cross-sell services.* If increasing service fees is not an appropriate decision given the nature of competition, firms should consider cross-selling other services. For example, banks benefit not only from selling their own products, but also from earning commissions from selling complementary products of other financial institutions, such as traveler's checks.

4. *Standardization and customization.* Standardizing some regular services reduces time spent on these tasks without affecting the quality of the service. The essence of standardization is to utilize the same knowledge in different applications in order to extract a maximum return from it. At the other extreme is customizing services provided to individual clients. Some firms are better at customizing services for each client and receiving a premium price. If clients understand the value of customized services, the firm can increase profitability.

5. *Train personnel.* It is the talent of the firm's personnel that creates value, not their time. Training the service providers and keeping them on the forefront of their practice is a long-term strategy to enhance customer satisfaction. For many professions, customer satisfaction is more important in their selection of a service provider than is price.

Pricing for Export Marketing

Export pricing has become an increasingly important aspect of marketing strategy throughout the world. Pressures brought about by increasing trade liberalization, domestic market saturation, increased price transparency due to the Internet, opening previously protected markets, and other pressures noted in Chapter 1 have made it increasingly difficult for multinational corporations to manage prices across markets. Despite such pressures on managing international business activities, little written information exists on export pricing. In this section we identify some of the problems and issues associated with export pricing.

Export pricing decisions are very complex because they require adapting a number of domestic variables and considering many new variables. Many of these new variables are beyond the ability of the firm to influence directly, but firms must consider them when developing export pricing strategies and tactics. We present six variables that must be considered.

Product

A product that has a technological edge, thereby limiting the number of local or foreign competitors, enhances pricing flexibility. In addition, if the importing country has few import barriers or other regulations, pricing flexibility is further enhanced. On the other hand, when foreign competitors can use low price as an entry tactic, pricing flexibility is diminished. In addition, situations in which the raw materials used to produce the product are subject to market price fluctuations require increased price review and flexibility. Essentially, then, the amount of pricing flexibility or discretion a firm has in exporting depends on the degree to which the product has a competitive advantage in terms of value delivered, the amount of government controls, and the presence or lack of price-oriented competition from other exporting countries.

Location of Production

Many companies have built production and assembly operations abroad to take advantage of raw material sources, lower labor costs, and favorable exchange rates. One of the issues of multinational production plants is how to price products transferred from one division in one country to another division in another country. This issue of international transfer pricing will be discussed later. Another issue that is discussed later involves gray markets that come about when a firm produces in one country but uses differential pricing when it exports to multiple other countries.

Environmental Factors

Environmental factors also affect export pricing. Market entry and effectiveness of prices hinge on economic factors such as exchange rates, rates of inflation, and governmental price controls. Because several of these factors are cyclical in nature, many firms build compensating adjustments into their pricing. When an exporter's own currency is undervalued, a pricing advantage exists; when it is overvalued, the exporter faces a pricing burden. For example, when the U.S. dollar weakens relative to the Japanese yen, significant erosion of Japan's pricing advantage in the U.S. market occurs. Of course, when the U.S. dollar is strong relative to the yen, then the Japanese exporters have a relative price advantage in the U.S. market (see Box 20.4).

Today, all major currencies float freely relative to one another, making it difficult to forecast the value of any one

AUTOMAKERS DISAGREE ON WHO HAS A PRICING ADVANTAGE — BOX 20.4

Early in 2002, the world's economies were struggling and the economies of some countries were in recession. One outcome of this economic situation was that the Japanese yen was relatively weak in comparison to the U.S. dollar. Indeed, the president of General Motors' North American automotive operations claimed that Japanese automakers had enjoyed a 30 percent cost advantage over the previous three years due to the weak value of the yen. He estimated that the Japanese had an average cost advantage of $3,400 per vehicle because of the low value of the yen. At the time he made this public statement, the yen had fallen to a three-year low of ¥133.5/$1. He went on to indicate that with a cost advantage of $3,400, the Japanese had considerable flexibility to lower prices, increase profits, or put more money into other marketing activities.

However, the general manager of Toyota countered by saying that two-thirds of the 1.5 million vehicles that Toyota had sold in the United States the previous year were built in the United States, with an average domestic content of 75 percent. "Toyota makes money in the U.S. because of its products, not foreign-exchange rates," he said. "If you want to be successful in the marketplace, you have to build good products....We weren't complaining when the yen was at ¥80/$1. Some people should stop complaining and start competing."

The president of Ford Motor Co. supported GM, saying "What they're doing is taking back better profit from this country, and I think they can be called windfall profits."

Source: Jim Mateja and Rick Popely, "GM Exec Contends Weak Yen Providing Hefty Pricing Edge," *Chicago Tribune* (February 8, 2002), Section 3, 2.

currency. It is important to understand the effect of currency fluctuations on a product's profitability and the product's competitive position in a foreign market. For example, assume a U.S. company sells products and materials to its sales division in another country in U.S. currency. The foreign sales division sells the product to its customers in that country. Assume that these customers have a fixed price agreement in that country's currency (FC) of FC55,000. As Table 20.2a shows, if the exchange rate is FC5/$1, the foreign sales division earns a profit margin of FC5,000 per sale.

However, if the U.S. dollar weakens relative to the FC to an exchange rate of FC4.5/$1, then the cost in the FC decreases and the foreign sales division earns a profit of FC10,000 per sale (Table 20.2b). But if the dollar strengthens relative to the FC to an exchange rate of FC5.5/$1, then the cost in FC increases and the foreign sales division has no profit margin. Thus with a fixed transfer price to the subsidiary and a fixed foreign customer price, the operating profits of the foreign sales division fluctuates with the currency exchange fluctuations.

TABLE 20.2 **Effect of Exchange Rates on Profit Margins**

Product Cost ($)	Exchange Rate	Foreign Currency Cost (FC)	+ Profit Margin (FC)	= Price (FC)
a. 10,000	FC5/$1	50,000	5,000	55,000
b. 10,000	FC4.5/$1	45,000	10,000	55,000
c. 10,000	FC5.5/$1	55,000	0	55,000

Now suppose the foreign sales division competes directly with a firm that has a manufacturing facility in the foreign country. When the dollar weakens relative to the FC, as in Table 20.2b, if there is no fixed price agreement the sales division has some pricing flexibility relative to its competitors. For example, it could lower its price by FC5,000 and still make a profit margin of FC5,000.

However, when the dollar becomes stronger as in Table 20.2c, then this pricing flexibility disappears, and the sales division may have to raise its price to obtain a profit margin. Because the local competitor does not have this currency exchange problem, it may now have a pricing advantage. Thus, many companies insist that terms of trade be in the selling company's national currency. Also, many companies engage in hedging in the money market. Especially when writing long-term contracts, companies must factor into the contract changes in the currency exchange rates as well as inflation. Otherwise, the company may end up providing large and unintended discounts (see our earlier discussion in Chapter 16 about reviewing quantity discount structures due to inflationary effects).

Attitude toward Export Marketing

Many small and medium-sized U.S. companies view exporting as a cure for excess production or as a safeguard against difficulties in the domestic market. As a result, top management does not put much effort into the exporting aspect of the business. Many export managers therefore use relatively simple pricing approaches such as full costing as opposed to a more customer-oriented value approach.[12] Pricing tends to

---

[12]Nikolaos Tzokas, Susan Hart, Paraskevas Argouslidis, and Michael Saren, "Industrial Export Pricing Practices in the United Kingdom," *Industrial Marketing Management 29* (May 2000), 191–204; Barbara Stottinger, "Strategic Export Pricing: A Long and Winding Road," *Journal of International Marketing 9,* no. 1 (2001), 40–63; Mary Anne Raymond, John F. Tanner Jr., and Jonghoon Kim, "Cost Complexity of Pricing Decisions for Exporters in Developing and Emerging Markets," *Journal of International Marketing 9,* no. 3 (2001), 19–40.

be inflexible and problems often develop because of this approach.

On the other hand, successful exporting companies tend to be flexible in their pricing and are likely to use an adaptive, incremental pricing strategy. This approach ignores domestic marketing and promotion costs, along with domestic overhead costs and fixed plant and equipment costs. It views exports as incremental business and considers only relevant costs (variable and fixed) of the international business. Consequently, these companies are highly flexible in their pricing and are able to adapt to changing competitive and environmental conditions in different countries.

Distribution System

The channels of export distribution have an important effect on pricing control. If a firm transfers its products to a subsidiary operating in another country, greater pricing control exists than if it uses an independent distributor. Executives have reported that distributors often mark up the prices substantially beyond the manufacturer's intent—up to 200 percent in some instances. This problem is compounded if the firm uses several levels of distributors in reaching its final foreign market. Hence many firms use as direct a method of distribution as possible.

Distribution costs are also affected by the size of the distribution system, which in many countries is underdeveloped relative to North America. Many distributors and retailers are small businesses and do not trade in the same volumes.[13] Transportation costs of moving goods to other countries and associated costs of packing, handling, and insurance are standard in the export business. Because import tariffs and taxes are based on the total landed costs, these additional transportation and associated costs further escalate the final price in international markets. *Price escalation* refers to the higher prices for the same goods in international markets relative to domestic markets. These higher prices reflect additional shipping costs, tariffs, taxes, larger distributor margins, longer distribution channels, and exchange rate fluctuations.

Gray Markets

Imagine yourself to be a Japanese tourist visiting the United States. You find a Japanese-made camera in the store that is

---

[13]Philip R. Cateora, *Strategic International Marketing* (Homewood. IL.: Dow Jones-Irwin, 1985), 199.

sold at a lower price than it is in Japan. Then you find a famous Scottish whiskey, also sold at a much lower price than in Japan. You buy these things and wonder to yourself: "If I can start a business buying these products here and shipping them back to Japan, I would soon be a rich person." This example illustrates the basic concept of a *gray market,* which is defined as parallel distribution of genuine goods by intermediaries other than authorized channel members. In the international context, gray marketing refers to the importation of genuine goods into a country by an intermediary other than the authorized distributors in that country. Gray marketers buy goods from another country—from an authorized distributor, consumers, or sometimes directly from the manufacturer—at a price lower than the prevailing price in the importing country. Because gray markets coexist with the authorized distribution of goods, the gray market system is also referred to as "parallel importation." As Figure 20.1 illustrates, parallel importation can occur in three ways:[14]

1. *Parallel importation*: Gray marketer (unauthorized distributor) buys the product in country 1 where the product is made and sells it in another country (3).

2. *Reimportation*: Gray marketer buys the product in country 2 and sells it back to the country where the product is made.

3. *Lateral gray importation*: Gray marketer buys and sells in two countries, neither of which is the country of product origin.

It is important to distinguish gray markets from black markets. A gray market is not necessarily illegal per se, as is a black market, because the merchandise sold is genuine goods, not counterfeits, and the import and export procedure typically is legally proper.

Extent of Gray Market Activity

Gray marketing occurs not only for consumer products, but also industrial products. The products most likely to be involved in gray marketing are premium brands of automobiles, cameras, watches, computers, perfumes, wine, champagne, glassware, tires, and construction equipment. Industrial sources estimate that about 10 percent of personal computer

[14]Gert Assmus and Carsten Wiese, "How to Address the Gray Market Threat Using Price Coordination," *Sloan Management Review 36* (Spring 1995), 31–41.

FIGURE 20.1   Gray Markets

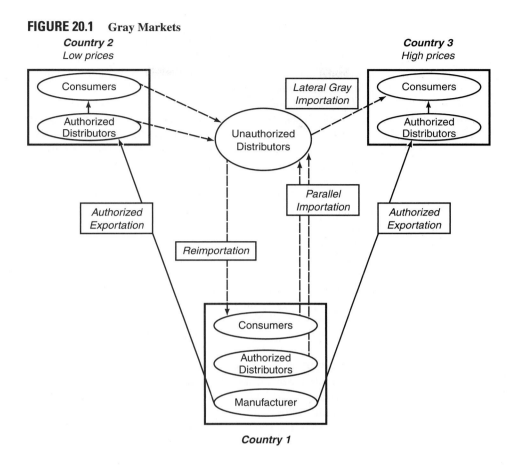

sales and 20 percent of electronic copier sales are accounted for by unauthorized channels in the United States. In 1996, estimates placed the total value of products distributed in the United States through gray market channels at $10 billion.[15] Gray market activity is also a worldwide phenomenon, occurring in developing countries and in many developed countries typically considered to be safe and stable.[16]

Management Concerns with Gray Markets

Managers are concerned with gray markets for several reasons. Gray market activities increasingly affect

[15]S. Tamer Cavusgil and Ed Sikora, "How Multinationals Can Counter Gray Market Imports," *Columbia Journal of World Business 23* (Winter 1988), 75–85.
[16]Matthew B. Myers and David A. Griffin, "Strategies for Combating Gray Market Activity," *Business Horizons 42* (November–December 1999), 2–8.

1. *Profitability:* Since identical lower-priced items are available through gray market channels, some customers who would otherwise be willing to pay a higher price buy the products in the gray market, thereby decreasing the profits of the manufacturer and the authorized dealer.

2. *Brand name:* As discussed in earlier chapters, price is not only a measure of sacrifice, but also a signal of quality and therefore value. Premium-priced brands that are marketed at much lower prices in gray markets send out a signal of lower quality for the brand and make it difficult to position the brand as a premium, high-quality brand.

3. *Manufacturer–distributor–customer relationships:* These relationships could become strained because the interests of the parties involved as affected by gray market activities are different. The degree and direction of the impact of gray marketing on manufacturers and distributors are different. For example, a distributor in a low-price market may benefit from gray marketing because he sells a large volume to gray market brokers, whereas the distributor in the high-price market will find sales reduced due to the competition from the lower-price gray market product. The manufacturer may be either better or worse off with gray marketing depending on the relative size of the new low-price market segment that buys the gray market products and the amount of cannibalized sales in the original higher-priced market segment.[17] No matter what the degree of impact is on these different parties, the gray market activity may strain their relationship because of distrust and skepticism toward each other. Moreover, the authorized distributor–customer relationship may also be strained if the customer purchases from the gray market distributor.

4. *Legal liability:* Should a manufacturer be responsible for a product if it is not sold through authorized channels? Should the company be liable if a machine causes an accident in the United States because it does not meet the safety standards there when the machine was actually built for countries with lower standards? Gray market activities create

---

[17]B. Rachel Yang, Reza H. Ahmadi, and Kent B. Monroe, "Pricing in Separable Channels: The Case of Parallel Imports," *Journal of Product & Brand Management Featuring Pricing Strategy & Practice 7,* no. 5 (1998), 433–40; Reza Ahmadi and B. Rachel Yang, "Parallel Imports: Challenges from Unauthorized Distribution Channels," *Marketing Science 19* (Summer 2000), 279–94.

a potential for legal problems, especially when the products fail to meet legal requirements.

5. *Marketing strategy:* Multinational companies usually have developed marketing strategies on a global level. However, the product movement caused by gray market activities may disrupt execution of strategy, thereby reducing the company's ability to control its global strategy and meet profit targets.

Despite these concerns, gray market activity may be beneficial to firms if it occurs in markets where there are a high percentage of price-insensitive customers and a market segment that is price sensitive that would not buy the product at the prevailing high price.[18] In an ideal situation, authorized distributors would keep their customers who are willing to pay a high price for reasons such as better service, product warranty, and prestige, or they may even be able to charge a higher price because they do not need to service the price-sensitive segment anymore. The gray marketer distributor would serve the segment that is willing to pay the lower price. This low-price segment in effect represents incremental sales to the manufacturer with minimal harm to the authorized distributors. Thus, the ultimate effect of gray marketing is the difference between the profit gain due to the newly acquired low-price customers and the profit loss from those customers who shifted from the high-price to the low-price products. This trade-off between sales gained and lost is why some manufacturers tolerate gray marketing to some extent in certain markets.

Why Do Gray Markets Occur?

The fundamental reason gray markets occur is that there is a significant price difference for the same product across markets. As long as the price difference is large enough to offset costs in sourcing, transporting, and importing goods by gray marketers, there is an incentive for gray marketing to occur. Such price differences may occur because

1. Some multinational companies aggressively price products differently depending on the relative degree of price sensitivity in individual national markets. For example, one pharmaceutical company, using Germany

---

[18]David Champion, "The Bright Side of Gray Markets," *Harvard Business Review 76* (September–October 1998), 19, 22.

as its standard of comparison, sold the same product in Spain 20 percent higher and in France 40 percent lower.

2. Fluctuations in the monetary exchange rate may result in widening price differences between different markets. The strong U.S. dollar in the 1980s led to an increase of gray market products into the country. When other currencies grew stronger, the United States gradually became a source country for some gray market products.

3. The inability of a multinational company to synchronize demand and supply in various national markets may lead to shortages of a product in some markets, eventually resulting in an increase in the price level in the undersupplied country and wider price difference between the countries.

Some other conditions that facilitate the growth of gray markets include these:

1. Customer demands across the world are becoming more similar due to the convergence of culture and economy. Products made for a specific market may also be desired by consumers in other markets.

2. Lowered trade barriers makes the importation of gray market products easier and less costly.

3. The use of information technology facilitates information flow about prices and markets, enabling gray market brokers to recognize more business opportunities and give customers easier access to gray market products.

Handling the Gray Market Threat

When a company first encounters a gray market situation, management must remember that allowing this alternative channel to exist might have positive implications. As just described, a gray market channel might provide a way to reach a low-price segment that otherwise might not be served (see a similar point on focused price reductions in Chapter 15). Yet firms often respond by attempting to remove the price difference that leads to a gray market activity or by seeking legal protection.

Unfortunately, neither remedy may be successful, although Box 20.5 illustrates one attempt to gain legal protection that worked. A price difference may be a necessary part of the firm's marketing strategy, or it may be caused by fac-

LEVI STRAUSS DEFENDS ITS BRAND NAME

BOX 20.5

In November 2001, Europe's highest court supported Levi Strauss & Company in its battle to prevent gray marketers from selling Levi jeans at discount prices. Levi Strauss had gone to court to prevent Tesco, Britain's biggest supermarket chain, from selling Levi blue jeans at discount prices. Tesco's practice was to buy goods such as Levi jeans, Nike sneakers, and Calvin Klein underwear at lower prices in other countries and then to sell them at prices below "regular" prices in Britain. For example, Levi's 501 jeans typically retailed for about $80 a pair in Levi Strauss's London outlet, but only for about $40 in the United States—the price that Tesco charged in London. Tesco used low-priced Levi jeans to attract shoppers to their stores and sold about 10,000 pairs of Levi jeans a month.

The European Court of Justice in Luxembourg ruled that trademark owners must grant permission unequivocally before goods made outside the European Economic Area could be sold within the European Union. Levi Strauss had claimed that it had the right to decide the way it wanted to distribute its products to meet the needs of its customers. This right included the practice of selling same or similar goods at very different prices to outlets in different countries. The Court agreed with Levi Strauss and ruled against Tesco. In the meantime, Tesco indicated that it would petition to get the law changed and announced that it would begin offering gray market name-brand hi-fi systems.

Source: Alan Colwell, "Court Backs Levi Strauss on Pricing," *New York Times on the Web* (November 21, 2001).

tors outside the control of the company. For companies with sales in many parts of the world, a price difference may be simply indispensable. Legal protection or government intervention rarely works because gray markets are not necessarily illegal. For example, in Europe, rulings forbid limitations of free trade between and among member states. These rulings actually established the legality of all kinds of gray imports among European Union members. In the United States, gray markets can be legally restrained in only a few instances. Nevertheless, companies have come up with both reactive and proactive ways to respond to the gray market threat.

Reactive methods have included price reductions, supply interventions, and buying out the gray market distributors. As indicated above, simply reducing prices has limitations, and it usually does not address the source of the gray market activity. One way to narrow the price differences across markets would be to reduce prices in some markets while increasing prices in others. The net effect would be to reduce the magnitude of the price differences between the various markets.

An alternative to reducing prices is to help the authorized distributors determine ways to create value that justify a higher price. For example, the manufacturer and authorized distributors can communicate to potential customers the service disadvantage of buying from gray marketers. Authorized distributors can provide more comprehensive services or other features that add value to the product offering. One Caterpillar dealer expanded its short-term rental fleet, modified certain products to differentiate them from gray market products, and created a "cafeteria style" service menu to meet its customers' different service and maintenance needs.

The supply intervention method requires the manufacturer to coordinate with its distributors to prevent the gray marketers from obtaining a supply of the firm's products. Firms that have strong centralized power and a close relationship with distributors may find this approach easier to implement than firms with a decentralized decision-making process and a loose distributor network. Another approach would be to provide an incentive system that rewards distributors who participate in the effort to discourage gray marketers. If the firm's incentive system is based on total sales volume in each geographic market, however, this coordination against gray market activity may not succeed.

An alternative tactic is to intervene with the supply of spare parts, rather than the products themselves. To implement this tactic, manufacturers use a slightly different design for important parts across geographic markets or control the amount of spare parts to each market. The authorized distributors provide spare parts only to those customers who purchased the original equipment from them. Or the manufacturer may set a global price on spare parts so that the gray marketers have no economic incentive to provide spare parts. Thus buyers would find gray market products less appealing for fear of not being able to obtain necessary spare parts and the net result is that potential gray market customers would rather source from the authorized dealer for the sure supply of parts in the future.

If the company thinks the gray market activity is only a one-time phenomenon, it may choose to buy the gray market products from gray marketers to protect the brand image and prevent customers from becoming accustomed to the idea of sourcing from a gray market. An extreme version of the buyout method is to acquire the gray market distributors themselves. Such an acquisition is usually costly and complicated and few firms have attempted this approach. However, such an acquisition might curtail the gray market activity while simultaneously expanding the distribution network.

As part of a proactive response to the gray market threat, the firm should develop an information system between the manufacturer and its distributors. Such an information system would help to

- Coordinate price decisions.

- Monitor price differences and detect gray market activities.

- Learn the profile of gray market customers and facilitate designing an effective marketing campaign to reach this specific market segment.

- Coordinate countermovements in promotion and advertising to fight gray market activities.

- Monitor product purchase origins for each product (by using bar codes or product codes) so service can be provided only for products bought from authorized dealers.

Another proactive approach would be to help authorized distributors build the image of the brands. As Chapter 8 explained, brand equity is exemplified not only in the product itself, but also in its advertising, venue of purchase, and after-sales service. By developing a positive image for the product and authorized dealers, the authorized channel enhances customers' perceptions of value.

Additional Pricing Issues

Selling in international markets continues to lead to new pricing issues. In some situations, importing countries do not have the cash to purchase needed capital equipment, or have severe restrictions against money flowing across their national borders. Two strategies to resolve these issues are leasing arrangements and countertrading. A third issue that has emerged, particularly as newly developing countries (NDCs) attempt to make significant progress in world trade, is "dumping" or selling products below cost in international markets. We briefly discuss these three issues next.

Leasing

One way to alleviate the high cost of purchasing capital equipment, particularly for foreign firms that do not have strong financial capability, is leasing. Leasing in international markets is similar to leasing in the United States. Leases typically run for one to five years, have either monthly or annual payments, and include servicing, repairs, and replacement parts. In countries beset with rampant inflation, lease contracts can result in losses as the lease period goes on. Leases can also be affected by currency devaluation, political turmoil, and, in cases of expropriation, even outright loss of the equipment. However, despite these disadvantages, leasing remains an important aspect of international pricing.

Countertrades

Countertrade covers those transactions where payment is made in kind rather than in currency. It has become a popular method of payment in Eastern European countries, China, and some developed countries. Countertrade includes four types of transactions: barter, compensation deals, counterpurchase, and buy-back.

Barter is the direct exchange of goods in a transaction. Perhaps one of the most notable barter transactions was the agreement between Occidental Petroleum and the Soviet Union. Occidental Petroleum agreed to ship superphosphoric acid to the Soviet Union in exchange for ammonia urea and potash for 20 years, at an estimated deal value of $20 billion. Such a barter situation requires that the exporting company, in this case Occidental Petroleum, must be able either to use the acquired products or to find markets for them. PepsiCo swapped billions of dollars of cola syrup for Stolichnaya vodka from Russia. Coca-Cola, Phillip Morris, and McDonald's are other firms that trade services, products, or excess inventory.[19] Obviously, a problem with barter is establishing the relative value of the goods being exchanged, and firms involved in bartering often rely on barter houses to establish the value of the goods and to locate potential buyers for them.

In a *compensation deal*, part of the payment is in currency and part is in goods. The basic advantage of a compensation deal is that it provides an immediate cash settlement for a portion of the transaction. The remainder of the cash comes from sale of the goods received as a part of the compensation deal.

[19]Genevieve Buck, "Barter Power Burgeons," *Chicago Tribune* (December 18, 1997), Section 3, 1, 4.

Counterpurchase involves two transactions. First the selling company negotiates a cash settlement for the goods being exported. Then, in a separate contingent transaction, the company agrees to purchase goods from the buyer equal to the amount of the initial sale. For example, McDonnell Douglas agreed to buy Yugoslavian goods in exchange for a sale of 22 DC-9 airplanes, worth $100 billion, to Yugoslavia. McDonnell Douglas then arranged to sell the goods, such as hams, glassware, and leather goods, to department store buyers.

In a product *buyback agreement*, the seller agrees to buy back, at a later time, output produced with the equipment originally sold. For example, a clothing manufacturer may agree to buy back a certain amount of the clothing produced in a plant established in the foreign country by the manufacturer. In effect, the exporting firm transfers technology (a manufacturing plant) to a foreign country and then agrees to buy some portion of the plant's output when it is fully operational. However, a major problem has surfaced with such arrangements: Eventually the foreign plant produces goods that directly compete with the manufacturer's own goods in world markets. This particular problem plagues U.S. automobile parts manufacturers—plants established in Asian countries now compete directly with the U.S. companies for the sale of automobile parts.

Dumping

As the preceding discussion implies, prices in export markets are often different from those in domestic markets for the same products. *Dumping* is defined as the practice of selling products in foreign markets at prices lower than what the products sell for in the home markets. Most countries have legislation against dumping and when it is determined that dumping has occurred, a countervailing duty (tax) is imposed to effectively raise the import price of the product. However, there is increasing pressure to phase out these antidumping laws in exchange for stricter limits on government subsidies to industries in their countries.[20]

International Transfer Pricing

As noted, one practice in global marketing is multinational companies' development of manufacturing and marketing

---

[20]Ronald E. Yates, "Dump Anti-Dumping Laws, Critics Say," *Chicago Tribune* (September 14, 1992), Section 4, 1, 4.

subsidiaries in foreign countries. Depending on the relative advantages, a multinational company (MNC) might produce the products at home and export them to foreign markets, produce the products in foreign countries for sale in the producing country, or produce in a foreign country for sale in the home country or other countries.

Subsidiary managers must have the capability of making decisions that allow them to maximize the profits their operations contribute to the MNC. That is, such managers must be able to decide what products to produce and sell in their markets, what prices to charge their customers as well as other subsidiaries of the MNC, what resources to acquire, and so on. In this way the manager is held accountable for the relative success of the subsidiary. However, delegating this authority creates an important dilemma for the MNC. When a product is transferred from one subsidiary or division to another, what price should be used for the transfer? Should the transfer price be the prevailing world market price? Should the transfer be at full cost, variable cost, cost plus some markup, or opportunity cost?

A *transfer price* is the price the selling department, division, or subsidiary charges another buying department, division, or subsidiary of the same organization for a product or service. A transfer price can be determined by several methods. By using one of the cost methods (full, variable, or cost plus), the product can be transferred at either actual or standard costs. Using the market price method, the transfer price is what an external party pays for similar quantities of the product. A negotiated transfer price is determined by a bargaining process between the buying and selling divisions. The choice of the appropriate transfer pricing method should consider the effect the method has on the firm's overall profit level, how well it allows for an evaluation of subsidiaries and their managers, its effect on the decision making of top management, and the degree it promotes autonomy for the subsidiary or division.

International transfer pricing occurs when the buying and selling divisions are in different countries. Moving products across national borders creates additional complexities that must be considered. One important issue is the taxes to be paid to both the exporting country and the importing country. For example, suppose that an MNC foreign firm has a subsidiary in the United States. If the corporate income tax in the United States is higher than in the foreign home country, then setting a high transfer price for products transferred to the subsidiary in the United States will lower the MNC's tax liability in the United States.

As Figure 20.2A shows, assume the manufacturing cost of a product to be shipped to the United States is $200. The unit is sold to the manufacturer's wholly owned subsidiary in the United States at $600. This subsidiary then sells it to a retailer at cost (including advertising and shipping of $100), or $700. The net effect is that the subsidiary in the United States shows no profit and pays no corporate income tax.

On the other hand, if the foreign manufacturer wishes to minimize corporate income tax in its home country, it might price as shown in Fig. 20.2B. Here, the product is transferred to the subsidiary at a price of $300. The subsidiary sells the product to the U.S retailer for $700 and shows a $300 profit that is subject to U.S. corporate income tax. It has been estimated that foreign-owned MNCs avoid more than $45 billion a year in U.S. taxes by transfer pricing strategies.[21] Moreover, U.S. firms with similar pricing practices may avoid more than another $50 billion in taxes a year.[22] Of course, national tax authorities, being aware of such possibilities, try to restrict such options.

A second problem arises when a country restricts the movement of cash from its borders. Such a situation may require multiple transfers in order to get the subsidiary's profits into the MNC's home country.

A third complication is the existence of high import duties, tariffs, or custom fees. A subsidiary can reduce the MNC's import duties by lowering the transfer price when exporting to a subsidiary in a high-tariff country. Because of the possibility of firms reducing their tax and tariff payments through transfer pricing, governments watch such activities very carefully.

To develop an appropriate international transfer pricing policy, it is important that the transfer pricing policy[23]

1. Allow for proper profit measurement of the subsidiary or division's operations.

2. Provide correct information as a guide to top-level management decisions.

---

[21]"Here Comes the Great Global Tax War," *Business Week* (May 30, 1994), 55–56.
[22]Gail DeGeorge, "Who Pays $25,000 for a Fax Machine? You," *Business Week* (March 21, 1994), 8.
[23]Wagdy M. Abdallah, *International Transfer Pricing Policies* (New York: Quorum Books, 1989).

FIGURE 20.2   **Profit and Tax Effects of International Transfer Pricing**

A. **High Transfer Price**

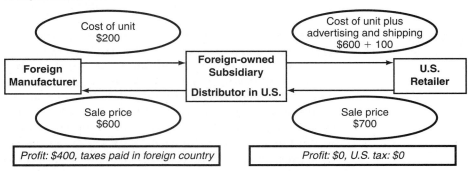

B. **Low Transfer Price**

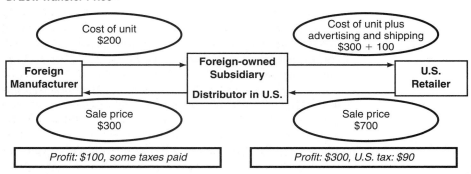

3. Lead to an increase in the firm's overall profit rate.

4. Motivate divisional or subsidiary managers to become as efficient as possible and to maximize their contributions to the corporation' overall profits.

5. Minimize international transaction costs by minimizing tax liabilities, tariff obligations, unfavorable exchange rates, and conflict with governmental agencies in all countries.

As with any pricing policy, a transfer pricing policy should be developed with specific behavioral and profit objectives in mind. Such a policy must be flexible but at the same time have a solid analytical basis. This is especially important because a transfer price audit by the government is an expensive and time-consuming process and may result in assessed penalties beyond the amount of determined tax obligations.[24]

Summary

This chapter has extended the discussion of developing profitable pricing strategies and tactics to areas that have not received much attention. Even though services have become dominant in many economies, there has been relatively little discussion on appropriate pricing methods for them. Earlier sections of this book applied some of the principles to services. For example, Chapter 8 developed contingency value pricing for an engineering consulting firm, and Chapter 15 discussed pricing hotel rooms and yield management as used by airlines and hotels. This chapter addressed additional issues of service pricing. These underlying principles of pricing remain the same whether the service organization is profit oriented or is a not-for-profit organization. Chapter 22 will summarize these principles, but it should be apparent from the perspective developed in this book that pricing must be carefully developed by all organizations, regardless of profit motivation. Organizations must move from tradition as a basis for setting prices to a careful analysis of the customers being served, their value perceptions and reasons for purchasing, the organization's relevant costs of meeting these needs, the organization's pricing objectives, and the organization's competitive market position. Service organizations, such as the financial services and educational services institutions also must be aware that they are providing multiple service lines to different price-market segments and carefully consider unbundling their service offerings. Price competition does not mean simply meeting or beating lower prices of competitive offerings. A price reduction strategy as a means of competing is successful only if it meets some very restrictive requirements (see Chapters 11 and 13). Unless these price reductions are focused and offered to specific price-sensitive markets, the net result is likely to be lower profits than before or less resulting revenue than needed to cover operational costs. Focusing on the value–price relationship of service offerings rather than simply minimizing the price charged will be of more long-run significance.

[24]John P. Fraedrich and Connie Rae Bateman, "Transfer Pricing by Multinational Marketers: Risky Business," *Business Horizons* (January–February 1996), 17–22.

Finally, this chapter discussed issues of export pricing in international markets and transfer pricing. The underlying principles of pricing for export are the same as those prescribed for domestic product and service pricing, although international marketing and pricing add additional complexities that need to be considered.

Discussion Questions	1. Summarize the unique differences between producing and marketing (*a*) services as opposed to products, (*b*) products in domestic markets as opposed to foreign markets, and (*c*) products for other divisions or subsidiaries of a firm.

1. Summarize the unique differences between producing and marketing (*a*) services as opposed to products, (*b*) products in domestic markets as opposed to foreign markets, and (*c*) products for other divisions or subsidiaries of a firm.
2. Using the differences developed in the answer to question 1, explain the implications for developing pricing strategies and prices for services, for export marketing, and for interdivisional product transfers.
3. What are the similarities for pricing products, services, and pricing for export as opposed to the differences developed in the answer to question 2?
4. Go to a bank or other financial institution and obtain information on all of the services the institution provides to its customers and the various prices, fees, charges, or balance requirements associated with these services. Are any services bundled for a specific package or bundle price?
5. What is gray marketing? Why does gray marketing occur? Is gray marketing always something a firm should seek to avoid? What are some ways to combat gray marketing?

Suggested Readings

Assmus, Gert, and Carsten Wiese: "How to Address the Gray Market Threat Using Price Coordination," *Sloan Management Review 36* (Spring 1995), 31–41.

Berry, Leonard L., and Manjit S. Yadav: "Capture and Communicate Value in the Pricing of Services," *Sloan Management Review 37* (Summer 1996), 41–51.

Fraedrich, John P., and Connie Rae Bateman: "Transfer Pricing by Multinational Marketers," *Business Horizons* (January–February 1996), 17–22.

Myers, Matthew B., and David A. Griffith: "Strategies for Combating Gray Market Activity," *Business Horizons 42* (November–December 1999), 2–8.

Yang, B. Rachel, Reza H. Ahmadi, and Kent B. Monroe: "Pricing in Separable Channels: The Case of Parallel

Imports," *Journal of Product & Brand Management Featuring Pricing Strategy & Practice 7*, no. 5 (1998), 433–40.

CHAPTER TWENTY-ONE

Pricing on the Internet

Analysts have predicted that online sales will increase from $48 billion in 1998 to $1.8 trillion by 2003. The worldwide Internet population of 445.9 million in 2002 was projected to grow to 709.1 million by 2004. Americans spent $2.6 billion online during the first week of December 2001, an increase of 91 percent from the estimated $1.4 billion spent during an average week in November 2001.[1]

Accompanying this rapid growth of online sales and the Internet population has been an emphasis on lower prices on the Internet than in conventional outlets. In part, this assumed consequence of the increased use of the Internet for e-commerce is based on the expectation that Internet purchasing will reduce distribution costs and make buyers' search for product and price information easier and perhaps costless. Some of this belief has resulted from the way some of the early dot com online businesses started. For example, in 1998, Buy.com, a shopping bot, provided online buyers with product and pricing information for approximately 30,000 products. Buy.com's management assumed that buyers would search or browse other sites to obtain product information, but that they would purchase the product from Buy.com at the lower price.[2]

Buy.com's approach epitomizes the theory that the Internet will drive down prices to competitive levels and strengthen buyer power. Many other online businesses adopted this

[1] "The World's Online Population," http://cyberatlas.internet.com, (February 1, 2002); "E-Commerce Numbers Add Up in December," http://cyberatlas.internet.com, (December 17, 2001).

[2] J. William Gurley, "Buy.com May Fail, But if It Succeeds, Retailing May Never Be the Same," *Fortune 139* (January 11, 1999), 150–52.

theory and continued to reduce prices to meet the assumed buyers' quest for the lowest price available. In some respects, what has occurred is an example of a self-fulfilling prophesy. That is, given these assumptions and beliefs that the Internet would lead to perfect competition, many online companies set prices below consumers' value-based prices. And, of course many online dot com companies failed and no longer exist.

Can the Internet Lead to Perfectly Competitive Prices?

In Chapter 2 we pointed out that traditional economic theory assumes that buyers and sellers have perfect information about prices, their own tastes and preferences, and a budget or income available for purchasing goods and services. In addition, a perfectly competitive market is characterized by many independently acting buyers and sellers, homogenized products, and relatively easy entry and exit of firms.

Moving toward Perfect Information

As we saw in Chapter 3, the quality of the attributes of some goods can be assessed prior to purchase, and we call these products search products. Examples of search products include books, CDs, brand-name hard goods, airline tickets, toys, pet supplies, and standard industrial supplies. Indeed, one survey indicated that online shoppers purchased more books and videotapes on line than in stores.[3] In a study of prices for DVD titles, prices of pure Internet retailers were lower by an average of $3.27 in comparison to retailers who sold both online and in retail stores. Moreover, the spread of prices for pure Internet sellers was considerably lower than the prices for the multichannel retailers.[4] Buyers perceive less risk in buying products that they believe vary little in quality across alternative sellers, including online sellers. If there is little perceived quality variation across sellers, then buyers are more likely to minimize the price paid for such items.

However, as Chapter 3 pointed out, search for the lowest price from alternative sellers in traditional shopping can be time consuming and require substantial effort. Most

---

[3]"Survey: More Buying Books, Video On-line Than in Stores," *Chicago Tribune* (January 11, 2000), Section 4, 2.

[4]Fang-Fang Tang and Xiaolin Xing, "Will the Growth of Multi-Channel Retailing Diminish the Pricing Efficiency of the Web?" *Journal of Retailing 77* (Autumn 2001), 319–33.

busy people do not have the time or the willingness to visit multiple outlets seeking the lowest price for a considered purchase. Thus, searching online for the lowest prices for these types of products can be convenient, quick, and comparatively costless. Search engines called shopbots provide "one-click" Internet access to price and product information from a relatively large number of competing sellers. According to estimates, shopbots can reduce buyer search costs for product and price information at least 30-fold in comparison to telephone shopping and searching retail stores in person.[5] Shopbots collect and provide information on a variety of product and retailer characteristics and usually rank the retailers on a characteristic specified by the shopper, such as price or shipping costs and time.

These search engines and demand aggregation sites, or Web aggregators, help to reduce asymmetric information between buyers and sellers (see Chapter 4) by providing searches that compile product and pricing information. By reducing this asymmetry in information, they provide buyers with additional influence in the negotiating process, increase buyers' ability to make informed decisions, and reduce transaction costs. These aggregators also connect individual buyers for the same product into buying groups and help them obtain volume discounts. General Electric Co. was able to reduce its purchase costs by 20 percent on more than $1 billion of purchases of operating materials by pooling orders from divisions worldwide.[6] Thus the ability of the Internet and information technology to reduce the amount of asymmetric information helps increase buyer power.

Many Independent Buyers and Sellers

As mentioned, online sales have been increasing rapidly, the worldwide Internet population has been growing dramatically, and there has been an influx and exit of online sellers and intermediaries. One consequence of this growth and market instability is a wide variety of choices for buyers. Such a variety of choices online further enhances buyers' power, including their ability to pool resources and purchase in volume. Moreover, the Internet eliminates local and

[5]Erik Brynjolfsson and Michael D. Smith, "Frictionless Commerce? A Comparison of Internet and Conventional Retailers," *Management Science 46* (April 2000), 563–85.
[6]Robert D. Hof, "The Buyer Always Wins," *Business Week e.Biz* (March 22, 1999), EB 26–28.

regional protections for sellers because buyers can literally buy from anyone in any region of the world (see Chapter 20). The direct supplier–buyer relationship in Internet transactions also reduces or eliminates the various intermediaries in traditional distribution systems. Moreover, the information intermediary may take a smaller percentage of the final selling price for the information service provided (perhaps 10 percent as opposed to the 40 to 50 percent traditional intermediary margins). Finally, a growing number of information intermediaries, manufacturers, distributors, and retailers provide buyers with access to buying on the Internet. Each of these trends increases competitive pressure and keeps pressure on prices to be relatively low, as would be expected from traditional economic theory.

Moving from Differentiated to Homogeneous Markets

The increased popularity of shopbots and aggregation sites has many online sellers fearing that their products will be perceived as homogeneous offerings, as compared to those of competing products, and price wars may erupt. Before the arrival of shopbots, online businesses maintained higher prices due to the lack of perfect information between buyers and sellers and the added convenience that buyers received from purchasing products online rather than in conventional retail outlets. Shopbots have weakened the ability of online firms to charge higher prices by reducing the effects of imperfect information and by giving online buyers increased convenience through technology that searches a variety of sites for pricing and product information.

In other words, many believe that the Internet, in effect, will homogenize products, resulting in price competition. As traditionally differentiated markets move towards commodity markets through consumers' use of shopbots and aggregators, previously differentiated markets will be defined by (1) a reduction in buyers' incremental costs of obtaining price and product information; (2) the inability, in theory, of sellers to easily "obscure their quoted prices" as third-party aggregators demonstrate competing prices side by side; and (3) equilibrium's positive effect on buyers through increased price competition and a reduction of sellers' market power.[7]

---

[7]Yannis Bakos, "Reducing Buyer Search Costs: Implications for Electronic Marketplaces," *Management Science 46* (December 1997), 563–85.

Are Prices Lower on the Internet?

Although there is evidence that prices for some types of products on the Internet are lower than in traditional retail outlets, nevertheless it remains inconclusive as to whether this assumed perfect competition consequence will materialize as believed. For example, one study found that prices for books and CDs on the Internet were 9 to 16 percent lower than prices in conventional outlets depending on whether taxes, shipping, and shopping costs were included in the price. The majority of books sold over the Internet were sold by Amazon.com, Barnes & Noble.com, and Borders.com, and these stores had similar prices. Yet online book sellers, to various degrees, had successfully pursued a differentiated strategy on dimensions of brand, price, and assortment. Even though it would be expected that Internet shoppers who use a shopbot would be the most price-sensitive buyers, they still seemed to use brand name as a signal of service quality and were willing to pay more for a book from one of these three retailers.[8]

Although the above evidence suggests that prices are lower on the Internet, it is not clear that prices are consistent with the expectations based on perfect competition. Other research exists that dispells the belief that the Internet leads to perfect competition. As the above research on a supposedly commodity product, books, indicates, competing on the Internet does not necessarily force online firms to lower prices. Furthermore, although price is an important factor in a buyer's purchasing decisions, a variety of other attributes including customer support, on-time delivery, shipping and handling, product content, privacy policies, ease of ordering, product information, Website navigation and locks, and product selection are rated more heavily in the purchasing decision than price. In addition, a McKinsey study discovered that the majority of online buyers do not actively search competing sites to find the best deal: 89 percent of online book buyers purchase from the first site they visit, as do 84 percent of those buying toys, 81 percent buying music, and 76 percent buying electronics. Given the fact that

[8]Karen Clay, Ramayya Krishnan, and Eric Wolff, "Prices and Price Dispersion on the Web: Evidence From the Online Book Industry," *The Journal of Industrial Economics 46* (December 2001), 521–39; Brynjolfsson and Smith, "Frictionless Commerce"; Michael D. Smith and Erik Brynjolfsson, "Consumer Decision-Making at an Internet Shopbot: Brand Still Matters," *The Journal of Industrial Economics 46* (December 2001), 541–58.

online consumers do not actively search competing sites, it is not surprising that online retailers often set higher prices than those of their competitors.

Why the Internet May Not Lead to Lower Prices

The belief that the Internet will move electronic markets towards a perfectly competitive market seems logical if it is assumed that imperfect information within the exchange relationship will decrease, that consumers will become increasingly price sensitive, and that the usage of shopbots will drive differentiated markets towards homogenization and price competition. However, studies have found that the majority of consumers are not as price sensitive as expected and they do not actively search competing sites before making a purchase decision.

Furthermore, although shopbots, in theory, should reduce information asymmetry and reduce consumer search costs, they really do not conveniently assist consumers in finding lower prices. To make accurate price comparisons online, consumers must have available not only the price of the product but also the shipping fees, sales tax, and other offer or transaction information. To collect and study all of this information requires time and outweighs the perceived reduction in search costs of online purchases. As the number of businesses online increases, so will the information provided through shopbots, creating an information overload for consumers. As the information provided to consumers increases, they will reduce search costs by adopting decision shortcuts or heuristics (see Chapters 3 and 6).[9] These shortcuts may take the form of purchasing from a recognized and trusted site even though the prices on that site may be higher than those of competing sites. This decision to purchase from a recognized name may explain why online bookstores such as Amazon.com, Barnes & Noble.com, and Borders.com can charge higher prices than the competition and still generate significant sales.

Online consumers' tendency to purchase recognized brands or from reputable stores and recent events within the electronic commerce industry demonstrate that entry and exit costs are not low. To attract consumers to a site amidst all the online clutter requires extensive marketing and advertising

[9]Rajneesh Suri, Mary Long, and Kent B. Monroe, "The Impact of the Internet and Consumer Motivation on the Evaluation of Prices," *Journal of Business Research 55* (2001), 1–12.

expenditures. To remain in business and earn a profit with these significant marketing and advertising expenditures, online retailers must achieve high gross margins. High entry and exit barriers, as shown through the need to maintain high gross margins while increasing advertising expenditures, further explain the inability of the Internet retailers to lower prices. It is unlikely that the Internet will create a perfectly competitive market because the products sold, even books, are not commodities. Consumers find buying from Amazon.com or Barnes & Noble.com is different because the interface and after-sales services are different.

Leveraging Pricing Opportunities on the Internet

The Internet provides a new channel for conducting business. It creates an electronic marketplace where buyers and sellers meet, gather information, submit bids, agree on orders, keep track of the orders being processed, and complete the transaction electronically. This virtual marketplace provides opportunities for online companies to be profitable if they develop and implement the right pricing strategies.

Research and Testing Capabilities

In traditional retail outlets sellers must undergo expensive and costly research in terms of time and resources to better understand the effects of pricing decisions on consumer purchases. However, through programs such as clickstream data that track current online sessions and cookies that track buying histories, the Internet offers online businesses the opportunity to research consumer purchasing behaviors and test pricing decisions in real-time with minimal costs.

For example, Zilliant tested various pricing strategies for its software services online by first reducing the price of four different products by 7 percent. The price reduction resulted in an increase in sales volume of 5 percent to 20 percent for three of the products, but unfortunately did not override the costs of implementing the lower price. However, Zilliant did discover that sales for the fourth product doubled. Further analysis of the data for the fourth product uncovered a new segment that the company had not targeted in the past—high schools and universities. As a result, Zilliant tailored a website with special prices to meet the needs of this new segment.[10]

---

[10]Walter Baker, Mike Marn, and Craig Zawada, "Price Smarter on the Net," *Harvard Business Review* 79 (February), 122-7.

Customer Segmentation

The Internet provides a way to not only test different pricing tactics but to also discover new market segments. An increasing number of online businesses have realized this segmentation benefit of the Internet and have adopted research techniques to categorize customers based upon their desired product features, previous purchase behaviors, and accepted price ranges.

Understanding each customer segment enables segment-specific prices or promotions. For example, United Airlines' electronic commerce division provides numerous benefits to the company. First, the division's unique online reservation system has eliminated an average of $1.3 billion in conventional transaction costs (such as travel agent commissions and booking fees). In addition, the online reservation system has enabled United Airlines to provide customers with efficient and timely customer service. However, more importantly, United Airlines' online reservation system and its tracking software have uncovered eight distinct customer segments ranging from price-sensitive consumers who prefer booking tickets through Priceline.com to business travelers requiring last-minute reservations.[11]

Dynamic Pricing

The ability to better segment consumers through Internet tracking technology has led to an increased usage of dynamic pricing practices by online businesses. The Internet provides marketers with the ability to offer special deals tailored specifically for individual consumers on all types of products and services from theater tickets to bank loans to a variety of merchandise. The Internet offers businesses a way to test prices, discover new segments, and continuously change prices based upon customer preferences.

One of the important advantages of the Internet is that it provides a way for firms to move from fixed prices to variable pricing. Previously, most firms changed list prices infrequently because the cost of implementing a price change throughout the distribution system could be quite high. (The cost of implementing a price change is referred to as a *menu cost*.) For firms with a large product or service offering, it would take months for price changes to filter throughout the

[11]John Schmeltzer, "United Airlines Moving to Get Friendlier with Web Commerce," *Chicago Tribune* (January 11, 2000), Section 4, 2.

distribution system. The Internet reduces the menu cost and the time to change prices. Thus there is no longer an excuse for not changing prices when they need to be changed. Moreover, increasing digitization of many aspects of businesses makes it much more feasible to tailor prices to segments or even individual customers.[12]

It should be clear that transparency and efficiency go both ways. If it is easy for buyers to compare prices on the Internet, so is it relatively easy for companies to track buyers' behavior and adjust prices accordingly. Just as it is easy for a price-conscious buyer to find a low price via the Internet, the Web increases the chances for the firm to find a buyer willing to pay a higher price. Online companies can store large amounts of customer information such as past shopping behavior, demographics, and preferences and can capture consumer surplus more easily by charging different price-sensitive customers different prices. Moreover, because effective pricing requires access to historical data and customer insights generated over time, it becomes difficult for new entrants to replicate dynamic pricing capabilities. Online companies with a large customer base have a competitive advantage over new entrants because customer data are a valuable resource for generating sales and profits and it takes time for the new firms to accumulate sufficient relevant information to be effective.[13]

Product Differentiation

To decrease online buyers' sensitivity to price, sellers must differentiate their products and brand. For example, Dell computer has differentiated itself from other PC manufacturers by offering online consumers the opportunity to choose a particular bundle of features. In essence, customers design their own computer and determine a price relative to the bundle of features they want. In effect, the buyer becomes a price maker as well as a price taker.

A study of online wine sales discovered that price sensitivity for wines common to online stores increased when cross-store price comparisons were made easy. However, easy cross-store price comparisons had no effect on price

---

[12]Leyland F. Pitt, Pierre Berthon, Richard T. Watson, and Michael Ewing, "Pricing Strategy and the Net," *Business Horizons 44* (March–April 2001), 45–54; Gordon A. Wyner, "New Pricing Realities," *Marketing Research* 13 (Spring 2001), 34-5.
[13]Ajit Kambil and Vipul Agrawal, "The New Realities of Dynamic Pricing," *Outlook,* no. 2 (2001).

sensitivity for unique wines. Moreover, when cross-store quality comparisons were made easier for the common wines, price sensitivity decreased.[14] Therefore, to avoid the theoretical commoditization effects of shopbots, sellers must provide differentiating features and information to prevent declining prices or price wars.

Develop Brand Loyalty

As we have indicated earlier, research indicates that few people really do search extensively on the Web before they buy. Because of security concerns, surfers tend to be brand loyal to certain websites with which they have had good experiences. Consumers may not take the risk of searching for products with better attributes; instead they remain with familiar products and websites. This behavior results in increased consumer loyalty, which permits firms to increase their prices. For example, most customers of Amazon.com are loyal even though Amazon.com has higher prices than some other online book retailers. Consumers are prepared to pay more to use a reputable seller and will pay more for a seller they have visited previously. Developing a reputable brand name and receiving a price premium for the products is the same pricing strategy as in the brick-and-mortar world (see Chapter 4).[15]

Include Shipping and Handling in the Profitability Analysis

As a way to attract buyers, some online companies charge a relatively low price on the product but add a shipping and handling fee that is greater than the actual cost of shipping and handling. Estimates indicate that nearly half of the biggest 50 online retailers make a profit beyond actual merchandise sales by charging shipping fees in excess of cost.[16] Although shipping and handling fees can be a source of income, this practice may be perceived to be unfair. Moreover, the attempt to use shipping and handling as a source of profits assumes that buyers do not pay attention to these charges.

[14]John G. Lynch and Dan Ariely, "Wine Online: Search Costs Affect Competition on Price, Quality, and Distribution," *Marketing Science 19* (Winter 2000), 83–103.
[15]Simon Latcovich and Howard Smith, "Pricing, Sunk Costs, and Market Structure Online: Evidence From Book Retailing," *Oxford Review of Economic Policy 17* (Summer 2001), 217–34.
[16]Andrea Orr, "E-Tailers Shifting to For-Profit Shipping to Bolster Bottom Line," *Chicago Tribune* (June 17, 2001), Section 5, 4.

However, if shoppers come to believe that shipping charges are a "rip-off," they are likely to abandon their virtual shopping carts.[17] Part of this problem of how shipping charges are perceived results because the majority of start-up Internet stores provided free shipping even for very bulky items like dog food and cat litter. Of course, many of these dot.com retailers did not survive, and those that have are trying to catch up now by charging for shipping and handling. E-retailers seem to prefer to set a flat shipping rate as opposed to a weight-based shipping charge because such a rate reduces the need to calculate the shipping and handling charge for each order. However, such an approach leads to some real difficulties. Consider the example of CD retailer CDNow, which set a $2.99 fee for shipping and handling for the first CD in an order, and 99 cents for each additional CD. An order of 200 CDs from CDNow would lead to a shipping and handling charge of $200, even though the shipping cost to the company would be $28.[18] Box 21.1 provides another illustration of the problems that shipping and handling fees can create when not made transparent.

Create or Participate in Electronic Marketplaces

The Internet can be used to build up a community for buyers and sellers or electronic marketplaces where a group of buyers and sellers interact to trade, consolidate sales, and set prices for transactions. In January 2002, 26 percent of organizations bought goods or services via online marketplaces.[19] These exchanges function by allowing buyers to make an "offer to buy" a specific item, for example, a type of steel, and sellers to make an "offer to sell." The Internet then provides a mechanism for the buyer to learn of current posted product offerings and the seller to learn of current product requests. If the item that buyers are seeking is listed in the product offerings, they can select a seller and submit a bid. Then the seller and buyer can negotiate to arrive at an agreeable set of terms for the transaction. Similarly, sellers can learn of buyers seeking a product and submit an offer to

[17]Ellen Neuborne, "Break It to Them Quickly," *Business Week e.biz* (October 29, 2001), EB 10.
[18]Orr, "E-Tailers Shifting to For-Profit Shipping."
[19]Robert J. Dolan and Youngme Moon, "Pricing and Market Making on the Internet," *Journal of Interactive Marketing 14* (Spring 2000), 56–73; "Online Purchasing Increases in Q4 2001," http://cyberatlas.internet.com (January 30, 2002).

AMAZON.COM CREATES A BEST SELLER

BOX 21.1

During the period of June 20 through July 3, 2001, Amazon.com offered a promotion for free shipping if the customer bought two or more items from the book, CD, video, or DVD categories. At that time the usual shipping and handling charges were $3.49 for the first item and 99 cents for each additional item. During this promotion, the shipping cost for one item was $2.49, but it was eliminated if the customer bought another item with the order. Unfortunately, this promotion created several problems.

First, Amazon sold a number of items that were regularly priced at 49 cents or $1. Once customers learned that they could order one of these relatively inexpensive items along with the item they wanted and shipping would be free, they quickly took advantage of the offer. Customers found out that *The Book of Hope* was one of the least expensive books at Amazon and passed the information along on the Internet. These customers ended up saving a net of $2 by ordering *The Book of Hope*

along with the item of interest. By July 1, *The Book of Hope* was number 11 on Amazon's best-seller list!

Second, during the promotion Amazon changed prices on many items, in many cases increasing prices. Although an Amazon spokesperson claimed that customers saved an average of 4 to 9 percent, a comparison by *The Wall Street Journal* for an order of five specific books found that even with free shipping, the total cost of the order was 14 percent higher. Interestingly, Amazon customers were more unhappy with the way Amazon disclosed the price changes than by the changes themselves. Customers felt that the free shipping promotion was simply a way to disguise a price increase.

Sources: Patrick T. Reardon, "Book According to Mammon," *Chicago Tribune* (July 11, 2001), Section 2, 3; Nick Wingfield, "Amazon.com's Free-Shipping Promotion Has Customers Crying, 'Price Increase,'" *The Wall Street Journal* (June 27, 2001), A3.

one or more of these buyers, which they can accept, reject, or negotiate.

Innovative Internet Pricing Models

The Internet also has led to some innovative pricing models. In this section we will review a few pricing models that had been successful in early 2002.

eBay's Trading Platform

In September 1995, eBay founder Pierre Omidyar, attempting to help his girlfriend trade Pez dispensers, began a basic website called Auction Web. But his vision was more than just to help her sell this product. What he had in mind was to create an exchange market for a range of goods that was powered by individuals, not large corporations. He designed an Internet auction site that used the mechanism of a Dutch auction (see Chapter 19) to allow relatively small sellers to sell collectibles in a much wider market. As Box 21.2 indicates, eBay has grown rapidly both in sales and in the community of sellers who regularly use the website to sell their products. The goal of eBay's management was "to build the world's largest online trading platform where practically anyone can trade practically anything."[20]

The business model eBay used was quite unique. eBay was able to open auctions to a much broader public while reducing transaction costs so that it was feasible to auction even low-priced items. As he had intended, Omidyar had created an entirely new market. Whereas many other Internet companies primarily borrowed something that existed off-line and translated it into an online version, he developed something that could not be done in the real world. Sellers are attracted to eBay because there is a large number of potential buyers, and buyers are attracted to eBay because of the broad selection of goods listed on there. The company generates revenues in two ways. Listing and special placement fees—the fees sellers pay for listing their items—account for approximately 45 percent of eBay's total revenue, and final value fees—a percentage of the final sale price of the item—accounted for 55 percent. As the size of its community grew, profits grew also. In addition, the eBay community provides a feedback system in which buyers and sellers can rate each other. eBay also tracks customers' information to improve its services and find other business opportunities.[21] Box 21.2 provides some additional information about eBay and the challenge it faces to meet its growth objectives.

Priceline's Reverse Auctions

Priceline, which specializes in bidding/reverse auctions, has become another successful business model. Priceline allows buyers to specify product requirements and the amount they are willing to pay and then make corresponding offers to the participating sellers, reversing the traditional functioning of retail markets. The novelty of Priceline's model is that it is the buyers who post the prices they are willing to pay. Moreover, it is the buyers who provide the specifications of the items they wish to buy. Then, if no one is willing to sell at

---

[20]Erick Schonfeld, "eBay's Secret Ingredient," *Business 2.0* (March 2002), 52–58.
[21]Stephen P. Bradley and Kelly A. Porter, "eBay, Inc." *Journal of Interactive Marketing,* (Autumn 2000), 73–97.

IS THIS THE EBAY ERA?   BOX 21.2

Revenue for eBay, the number 1 online auction site, grew from less than $100 million in 1998 to about $750 million in 2001. Meg Whitman, CEO of eBay, predicted that its revenues would reach $3 billion by 2005. By the end of 2001, the eBay community had reached 38 million and was adding more than 2 million a month. This widespread customer network and low cost of conducting business on the site has attracted traditional companies to enter into the cyber auction marketplace. Large firms such as JC Penney, Xerox, IBM, and Disney have all moved into eBay, signaling that the next stage of development for this site has begun.

For eBay, the entry of big businesses should enhance its revenues. But this strategy could alienate its longtime clients, most of whom were part-time sellers. These individuals were afraid that the entry of major companies would put pressure on bidding prices. At the same time, the entry of big businesses also encourages eBay to move more of its transactions to fixed pricing, rather than auctions primarily because some full-time sellers need the fixed-pricing option to protect their margins.

The attraction of eBay's bidding model is that it gives buyers an opportunity to pay the price at which they value the item. Simultaneously, it gives sellers an opportunity to receive the price from the buyer who values the item the most. While moving away from the auction bidding model would shake the foundation of eBay, many buyers and sellers ask for fixed pricing for different reasons, from accelerating transactions to the purely psychological comfort of knowing the price for sure.

It is also too early to say whether it was a good idea for big companies to join eBay or provide auctions on their own websites. eBay is in the middle of online and off-line commerce and also in the middle of fixed pricing and flexible pricing at this stage of its development. Is this the beginning of eBay's era or is it the prelude of its demise?

Sources: Robert D. Hof, "The People's Company," *Business Week, e.biz* (December 3, 2001), 15; Leslie Walker, "Big Business Making Foray into eBay," *Chicago Tribune* (July 23, 2001), Section 4, 8.

the posted price and specifications, the buyers may raise the price until at least one seller agrees to the price.

For example, Priceline allows consumers to specify when and where they want to fly and what price they are willing to pay. Priceline then searches its supplier database to determine the minimum price a cooperating airline is willing to fly someone between the points specified by the buyer. If there is an airline willing to fly someone on that date between the specified points for a price at or below the buyer's specified price, a sale occurs. If there is an airline willing to sell the seat at a price below what the buyer has specified, Priceline receives a commission and the difference between the buyer's willingness to pay price and the airline's willing to supply price. On July 31, 2001, Priceline posted its first-ever profit, and excluding one-time gains and losses,

Priceline.com reported a pro forma profit of $3.3 million, or 1 cent a share for the last quarter of 2001.[22]

For the Priceline model to work, a flexible customer base is required. Buyers must be willing to accept different brand names, products, or features. The second requirement for the model to work is that there must be suppliers who either have excess inventory or perishable assets. That is, buyers must be flexible and willing to purchase items that suppliers either have had difficulty selling or that will soon be unavailable for sale.

There are concerns about the viability of the Priceline model. Is this model only a way to sell excess supply or out-of-season inventory? Does it lead to selling an unbranded, product or service of unknown quality? The model does not provide the seller with important information about its customer, and the seller cannot withdraw from the deal if it underprices the product. On the other hand, buyers can make only one bid for an item at a time, preventing them from obtaining price information within the specific transaction. If buyers are not very knowledgeable about prices for a particular product or service, they might submit either frivolously low prices or much higher prices than necessary. This difference in knowledge about prices and the category-level retail pricing practices has important implications not only for the bid success of consumers and the willingness of sellers to supply products and services for sale, but ultimately for the actual success of the Priceline model.[23]

Legal Issues in Internet Pricing

The rapid development of the Internet and the resulting growth of e-commerce have been revolutionizing the ways transactions are conducted. Though it is true that better informed buyers may have more bargaining power, the same amount of information, if not more, is also available to sellers, which makes price-fixing, price discrimination, and predatory pricing easier as well. In this section, we briefly

[22]"Priceline Shocker: Black Ink," *Business Week* (August 13, 2001), 40; "Priceline.Com Tops Forecast for Quarter, but Its Shares Fall," *New York Times* (www.nytimes.com), (February 5, 2002).

[23]P. K. Kannan and Praveen K. Kopalle, "Dynamic Pricing on the Internet: Importance and Implications for Consumer Behavior," *International Journal of Electronic Commerce 5* (Spring 2001), 63–83; Dolan and Moon, "Pricing and Market Making on the Internet"; Peter Coy, "A Revolution in Pricing? Not Quite," *Business Week* (November 20, 2000), 48–49.

review some of the emerging legal issues related to pricing on the Web.[24]

Price-Fixing

Horizontal Price-Fixing

The rapid and inexpensive exchange of information among sellers makes it easier for them to coordinate and to find a set of prices everyone can agree on. More importantly, once a price agreement is reached, no competitor has an incentive to deviate from the agreement because any single deviation on price would be easily discovered by others. Thus the deviant seller would be unlikely to be able to increase sales by secretly reducing price.

Even if it makes economic sense for the parties involved to reach a parallel price agreement, the courts still need additional information to be able to infer price-fixing. Three indicators are usually used. First, firm behavior might be more complex than would be plausible if the outcomes had been reached absent the forbidden process, as through mere leader-follower behavior. For example, if a company raised price universally by 5 percent to follow the industry leader, it would be considered reasonably explicit leader-follower behavior. However, if a firm adopts a more complex price structure of a competitor, which is less likely to be a simple response to either industry leaders or competitors, then the process would be in question. A second indication is whether the company's explanation of its pricing behavior makes business sense. For example, if a company is questioned about whether it posts prices on its website to communicate to its competitors, it can argue that the prices are for potential customers rather than competitors, and this is a very reasonable argument. The third indicator is whether the rivals had an opportunity to communicate and whether they did in fact communicate.

Airline pricing illustrates the horizontal price-fixing issue. Over a multiyear period, the leading airlines used a

---

[24]For additional reading see Jonathan B. Baker, "Identifying Horizontal Price Fixing in the Electronic Marketplace," *Antitrust Law Journal 65* (1996), 41–55; David A. Balto, "Emerging Antitrust Issues in Electronic Commerce," *Journal of Public Policy and Marketing 19* (Fall 2000), 277–86; Albert A. Foer, "E-Commerce Meets Antitrust: A Primer," *Journal of Public Policy and Marketing 20* (Spring 2001), 51–63; Maureen A. O'Rourke, "Shaping Competition on the Internet: Who Owns Product and Pricing Information?" *Vanderbilt Law Review 53* (November 2000), 1965–2006.

computer system to collect prices and send them to its reservation system to set price. All three indicators of price-fixing were present. First, the conduct was too complex to have been arrived at other than through an illegal process. Second, claims of legitimate business justification were unconvincing because the computer system employed records of price information ordinary consumers could not understand or use, but that were useful to other airlines. Third, there was a great deal of communication among the airlines. Though there was no evidence of a physical agreement document, the court still ruled this was illegal price fixing.

Vertical Price-Fixing

Vertical price-fixing is more complicated in e-commerce than in traditional commerce. Manufacturers sometimes put restraints on prices of the items distributed via the Internet. While vertical price-fixing is illegal per se in traditional commerce, some manufacturers argue that it is necessary to prevent online distributors from free riding on the promotion efforts of brick and mortar distributors and offering lower prices. For example, manufacturers can reach cooperative minimum advertised price (MAP) agreements with online distributors. The Federal Trade Commission has not ruled that MAP is per se illegal, so long as it does not become a form of actual resale price maintenance. However, if the manufacturer tries to extend MAP to all online items, or to fix price on items that are not in the MAP agreement, it likely would be considered illegal vertical price-fixing.

Predatory Pricing

Predation means that a firm can eliminate a smaller competitor by using its deeper resources to undercut the competitor's price, thereby taking away the competitor's customers. When the competitor has been eliminated, the firm can raise its price, recover the cost of the predatory behavior and then make larger profits than was possible before. The traditional method of identifying predation is that the predatory price must be lower than the firm's own marginal cost, and the cost of the predatory behavior must be likely to be recouped in the same market after competitors leave. This requirement of recoupment raises a question in e-commerce. As we know, the marginal cost of most digital products (whether physical products or information products) approaches zero. So the traditional method concerning pricing below marginal costs, and therefore sustaining a cost to drive out a rival, does not help to identify predatory pricing in the e-commerce age.

Recent cases show the courts' evolving understanding of this issue. In the Microsoft Explorer bundling case, the court took the position that recoupment of investment in this case should not be measured in terms of a later intention to raise price of the browser, but rather in terms of Microsoft's belief that it needed to destroy Netscape lest Netscape become a platform for a competing operating system. As shown by the case, the court did not use marginal cost as an indicator for determining predation because it has become meaningless in many e-commerce scenarios. The court also broadened the scope of investment recoupment: Any possible gain in the form of reputation, brand equity, market power, or increase in sales of other products would be considered benefits from predatory pricing, rather than only the direct gain from the product that was priced lower to drive away competitors.

Price Discrimination

Technology has made it relatively easy for e-commerce sites to sort customers into different price zones and set a different price for the same product. Price discrimination involving only end users is not covered by the Robinson-Patman Act. However, firms should still be cautious about discriminating between individual customers on the basis of price. Firms must realize that the Internet has made it easier to practice price discrimination, but at the same time, it also keeps customers better informed and equips them with ways to fight back.

The Robinson-Patman Act does govern price discrimination in business to business transactions, whether online or off-line. No case about price discrimination in business-to-business e-commerce has been reported yet. However, the traditional standard used to identify price discrimination also should be applicable to online business-to-business transactions. That is, price discrimination that lessens competition and cannot be justified by one of the affirmative defenses would be considered illegal.

Summary

Initial online pricing analysis supported the idea that the Internet would create a perfectly competitive market. The assumed increase in information flow between buyers and sellers combined with the commoditization effects of shop-bots were to have resulted in lower online prices. Although there is some evidence to support this theory of the Internet creating perfect competition, more extensive research has found that online prices are not uniformly decreasing. In fact, in some cases online prices are higher than those of conventional retail outlets.

Given that the Internet is not creating a state of perfect competition by forcing prices downward, pricing managers must understand how to use Internet technology to improve upon their pricing decisions. Now more than ever, through the use of Internet technology, managers are efficiently and effectively able to test pricing schedules and customer behaviors, segment their customers, continuously maintain and update prices, and differentiate their product and price offerings. In conclusion, the Internet is moving towards a completely different direction than previously thought. Instead of uniformly low prices, online firms are using the Internet to create a market where uniform prices are increasingly rare.

The pricing principles developed in this book and summarized in Chapter 22 apply equally to pricing on the Internet. Moreover, as indicated in Chapter 1 and repeated in Chapter 22, managers must continuously confront their assumptions and beliefs about how customers behave. The way that pricing works is exceedingly complex and must be understood if dot com firms are to succeed. That so many dot com firms failed in the early days of the Internet is a clear warning that there is no easy way to Internet success except through careful consideration and application of the pricing principles developed in this book.

Discussion Questions

1. a. Briefly outline the argument that the Internet would push prices to perfect competition levels.
   b. What are some counterarguments to the argument you outlined in *a*?
   c. What is the evidence to date on these arguments?

2. What are some of the important pricing opportunities that the Internet provides for firms?

3. Select a product that you are interested in buying and visit several price comparison websites. Write a brief report on your comparisons of these sites. What features do they provide? What information would you like to receive from these sites that was not available?

4. Assume that you have been appointed pricing manager for a retail store's online site. What pricing principles would you believe are the most important? How would you try to leverage the opportunities that the Internet offers to pricing managers?

Suggested Readings

Baker, Walter, Mike Marn, and Craig Zawada: "Price Smarter on the Net," *Harvard Business Review 79* (February 2001), 122–27.

Dolan, Robert J., and Youngme Moon: "Pricing and Market Making on the Internet," *Journal of Interactive Marketing 14* (Spring 2000), 56–73.

Foer, Albert A.: "E-Commerce Meets Antitrust: A Primer," *Journal of Public Policy & Marketing 20* (Spring 2001), 51–63.

Kannan, P. K., and Praveen K. Kopalle: "Dynamic Pricing on the Internet: Importance and Implications for Consumer Behavior," *International Journal of Electronic Commerce 5* (Spring 2001), 63–83.

Pitt, Leyland, Pierre Berthon, Richard T. Watson, and Michael Ewing: "Pricing Strategy and the Net," *Business Horizons 44* (March–April 2001), 45–54.

Michael D. Smith and Erik Brynjolfsson: "Consumer Decision-Making at an Internet Shopbot: Brand Still Matters," *The Journal of Industrial Economics 46* (December 2001), 541–58.

Suri, Rajneesh, Mary Long, and Kent B. Monroe: "The Impact of the Internet and Consumer Motivation on the Evaluation of Prices," *Journal of Business Research 55* (2001), 1–12.

Wyner, Gordon A.: "New Pricing Realities," *Marketing Research 13* (Spring 2001), 34–35.

Recommendations

This last section of the book offers some prescriptions for improving pricing decisions. Chapter 22 begins by outlining four basic rules for developing a positive approach to pricing. These rules summarize the analytical prescriptions contained in Chapters 2 through 13. The chapter also discusses the different types of information a firm can use when considering the profit implications of pricing alternatives and suggests when it is appropriate to use each.

The chapter recommends that pricing be included in a firm's marketing planning in an adaptive manner. An adaptive or flexible approach to pricing is necessary to help both profit and not-for-profit organizations adjust to current and future economic pressures. Finally, the chapter provides a set of guidelines for developing and maintaining an effective approach to solving pricing problems.

CHAPTER TWENTY-TWO

Guidelines for Better Pricing Decisions

This book has systematically presented the factors to consider when setting price and has shown how pricing alternatives can be developed and analyzed. As Chapter 1 observed, many contemporary pricing practices are reactions to environmental pressures that have evolved over a number of years. In reaction to these environmental pressures, we have witnessed a near-revolution in pricing practices with implications for capital spending, the inflation rate, the development of global markets, and the application of regulatory and legal policies.

This book has not emphasized descriptions of current or past pricing practices. Rather, we have sought to outline and prescribe approaches to setting prices that reflect the current and future realities of a modern global economy. Indeed, many businesses have changed their approach to pricing. Perhaps the foremost change has been the elevation of the pricing decision to a more central position in corporate headquarters. Business organizations are also establishing strategic pricing groups, and service organizations are recognizing the importance of price for their success. Moreover, price has been recognized as a key influence on investment decisions because of the direct link between price and net cash flow into the organization.

This chapter reviews some of the basic prescriptions for improving an organization's pricing function and presents a set of guidelines for developing and maintaining an effective organizational approach to solving pricing problems. The chapter first summarizes the analytic framework provided in

Chapters 2 through 13, then presents some criteria for making pricing decisions. It concludes with a set of guidelines for improving the pricing function of the organization.

Four Basic Rules for Pricing

The four rules discussed next are intended to capture the essence of the analysis necessary to determine and evaluate pricing alternatives. The order in which the rules are presented does not imply a hierarchy of importance—each rule is equally important.

Know Your Costs

The initial prescription is to determine the basic cost data necessary for the pricing decision. As Chapters 10 and 11 explain, it is necessary to know which costs vary directly with changes in levels of activity, and the underlying causes of the changes in costs. It is also necessary to identify the costs that are directly related to the product being costed, but do not vary with activity levels—direct period or fixed costs. Furthermore, marketing and distribution costs should be objectively traced to the products and not simply lumped into a general overhead category.

Valid cost data provide an objective basis for choosing between pricing alternatives, determining discounts, and establishing differential pricing alternatives. Furthermore, objective cost studies that are completed before the pricing decisions provide the firm with a valid legal justification for its price structure. The costing approach developed in this book provides a mechanism for obtaining objective, valid cost data. It is based on the idea of considering the relevant activities and functions performed by the various operating units, and not on production plus all other costs. As Chapter 11 indicates, this activity accounting approach is recognized today as closer to the realities of the modern business enterprise. Finally, when it is necessary to develop full-cost data, the firm should avoid arbitrary allocation formulas based on inappropriate allocation bases. Again, well-executed cost studies usually provide a more valid way of assigning period expenses not directly related to the appropriate activity levels.

Moreover, as shown in Chapter 13, the experience curve can be a valuable analytical tool for understanding the dynamics of a product's, firm's, or industry's costs. However, the experience curve is limited in its usefulness and requires careful monitoring and estimating of the firm's costs over the various activities and functions performed.

Know Your Demand

This second prescription suggests that the firm fully understand the factors influencing the demand for its products and services. Demand analysis is not as objective or as quantifiable as cost analysis, but it is critical. The discipline of consumer research has provided considerable information on consumer behavior and has begun to provide information on industrial buying behavior. From the perspective of this book, the key question is the role of price in the purchaser's decision process. As Chapters 5 through 8 indicated, price and price differentials influence buyer perceptions of value. In fact, many companies have achieved positive results from differentially pricing their products and services. A vice president of a large data processing company observed, "We try to find a market position where our product has a unique application."

Coupled with knowing how price influences buyers' perceptions of value, it is necessary to know how buyers use the product or service. Is the product used as an input in the buyer's production process? If so, does the product represent a significant or insignificant portion of the buyer's manufacturing costs? If the product is a major cost element in the buyer's production process, then small changes in the product's price may significantly affect the buyer's costs and the resulting price of the manufactured product. If the final market is sensitive to price increases, then a small price increase to the final manufacturer may significantly reduce demand to the initial seller of the input material. Thus, knowing your buyers means understanding how they react to price changes and price differentials, as well as knowing the relative role price plays in their purchase decisions. As prescribed in Chapter 1, the successful proactive pricer targets the relevant purchasing decision maker.

Furthermore, as suggested in Chapters 16 through 18, the seller should know the different types of distributors and their function in the distribution channel. This is particularly important when the manufacturer sells both to distributors and to the distributors' customers.

Know Your Competition and Your Market

In addition to the influence of buyers, a number of other significant market factors influence demand. It is important to understand the operations of both domestic and foreign competitors, their rate of capacity utilization, and their products and services. As Chapter 11 describes, the current rate of capacity influences product supply. In many markets, the dynamic interaction of supply and demand influences prices. Moreover, changes in capacity availability due to capital investment programs will influence supply and prices.

A second important aspect of knowing the market is the need to determine price–volume relationships. Chapter 9 discussed methods of estimating demand and behavioral influences on demand. Chapters 14 and 19 showed the importance of knowing price–volume relationships when setting prices or determining competitive bids. Finally, as shown in Chapter 11, when resources or capacity are scarce, knowing price–volume relationships facilitates the use of price to allocate these scarce resources over products and to customers.

Know Your Objectives

Many firms stress the profit objective of return on investment. Other firms stress the objective of maintaining specified profit margins. Still other firms seek to achieve market-share goals. As Chapter 11 shows, it is not necessary for each product to maintain the same profit margin in order to achieve a particular return on investment. Similarly, different margins on products may still produce an overall desired corporate profit goal. Finally, firms stressing market share may utilize the experience curve factor developed in Chapter 13 and build profits by reducing prices.

The important point to remember is that differences in corporate profit objectives eventually will lead to differences in prices and in the way price influences actual profits. Thus imitating or following the pricing practices of other companies is not necessarily in the best interests of any firm. Ultimately, regardless of the financial goal, profits or breakeven, the pricing objective is behavioral in nature. That is, whether buyers buy more, whether nonbuyers now decide to buy, whether buyers decide to purchase less frequently but in greater volume per order, or whether buyers decide to pay earlier is influenced by the prices and price structure of the seller. Further, the degree that distributors and dealers are cooperative and motivated to sell the firm's products depends largely on the financial incentives that the suppliers' prices and price structure provide. The salespeople's motivation to help the firm achieve its financial objectives depends on their understanding and acceptance of the pricing strategy the firm follows. Price has an important role in developing incentives for distributors, salespeople, and buyers to perform in ways that will be beneficial to the firm. Thus it is important that the seller develop a positive attitude toward pricing that will lead to a proactive pricing approach.

Criteria for Pricing Decisions

Following the preceding four rules should enable a firm to have a balanced approach to pricing. That is, costs, demand, competition, and corporate profit objectives will all have a place in the analysis. Hence, when a firm is operating at normal capacity and internal and external environmental factors are stable, prices can be determined with a degree of confidence. However, as observed throughout the book, the current and future economic environment has made pricing a more complex and important decision. The price setter, therefore, must develop a more analytical decision process.

This text has emphasized a contribution approach to pricing. A contribution analysis produces several types of data: profit–volume ratio, contribution dollars, contribution per scarce resource unit, and target selling price. This section evaluates the appropriateness of each of these types of data for situations in which a firm is not operating under normal conditions.

When Operating below Normal Capacity

As we suggested when discussing whether to submit a bid and at what price in Chapter 19, a firm operating at 55 percent capacity needs additional business that can make some contribution to overhead and profits. Hence maximizing contribution dollars represents the key criterion for pricing new orders or for increasing the demand for existing products. Management's primary concern should be to generate enough contribution dollars to bring the firm's operating level above the breakeven point. Thus the key pricing decision criterion is to maximize contribution per sales dollar generated.

By using either a minimum PV ratio or gross margin, a firm may discourage business because its prices are too high. Adhering to a target selling price also may lead to overpricing the market. When operating below normal capacity, the goal is to generate sufficient product volume to cover all costs and also earn a profit. By stressing the dollars of contribution earned per sales dollar, the firm is in a position to achieve some minimal level of profits.

When Operating at or Near Maximum Capacity

When a firm is operating at capacity, its situation is essentially the same as when resources are scarce. And, as demonstrated in Chapter 11, the appropriate decision criterion is to maximize the contribution per scarce resource unit. Any other criterion may produce lower contributions to profit.

When Operating at Normal Capacity

Under normal operating conditions, a firm should seek primarily to maximize dollar contributions consistent with target return on investments. As Chapter 11 shows, because of the different ways variable and fixed capital are mixed to produce different products, it is not necessary for each product to have equal profit–volume ratios or contribution margins. Because there are no scarce resource constraints in normal circumstances, the CPRU criterion is also inappropriate.

Summary

There is no one right way to determine price. Pricing simply cannot be reduced to a formula—there are too many interacting factors. Successful pricing requires considering all internal and external factors and adapting to changes as they occur. Successful pricing is adaptive pricing.

Adaptive Pricing

Adaptive pricing explicitly recognizes the role of costs, corporate goals, and competition, as well as the effect of price and the total interaction of the marketing mix variables on demand when making pricing decisions. Moreover, adaptive pricing provides a formal mechanism to adapt to environmental changes.

Adaptive pricing requires the formal use of (1) plans and standards of controls, (2) review and analysis of deviations between planned and actual results, and (3) an information feedback system for revision of plans, standards, and policies. The decision to commit resources involves analyzing a variety of variables that interact with price: (1) product characteristics, (2) price–product quality relationships, (3) the distribution organization for marketing the products,

(4) advertising and other communicative efforts, and (5) the quality and nature of services to offer with the products.

Changes in demand, legal and regulatory changes, and changes in competitor strategies and products influence the firm to develop adaptive policies with respect to product, quality, price, personal selling, advertising, and service. These decisions influence the quantity and type of fixed investments and the level and behavior of other costs. The decision process involving these variables must consider several alternative dimensions for each variable. To limit the costs of generating, processing, and transmitting information, goals and tasks are determined for each of several levels in the firm. That is, operating divisions are given targets to reach for, and if these targets are reached, the overall position of the firm is enhanced. For example, a product manager may be given a market share target determined by considering the market potential and the managerial judgment of the share of the market the product may be expected to capture. Given the market potential and the target market share, the expected sales volume can be determined, which allows determining the necessary capacity and, therefore, necessary investment.

The major features of adaptive pricing are that it

1. Explicitly considers demand and the responsiveness of demand to the marketing mix variables.

2. Recognizes the constraining influences of competitive products and services and legal and regulatory forces.

3. Considers the necessity to develop a mechanism for adapting to changing market and environmental forces.

Thus a pricing goal per se exists only in the context of an adaptive marketing plan. The adaptive marketing plan should determine investments and cost behavior rather than existing investments and cost behavior determining pricing and marketing decisions.

Principles of Pricing Management

Throughout the book, we have developed a number of important principles for pricing management. The following list summarizes some of the most important principles.

1. The more that competitors and customers know about your pricing, the better off you are. To avoid misinter-

pretations, create appropriate and correct signals about intentions and the quality of products and services. In an information age, it is necessary to be transparent about prices and the value of a firm's offerings.

2. In highly competitive markets, the focus should be on those market segments that provide opportunities to gain competitive advantage. Firms must focus externally on relevant markets, carefully consider the benefits that customers are seeking, and evaluate how they comparatively are providing those benefits. Such a focus leads to a value-oriented pricing approach.

3. Pricing decisions should be made within the context of an overall marketing strategy that is embedded within a business or corporate strategy.

4. Successful pricing decisions are profit oriented, not sales volume or market share oriented. Price should not be used as a competitive weapon.

5. Prices should be set according to customers' perceptions of value.

6. Pricing for new products should start as soon as product development begins. Getting an early start on the pricing of new products facilitates early identification of unprofitable ideas and will help identify different product variations for specific market segments.

7. The relevant costs for pricing are the incremental avoidable costs. Pricing managers should avoid using average total or average variable costs, unitizing fixed costs, and using fully allocated cost systems.

8. A price may be profitable when it provides for incremental revenues in excess of incremental costs.

9. A central organizing unit should administer the pricing function. Generally, it is better to avoid letting salespeople set price, especially without access to profitability information and specific training in pricing and revenue management. A central, top-level management unit should also control authority to reduce prices.

10. Pricing management should be viewed as a process and price setting as a daily management activity, not a once-a-year activity. Prices should not be established

during the budgeting process, but before budgeting and with a clear market, customer, and value-oriented focus.

Providing a Basis for Effective Pricing Decisions

The discussion in Chapter 1 detailed reasons why many firms' current pricing strategies may be incorrect. Firms can develop strategies that may be more consistent with the actual decision environment.

Determine Consistent Objectives

As already suggested, objectives such as improving margins, avoiding bottlenecks, and improving cash flows may not be mutually consistent. Chapter 11 showed that focusing on high-margin products may increase bottlenecks because of the resources required and may lead to cash flow reductions because of the sales decline of low-margin, high-volume products. A clear and consistent statement of pricing objectives is necessary as a basis for appropriate pricing strategies.

In addition, the impact of short-run objectives on long-run profits must be recognized. When identifying "weak" products, managers should consider potential sales growth and the annual cash flow generated per dollar of assets invested in the product. Further, if shortages are expected to persist in the long run, the appropriate objective would be to maximize contributions per critical resource unit.

Establish a Pricing Research Program

The effects of price changes and price differences on buyer behavior is the least understood and the least studied area of marketing research. As Chapters 3 through 8 show, the lack of appropriate information in this area has led to many inappropriate pricing strategies. To understand the profit implications of these price effects, a pricing research program also should be able to provide information on the cost effects of price changes. (See Chapter 9.)

Demand Effects of Price Changes

The objective of research in this area is to determine the sensitivity of the market to price changes and price differences. Clearly, the seller should know the sensitivity of buyers to price changes, but the seller should also know the sensitivity of buyers' customers to price changes. The seller should be concerned about how buyers use price in their purchasing decisions, whether they assume quality on the basis of price, and whether perceived end prices affect the evaluation of the product line. Further, considerations of cross-elasticity of demand for the product line, including the behavioral perception of complementarity, should be investigated. (See Chapters 2–9.)

Cost Effects of Price Changes

Whereas the effect of price changes on demand concerns market or external reactions, the cost effects of price changes are internal considerations. As Chapter 11 discussed, a multiple-product firm has cost and demand interdependencies. Dropping low-margin products or curtailing volume by increasing prices can have unanticipated results. First, eliminating a product shifts its common cost burden to other products. Second, severe reductions in output demand may remove the firm's eligibility for quantity discounts when purchasing production inputs. Therefore, it is important that the firm properly classify costs into those costs that are tangibly traceable to and generated by a given product and those costs that are common. Furthermore, since for pricing purposes only future costs are relevant, the firm must develop adequate bases for forecasting future costs. (See Chapters 9 and 13.)

Develop an Information System for Pricing

A recurring theme throughout this book is the availability of relevant information for pricing management. Clearly, managers must routinely assemble information that would be useful for developing pricing strategy and tactics, as well as for defenses against alleged illegal pricing practices. (See Chapter 18 for guidelines on information needed for such defenses.) It is difficult to collect information post hoc that is relevant to a regulatory or legal concern and convince public policy officials that management acted in good faith or is making valid claims about the future effects of a particular action. Indeed, if prior and current decisions are being made without the relevant information supporting them, what is the probative value of the post hoc information offered to justify the decisions? However, even more importantly, routinely collecting, analyzing, and using such information is simply wise managerial practice.

Managing prices well can improve profitability. An important resource in a pricing management program is information on past price, market, and competitor performance. Capturing past price, quantity, and cost data will be efficient and effective if management plans well and sets up a system to support data collection, analysis, and dissemination to management personnel. In general, it is best to have a substantial history of price, quantity, and cost data over an appropriate observation period, which is generally consistent with the relative frequency of price changes, whether monthly, quarterly, or yearly. To be able to perform useful analyses of the data, it is best to have 20 or 30 data points, although useful patterns often emerge with a much smaller number of data points.

The following list outlines the minimum requirements for an effective pricing information system. Relevant data should be collected for each business segment (product or product line, customer or customer group, sales territory, alternative distribution systems, salespeople, store or facility) and cross-classified by meaningful categories. Minimally, a pricing information system should

1. Include price and quantity information by product, customer, and other meaningful business segments.

2. For product profitability analysis, group similar products into categories or product lines using weighted averages based on the relative revenue mix of the products.

3. Include all important (high-volume) products, but remember that today's low-volume product may be tomorrow's high-volume product.

4. For customer profitability analysis, group similar customer segments into categories by their behavior. For each segment, develop measures of contributions to profit from product or service revenues as well as the costs incurred to serve the segment.

5. Include activity-based cash costs. (Avoid all arbitrarily allocated costs that are based on various rules or formulas.) These cash costs should be classified into their variable and fixed components.

6. Include actual transaction prices after all discounts and allowances.

7. As much as feasible, include a similar database for major competitors (as defined by customers).

8. Include information on all other variables that influence sales of the products, including relevant economic

variables, level of marketing and sales efforts, and similar efforts of competitors.

9. Track price, volume, and cost data in both current and deflated dollars. Use an indexing system to observe relative changes or differences in data that are complex and subject to fluctuations.

Reengineering the Pricing Process

When organizations recognize that their approach to pricing needs to be changed to reflect the analysis and prescriptions presented in this book, the question often is how to do so. That is, how do we move from setting prices periodically to a process that has potential for improving revenue management and profitability? Often some of the best strategies fail because the decision-making process fails to facilitate the strategic objectives. *How* decisions are made often determines what decisions are made. To establish a more effective pricing process may require reengineering how prices are set and managed within the organization. This section provides an outline of how to accomplish such a change.

Establish Clear Goals

To help establish the goals to be accomplished by reengineering the pricing process, the following key questions should be answered:

1. What is the pricing strategy?

2. How does the pricing process hinder or support implementing the strategy?

3. Who are the custodians of value in the price decision process?

4. How does the pricing decision impact the performance of other units of the organization?

5. How do these units participate in the pricing process?

6. What effect does the process have on price administration and implementation?

7. How does the pricing process affect customers?

Document the Existing Process

When determining how pricing is currently being managed, the following questions must be answered. Many decisions that have not been considered as pricing related must be covered when answering these questions (such as free services, extended warranties and guarantees, various discounts, promotions and advertising allowances, freight, and transportation and shipping adjustments).

1. Who makes the decisions?

2. How are the decisions made?

3. What information is used?

Best Practices Study

After reviewing the current pricing system in its entirety, alternative pricing processes for the organization must be developed. At this stage, it would be useful to do a best practices study to determine how other organizations have converted to a pricing process and how they have succeeded. It is important to remember that an organizational change such as reengineering pricing will be disruptive and will require some challenges to current beliefs, attitudes, and practices. Thus it is important to include all important stakeholders in the process of developing alternative pricing processes.

Establishing the New Pricing Process

When creating the new pricing process, a number of important decisions must be made, including

1. Who will make the pricing decisions?

2. Structurally, at what level will pricing and revenue management be within the organization?

3. What will be the structure of the pricing unit?

4. What sources of information will be used when setting or changing prices?

5. When will pricing decisions be made?

6. Who will have authority to adjust prices and allowances? Within what limits of discretion?

7. What types of decisions will the pricing unit make?

8. What ongoing training and updating of skills will be provided personnel involved with pricing?

Guidelines for Better Pricing Decisions

The purpose of this book has been to develop a consistent, analytical approach to pricing. Our emphasis has been on developing positive attitudes toward the pricing decision and to demonstrate that price is a critical decision variable in the marketing mix. We have also shown how appropriate pricing strategies can be developed with the help of adequate information and analysis. The following guidelines can help organizations improve their pricing decisions.

Set Consistent Objectives

1. Make sure that operating objectives are clearly stated, operational, and mutually consistent.

2. When there are several objectives, develop priorities or otherwise clarify the relationships between the objectives.

3. Make sure that everyone concerned with a pricing decision, at any level in the firm, understands the relevant objectives.

4. Translate the operating and financial objectives into buyer and market behavioral objectives.

Identify Alternatives

1. Identify enough alternatives to permit a sensible choice between courses of action.

2. Avoid traditional thinking; encourage creativity.

3. Consider all feasible alternatives regardless of past success or failures.

Acquire Relevant Information

1. Be sure that information about customers, distributors, and competitors is current and reflects both their current and future situations.

2. Make sure information applies to the future, and is not just a report of the past.

3. Involve market research people in the pricing problem.

4. Make sure cost information identifies which costs will be affected by a particular pricing alternative.

5. Communicate with and involve accounting people with the cost aspects of a pricing decision.

6. Analyze the effect a particular alternative will have on scarce resources, inventories, production, cash flows, market share, volume, and profits.

Make the Pricing Decision

1. Make full use of the information available.

2. Correctly relate all the relevant variables in the problem.

3. Use sensitivity analysis to determine which elements in the decision are most important.

4. Consider all human and organizational problems that could occur with a given pricing decision.

5. Consider the long-run effects of the pricing decision.

6. Base the pricing decision on the life cycle of each product.

7. Consider the effect of experience in reducing costs as the cumulative production and sales volume increases.

Encourage Feedback and Maintain Control

1. Develop procedures to ensure that pricing decisions fit into the firm's overall marketing strategy.

2. Provide a feedback mechanism to ensure that all who should know the results of individual price decisions are fully informed.

To summarize, pricing decisions should be logically made and should involve rigorous thinking, with minimum interference from human and organizational factors. The future must be considered, not the past. Finally, pricing decisions should be made within a dynamic, long-run marketing strategy.

Discussion Questions

1. Assume that you are the pricing administrator for a corporation and you wish to implement the four basic rules for pricing given in this chapter. What steps would you take to put these rules into action?

2. Comment on the applicability of the following types of data for pricing purposes:

   a. Profit–volume ratio.

   b. Contribution dollars.

   c. Contribution per scarce resource unit.

   d. Target selling price.

3. What is "adaptive pricing"?

4. Review the "Guidelines for Better Pricing Decisions" given in this chapter. Explain the rationale for each guideline.

absolute price thresholds   The lowest and highest prices that buyers are willing to pay for a particular good or service. See also *acceptable price range, reservation price, differential price threshold.*

acceptable price range   Those prices that buyers are willing to pay for a good or service.

activity-based costing   A cost accounting system that ties actual costs to the direct performance and value of activities. Costs are traced and assigned to specific activities rather than by formula.

adaptation-level price   The price a buyer uses as the basis of a comparison with a product or service's actual price. See also *reference price.*

adaptation-level theory   Assumes that stimuli are judged with respect to internal norms (*adaptation levels*) representing the combined effects of present and past experiences. Stimuli are perceived as members of categories and are evaluated relative to the individual's adaptation level for that category.

advance purchase discount   Discount given to customers who purchase or make reservations early.

anchoring effect   The result when buyers make comparisons of prices or products against a reference price or product. The comparison typically is weighted towards the reference price creating a bias, which is termed the anchoring effect.

anchoring prices   Prices used by individuals to make perceptual judgments about other prices.

approximation process   The process by which Arabic or verbal numerals are first converted into an internal magnitude representation. The input mode, such as dollars or ounces, is then ignored and the numerical quantities are represented and processed similarly to other physical magnitudes such as size.

assimilation-contrast effects   When comparing prices against a reference price, buyers first judge whether the price being evaluated belongs in the same category as the reference price. If the price is judged to be in the same price category as the reference price, then the buyer judges that it is similar (assimilation effect). If the buyer judges that the price belongs to another price category, then the buyer evaluates it as different (contrast effect).

asymmetric competition   The situation when buyers respond differently to similar price changes of different competitors. A dominant competitor (brand) may induce buyers of other brands to switch to it with a price promotion, but price promotions by the other brands may not induce buyers of the dominant brand to switch.

asymmetric information   Occurs when one party to a transaction has more information than the other.

auction   A form of selling in which buyers bid the price they are willing to pay to acquire a product or service. Normally, the buyer who bids the highest price is given the opportunity to buy the item.

average revenue   Total revenue divided by the number of units sold.

average total cost   Total cost divided by the number of units produced and sold.

average variable cost   Total variable cost divided by the number of units produced and sold.

barter   The practice of exchanging goods and services for other goods and services rather than money.

basing-point pricing   A variation of delivered pricing. The basing point is a city is from which transportation charges are determined. But in basing-point pricing the product actually may be shipped from a city other than the basing point. See also *multiple basing-point pricing system.*

begrudging expenditure   For some products or services, buyers prefer not to make the expenditure, even though it may be a necessary purchase.

bond   Capital assets or secured monies that are forfeited if the bonded party fails to perform as promised.

bottlenecks   Constraints that slow up or halt production or distribution of a product. The scarcity of resources, such as equipment, skilled labor, or raw material, can effectively slow down the process.

breakeven analysis   A method of examining the relationships between fixed costs, variable costs, volume, and price. The objective of the analysis is to determine the breakeven point at alternative prices and a given cost structure.

breakeven point   The sales volume at which total revenues are equal to total costs.

buy-back agreement   The seller agrees to buy back, at a later time, output produced with the equipment originally sold.

buyers' costs   The costs that buyers incur when acquiring and using products and services, including the price of the item being acquired, information search, shipping, transportation and installation, and postpurchase costs that may affect buyers' perceptions of value of the item being acquired.

buy-response curve   A curve depicting the frequency distribution of acceptable prices for a product. The midpoint price of the buy-response curve provides an estimate of the price likely to be judged most acceptable, as well as the proportion of buyers likely to consider buying the product at that price.

cash costs   Costs that can lead to cash outlays, also known as *out-of-pocket cost.*

cash discount   A reward for the payment of an invoice or account within a specified amount of time.

cash on delivery   Commonly referred to as C.O.D. The practice of collecting for the price of the merchandise plus the relevant transportation charges at the time of delivery.

Clayton Antitrust Act (1914)   Specifically outlawed discrimination in prices, exclusive and tying contracts, intercorporate stockholdings, and interlocking directorates "where the effect . . . may be to substantially lessen competition or tend to create a monopoly."

closed auction   An auction in which bidders submit offers simultaneously, and the bidtaker evaluates the offers.

cognition   The mental process of interpretation and decision making, including the beliefs and meanings they create.

common costs   Costs that cannot be traced to a product or segment (similar to overhead costs).

compensation deal   A countertrade in which a part of the payment is in currency and a part is in goods.

competitive bidding   Firms submit offers (or bids) that detail the services and product specifications to be offered at a stated price.

competitive signal   Information provided by one seller to other competing sellers in the market, which the other sellers can use to make inferences about the behavioral intentions of the seller sending the signal.

competitors' costs   Those costs that a competing firm incurs when producing, marketing, and distributing a product in competition with a firm's product or service.

conjoint analysis   A research method used to determine prospective buyers' relative preferences for different product attribute combinations, including price. See *trade-off analysis.*

consumers' surplus   The difference between the maximum price that consumers are willing to pay and the lower amount they actually pay. See *value-in-use.*

contingency pricing   The setting of a price based either on actual costs incurred after the service has been performed or the product produced or on the measured value the buyer realizes because of the service or product.

contribution   The amount of revenue remaining from the sale of a product or service after the direct and indirect costs related to the product or service have been deducted.

contribution per resource unit   The amount of revenue left from the sale of a product or service after the direct and indirect costs related to that product or service have been deducted, divided by the number of resource units used to produce the product or service.

contribution pricing   A method of determining the price of a product or service through a relation between the direct or indirect traceable costs and the relevant costs of production and sale of the product or service.

cost   Money expended to produce a product or service. See specific cost category definitions.

cost-plus pricing   A method of determining the price of a product or service that uses direct, indirect, and fixed costs whether related to the production and sale of the product or service or not. These costs are converted to per-unit costs for the product, and a predetermined percentage of these costs is then added to provide a profit margin. The resulting price is cost per unit plus the percentage markup.

counterpurchase   A form of countertrade in which the selling firm agrees to purchase, at a later time, goods from the buyer equal to the amount of the original sale.

countertrade   The practice of requiring some of the payment for products or services to be in other products or services rather than money.

coupon   A document that entitles the holder to a reduced price or to a stated amount off the actual purchase price of a product or service.

coupon face value   The percentage off the regular price expressed in dollars and cents.

coupon redemption   The use of a seller's value certificate at the time of purchase to obtain either a lower price or greater value than normal. Also, the act of accepting a seller's certificate by a retailer or other intermediary.

credence products and services   These products have attributes that buyers cannot evaluate confidently even after one or more purchases. See also *experience products and services* and *search products and services.*

credit   The transfer of a product or service in return for the promise of payment at a later time.

cross-price elasticity   Measures the responsiveness of demand for a product to a change in price of another product.

cue   Any informational stimulus about or relating to the product, service, or purchase context.

cumulative quantity discount   A reduction in the price to be paid for purchases that exceed a given level of volume over a specified period of time. Also called a *deferred discount* or a *patronage discount.*

delivered pricing   The practice of quoting a price that includes both the list price and the transportation costs from a basing point to the buyer. The prices are quoted as f.o.b. destination, meaning the manufacturer bears the responsibility of selecting and paying for the method of transporting the product.

demand   The amounts that buyers would be willing to purchase at a corresponding schedule of prices.

demand-oriented pricing   A method of pricing in which the seller attempts to set the price at the level that the intended buyers are willing to pay. Also called *value-oriented* or *value-in-use pricing.*

depreciation   An accounting charge that reduces the cost of an asset, such as a factory or a machine tool, over its useful life. This charge does not require cash outlays.

derived demand   The demand for one product that is derived from the purchase of another. The demand for industrial products is created by the purchase of consumer products that use or incorporate industrial products in them or in their manufacture.

differential pricing   The pricing strategy of offering a different price to different market segments.

differential threshold   The difference in price between alternative choices necessary before a buyer will switch to the other choice. See also *absolute price thresholds.*

direct costs   Fixed or variable costs incurred by and solely for a particular product, department, program, sales territory, or customer account. Also called *traceable* or *attributable costs.*

direct fixed costs   Costs that are incurred by and solely for a particular product or segment but that do not vary with an activity level.

direct variable costs   Costs that vary directly with an activity level.

discount   A reduction in price.

discrete choice modeling   This approach allows the measuring of brand-specific price elasticities as well as brand cross-price elasticities. The modeling involves developing

choice sets that show products available in the market, along with their descriptions.

distance effect   It indicates that the time required to compare two numbers is an inverse function of the numerical distance between them. See also *magnitude effect.*

dual-function discount system   Reduction in price granted distributors or dealers who perform different marketing functions for the manufacturer. For example, one channel of distribution may consist of wholesalers and retailers, while another channel used by the same manufacturer may consist only of retailers. In the latter channel, some of the functions performed by the retailers may be of a wholesaling nature, hence these retailers are performing a "dual function" for the manufacturer.

dumping   The practice of selling products in foreign markets at prices lower than what the products are sold for in the home markets.

Dutch auction   A form of auction in which the auctioneer (or an electronic device) starts with a high price and successively announces a lower price until a bidder bids and wins the lot for sale.

economies of scale   The saving derived from producing and selling a large number of units; for example, in a situation where all inputs are doubled, output may be more than doubled.

elasticity   The degree of change in one economic variable in response to a change in another economic variable.

end prices   The prices of the lowest and the highest priced products in a product line.

English auction   A form of auction in which the highest bidder among potential buyers, or the lowest bidder among potential sellers, is the winner.

exchange   The act of relinquishing something for something else of equal value.

experience attribute   A product attribute that can be evaluated only after purchase and use.

experience curve The reduction in costs per unit that occurs when production, marketing, and distribution increase cumulatively. Typically, these cost reductions occur because of learning effects, economies of scale, and improvements in technology.

experience-curve pricing A method of pricing in which the seller sets the price sufficiently low to encourage a large sales volume in anticipation that the large sales volume would lead to a reduction in average unit costs. Generally this method of pricing is used over time by periodically reducing price to induce additional sales volumes that lead to lower per-unit costs.

experience products and services These products have attributes that can be evaluated only after purchase and use. See also *credence products and services* and *search products and services.*

Federal Trade Commission Act (1914) Placed a blanket prohibition against "unfair methods of competition" and created the Federal Trade Commission to enforce it.

financial leverage The use of debt to finance the operations of an organization. More formally, the degree to which operating profits before interest and taxes change relative to a change in operating profits before taxes. See also *operating leverage.*

flat-rate pricing A fixed price is charged regardless of levels of volume or other characteristics of service for which costs vary with some measure of usage.

F.O.B. origin pricing A method of pricing where the seller quotes prices from the point of shipment.

F.O.B. with freight allowed A form of delivered pricing in which the buyer arranges and pays for the transportation, but deducts these transportation costs from the invoice total and remits the net amount.

focused price reduction Selectively reducing price to specific market segments or accounts, as opposed to an across-the-board price reduction.

forward buying The practice of buying excess amounts of the merchandise offered on deal, relative to actual demand, and selling some units at full price after the deal period is over.

framing Establishing the mental context in which alternatives are evaluated before a choice is made.

free-on-board (f.o.b.) Quoted price without delivery. It is the buyer's responsibility to select the mode of transporting the goods, choose the specific carrier, handle all claims, and pay all shipping charges.

full-cost pricing An approach whereby prices are determined after all costs have been allocated.

functional discount Payment to independent retailers and wholesalers for performance of certain marketing functions that would otherwise be performed by the manufacturer. See *trade discount.*

gray market A market formed by parallel distribution of genuine goods by intermediaries other than authorized channel members.

income effect The increase or decrease in a consumer's real income as a result of the change in the price of a good or service.

income elasticity of demand The responsiveness of the quantity demanded of a product or service to a change in personal income.

indirect traceable costs Costs that are not incurred solely for a particular activity but that can be traced through reasonably objective means in part to the activity for which they are incurred.

invoice price Price after usual volume, trade, and cash discounts.

lateral gray market Gray marketer buys and sells in two countries, neither of which is the country of product origin.

leverage   The degree to which a change in sales volume leads to a subsequent change in a company's operating profits and financial performance of a company.

life-cycle costs   The costs of a durable good over its entire operating or useful life.

list price   The selling price for an item before any discounts or reductions in price.

loss leader pricing   Featuring items priced below cost or at relatively low prices to attract customers to the seller's place of business.

magnitude effect   Indicates that, for equal numerical distance, it is easier to discriminate small numbers (for example, 1 versus 2) than larger numbers (for example, 8 versus 9). See also *distance effect.*

margin   The difference between the selling price and total unit costs for an item.

marginal cost   The change in total cost resulting from producing and marketing one additional unit.

marginal revenue   The change in total revenue resulting from producing and marketing one additional unit.

markdown   The amount of a reduction from the selling price.

marketing profitability analysis   A study of the organization's entire marketing and distribution function to determine the profitability of different market or sales segments, such as products, customers, territories, and sales order sizes.

markup   The amount of an increase in price over total unit costs.

maximum acceptable price   The highest price a buyer is willing to pay for a product or service. Also called *reservation price.*

mixed bundling   The practice of offering for sale two or more products or services either at individual prices or for one single price. See also *price bundling.*

mixed-leader bundling   The price of a second product is discounted if the first product is purchased at full price.

mixed-joint bundling   A single price is set for a combined group of products or services.

most-favored-customer pricing   The practice that guarantees a customer the lowest prices the seller offers to anyone.

multiple basing-point pricing system   A method of pricing in which several locations are designated as basing points and the price is determined by the point that yields the lowest delivered cost to the buyer.

multiple-zone pricing system   A pricing system in which prices are uniform within two or more delivery zones. See also *single-zone pricing.*

noncumulative quantity discount   A discount granted for volume purchased (measured either in units or dollars) at a single point in time. See also *quantity discount.*

nonlinear pricing   Situation when a price structure leads to a change in average per-unit price as volume sold (ordered) increases.

nonprice competition   The competition among firms on the basis of variables other than price, such as quality, brand, assortment, or services.

odd-even pricing   A form of psychological pricing suggesting buyers are more sensitive to certain final digits. In odd pricing, the price ends in an odd number (e.g., 1, 3, 5, 7, 9), or just under a round number (e.g., 99, 98). In even pricing the price ends in a whole number or in tenths (e.g., $5.00, $5.10, $5.90).

open auction   A form of auction in which prices are publicly announced and bidders are able to indicate their willingness to transact at specific prices.

operating leverage   The degree to which operating profits change in response to a change in sales volume. See also *financial leverage.*

opportunity costs   The amount of revenues forgone by not pursuing the next best alternative.

parallel pricing   Following the pricing practices of other organizations, particularly competitors.

parallel importation   Gray marketer buys the product in the country where the product is made and sells it in another country.

patronage discount   Offering a price reduction based on previous customer relationship or preferred customer standing.

penetration pricing   The strategy of setting a product's price relatively low in order to generate a high sales volume. See also *skimming.*

per se rules   Rules that define clear-cut business violations.

perceived acquisition value   The buyers' perceptions of the relative worth of a product or service. It is formally defined as the subjectively weighted difference between the most a buyer would be willing to pay for the item less the actual price of the item.

perceived quality   The amount of quality buyers believe a product or service has. Perceived quality is usually based on some information or cues about the product, for example, its price or brand name.

perceived transaction value   The perceived benefits or gain from taking advantage of an offer or deal.

perceived-value pricing   A method of pricing in which the seller sets price at the level that the intended buyers value the product. See also *value-oriented pricing* and *demand-oriented pricing.*

perception   The cognitive impression that is formed of "reality," which influences the individual's actions and behavior.

phantom freight   In basing-point pricing, when the seller quotes a delivered price that includes a freight charge greater than the actual transportation costs.

predatory pricing   The practice of selectively pricing a product below that of competition to eliminate competition while pricing the product higher in markets where competition is relatively weaker.

preemptive pricing   Setting low prices to discourage competitors from entering the market.

price   The formal ratio that indicates the quantity of money, goods, or services needed to acquire a given quantity of goods or services.

price awareness   The degree to which buyers are knowledgeable of the prices of alternative products and services that they are interested in buying.

price bundling   The practice of offering two or more products or services for sale at one price.

price consciousness   The degree to which buyers are sensitive to differences in price between alternative choices. Generally, a price-conscious person seeks to minimize the price paid for an item.

price discrimination   The practice of charging different buyers different prices for the same quantity and quality of products or services.

price elasticity of demand   A measure of the sensitivity of demand to changes in price.

price fixing   The illegal practice of two or more sellers agreeing on the price to charge for similar products or services.

price judgment   Individual's assessment of whether a price is too low, acceptable, or too high.

price leader   In competitive situations, the seller who normally initiates price changes in the market. In some instances, the leader announces the price change after other competitors have made price changes. In this situation, the other competitors then adjust their prices to match those of the price leader.

price-market segmentation   The strategy recognizing that different buyers will have different degrees of sensitivity to price differences, price changes, and price levels.

price promotion   Advertising a price for a product or service. Usually, the price being promoted is a reduction from a previously established price.

price–quality relationship   The degree to which product or service quality covaries with price.

price–quality tiers   Many product lines consist of different models or versions of the basic product, each with different performance capability and differing prices, called price–quality tiers.

price sensitivity meter   A research method for establishing the range of prices that buyers are willing to pay for a product or service. See also *acceptable price range.*

price structure   Some combination of the time and conditions of payment, the nature of discounts to be allowed the buyer, and where and when the buyer takes title.

price–value map   Illustrates the way customers in a value segment trade off perceived benefits against perceived price.

proactive pricing   The managerial practice of deliberately analyzing the factors that influence prices before setting prices. Normally, a proactive pricer establishes specific objectives to be accomplished by the prices and then proceeds in the development of specific prices.

product life cycle   The stages that a product is thought to go through from birth to death: introduction, growth, maturity, saturation, and decline.

product line   A group of products sold by an organization to one general market. The products have some characteristics, customers, or uses in common and may also share technologies, distribution channels, prices, and services.

product-line pricing   Setting prices for all items in a product line.

profit analysis   An analysis for determining the effect of costs, prices, and volume on profits.

profit–volume (PV) ratio   The dollar contribution per unit divided by the per-unit price. The profit–volume ratio indicates the rate at which fixed costs are recovered and, after the breakeven point has been reached, the rate at which profits are earned as sales volume increases.

promotional discount   A reduction in price given to wholesalers and retailers in return for providing some promotion for the product.

purchase acceleration   Occurs when customers buy larger quantities when the brand is promoted or purchase the brand sooner than normal.

quantity discount   A reduction in price for volume purchases, either in a single purchase or over a period of time. See also *cumulative quantity discount* and *noncumulative quantity discount.*

rebate   A return of a portion of the purchase price in the form of cash by the seller to the buyer.

redemption rate   The number or percentage of sales promotion offers that consumers or retailers act on out of the total number possible.

reference price   The price that buyers use to compare the offered price of a product or service. The reference price may be a price in a buyer's memory or the price of an alternative product.

refund   A return of the amount paid for an item.

reimportation   Gray marketer buys the product in a country where the product is sold but not manufactured, and sells it back to the country where the product is manufactured.

reservation price   The highest price a buyer is willing to pay for a product or service. See also *absolute price thresholds, maximum acceptable price.*

Robinson-Patman Act (1936) An amendment to the Clayton Act that prohibits price discrimination where the effect "may be substantially to lessen competition or create a monopoly"; prohibits payments of broker's commission where an independent broker is not employed; forbids sellers to provide allowances or services to buyers unless these are available to all buyers on "equally proportional terms"; and prohibits a buyer from inducing or receiving a prohibited discrimination in price.

rule of reason A basis for determining the legality of business practices using relevant evidence.

sacrifice The sum of all costs that customers incur to acquire and use a product or service.

search products and services Products with purchase-determining attributes that buyers can readily evaluate before purchase. See also *experience products or services* and *credence products or services.*

search attribute Product attributes that can be readily evaluated before purchase.

segmentation strategy The strategy of subdividing a market into distinct subsets of customers that behave in the same way or have similar needs.

seller's costs The costs that the seller incurs to provide the products or service to the buyer.

seller's pricing discretion The difference between the direct variable costs of producing, marketing, and distributing the product and the highest price that buyers are willing to pay for the product.

semantic congruency effect When judging which number in a pair is larger, people find the task easier when both numbers are large than when both are small. The opposite is true when people have to decide which item is smaller. See also *size congruity effect.*

semivariable costs The costs that are incurred in a lump amount before any business activity can begin; they vary with volume once the activity is under way.

Sherman Anti-Trust Act (1890) Prohibits contracts, combinations, and conspiracies that restrain interstate or foreign trade as well as monopolization, attempts to monopolize, and conspiracies to monopolize.

signal A piece of information that can be revealed to the market at some cost to the provider. It is an observable, alterable characteristic that may affect buyers' assessment of product quality.

single-zone pricing Setting one price for all buyers regardless of their distance from the seller.

size congruity effect When people are trying to determine which of two numerals is larger, it is an easier task if the larger of the compared numerals is displayed in larger font size. Similar results occur when people are trying to determine the smaller of compared numerals and the smaller numeral is displayed in smaller font size. See also *semantic congruency effect.*

skimming The pricing method of attempting to first reach buyers who are willing to purchase at a high price before marketing to more price-sensitive customers. See also *penetration pricing.*

total revenue Price per unit multiplied by sales volume and summed over all products and services.

trade discount The discount allowed to independent wholesalers and retailers from list price based on a distributor's place in the distributive sequence. See *functional discount.*

trade-off analysis Research approach designed to determine the relative value buyers place on different factors or attributes of alternative offerings. See also *conjoint analysis.*

transfer pricing Pricing goods and services that are sold to controlled entities of the same organization, for example, movements of goods and services within a multinational or global corporation.

two-block pricing   A fixed price per unit is charged until the quantity price break point is reached. Then the quantity discount is applied to all units purchased *after* the break point.

uniform two-part pricing   A fixed price for the service is charged regardless of whether any units are used. Once the customer uses the product or service, then a uniform per-unit price is applied.

utility   The usefulness consumers receive from buying, owning, or consuming a product.

value analysis   An analytical procedure to study the costs versus the benefits of a currently purchased material, component, or design in order to enhance the benefit–cost ratio as much as possible. Also called *value engineering* or, when performed by a seller, *value-in-use analysis.*

value-in-exchange   The amount of money or goods actually paid for a product or service.

value-in-use   The amount of money or goods that buyers would be willing to pay for a product or service. Value-in-use is always greater than value-in-exchange. See *consumers' surplus.*

value-oriented pricing   An approach to pricing products that begins with establishing what the target market would be willing to pay for the projected performance level of the product. Then once the target price has been established, it is the task of the development process to design the product that will have a target cost that provides sufficient profit margins to the firm as well as to distributors.

warranty   A statement or promise made to the customer that a product being offered for sale is fit for the purpose being claimed. The promise concerns primarily what the seller will do if the product performs below expectations or turns out to be defective in some way.

Wheeler-Lea Act   An amendment to the Federal Trade Commission Act that broadens the FTC's purpose to include protection of the public from deceptive business practices. It also prohibited false and misleading advertising and provided more stringent penalties and enforcement procedures.

winner's curse   The situation when one wins the item or contract, but makes below normal or negative profits.

yield management   The practice of pricing to maximize the amount of revenue received per unit sold. Commonly associated with the pricing practices of airlines, hotels, and other sellers of "perishable" assets.

SUBJECT INDEX